THE
IMMIGRANT LABOR PRESS
IN NORTH AMERICA,
1840s–1970s

THE
IMMIGRANT LABOR PRESS
IN NORTH AMERICA,
1840s–1970s
An Annotated Bibliography

VOLUME 3: MIGRANTS FROM SOUTHERN
AND WESTERN EUROPE

Edited by **Dirk Hoerder**
Christiane Harzig, *Assistant Editor*

Bibliographies and Indexes in American History, Number 8

GREENWOOD PRESS
New York • Westport, Connecticut • London

Library of Congress Cataloging-in-Publication Data
(Revised for vols. 2 and 3)

Hoerder, Dirk.
  The immigrant labor press in North America,
1840s-1970s.

  (Bibliographies and indexes in American history,
0742-6828 ; no. 4, 7-8)
  Includes indexes.
  Contents: v. 1. Migrants from northern Europe —
v. 2. Migrants from eastern and southeastern Europe —
v. 3. Migrants from southern and western Europe.
  1. American newspapers—Foreign language press—
Bibliography. 2. American periodicals—Foreign
language press—Bibliography. 3. Canadian newspapers
—Foreign language press—Bibliography. 4. Canadian
periodicals—Foreign language press—Bibliography.
5. Press, Labor—United States—Bibliography.
6. Press, Labor—Canada—Bibliography. I. Harzig,
Christiane. II. Title. III. Series: Bibliographies
and indexes in American history ; no. 4, etc.
  Z6953.5.A1H63 1987   016.0704'4933188'0973   87-168
  [PN4884]
  ISBN 0-313-24638-6 (lib. bdg. : v. 1 : alk. paper)
  ISBN 0-313-26077-X (lib. bdg. : v. 2 : alk. paper)
  ISBN 0-313-26078-8 (lib. bdg. : v. 3 : alk. paper)

British Library Cataloguing in Publication Data is available.

Library of Congress Catalog Card Number: 87-168
ISBN: 0-313-26078-8
ISSN: 0742-6828

First published in 1987

Greenwood Press, Inc.
88 Post Road West, Westport, Connecticut 06881

Printed in the United States of America

The paper used in this book complies with the
Permanent Paper Standard issued by the National
Information Standards Organization (Z39.48-1984).

10 9 8 7 6 5 4 3 2 1

Contents

User's Guide

Each language section consists of the following parts:

First some **general information** about the language section is given.

The **introduction** includes a survey of the development of the labor and radical press as related to the development of the working-class section of the ethnic group.

The **annotated bibliography** contains all periodicals which appeared more than once a year alphabetically according to title. Whenever material is available a short description of the periodical is included as well as the basic bibliographic information. (See below for details.) For some ethnic groups appendices list annuals or other closely related types of publications, which - for reasons explained in each case - are of particular importance for the group concerned.

The **index** section consists of (1) a complete alphabetical title index including alternative titles and references to related publications, (2) a geographical index of periodicals according to place of publication, and (3) a chronological index of periodicals according to first year of publication.

1. General Information

This part informs about

- the cooperating language specialist(s);
- the area where the language was spoken in 1910. This is also shown on a map in the respective volume's introduction;
- an explanation of the library and depository symbols used in the section;
- and contains a bibliography which also lists all special language and area bibliographic aids used during the compilation of this section. (General bibliographies used for all language groups are listed in the introduction of the complete bibliography.)

2. Introduction

These essays give information about

- the number of immigrants in ten-year periods from (a) official U.S. and Canadian statistics, (b) statistics of the country or area of origin when available, (c) remigration statistics when available;
- the working-class section of the ethnic group including social status in the culture of origin, reasons for migration, main fields or occupation in the country of arrival, main labor/ethnic organizations, estimate of the relative size of the working class as compared with the other classes of the respective ethnic group;
- the development of the press of the group, particularly the working-class press.

For further information see the reference books by Wayne Charles Miller, the *Harvard Encyclopedia of American Ethnic Groups*, the Oceana "Chronology & Fact Book" Series, and the Gale "Ethnic Studies Information Guide" Series, as well as the Bibliography in volume I. of this publication.

3. Annotated Bibliography

The bibliographic information included for each periodical lists:

3.1 Information related to the title

- Title and title variants and changes
- Important subtitles displayed on masthead
- English translation of title
- Title transliteration where applicable

3.2 Place(s) and dates of publication

- place of publication
- date of first issue
- date of last issue, if defunct

3.3 Language(s) other than main language

3.4 Other publication data

- Frequency of publication
- Supplements, weekly and Sunday editions
- Production process if other than printing
- Statement about related publications
- Circulation figures if obtainable

3.5 Institutions and persons responsible for publication

- Sponsoring organization(s), if any
- Name of first editor(-in-chief) and changes
- Name of first publisher and changes

3.6 State and form of preservation of a periodical

3.7 Libraries and other depositories of the periodical and extent of holdings

3.8 Short description of contents, political affiliation, ideological orientation, form of presentation

Periodicals which are known to have been published but of which no copies have been preserved are included with information as complete as possible gained from other sources. Publications undergoing a change of title or place of publication but continuing in volume numbering will be treated as one periodical. Listing will usually be according to first title and first place of publication with a short description of all changes which occured. Periodicals which were temporarily labor-oriented are included for the radical period only.

3.1 *Title*

Title listings (in capital letters) include all diacritical marks in the original. Two identical titles published in the same place are distinguished by roman numerals in parentheses: (I). Title changes, including minor variations, are listed in the short description and included in the title index. Subtitles are included if regularly used or if important for identification. Changes in subtitles or mottoes, even if the latter were part of the periodical's masthead, are not listed. Title translation follows American-English spelling unless the translation was part of the official title and used British-English spelling. Transliteration follows international rules. The original title in non-Roman letters is placed at the beginning of the short description. All the periodical titles are printed in italics and all the translations are given in square brackets.

3.2 *Place and Dates of Publication*

The headline of each bibliographic entry contains the first place of publication by town or city, preceded by the state or province in official abbreviation. Changes in the place of publication are listed in the short description.

Canadian Provinces

A	Alberta	NS	Nova Scotia
B	British Columbia	O	Ontario
M	Manitoba	PE	Prince Edward Island
NB	New Brunswick	Q	Quebec
NF	New Foundland	S	Saskatchewan

U.S. States

AL	Alabama	MT	Montana
AK	Alaska	NE	Nebraska
AZ	Arizona	NV	Nevada
AR	Arkansas	NH	New Hampshire
CA	California	NJ	New Jersey
CO	Colorado	NM	New Mexico
CT	Connecticut	NY	New York
DE	Delaware	NC	North Carolina
DC	District of Columbia	ND	North Dakota
FL	Florida	OH	Ohio
GA	Georgia	OK	Oklahoma
HI	Hawaii	OR	Oregon
ID	Idaho	PA	Pennsylvania
IL	Illinois	PR	Puerto Rico
IN	Indiana	RI	Rhode Island
IA	Iowa	SC	South Carolina
KS	Kansas	SD	South Dakota
KY	Kentucky	TN	Tennessee
LA	Louisiana	TX	Texas
ME	Maine	UT	Utah
MD	Maryland	VT	Vermont
MA	Massachusetts	VA	Virginia
MI	Michigan	WA	Washington
MN	Minnesota	WV	West Virginia
MS	Mississippi	WI	Wisconsin
MO	Missouri	WY	Wyoming

The title line indicates first and last year of publication. If a general periodical became a labor periodical for part of its existence only this period is listed and the publication dates are given in paranthesis: (1884-1887). The dates of the first and last issue - if known - are always listed in the sequence day - month - year with the following abbreviations for the months:

Ja	January	My	May	S	September
F	February	Je	June	O	October
Mr	March	Jl	July	N	November
Ap	April	Ag	August	D	December

3.3 *Additional Languages*

If a periodical appealed to more than one language group the second (and further) language(s) used are listed as "additional languages." Any such periodical is described only once in this bibliography under its main language, but the title index of each additional language group contains cross references. The regular or frequent appearance of articles in "artificial" languages - Esperanto, Ido, Volapük - is noted in the short description. Dates are given if the periodical was temporarily multi-lingual. Conversion from non-English to English, at least in parts of each issue, is noted in the short description.

3.4 *Other Publication Data*

Frequency of publication, production process if other than printed, related publications and supplements, circulation figures are included in this category.

General symbols:

c.	circa = approximately
+	to date
//	following dates: definitely ceased publication
?	uncertain, lacks proof
[ ]	incomplete holdings - used with depository symbols

Abbreviations to indicate frequency of publication:

a	annually	sm	semimonthly	sw	semiweekly
sa	semiannually	m	monthly	3/w	three times a week
q	quarterly	bw	biweekly	d	daily
bm	bimonthly	w	weekly	ir	irregularly

Abbreviations to indicate related publications:

c	continuation of	m	merged with	s	superseded by

"Supplements" include not only additional sections of a periodical but also Sunday editions and weeklies.

The production process for the vast majority of periodicals is, of course, printing. A few were mimeographed. No handwritten and handcopied periodicals are listed.

Circulation figures are listed when available. The style is: "1880: 5500" - meaning a circulation of 5500 in the year 1880.

3.5 *Institutions and Persons Responsible for Publication*

An editor is the person in charge of a periodical's regular contents. The publisher is the person (or company) which owns the periodical - however for a large part of the labor press at the turn of the century publisher and editor were one person or one labor organization (e.g. "Workingmen's Printing Club"). The sponsoring organization is a party, a union or any other type of working-class organization. Note: A periodical was often the official (=sponsored) organ for only a limited period of its existence. Changes in editorship, ownership and sponsorship are noted in the short description.

3.6 *State and Form of Preservation of a Periodical*

This section provides information in so far as it is available, on how completely a periodical has been preserved and in which form (original, microform) it is available to users.

Abbreviations indicating state of preservation:

1:    complete
2:    almost complete = scattered issues missing
3:    incomplete
4:    very incomplete
5:    scattered issues only
6:    fragment only
7:    lost altogether

[ ] indicate that a library has incomplete holdings:

Example: Usa-NN (3:1880-[1883-1885]-1886,o) means that the library USA-NN has incomplete holdings, that the years 1880-1882 and 1886 are complete while the holdings for 1883-1885 are incomplete and that the original is available.

Abbreviations indicating form of preservation:

o	original	mm	microfilm master
oub	original, unbound	mn	microfilm, negative
ob	original, bound	mp	microfilm, positive
m	microfilm	mf	microfiche

3.7 *Symbols of Libraries and Other Depositories*

Each country has developed an official system of symbols to designate by a few letters or figures (or a combination of both) its libraries and archives (=depositories). For each country the official symbols have been used. To distinguish between countries the depository symbols have been prefixed by the internationally adopted combination of letters to designate nationality of automobiles. For commercial publishers the additional prefix "&" is used. The prefix "§" indicates a private collection to which access might be restricted and "<" stands for an abbreviation used but developed by the respective cooperating language specialist or the editors.

Examples:

Usa-N	New York State Library, Albany, New York, U.S.A.
Usa-N(1,mm)	*ibid.*, complete holdings, microfilm master
Usa-N(2: 1885-[1887-1893]-1905,o)	*ibid.*, almost complete holdings, with scattered issues missing for the volumes 1887 to 1893, original

D-212   Institut für
                                               Auslandsbe-
                                               ziehungen, Bibliothek
                                               [Institute for Foreign
                                               Relations, Library],
                                               Stuttgart, Germany,
                                               Fed. Rep.

Depositories with very incomplete, scattered or fragmentary holdings (categories 4-6) have not been listed whenever more complete collections are available. Since many depositories are so short of staff that they cannot answer queries a library listing without square brackets does not necessarily indicate complete holdings.

List of nationality prefixes:

Al	Albania	I	Italy
Aus	Australia	L	Luxembourg
A	Austria	M	Malta
B	Belgium	Mex	Mexico
Bg	Bulgaria	Nl	Netherlands
Cdn	Canada	Nz	New Zealand
C	Cuba	N	Norway
Cs	Czechoslovakia	Pak	Pakistan
Dk	Denmark	Pl	Poland
Sf	Finland	P	Portugal
F	France	R	Romania
Ddr	Germany, Dem. Rep.	Su	Soviet Union
D	Germany, Fed. Rep.	Es	Spain
Gb	Great Britain	S	Sweden
Gr	Greece	Ch	Switzerland
H	Hungary	Tr	Turkey
Is	Iceland	Usa	United States
Irl	Ireland (Eire)	Yu	Yugoslavia
Il	Israel		

3.8 *Short Description and Political Category*

Whenever possible the periodicals are classified as "labor union," "reform," "social-democrat," "socialist," "communist," "syndicalist," "anarchist." Party or union affiliation are indicated after the category with the usual initials, e.g. SLP for Socialist Labor Party. The category "radical" is used for anti-capitalist and pro-worker periodicals. Some cooperating language specialists have used further categories appropriate to the political development of the respective ethnic group.

The short description notes changes in title, editorship etc. It contains a summary of the periodical's main themes and describes the predominant form of reporting (newsnotes, analytical essays, library or theoretical pieces). It closes with bibliographic references only when the cited works contain additional information or when the information has been taken unchecked from the cited works because the periodical was not available to the cooperating language specialist.

4. Indices

The *title index* is organized alphabetically according to original, i.e. usually the non-English title. In addition it contains all alternative titles and title changes as well as periodicals mentioned in the description (see). "See also" refers to related publications also listed in the bibliography. Periodicals published in more than one language are cross-referenced in the indices of all language groups to which they were addressed. In case of languages using non-Roman alphabets, the index is alphabetical according to transliterated title.

The *place index* is organized alphabetically according to country (Canada, United States), province or state, town or city.

The *chronological index* lists periodicals according to first year of publication and, in chart form, shows length of publication. Dates are given on the first two lines. Decades are followed by the year date on the second line. For technical reasons the chronological index does not always list the complete name of the periodical.

Note: While the cooperating language specialists have taken great pains to collate as complete a bibliography as possible the ephemeral character of much of the press, the poor state of preservation, and problems of categorization explain omissions and oversights. Any scholar knowing of additional titles is invited to send the information to the Bremen coordinating office, Prof. Dr. Dirk Hoerder, University of Bremen, D-2800 Bremen, Federal Republic of Germany.

MIGRANTS FROM SOUTHERN EUROPE

The Press of Labor Migrants From South European Countries: Introduction

by Dirk Hoerder

Emigration and labor migration from southern Europe concerns the Iberian and Italian peninsulas, i.e. the territories of present-day Portugal, Spain and Italy. Although Greece geographically is a southeast European country, for a number of reasons, it has often been classified as a south European country. From the point of view of labor migration Greek developments are similar to Bulgaria and other countries in that area and it is therefore dealt with in that section. The population of each peninsula is relatively homogeneous. Early patterns of conquest and migration influenced later migrations less than in eastern and southeastern Europe. On the Iberian peninsula Arab domination was pushed back during the eighth-thirteenth centuries (*reconquista*) and the areas were settled again from the north (*repoblación*). Expulsions occurred in 1492 and 1501 when the Jews and the remaining Arabs had to leave, to the detriment of agriculture, crafts and commerce. About a century later, the christianized Arabs (Moriscos) were expelled (1568-70 from Granada, 1609-11 from the rest of Spain). This agrarian and artisanal population of approximately 600,000 was not replaced by immediate in-migration. The mercantile activities of the Jews were taken over at least in part by migrants from the Spanish Netherlands. None of these migrations led to an ethnically mixed multilingual permanent settlement pattern comparable to the east European situation.

The patterns of colonization from the fifteenth century onward determined patterns of population outflow that lasted into the nineteenth and twentieth centuries. Portugal and Spain as the first large Atlantic seapowers before the rise of the Netherlands and later France and England sent considerable numbers of migrants to Central and South America. Portugal imported slaves in large numbers and temporarily controlled this type of forced labor migration in the Atlantic world. The Italian territory covered by present-day Italy was divided into a number of smaller units - a few of them belonging to Spain - with Venice and Genoa as the leading city states that dominated trade in the eastern and western halves of the Mediterranean. Accordingly Italian migration was originally limited to the establishment of mercantile settlements while the Portuguese population of two million declined by fifty percent during the first half of the sixteenth century because of emigration to the colonies and losses due to the permanent colonial wars. Emigration from Portugal and Spain continued to be directed toward Central and South America into the modern period: from 1916-54 1.3 million Spanish people left their home country - but almost 0,9 million returned. From Portugal almost 1.2 million people left for Brazil between 1901 and 1940. "International" communities as found in eastern Europe and in a few north European planned towns are few in the South. One example is Livorno, the massive expansion of which in the second half of the sixteenth century attracted Catholics from England, Jews and Arabs from Spain, French merchants from Marseille and many others.

The modern states of Spain and Portugal were re-established at the Congress of Vienna in 1815. As a consequence of the Napoleonic wars both countries lost their hold over their Central and South American colonies - one reason why later labor migration was directed toward North America. Italy did not become a unified state until the 1860s, at the end of the *risorgimento*.

Linguistically each of the three states has its own language. (See Figure 1) All three have numerous dialects, some of which are not mutually understandable. The populations of the areas where minority languages were spoken did not make a numerically significant contribution to emigration to North America. (See Figure 2) None of them developed a labor press, or - with the exception of the Basques - a general press. The southeast European population shifts led to some linguistic islands of languages from this area in Italy, but they are of no relevance for emigration.[1]

In view of the traditional maritime orientation of Portugal and Spain little intra-European migration came from these areas. Only along the Spanish border to France did a seasonal northward migration of grapepickers develop. In the case of Italy, internal migration, seasonal labor migration to European countries and as far as Argentina as well as permanent emigration increased noticeably after unification. Though there are no statistics available for the preceding decades, it is evident that only relatively small numbers left Italy for North and South America, Northern Africa or other parts of Europe. Migration from the South to the industrializing North was beginning. Internal migration was particularly widespread in the building trades. Bricklayers developed a language of their own - not to keep newcomers out of the trade but because many Italian dialects are mutually unintelligible. Italian migration was partly one of specialized callings; the Italian colony in Glasgow developed from the 1870s to the 1920s as a community of icecream vendors and later as merchants. Italian tilelayers were in demand all over Europe. Most Italian migrants, however, were unskilled workers. In Switzerland they had replaced the Germans as the largest group of labor migrants by the turn of the century. They also made up the largest group of in-migrants to France and in Germany they were the leading ethnic group of labor migrants until Polish laborers were admitted in the 1890s. Italians dominated a few crafts, but came mainly as unskilled construction workers. At the turn of the century Italian labor migration in Europe was "naturally" seasonal since civil engineering and building came to a standstill during the winter and unemployment forced workers to return home. Up to World War One Italian migration to European countries remained larger than that to North America.[2] Emigrant aid societies were established by the government and by the socialist parties to further their social and economic position and to involve them in the labor movement. Since Italians had repeatedly been recruited as strikebreakers, antialien sentiments among the working classes were growing and the socialist parties and trade unions tried to counter this development.[3] From the 1870s to the beginning of the Great Depression of the 1930s about 17 million Italians left their country. Perhaps half of them returned. Migration to the United States began during the 1850s and 1860s with about 10,000 immigrants per decade. About one million persons came during the next three decades, another three million from 1900-1920 and half a million during the twenties, but only 70,000 during the Depression decade. At the turn of the century only one sixth of the migrants came from the industrializing North, the rest from the agrarian South. During the first two decades of the century about 55 percent of the migrant workers returned and during the Depression decade the backward stream was larger than the move outward. Most Italian labor migrants concentrated in the Pennsylvania, New Jersey, New York and southern New England areas. Italian migration to Canada began later and remained small. During the 1920s and 30s the Italian-Canadian group numbered about 120,000 persons. The Italian migrants established one of the most vibrant labor movements in North America and were singled out in the United States for special pro or rather

Figure 1   Romance Languages

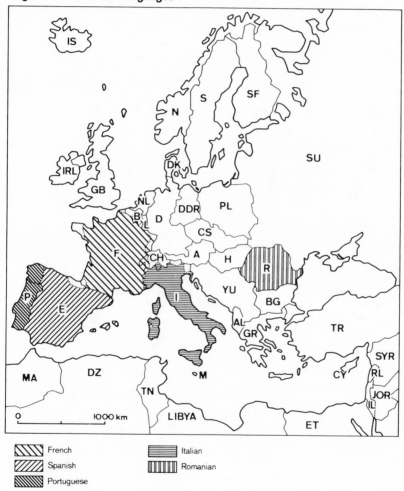

	French		Italian
	Spanish		Romanian
	Portuguese		

Figure 2 Linguistic Minorities in the West and South European
         Romance Areas

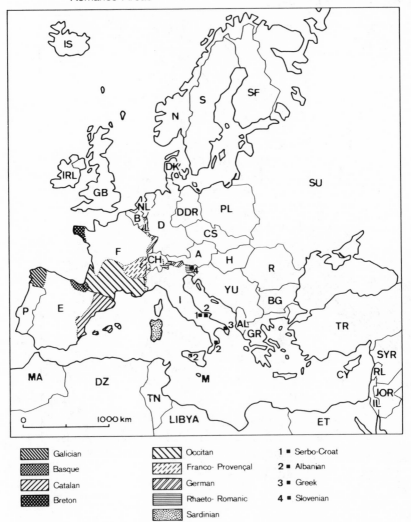

Galician		Occitan	**1** ■	Serbo-Croat
Basque		Franco- Provençal	**2** ■	Albanian
Catalan		German	**3** ■	Greek
Breton		Rhaeto- Romanic	**4** ■	Slovenian
		Sardinian		

persecution in the case of Sacco and Vanzetti.

Comparatively few of the people who emigrated overseas from Portugal and Spain went to North America. There were no more than 5,000 from Portugal up to 1870. About 60,000 came from 1871 to 1900, to be followed by another 160,000 during the first two decades of the twentieth century. Thereafter immigration dropped to 30,000 during the twenties and to 3,000 during the Great Depression. Spanish immigration remained below 10,000 per decade up to 1900, with a total of about 40,000 arrivals from 1820 to 1900. The next three decades witnessed a sharp rise from 28,000 to 69,000 and then an equally sharp decline to 29,000. During the Depression decade figures dropped to 3,000. Both nationalities therefore belong to the smaller immigrant groups.

The Portuguese Americans came from northern Portugal, the Azores and the Cape Verde Islands and clustered in a few New England towns, California and Hawaii. Partly as a result of its small size this conservative community did not develop a labor press of its own.[4] The general Portuguese-language press, however, is surprisingly large even though some of the periodicals may have been directed at Portuguese-speaking immigrants from Brazil. Originally a number of newspapers were published by priests and former printers - just as is the case with many other immigrant groups.

For the Spanish immigrant community the picture is quite different. (See below for Spanish-Puerto Rican, Spanish-Cuban and Spanish-Mexican migrants.) Since the 1890s a labor movement had begun to develop in Spain, an anarchist-oriented one centered in Barcelona, a Marxist-oriented one centered in Madrid. Of the workers who emigrated, about 134,000 arrived in the United States between 1890 and 1930. Many of them came indirectly via the (former) Spanish possessions of Puerto Rico and Cuba. Spanish migrant workers' colonies developed in Florida (Tampa, Ybor City), New York and later in a few other towns. Thousands of Spanish migrants were cigarmakers who moved from Spanish to Cuban and U.S. mainland centers. Linked with Cuban and Puerto Rican workers by their language, they were nevertheless divided hierarchically with the Spanish-European migrants occupying the top positions.

The Spanish-American radical press published by migrants from Europe belongs to two distinct periods and camps. From 1891 to 1914 eight anarchist labor periodicals were established, three of them lasting a year or less, two more than a decade and one for almost fifty years.[5] They were published in New York (including Brooklyn) and Tampa. While in the case of the German-American labor movement, anarchism was a temporary stage of development particular to the 1880s, for the Spanish Americans - as for the Italian Americans - it represented a long-lasting brand of working-class thought.

European events spawned the second "cluster" of Spanish-American periodicals. In 1923 a military dictatorship took control in Spain and in the same year a democratic and antifascist paper was established in the United States. Three others followed in the period up to 1940. The last two periodicals representing a free Spain were of communist or socialist leaning and appeared in the forties.[6] All six were published in New York including Brooklyn - which had also been the center of German exiles from fascism since the 1930s.

A third group of Spanish-language periodicals (six separate publications) is significantly different. All of these are union papers directed toward Spanish and Latin-American immigrants from Puerto Rico, Cuba and in one case other Spanish-speaking countries. They appeared from 1906 till 1981 and represented the cigarmakers (*El International*, Ybor City, 1906-26) and the garment workers (*Justicia*, New York, 1914-81). The Industrial Workers of the World published *Solidaridad* (New York, 1918-30). During the thirties and forties local labor organizations in New York and Chicago published *El Obrero* (New York, 1931-32), *Noticias de la UCAPAWA* (New York, 1939-49) and *Obrero de la carne* (Chicago, 1946-48). Two additional publications were issued in Washington *(Noticiario Obrero Norteamericano)* and by the CIO in New York (*Boletino Latino Americano de CIO*).

These publications addressing a Spanish-speaking labor force of differing ethnic or cultural origin provide the link to publications in Spanish aimed mainly at Puerto Rican or Mexican-American (Chicano) workers. Similarly, the last of the newspapers to be founded by the Spanish immigrants from Europe, *Liberación*, was at first only addressed to these immigrants, but later it tried to reach Puerto Rican and Latin-American Spanish-speaking workers in general. Several Puerto Rican publications of the 1890s and 1900s give important information on early labor migration to the United States. About half a dozen labor periodicals published on the island and two published in New York during the 1930s have also been discovered.

The Spanish-language Mexican-American (Chicano) press had its heyday during the first two decades of this century. It was aimed at Mexicans living in the United States as well as at opponents of the Diaz regime and Social Revolutionaries in Mexico. All of these papers can be classified as anarchist. One of them was a feminist periodical. From 1915 to 1919 the IWW issued two Spanish-language periodicals in Los Angeles. A general labor periodical came out in San Antonio, Texas in 1919. Thereafter no labor or radical periodicals could be found until the struggle of the farm workers began in California during the 1960s.

The Italian-language labor press began a continuous rise in the early 1890s (formative period 1888, 1892-1907). It maintained a high level of activity from 1908 to the mid-forties with temporary setbacks during World War One and the early depression years. After a steep decline in the late forties it maintained an even level through the fifties. Then another slow decline set in and at present only two periodicals are still being published. (See Table) While the early growth is due wholly to labor migration and the creation of Italian-American communities, the continuously large number of publications is explained by the early coming of fascism in Italy: Mussolini took power in 1922 and four years later parties and unions were made illegal. The political emigration of this period was largely working-class. Furthermore - and contrary to the situation of the later German exiles - the middle-class Italian-American community as well as parts of the working class viewed fascism at least in its early stages in a positive light. "Order" in Italy increased the respect of the mainstream society for the Italian ethnic community in the United States. Thus even refugee intellectuals and the few bourgeois opposition circles had to integrate into the larger working-class antifascist movement to avoid complete isolation.

Like its Spanish-American counterpart, the Italian labor movement had a strong anarchist wing throughout its history. This explains a peculiar characteristic of its press - its shortlivedness. Anarchists, who believed in the supreme power of education through the written and spoken word, went on lecture tours through the United States and founded periodicals wherever they happened to be, many of which published only a few issues.[7] The belief of anarchists in the power of education fitted well into the "spirit of the times." American social reformers collected and published statistics about poverty as well as poor working and living conditions in the firm belief that the powerful impression made by this data on Congress would lead to reform legislation. While the social reformers had to learn to lobby because the facts alone were not sufficient education for the political authorities, some anarchists switched to "propaganda by deed," i. e. the assassination of political leaders who headed a deeply inhuman system of exploitation and oppression. They too, fitted in with the "spirit of the times." Mainstream American society resorted to similar means to punish those at the bottom of the social scale: Italians were lynched in New Orleans in 1891, there was a riot against Greeks in South Omaha in 1909 and members of the IWW were molested, arrested and lynched on a number of occasions.

The following analysis of the Italian-American labor press will concentrate on the United States since immigration to Canada came later and remained comparatively small. Less than ten papers appeared there. In the United States of the total of about 190 periodicals seventy-two appeared in New York, another twenty in the surrounding area and a further ten in Philadelphia. Fifteen publications came from New England to which some skilled workers went in chain migrations from specific Italian areas to specific labor markets. Eleven publications came from the western Pennsylvania/New York state area. Thirty-two were published in the North Central area from Cleveland to Duluth, with Chicago (21) producing the lion's share. Three other minor centers are the mining areas of Colorado, Utah and Wyoming with twelve publications, the San Francisco Italian community with nine publications and the Tampa, Florida cigarmakers with five publications.

More than half of the Italian labor press appeared for less than two years. Another third survived from ten to fourteen years with heavy clustering in the lower time brackets and an average duration of only five and a half years. About one tenth which existed for more than 15 years, about 40 years on average, formed a "core press" similar to that of the German-American community. They show a wide geographic distribution and represent the major political divisions in the Italian-American labor movement.

Italian Periodicals Existing for More Than 15 Years			
1895-1920	*Mastro Paolo*	PA Philadelphia	labor
1896-1946	*Il Proletario*	NY New York	socialist
1897-1930	*Critica*	CA San Franc.	republican
1897-1926	*Unione*	CO Pueblo	labor
1902-1927	*Il Lavoratore Italiano*	CO Trinidad	labor union
1903-1919	*Cronaca sovversiva*	VT Barre	anarchist
1904-1948	*El International*	FL Tampa	labor union
1906-1955	*Risveglio*	CO Pueblo	reform
1907-1933	*Corriere di Chicago*	IL Chicago	socialist
1910-1967	*Corriere del populo*	CA San Franc.	socialist
1914-1932	*Lavoro*	NY New York	labor union
1914-1933	*United Mine Workers'J.*	IN Indianapolis	lab. union
1916-1946	*Martello*	NY New York	anarchist
1919+	*La Giustizia*	NY New York	labor union
1921+	*Parola del Populo*	IL Chicago	socialist
1922-1971	*Adunata dei refrattari*	NY New York	anarchist
1938-1967	*Controcorrente*	MA Boston	anarchist
1963-1979	*La Tribuna italiana*	Q Montreal	socialist

Major periods of change in the Italian-American press were the years from 1908 to 1919 with 80 periodicals founded and 74 closed down and the year of 1938 with ten periodicals founded and ten closed down. But the major dividing line of the press is 1922/23 - the advent of fascism in Italy. (See Figure 3)

Before 1923 the Italian-American radical press can be divided according to political and union affiliation into the large but internally divided anarchist section (51 publications), a socialist section (30), a general labor and labor union section (25), the syndicalist (3) and communist (1) sections, and finally a group of radical, pro-labor, republican and reform periodicals (7). Many of the journals that continued beyond 1922 became antifascist. The anarchist periodicals, which remained relatively numerous in the period from 1923 to 1946, can be divided into individualist, antiorganizational and federational publications. The socialist papers show a certain affinity to the Socialist Party (SP). The differences between SP and SLP were of limited interest to the Italian Americans. They established an Italian Socialist Federation, which united members of both parties, though it was sometimes affiliated with one or the other, mostly with the SP. Doctrinal differences never divided the Italian socialists as they did other groups. The Italian anarchists, on the other hand, established perhaps fifty percent of their periodicals in order to oppose other anarchist modes of thought rather than to address the migrant workers community as a whole. The labor press was directed mainly toward garment workers and cigarmakers. In a number of instances these journals also addressed other ethnic groups or fought against their dominating influence within a specific union.

A major difference compared with the left and labor press of other ethnic groups was the large number of connections the Italians had with their country. Not only did perhaps half of the Italian-American community remigrate, but a number of socialist and anarchist periodicals were closely tied to left parties, trends and events in Italy. Involuntarily this tradition was continued by the Italian communists in the 1923-46 period because their periodical publications had to be transferred to free countries, first France and later the United States. But this became an exile press which only began to consider the migrant audience in a secondary phase, when clandestine distribution of the press in Italy became more and more difficult.

In the period 1923-46 the major political and organizational differences continued, with the following types and numbers of publications appearing: anarchist (16), labor and labor union (7), socialist (4), communist including the exile press (5), reform (1). With the exception of a few anarchist publications devoted to internal polemics, many of these periodicals were antifascist. Additionally, an almost equal number of primarily antifascist periodicals were founded, the last one in 1946 to help returning exiles to re-adjust to the old society. Of the labor periodicals a number were devoted to struggles of left rank-and-file unionized immigrants against an increasingly conservative or corrupt, usually Anglo leadership.

After the war the ubiquitous AFL "free trade unionism" publication was also published in Italian.

The Italian ethnic press continued in 1948 with one new labor, socialist and communist publication each in addition to those that had survived the hardship of war and profascist attitudes. In Canada an antifascist press had made its appearance in the 1923-46 period. (Seemingly no Italian labor and radical periodicals existed before that date in Canada). After the war four labor, socialist and prolabor papers were published.

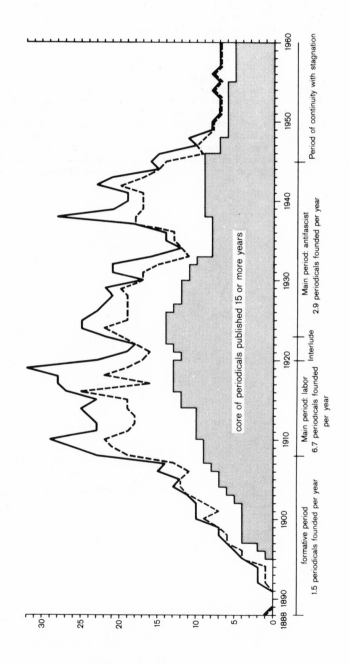

Figure 3   Italian-North American Labor and Radical Periodicals Founded and Closed Down by Years 1888 - 1960

——— Number of periodicals founded in addition to those existing in the previous year (= gross number of periodicals)

- - - Gross number of periodicals minus those that closed down in the same year (= net number of periodicals)

formative period
1.5 periodicals founded per year

Main period: labor
6.7 periodicals founded
per year

Interlude

Main period: antifascist
2.9 periodicals founded per year

Period of continuity with stagnation

core of periodicals published 15 or more years

While the basic dividing line of the Italian-American press was imposed by events in Italy, the boom in newly-founded periodicals from 1915 to 1919 stemmed from opposition to the war, from the need to speak out against the anti-radical persecutions by the so-called Department of Justice and other organizations and from the need to publish banned periodicals under new titles.

In summary it may be said that the press of the south European labor migrants - similar to that of those workers coming from western European countries and Germany - do not form a coherent set of publications. The press of each group was determined by characteristics particular to the individual ethnic groups and conditions in the home countries. The Spanish and Italian-American movements shared a strong tendency toward anarchist thought and long resistance to fascism and dictatorship. While a few remnants of the Italian-language radical press continue publication, the Spanish-language press has changed its character and background totally and now addresses migrants from Central (and South) America.

Notes

1. For a concise survey of Italian dialects, influence of contiguous languages and language "islands" see e.g. *Encyclopedia Americana* (New York, 1965), vol. 15, pp. 496-500.

2. Domenico Demarco, "L'émigration italienne de l'Unité á nos jours: profil historique," in *Les migrations internationales de la fin du XVIIIième siècle á nos jours* (Paris, 1980), pp. 595-614; Bruno Bezza, ed., *Gli italiani fuori d'Italia* (Milan, 1983).

3. Maurizio Punzo, "La Societa'" umanitaria e l'emigrazione. Dagli inizi del secolo alla prima guerra mondiale," pp. 119-144 in Bezza, ed., *Gli italiani.*

4. The Pan American Committee of Meat Workers published the *Obrero de la carne* (IL Chicago, 1946-48) in Spanish, English and Portuguese.

5. By first year of publication the eight Spanish-language anarchist periodicals were *El Despertar*, New York, 18911902; *El Esclavo*, Tampa, 1894-1898; *La Voz del Esclavo*, Tampa, 1900; *Doctrina Anarquista-Socialista*, Paterson, 1905; *Cultura Proletaria*, New York, 1910-1959; *Cultura Obrera*, Brooklyn, 1911-1923; *Brazo Y Cerebro*, New York, 1912-1914; *El Obrero Industrial*, Tampa, 1914.

6. By first year of publication the six periodicals of this group were *Espana Nueva*, 1923-1942; *Espana Republicana*, 1931-1935, *Frente Popular*, 1937-1939, continued by *Espana Libre*, 1939-1977; and *Pueblos Hispanos*, 1943-1944, continued by *Liberación*, 1946-1949.

7. Some scholars speak of "Single issue periodicals." These are not documented in the bibliography.

Italians

Language

Italian

Area covered

Italy

Compiled by

Annamaria Tasca

Istituto Nazionale per la storia del movimento di liberazione in Italia Milan, Italy

Acknowledgements

In recent years the Istituto Nazionale per la storia del movimento di liberazione in Italia has been collecting the Italian antifascist press published abroad. These library holdings have formed the basis for the compilation of this bibliography. In addition to the 'Fondo a Prato' held by the Istituto Nazionale, we refer especially to the microfilms reproducing the periodicals held by the Archivio centrale dello stato, Rome, the Fondazione Feltrinelli, Milan, the Fondazione Basso/ISSOCO, Rome and the Internationaal Instituut voor Soziale Geschiedenis, Amsterdam. Specialists, cooperating with the Istituto Nazionale on the present research have identified and described additional newspapers. We would like to thank the libraries, archives, historical institutions and centers both in Europe and North America that have allowed the cooperating specialists to consult their holdings.

We also want to thank Gianfausto Rosoli, of the Centro Studi Emigrazione, Rome, who, in allowing us to consult the 'Catalogo collettivo della stampa periodica italo americana (1836-1980)' by Pietro Russo (Roma, edizione provvisoria, 1983), has enabled us to find in a comparatively short time the newspapers held in Italian and American depositories. From Russo's catalogue we have also derived all information concerning the holdings we could not visit ourselves.

The Istituto Nazionale is grateful to Bruno Cartosio, University of Milan, both for his valuable cooperation and for sharing the results of his previous work on the Italian-American labor press. Many thanks also to Rossella Di Leo (Centro Studi Liberatari Pinelli, Milan) for her kind cooperation.

Cooperating specialists: Annamaria Tasca, editor; Luigi Bruti Liberati, responsible for the Italian-Canadian material; Adriana Dada, Nicoletta Serio for depositories in Italy; Laurette Fiocchi, Susanna Garroni, Wayne Heimbach for depositories in the United States; Sergio Sgaramella for depositories in Canada. To them all goes the gratitude of the Istituto Nazionale.

Depositories

Canada:

Cdn-OONL   National Library, Bibliothèque
           Nationale, Ottawa, O.

Italy

I-ACS   Archivio centrale dello stato, Roma.
I-BAB   Biblioteca e archivio Berneri, Pistoia.
I-BABo   Biblioteca dell'Archiginnasio, Bologna.
I-BAMi   Biblioteca Ambrosiana, Milano.
I-BCM   Biblioteca communale, Milano.
I-BMN   Biblioteca "Max Nettlau," Bergamo.
I-BNB   Biblioteca nazionale braidense, Milano.
I-BSMC   Biblioteca di storia moderna e contemporanea, Roma.
I-BUB   Biblioteca Università Bocconi, Milano.
I-CSLP   Centro studi liberatari Pinelli, Milano
I-FF   Fondazione Giangiacomo Feltrinelli, Milano.
I-IG   Istituto Gramsci, Roma.
I-INSML   Istituto nazionale per la storia del movimento di
           liberazione in Italia, Milano.
I-ISRT   Istituto storico della resistenza in Toscana, Firenze.
I-ISSOCO   Fondazione Lelio e Lisli Basso-ISSOCO, Roma.
I-ISTAM   Istituto di studi americani, Firenze.

Netherlands:

Nl-IISG   Internationaal Instituut voor Soci-
           ale Geschiedenis, Amsterdam.

United States:

Usa-CMS   Center for Migration Studies, Staten Island, NY.
Usa-CoP   Pueblo Regional Library, Pueblo, CO.
Usa-CSt-H   Stanford University, Hoover Institute on War,
              Revolution and Peace, Stanford, CA.
Usa-CtY   Yale University, New Haven, CT.
Usa-CU   University of California, Berkeley, CA.
Usa-CU-BANC   University of California, Bancroft Library, Berke-
              ley, CA.
Usa-DCL   U.S. Library of Congress, Washington, DC.
Usa-DL   U.S. Department of Labor Library, Washington, DC.
Usa-FU   University of Florida, Gainsville, FL.
Usa-ICHi   Chicago Historical Society, Chicago, IL.
Usa-ICRL   Center for Research Libraries, Chicago, IL.
Usa-IU   University of Illinois, Urbana, IL.
Usa-MB   Boston Public Library, Boston, MA.

§Usa-McP	Micro Photo Division, Bell and Howell Company, Wooster, OH.
Usa-MdBJ	Johns Hopkins University, Baltimore, MD.
Usa-MH	Harvard University, Cambridge, MA.
Usa-MiU	University of Michigan, Ann Arbor, MI.
Usa-MnU-I	University of Minnesota, Immigration History Research Center, St.Paul, MN.
Usa-NBM	Medical Research Library of Brooklyn, NY.
Usa-NjP	Princeton University, Princeton, NJ.
Usa-NN	New York Public Library, New York, NY.
Usa-NNC	Columbia University, New York, NY.
Usa-NNC-CI	Casa Italiano, Columbia University, New York, NY.
Usa-NNN	New York Academy of Medicine, New York, NY.
Usa-OU	Ohio State University, Columbus, OH.
<Usa-PPBI	The Emily G. Balch Institute for Ethnic Studies, Philadelphia, PA.
Usa-RHi	Rhode Island Historical Society, Providence, RI.
Usa-UU	University of Utah, Salt Lake City, UT.
Usa-WHi	State Historical Society of Wisconsin, Madison, WI.

Introduction

Between 1896 and 1976 more than 26 million people left Italy and emigrated to European and non-European countries. Over 6 million Italians went to the United States and Canada, and most of them, that is about 3 million, left Italy for the United States between 1900 and 1915.

Expatriations to the United States and Canada 1876-1976		
Years	to Canada	to the U.S.
1876-80	139	13,235
1881-85	1,059	74,758
1886-90	5,213	170,472
1891-95	2,344	206,596
1896-00	3,571	307,731
1901-05	19,654	998,352
1906-10	45,451	1,331,099
1911-15	71,134	1,054,701
1916-20	12,494	512,081
1921-25	20,655	225,969
1926-30	11,144	193,192
1931-35	2,077	66,220
1936-40	1,392	48,416
1941-45	-	-
1946-50	15,590	66,068
1951-55	10,5541	88,952
1956-60	123,791	104,507
1961-65	8,0714	65,174
1966-70	88,078	101,787
1971-76	23,496	55,022

Source: Gianfousto Rosoli, ed., *Un secolo di emigrazione italiana: 1876-1976* (Roma: Centro studi emigrazione, 1978), pp. 353-355.

The Italians who migrated to the United States after 1880 went to form, with Slavs and East European Jews, the so-called new immigration, which added to the old one, formed by British, Irish, German and Scandinavian workers. While in the preceding years the migratory flux from Italy, mostly from the Northern regions of Veneto, Friuli, Piedmont and Lombardy, had been mainly directed to South America, since 1880 the Italians who left Italy to find "pane e lavoro" (bread and work) in the New World came mainly from the south of Italy, that is from Campania, Calabria, Abruzzi e Molise and Sicily. The great majority of immigrants were unskilled workers, peasants in the mother country, used to be paid very little money for their daily work. Large part of the "meridionali" (people from the South) who left Italy at the turn of the century were illiterate and with little knowledge of western political structures. They emigrated mainly in order to earn some money and possibly return to their native village and buy some land. The first decades of massive immigration to the United States from the South saw the Italians employed as manual laborers in heavy, often seasonal jobs such as railroad or building construction. Their immigration was often temporary and limited to working men: this was one of the reasons for the reluctant participation of the immigrants in American life and for the strong links they kept with the mother country, which increased both ethnic prejudices against them and their isolation.

In fact, a peculiarity of the first Italian immigration was the so-called "padrone system." The *padrone*, or "boss," was an Italian who put the new immigrants in touch with the new country, representing the only link with America, purchasing the jobs, lending money, renting rooms.

Remigration from the United States and Canada 1905-1976*		
Years	from Canada	from the U.S.
1906-10	-	637,351
1911-15	13,163	602,998
1916-20	5,317	160,393
1921-25	4,194	216,474
1926-30	2,560	152,929
1931-35	1,367	70,548
1936-40	548	26,832
1941-45	-	206
1946-50	329	15,637
1951-55	3,163	15,164
1956-60	8,511	18,707
1961-65	730	1601
1966-70	10,794	10,885
1971-75	18,305	28,124

* data are available only after 1905

Source: Gianfausto Rosoli, ed., *Un secolo di emigrazione italiana 1876-1976* (Roma: Centro studi migrazione, 1978), pp.373-74.

Though the large majority of immigrants was formed by peasants from the South of Italy, other social classes contributed to the Italian-American colony, too. Among the immigrants there was also a number of artisans, tradesmen and industrial workers, those from the South being mainly tailors, barbers or shoemakers, while textile workers and marble cutters mainly came from the regions of Piedmont and Tuscany. Another small number of immigrants was constituted by intellectuals who had accomplished their studies but could not find employment in Italy. To complete an outline of the social composition of Italian immigrants, we must remember that there was a minority of radical leaders, bound to emigrate owing to political repression which had followed the popular riots of Sicily in 1894 (the so-called "fasci siciliani") or the upheavals in Milan in 1898, both repressed in blood by the authorities. Other Italian radicals used to go to the United States on "propaganda tours," in order to spread their radical ideas among the Italians. This partly accounts for the fact that Italian radicalism was, in those years, the reflection of the Italian left, more closely bound to Italian political events than to those in the United States and torn by the same ideological divisions that prevented Italian radicals from realizing political unity.

After 1900, the Italians who migrated to the United States began to have access to industrial occupations, and to have a more active part in American society and life. This fact, transforming the character of Italian immigration from temporary to permanent, also meant the immigration to the United States of the immigrants' families and created the preliminary conditions for the existence of a consistent ethnic community.

The characteristics of the Italian participation in the American labor movement are, obviously, strictly connected with the quality of immigration itself.

The unskilled immigrants of the late 19th century, badly exploited and working in isolated places such as quarries and on railroads had little chance to develop class consciousness. Often they were used as strike-breakers, thus deserving the despise of labor unions. While the unskilled rarely participated in the unions, quite a number of Italian artisans joined the labor unions of the Knights of Labor or the American Federation of Labor. The strenuous efforts of the Italian radicals, who exerted a strong influence on their fellow-countrymen, began to bring some results, especially in the fields of activity in which the Italians were more numerous.

Paterson, NJ, a textile center housing many workers from Piedmont, and Barre, VT, housing marble cutters from Tuscany, became important centers of radicalism. Another field in which skilled Italian workers were quite numerous were the coal, iron and copper mines; the Italian settlements in the mining states such as Pennsylvania, Ohio, Montana and Colorado became socialist strongholds, giving a remarkable contribution to the United Mine Workers, taking active part in several strikes.

The foundation of the Industrial Workers of the World (IWW) marked a turning point in the history of the Italian participation in the American labor movement. In fact the IWW, with its revolutionary ideals of class struggle, general strike and one large union, attracted the Italian radicals, who played a very important role in the two great strikes organized by the IWW, in Lawrence, MA (1912) and in Paterson, NJ (1913). After 1914, when the influence of the IWW began to decline in the eastern and mid-western states, many Italian socialists and "wobblies" active in the garment industries entered the unions in those fields, contributing to the new socialist orientation and industrial organization of both the old International Ladies Garment Workers Union and the new Amalgamated Clothing Workers of America.

World War One and the American participation in it had a considerable impact on Italian labor. The shortage of labor it necessarily implied and the reduction of immigration from Europe, marked a considerable step in the integration of Italian workers in the American industrial structure and, consequently, in their participation in labor organizations. The turning point in the history of Italian emigration, which completely changed both its quality and quantity, were the Immigration Quota Acts of 1921 and 1924 which, fixing at 3850 units per year the number of Italians allowed to enter the United States, sharply reduced the migratory flux.

The Italian political situation after the seizure of power by Mussolini in 1922 and the suppression of political parties in 1926 also accounted for the quality of immigration from Italy. From 1922 onward, the immigrants were mainly opponents of the fascist regime, that is politically conscious persons compelled to leave Italy and eager to struggle against dictatorship and in defense of the workers' rights. The Italians in the United States were, in the meantime, undergoing a process of Americanization: the time of the "birds of passage" was over, and the new American-born generation was taking part in American political and social life. Owing also to the policy of Americanization carried on by the American government under the Roosevelt' administration, the sons of the poor emigrants of the turn of the century came to occupy political positions and, most significantly, were now an active part of the organized working class.

What has been called the "third wave" of Italian immigration to the United States took place during World War Two: to the "fuorusciti" (a term used by fascist propaganda to label those who had left the country, "political exiles.") of the interwar years were added, at the outbreak of war, other political enemies of Mussolini, who had sought refuge in other European countries, especially in France. With their return to Italy at the end of the war the American "adventure" of so many Italians can be considered definitely closed.

The Italian Labor Press in the United States

The quick overview we have given at the characteristics of Italian immigration to the United States was necessary to build the framework within which to interpret the press produced by Italian workers. The importance of newspapers as a necessary source to study the political and social life of the ethnic community is nowadays universally known. Papers often represent a significant if not the only means to reconstruct the history of the Italian Americans, their activities and their relationship with American society, besides their ties to the mother country and their incidence on the relations between Italy and the United States. A survey of the great number of papers published by Italian immigrants in the years between the last decades of the 19th century and the end of World War Two immediately brings one thing to mind: the great number does not necessarily mean completeness but is, on the contrary, a demonstration of the poverty of the immigrants and of the complexity of divisions within their social fabric. The workers' papers were extremely poor, constantly on the verge of economic failure and were, during World War One and in the postwar years, subject to repression on the part of government authorities. The few available data concerning the circulation of the Italian-American press cannot but confirm the characteristics of poverty and instability mentioned above. Moreover, the irregularity of publication made the radical press little appealing to advertisers and, besides that, radical papers themselves selected the advertisers owing to ideological reasons. Radical papers had then to be supported by the parties and by the organizations they represented, besides being financed by their own readers and "friends," poor workers but also sympathizers who, even if they were not members of parties or organizations, gave money to support them. A significant example of this situation is *Il Proletario*, started in 1896, suspended in 1897 for lack of money and revived in 1898 when it could be financed by an association called "Aderenti al Proletario," whose members regularly contributed to the paper. That notwithstanding, in the following years, the newspaper was be forced again to suspend publication. Besides papers lasting for many years, such as *Il Proletario*, *La Parola dei Socialista*, or *Cronaca Sovversiva*, there was a large number of papers which lasted a few years or a few months, or which published a few issues only. The anarchists often published single issues (not included in this bibliography) for special occasions, such as anniversaries or celebrations. Some papers, lasting a few issues, are the expression of the need felt by the Italians to make their voice heard on special occasions, such as struggles or strikes. An example of this kind of paper is the *Bollettino dello sciopero dei sarti*, published in Chicago in 1910 by the Italian Committee of the United Garment Workers, which lasted only through the tailors' struggles, but is quite significant as it reflects the political growth of a specific section of the working class. Other short-lived papers are quite interesting as they are entirely bound to the activity of a single person. This is the case of the anarchist Giuseppe Ciancabilla, who in 1899 gave up the editorship of *La Questione Sociale* published in Paterson, NJ since 1885 and founded *L'Aurora*, in West Hoboken, NJ. *L'Aurora* then moved with its editor to Spring Valley, IL, to cease publication when Ciancabilla shared the editorship of *La Protesta Umana*, founded in Chicago in 1902. *La Protesta Umana* followed Ciancabilla when, owing to bad health, he was compelled to move to San Francisco, where it died shortly after its editor, in 1904. Besides the papers published on special occasions, or being the result of the political activity of single persons, many other newspapers were the result of the activities of substantial sections of Italian communities in different cities. This is the case of papers such as *La Fiaccola*, published in Buffalo in 1902-1912, by the Italian socialists and being the end product of several initiatives such as consumers' cooperatives, schools or credit cooperatives. Other examples of papers representing the life and activities of entire communities are those published in Colorado, where there was a strong Italian community among the miners, such as *L'Unione*, Pueblo 1897 and *Il Risveglio*, Denver 1906, official organ of mining districts 15 and 22. These papers are, in fact, the expression of the Italian participation in the miners' struggles of the prewar years. Another center where the Italian community expressed itself through significant papers was Barre, VT, divided as it was between the socialists, who temporarily published *La Cooperazione*, and the anarchists, who published *La Cronaca Sovversiva*, one of the most important Italian-American anarchist periodicals and the less important and short-lived *Il Contropelo* and *Il Corriere Libertario*. The irreconcilable differences separating the anarchists and the socialists were not limited to the town of Barre, but were, on the contrary, one of the characteristic aspects of Italian radicalism in the United States.

As we have already pointed out, most of the people who migrated to the United States left Italy with the intention of returning home, which, in fact, nearly half of them did. Another element to be taken into consideration is the profound isolation suffered by the immigrants, their difficulty in becoming active in the American labor movement. In the first decade of the century, the only political and ideological common ground for Italian radicals was Italy. The ties with the mother country deeply conditioned the American activities of anarchists and socialists, reproducing, on an American background, the problems and debates tearing the Italian left. The Italian anarchist leaders, in fact, extensively travelled to the United States, starting journals, publishing pamphlets, travelling on propaganda tours, organizing debates. Among them, we must mention Francesco Saverio Merlino, who started *Il Grido del Popolo* in New York in 1892, or Pietro Gori, who was among the founders of *La Questione Sociale*, in Paterson, NJ, 1899. The high number of anarchist mastheads does not, as a matter of fact, account for their strong presence in the labor movement but is evidence, on the contrary, of the lack of cohesiveness, of the divisions tearing from the inside the anarchist movement. On the ideological side, the most significant anarchist groups, in continuous struggle among themselves, were the antiorganizational group, the federalist or organizational one, and the individualistic one. The most diffused was the first one, refusing to accept any form of organizational structure, and believing in the common conscience as the means to constitute an anarchist community. It was supported by Luigi Galleani, who founded and directed *La Cronaca Sovversiva*, and later by *L'Adunata dei Refrattari* (1922), which intended to propagate its ideals. The most significant papers of the organizational group, inspired by Errico Malatesta, who tried to create organizational structures on a federal basis, were *Il Grido degli Oppressi* and *La Questione Sociale*. Among the few, scarcely important papers following the individualistic theories inspired by Max Stirner and sustaining the necessity of individual action, we must mention *Sorgiamo!* and *La Gogna*. A common characteristic of the anarchist papers, whatever their position inside the movement, was to be mostly theoretical papers, mainly devoted to debates and reporting essays and news on the Italian and European anarchist movements, with little attention paid to American politics. More than other radical periodicals, the anarchist press suffered from the restrictive laws of the war and postwar years, when many anarchists were also arrested and deported to Italy.

The socialists and their ties with the mother country exerted a considerable influence on Italian immigrants, too. The Socialist Party had been founded in Italy in 1892, separating the socialists from the anarchists, and needed cadres and representatives. This was the reason why, with the exception of Luigi Menotti Serrati, the main Italian socialist leaders did not cross the ocean to propagate their ideas as the anarchists did. Even so, they strongly influenced the Italian socialists in the United States, who depended on Italy for their theoretical guidelines. One of the two most important socialist mastheads, *Il Proletario*, was, at least in the years following its foundation in 1896, under direct Italian influence, and it became the official organ of the newly created Italian Socialist Federation in 1911 which - at times - was the Italian section of the SLP. During the editorship of Carlo Tresca, begun in 1904, the paper started to become really Italian-American, propagating the principles of revolutionary industrial unionism. *Il Proletario* became in fact, after the foundation of the IWW in 1905, first the sustainer and later the official organ of the Italian section of the new working-class organization, closely following its activity until 1916. It was in the IWW, a true revolutionary movement of the working class in the United States, that Italian workers could break their isolation and join the workers of all nationalities. Not all the socialists of the Italian Socialist Federation were willing to adhere to the IWW: among them Giuseppe Bertelli left *Il Proletario* in 1907, leaving New York for Chicago and organizing an Italian branch of the American Socialist Party. It was in Chicago in 1907 that Bertelli founded *La Parola dei Socialisti*, which became the organ of the moderate socialist wing.

A turning point in the history of Italian immigration and consequently, of its radical wing was represented, as we have seen, by World War One. During the war and in the postwar years, a sharp reduction of European immigration to the States took place and, alongside with it, an increasing request for work and the consequent steady introduction of Italian workers in the ranks both of the skilled workers and of the labor unions. The process of Americanization taking place in those years deeply affected the Italian-American labor press. The Washington administration wanted, in fact, to control the press and to rally it to the support of the war effort. While the large Italian-American commercial press rapidly became a vehicle of the American ideology and a medium for the diffusion of the government's viewpoint, thus contributing to the ongoing process of Americanization, the radical press underwent harsh repression. The Italian left (both socialists and anarchists were, on this occasion, on the same line) firmly opposed the war. This opposition, which did not cease after the entry of the United States into the war in April 1917, provided the authorities with the excuse for their repression of the radical press. Most radical papers underwent remarkable difficulties, some were compelled to cease publication, others could survive owing to the personal efforts of their sustainers. Many papers were denied the use of the mail by the Department of the Post Office: among them the anarchist *Cronaca Sovversiva* was obliged to discontinue publication while others, such as the IWW paper *Il Proletario* or the socialist *La Parola dei Socialisti* were temporarily compelled to suspend publication and to change their mastheads several times.

In the years following the war, during the "Red Scare" of 1919-1920, many radical leaders were deported to Italy, others left voluntarily, others underwent severe persecutions. Notwithstanding some successful activities, such as the participation in the Lawrence strike of 1919, the beginning of the 1920s saw the Italian radicals in quite a difficult condition. Both the anarchists and the socialists, whose press had been ground for political debates and struggles, were scattered and decimated by schisms. The original Italian Socialist Federation, founded in 1902, was dissolved in 1921: some of its leaders and members had entered other organizations such as garment unions (ILGWU or ACWA), or retired to private life. Others became members of the newly formed communist party (Workers Party of America), founded in 1921, whose official organ, *Alba Nuova*, followed in 1924 by *Il Lavoratore*, immediately became one of the most significant voices of the Italian left. Also the paper of the dissident socialist federation adhering to the Socialist Party, now *La Parola del Popolo*, had to suspend publication in 1929, to come out again in 1933. A symbol of the persecutions suffered by radicals in general and particularly by the anarchists were Bartolomeo Sacco and Nicola Vanzetti, who, arrested in 1920 on the charge of murder were finally sentenced to death in 1927. Their vicissitudes took large part in the radical press and the campaign to save them was one of the unifying themes of the Italian left, originating an official defense committee, proposed by Carlo Tresca then of *Il Martello*, while only *L'Adunata dei Refrattari* founded a committee of their own. The two most important anarchist papers of the interwar years were, in fact, sharply opposed to each other: Tresca's *Il Martello* was favorable to the alliance with other trade unions and democratic forces, while *L'Adunata dei Refrattari*, being opposed to any kind of cooperation on principle was isolated from the other Italian radicals.

The seizure of power by Mussolini in 1922 had brought a considerable political immigration, which strengthened the radical and antifascist forces in the United States in the twenties and thirties. Among the most important political exiles of these years we may quote the socialists Serafino Romualdi and Carmelo Zito, or the communist Vittorio Vidali (under the pseudonym Enea Sermenti). This new wave of politicized immigrants reinforced Italian radicalism, creating a common ground of involvement and struggle. Even if divided by ideological conflicts, socialists and communists, republicans and anarchists were united in their fight against the fascist regime. The Italian-American community had, in general, favorably accepted fascism and its propaganda as it revalued, in the eyes of many, the international role of Italy giving a new dignity to the Italians abroad. In addition to the official publications of the fascist government (*Il Grido della Stirpe*, *Giovinezza*) most Italian-American commercial papers were openly favorable to Mussolini, at least until the outbreak of World War Two, and largely contributed to influence public opinion. The most important of them were the widely diffused *Il Progresso Italo-americano*, *Il Corriere d'America*, *Bollettino della sera*.

American authorities openly sustained pro-fascist organizations and papers, which obviously increased the difficulties antifascists had to face. Perhaps the most significant moment in the antifascist struggle is represented by the Antifascist Alliance of North America, whose Manifesto was published in the New York paper *Il Nuovo Mondo* in August 1926. Among those who signed the Manifesto were, besides such unions as ACWA and ILGWU, antifascist papers of various tendencies: *Il Lavoratore*, *Il Martello*, *La Scopa*, *Il Lavoro*, *Giustizia* and *Il Nuovo Mondo*. *Il Nuovo Mondo*, a labor antifascist daily, had started publication in New York in 1925 but had to cease publication in 1930, owing mainly to internal and economic difficulties, and was substituted by *Stampa Libera*. The short-lived *Il Nuovo Mondo* is a clear example of the internal struggles tearing the antifascist groups, soon undermining the temporary unity reached by the Antifascist Alliance. But also the determination of the

Italian-American conservatives to silence the voice of antifascism had a role in its demise.

As antifascism is, in the late 1920s and in the 1930s, the central motif of American radicalism becoming the distinctive element of the radical press, an identification of the antifascist press with the workers' press is quite inevitable. The defense of democracy against dictatorship automatically became the defense of the exploited against the exploiters, and of the struggles of workers to obtain better living conditions. It must be said that the antifascist press, especially with the new wave of political exiles, the "fuorusciti" who reached the United States at the outbreak of World War Two, was often more concerned with international politics, the international role of Italy and her future after the end of the war than it was with the American and labor scene. Besides informing on the Italian situation, the Italian-American antifascist press also fulfilled the important task of establishing connections and mobilizing public opinion also outside the United States, as it happened for the Sacco and Vanzetti trial or during the Spanish Civil War in 1936.

Again, even if on different terms than before World War One, the ties with the mother country deeply affected the Italian immigrants. After the international events which lead to the outbreak of World War Two, the antifascists in the United States felt it their task to inform both Italian Americans and Americans of facts and events the official press did not mention, and convince the Americans that the struggle against fascism was a struggle for democracy. With the American intervention in the war, the antifascist press became more and more engaged in the political struggle, producing papers that were the organs of parties and organizations but also independent ones, open to different contributions. Among the Italian intellectuals who contributed to antifascist papers were people as different as Gaetano Salvemini (a leftist university professor), Luigi Sturzo (a Catholic), Carlo Sforza (a nobleman), Max Ascoli (a pro-labor man), Aldino Felicani (an anarchist), Giuseppe Berti (a communist), Mario Lupis (a liberal radical). The antifascist papers also set the stage for the debates on the postwar assessment of Italy. They were the place where, among the different groups and within them, were foreshadowed the alliances and the alignments that would lay the basis of the relationship between Italy and the United States in the postwar period. One of the most active antifascist organizations, collecting intellectual democratic exiles, was the Mazzini Society, so called after the name of the republican leader of the Italian Risorgimento in the 19th century. Founded by Max Ascoli, it intended to rally non-communist exiles, establishing also contacts with the American administration. After trying to use the monthly *Il Mondo* as its organ, it published first the bulletin *Mazzini News*, then, since 1942, the weekly *Nazioni Unite*. Though strenuously fighting both fascism and the Italian-American "prominenti," first among them Generoso Pope, editor of *Il Progresso Italo-americano*, the Mazzini Society was deeply anticommunist, even after the Nazi aggression on the Soviet Union. Internal debates, especially on the Mazzini's ties with the American Department of State, brought it to an end in 1946.

Another republican/antifascist paper was *La Legione dell'Italia del Popolo*, edited by Randolfo Pacciardi, which tried to create a unified front including the communists, often isolated from the other antifascists. On its part, the communist press acquired greater importance with the publication in 1939 of *L'Unita del Popolo*, edited by Ambrogio Donini, which had the task of keeping the Italian-American community informed of the war and of Italy, while the ideological organ of the Italian Communist Party was *Lo Stato Operaio*, transferred to the United States from France in 1940.

Having been, as we have seen, so closely bound to the fight against fascism and to the consequences of the war, the Italian-American political press had no reason for existing after the end of World War Two. Its contributors returned to Italy, and the major papers of the war period ceased publication. Only a few of them survived, even if with no significant political role. Among them the old *La Parola del Popolo*, a social-democratic information review still published in Chicago, and *L'Adunata dei Refrattari*, ceased in 1971, which had little influence on the Italian-American community. With World Two Two the rich flow of the press published by Italian workers in the United States, slowly begun during the late 19th century, had definitely come to an end.

The Italian Labor Press in Canada

Italian immigration to Canada is not much different from the one directed toward the United States, but it becomes numerically significant later. Before World War One and during the interwar years, the Italian-Canadian community was relatively small, numbering about 120,000 people. Though police reports in the archives in Rome mentioned some labor leaflets before the 1920s no further information on them could be obtained. Therefore the scope of these notes is limited to the years between the advent of fascism in Italy in 1922 and its fall in 1945.

The antifascists were only a slight minority. In fact fascist officials, though at first extremely cautious in their work among Italian Canadians, to avoid arousing suspicions from federal authorities, in a few years gained a strong hold on the immigrant community. Most mutual-benefit associations, among them the powerful "Order of the Sons of Italy," fell under fascist control, directly or indirectly; Italian-language newspapers turned into mouthpieces of the regime or disappeared. At the same time antifascist action was seriously hampered since the "Red Scare psychology" of the 1920s had developed an atmosphere of suspicion surrounding any form of worker activities. Moreover, inner dissent between socialists and communists tore the Italian leftists apart.

Owing to this situation Italian-Canadian antifascists were confronted with a very difficult task as can be easily inferred from the case of *Il Risveglio Italiano* of Montreal. When the young antifascist Antonino Spada, who was in Canada on a student visa, started in 1926 the newspaper *Il Risveglio Italiano*, the experiment lasted only four months. Yielding to pressure from the Italian Consul General the Department of Immigration suppressed the paper and placed its editor under order of deportation. Eventually Spada avoided this fate as a result of a petition signed by several thousand people; nonetheless, the paper had to stop publication.

This was a substantial fascist victory since Montreal had the largest Italian community of the Dominion. Then the task of spreading antifascist propaganda rested on the shoulders of Italian militant workers of Toronto. In this city a "Matteotti Club" had been established in 1926 as a protest against the assassination of the Italian socialist leader Giacomo Matteotti by fascists in Rome in 1924, but the first real sign of cooperation among different wings of antifascists came in 1928 with the foundation of the "Mazzini Club," among whose supporters there were both socialists and communists. It was the "Mazzini Club" which gave birth in 1933 to the socialist newspaper *La Voce Operaia*. Being the expression of left wing workers, the paper was socialist in outlook and uncompromisingly anticapitalist but it declared itself independent of any political parties as stated in the editorial published in the first issue of July 29, 1933.

At the beginning of the 1930s fascist activities in Canada reached their peak; after the posting of new fascism-imbued consuls in Ottawa, Montreal and Toronto large-scale propaganda began to flood the country. Italian officials could take advantage of the fact that the fascist regime was by then internationally recognized as a factor of stability in the European balance of power and as a stronghold against communism. As a result, blackshirts could march openly in Canadian streets and huge meetings were held with the participation of both Italian and Canadian authorities. Probably these growing activities were fostered by the friendly attitude of the new conservative Premier R.B. Bennett, in charge from 1930 to 1935, who considered Italian-Canadian fascists as law-abiding citizens fighting against communism.

La Voce Operaia tried to counteract fascist propaganda in many ways. It published news and reports about Italy which would never have appeared in other newspapers; thus it clashed with *Il Bollettino Italo-Canadese*, mouthpiece of the Italian vice-consulate in Toronto. Moreover, it exposed schemes and frauds of local fascists who were trying to gain control of all Italian mutual-benefit associations. In this task the paper scored some success, at least to the extent that it showed that the opposition's voice was still alive, in spite of overwhelming fascist power.

Unfortunately *La Voce Operaia* had to discontinue its publication in the spring of 1935, just at the eve of Mussolini's aggression on Ethiopia. This was a turning point in Italian-Canadian history since for the first time Canadians came to realize that fascist ruthlessness could be used also against western democracies. Thus, in the crucial months of the Ethiopian campaign antifascists lacked a newspaper which could counteract fascist propaganda among Italian Canadians. In fact, after 1936, fascism lost part of its popularity among Canadians, but it gained new support from Italian immigrants who were proud of the new Roman empire built by Mussolini in Africa.

A new antifascist Toronto newspaper, *Il Lavoratore*, began its regular publication in March 1936, as a result of an initiative taken by local Italian communists. That notwithstanding, the paper was open to collaboration with other political forces since it followed the Popular Front's line adopted by Comintern in 1936. *Il Lavoratore* fostered a wide antifascist alliance, supporting both the Cooperative Commonwealth Federation (pro-labor party founded in 1933) and the Canadian Communist Party. With regard to foreign policy it tried to make people aware of the growing Nazi-fascist menace, embodied in such aggressions as those against republican Spain, Austria and Czechoslovakia. Eventually *Il Lavoratore* had to be discontinued in September 1938, due to the rising disputes among the groups involved but a few weeks later a new organ, *La Voce degli Italo-Canadesi*, started its publication. The paper tried to pursue the line of large antifascist coalitions, enlisting among its supporters small businessmen, merchants and professional people.

This new line, however, did not last long. In fact, after the signing of the Nazi-Soviet non-aggression pact of August 1939, and the outbreak of World War Two, *La Voce* aligned itself with the communist position of non-intervention in what was considered to be a capitalistic war. As a result most non-communists withdrew their support and in spring 1940, the paper was closed by Canadian authorities. During its short-lived existence, however, *La Voce* led an effective struggle against local fascists who were still propagating fascist ideas among the Italian-Canadian community. Less effective was its attempt to avoid hard wartime measures against Italian Canadians; at the beginning of 1940 the feeling that Mussolini would soon get into war on Hitler's side created a mounting anti-Italian sentiment, foreshadowing what happened in June 1940, when several hundred Italian-Canadian "enemy aliens" were arrested and taken to internment camps.

During the war years Italian antifascists were confronted with an extremely difficult task; the immigrant community was still shocked by the internments and the antifascist front was badly split after the outlawing of the Canadian Communist Party in 1940. It was only in 1941, after the Nazi attack on Russia, that a change took place. Now all antifascists could freely cooperate against a common foe; moreover, Canadian authorities were beginning to realize the importance of Italian-Canadian support to the war effort. As a consequence a number of initiatives flourished, among which were the foundation of a "Free Italy Movement" and of a "Mazzini Society of Canada." In this new political climate protestant minister Augusto Bersani was able to launch in spring 1942, the paper *La Vittoria* which was at the beginning an unofficial organ of the "Mazzini Society." Shortly afterwards Bersani turned the paper over to a group headed by the Italian Communist Ennio Gnudi, who had just moved from New York to Toronto. This change was not praised by Canadian authorities, but in general the paper continued to pursue a non-sectarian political line, except for the harsh polemic against right-wing antifascists who supported the new monarchical Badoglio government established in Italy after 1943. After the Italian armistice *La Vittoria* maintained that it was the supreme duty of the allies to sweep away all remnants of the fascist regime and to give free hand to antifascists in the administration of freed Italy. Eventually *La Vittoria* was discontinued at the end of 1943, due to lack of funds and support from Canadian officials.

Bibliography

United States

Andreucci, Franco, and Detti, Tommaso.

> *Il movimento operaio italiano. Dizionario biografico 1853-1943* [The Italian Workers' Movement. A Biographical Dictionary 1853-1943]. 5 vols. Roma: Editori Riuniti, 1979.

N.W. Ayer and Son's Directory.

> *Newspapers and Periodicals.* Philadelphia, annually 1890-1930.

Bettini, Leonardo.

> *Bibliografia dell'anarchismo* [A Bibliography of Anarchism]. Vol. 1, part 1. Periodici e numeri unici anarchici pubblicati all'estero [Anarchist Periodicals and Single Issues Published Abroad]. Firenze: CP Editrice, 1976.

Bianco, Carla, and Anguili, E.

> *Emigrazione. Una ricerca antropologica sui processi di acculturazione relativi all'emigrazione italiana negli Stati Uniti* [Migration. An Anthropological Research on the Cultural Processes Concerning the Italian Emigration to the United States]. Bari: Dedalo, 1980.

Boyd, Caroli Betty.

> *Italian Repatriation from the United States 1900-1914.* New York: CMS, 1973.

Calvi, Giulia.

> *Societa industriale e cultura operaia negli Stati Uniti 1880-1917* [Industrial Society and Workers' Culture in the United States 1880-1917]. Roma: Bulzoni, 1979.

Cartosio, Bruno.

> "Gli emigrati italiani e l'Industrial Workers of the World" [The Italian Emigrants and the IWW]. In *Gli italiani fuori d'Italia*, edited by Bruno Bezza, pp. 359-95. Milano: Angeli, 1983.

> "Italian Workers and Their Press in the United States." In *The Press of Labor Migrants in Europe and North America*, edited by Christiane Harzig and Dirk Hoerder, pp. 423-443. Bremen, 1985,

Cerrito, Gino.

> "Sull'emigrazione anarchica italiana negli Stati Uniti d'America" [On the Italian Anarchist Emigration to the United States]. *Volontà* (1969), pp. 269-276.

Chicago Public Library.

> Work Projects Administration (WPA). *Bibliography of Foreign Language Newspapers and Periodicals Published in Chicago.* Compiled by Chicago Public Library Omnibus Project. Chicago, 1942.

Ciuffoletti, Zeffiro.

> *Degl'Innocenti Maurizio. L'emigrazione nella storia d'Italia 1868-1975* [Emigration in the History of Italy]. 2 vols. Firenze: Vallecchi, 1978.

Cordasco, Francesco, and Lagumina, Salvatore.

Italians in the United States. A Bibliography of Reports, Texts, Critical Studies and Related Materials. New York: Ovide Editions, 1972.

Cutter, Margot and Thompson, Margaret.

A Survey of the Italian Language Press in the United States. Princeton, NJ, 1942.

Dadà, Adriana.

"Contributo metodologico per una storia dell' emigrazione e dell'antifascismo italiano negli Stati Uniti" [A Methodological Contribution to the History of Italian Emigration and Antifascism in the United States]. *Annali dell'Instituto di Storia. Facoltà di magistero*. University of Florence, no. 1 (1979), pp. 197-218.

De Ciampis, Mario.

"Storia del movimento socialista rivoluzionario italiano" [A History of the Italian Socialist Revolutionary Movement]. In *La parola del popolo*. 50th Anniversary 1908-1958, Dec. 1958/Ja 1959, pp. 136-163.

Delzell, Charles F.

Mussolini's Enemies. Princeton, NJ: Princeton University Press, 1961.

Diggins, John P.

Mussolini and Fascism: A View from America. Princeton, NJ: Princeton University Press, 1972.

Dore, Grazia. ed.

Bibliografia per la storia dell'emigrazione italiana in America [A Bibliography for the History of Italian Emigration to America]. Roma: Tipografia del Ministero degli Affari Esteri, 1956.

Fedeli, Ugo.

"Giornali, riviste, numeri unici anarchici" [Anarchist Papers, Reviews, Single Issues]. *Movimento operaio*, no. 11/12 (1950).

Fenton, Edwin.

Immigrants and Unions: A Case Study: Italians and American Labor 1870-1920. New York: Arno Press, 1975.

Fink, Gary, ed.

Biographical Dictionary of American Labor. Westport, CT: Greenwood Press, 1984.

Foester, Robert F.

The Italian Emigration of Our Times. Cambridge, MA: Harvard University Press, 1924.

Foner, Philip S.

History of the Labor Movement in the United States. 5 vols. New York: International Publisher, 1955.

Gutman, Herbert G.

Work, Culture and Society in Industrializing America. New York: Vintage Books, 1977.

Iorizzo, Luciano J., and Mondello, Salvatore.

The Italian Americans. New York: Twayne Publishers, Inc., 1971.

La Gumina, Salvatore, ed.

Ethnicity in American Political Life: The Italian American Political Experience. New York: AIHA, 1969.

Laslett, John H.M.

Labor and the Left. A Study of Socialist and Radical Influences in the American Labor Movement 1881-1924. New York, London: Basic Books Inc. Publishers, 1970.

Legnani, Massimo.

"La stampa antifascista 1922-1943" [The Antifascist Press 1922-1943]. In *La stampa italiana nell'età fascista*, edited by Valerio Castronovo and Nicola Tranfaglia. Bari: Laterza, 1988.

Livi, Bacci Massimo.

L'immigrazione e l'assimilazione degli italiani negli Stati Uniti secondo le statistiche demografiche americane [Immigration and Assimilation of the Italians in the United States According to American Demographic Statistics]. Milano: Giuffré, 1961.

Lopreato, Joseph.

Italian Americans. New York: Random House, 1970.

Martellone, Anna Maria.

"La presenza dell'elemento etnico italiano nella vita politica degli Stati Uniti dalla non partecipazione alla post-etnia" [The Presence of the Italian Ethnic Element in the Political Life From Non-Participation to Post-Ethnicity]. In *Gli italiani fuori d'Italia*, edited by Bruno Bezza, pp. 349-358. Milano: Angeli, 1983.

Martellone, Anna Maria, ed.

La 'questione' dell'immigrazione negli Stati Uniti [The 'Question' of Immigration to the United States]. Bologna: Il Mulino, 1980.

McBride, Paul M.

The Italians in America. An Interdisciplinary Bibliography. Ithaca: AIHA, 1976.

Migone, Gian Giacomo.

Gli Stati Uniti e il fascismo [The United States and Fascism]. Milano: Feltrinelli, 1980.

Molinari, Augusta.

"I giornali delle comunità anarchiche italo-americane" [The Papers of the Italian-American Anarchist Communities]. *Movimento operaio e socialista*, no. 1/2 (1981), pp. 117-130.

Montana, B. Vanni.

Amarostico. Testimonianze euro-americane [Amarostico. A European-American Witness]. Livorno: Bastogi, 1975.

Nelli, Humbert S.

Italians in Chicago 1880-1930. A Study in Ethnic Mobility. London, New York: Oxford University Press, 1970.

Ortoleva, Peppino.

"Una voce dal coro: Angelo Rocco e lo sciopero di Lawrence del 1912" [A Voice From the Choir: Angelo Rocco and the Lawrence Strike in 1912]. *Movimento operaio e socialista*, no. 1/2 (1981), pp. 5-32.

Paoli, Gumina Deanna.

The Italians of San Francisco 1850-1930. New York: CMS, 1978.

La Parola del Popolo.

[The Voice of the People]. 50th Anniversary 1908-1958, Dec. 1958/Ja. 1959.

Pozzetta, George E. ed.

Pane e lavoro. The Italian-American Working Class. Toronto: MHSO, 1980.

Revolutionary Radicalism.

Revolutionary Radicalism.Its History, Purpose and Tactics. Report of the Joint Legislative Committee Investigating Seditious Activities. Filed 24 April 1920 in the Senate of New York. 4 vols. Vol. 2, part 1, pp. 2003-06. Albany, NY: J.B. Lyons Co., 1920.

Romualdi, Serafino.

"Uomini, forze ed eventi nella Local 89" [Men, Forces and Events in Local 89]. *Local LXXXIX,* XV Anniversary ILGWU. New York, 1934.

Rosoli, Gianfausto, ed.

Un secolo di emigrazione italiana 1876-1976 [A Century of Italian Emigration]. Roma: CSER, 1978.

Russo, Pietro.

Catalogo collettivo della stampa periodica italo americana 1836-1980 [Catalogue of the ItalianAmerican Periodical Press]. Edizione provvisoria. Roma: Centro Studi Emigrazione, 1983.

Russo, Pietro.

"La stampa periodica italo americana" [The Italian-American Periodical Press]. In *Gli italiani negli Stati Uniti* [The Italians in the United States]. Firenze: ISTAM, 1972.

Salvemini, Gaetano.

Memorie di un fuoruscito [Memories of a 'fuoriuscito' (exile)]. Milano: Feltrinelli, 1960.

Sori, Ercole.

L'emigrazione italiana dall'Unità alla seconda guerra mondiale [The Italian Emigration From the 'Unità' to World War Two]. Bologna: Il Mulino, 1979.

Tirabassi, Maddalena.

"La Mazzini Society 1940-1946. Un' associazione degli anti fascisti italiani negli Stati Uniti" [The Mazzini Society, 1940-1946. An Association of the Italian Antifascists in the United States]. In *Italia e America dalla grande guerra a oggi* [Italy and America form World War One to Our Days]. Padova: Marsilio, 1976.

Tomasi, Lidio F.

The Italians in America: the Progressive View 1891-1914. New York: Center for Migration Studies. 1972.

Tomasi, Silvano M., ed.

Perspectives in Italian Immigration and Ethnicity. New York: Center for Migration Studies, 1977.

Tomasi, Silvano M., and Engel, M.H., ed.

The Italian Experience in the United States. New York: Center for Migration Studies, 1970.

Torregrossa, Antonietta.
"Antonio Crivello." In *La Parola del Popolo*, 50th Anniversary 1908-1958, Dec. 1958/Ja 1959.

U.S. Library of Congress.
Union List of Serials in the Libraries of the United States and Canada. 5 vols. New York: H.W. Wilson Comp., 1965.

Varsori, Antonio, ed.
L'antifascismo italiano negli Stati Uniti durante la seconda guerra mondiale. [Italian Antifascism in the United States during World War Two]. Roma: Archivio Trimestrale, 1984.

Vecoli, Rudolph J.
"Anthony Capraro and the Lawrence Strike of 1919." In *Pane e lavoro. The Italian-American Working Class*, edited by George E. Pozzetta. Toronto: MHSO, 1980.

"The Italian Immigrants in the United States Labor Movement from 1880 to 1929." In *Gli italiani fuori d'Italia*, edited by Bruno Bezza. Milano: Angeli, 1983.

Vecoli, Rudolph J, ed.
Italian-American Radicalism: Old World Origins and New World Developments. New York: American-Italian Historical Association, 1973.

Velikonja, Joseph.
Italians in the United States. Bibliography. Carbondale, IL: Southern Illinois University, 1963.

Venturini, Nadia.
"Le comunità italiane negli Stati Uniti fra storia sociale e storia politica" [The Italian Communities in the United States Between Social and Political History]. *Rivista di storia contemporanea*, no. 2 (1984), pp. 189-218.

Vezzosi, Elisabetta.
"La Federazione Socialista Italiana del Nord America tra autonomia e scioglimento nel sindacato industriale 1911-1921" [The Italian Socialist Federation of North America Between Autonomy and Fusion in the IWW 1911-1921]. *Studi emigrazione*, no. 73 (1984), pp. 81-109.

Wasserman, Paul, and Morgan, Jean.
Ethnic Information Sources of the United States (Detroit: Gale Research Co., 1976.

Wynar, Lubomyr R. and Wynar, Anne F, ed.
Encyclopedic Directory of Ethnic Newspapers And Periodicals in the United States. Littleton, CO: Libraries United Inc., 1976.

Yans-McLaughlin, Virginia.
Family and Community. Italian Immigrants in Buffalo 1880-1930. Urbana: University of Illinois Press, 1982.

Canada

Bruti Liberati, Luigi.

Il Canada, l'Italia e il fascismo 1919-1945 [Canada, Italy and Fascism 1919-1945]. Roma: Bonacci, 1984.

"La comunita italo-canadese." In *Gli italieni fuori d'Italie*, edited by Bruno Bezza, pp. 397-418. Milano: Angeli, 1983.

Hann, R.G., and Kealey, G.S.

Primary Sources in Canadian Working Class History, 1860-1930. Kitchener, O: Dumont Press Graphix, 1973.

Harney, Robert F.

Dalla Frontiera alle Little Italies. Gli italiani in Canada 1800-1945 [From the Frontier to the Little Italies. The Italians in Canada, 1800-1945]. Roma: Bonacci, 1984.

MacLaren, Duncan.

Ontario Ethnic Cultural Newspapers 1835- 1972: An Annotated Checklist. Toronto: University of Toronto Press, 1973.

Principe, Angelo.

Italo-Candadian Antifascist Press in Toronto, 1922-1960. Vol. 1. Proceedings of the Italian Section, Northeast Modern Language Association Conference, 20-22 March 1980.

The Italo-Canadian Press

The Italo-Canadian Press in Toronto 1922- 1940. Nemla Italian Studies, vol. IV, 1980.

Spada, Antonino.

The Italians in Canada. Ottawa, Montreal: Riviera Printers, 1969.

Annotated Bibliography

ABRUZZO E MOLISE	CO Pueblo	1924-1926

Title trans.:	Name of a region in Central Italy	*First issue:*	1 Ja 1924
Subtitle:	Gazzetta settimanale diretta da V. Massari	*Last issue:*	31 D 1926
Add. lang.:		*Vols. (nos.):*	VII(1) - IX(52)
First editor:	Vincenzo Massari	*Frequency:*	w
First publ.:		*Preservation:*	2
Related pubs.:	c *Marsica Nuova*, s *L'Unione*	*Supplements:*	
Circulation:		*Category:*	antifascist

Depositories: I-ISTAM (2,m); Usa-CoP (2); Usa-CU-BANC (2); Usa-ICRL (2,m); Usa-IU (2); Usa-MH (2); Usa-OU (2)

Subtitle translation: A Weekly Gazette Directed by V. Massari.

Printed by the Abruzzi community, this newspaper mainly dealt with the social, political and administrative life in the Italian region of the Abruzzi and in the Abruzzi settlement in the United States.

L'ADUNATA DEI REFRATTARI	NY New York	1922-1971

Title trans.:	The Call of the Refractaires	*First issue:*	14 Ap 1922
Subtitle:	Pubblicazione quindicinale	*Last issue:*	15 Ap 1971
Add. lang.:		*Vols. (nos.):*	I(1)-L(4)
First editor:	Costantino Zonchello	*Frequency:*	bw,w,m
First publ.:		*Preservation:*	1
Related pubs.:		*Supplements:*	
Circulation:		*Category:*	anarchist

Depositories: Usa-NN (2,m); Usa-MnU-I (2); Nl-IISG (1); I-ISSOCO (2); I-ISTAM (2); I-BMN (2)

Subtitle translation: A Biweekly Publication.

The English title of the paper also appeared on the masthead. This was one of the most interesting Italian-American anarchist publications both for its duration and for its wide international circulation among anarchists. Like most anarchist papers, it dealt mainly with ideological topics and devoted more space to political comments on the international situation than to North American events. Its principles were those of Galleani's *Cronaca Sovversiva* [Subversive Chronicle], that is to say that it encouraged solidarity among anarchists and individual action as opposed to planned organization. This policy aroused criticism, particularly from the contributors of *Il Martello* [The Hammer] edited by Carlo Tresca. In the twenties *L'Adunata* formed an unofficial committee in defense of Saco and Vanzetti (the official committee being promoted by its leading spirits Tresca and Felicani). The paper was edited by Costantino Zonchello until 1925, when he resigned "for personal reasons." Since 1924 his management of *L'Adunata* had been strongly under attack (e.g. from *La Sferza* [The Lash], *Il Pensiero* [The Thought], *Il Bohemien*

[The Bohemian].

L'Adunata backed the Antifascist Alliance of North America but in the late thirties it was charged with having published the names of Italian-American antifascists, thus denouncing them to the police.

In 1927 its editor was Ilario Margarita, who founded *L'Aurora* [The Dawn] in early 1928. Margarita was replaced in 1928 by Max Sartin, who published "Rivoluzione e controrivoluzione. Manifesto dei gruppi anarchici del Nord America" [Revolution and Counter-revolution. Manifesto of the Anarchist Groups of North America] (New York 1944), that gave information on the groups supporting *L'Adunata*. In 1944-1945 the paper published three special issues designed to be secretly introduced into Italy. Notwithstanding the fierce polemics that for different reasons followed its publication, in the following years *L'Adunata* was to become the only Italian-American anarchist paper. It ceased publication in 1971.

L'AGITAZIONE		MA Boston	1920-1925
Title trans.:	Agitation	*First issue:*	? D 1920
Subtitle:	Organo del Comitato di difesa pro Sacco e Vanzetti	*Last issue:*	F 1925
Add. lang.:		*Vols. (nos.):*	I(1)-IV(1)
First editor:	Aldino Felicani	*Frequency:*	bw, ir
First publ.:		*Preservation:*	2
Related pubs.:	s *La Protesta Umana*	*Supplements:*	
Circulation:		*Category:*	anarchist

Depositories: Nl-IISG (2,o); I-INSML (2:[1922-25],mp)

Subtitle translation: The Organ of the Sacco and Vanzetti Defense Committee.

The organ of the committee organized by the anarchist Carlo Tresca with the support of most of the radical press, this bulletin was entirely dedicated to the defense of the two anarchists, reporting on the trial against them, raising funds and organizing meetings. Its work was continued by *La Protesta Umana* [Human Protest] in 1926.

ALBA		PA Pittsburgh	1929-1931
Title trans.:	Dawn	*First issue:*	1 Jl 1929
Subtitle:	Periodico libertario redatto da operai	*Last issue:*	Jl/Ag 1931
Add. lang.:		*Vols. (nos.):*	I(1)-III(5-6)
First editor:	Francesco Russo	*Frequency:*	ir
First publ.:		*Preservation:*	1
Related pubs.:		*Supplements:*	
Circulation:		*Category:*	anarchist

Depositories: Nl-IISG (1,o); I-INSML (1,mp)

Subtitle translation: Libertarian Periodical Edited by Workers.

This was founded in order to create a discussion forum for North American anarchists in answer to the internal struggles that ravaged the anarchist movement. It asked its contributors not to be too insulting in their language and allusions. It published information about activities on behalf of political victims, i.e. the appeals of the "Comitato Libertario pro V.P. (vittime politiche)" and of the "Comitato Internazionale Libertario" [Libertarian Committee for Political Victims and International Libertarian Committee] of Westfield. It reproduced abstracts of the writings of Eliseo Reclus, Max Nettlau and Kropotkin and gave information about political persecutions in Italy and in the Soviet Union.

It was mainly antifederalist and criticized the anarcho-syndicalism of Camillo Berneri, but it was also against individualism.

L'ALBA NUOVA	NY New York	1921-1924

Title trans.:	The New Dawn	*First issue:*	S 1921
Subtitle:	Organo della federazione dei lavoratori italiani d'America aderente al Workers Party of America	*Last issue:*	10 My 1924
Add. lang.:		*Vols. (nos.):*	I(1)-IV(17)
First editor:	Antonio Capraro	*Frequency:*	m, w
First publ.:	Mario Rapisardi Literary Society	*Preservation:*	2
Related pubs.:	s *Il Lavoratore*	*Supplements:*	
Circulation:		*Category:*	communist

Depositories: Usa-DLC (2); Usa-MH (2); Usa-NN (2); Nl-IISG (5:[1922-23],o); I-INSML (5:[1922-23],m)

Subtitle translation: The Organ of the Federation of the Italian Workers of America Affiliated to Following the Workers Party of America.

This newspaper was the organ of the Italian Section of the Communist Workers Party of America (founded in 1921). It was published by the Mario Rapisardi Literary Society, an association which bore the name of the Calabrian poet who was so famous among Italian Americans and who made the unrealistic suggestion that the center become an "intellectual center of the Italian-American proletariat spiritually tied to the American proletariat."

The paper published appeals and bulletins of the Italian section of the Friends of Soviet Russia, information on the labor-union movement and on the various sections of the party. It was the first communist inspired review which led the way to the founding of the daily *Il Lavoratore* [The Worker] in 1924.

L'ALBA SOCIALE   FL Tampa   1901

Title trans.:	The Social Dawn	*First issue:*	15 Je 1901
Subtitle:	Periodico socialista-anarchico	*Last issue:*	15 Ag 1901
Add. lang.:		*Vols. (nos.):*	I(1)-I(5)
First editor:		*Frequency:*	bw
First publ.:		*Preservation:*	1
Related pubs.:		*Supplements:*	
Circulation:		*Category:*	anarchist

Depositories: Nl-IISG (1,o); Usa-MnU-I (1,m); I-CSLP (1,m)

Subtitle translation: Socialist-Anarchist Periodical.

This short-lived paper covered with particular emphasis the news of the death in jail of Gaetano Bresci (the anarchist who killed Humbert I, King of Italy). Antimilitarist and anticlerical in its approach, it gave information on the radical movement in the United States and Europe, mainly in Italy. It published essays of the most famous anarchist writers such as Bakunin and Kropotkin.

L'ALLARME   IL Chicago   1915-1917

Title trans.:	The Alarm	*First issue:*	1 N 1915
Subtitle:	Contro ogni forma di autorità e di sfruttamento	*Last issue:*	1 Ap 1917
Add. lang.:		*Vols. (nos.):*	
First editor:	Umberto Postiglione	*Frequency:*	ir
First publ.:		*Preservation:*	3
Related pubs.:		*Supplements:*	
Circulation:	1915: 2000; 1916: 6000	*Category:*	anarchist

Depositories: I-CSLP (3,m); I-BMN (3,o); I-ISTAM (3); Usa-MnU-I (3)

Subtitle translation: Against Any Form of Authority and Exploitation.

This paper was mainly used for propaganda and it was distributed free of charge among proletarians. It did not publish correspondence. All articles were written in a very simple form intended for the enhancement of proletarian culture. The main focus was on the European war, considered a scourge for the workers' movement.

L'ANARCHIA		NY New York	1918-1919

Title trans.:	Anarchy	*First issue:*	23 N 1918
Subtitle:		*Last issue:*	N 1919
Add. lang.:		*Vols. (nos.):*	I(1)-II(10)
First editor:	Costantino Zonchello ?	*Frequency:*	ir
First publ.:		*Preservation:*	2
Related pubs.:		*Supplements:*	
Circulation:		*Category:*	anarchist

Depositories: Nl-IISG (2,o); Usa-MnU-I (2,m); I-BABo (2)

This newspaper started with the aim of assuming the political role of *Cronaca Sovversiva* [Subversive Chronicle] forced to cease publication owing to the laws on the control of the press. *L'Anarchia* also had problems as a result of these laws and had to change its title twice. In fact, in December 1918 *L'Anarchia* was printed with the title *Il Diritto* [The Right]. The readers were informed that any explanation of this change would be counterproductive and dangerous, but that *Il Diritto* "is the son of *L'Anarchia* and the comrades know what this means." The paper changed its title once more in November 1919 and became *Il Refrattario* [The Refractary]. Under all of its titles the paper carried on the propaganda started by *Cronaca Sovversiva* against any form of organization and, consequently, any form of bureaucratization of the anarchist movement. Besides that, it condemned the prosecution of so-called subversives in the United States and the use made of the immigration laws to deport them or prevent them from entering. The paper also provided coverage on the international political situation.

L'ANARCHICO		NY New York	1888

Title trans.:	The Anarchist	*First issue:*	1 Ja 1888
Subtitle:	Organo del Gruppo Socialista-Anarchico Rivoluzionario Italiano "Carlo Cafiero"	*Last issue:*	30 Je 1888
Add. lang.:		*Vols. (nos.):*	I(1)-I(6)
First editor:		*Frequency:*	ir
First publ.:		*Preservation:*	2
Related pubs.:		*Supplements:*	
Circulation:		*Category:*	anarchist

Depositories: I-CSLP (2,mn); Nl-IISG (2,o); Usa-MnU-I (2,m)

Subtitle translation: The Organ of the Italian Socialist-Anarchist Revolutionary Group "Carlo Cafiero."

The first Italian anarchist paper in the United States this emerged following an extraordinary meeting of the Italian anarchists in New York City who were members of the group "Carlo Cafiero." The main issues dealt with in the paper were the nativist reactions against immigrant workers and the repressive legislation against anarchists and radicals. Special attention was devoted to the automation process then being introduced in the American industrial system: in a capitalist society technological developments were considered to serve only individual profit.

L'APPELLO	OH Cleveland	1916-1917

Title trans.:	The Call	*First issue:*	15 Mr 1916
Subtitle:	Periodico mensile di propaganda anarchica	*Last issue:*	Ag 1917
Add. lang.:		*Vols. (nos.):*	I(1)-II(5)
First editor:	Calogero Speziale	*Frequency:*	m
First publ.:	Ugo Balzano	*Preservation:*	3
Related pubs.:		*Supplements:*	
Circulation:		*Category:*	anarchist

Depositories: Usa-MnU-I (3); Nl-IISG (3); I-ISTAM (3,m)

Subtitle translation: A Monthly Periodical for Anarchist Propaganda.

Publisher after Ugo Balzano was Antonio Pistilli (May 1917). The paper was distributed free of charge. The leading articles were written by Ateo Rivolta (probably the pseudonym of Calogero Speziale). Speziale was a Sicilian immigrant who before World War One was a leading spirit of the anarchist group in Detroit. After *L'Appello* ceased publication, Speziale started a new publication, *La Campana* [The Bell]. As far as the anarchist movement was concerned, the paper supported individualism rather than organization. It regularly featured articles on the lynchings and murders of proletarians under the heading "Free Country." It was violently critical of the foreign policy of Wilson's administration and called for a general strike against the American intervention in the European war. It welcomed the February revolution: the new government was a bourgeois one but at least the Russian workers were trying to throw off the yoke and, according to the paper, the proletarian revolution was just ahead.

L'ASCESA DEL PROLETARIATO	PA Wilkes Barre	1908-1910

Title trans.:	The Rise of the Proletariat	*First issue:*	1 O 1908
Subtitle:		*Last issue:*	15 S 1910
Add. lang.:		*Vols. (nos.):*	
First editor:		*Frequency:*	bw
First publ.:	Alberico Molinari	*Preservation:*	2
Related pubs.:		*Supplements:*	
Circulation:		*Category:*	socialist

Depositories: Usa-MnU-I (2,mp)

The aim of this paper was "to arm the brain" with socialist politics and theory before unleashing the rage necessary for socialist action. It discussed issues such as evolution and business unionism and it had a series for women on how to raise strong, rational and socialist children. It supported the use of the general strike as long as it involved disciplined action. It contained very little news although there were articles on the miners' union. Though the paper was founded by SP members, it was not the official organ of the Italians in the Socialist Party.

L'ASINO		NY New York	1908-1910

Title trans.:	The Donkey	*First issue:*	5 Jl 1908
Subtitle:		*Last issue:*	27 F 1910
Add. lang.:		*Vols. (nos.):*	
First editor:		*Frequency:*	w
First publ.:	Asino Publishing Co.	*Preservation:*	2
Related pubs.:		*Supplements:*	
Circulation:		*Category:*	socialist

Depositories: Usa-MnU-I (5:[1910],oub)

This was an anticlerical literary paper which discussed the ideas of Mazzini, Marx and Italian workers' leaders such as Andrea Costa.

L'AURORA		NJ West Hoboken	1899-1901

Title trans.:	The Dawn	*First issue:*	16 S 1899
Subtitle:	Periodico anarchico	*Last issue:*	14 D 1901
Add. lang.:		*Vols. (nos.):*	I(1)-III(60)
First editor:	Giuseppe Ciancabilla	*Frequency:*	bw, w
First publ.:		*Preservation:*	2
Related pubs.:		*Supplements:*	
Circulation:		*Category:.*	anarchist

Depositories: I-CSLP (2,mn); Nl-IISG (2,o); Usa-MnU-I (2,m)

Subtitle translation: An Anarchist Periodical.

This paper was founded by Giuseppe Ciancabilla with the main purpose of counteracting the propaganda in favor of organization carried on by Errico Malatesta, the famous Italian anarchist leader who had become the editor of *La Questione Sociale* [The Social Question] during his stay in the United States in 1899-1900. Being what has been called a "one man paper," *L'Aurora* followed Ciancabilla to Yohoganny, PA, when he was compelled to leave New Jersey for political reasons in 1900. It also moved with its editor when he moved to Spring Valley, IL, in December 1900.

L'Aurora gave wide coverage to the killing of King Humbert I of Italy by the anarchist Umberto Bresci in July 1900, violently criticizing the Italian socialists and radicals who had condemned the assassination. Like most anarchist papers, *L'Aurora* was mainly theoretical in its approach, giving only occasional news on the workers' movement in the United States and Italy.

L'AURORA   MA Boston   1928-1930

Title trans.:	The Dawn	*First issue:*	15 F 1928
Subtitle:	Pubblicazione quindicinale	*Last issue:*	2 My 1930
Add. lang.:		*Vols. (nos.):*	I(1)-III(2)
First editor:	Ilario Margarita (pseudonym Ilario di Castelred)	*Frequency:*	bw, ir
First publ.:		*Preservation:*	2
Related pubs.:		*Supplements:*	
Circulation:		*Category:*	anarchist

Depositories: Nl-IISG (2,o); I-INSML (2,mp); I-ISTAM (2); Usa-MnU-I (2,m); Usa-NN (2)

Subtitle translation: A Biweekly Publication. In January 1929 the subtitle changed to: A Journal of Criticism and Ideas.

This paper published theoretical essays, besides providing news about the international workers' movement and local news coverage.

AURORA SOCIALISTA   UT Salt Lake City   1910; 1913-1914

Title trans.:	Socialist Dawn	*First issue:*	1910
Subtitle:		*Last issue:*	1014
Add. lang.:		*Vols. (nos.):*	
First editor:		*Frequency:*	w
First publ.:		*Preservation:*	7
Related pubs.:		*Supplements:*	
Circulation:		*Category:*	socialist ?

Depositories:

No further information could be obtained.

Source: Russo, *Catalogo collettivo*.

AVANTI !   IL Chicago   1918-1921

Title trans.:	Forward	*First issue:*	1 O 1918
Subtitle:		*Last issue:*	1 O 1921
Add. lang.:		*Vols. (nos.):*	VI (31)
First editor:	Girolamo Valenti	*Frequency:*	m, w, bw
First publ.:		*Preservation:*	3
Related pubs.:	c *La Parola dei Socialist*, c *La Parola Proletaria*, c *La Fiaccola*, s *La Parola del Popolo*, s *La Parola*	*Supplements:*	
Circulation:	3500-5000	*Category:*	socialist-ISF

Depositories: Usa-ICRL (3,mp)

This was the official organ of the Italian Socialist Federation which was part of the Socialist Party of America. It mainly covered current international events and attempted to give some political background information especially on events in Germany and Italy. Educational topics included the meaning of socialism and the role of women in society. Its United States coverage often had to do with political prisoners such as Tom Mooney or with the struggle in the mines. It ran a number of articles opposing the arrival in the United States of an Italian union delegation which had been invited by the AFL.

L'AVANTI		NJ Newark	1904-1906

Title trans.:	The Forward	*First issue:*	18 Je 1904
Subtitle:	Giornale Socialista Italo-Americano	*Last issue:*	6 Ja 1906
Add. lang.:	English	*Vols. (nos.):*	
First editor:	Teofilo Petriella	*Frequency:*	w, sw
First publ.:	The Newark Socialist Cooperative	*Preservation:*	3
Related pubs.:		*Supplements:*	*Forward!*
Circulation:		*Category:*	socialist-SP

Depositories: Usa-NN (3,m)

Subtitle translation: Italian-American Socialist Journal.

A former contributor to *Il Proletario* and a member of the Socialist Party of America, Petriella began the publication of *L'Avanti* relying on his own finances and on the cooperation of the Newark SP club. The paper reported on SP political campaigns, on Italian rank and file SP drives and on the conflicts between Italian members of the SLP and SP. In addition, the paper's editorials often denounced the maneuvers of the Catholic Church and political and moral deficiencies of the Newark Italian community leaders. Its columns welcomed and sought correspondence from Italians actively participating in the American working-class movement. Economic problems prevented its publication by the end of March 1905. It reappeared as a semimonthly in Cleveland, Ohio in July of the same year but was discontinued in January 1906. On 22 December 1904 the paper published and American supplement.

AVANTI !		PA Philadelphia	1895-1896

Title trans.:	Forward	*First issue:*	? 1895
Subtitle:		*Last issue:*	? 1896
Add. lang.:		*Vols. (nos.):*	
First editor:	Giusto Calvi ?	*Frequency:*	
First publ.:		*Preservation:*	7
Related pubs.:	s *Il Proletario*	*Supplements:*	
Circulation:		*Category:*	socialist

Depositories:

In 1895, Giusto Calvi, an exile following the Fasci siciliani [period of rural uprisings], launched *Avanti* in Philadelphia which was succeeded by *Il Proletario* [The Proletarian] in Pittsburgh.

Source: Vecoli, "The Italian Immigrants," p. 272.

L'AVVENIRE		NY New York	1943-1944
Title trans.:	The Future	*First issue:*	25 D 1943
Subtitle:	Quindicinale di propaganda. Organo libertario della vecchia guardia	*Last issue:*	11 Ja 1944
Add. lang.:		*Vols. (nos.):*	
First editor:	La vecchia guardia del gruppo "Carlo Tresca già gruppo del *Martello*	*Frequency:*	bw
First publ.:	La vecchia guardia del gruppo "Carlo Tresca" già gruppo del *Martello*	*Preservation:*	5
Related pubs.:		*Supplements:*	
Circulation:		*Category:*	anarchist

Depositories: I-INSML (5:[1944]; Usa-MnU-I (5:[1943-44])

Subtitle translation: A Biweekly of Propaganda. The Anarchist Organ of the Old Guard.

This paper was published and edited by "the old guard of the group "Carlo Tresca," formerly named after *Il Martello*." It published theoretical essays on anarchism (Errico Malatesta, Pierre-Joseph Proudhon) and provided international and local news coverage. It commemorated the anarchist Carlo Tresca , one of the founders of the paper *Il Martello* [The Hammer] who was murdered in 1943 by unknown killers.

L'AVVENIRE		PA New Kensington	1910-1917
Title trans.:	The Future	*First issue:*	10 Ag 1910
Subtitle:	An Italian Weekly Newspaper	*Last issue:*	7 Jl 1917
Add. lang.:		*Vols. (nos.):*	
First editor:	Carlo Tresca	*Frequency:*	w
First publ.:	C. De Gregoriis	*Preservation:*	5
Related pubs.:		*Supplements:*	see below
Circulation:		*Category:*	anarchist

Depositories: Usa-MnU-I (5:[?]); I-ISTAM (5:[1916-17]); I-BSMC (5:[?]); I-ACS (5:[1916-17])

The founder of this paper was the well-known Italian anarcho-syndicalist Carlo Tresca, previously contributor to *Il Proletario* [The Proletarian] who started three publications in the following order: *La Plebe* [The Populace], *L'Avvenire* [The Future], *Il Martello* [The Hammer]. *L'Avvenire* gave voice to the problems of Italian immigrant workers and took part in the struggles of all immigrant workers. After the arrest of Tresca (charged with murder together with others during the strikes in Minnesota in 1917) *L'Avvenire* led a campaign on behalf of its editor and published abstracts in favor of Tresca from a number of European and Russian newspapers in the original language of publication. On 15 December 1916 it published as a supplement a calendar on strikes in Minnesota. Among the contributors of the paper were Vincenzo Vacirca (editor of *L'Internazionale*), Paolino Fragale, Frank Bellanca,

Vincenzo Fazio. The paper was suppressed by the American authorities in 1917, although Tresca was not prosecuted.

Source: Andreucci/Detti, *Il movimento operaio italiano*, vol. V, p. 98-99.

L'AVVENIRE	OH Steubenville	1909-1910

Title trans.:	The Future	*First issue:*	24 Jl 1909
Subtitle:		*Last issue:*	9 Jl 1910
Add. lang.:		*Vols. (nos.):*	
First editor:		*Frequency:*	w
First publ.:	G. Zavarella	*Preservation:*	6
Related pubs.:		*Supplements:*	
Circulation:		*Category:*	socialist

Depositories: Usa-MnU-I (6:[1910],m)

This paper had a branch office in Pittsburgh, PA, and contained information on mine workers' strikes as well as articles of a more general nature which were anticlerical and antimilitarist. Carlo Tresca was connected with the administration of the paper and he also wrote some articles.

L'AZIONE	VT Barre	1913-?

Title trans.:	Action	*First issue:*	1913
Subtitle:	Settimanale di Critica e di Propaganda Rivoluzionaria	*Last issue:*	?
Add. lang.:		*Vols. (nos.):*	
First editor:	Felice Guadagni	*Frequency:*	w
First publ.:		*Preservation:*	6
Related pubs.:		*Supplements:*	
Circulation:		*Category:*	syndicalist-IWW

Depositories: Usa-NN (6:[1913],o)

Subtitle translation: Revolutionary Weekly of Critique and Propaganda.

The founder and editor of this paper had written for *Il Proletario* [The Proletarian] in the early part of 1913, but had left his previous assignment under the charge of having mishandled the paper's funds. From the only issue of *L'Azione* (4 October 1913) that has apparently survived it is possible to gather that the paper expressed the concerns and ideas of some of the Italians who were actively involved in the syndicalist branch of the IWW. It contained harsh polemical articles against the socialists and focused on the trials against some Italian strikers. The section called "Dai Campi d'Azione" [From the Fields of Action] was dedicated to news of labor struggles and correspondence from Italian militants.

Source: De Ciampis, "Storia del movimento socialista," p. 159.

L'AZIONE   NY New York   1941-1942

Title trans.:	Action	*First issue:*	24 N 1941
Subtitle:	Organo quindicinale della democrazia repubblicana italiana	*Last issue:*	15 Jl 1942
Add. lang.:		*Vols. (nos.):*	I(1)-II(15)
First editor:	Aurelio Natoli	*Frequency:*	bw
First publ.:		*Preservation:*	1
Related pubs.:		*Supplements:*	
Circulation:		*Category:*	antifascist

Depositories: I-INSML (2:[1941-42]); Usa-NN (1)

Subtitle translation: The Biweekly Organ of the Italian Republican Democracy.

This paper was founded by a group of Italian antifascist exiles, but was not the official organ of any particular association. It declared that it intended to destroy the legend (created abroad by the fascists) that all Italians were fascists, to establish political and economic democracy and to make a free Italy part of a future "Republican Federation of the United States of Europe." To this end, *L'Azione* featured news and articles on international and American politics, besides reporting on the activities of Italian-American democratic associations. Though this was more of a bourgeois newspaper, it identified with the workers' movement, which was the unifying element in the antifascist struggle.

IL BALILLA   MA Lynn   1912

Title trans.:		*First issue:*	5 Je 1912
Subtitle:	Quindicinale di propaganda libertaria ai fanciulli	*Last issue:*	15 Ag 1912
Add. lang.:		*Vols. (nos.):*	I(1)-I(3)
First editor:		*Frequency:*	bw,ir
First publ.:	Maria R. Galleani	*Preservation:*	1
Related pubs.:		*Supplements:*	
Circulation:		*Category:*	anarchist

Depositories: Nl-IISG (1,o); Usa-MnU-I (1,m)

Subtitle translation: A Biweekly of Libertarian Propaganda for Children

This paper was founded with the aim of supplementing *Cronaca Sovversiva* [Subversive Chronicle] with a paper containing educational propaganda, but the enterprise did not succeed. The periodical addressed boys and adults who still lived in "intellectual childhood," but it published long-winded articles which were difficult to understand. *Il Balilla* intended to publish educational short stories and poems and to inform its readers about the reality of everyday life in order to show the falseness of religious, political and moral conventions. Among the themes dealt with in the few issues of *Il Balilla* were war and antimilitarism.

IL BARBIERE MODERNO	NY New York	1914-?

Title trans.:	The Modern Barber	*First issue:*	1914
Subtitle:	Organo ufficiale della società di benevolenza barbieri italiani dello Stato di New York	*Last issue:*	
Add. lang.:		*Vols. (nos.):*	
First editor:		*Frequency:*	w, m
First publ.:		*Preservation:*	6
Related pubs.:		*Supplements:*	
Circulation:		*Category:*	labor

Depositories: I-INSML (6:[1943])

Subtitle translation: The Official Organ of the Italian Barbers' Benevolent Society in the State of New York

The only available issue contains general news on the war in Europe besides information on the activities of the Barbers' Benevolent Society.

IL BOHEMIEN	NY New York	1925

Title trans.:	The Bohemian	*First issue:*	Mr 1925
Subtitle:	Pubblicazione periodica	*Last issue:*	
Add. lang.:		*Vols. (nos.):*	
First editor:	Nicola Caporale	*Frequency:*	
First publ.:		*Preservation:*	7
Related pubs.:		*Supplements:*	
Circulation:		*Category:*	anarchist

Depositories:

Subtitle translation: A Periodical Publication

This was a pamphlet published by the individualist anarchist Caporale in order to defend himself against charges made by *L'Adunata dei Refrattari* [The Call of the Refractaires]. It provides evidence of the internal polemics of the anarchist movement in the United States.

Source: Bettini, *Bibliografia dell'anarchismo*, p. 218.

BOLLETTINO (I)		IL Chicago	1926-1933

Title trans.:	Bulletin	*First issue:*	? 1926
Subtitle:		*Last issue:*	? 1933
Add. lang.:		*Vols. (nos.):*	
First editor:	see below	*Frequency:*	
First publ.:		*Preservation:*	7
Related pubs.:		*Supplements:*	
Circulation:		*Category:*	socialist-ISF

Depositories:

This was published by the Federazione Italiana del Socialist Party of America [Italian Federation of the SP].

Source: Russo, *Catalogo collettivo.*

BOLLETTINO (II)		IL Chicago	1931-1933

Title trans.:	Bulletin	*First issue:*	? 1931
Subtitle:		*Last issue:*	? 1933
Add. lang.:		*Vols. (nos.):*	
First editor:	Giovanni Pippan ?	*Frequency:*	
First publ.:		*Preservation:*	7
Related pubs.:		*Supplements:*	
Circulation:		*Category:*	labor

Depositories:

The organ of the "Lega italiana dei panettieri e distributori del pane" [Italian League of Bakers and Bread Distributors], this paper was founded by Giovanni Pippan, the League's secretary. Pippan had emigrated to the United States from Italy to escape fascist prosecution. He became a labor organizer in southern Illinois, Chicago and New Jersey and cooperated with several labor papers. He was killed in Chicago in 1933 (presumably by fascists).

Source: Andreucci/Detti, *Il movimento operaio italiano*, vol. IV, p. 158-159.

BOLLETTINO D'INFORMAZIONE		NY New York	1938

Title trans.:	Information Bulletin	*First issue:*	5 My 1938
Subtitle:		*Last issue:*	
Add. lang.:		*Vols. (nos.):*	
First editor:		*Frequency:*	
First publ.:		*Preservation:*	7
Related pubs.:		*Supplements:*	
Circulation:		*Category:*	antifascist

Depositories:

This paper was edited by the "Comitato italiano antifascista" [Italian Antifascist Committee].
Source: Russo, *Catalogo collettivo*.

IL BOLLETTINO DE L'ERA NUOVA	NJ Paterson	1919

Title trans.: The Bulletin of the New Age	*First issue:*	1 Mr 1919
Subtitle:	*Last issue:*	10 My 1919
Add. lang.:	*Vols. (nos.):*	I(1)-I(5)
First editor:	*Frequency:*	ir
First publ.:	*Preservation:*	1
Related pubs.: c *L'Era Nuova*	*Supplements:*	
Circulation:	*Category:*	anarchist

Depositories: Nl-IISG (1); Usa-MnU-I (1,m)

After the suppression by the American authorities of *L'Era Nuova*, an anarchist-syndicalist paper, five more issues appeared in 1919 with this new title.

BOLLETTINO DEL COMITATO	NY New York	1938

Title trans.: Bulletin of the Promoting Committee of *Il Popolo*	*First issue:*	4 S 1938
Subtitle:	*Last issue:*	
Add. lang.:	*Vols. (nos.):*	
First editor:	*Frequency:*	
First publ.:	*Preservation:*	7
Related pubs.: s *Il Popolo*	*Supplements:*	
Circulation:	*Category:*	antifascist

Depositories:

The complete title of the paper was *Bollettino del comitato promotore de Il Popolo*. No further information could be obtained.
Source: Russo, *Catalogo collettivo*.

BOLLETTINO DELLO SCIOPERO DEI SARTI	IL Chicago	1910

Title trans.: The Tailors' Strike Bulletin	*First issue:*	10 N 1910
Subtitle:	*Last issue:*	11 D 1910
Add. lang.:	*Vols. (nos.):*	s.a. (1)-s.a.(4)
First editor: Emilio Grandinetti	*Frequency:*	ir
First publ.:	*Preservation:*	1
Related pubs.:	*Supplements:*	
Circulation:	*Category:*	labor union

Depositories: I-ISTAM (1,m); Usa-MnU-I (1,m)

Published by the Italian Committee of the United Garment Workers, this paper dealt with the 1910 strike in the textile industry. Involving 41,000 workers in Chicago, this strike marked a new class consciousness among workers in this sector and prepared the way for a new labor union, the Amalgamated Clothing Workers of America. In this union the Italian element was of fundamental importance. The bulletin was edited by Emilio Grandinetti, a socialist leader and coeditor of *La Parola del Popolo* [The People's Word]. Although many of the strikers were women workers the paper did not address women's issues.

Source: Cartosio, "Italian Workers and Their Press," p. 427-28.

BOLLETTINO MENSILE ...	NY New York	1932

Title trans.:	Monthly Bulletin of the GL Federation of North America	*First issue:*	1932
Subtitle:		*Last issue:*	
Add. lang.:		*Vols. (nos.):*	
First editor:	Roberto Bolaffio	*Frequency:*	
First publ.:		*Preservation:*	7
Related pubs.:		*Supplements:*	
Circulation:		*Category:*	antifascist

Depositories:

The complete title of the paper was *Bollettino mensilie della federazione giustizia e livertà del Nord America*.

Salvemini writes in his memoirs that "In the issue of 24 September 1932 of the 'Bollettino mensile della federazione Giustiuzia e Liberta del Nord America' edited in New York by Roberto Bolaffio, I explained the aims of Giustizia e Liberta."

Source: Salvemini, *Memorie di un fuoruscito*, p. 119.

LA CAMPANA	MN Minneapolis	1917

Title trans.:	The Bell	*First issue:*	O 1917
Subtitle:	Giornale anarchico	*Last issue:*	
Add. lang.:		*Vols. (nos.):*	I(1)
First editor:		*Frequency:*	ir
First publ.:	Calogero Speziale	*Preservation:*	1
Related pubs.:		*Supplements:*	
Circulation:		*Category:*	anarchist

Depositories: I-CSLP (1,m); I-BMN (1,o); Usa-MnU-I (1)

Subtitle translation: Anarchist Journal

This was probably the only Italian-language anarchist paper ever published in Minnesota. The only available issue intended to give the true version of an 'incidence' (as it was officially called) which took place in a church during a Sunday sermon in Milwaukee, WI, when two Italian anarchists were killed by the police.

Source: Bettini, *Bibliografia dell'anarchismo*, pp. 206-07.

CHANTECLAIR	NY Bronx	1942-1945

Title trans.:	Chanteclair	*First issue:*	O 1942
Subtitle:	Mensile antifascista	*Last issue:*	Mr 1945
Add. lang.:		*Vols. (nos.):*	I(1)-III(19)
First editor:	Virgilio Gozzoli (pseud. 'Vir')	*Frequency:*	m,ir
First publ.:		*Preservation:*	1
Related pubs.:		*Supplements:*	
Circulation:		*Category:*	antifascist/ anarchist

Depositories: I-INSML (1); I-FF (2:[1942-45]); Nl-IISG (1)

Subtitle translation: Antifascist Monthly

After 1944 Tintino Rasi (pseud. Gold O' Bay) became coeditor. Entirely dedicated to the antifascist struggle, this paper discussed political themes and reported on the war in Europe, particularly on the Italian situation. A popular publication entirely written by its editors, it also contained parts of dramas, didactic articles and poems all devoted to antifascist propaganda.

CI VAIU	NY Brooklyn	1929

Title trans.:	I go there	*First issue:*	15 Je 1929
Subtitle:	Ogni mese	*Last issue:*	
Add. lang.:		*Vols. (nos.):*	I(1)
First editor:		*Frequency:*	m
First publ.:		*Preservation:*	5
Related pubs.:		*Supplements:*	
Circulation:		*Category:*	antifascist

Depositories: Nl-IISG (5,o); I-INSML (5,mp)

Subtitle translation: Every Month

The title is in southern Italian dialect. This was a popular magazine which claimed that it had no specific program. It published satires of fascism, poems, dialogues etc. as well as local news.

COGITO, ERGO SUM		CA San Francisco	1908
Title trans.:	I Think, Therefore I Am	*First issue:*	15 S 1908
Subtitle:		*Last issue:*	15 N 1908
Add. lang.:	French, Spanish	*Vols. (nos.):*	I(1)-I(3)
First editor:	Carlo Dalboni	*Frequency:*	m
First publ.:		*Preservation:*	1
Related pubs.:		*Supplements:*	
Circulation:		*Category:*	anarchist

Depositories: Nl-IISG (1,o); I-CSLP (1,m)

The political position of this short-lived paper was completely isolated from that of the other anarchist groups. In the article 'Individualismo e anarchismo' [Individualism and Anarchism] its editor, Carlo Dalboni, expressed his theories according to which it was impossible to change the structure of society; therefore, the only solution could be found in a process of individualistic achievement and improvement.

Source: Bettini, *Bibliografia dell'anarchismo*, pp. 186-87.

COLTURA POPOLARE		CA San Francisco	(?) 1937-1938
Title trans.:	Popular Culture	*First issue:*	? 1937
Subtitle:		*Last issue:*	1938
Add. lang.:		*Vols. (nos.):*	
First editor:	Giuseppe Facci	*Frequency:*	
First publ.:		*Preservation:*	5
Related pubs.:		*Supplements:*	
Circulation:		*Category:*	antifascist

Depositories: I-ACS (5:[1938],o); I-INSML (5:[1938],mn)

The only existing issue is that of January 1938. Its main focus was to give information on the Italian fascist regime and on Italian antifascist activity. It also contained news on the efforts to counteract fascist propaganda in San Francisco. Moreover, the paper kept its readers up to date on the Spanish Civil War.

LA COMUNE		PA Philadelphia	1910-1915

Title trans.:	The Commune	*First issue:*	Je 1910
Subtitle:	Organo di difesa proletaria	*Last issue:*	Jl 1915 ?
Add. lang.:		*Vols. (nos.):*	I(1)-VI(1)
First editor:		*Frequency:*	m, bw
First publ.:		*Preservation:*	3
Related pubs.:		*Supplements:*	
Circulation:		*Category:*	anarchist

Depositories: Nl-IISG (3); Usa-MnU-I (3,m)

Subtitle translation: Organ of Proletarian Defense
Editor in 1915: Erasmo Abate.
Source: Bettini, *Bibliografia dell'anarchismo*, pp. 189-90.

LA CONQUISTA		PA Philadelphia	1915 ?-1921

Title trans.:	The Conquest	*First issue:*	1915
Subtitle:		*Last issue:*	23 Ag 1921
Add. lang.:		*Vols. (nos.):*	
First editor:		*Frequency:*	w
First publ.:	Unione Lavoratori Italiani	*Preservation:*	7 ?
Related pubs.:		*Supplements:*	
Circulation:		*Category:*	labor

Depositories:

This paper was published by the Union of Italian Workers.
Source: Russo, *Catalogo collettivo*.

IL CONTRAVVELENO		NY New York	1929

Title trans.:	The Antidote	*First issue:*	1929
Subtitle:	Serve contro il tossico fascista	*Last issue:*	
Add. lang.:		*Vols. (nos.):*	I
First editor:	Marco Ottonieri	*Frequency:*	w
First publ.:		*Preservation:*	5
Related pubs.:		*Supplements:*	
Circulation:		*Category:*	antifascist

Depositories: I-ACS (5,o); I-INSML (5,mn)

Subtitle translation: To Be Used Against Fascist Poison
A satirical newspaper of antifascist propaganda, the only available issue published comments on the Italian situation.

LA CONTROCORRENTE   MA Boston   1938-1967

Title trans.:	The Countercurrent	*First issue:*	1 Jl 1938
Subtitle:	Pubblicazione dedicata alla lotta contro il fascismo	*Last issue:*	Winter 1967
Add. lang.:	English	*Vols. (nos.):*	I(1)-XIII(2); n.s. XIV(1)-XXIII(3)
First editor:	Anita Paolini	*Frequency:*	m, bw
First publ.:	Aldino Felicani	*Preservation:*	2
Related pubs.:		*Supplements:*	
Circulation:		*Category:*	antifascist/anarchist

Depositories: Nl-IISG (2); I-ISTAM (2,m); I-BAB (2) Usa-MH (2); Usa-NN (2)

Subtitle translation: A Publication Devoted to the Struggle against Fascism

The review was directed by Aldino Felicani, an anarchist who was active in the 1920s in the struggle for the defense of Sacco and Vanzetti. Felicani maintained his interest in this case throughout both series of the paper, even promoting a committee for their rehabilitation.

The paper's first series (from 1938 to 1951) mainly dealt with the struggle to bring about the fall of the fascist regime and with the problem of Italy's reconstruction after its liberation. Some of the paper's contributors were famous antifascists like Gaetano Salvemini and Enzo Tagliacozzo. From the very beginning it supported the union of all genuine antifascist causes, either Italian or Italian-American and was against Anglo-American policies in Europe and Italy and for the sovereign rights of the Europeans.

After the war it promoted a campaign to help the case of Carlo Tresca. He was assassinated in 1943 but no suspects or motives were found by the police.

A second series was published starting July-August 1956 and its goal "to hold the banner of resistance and warfare high up against the forces of darkness and intolerance, to gather around it all those who loathe suppression of free thought, to gather around it good natured men and those who toil for the banning of oppression, wars, dictatorships and any type of authority of man over man." This second series, full of evocative and commemorative articles, is less penetrating in its analysis of the Italian and Italian-American situation. Starting in 1939 it also published a section in English entitled *The Countercurrent*, Against all Fascism Everywhere.

IL CONTROPELO   VT Barre   1911-1912

Title trans.:	Counterpoint	*First issue:*	F 1911
Subtitle:	Giornale Libertario	*Last issue:*	Mr 1912
Add. lang.:		*Vols. (nos.):*	I-II
First editor:		*Frequency:*	m
First publ.:		*Preservation:*	2
Related pubs.:		*Supplements:*	
Circulation:		*Category:*	anarchist

Depositories: I-CSLP (2,m); Nl-IISG (2,o); Usa-MnU-I (2,m)

Subtitle translation: A Libertarian Journal

This paper was strongly polemical against *Cronaca Sovversiva* [The Subversive Chronicle] and its editor Luigi Galleani. In every issue items could be found referring to financial scandals allegedly involving Galleani. The paper was pro-individualistic. It gave information about the Italian political situation (the Libyan war) and the Mexican revolution.

CONTRO-VELENO	PA Philadelphia	1918

Title trans.:		*First issue:*	1918
Subtitle:		*Last issue:*	
Add. lang.:		*Vols. (nos.):*	
First editor:		*Frequency:*	
First publ.:		*Preservation:*	7
Related pubs.:		*Supplements:*	
Circulation:		*Category:*	labor

Depositories:

No further information could be obtained.

Source: Ayer, *Newspapers and Periodicals*, 1918.

IL COOPERATORE	CO Pueblo	1918-1919

Title trans.:	The Cooperator	*First issue:*	15 O 1918
Subtitle:		*Last issue:*	15 Mr 1919
Add. lang.:		*Vols. (nos.):*	I(2)-II(1)
First editor:	Vincenzo Massari	*Frequency:*	sm
First publ.:		*Preservation:*	2
Related pubs.:		*Supplements:*	
Circulation:		*Category:*	socialist

Depositories: I-ISTAM (2,m); Usa-CoP (2,m)

"A Cooperation and Mutual Assistance Monitor," this was the official organ of the Pueblo Cooperative Association Mercantile Co. The secretary of the cooperative which had been promoted by the Italian Socialist Section, was Vincenzo Massari, the director of the newspaper. Besides keeping Italian-American cooperators informed and printing theoretical articles on cooperation and socialism, the periodical kept track of the development of cooperatives in other countries and supported the International Cooperative Alliance.

LA COOPERAZIONE	VT Barre	1911

Title trans.:	Cooperation	*First issue:*	10 My 1911
Subtitle:	see below	*Last issue:*	10/25 S 1911
Add. lang.:		*Vols. (nos.):*	I(1)-I(9/10)
First editor:	Gioacchino Artoni	*Frequency:*	bm
First publ.:	Louis Barberi	*Preservation:*	3
Related pubs.:		*Supplements:*	
Circulation:		*Category:*	socialist/
			cooperativist

Depositories: I-ISTAM (3,m); Usa-MnU-I (3,m)

Subtitle: Giornale bimensile dedicato alla propaganda in favore della cooperazione, mutua assistenza, assicurazione, case del popolo, banche popolari e problemi dell'emigrazione.

Subtitle translation: A Bimonthly Paper Dedicated to Propaganda in Favor of Cooperation, Mutual Assistance, Insurance, Workman's Recreational Clubs, People's Banks and Immigration Problems.

This periodical was founded following a decision taken by the Board of Directors of the Consumers Cooperative of Barre, VT, to set up within six months a "Federation of Italian Consumer Cooperatives in the United States and a central deposit of the same." The periodical contributed to the consolidation process of cooperatives in the United States. From 2-4 September 1911 a meeting of Italian cooperatives was held in West Hoboken, NJ, to discuss the formation of a cooperative federation.

IL CORRIERE DEL POPOLO	CA San Francisco	1910-1967

Title trans.:	The People's Messenger	*First issue:*	1910
Subtitle:		*Last issue:*	1967
Add. lang.:		*Vols. (nos.):*	
First editor:	Pedretti Brothers	*Frequency:*	bw, w, m
First publ.:	Pedretti Brothers	*Preservation:*	2
Related pubs.:		*Supplements:*	
Circulation:		*Category:*	socialist

Depositories: Usa-MnU-I (2:[1920-62],mp); Usa-ICRL (3:[1921-38]); Usa-IU (2:[1910-67]); §Usa-McP (2:[1910-67],m); <Usa-PPBI (2:[1910-67])

Editors after the Pedretti Brothers were V. Busalacchi and Carmelo Zito. In 1944 an East Coast Office was organized with G.D. Procopio as coeditor.

During World War One and the 1920s this paper mainly published news of Italian politics although much coverage was given to such issues as the cases of Sacco and Vanzetti as well as Tom Mooney. The readership of the paper was mainly on the Pacific Coast and there was a separate page advertising events among the Italian community in California. The politics of the paper were social democratic and it sided with the non-communists in the split within the Italian Socialist Party. It often reprinted articles from the Italian socialist press to explain Italian politics.

Il Corriere closely followed the growth of fascism in Italy and was critical of the Italian political parties for not adequately fighting the rise of fascism. The paper also called for a non-fascist reconstruction of Italy without the monarchy.

Another point of interest was the periodic mentioning of the organizational and political positions of Freemasons both in the United States and in Italy. After World War Two the paper followed the anticommunist politics of the AFL both nationally and internationally.

IL CORRIERE DI CHICAGO		IL Chicago	1907-1933

Title trans.:	The Chicago Messenger	*First issue:*	? 1907
Subtitle:	Giornale settimanale politico scientifico	*Last issue:*	1933
Add. lang.:		*Vols. (nos.):*	I(1)-?
First editor:	Emilio Grandinetti	*Frequency:*	w, m, bm
First publ.:		*Preservation:*	5
Related pubs.:		*Supplements:*	
Circulation:		*Category:*	socialist

Depositories: I-ISTAM (5:[1907-17],m); Usa-MnU-I (5:[1907-1917],m)

Subtitle translation: A Weekly Political and Scientific Paper

From the few issues available, it seems that this periodical was inspired by socialist and trade-unionist ideals. The label of the Industrial Workers of the World appears in the first issue. It was directed by Emilio Grandinetti and Rosalino Pascuzzi.

CORRIERE LIBERTARIO		VT Barre	1914-1915

Title trans.:	The Libertarian Courier	*First issue:*	1 Ag 1914
Subtitle:	Settimanale di propaganda libertaria	*Last issue:*	1 Mr 1915
Add. lang.:		*Vols. (nos.):*	I(1)-II(10)
First editor:	Vincenzo Panizza	*Frequency:*	w
First publ.:		*Preservation:*	3
Related pubs.:		*Supplements:*	
Circulation:		*Category:*	anarchist

Depositories: I-CSLP (3,mm); Nl-IISG (3); Usa-MnU-I (3,m)

Subtitle translation: A Weekly of Libertarian Propaganda

This paper published abstracts from anarchists such as Peter Kropotkin and Max Stirner. Strongly antimilitarist, it maintained this position in the years of World War One. It also gave wide coverage to strikes in the United States.

LA CRITICA   CA San Francisco   1897-1930?

Title trans.:	Criticism	*First issue:*	1897
Subtitle:	Giornale indipendente	*Last issue:*	1930 ?
Add. lang.:		*Vols. (nos.):*	
First editor:		*Frequency:*	bw, w
First publ.:		*Preservation:*	5
Related pubs.:		*Supplements:*	
Circulation:		*Category:*	antifascist

Depositories: I-INSML (5:[1928,1930],mn); I-ACS (5:[1928,1930],o)

Subtitle translation: An Independent Newspaper

Information on this paper which was founded in 1897 is based on three issues, published in 1928 and 1930 when its editor was G. Mancini. It was a republican and antifascist paper and published articles on the antifascist movement in Italy and in Europe.

CRONACA SOVVERSIVA   VT Barre   1903-1919

Title trans.:	The Subversive Chronicle	*First issue:*	6 Je 1903
Subtitle:	Ebdomadario anarchico di propaganda rivoluzionaria	*Last issue:*	Mr 1919
Add. lang.:		*Vols. (nos.):*	I(1)-XVII(1)
First editor:	Luigi Galleani	*Frequency:*	w
First publ.:		*Preservation:*	2
Related pubs.:		*Supplements:*	*Il Balilla*
Circulation:		*Category:*	anarchist

Depositories: Usa-DLC (2,m); Usa-MnU-I (2,m); Usa-MB (2,m); I-ISTAM (2,m); I-BABo (2); I-BAB (2); Nl-IISG (2,o)

Subtitle translation: An Anarchist Weekly of Revolutionary Propaganda

This paper was mainly devoted to theoretical considerations against militarism and unionism and in favor of antiorganizational anarchism. It fiercely opposed any form of political and syndicalist organization. It published essays by Kropotkin, Nettlau, Malatesta and Faure. Its editor, the well-known anarchist Luigi Galleani, published it in Barre, VT, until February 1912; he then moved to Lynn, MA, where he lived until he was deported to Italy in 1919. Though it was prosecuted during World War One because of its strong antimilitarism, the periodical was widespread among Italian immigrants and helped to introduce them to American society. Its defense of violence must be seen in the context of the blatant exploitation of Italian workers in North America and the federal persecution of so-called subversives in general. The paper had to discontinue legal publication in 1918 because of the laws of the press, though two more illegal issues were published in 1919. Its message had a very strong influence on the Italian-American anarchists and many publications claimed to be its heir.

Source: Cartosio, "Italian Workers and Their Press in the United States," p. 452

LA DIANA	NY New York	1923

Title trans.:	The Reveille	*First issue:*	15 S 1923
Subtitle:	Organo ufficiale dell'Alleanza Operaia Antifascista del Nord America	*Last issue:*	
Add. lang.:		*Vols. (nos.):*	
First editor:		*Frequency:*	bw
First publ.:	Avanti Publ. Co.	*Preservation:*	5
Related pubs.:		*Supplements:*	
Circulation:		*Category:*	antifascist

Depositories: Nl-IISG (5,o); I-INSML (5,mp); I-ACS (5,o)

Subtitle translation: Official Organ of the Antifascist Workers' Alliance of North America (AWA)

This paper started publication five months after the formation of the Alliance. The AWA was founded in April 1923 as a result of an appeal made by the Camera del Lavoro Italiana [Italian Chamber of Work] which was an all-inclusive labor organization of Italian workers organized by Frank Bellanca in 1913 in New York. The AWA had a bureau of propaganda that promoted debates on fascism within North American trade unions, clubs and circles. Its federal organizer was Leonardo Frisina. *La Diana* aimed at forming a united proletarian front among Italian Americans. The paper viewed fascism as a kind of fierce bourgeois reaction and gave information on antifascist activities and fascist policy.

LA DIFESA	IL Chicago	1918

Title trans.:	The Defense	*First issue:*	1 My 1918
Subtitle:		*Last issue:*	23 N 1918
Add. lang.:		*Vols. (nos.):*	
First editor:	Angelo Faggi	*Frequency:*	w, ir
First publ.:	Industrial Workers of the World	*Preservation:*	2
Related pubs.:	c *Il Proletario,* s *Il Nuovo Proletario*	*Supplements:*	
Circulation:		*Category:*	syndicalist-IWW

Depositories: Usa-NN (2,m); Usa-MnU-I (2,m); I-ISTAM (2,m)

This was the name *Il Proletario* took after the 1917 raids by the Department of Justice on the IWW when the IWW papers were prohibited from using second class mailing rates. Thus the paper could not be sent by mail and so it was delivered by hand most of the time. Its pages were devoted almost exclusively to news of IWW trials and of rallies held to raise defense funds. The Italian Bakers' Federation of New York City was the only active IWW local of Italians reporting to the paper.

Sources: De Ciampis, "Storia del movimento socialista," p. 163; Fenton, *Immigrants and Unions*, p. 188.

LA DIFESA	NY New York	1923-1924

Title trans.:	The Defense	*First issue:*	F 1923
Subtitle:	Foglio di educazione e di lotta	*Last issue:*	15 Jl 1924
Add. lang.:		*Vols. (nos.):*	I(1)-II(29)
First editor:		*Frequency:*	bw
First publ.:		*Preservation:*	4
Related pubs.:		*Supplements:*	
Circulation:		*Category:*	antifascist/ anarchist

Depositories: Nl-IISG (4,o); I-ISTAM (4,m); I-CSLP (4,m)

Subtitle translation: Paper of Education and Struggle

This publication was mainly devoted to antifascist propaganda and provided comments on contemporary Italian events and on the political situation of the Italian-American community in New York. It also recalled past events of particular significance for its ideological propaganda such as the Commune of Paris. *La Difesa* was supported by the Circolo operaio di Coltura Sociale [Workers' Circle for Popular Culture] of New York and was possibly edited by G. Marascia.

LA DIFESA DE *IL LAVORATORE*	NY New York	1931

Title trans.:	The Defense of *The Worker*	*First issue:*	Ja 1931
Subtitle:	Bollettino quindicinale edito dal Bureau italiano del CC	*Last issue:*	
Add. lang.:		*Vols. (nos.):*	
First editor:		*Frequency:*	bw
First publ.:		*Preservation:*	5
Related pubs.:	c *Il Lavoratore* (Chicago)	*Supplements:*	
Circulation:		*Category:*	communist

Depositories: I-ACS (5,o); I-INSML (5,mp)

Subtitle translation: Biweekly Bulletin edited by the Italian Bureau of the Central Committee

The bulletin was mimeographed. Its aim was to collect funds to restart publication of *Il Lavoratore*, the official organ of the Communist Party. The Central Committee of the Party had in fact decided to discontinue its publication for three months. The bulletin also tried to inform its readers about the activities of the Communist Party among Italian Americans. It fostered a change in the policy of the party, i.e. the entry of communist activists into larger popular associations.

DOMANI	NY Brooklyn	1919

Title trans.:	Tomorrow	*First issue:*	30 Mr 1919
Subtitle:	Rivista quindicinale di critica del movimento sovversivo	*Last issue:*	15 O 1919
Add. lang.:		*Vols. (nos.):*	I1(1)-II(10)
First editor:	Roberto D'Elia	*Frequency:*	bw
First publ.:		*Preservation:*	1
Related pubs.:		*Supplements:*	
Circulation:	1000	*Category:*	anarchist

Depositories: I-ISRT (1); Usa-MnU-I(1); Usa-MB (1, m); Nl-IISG (1,o)

Subtitle translation: Biweekly Review of Criticism of the Subversive Movement

This was an anarchist propaganda periodical which, like many anarchist papers, was isolated from United States reality. America was in fact drastically defined as: "Free America...the slaughter house of all freedoms." It was much more up to date on the Italian situation, publishing the resolutions of the constituent Congress of the Communist-Anarchist League of Italy. It also serialized Maxime Leroy's essay on Max Stirner.

Source: *Revolutionary Radicalism*, pp. 2003-06.

LA DOMENICA	NY Rochester	(1912)

Title trans.:	Sunday	*First issue:*	(1912)
Subtitle:		*Last issue:*	
Add. lang.:		*Vols. (nos.):*	
First editor:	Girolamo Valenti	*Frequency:*	w
First publ.:		*Preservation:*	7
Related pubs.:		*Supplements:*	
Circulation:		*Category:*	socialist

Depositories:

This weekly was published by Girolamo Valenti, who had migrated to the United States in 1911. It was close to the Italian Socialist Federation of the Socialist Party of America.

Source: Andreucci/Detti, *Il movimento operaio italiano*, vol. V, p. 171.

L'EMANCIPAZIONE	CA San Francisco	1927-1932

Title trans.:	Emancipation	*First issue:*	Ja 1927 ?
Subtitle:	Periodico libertario del West	*Last issue:*	O 1932
Add. lang.:	English	*Vols. (nos.):*	I(1)-VI(4)
First editor:	Vincenzo Ferrero	*Frequency:*	m
First publ.:		*Preservation:*	1
Related pubs.:	s *Man!*	*Supplements:*	Golgota (28 Ag 1927)
Circulation:		*Category:*	anarchist

Depositories: Nl-IISG (1,o); I-INSML (1,mp)

Subtitle translation: The Libertarian Periodical of the West

This paper was addressed to Russian, Jewish and Italian-American anarchists; therefore it was published both in Italian and in English. It debated theoretical issues such as anarchism, organization and antiorganization, insurrection and revolution as well as fascism. It called for the support of Tom Mooney and Ray Billings and commemorated murdered anarchists. *L'Emancipazione* discussed widely the foreign policy of the Soviet Union as well as the persecution of communists in the USSR. Its last issue announced that *L'Emancipazione* was to be replaced by *Man!*, a publication in English based on the same principles as *L'Emancipazione*. This happened because of a financial deficit, the decrease in Italian immigration and the decision to support *L'Adunata dei Refrattari.*

ERA NUOVA	NJ Paterson	1908-1917

Title trans.:	New Age	*First issue:*	13 Ja 1908
Subtitle:	Periodico settimanale	*Last issue:*	29 O 1917
Add. lang.:		*Vols. (nos.):*	I(1)-X(455)
First editor:	Camillo Rosazza	*Frequency:*	w
First publ.:	Camillo Rosazza	*Preservation:*	1
Related pubs.:	s *Il Bollettino de l'Era Nuova*	*Supplements:*	
Circulation:		*Category:*	anarchist

Depositories: Nl-IISG (1); Usa-MnU-I (1,m)

Subtitle translation: A Weekly Periodical

This paper was intended to be "the cry of anguish of the poor miner buried in the bowels of the earth, of the miserable weaver spitting blood on her loom, of the wretched bricklayer scorched by July's scalding sun; a voice of protest for the oppressed, the disdained, the rejected, the parasites who yearn for a new life, who claim a place at the grand banquet by them laid."

In accordance with its pre-established program this anarchist and syndicalist periodical dealt not only with Italian-American labor problems, but also with international labor problems. Of the anarchist organizational tendency, the periodical published articles by Luigi Fabbri, Errico Malatesta and Luigi Bertoni. In 1908 it supported the idea of founding an Anarchist-Socialist Federation in reaction to the disintegration of the anarchist movement in the United

States as a result of the individualist and antiorganizational tendencies fostered by Galleani and his supporters.

In 1913 *Era Nuova* became involved in the struggles of Paterson's weavers and published excellent reports. It also kept close track of other struggles within the U.S. workers' movement, siding with the IWW against the unionist AFL.

During the war it campaigned vigorously against militarism. In 1917 publication ceased due to the persecution of foreign radicals by the political and postal authorities. Later five more issues appeared under the title *Bollettino de l'Era Nuova*.

ERESIA DI OGGI E DI DOMANI		NY Bronx	1928-1932
Title trans.:	Heresy of Today and Tomorrow	*First issue:*	Ap 1928
Subtitle:	Per l'affrancamento dell'individuo	*Last issue:*	Ja 1932
Add. lang.:		*Vols. (nos.):*	
First editor:	Ciriaco Arrigoni (pseudonym Brand, Harry Goni)	*Frequency:*	m, ir
First publ.:	Joe Conti	*Preservation:*	1
Related pubs.:		*Supplements:*	
Circulation:		*Category:*	anarchist

Depositories: Usa-NN (1); Nl-IISG (1); I-INSML (1); I-BMN (1); I-BAB (1);

Subtitle translation: For the Liberation of Man

The title after 1928 is sometimes *Eresia*. The publishers after Conti were Amadeo Fulvi and A. Pirani. This was an individualist review which was mostly theoretical and literary; among its contributors were many individualist anarchists, both European and American (E. Armand, Pietro Bruzzi, E. Bertrand, Ugo Fedeli, Henry Ner (pseudonym Han Ryner). Particularly significant was the debate carried on in its columns on the themes of expropriation and the ideology of illegal action. It ceased publication temporarily between March 1929 and October 1931.

LA FIACCOLA		NY Buffalo	1909-1912
Title trans.:	The Torch	*First issue:*	? ? Ag 1909
Subtitle:	Weekly Italian Newspaper for Emancipation of the Working Class	*Last issue:*	1 D 1912
Add. lang.:		*Vols. (nos.):*	I(1)-IV(40)
First editor:	Giacomo Battistoni	*Frequency:*	w, m
First publ.:		*Preservation:*	1
Related pubs.:		*Supplements:*	
Circulation:		*Category:*	socialist-ISF

Depositories: I-ISTAM (1,m); Usa-CMS (1); Usa-MnU-I (1,m)

This was the organ of the Italian section of the Socialist Party of Buffalo, NY, which had been founded in 1907. It took a general interest in the progress of party life, particularly in the Italian section and the Consumer's Cooperative in Buffalo. It also had a peculiar and interesting column with a list of the letters written by Italians and to be found at Buffalo Post Office.

LA FIACCOLA	IL Chicago	1918

Title trans.:	The Torch	*First issue:*	12? Ja 1918
Subtitle:	A Bulletin of Current Events	*Last issue:*	6 Jl 1918
Add. lang.:		*Vols. (nos.):*	I(1)-I(25)
First editor:	Girolamo Valenti	*Frequency:*	
First publ.:		*Preservation:*	2
Related pubs.:	c *La Parola dei Socialisti*, c *La Parola*	*Supplements:*	
	Proletaria, s *Avanti*, s *La Parola del*		
	Popolo, s *La Parola*		
Circulation:		*Category:*	socialist-ISF

Depositories: I-ISTAM (2,m); Usa-CoP (2)

When postal subscription rights were taken away from *La Parola dei Socialisti* [The Socialist's Word], the latter changed its name to *La Parola Proletaria* [The Proletarian's Word], then to *La Fiaccola*. Starting from no. 18 *La Fiaccola* moved to Chicago and changed its format (from magazine to newspaper). The official organ of the Italian Socialist Federation of the Socialist Party of America, the paper was very active in calling for the recognition of the Russian socialist government. Its areas of major influence were New York, Massachusetts, Pennsylvania, and Illinois. In 1918 it became *Avanti* [Forward] then, in 1921 *La Parola del Popolo* [The People's Word].

Source: Vezzosi, "La Federazione Socialista," p. 90.

FORZE NUOVE	O Toronto	1972-1978

Title trans.:	New Forces	*First issue:*	S 1972
Subtitle:		*Last issue:*	Je 1978
Add. lang.:		*Vols. (nos.):*	VII
First editor:	Odoardo Di Santo	*Frequency:*	m, ir
First publ.:		*Preservation:*	1
Related pubs.:		*Supplements:*	
Circulation:		*Category:*	progressive/
			pro-union

Depositories: Cdn-OONL (1,m)

Subsequent editor: Angelo Principe. This was one of the best attempts made in Toronto to produce an articulate and progressive periodical in Italian. The editorial committee took full financial responsibility for starting and maintaining *Forze Nuove* for years. Its contents included investigations and denouncements of social, economic and political aspects of Canadian society. Its position was close to the New Democratic Party.

LA FRUSTA DEI CLOAK MAKERS		NY New York	1922-1924

Title trans.:	The Whip of the Cloakmakers	*First issue:*	1922
Subtitle:		*Last issue:*	5 S 1924
Add. lang.:		*Vols. (nos.):*	I(1)-III(5)
First editor:	Luigi Rea, Pasquale Fugetta	*Frequency:*	m
First publ.:		*Preservation:*	5
Related pubs.:		*Supplements:*	
Circulation:		*Category:*	labor union

Depositories: Nl-IISG (5,o); I-INSML (5,mp)

This monthly publication was started by the group "Gli Insorti" [The Insurgents]. The group was formed by nine workers expelled from Local 48 of the ILGWU for their criticism of the management of the funds and cooperatives of Local 48. They founded the paper in order to express their opinions and to publish details of their charges against the managers of Local 48. Their protest aroused solidarity among members of the Amalgamated Clothing Workers of America.

GERMINAL (I)		IL Chicago	1913

Title trans.:	Germinal	*First issue:*	7 S 1913
Subtitle:	Periodico di Propaganda Anarchica	*Last issue:*	
Add. lang.:		*Vols. (nos.):*	I(1)
First editor:	Umberto Postiglione	*Frequency:*	
First publ.:		*Preservation:*	1
Related pubs.:		*Supplements:*	
Circulation:		*Category:*	anarchist

Depositories: Nl-IISG (1,o); Usa-MnU-I (1,m); I-CSLP (1,m)

Subtitle translation: Periodical of Anarchist Propaganda

The publication of this paper was fostered by the "Gruppo di Propaganda Anarchica" [Group for Anarchist Propaganda] of Chicago. It aimed at increasing the knowledge of Italian immigrants about politics by publishing clearly written articles on war, religion, politics and poems such as those of Gori and D'Annunzio. It was discontinued after the first issue due to lack of funds. Two years later its editor Umberto Postiglione became the editor of *L'Allarme*.

GERMINAL (II)	IL Chicago	1926-1930

Title trans.:	Germinal	*First issue:*	1 Ap 1926
Subtitle:	Mensile anarchico di propaganda	*Last issue:*	1 My 1930
Add. lang.:		*Vols. (nos.):*	I(1)-V(5)
First editor:	Erasmo Abate	*Frequency:*	m, bw
First publ.:		*Preservation:*	1
Related pubs.:		*Supplements:*	
Circulation:		*Category:*	anarchist

Depositories: Usa-NN (1); Nl-IISG (1); I-FF (3:[1926-28])

Subtitle translation: An Anarchist Monthly of Propaganda

Editors after Abate: Armando Tiberi and Carlo Pagella, then (May 1928) Silvestro Spada. This paper published theoretical articles on fascism, anarchism, relations between women and men, news from the United States and information on international politics. It also published many articles on antifascism and anarchism, denouncing antifascist Garibaldinism as a politically fraudulent undertaking. *Germinal* cautiously opposed alliances against fascism which were supposed to be dangerous to the anarchist cause and proposed instead free organization of the anarchist movement. It also criticized the antiorganizational policy of *L'Adunata dei Refrattari* that refused to take part in the North American Anarchist Conference held in Pittsburgh.

IL GIORNALE DELL'UNIONE DEI MINATORI	IN Indianapolis	1917 ?

Title trans.:	The Journal of the Miners' Union	*First issue:*	1917 ?
Subtitle:		*Last issue:*	
Add. lang.:		*Vols. (nos.):*	
First editor:		*Frequency:*	w
First publ.:		*Preservation:*	7
Related pubs.:		*Supplements:*	
Circulation:		*Category:*	labor union

Depositories:

No further information could be obtained.

Source: Russo, *Catalogo collettivo.*

LA GIOVANE ITALIA	NJ West Hoboken	1898

Title trans.:	Young Italy	*First issue:*	1898
Subtitle:		*Last issue:*	
Add. lang.:		*Vols. (nos.):*	
First editor:	Giacinto Piccoli	*Frequency:*	
First publ.:		*Preservation:*	7
Related pubs.:	m *Il Proletario*	*Supplements:*	
Circulation:		*Category:*	republican

Depositories:

Founded by the Italian republican Giacinto Piccoli in 1898, this paper merged with *Il Proletario* in the same year.

Source: De Ciampis, "Storia del movimento socialista," p. 138.

LA GIOVENTU LIBERTARIA	OH Cleveland	1914

Title trans.:	Libertarian Youth	*First issue:*	23 Ap 1914
Subtitle:		*Last issue:*	1914?
Add. lang.:		*Vols. (nos.):*	I(1)-I(3)
First editor:	Aldino Felicani	*Frequency:*	w
First publ.:		*Preservation:*	1
Related pubs.:		*Supplements:*	
Circulation:		*Category:*	anarchist

Depositories: Usa-MnU-I (1)

The editor of *La Gioventù Libertaria* was an Italian political refugee who had been obliged to leave his native country because as the editor of *Rompete le File* [Break the Lines] in Bologna, he had fiercely opposed Prime Minister Giolitti's foreign policy during the Libyan war. The publication of *La Gioventù Libertaria* was at first welcomed by many North American anarchists and was supported by the "Circolo studi sociali" [Circle for Social Studies] of Cleveland. Soon after publication of the first issue, Felicani realized that his revolutionary unionist perspective would not be accepted and supported by people in Cleveland and in North America in general, where the antiorganizational position was widespread. The publication of the paper ceased after three issues.

Source: Bettini, *Bibliografia dell'anarchismo*, p. 194.

LA GIUSTIZIA	NY New York	1919+

Title trans.:	Justice	*First issue:*	18 Ja 1919
Subtitle:	Organo Ufficiale della ILGWU	*Last issue:*	
Add. lang.:		*Vols. (nos.):*	I +
First editor:	S. Yanofski (ass. ed. Raffaele Rende)	*Frequency:*	w, m
First publ.:	ILGWU	*Preservation:*	1
Related pubs.:	m *Lotta di Classe,* c *L'Operaia*	*Supplements:*	
Circulation:	1942: 40,000, 1974: 51,000	*Category:*	labor union- ILGWU

Depositories: Usa-NN (1,m); Usa-MnU-I (1,); I-ISTAM (1,m)

Subtitle translation: Official Spokesman of the ILGWU

From its inception, it was the aim of this paper to be an educational journal on politics and unionism and to inform its readers about union matters. The paper catered especially to women workers who were numerous in the garment trade. In its early years *La Giustizia* covered a wide variety of issues including the activities of the Sons of Italy, a powerful ethnic organization of which several members were active in the organizational drives of the garment industry. The paper also gives an insight into the struggles that affected the Italian Chamber of Labor in New York, since some of the Italian ILGWU leaders were also on its Executive Board. While carefully following the activities of the Socialist Party in Italy, of the Soviet Revolution and of the Third International, the paper usually supported SP candidates and at times other candidates who were strongly in favor of labor interests during United States electoral campaigns. The paper also flirted sporadically with the Communist Workers' Party of America and the American Labor Party. In the 20s and 30s the paper expressed strong antifascist feelings and actively campaigned for the defense of those Italians who were persecuted for political reasons, such as Sacco and Vanzetti. Luigi Antonini's meeting with Roosevelt to try to prevent Italians from being labelled as "enemy aliens" was also reported. When World War Two ended *La Giustizia* covered workers' conditions in Italy and strove to create contacts between American unionism and the newly reorganized Italian workers' movement. In 1984 the paper was still listed as one of the official organs of the ILGWU.

Sources: Cutter/ Thompson, *A Survey of the Italian Language Press.* Fink, *Bibliographical Dictionary of American Labor,* p. 90. Wynar/Wynar, *Encyclopedic Directory of Ethnic. Newspapers*

LA GOGNA	Il Kensington	1909

Title trans.:	The Pillory	*First issue:*	N 1909
Subtitle:	Organo polemico, satirico, spregiudicato	*Last issue:*	
Add. lang.:		*Vols. (nos.):*	I(1)
First editor:		*Frequency:*	
First publ.:		*Preservation:*	1
Related pubs.:		*Supplements:*	
Circulation:		*Category:*	anarchist

Depositories: Usa-MnU-I (1,m)

Subtitle translation: A Polemical, Satirical, Unprejudiced Organ

This was one of the few Italian-American papers representative of individualist anarchism according to the theories of Max Stirner.

Sources: Bettini, *Bibliografia dell'anarchismo*, p. 189. Molinari, "I giornali delle comunità ," p. 118.

GRIDO ANTIFASCISTA	Il Chicago	?

Title trans.:	The Antifascist Cry	*First issue:*	
Subtitle:		*Last issue:*	
Add. lang.:		*Vols. (nos.):*	
First editor:		*Frequency:*	
First publ.:		*Preservation:*	?
Related pubs.:		*Supplements:*	
Circulation:		*Category:*	antifascist

Depositories:

No further information could be obtained.

Source: Russo, *Catalogo collettivo.*

IL GRIDO DEGLI OPPRESSI	NY New York	1892-1894

Title trans.:	Cry of the Oppressed	*First issue:*	5 Je 1892
Subtitle:	Pubblicazione dei gruppi comunisti anarchici di N.Y. e dintorni	*Last issue:*	13 O 1894
Add. lang.:		*Vols. (nos.):*	I(1)-III(8)
First editor:	Francesco Saverio Merlino	*Frequency:*	bw,w
First publ.:		*Preservation:*	2
Related pubs.:		*Supplements:*	
Circulation:		*Category:*	anarchist

Depositories: Usa-MnU-I (2,m); Usa-NN (2,m); I-BAB (2)

Subtitle translation: A Publication of the Communist Anarchist Groups of New York and District

One of the oldest voices of the Italian-American anarchists, this paper was founded by the Italian anarchist Francesco Saverio Merlino who had come to the United States on a propaganda tour. It was edited by the group "Gli Oppressi" [The Oppressed] of New York, two of whom, Vito Solieri and Zuigi Raffuzzi, were contributors to the paper. In 1893 it moved to Chicago where it attracted a wider readership. It devoted much space to the denunciation of the exploitation of Italian immigrants by prominenti and bosses. It tried to enforce the federalist-antiorganizational trend in the anarchist movement, but its editor soon realized that the antiorganizational position was too widespread for there to be enough support for the continuation of the publication.

IL GRIDO DEL POPOLO   CO Denver   1907-1910

Title trans.:	The Cry of the People	*First issue:*	9 D 1907
Subtitle:		*Last issue:*	
Add. lang.:		*Vols. (nos.):*	
First editor:	Il Folletto	*Frequency:*	w
First publ.:		*Preservation:*	6
Related pubs.:		*Supplements:*	
Circulation:		*Category:*	labor union

Depositories: Usa-MnU-I (6:[1907],oub)

This claimed to be the only newspaper in the western states devoted to the interests of the Federation of Miners. It contained news of workers including events in the United Mine Workers and the Western Federation of Miners. However, there was less discussion about Italians as workers than as Italians. In 1907 ownership was transferred to S. Mancini although Il Folletto continued as editor. In 1907 *Corriere del Wyoming* was added to the masthead as both Denver and Rock Springs, WY, were given as the places of publication.

IL GRIDO DELLA FOLLA   NY New York   1916

Title trans.:	The Cry of the Crowd	*First issue:*	20 My 1916
Subtitle:	Giornale quindicinale di propaganda e critica rivoluzionaria	*Last issue:*	15 Je 1916
Add. lang.:		*Vols. (nos.):*	I
First editor:	Pietro Saviotti, Antonio Maffei	*Frequency:*	bw
First publ.:		*Preservation:*	1
Related pubs.:		*Supplements:*	
Circulation:		*Category:*	anarchist

Depositories: I-CSLP (1,mm); Nl-IISG (1,o); Usa-MnU-I (1,m)

Subtitle translation: Biweekly Newspaper for Revolutionary Propaganda and Criticism

This very short-lived periodical supported proletarian violence as a means to hasten the outbreak of revolution and to sabotage the bourgeois system. It criticised Italian patriotism in North America during World War One.

LA GUARDIA ROSSA	NY New York	1919-1921

Title trans.:	The Red Guard	*First issue:*	My 1919
Subtitle:	Compilato da Carlo Tresca a cura della Libreria Rossa	*Last issue:*	My 1921
Add. lang.:		*Vols. (nos.):*	s.a.(2)-s.a.(4)
First editor:	Carlo Tresca	*Frequency:*	ir
First publ.:	Carlo Tresca	*Preservation:*	2
Related pubs.:		*Supplements:*	
Circulation:		*Category:*	anarchist

Depositories: I-ISTAM (2,m); Usa-MnU-I (2); Usa-NN (2,m)

Subtitle translation: Compiled by Carlo Tresca and Edited by the Red Bookshop

The five issues of this paper, usually published on 1 May as special editions of the periodical *Il Martello*, are of a monographic nature and deal with workers' struggles and propaganda. The fourth issue of May 1920, has the subtitle 'Il terrore bianco in America' [White Terror in America] and is dedicated to the cruel oppression of the workers' movement in the United States after the war. (Also known as the Red Scare).

L'IDEA	NY New York	1923

Title trans.:	The Idea	*First issue:*	1 O 1923
Subtitle:	Rivista Politico-sociale	*Last issue:*	16 N 1923
Add. lang.:		*Vols. (nos.):*	
First editor:	Arturo Di Pietro	*Frequency:*	sm
First publ.:	La Rinascenza Publishing Society	*Preservation:*	6
Related pubs.:		*Supplements:*	
Circulation:		*Category:*	antifascist

Depositories: Usa-MnU-I (6,oub)

Subtitle translation; A Political Social Review

This fairly conservative magazine was antifascist and also gave information on Freemasonry activities.

L'INEVITABILE	NY New York	1920

Title trans.:	The Inevitable	*First issue:*	1920
Subtitle:		*Last issue:*	
Add. lang.:		*Vols. (nos.):*	
First editor:		*Frequency:*	
First publ.:		*Preservation:*	7
Related pubs.:		*Supplements:*	
Circulation:		*Category:*	anarchist

Depositories:

This was published only for a few months in 1920.
Source: Fedeli, "Giornali, riviste, numeri unici anarchici," p. 346.

EL INTERNACIONAL	FL Tampa	1904-1948

Title trans.:	The International	*First issue:*	30 Ja 1904
Subtitle:		*Last issue:*	1948
Add. lang.:	Spanish	*Vols. (nos.):*	
First editor:		*Frequency:*	w
First publ.:		*Preservation:*	2
Related pubs.:		*Supplements:*	
Circulation:		*Category:*	labor union

Depositories: Usa-FU (2,m)

The union paper of the cigarworkers, this devoted more and more space to Italian-language articles as the years progressed.
Source: Russo, *Catalogo collettivo.* Pozzetta, *Pane e Lavore*, p. 35.

L'INTERNAZIONALE	MA Boston	1917

Title trans.:	The International	*First issue:*	19 My 1917
Subtitle:		*Last issue:*	2 Je 1917
Add. lang.:		*Vols. (nos.):*	
First editor:	Vincenzo Vacirca	*Frequency:*	w
First publ.:		*Preservation:*	5
Related pubs.:		*Supplements:*	
Circulation:		*Category:*	socialist

Depositories: Usa-MnU-I (5); Usa-CoP (5); I-ISTAM (5,m); I-BSMC (5)

Vincenzo Vacirca, the founder of this paper, was an outstanding radical leader who co-operated with Carlo Tresca, the Socialist Party of America and the Amalgamated Clothing Workers of America. The paper provided information on the Bolshevik revolution and on Leninism. Clara P. Vacirca wrote on Russian women during the revolution. It published news from Italy and held a pacifist position during World War One.

L'INTERNAZIONALE	PA Philadelphia	1909

Title trans.:	The International	*First issue:*	1 Ja 1909
Subtitle:	Rivista quindicinale illustrata di politica, scienza e arte	*Last issue:*	15 Mr 1909
Add. lang.:		*Vols. (nos.):*	I(1)-I(6)
First editor:	Ludovico Caminita	*Frequency:*	bw
First publ.:		*Preservation:*	1
Related pubs.:		*Supplements:*	
Circulation:		*Category:*	anarchist

Depositories: Nl-IISG (1,o); Usa-MnU-I (1,m)

Subtitle translation: A Biweekly Illustrated Review of Politics, Science and Art
Source: Bettini, *Bibliografia dell'anarchismo*, p. 187.

INTESA LIBERTARIA	PA Philadelphia	1939

Title trans.:	Libertarian Alliance	*First issue:*	15 Ap 1939
Subtitle:	Organo dei gruppi Nord-americani	*Last issue:*	1 Je 1939 ?
Add. lang.:		*Vols. (nos.):*	I(1)-I(4)
First editor:	Mario Zucca	*Frequency:*	bw
First publ.:		*Preservation:*	1
Related pubs.:		*Supplements:*	
Circulation:		*Category:*	anarchist

Depositories: I-INSML (1,mp); Nl-IISG (1,o)

Subtitle translation: The Organ of the North American Groups
The decision to begin publication of this paper was made during the Anarchist
Meeting of North America held in New York on 1-2 April 1939 in order to promote once again the solidarity and internal harmony of the anarchist movement. *Intesa Libertaria* was in fact intended to foster new solidarity inside
the anarchist movement and to promote the action necessitated by the serious international situation. It published many articles on persecutions in the
Soviet Union and Europe, with particular attention to France and Spain. One
devoted contributor was Ezio Taddei. Its internal harmony was very short-
lived and it ceased publication after a few issues.

L'ITALIA D'OGGI   NY New York   1945

Title trans.:	Italy Today	*First issue:*	1 Ja 1945
Subtitle:	Bollettino settimanale d'informazione sull'Italia e sui problemi italiani	*Last issue:*	30 Je 1945
Add. lang.:		*Vols. (nos.):*	I(1)-I(9)
First editor:	Michele Sala	*Frequency:*	w
First publ.:		*Preservation:*	1
Related pubs.:		*Supplements:*	
Circulation:		*Category:*	antifascist

Depositories: Usa-MH (1); Usa-NjP (1); I-IG (1)

Subtitle translation: Weekly Bulletin of Information on Italy and on Italian Problems

This bulletin aimed at providing information on Italian political, economic and social life in defense of the interests of American and Italian workers. Contributions to the paper came from Italian socialists, communists and catholics who were at that time in the United States.

Its column "La settimana" [The Week] was written by Giuseppe Berti and Ambrogio Donini who were both Italian communist intellectuals.

L'ITALIANA   NY Rochester   1938-1943

Title trans.:	The Italian Woman	*First issue:*	S 1938
Subtitle:	Rivista della Donna Italiana. la vera Amica della Famiglia	*Last issue:*	Jl 1943
Add. lang.:		*Vols. (nos.):*	
First editor:	Anna Ponari-Rizzo	*Frequency:*	m
First publ.:	Eleonora Duse Italian Women's Club	*Preservation:*	1
Related pubs.:		*Supplements:*	
Circulation:		*Category:*	educational/ socialist?

Depositories: Usa-NN (1,m); I-INSML (5:[1941-42])

Subtitle translation: Italian Woman's Review. The True Family Friend

This was a small mimeographed journal that called itself a "monthly review for popular education." The publishing club claimed 350 members in January 1942 and thus it can be assumed that this was also the paper's approximate circulation. Addressing primarily women, it clearly tried to relay progressive if not outspokenly socialist ideas, while carrying on the task of education in politics and unionism. In content *L'Italiana* covered a wide range of topics including international and national news, science, sports and health. The journal openly supported the Workers' Party of America, criticism of anti-semitism and racism and opposition to wars in general and specifically to the Italian wars in Abyssinia and Spain. During election periods the paper supported Socialist candidates and in 1941 it favored the American Labor Party. Sections of the paper called "La Donna Moderna" [Modern Women], "La Pagina delle Lettrici" [The Women's Pages] where letters from women or issues raised by them were discussed and "Notiziario della Comunita' di Rochester" [Rochester Community News] offered insights into the life of the Italian community of the area, but they appeared at irregular intervals. Strongly antifascist, *L'Italiana* was critical of the Mazzini Society and favored the Alleanza Garibaldi.

L'ITALIANO	CO Denver	1912

Title trans.:	The Italian	*First issue:*	29 S 1912
Subtitle:		*Last issue:*	
Add. lang.:		*Vols. (nos.):*	
First editor:		*Frequency:*	w
First publ.:	Domenic Lepore	*Preservation:*	6
Related pubs.:		*Supplements:*	
Circulation:		*Category:*	labor

Depositories: Usa-MnU-I (6,oub)

This paper had articles of general interest to labor such as the defense of labor leaders Joseph Ettor and Arturo Giovannitti, the IWW leaders jailed during the Lawrence strike in 1912. The paper was critical of the Temperance Society and its call for abstinence from liquor but *L'Italiano* recognized the danger of alcohol for the working class and favored moderation.

LA JACQUERIE	NJ Paterson	1919

Title trans.:	The Jacquerie	*First issue:*	1919
Subtitle:		*Last issue:*	15 D 1919
Add. lang.:		*Vols. (nos.):*	I(1)-I(2)
First editor:	Ludovico Caminita	*Frequency:*	
First publ.:		*Preservation:*	7
Related pubs.:		*Supplements:*	
Circulation:		*Category:*	anarchist

Depositories:

The few issues of this paper met with serious difficulties owing to the reaction against anarchists. The paper ceased publication after the arrest of Caminita and of the whole editing staff in 1920.

Source: Bettini, *Bibliografia dell'anarchismo*, p. 210-211.

LADIES' GARMENT WORKER NY New York 1910-(1911)

Title trans.:		*First issue:*	1 Ap 1910
Subtitle:		*Last issue:*	D 1918
Add. lang.:	Yiddish	*Vols. (nos.):*	I-IX, no. 12
First editor:		*Frequency:*	m
First publ.:	International Ladies' Garment Workers' Union	*Preservation:*	3
Related pubs.:	s *Justice*	*Supplements:*	
Circulation:		*Category:*	labor union-ILGWU

Depositories: Usa-NN (3:[1910-18],o,ob); Usa-CU (4:[1910-18]); Usa-DL (3:[1910-18]); Usa-MdBJ (3:[1910-18])

A successful strike in New York among the women workers in the trade, in which Italian women also participated, and plans for another to be held in August 1910 (?) prompted the International Ladies' Garment Workers' Union to issue a section of its official journal also in the Italian language. In this section several articles pointed out the advantage of unionism and the union autonomy the Italians would have enjoyed under the ILGWU banner if they had joined in a meaningful number. Other articles reported on the activities of locals already organized. The paper also stressed the need for a policy of mutual understanding if not of compromise with the employers, as opposed to a policy of more radical and allegedly self-defeating union demands. In May 1911 the paper discontinued its Italian section becoming an English and Yiddish union paper under the editorship of John A. Dyche until 1918. (It is particularly difficult, if not impossible to identify the contributors to the Italian section since the majority of its articles went unsigned.)

IL LAVORATORE IL Chicago 1924-1931

Title trans.:	The Worker	*First issue:*	? Je 1924
Subtitle:	Giornale Quotidiano dei Lavoratori	*Last issue:*	(?) 26 S 1931
Add. lang.:		*Vols. (nos.):*	XII (18)
First editor:	Antonio Presi	*Frequency:*	d, w, ir
First publ.:	Il Lavoratore Publ. Co.	*Preservation:*	2
Related pubs.:	c *Il Lavoratore* (Trieste, Italy), m *Alba Nuova* Chicago,	*Supplements:*	
Circulation:		*Category:*	communist

Depositories: Usa-NN (2,m); Usa-NNC (2))

Subtitle translation: The Workers' Daily Paper

This paper was managed by the Italian Federation of the Workers' Party of the U.S.A. which at the time largely consisted of a group of exiled Italian communists originally connected with *Il Lavoratore* of Trieste. The earliest American issues of *Il Lavoratore*, when it was still edited by Antonio Presi of *Alba Nuova* [The New Dawn], are a clear manifestation of this group's efforts to acquire a foothold in the Italian community at large. In March 1925 *Il*

Lavoratore appeared in New York as a weekly, under the editorship of G. Cannata. The subtitle became "Official Italian Language Journal of the Workers' Party of America." By 1926 the name of the editor had disappeared, to be replaced by the more anonymous "Italian Federation of the Workers' Party of America." The paper contributed articles to the clandestine edition of the Italian *Unità* [Unity] and it kept in touch with Italian exiles in other countries. It regularly described what was considered rank and file activity within different areas of the organized labor movement and sharply criticized the official leaders of various organized unions. The paper also made a point of denouncing the existing collaboration between the Mussolini government and United States institutions, and strove to unite the progressive forces of the Italian immigration in the defense of those Italians in the United States who were persecuted for political reasons. Nevertheless, it seldom abated its harsh polemics against the socialists and other independent radicals. Among its contributors were A. Leoni, Giovanni Germanetto, Nino Capraro, Giovanni Pippan, Enea Sormenti (pseudonym of Vittorio Vidali) and Tommaso De Fazio.

IL LAVORATORE		NY New York	1913
Title trans.:	The Worker	*First issue:*	Ja 1913
Subtitle:	Organo mensile della lega ebanisti e affini di New York	*Last issue:*	
Add. lang.:		*Vols. (nos.):*	
First editor:		*Frequency:*	m
First publ.:		*Preservation:*	7
Related pubs.:		*Supplements:*	
Circulation:		*Category:*	labor

Depositories:

Subtitle translation: The Monthly Organ of the League of Ebonists and the Like of New York

Source: Russo, *Catalogo collettivo*.

IL LAVORATORE		O Toronto	1935-1938
Title trans.:	The Worker	*First issue:*	4 D 1935
Subtitle:	Organo di rivendicazioni dei lavoratori italiani del Canada	*Last issue:*	17 S 1938
Add. lang.:		*Vols. (nos.):*	I(1)-III(14)
First editor:	Giuseppe Frattini	*Frequency:*	bw
First publ.:		*Preservation:*	1
Related pubs.:		*Supplements:*	
Circulation:		*Category:*	antifascist

Depositories: Cdn-OONL (1)

Subtitle translation: The Organ of Revenge of the Italian Workers of Canada

This paper began regular publication in March 1936 but a special issue was published in December 1935 as a political platform to be discussed at an antifascist conference held later that month. The initiative to publish the paper was taken by members of the Italian Communist Club of Toronto but it followed the Popular Front's policy supporting wide antifascist alliances. In Canadian politics it supported both the Canadian Communist party and the Cooperative Commonwealth Federation (pro labor party). In foreign affairs the paper warned against the aggressive policies of Hitler and Mussolini and gave wide information on the Spanish Civil War and the activities of the International Brigades.

IL LAVORATORE   Q Montreal   1970-1974

Title trans.:	The Worker	*First issue:*	16 My 1970
Subtitle:	Organo del movimento progressista italo-quebecchese	*Last issue:*	S 1974 ?
Add. lang.:		*Vols. (nos.):*	I(1)-V(8)
First editor:	Bruno Cartosio	*Frequency:*	m
First publ.:	Vincenzo Vincelli	*Preservation:*	1
Related pubs.:		*Supplements:*	
Circulation:	1000	*Category:*	labor

Depositories: private collection

Subtitle translation: The Organ of the Progressive Italian-Quebequian Movement

This paper was published during 1970 as an instrument for the political mobilization of the Italian community in Montreal. Started by Bruno Cartosio with Anfonso Caramazza and others, in 1971 it was continued by Caramazza himself with Antonio Ranellucci and Giuseppe Sciortino and others. The principal aim of the paper was to introduce left-wing politics among the Italian immigrants and to break their isolation especially in relation to French-speaking workers. The main themes dealt with were workers' and syndicalist struggles, a protest against a tax on property imposed by the Catholic Church within the Italian community, Italian and international politics.

IL LAVORATORE ITALIANO   CO Trinidad   1902-1927

Title trans.:	The Italian Worker	*First issue:*	1902
Subtitle:		*Last issue:*	1927
Add. lang.:		*Vols. (nos.):*	XXVI
First editor:	J. Simpson	*Frequency:*	w, bm
First publ.:	Carlo Demolli	*Preservation:*	3
Related pubs.:	s *Italian American*	*Supplements:*	
Circulation:	2500	*Category:*	labor union

Depositories: Usa-MnU-I (5:[1904-06],xerox),(3:[1906-27],mf); Usa-ICRL (3:[1917-27],ob); I-ISTAM (5)

While this paper was published in Trinidad, CO, it was the official organ of District 15 of the United Mine Workers of America; by 1906 it was related to the Western Federation of Miners, whose official organ it was until 1909. In 1906 Edouardo Caffaro, who had become the paper's editor, moved it to Pittsburgh, KA, partly because of pressure from the Colorado mining interests. Caffaro remained editor and publisher until 1927 when he sold the paper.

While the paper was in Colorado it described and discussed the series of strikes and acts of violence that were part of the life of the Mine Workers' Union in Colorado and Utah. It analyzed the employers' "Citizens Alliance" by comparing it to the Camorra and Mafia and it carried continuing appeals for lists of the names of scabs working during strikes. Politically it denied being an anarchist publication and claimed that Carlo Demolli had ceased to be its publisher in 1903, although, he continued to write for the paper for a considerable number of years.

After the paper left Colorado it became much less agitational although it continued to provide politically educational articles on such topics as militarism and fascism. The content of the paper also became more literary, although, even the Colorado paper had serialized Zola's *Germinal*, a novel about miners.

Source: Ayer, *Newspapers and Periodicals*, p. 1312.

IL LAVORO (I)		NY New York	1914-1932

Title trans.:	Labor	*First issue:*	? 3 Ja 1914
Subtitle:	Per la Organizzazione e La Lotta di Classe	*Last issue:*	
Add. lang.:		*Vols. (nos.):*	I-XX
First editor:	Francesco (Frank) Bellanca	*Frequency:*	w
First publ.:	The General Office of the Amalgamated Clothing Workers of America	*Preservation:*	3
Related pubs.:		*Supplements:*	
Circulation:	5000	*Category:*	labor union-ACWA/ antifascist

Depositories: Usa-CMS (3:[1916-30],m); Usa-NN (3:[1916-32],m)

Subtitle translation: For Organization and Class Struggle

This paper was founded with the intention of being the spokesman for the considerable group of Italian workers within the ACWA (mainly women), their means of contact and debate with Italian workers still affiliated with the AFL and a powerful instrument for the appreciation of industrial unionism and socialist ideas. In 1919 the paper emphasized its educational function by aiming at being "read, re-read and thought over." The subtitle was changed into "Rivista Popolare di Questioni Sociali" [People's Review of Social Issues] and the number of editorials concerning political, cultural and behavioral topics was increased. Yet it never ceased to devote its attention to the strikes that were occurring and often organized effective material support for the strikers. Fiercely opposed to the war, the paper eagerly condemned the persecution of radicals and the unjustified violence of the institutions against many Italians who were active in the workers' movement. In the early years of the Soviet Revolution *Il Lavoro* expressed positive feelings toward its achievements.

As soon as fascism started making inroads in the Italian government, the paper became involved in antifascist activities and began to mobilize workers against the deportation of Italians and other foreigners for political reasons. Communications from the Italian Federation of the Workers' Party often appeared in its pages. *Il Lavoro* published articles written by such authors as Raffaele Rende, Luigi Antonini, Frank Bellanca, Arturo Giovannitti, Leonardo Frisina, Joe Angelo, Gioacchino Artoni, C. Corti, Paolo Fortiguerra, G. Procopio and D. Ruggero. With the harshening of the depression the Italian paper seemed to soften its militant criticism; unemployment drastically reduced union membership. Thus during its last few years of publication *Il Lavoro* dwelt more upon the problems of the workers in the United States than on international and ideological issues.

Source: Foner, *History of the Labor Movement*, pp. 256-264.

IL LAVORO (II)		NY New York	1956-1957

Title trans.:	Labor	*First issue:*	Ap 1956
Subtitle:		*Last issue:*	Ap 1957
Add. lang.:		*Vols. (nos.):*	I-II(4)
First editor:		*Frequency:*	m
First publ.:	American-Italian Labor Alliance	*Preservation:*	2
Related pubs.:		*Supplements:*	
Circulation:		*Category:*	labor union

Depositories: Usa-NN (2,mn)

The name of this paper was chosen on purpose to recall the well-known *Il Lavoro* published from 1914-1930. It may be assumed that this new periodical was established by those Italians who had been active in the ACWA.

LA LEGIONE DELL'ITALIA DEL POPOLO		NY New York	1942-1946

Title trans.:	The Italian People's Legion	*First issue:*	22 O 1942
Subtitle:		*Last issue:*	7 D 1946
Add. lang.:		*Vols. (nos.):*	I(1)-V(49)
First editor:	Randolfo Pacciardi	*Frequency:*	sm,m
First publ.:	Italian People's Union	*Preservation:*	3
Related pubs.:		*Supplements:*	
Circulation:		*Category:*	antifascist

Depositories: I-BNB (3); I-ISTAM (3,m); Usa-NN (3); Usa-MnU-I (3)

The organ of the American Federation of the Republican Party in Italy, this paper was directed by Randolfo Pacciardi, who had fought on the Republican side during the Spanish Civil War. Its goal was to unite the Italians living in the United States in order to fight as an independent legion side by side with the Allies against Mussolini's Italy. According to the resolutions taken at the Congress of Antifascist Organizations of the two Americas held in Montevideo in August 1942, this legion was to be flanked by an "Italian National Council," representing "Free Italians" at the United Nations.

On 16 August 1943 the periodical changed its name to *L'Italia Libera / La Legione dell'Italia del Popolo.* From 16 January 1944 the periodical was directed by an editorial staff which included Walter Toscanini, Nicola Chiaromonte and Roberto Bolaffio. Among its contributors were Giuseppe Antonio

Borgese, Giorgio La Piana, Randolfo Pacciardi, Luigi Sturzo, Gaetano Salvemini and Enzo Tagliacozzo. Strongly opposed to the Italian monarchy, it supported both the future constitution of the republic in Italy and the "Comitato
di Liberazione Nazionale" [National Liberation Committee] formed by the
Italian antifascist parties. It also criticized Allied policies and accused them
of stifling mass participation in the fight against Nazi-fascism.

Sources: Varsori, *L'antifascismo italiano*, passim. Tirabassi, *La Mazzini
Society*, passim.

IL LIBERATORE	NY New York	1919 ?

Title trans.:	The Liberator	*First issue:*	1919 ?
Subtitle:		*Last issue:*	
Add. lang.:		*Vols. (nos.):*	
First editor:		*Frequency:*	
First publ.:		*Preservation:*	7
Related pubs.:		*Supplements:*	
Circulation:		*Category:*	anarchist

Depositories:

No further information could be obtained.

Source: *Revolutionary Radicalism*, pp. 2003-06.

LA LIBERTA	NY New York	1902

Title trans.:	Freedom	*First issue:*	1 My 1902
Subtitle:	Pubblicazione anarchica. A cura del Club Indipendente	*Last issue:*	24 My 1902
Add. lang.:		*Vols. (nos.):*	I(1)-I(2)
First editor:	Rocco Montesano (pseud. Carlo Prato)	*Frequency:*	ir
First publ.:		*Preservation:*	1
Related pubs.:		*Supplements:*	
Circulation:		*Category:*	anarchist

Depositories: Nl-IISG (1,o); Usa-MnU-I (1,m); I-CSLP (1,m)

Subtitle translation: Anarchist Publication. Edited by the Independent Club

This paper was founded by Rocco Montesano, previously an active contributor
to *L'Aurora* [The Dawn] edited by Giuseppe Ciancabilla. Its publication was
supported by several North American groups. Notwithstanding their support,
it had a very short life. *La Liberta* aimed at counteracting the campaign carried on by the federal authorities against anarchists after the death of
McKinley in 1901.

Source: Bettini, *Bibliografia dell'anarchismo*, p. 181.

LA LOTTA	NY New York	1909

Title trans.:	The Struggle	*First issue:*	9 Ja 1909
Subtitle:	Settimanale socialista	*Last issue:*	28 Ag 1909
Add. lang.:		*Vols. (nos.):*	I(1)-I(28)
First editor:		*Frequency:*	w
First publ.:		*Preservation:*	6
Related pubs.:		*Supplements:*	
Circulation:		*Category:*	socialist

Depositories: I-ISTAM (6,m); Usa-WHi (6); Usa-MnU-I (6,m)

Subtitle translation: A Socialist Weekly

The only issue found, that of 1 May 1909, contains a long article with a list of the victims of the repression of the riots of May 1898 in Milan.

LA LOTTA	NY New York	1918-1919

Title trans.:	The Struggle	*First issue:*	1918
Subtitle:		*Last issue:*	1919
Add. lang.:		*Vols. (nos.):*	
First editor:	Girolamo Valenti ?	*Frequency:*	
First publ.:		*Preservation:*	7
Related pubs.:		*Supplements:*	
Circulation:		*Category:*	socialist

Depositories:

This was published by Girolamo Valenti for the Italian socialists in the state of New York.

Source: Andreucci/Detti, *Il movimento operaio*, vol. V, p. 171.

LA LOTTA DI CLASSE (I)	NY New York	1912-1917

Title trans.:	The Class Struggle	*First issue:*	3 F 1912
Subtitle:	Organo Ufficiale della Cloak and Skirt Makers Union of New York	*Last issue:*	28 D 1917
Add. lang.:		*Vols. (nos.):*	
First editor:	Arturo Caroti	*Frequency:*	w
First publ.:	Joint Board of the Cloak and Skirt Makers Union of New York	*Preservation:*	2
Related pubs.:	m *L'Operaia*, s *La Giustizia*	*Supplements:*	
Circulation:		*Category:*	labor union/ socialist

Depositories: Usa-NN (2,m); Usa-MnU-I (2,m)

Subtitle translation: The Official Spokesman of the Cloak and Skirt Makers Union of New York

This paper seems to have been published with the main purpose of allowing Italian workers some input in the conflict between the moderate leadership of the ILGWU and its more militant rank and file. The paper was also instrumental in the exertion of more meaningful pressure by Italian workers on the Joint Board of the Cloak and Skirt Makers' Union. Outspokenly socialist, *La Lotta Di Classe* favored an active union involvement in politics and sought to downplay narrow corporative or ethnic claims in the wider contest of the working-class struggle. In the hope of a better understanding, *La Lotta Di Classe* took the lead in expressing the Italian workers' uneasiness about Jewish hegemony over the union leadership. After Arturo Caroti resigned from his editorial position in 1912, he was followed successively by Raimondo Canudo, Gasparre Sangiorgio and eventually Raffaele Rende. Luigi Antonini wrote occasionally for *La Lotta Di Classe* as did Gino Fazio, Augusto Bellanca and several other Italian union members active in different trades affiliated with the Joint Board of the Cloak and Skirt Makers' Union.

Source: Laslett, *Labor and the Left*, p. 112.

LOTTA DI CLASSE (II)   NY New York   1927

Title trans..	Class Struggle	*First issue:*	1 Ja 1927
Subtitle:	Organo dei lavoratori italiani progressisti dell'industria dell'ago	*Last issue:*	18 Je 1927
Add. lang.:		*Vols. (nos.):*	
First editor:	Ettore Frisina	*Frequency:*	w
First publ.:	Italian Trade Progressive Center	*Preservation:*	1
Related pubs.:		*Supplements:*	
Circulation:		*Category:*	labor union

Depositories: Usa-NN (1); Nl-IISG (5:[1927],o); I-INSML (5:[1927], mp)

Subtitle translation: Organ of the Progressive Italian Workers of the Needle Industry

This paper aimed at raising class consciousness and international solidarity among Italian-American workers. It claimed to work for "the organization of the disorganized workers," for workers' control over their unions and for the foundation of a "Party of Workers" against any kind of class collaboration. *Lotta Di Classe* proposed an "aggressive unionism" in answer to the policy promoted by Samuel Gompers of the AFL who was accused of being responsible for the corruption of the union movement. Notwithstanding its tough criticism of the policy of the IWW *Lotta Di Classe* supported campaigns such as the strike called by the general assembly of the Italian members of the IWW of Greater New York on behalf of Sacco and Vanzetti. The general secretary of *Lotta Di Classe* was Francesco Coco.

LOTTA OPERAIA	NY Utica	1913-1915

Title trans.:	Workers' Struggle	*First issue:*	1913
Subtitle:		*Last issue:*	1915
Add. lang.:		*Vols. (nos.):*	
First editor:		*Frequency:*	w
First publ.:		*Preservation:*	7
Related pubs.:		*Supplements:*	
Circulation:		*Category:*	socialist

Depositories:

No further information could be obtained.
Source: Ayer, *Newspapers and Periodicals.*

MARSICA NUOVA	CO Pueblo	1918-1925

Title trans.:	Marsica Nuova	*First issue:*	26 N 1918
Subtitle:	Organo ufficiale della Federazione Lucchese-Marsicana	*Last issue:*	18/25 D 1925
Add. lang.:		*Vols. (nos.):*	I(1)-VI(51/52)
First editor:	Vincenzo Massari	*Frequency:*	m, sm, w
First publ.:	Società Editrice Marsicana	*Preservation:*	2
Related pubs.:	s *Abruzzo e Molise,* m *L'Unione,* m *Il Risveglio*	*Supplements:*	
Circulation:		*Category:*	reform

Depositories: I-ISTAM (2,m); Usa-CoP (2,m); Usa-NN (2)

Subtitle translation: The Official Organ of the Marsicana Federation (an area of the Italian region of Abruzzi-Molise)

This paper dedicated a great deal of space to civil life in the Abruzzi-Molise region and to the Abruzzi settlement in the United States. It supported the Abruzzi farmers' claims for land and promoted fund raising for socialist initiatives in the region, such as the Workman's Recreational Club of Avezzano ("Casa del Popolo"). In 1924 it changed its title to *Abruzzi e Molise.* Its editor, Vincenzo Massari, was a miner's son and a contributor to several workers' papers in Colorado.

Source: Cartosio, "Italian Workers and Their Press," p. 451.

IL MARTELLO   NY New York   1916-1946

Title trans.:	The Hammer	*First issue:*	? 3 N 1916
Subtitle:	Giornale politico, letterario, artistico	*Last issue:*	1 My 1946
Add. lang.:		*Vols. (nos.):*	I(1)-XXXI(3)
First editor:	Luigi Preziosi	*Frequency:*	w, bw, ir
First publ.:	Luigi Preziosi	*Preservation:*	1
Related pubs.:		*Supplements:*	see below
Circulation:		*Category:*	anarchist

Depositories: Usa-MnU-I (1); Usa-NN (1,m); I-ISTAM (1,m); I-BAB (1)

Subtitle translation: A Political, Artistic and Literary Paper

After several changes in 1943, the subtitle finally became 'Quindicinale libertario fondato da Carlo Tresca' [Libertarian Weekly Founded by Carlo Tresca]. Its editors after Preziosi were Carlo Tresca (1916) and John Mancini (1943). Its publishers after Preziosi were Tresca (1918) and Il Martello Publishing Company (1927). Carlo Tresca ceased publishing *L'Avvenire* [The Future] in 1916. The paper published a number of supplements: *La guardia rossa, In memoria di Ettore Tresca* (February 1942), *Manet immota fides* (28 March 1943). *Il Martello* was one of the liveliest papers of the Italian-American workers' movement. It was in contact with the international movement and engaged in the everyday struggle for the civil and political rights of the immigrants. In sharp contrast with *L'Adunata dei refrattari* [The Call of the Refractaires], *Il Martello* deemed it necessary to cooperate with the other political and syndical forces, particularly after the rise of fascism in Italy. Among the promoters of the "Antifascist Alliance of North America," *Il Martello* kept good contacts with Italy, sending copies of the paper and leaflets there. Critical of the New Deal, it was seriously involved in the antifascist struggle during the Civil War in Spain together with other antifascist forces. After the end of the war, it reconsidered its relations with the other forces of the left, especially with the communists. It interrupted publication from January 1939 to February 1940 to give space to the unitary paper of the movement *L'intesa libertaria* [Anarchist Alliance]. After the murder of its editor Carlo Tresca by unknown persons in 1943, *Il Martello* reappeared for a few years, still engaged in the struggle against fascism.

MASTRO PAOLO   PA Philadelphia   1895-1920 ?

Title trans.:	Master Paul	*First issue:*	1895
Subtitle:	Giornale dei lavoratori italiani / Italian Weekly Humorous Newspaper	*Last issue:*	1920 ?
Add. lang.:		*Vols. (nos.):*	
First editor:		*Frequency:*	w
First publ.:	Giuseppe Bruno	*Preservation:*	5
Related pubs.:		*Supplements:*	
Circulation:		*Category:*	labor

Depositories: I-ISSOCO (5:[1903],o); Usa-MnU-I (5:[1903],m)

Subtitle translation: Newspaper of Italian Workers

From the only available issue, this is assumed to be a (profoundly anticlerical) popular newspaper. Besides covering international and Italian news, it reported on the activity of local labor unions and Italian clubs. It also published poems and a serial story.

IL MINATORE		IL Chicago	1919-1920 ?
Title trans.:	The Miner	*First issue:*	1919
Subtitle:		*Last issue:*	1920 ?
Add. lang.:		*Vols. (nos.):*	
First editor:	Girolamo Valenti	*Frequency:*	
First publ.:		*Preservation:*	7
Related pubs.:		*Supplements:*	
Circulation:		*Category:*	labor

Depositories:

This paper was published by Girolamo Valenti for the Italian workers in Illinois, Indiana and Wisconsin.

Source: Andreucci/Detti, *Il movimento operaio*, vol. V, p. 171.

IL MINATORE		CO Pueblo	?
Title trans.:	The Miner	*First issue:*	
Subtitle:		*Last issue:*	
Add. lang.:		*Vols. (nos.):*	
First editor:		*Frequency:*	
First publ.:		*Preservation:*	7
Related pubs.:		*Supplements:*	
Circulation:		*Category:*	labor

Depositories:

No further information could be obtained.

Source: Russo, *Catalogo collettivo*.

IL MINATORE	UT Salt Lake City	1908-1913

Title trans.:	The Miner	*First issue:*	11 Ja 1908
Subtitle:		*Last issue:*	1913?
Add. lang.:		*Vols. (nos.):*	
First editor:		*Frequency:*	w
First publ.:		*Preservation:*	4
Related pubs.:		*Supplements:*	
Circulation:		*Category:*	labor

Depositories: Usa-UU (4[?])

No further information could be obtained.
Source: Russo, *Catalogo collettivo*.

IL MINATORE ITALIANO	MN Duluth	1918

Title trans.:	The Italian Miner	*First issue:*	1918
Subtitle:		*Last issue:*	1918
Add. lang.:		*Vols. (nos.):*	
First editor:		*Frequency:*	
First publ.:		*Preservation:*	7
Related pubs.:		*Supplements:*	
Circulation:		*Category:*	labor

Depositories:

No further information could be obtained.
Source: Russo, *Catalogo collettivo*.

IL MONDO (I)	NY New York	1938-1946

Title trans.:	The World	*First issue:*	15 S 1938
Subtitle:	Rivista mensile di problemi internazionali	*Last issue:*	D 1946
Add. lang.:	English	*Vols. (nos.):*	
First editor:	Giuseppe Lupis, Umberto Gualtieri	*Frequency:*	m
First publ.:		*Preservation:*	1
Related pubs.:	Il Mondo	*Supplements:*	
Circulation:		*Category:*	antifascist

Depositories: Usa-CMS (1); Usa-MnU-I (1); I-ISTAM (2:[1938-46]); I-INSML (2:[1938-46]); I-FF (2:[1938-46])

Subtitle translation: A Monthly Review of International Problems

A cultural and political monthly, this played a very important role in informing the Italian Americans about international politics and about the Italian
situation during the years of World War Two. In the fight against fascism its
contributors included the most important antifascist exiles, among them

Guglielmo Ferrero, Carlo Sforza, Pietro Nenni, Gaetano Salvemini and Luigi Sturzo. Between 1940 and 1941 *Il Mondo* became the unofficial organ of the Mazzini Society (an antifascist organization founded by Italian exiles), supporting its political line and denouncing the press and the activities of the Italian-American groups favorable to fascism, especially Generose Pope and his daily paper *Il Progresso Italo Americano* [Italian-American Progress]. In these years *Il Mondo* had a very rich English section; in October 1941 a daily paper with the same title was also published. After breaking with the Mazzini Society, *Il Mondo* moved closer to socialist positions and favored unity of action with the communists. After the United States intervention in World War Two *Il Mondo* published articles on various international problems and, most of all, on the Italian situation.

IL MONDO (II)		NY New York	1941

Title trans.:	The World	*First issue:*	8 S 1941
Subtitle:	An Italian Daily with American Ideals	*Last issue:*	15 O 1941
Add. lang.:		*Vols. (nos.):*	I(1)-I(37)
First editor:	Giuseppe Lupis	*Frequency:*	d
First publ.:	Il Mondo Publishing Co., Inc.	*Preservation:*	1
Related pubs.:	Il Mondo	*Supplements:*	
Circulation:		*Category:*	antifascist

Depositories: I-INSML (1)

Published by the same editorial staff as the monthly review *Il Mondo* along the same political line, this paper wanted to be the "interpreter of the Americans of Italian origin" and "an organ of struggle...for the working class." It therefore contained coverage of international as well as American politics. Besides publishing union news and serializing Mazzini's life.

IL MOVIMENTO ANARCHICO		MA East Boston	1913

Title trans.:	The Anarchist Movement	*First issue:*	Je ? 1913
Subtitle:	Bollettino di critica e polemica pubblicato a cura del Gruppo Autonomo di E. Boston	*Last issue:*	
Add. lang.:		*Vols. (nos.):*	
First editor:		*Frequency:*	
First publ.:		*Preservation:*	7
Related pubs.:		*Supplements:*	
Circulation:		*Category:*	anarchist

Depositories:

Subtitle translation: Bulletin of Critique and Polemics Edited by the Autonomous Group of E. Boston

Source: Bettini, *Bibliografia dell'anarchismo*, p. 192.

NAZIONI UNITE	NY New York	1942-1946

Title trans.:	The United Nations	*First issue:*	5 Mr 1942
Subtitle:	Weekly later Semimonthly of the Mazzini Society	*Last issue:*	1 D 1946
Add. lang.:	English	*Vols. (nos.):*	
First editor:	Umberto Gualtieri	*Frequency:*	w, sm
First publ.:	Mazzini Society Inc.	*Preservation:*	2
Related pubs.:		*Supplements:*	
Circulation:		*Category:*	antifascist

Depositories: I-INSML (2); I-ISTAM (2); Usa-NN (2); Usa-MnU-I (2)

This replaced the English bulletin *Mazzini News* as official organ of the Mazzini Society (an association of Italian antifascist exiles). Until 15 July 1943 the fourth page of *Nazioni Unite* was entitled *Mazzini News* and was in English. After November 1944 it was divided into two sections, Italian and English. *Nazioni Unite* carried on a campaign started by *Mazzini News* which was intended to absolve the Italian people of responsibility for fascism and to provide information about the financial aid given to Mussolini by Britain and the United States; the paper provided information on Italian and international events and had a strongly anticommunist tone. The United States was regarded as a model of democracy; after 1943 *Nazioni Unite* criticized American politics in relation to Italy.

NIHIL	CA San Francisco	1909

Title trans.:	Nothing	*First issue:*	4 Ja 1909
Subtitle:	Individualista-anarchico	*Last issue:*	30 O 1909
Add. lang.:		*Vols. (nos.):*	I(1)-I(10)
First editor:	Adolfo Antonelli	*Frequency:*	ir
First publ.:	Michele Centrone	*Preservation:*	1
Related pubs.:		*Supplements:*	
Circulation:		*Category:*	anarchist

Depositories: Usa-MnU-I (1,m); Nl-IISG (1,o); I-CSLP (1,m)

Subtitle translation: The Individualist Anarchist

This publication devoted more space to international news (Italy, Mexico) than to the North American panorama. It was intended as propaganda for individualistic anarchism and paid little attention to contemporary events.

NOTIZIARIO INTERNAZIONALE	NY New York	1947-1974

Title trans.:	International News of the Free Syndical Movement	*First issue:*	1947
Subtitle:	Edito dal Comitato sindacati liberi dell'American Federation of Labor-Congress of Industrial Organizations (AFL-CIO)	*Last issue:*	Ja 1974
Add. lang.:		*Vols. (nos.):*	I(1)-XXVIII(6)
First editor:		*Frequency:*	m
First publ.:		*Preservation:*	1
Related pubs.:		*Supplements:*	
Circulation:		*Category:*	labor imperialist-AFL-CIO

Depositories: I-BCM (1:1947-58); I-BUB (1:1947-58)

Subtitle translation: Edited by the Free Syndicates Committee of AFL-CIO

The complete title of the paper was *Notiziario internazionale del movimento sindacale libero.* As its title and subtitle indicate, this was a newsletter intended for distribution outside the United States, being the official voice of the AFL-CIO. It covered international politics (from a strongly anti-Soviet position), besides reporting international and U.S. labor news. Though it is an Italian-language paper, it is no publication by Italian-American workers.

IL NOVATORE	NY New York	1910-1911

Title trans.:	The Innovator	*First issue:*	15 O 1910
Subtitle:	Rivista libera quindicinale per tutte le giovani energie che hanno qualche cosa di nuovo e geniale da dire	*Last issue:*	16 Ap - 1 My 1911
Add. lang.:		*Vols. (nos.):*	I(1)-II(8/9)
First editor:	Massimo Rocca	*Frequency:*	bw
First publ.:		*Preservation:*	1
Related pubs.:	Il Novatore Anarchico (Rome)	*Supplements:*	
Circulation:		*Category:*	anarchist

Depositories: Nl-IISG (1,o); Usa-MnU-I (1,m); I-CSLP (1,m); I-FF (1)

Subtitle translation: Free Biweekly Review for All Young People Who Have Something New and Ingenious to Say

This review was founded by Massimo Rocca under the pseudonym of Libero Tancredi in 1910 and it was discontinued in 1911 when he went back to Italy. Massimo Rocca had already systematically expressed his political views in Italy as editor of *Il Novatore Anarchico* in Rome. In his writings for *Il Novatore* Rocca asserted that war and violence were to be the catalysts of new energies and the destroyers of useless and incapable people. On his return to Italy, Rocca's views found expression in his propaganda in favor of "revolutionary nationalism." In 1919 he became an active fascist leader and supported fascism until 1925.

Source: Andreucci/Detti, *Il movimento operaio*, vol. IV, p. 356.

NUOVI TEMPI	NJ Paterson	1918

Title trans.:	New Times	*First issue:*	Mr 1918
Subtitle:	Periodico di dottrina e battaglia	*Last issue:*	
Add. lang.:		*Vols. (nos.):*	I(1)
First editor:		*Frequency:*	ir
First publ.:		*Preservation:*	5
Related pubs.:		*Supplements:*	
Circulation:		*Category:*	anarchist

Depositories: Usa-MnU-I (5,m); I-CSLP (5,m); Nl-IISG (5,o)

Subtitle translation: Periodical of Doctrine and Struggle

The only available issue was mainly devoted to the Russian Revolution. It expressed the wish that a proletarian revolution would follow the imperialist war.

IL NUOVO MONDO	NY New York	1925-1931

Title trans.:	The New World	*First issue:*	16 N 1925
Subtitle:	Quotidiano dei lavoratori italiani d'America	*Last issue:*	29 N 1931
Add. lang.:		*Vols. (nos.):*	I(1)-VII(282)
First editor:	Vincenzo Vacirca	*Frequency:*	d
First publ.:	Avanti News Co. Inc.	*Preservation:*	1
Related pubs.:	s *La Stampa Libera*	*Supplements:*	
Circulation:		*Category:*	antifascist

Depositories: I-ISTAM (1,m); Usa-DLC (1,m); Usa-NN (1,m)

Subtitle translation: The Daily of the Italian Workers in America

After years of attempts, on 16 November 1925 the antifascist and socialist movements succeeded in printing *Il Nuovo Mondo* the first antifascist daily to appear abroad. Financially it received contributions from Luigi Antonini's International Ladies' Garment Workers Union and it was supported by "Avanti News Co., Inc.," of which Matteo Siracusa was president, Frank Bellanca secretary and Giovanni Sala treasurer, all three of them famous antifascist and labor-union representatives. It was initially directed by Vincenzo Vacirca, a socialist and trade-unionist militant. Active in condemning fascist activities in Italy and in the United States, the paper was boycotted by the colonial press, banks and importers who soon discontinued advertising as a result of the pressure exerted by the fascist government who were wary of the newspaper becoming a dangerous antifascist voice abroad. The fascists, however, did not limit themselves to merely this, because in July 1927 they plundered the paper's printing office, forcing the local police to break into the offices and arrest the editors.

In 1929 the paper was torn by struggles between right and left factions of the workers' movement and by struggles between communists and socialists. From that date the paper became more moderate, so Valenti, the editor decided to move the main office to Chicago, where leftist ideas had more chance of success and support.

In their efforts to support the paper, the Italian Socialist Federation and its periodicals went into debt and were forced to sell the printing press and a workman's club ("Casa del Popolo") to pay off their debts. Life was difficult for the paper which often suspended publication. On 3 October 1931 it became *The Liberal and Independent Daily*, supported by an even more moderate group and directed by Philip Bongiorno. Meanwhile, the socialists had founded a new paper, *La Stampa Libera*.

IL NUOVO PROLETARIO		IL Chicago	1918-1919

Title trans.:	The New Proletarian	*First issue:*	30 N 1918
Subtitle:		*Last issue:*	N 1919
Add. lang.:		*Vols. (nos.):*	
First editor:	Angelo Faggi	*Frequency:*	w, ir
First publ.:	IWW	*Preservation:*	1
Related pubs.:	c *La Difesa*, s *Il Proletario*	*Supplements:*	
Circulation:	1000	*Category:*	labor-IWW

Depositories: Usa-NN (1,m)

As soon as the group of Italian militants who were originally involved in the publication of *Il Proletario* and *La Difesa* were able to reacquire mailing rights after the end of World War One, they re-established the paper under this new name. The first editor was Angelo Faggi, who had edited *La Difesa* until then. It was not long before he was deported and replaced by Antonio Presi, who remained the editor of *Il Nuovo Proletario* when the paper reverted to its original name of *Il Proletario*.

Sources: De Ciampis, "Storia del movimento socialista," p. 163; *Revolutionary Radicalism*, pp. 2003-06.

L'OPERAIA		NY New York	1915-1919
Title trans.:	The Working Woman	*First issue:*	? 9 Ja 1915
Subtitle:	An American Labor Weekly	*Last issue:*	11 Ja 1919
Add. lang.:		*Vols. (nos.):*	I-VII
First editor:	Alfredo Consiglio	*Frequency:*	w
First publ.:	Local 25 of the International Ladies Garment Workers'Union	*Preservation:*	3
Related pubs.:	s *La Giustizia*	*Supplements:*	
Circulation:		*Category:*	labor union- ILGWU / socialist

Depositories: Usa-CMS (3,mn); Usa-MnU-I (3,m)

One aim of this paper was to educate workers and encourage union principles and behavior. Particular attention was given to women workers through a special section called "La Pagina Della Donna" [The Woman's Page]. It also strove to keep its readers informed on debates and initiatives undertaken by the local executive committee and its Italian organization committee. Furthermore, the paper became instrumental in promoting the organization of an Italian ethnic local so as to participate more effectively in the struggle over union power affecting the union executive committee which was composed primarily of Jewish workers. During periods of contract renewals, the paper translated the local's demands into Italian and supported the organization of strikes to enforce them. It also reported strikes in other trades to promote workers' solidarity. Luigi Antonini was appointed editor in 1917, although he had unofficially occupied this position since the previous year. Outspokenly socialist, *L'Operaia*'s editorials against the war caused the suspension of its publication.

Sources: Romualdi, "Uomini, force ed eventi," p. 37; Torregrossa, "Antonino Crivello," p. 220.

L'OPERAIO		NY New York	1900-1906
Title trans.:	The Worker	*First issue:*	1900
Subtitle:		*Last issue:*	10 N 1906
Add. lang.:		*Vols. (nos.):*	
First editor:		*Frequency:*	
First publ.:		*Preservation:*	7
Related pubs.:		*Supplements:*	
Circulation:		*Category:*	labor

Depositories:

No further information could be obtained.
Source: Russo, *Catalogo collettivo.*

L'OPERAIO ITALIANO	PA Altoona	1910-1911

Title trans.:	The Italian Worker	*First issue:*	1910
Subtitle:		*Last issue:*	1911
Add. lang.:		*Vols. (nos.):*	
First editor:		*Frequency:*	
First publ.:		*Preservation:*	7
Related pubs.:		*Supplements:*	
Circulation:		*Category:*	labor

Depositories:

No further information could be obtained.

Source: Russo, *Catalogo collettivo*.

L'ORDINE	NY New York	1919-1920

Title trans.:	The Order	*First issue:*	31 O 1919
Subtitle:	Periodico di propaganda anarchica	*Last issue:*	16 F 1920
Add. lang.:		*Vols. (nos.):*	I(1)-I(7)
First editor:	Roberto Elia ?	*Frequency:*	bw
First publ.:		*Preservation:*	1
Related pubs.:		*Supplements:*	
Circulation:		*Category:*	anarchist

Depositories: I-BAB (1)

Subtitle translation: A Periodical of Anarchist Propaganda

This paper claimed to be the ideological heir of *Cronaca Sovversiva* [Subversive Chronicle]. It did not represent any particular section of the anarchist movement but only voiced the opinion of individual members. By contrast it kept up to date on anarchist activity in Italy. It published articles on military and naval expenses, North American capital, unionism (which it accused of collaborating with capital) and the persecution of anarchists in the United States. It was anticlerical and attacked both socialists and democrats.

L'ORDINE NUOVO	NY New York	1932-?

Title trans.:	The New Order	*First issue:*	(?) 1932
Subtitle:	Organo dei lavoratori italiani negli Stati Uniti d'America	*Last issue:*	
Add. lang.:		*Vols. (nos.):*	I
First editor:		*Frequency:*	sm
First publ.:	Ordine Nuovo Publishing Association	*Preservation:*	5
Related pubs.:		*Supplements:*	
Circulation:		*Category:*	labor union

Depositories: I-ACS (5:[1932]); I-INSML (5:[1932],mn); I-BSMC (5: [1932])

Subtitle translation: The Organ of the Italian Workers in the U.S.A.

Intended to be 'an instrument of struggle in the hands of Italian workers,' this paper featured news and articles on international politics and Italy, besides providing news coverage 'from factories and mines.'

L'ORGANIZZATORE	FL Tampa	1920

Title trans.:	The Organizer	*First issue:*	3 Ja 1920
Subtitle:		*Last issue:*	1920
Add. lang.:		*Vols. (nos.):*	
First editor:	G. Vaccaro	*Frequency:*	w
First publ.:		*Preservation:*	6
Related pubs.:		*Supplements:*	
Circulation:		*Category:*	labor union

Depositories: Usa-MnU-I (6,xerox)

This paper was connected with the Cigar Workers' Union and it identified with the Italian Socialist Federation of the Socialist Party. It was anticapitalist but not revolutionary.

IL PAESE	PA Philadelphia	1938

Title trans.:	The Country	*First issue:*	1938 ?
Subtitle:	L'unico giornale liberale che si pubblica in Pennsylvania	*Last issue:*	1938
Add. lang.:		*Vols. (nos.):*	
First editor:	Roberto D'Antonio	*Frequency:*	w
First publ.:	I-INSML (5,mn); I-ACS (5,o)	*Preservation:*	5
Related pubs.:		*Supplements:*	
Circulation:		*Category:*	antifascist

Depositories:

Subtitle translation: The Only Liberal Paper Published in Pennsylvania

The only available issue gives information on the Amalgamated Clothing Workers of America and on *Giovine Italia*, an antifascist paper published in Paris by Randolfo Pacciardi.

IL PALCOSCENICO	NY New York	1935-1936

Title trans.:	The Stage	*First issue:*	1935
Subtitle:		*Last issue:*	1936
Add. lang.:		*Vols. (nos.):*	
First editor:	Giuseppe Sterni	*Frequency:*	m
First publ.:		*Preservation:*	6
Related pubs.:		*Supplements:*	
Circulation:		*Category:*	labor

Depositories: Usa-MnU-I (6:[1936],oub)

The paper was the official publication of the League for the Betterment of Scenic Artists. It was a conservative journal which praised Italy's victory over Ethiopia and congratulated Mussolini. It also included a history of Italian theater as well as general history such as that of World War One.

LA PAROLA	IL Chicago	1937-1948

Title trans.:	The Word	*First issue:*	1937
Subtitle:		*Last issue:*	O 1938
Add. lang.:		*Vols. (nos.):*	
First editor:		*Frequency:*	w
First publ.:		*Preservation:*	1
Related pubs.:	c *La Parola dei Socialisti*, c *La Parola Proletaria*, c *La Fiaccola*, c *Avanti!*, c *La Parola del Popolo*	*Supplements:*	
Circulation:		*Category:*	socialist

Depositories: Usa-DLC (1); Usa-MnU-I (1); Usa-NN (1); I-ISTAM (1)

This was the title assumed between 1937 and 1948 by the socialist paper *La Parola dei Socialisti*.

LA PAROLA		O Toronto	1974-1977

Title trans.:	The Word	*First issue:*	1974
Subtitle:		*Last issue:*	1977
Add. lang.:		*Vols. (nos.):*	III
First editor:	Angelo Principe	*Frequency:*	m
First publ.:	Angelo Principe	*Preservation:*	7
Related pubs.:		*Supplements:*	
Circulation:	1000	*Category:*	progressive/ pro-union

Depositories:

The contents of this paper was focused on the working conditions of the working class in Toronto. Other articles reported on the political situation in Italy. It had a cultural page with books and movie reviews.

Source: Information was given by the editor.

LA PAROLA DEI DRESSMAKERS		NY Brooklyn	1937-1938

Title trans.:	The Voice of the Dressmakers	*First issue:*	S 1937
Subtitle:	Edited by the Italian Dressmakers Fair Play Committee	*Last issue:*	N 1938
Add. lang.:		*Vols. (nos.):*	
First editor:		*Frequency:*	
First publ.:		*Preservation:*	5
Related pubs.:		*Supplements:*	
Circulation:		*Category:*	labor union

Depositories: Nl-IISG (5:[1938],o); I-INSML (5:[1938],mp)

This paper was addressed to garment workers and urged them to clear the local unions of "dictators and racketeers." The paper called attention to the "continuous abuses perpetrated by certain officials of Local 25 ACW of A., and Local 48 and 89, ILGWU, all affiliated to the American Labor Party." In particular, *La Parola dei Dressmakers* requested the dismissal of Luigi Antonini, general secretary of Local 89. It fought "for democracy and freedom of the press" and provided information on labor. In 1938 the title became *The Voice of the Dressmakers*.

| LA PAROLA DEI SOCIALISTI | IL Chicago | 1908-1914 |

Title trans.: The Socialist's Word	*First issue:*	17 F 1908
Subtitle:	*Last issue:*	10 Ja 1914
Add. lang.:	*Vols. (nos.):*	I(1)-VII (286)
First editor: Giuseppe Bertelli	*Frequency:*	w
First publ.:	*Preservation:*	2
Related pubs.: s *La Parola Proletaria*, s *La Fiaccola*, s *Avanti*, s *La Parola del Popolo*, s *La Parola*	*Supplements:*	
Circulation:	*Category:*	socialist-SP

Depositories: I-ISTAM (2,m); Usa-MnU-I (2)

La Parola dei Socialisti was founded on 17 February 1908 by the socialist group headed by Giuseppe Bertelli. It was the "Italian-language organ of the Socialist Party of America" affiliated to the Socialist Party. It was opposed to the party's wing which supported strong labor unions and revolution, published *Il Proletario* and had strong ties with the Socialist Labor Party. The activity of the wing affiliated to the Socialist Party was based on Bertelli's great zeal and on his friendship with Malhon Berner, secretary-general of the Socialist Party. Bertelli financed the paper with his own funds. Directors of the paper were Alberico Molinari and Vincenzo Vacirca. During the war oppression affected the socialists and their newspapers when postal subscription facilities were withdrawn. Even *La Parola dei Socialisti* was no longer allowed to mail its issues and had to change its name first to *La Parola Proletaria*, then to *La Fiaccola* and finally to *Avanti!*. After Wilson's defeat, the paper appeared under the title *La Parola del Popolo* and had postal rights. *La Parola dei Socialisti* dealt with labor unionism, socialist and anticlerical propaganda, besides informing its readers about the Italian situation, and reporting from Italian socialist newspapers.

Sources: Vezzosi, "La Federazione Socialista Italiana," passim; *La Parola del Popolo*, passim; Andreucci/Detti, *Il movimento operaio*, vol. III, pp. 506-09.

| LA PAROLA DEL MEDICO | NY New York | 1916-1919 |

Title trans.: The Doctor's Word	*First issue:*	2 Ap 1916
Subtitle: A Monthly Review on Health Education directed by Dr. Petillo	*Last issue:*	Mr 1919
Add. lang.:	*Vols. (nos.):*	I(1)-5(3)
First editor: Ettore Tresca	*Frequency:*	m, bw
First publ.:	*Preservation:*	5
Related pubs.:	*Supplements:*	
Circulation:	*Category:*	pro-labor/ medical

Depositories: I-ISTAM (5); Usa-MnU-I (5:[1916-19?]); Usa-IU (5:[1916-19?]); Usa-NBM (5); Usa-NNN (5:[1916-19?])

This review was directed by Ettore Tresca, the Italian-American doctor, brother of Carlo, the anarchist who fought against fascism. It was a review on health and education, ecology, literary and social affairs; it had close links with left-wing circles in the Italian-American community and the Italian Hospital of New York.

LA PAROLA DEL POPOLO	IL Chicago	1921+

Title trans.:	The People's Word	*First issue:*	1921
Subtitle:		*Last issue:*	+
Add. lang.:		*Vols. (nos.):*	
First editor:	Girolamo Valenti	*Frequency:*	w, sw, m
First publ.:		*Preservation:*	1
Related pubs.:	c *La Parola dei Socialisti,* c *La Parola Proletaria,* c *La Fiaccola,* c *Avanti!,* s *La Parola*	*Supplements:*	
Circulation:		*Category:*	socialist

Depositories: Usa-MnU-I (1); I-BAMi (1); I-ISTAM (3:[1937+])

This paper was the organ of the Italian Socialist Federation of the Socialist Party of America, as were *La Parola dei Socialisti, La Parola Proletaria, La Fiaccola* and *Avanti!* before it. It was directed by Girolamo Valenti, then by Giuseppe Bertelli, Serafino Romualdi and Giovanni Pippan, who was later assassinated in Chicago. The paper covered political events outside the United States, especially those in Italy and the Soviet Union. It considered the USSR to be the first workers' state and it supported the dictatorship of the proletariat. It also fought for socialist unity both in the United States and within the international movement and identified itself with the Serrati wing of the Italian Socialist Party. *La Parola del Popolo* also gave wide coverage to events in the United States. Besides keeping up with the case of Sacco and Vanzetti, the paper also discussed events concerning the United Mine Workers, the railroad workers and the situation in the clothing industry. The paper also followed the rise of the Ku Klux Klan.

With the transfer of *Il Nuovo Mondo* to Chicago in 1930, the Italian Socialist Federation was forced to suspend publication of *La Parola del Popolo* for economic reasons. In 1937 the paper was given a new title, *La Parola,* under the direction of Serafino Romualdi, Domenico Saudino, Pietro Camboni and Egidio Clemente. In 1938 it moved to New York and was directed by Girolamo Valente. It carried on a struggle against fascism and for the resumption of democratic life in postwar Italy. After the war, *La Parola* was deprived of its director who returned to Italy in 1948. It was then reduced in format and finally ceased publication in October 1948. In January 1951 it resumed publication under the title *La Parola del Popolo* with the following subtitle: "Socialist Review of the Italian Americans in the United States." It was directed by Egidio Clemente in Chicago, where it is still published today. In the United States it represents the non-religious and socialist voice of the Italian-American community, having ties with democratic clubs in the country. It deals with international and national relations, literature and arts, science and commemoration of events in the history of the Italian-American and Italian workers' movements.

Sources: Vezzosi, "La Federazione Socialista Italiana," passim; *La Parola del Popolo,* passim; Andreucci/Detti, *Il movimento operaio,* vol. III, pp. 506-09.

LA PAROLA PROLETARIA		IL Chicago	1916-1917

Title trans.:	The Proletarian Word	*First issue:*	1 Ja 1916
Subtitle:		*Last issue:*	29 D 1917
Add. lang.:		*Vols. (nos.):*	IX(1)-X(52)
First editor:	Toni Lucidi	*Frequency:*	w
First publ.:		*Preservation:*	2
Related pubs.:	c *La Parola dei Socialisti*, s *La Fiaccola*, s	*Supplements:*	
	Avanti!, s *Parola del Popolo*, s *La Parola*		
Circulation:	4500	*Category:*	socialist-SP

Depositories: Usa-CoP (2,m); I-ISTAM (2,m); I-BSMC (2))

As it was the "Italian-language organ of the Socialist Party of America," this paper had to change its name owing to oppression during the war. In 1917 it changed its name to *La Fiaccola*.

IL PENSIERO		NY Buffalo	1915 ?

Title trans.:	The Thought	*First issue:*	1915 ?
Subtitle:		*Last issue:*	
Add. lang.:		*Vols. (nos.):*	
First editor:		*Frequency:*	
First publ.:		*Preservation:*	7
Related pubs.:		*Supplements:*	
Circulation:		*Category:*	socialist

Depositories:

This was a small journal published by the Italian socialists in Buffalo after the economic depression of 1914-15. It was against war and warmongers.

Source: Yans-McLaughlin, *Family and Community*, p. 123.

IL PENSIERO		NY New York	1938-1939

Title trans.:	The Thought	*First issue:*	20 O 1938
Subtitle:		*Last issue:*	18 Mr 1939
Add. lang.:		*Vols. (nos.):*	I(1)-II(3)
First editor:	Editorial Committee	*Frequency:*	bw
First publ.:	Gruppo 'Camillo Berneri'	*Preservation:*	1
Related pubs.:		*Supplements:*	
Circulation:		*Category:*	anarchist

Depositories: Nl-IISG (1,o); I-INSML (1,mp); I-CSLP (1,m)

This paper was formally edited by an editorial committee but in fact its first editor was Ezio Taddei who had just emigrated to the United States and who was a contributor to *L'Adunata dei Refrattari* [The Call of the Refractaires]. At the end of 1938, Taddei was charged with involvement with people considered non-anarchists by the 'Gruppo Camillo Berneri' (named after the Italian anarchist killed in Barcelona, Spain in May 1937) and removed from his position. On 17 November 1938 the group who were mainly represented by John Mancini, began to edit the paper. The aim of *Il Pensiero* was to organize financial and political support for French and Spanish political victims and refugees. In 1939 *Il Pensiero* started a campaign against *L'Adunata dei Refrattari* and its editor Max Sartin, accusing him of being "a betrayer of the people," and asserting that *L'Adunata* had more than once published the names of political refugees, thus revealing them to the police.

Source: Andreucci/Detti, *Il movimento operaio*, vol. V, p. 1.

IL PENSIERO OPERAIO	NJ Paterson	1893

Title trans.:	The Workers' Thought	*First issue:*	1893
Subtitle:		*Last issue:*	
Add. lang.:		*Vols. (nos.):*	
First editor:		*Frequency:*	
First publ.:		*Preservation:*	7
Related pubs.:		*Supplements:*	
Circulation:		*Category:*	labor

Depositories:

No further information could be obtained.

Source: Russo, *Catalogo collettivo*.

LA PLEBE	PA Philadelphia	1907-1908

Title trans.:	The Populace	*First issue:*	24 Ag 1907
Subtitle:	Italian Weekly Newspaper	*Last issue:*	26 S 1908
Add. lang.:		*Vols. (nos.):*	I(1)-II(38)
First editor:	Carlo Tresca	*Frequency:*	w
First publ.:		*Preservation:*	4
Related pubs.:		*Supplements:*	
Circulation:		*Category:*	socialist

Depositories: I-ISTAM (4,m); Usa-MnU-I (4,m)

Having left the management of *IL Proletario*, Carlo Tresca founded this periodical in which he used to spread anticlerical, antimilitarist and socialist ideals, "in a struggle against priests, proprietors and the Camorra." On 22 February 1908 Helga Tresca took over the management of the periodical because in his fight against corruption, Carlo Tresca had been condemned to serve three months in prison for writing an article against the Italian consul.

Source: Andreucci/Detti, *Il movimento operaio*, vol. V, pp. 97-99.

IL POPOLO	NY New York	1938-1939

Title trans.:	The People	*First issue:*	29 O 1938
Subtitle:	Organo dei progressisti italiani d'America	*Last issue:*	11 F 1939
Add. lang.:		*Vols. (nos.):*	I(1)-II(6)
First editor:		*Frequency:*	bw, w
First publ.:	Italian American Liberal Association, Inc.	*Preservation:*	5
Related pubs.:	c *Bollettino del Comitato promotore de Il Popolo*	*Supplements:*	
Circulation:		*Category:*	antifascist

Depositories: I-INSML (5); I-ISTAM (5)

Subtitle translation: An Italian-American Progressive Organ

A popular paper whose president was the pro-communist deputy Vito Marcantonio, it published writings by Italian communists (living in Italy) such as Felicita Ferrero and Emilio Sereni or by the socialist Francesco Frola, who was living in exile in Mexico. Besides providing international and Italian news coverage along a profoundly antifascist line, it regularly published surveys on the American workers' movement, life in the various Italian regions and correspondence from the various states. It contained large sections on sports, theater and problems of everyday life such as health and cooking.

Source: Andreucci/Detti, *Il movimento operaio*, vol. V, p. 172.

IL PROLETARIATO	NY New York	1919 ?

Title trans.:	The Proletariat	*First issue:*	1919 ?
Subtitle:		*Last issue:*	
Add. lang.:		*Vols. (nos.):*	
First editor:		*Frequency:*	
First publ.:		*Preservation:*	7
Related pubs.:		*Supplements:*	
Circulation:		*Category:*	anarchist

Depositories:

No further information could be obtained.

Source: *Revolutionary Radicalism*, pp. 2003-06.

IL PROLETARIO	NY New York	1896-1946

Title trans.:	The Proletarian	*First issue:*		1896 ?
Subtitle:	Organo dei Socialisti Italiani	*Last issue:*		My 1946
Add. lang.:		*Vols. (nos.):*		III-L
First editor:	Alessandro Mazzoli	*Frequency:*	tm, bm, w, bw, d, ir
First publ.:		*Preservation:*		3
Related pubs.:	c Avanti!, s La Difesa, s Il Nuovo Proletario, s Il Proletario, m La Giovane Italia	*Supplements:*		23 Ag 1902
Circulation:	1900: 3000; 1916: 7800	*Category:*		socialist/ SLP/ syndicalist-IWW

Depositories: I-ISTAM (2)); Usa-MnU-I (2,mn, mp,ou,); Usa-DLC (2); Usa-MH (2); Usa-MiU (2); Usa-NN (2); Usa-NNC (2); <Usa-PPBI (2); Usa-WHi (2)

Subtitle translation: Periodical of the Italian Socialists

Originally published by a workingmen's cooperative enterprise, this paper started out as a successor to *Avanti!*. Officially affiliated with the SLP in 1899, it regained its autonomy in 1902 when it became the official organ of the recently organized Italian Socialist Federation. In this organization SLP and SP allegiances coexisted and the paper reflected an intricate web of tensions and debates within and outside the Federation. Between 1911 and 1916 *Il Proletario* became a partisan of the IWW and strongly supported IWW strikes, especially when Italians were involved. It eventually became the official organ of the Italian sections of the IWW in 1921. It often campaigned for militants who were persecuted for their activities on behalf of the labor movement and took part in the IWW fight for "free speech." Because of its antiwar stands and of its cooperation with the IWW during the "Red Scare," *Il Proletario* was stripped of mailing rights. It then appeared as *La Difesa* and subsequently as *Il Nuovo Proletario* in Chicago. It regained its old name in 1920. From this period onward, *Il Proletario* strove for a strong antifascist unity among Italian immigrants beyond ideological differences. Nevertheless, its antagonism toward allegedly deceiving reformist workers' organizations, such as the ILGWU or the ACWA, never waned. While it regarded the Soviet revolution favorably, relations with the American Communist Party were often strained. During World War Two it supported American war efforts and also devoted its attention to the discussion of postwar plans concerning Italy. Most of the time *Il Proletario* concentrated on political comments, on debates concerning the organization of workers and correspondence from workers. At times there were educational sections aiming at women and articles on general culture and scientific knowledge. Its editors included famous names such as Dino Rondani, Giacinto Menotti Serrati, Carlo Tresca, Arturo Giovannitti, Edmondo Rossoni, Raimondo Fazio, Mario De Ciampis and many others.

Sources: Vezzosi, "La Federazione Socialista Italiana," p. 104; Cartosio, "Gli emigranti italiani," pp. 366-67; Cutter/Thompson, *A Survey of the Italian Language Press*, p. 66.

LA PROPAGANDA	IL Chicago	1908-?

Title trans.:	Propaganda	*First issue:*	7 Mr 1908
Subtitle:	Organo settimanale delle Sezioni socialiste del Nord Ovest	*Last issue:*	
Add. lang.:		*Vols. (nos.):*	
First editor:	Diagora De Bella	*Frequency:*	w
First publ.:	Italian Socialist Federation Branch of Chicago	*Preservation:*	5
Related pubs.:		*Supplements:*	
Circulation:		*Category:*	socialist-ISF

Depositories: I-ISSOCO (5:[1908],o); Usa-MnU-I (5:[1908],m);

Subtitle translation: The Weekly Organ of the North West Socialist Branches

The leading article of the first issue declared the objective of this newspaper: to provide news on the program and activities of the Socialist Party; to spread knowledge of socialist theory and practice among Italian immigrants and contribute to the awakening of their consciousness. In the few available issues general, international, national and local news coverage was provided. "La pagina degli operai" [the workers' page] contained local union news.

LA PROTESTA UMANA	CA San Francisco	1900

Title trans.:	Human Protest	*First issue:*	1 Mr 1900
Subtitle:	Periodico comunista-anarchico	*Last issue:*	S 1900
Add. lang.:		*Vols. (nos.):*	I(3)
First editor:	Enrico Travaglio	*Frequency:*	m
First publ.:		*Preservation:*	1
Related pubs.:	s *La Protesta Umana* (Chicago)	*Supplements:*	
Circulation:		*Category:*	anarchist

Depositories: Nl-IISG (1,o); Usa-MnU-I (1,m); I-ISTAM (1,m)

Subtitle translation: A Communist-Anarchist Periodical

Being profoundly antiorganizational, Travaglio, who had just emigrated to the United States, founded this periodical in order to spread knowledge about anarchism through the publication of abstracts from writings of Kropotkin, Mella, Raveggi, Ciancabilla. It lasted only a few months for lack of funds. In 1902 Travaglio succeeded in founding another *La Protesta Umana* together with Enrico Ciancabilla in Chicago, IL.

Source: Bettini, *Bibliografia dell'anarchismo*, p. 175.

LA PROTESTA UMANA   IL Chicago   1902-1904

Title trans.:	Human Protest	*First issue:*	F 1902
Subtitle:	Rivista mensile di scienze sociali, arte e letteratura	*Last issue:*	1 O 1904
Add. lang.:		*Vols. (nos.):*	I(1)-III(23)
First editor:	Enrico Travaglio, Giuseppe Ciancabilla	*Frequency:*	m, w
First publ.:		*Preservation:*	2
Related pubs.:	c *La Protesta Umana* (San Francisco)	*Supplements:*	
Circulation:		*Category:*	anarchist

Depositories: Nl-IISG (2,o); Usa-MnU-I (2, m); I-ISTAM (2,m)

Subtitle translation: A Monthly Review of Social Sciences, Art and Literature

Enrico Travaglio, editor of the short-lived *La Protesta Umana* published in San Francisco in 1900, succeeded in bringing the paper to new life in 1902 with the aid of Giuseppe Ciancabilla. The new *La Protesta Umana* was published in Chicago but at the beginning of 1903 Ciancabilla moved to San Francisco owing to his bad health and *La Protesta Umana* moved with him. When Ciancabilla died on 15 September 1904, the paper printed two more issues and then closed down on 1 October. The review published articles on theoretical issues, criticized unionism and defended individual terrorism. Many people contributed to *La Protesta Umana*; among them were Luigi Molinari, Giovanni Baldazzi and Raffele Valente.

Source: Cartosio, "Italian Workers and their Press," p. 429.

PROTESTA UMANA   MA Boston   1926-1927

Title trans.:	Human Protest	*First issue:*	Je 1926
Subtitle:	Bollettino del Comitato di difesa Sacco e Vanzetti	*Last issue:*	Ap 1927
Add. lang.:		*Vols. (nos.):*	I(1)-II(3)
First editor:		*Frequency:*	ir
First publ.:		*Preservation:*	1
Related pubs.:	c *L'Agitazione*	*Supplements:*	
Circulation:		*Category:*	anarchist

Depositories: Nl-IISG (1); I-INSML (1,mp)

Subtitle translation: The Bulletin of the Sacco and Vanzetti Defense Committee

Like its predecessor *L'Agitazione*, this bulletin was entirely dedicated to the defense of the two anarchists. It reported on the trial, raised funds and organized meetings.

QUADERNI ITALIANI	MA Boston	1942-1944

Title trans.:	Italian Notebooks	*First issue:*	Ja 1942
Subtitle:		*Last issue:*	1944
Add. lang.:		*Vols. (nos.):*	I(1)-(4)
First editor:	Bruno Zevi	*Frequency:*	ir
First publ.:		*Preservation:*	1
Related pubs.:		*Supplements:*	
Circulation:		*Category:*	antifascist

Depositories: I-ISTAM (2:[1942-44]); I-INSML (2:[1942-43]); Usa-DLC (1); Usa-NN (1); Usa-NNC (1); Usa-NNC-CI (1)

The four existing issues of this paper were published by a group of intellectual Italian antifascists (Aldo Garosci, Renato Poggioli, Enzo Tagliacozzo, Bruno Zevi) associated with the group "Giustizia e libertà " [Justice and Freedom]. The aim of *Quaderni Italiani* was in accordance with the political line of the GL group "to study the Italian situation, to examine the problems of reconstruction at the fall of fascism, to make the antifascist organizations acting in Italy known." Printed in two different editions, it was clandestinely sent to Italy as well as being distributed among Italian exiles all over the world.

LA QUESTIONE SOCIALE	NJ Paterson	1895-1908

Title trans.:	The Social Question	*First issue:*	15 Jl 1895
Subtitle:	Periodico socialista anarchico	*Last issue:*	21 Mr 1908
Add. lang.:		*Vols. (nos.):*	I(1)-XIV(419)
First editor:	Giuseppe Ciancabilla	*Frequency:*	bw, w
First publ.:		*Preservation:*	2
Related pubs.:		*Supplements:*	see below
Circulation:		*Category:*	anarchist

Depositories: Nl-IISG (2:[1895-1908]); Usa-MnU-I (2:[1895-1908]); I-ISSOCO (3:[1895-1904])

Subtitle translation: A Socialist-Anarchist Periodical

The publication of this paper was fostered by Pietro Gori, who had emigrated to the United States to attempt to support the organizational trend in the North American movement by organizing lectures and founding periodicals. In 1899 its editor, Giuseppe Ciancabilla, who had in the meantime become convinced of the impossibility of spreading organizational ideas in the United States and who had become a supporter of antiorganization, left the paper to found *L'Aurora* [The Dawn], in order to spread his new ideas. When Ciancabilla left, Errico Malatesta, an Italian anarchist who had emigrated to the United States on a propaganda tour, personally assumed the editorship of *La Questione Sociale*. The periodical had columns such as Rassegna settimanale Nord-americana [Weekly North American Review], Nel mondo minerario [In the Mining World] and La nostra stampa [Our Press]. The paper also published a number of supplements: *Al popolo italiano* [To the Italian People] (20 May

1899), *Umberto e Bresci* [Humbert and Bresci] (20 November 1900), *The Social Question. Supplement to La Questione Sociale* (30 April 1902)
Sources: Cartosio, "Italian Workers and Their Press," p. 434; Bettini, *Bibliografia dell'anarchismo*, p. 292.

LA QUESTIONE SOCIALE	NY New York	1914-1916

Title trans.:	The Social Question	*First issue:*	18 O 1914
Subtitle:	Periodico di propaganda anarchica	*Last issue:*	3 S 1916
Add. lang.:		*Vols. (nos.):*	I(1)-III(6)
First editor:	Aldino Felicani	*Frequency:*	w, ir
First publ.:		*Preservation:*	3
Related pubs.:		*Supplements:*	
Circulation:		*Category:*	anarchist

Depositories: NI-IISG (3); Usa-MnU-I (3,m)

Subtitle translation: A Periodical of Anarchist Propaganda
Publication of this review started in October 1914 to "unite revolutionary forces" against the cruelty of capitalism. Directed by Aldino Felicani, its main activity was centered on antimilitary issues throughout the duration of its existence. Having an organizational tendency, it was naturally opposed to *Cronaca Sovversiva* [Subversive Chronicle] the review directed by Luigi Galleani which supported the individualist tendency. Due to disputes between the two tendencies, *La Questione Sociale* suspended publication between April and August 1916.

LA RAGIONE NUOVA	RI Providence	1909-1910

Title trans.:	The New Reason	*First issue:*	Ja 1909
Subtitle:		*Last issue:*	S 1910
Add. lang.:		*Vols. (nos.):*	
First editor:	Luigi Nimini	*Frequency:*	m
First publ.:		*Preservation:*	5
Related pubs.:		*Supplements:*	
Circulation:		*Category:*	socialist

Depositories: Usa-RHi (5:[1909-10])

Luigi Nimini founded a socialist circle, The Karl Marx Circle, and published *La Ragione Nuova*.
Source: Vecoli, "The Italian Immigrants," p. 279.

LA REALTA' DEI PROBLEMI SOCIALI CONTEMPORANEI	MI Detroit	1932-1933

Title trans.:	The Reality of Social Contemporary Problems	*First issue:*		O 1932
Subtitle:		*Last issue:*		Ja 1933
Add. lang.:		*Vols. (nos.):*		(1)-(3)
First editor:	Domenico Zavattero	*Frequency:*		m, bm
First publ.:		*Preservation:*		5
Related pubs.:		*Supplements:*		See below
Circulation:		*Category:*		anarchist

Depositories: I-ISTAM (5); Nl-IISG (5)

Printed in Marseille, France, but also distributed through the "Self-Governing" book store of Detroit, MI, this antiestablishment leaflet was inspired by Galleani, who had been deported to Italy in 1919. It championed "new and more decisive methods of action" which were required by the reality of social oppression. It published a supplement *Manifesto ai compagni degli Stati Uniti* (1933) [A Manifesto to the Comrades in the United States].

IL RIBELLE	NY New York	1939

Title trans.:	The Rebel	*First issue:*	5 O 1939
Subtitle:	Organo del gruppo Camillo Berneri	*Last issue:*	?
Add. lang.:		*Vols. (nos.):*	
First editor:		*Frequency:*	ir
First publ.:		*Preservation:*	5
Related pubs.:		*Supplements:*	
Circulation:		*Category:*	anarchist

Depositories: I-ISRT (5); Nl-IISG (5); Usa-MnU-I (5)

Subtitle translation: The Organ of the Camillo Berneri Group

This anarchist propaganda paper of which only one issue was found, strongly criticized *L'Adunata dei Refrattari* [The Call of the Refractaires] and its contributors, accusing them of swindling and of authoritarian tendencies.

IL RISCATTO		IL Chicago	1914
Title trans.:	Redemption	*First issue:*	1 My 1914
Subtitle:	Per l'emancipazione operaia e la lotta di classe	*Last issue:*	21 O 1914
Add. lang.:		*Vols. (nos.):*	I(1)-I(10)
First editor:	Emilio Grandinetti	*Frequency:*	bw
First publ.:		*Preservation:*	4
Related pubs.:		*Supplements:*	
Circulation:	1914: 5000	*Category:*	labor union/ syndicalist

Depositories: I-ISTAM (4,m); Usa-MnU-I (4,m)

Subtitle translation: For Workers' Emancipation and Class Struggle

This paper was the organ of Local 358 of the Tailors' Industrial Union International and it favored amalgamation with the United Garment Workers Union of America to form a single tailors' union.

LA RISCOSSA		NY Brooklyn	1916-1917
Title trans.:	The Revolt	*First issue:*	Ja 1916
Subtitle:	Giornale libertario, antimilitarista, rivoluzionario	*Last issue:*	N 1917
Add. lang.:		*Vols. (nos.):*	I(1)-II(8)
First editor:		*Frequency:*	m
First publ.:		*Preservation:*	1
Related pubs.:		*Supplements:*	
Circulation:		*Category:*	anarchist

Depositories: I-CSLP (1,m); Nl-IISG (1,o); Usa-MnU-I (1,m)

Subtitle translation: A Libertarian, Antimilitarist, Revolutionary Journal

A strongly anticlerical paper, this dealt mainly with World War One and opposed Wilson's peace policy. It also published articles on strikes in Minnesota and on the arrest of Carlo Tresca.

LA RISCOSSA		FL Tampa	1936-1941

Title trans.:	The Revolt	*First issue:*	30 Ap 1936
Subtitle:	Contro la guerra, contro il fascismo.	*Last issue:*	30 Ag 1941
	Edito dal gruppo antifascista		
Add. lang.:	Spanish	*Vols. (nos.):*	I(1)-VI(8)
First editor:	Romeo Zenoni	*Frequency:*	ir, bw
First publ.:		*Preservation:*	2
Related pubs.:		*Supplements:*	
Circulation:		*Category:*	antifascist/ anarchist

Depositories: Nl-IISG (2,o); I-INSML (2,mp)

Subtitle translation: Against War, Against Fascism. Published by the Antifascist Group.

The main issue of this paper being propaganda against war and fascism, it supported the formation of a united front against fascism, maintaining at the same time that each group would remain intact inside the front. In October 1938 the paper was discontinued due to lack of funds. A second series was started in April 1939. The paper was distributed through the local "Centro Obrero" [Workers' Center] and was printed both in Spanish and in Italian; it provided international information as well as local political and labor news. Among its contributors were Alfonso Coniglio, F. Cavalli, Arturo Giovannitti. *La Riscossa* also published articles from other papers and abstracts from Galleani, Carlo Rosselli and others.

RISORGERE		NY New York	1931-1932

Title trans.:	Resurrection	*First issue:*	10 O 1931
Subtitle:	Bollettino mensile dei gruppi di Giustizia	*Last issue:*	15 D 1932
	e libertà		
Add. lang.:		*Vols. (nos.):*	I(1)-II(10)
First editor:		*Frequency:*	m
First publ.:		*Preservation:*	2
Related pubs.:		*Supplements:*	
Circulation:		*Category:*	antifascist

Depositories: I-ISRT (2); Usa-MH (2))

Subtitle translation: The Monthly Bulletin of the Groups "Justice and Freedom."

IL RISVEGLIO   CO Pueblo   1906-1955

Title trans.:	The Awakening	*First issue:*	18 Ja 1906
Subtitle:	Organo quotidiano indipendente delle colonie italiane negli S.U.	*Last issue:*	D 1955
Add. lang.:		*Vols. (nos.):*	I(?)-L(11)
First editor:	Vincenzo Massari	*Frequency:*	w, sw, d, m
First publ.:	Frank Mancini	*Preservation:*	2
Related pubs.:	m *L'Unione*	*Supplements:*	
Circulation:		*Category:*	reform

Depositories: Usa-CoP (2,m); I-ISTAM (2,m)

Subtitle translation: The Independent Daily Organ of the Italian Colonies in the United States.

This was a socialist-inspired independent periodical which had as a motto "united we stand, divided we fall." At the 1915 Louisville Convention of the United Mine Workers of America, it became "The Italian Organ of District n. 15 and 22, U.M.W.A." It mainly dealt with immigrants' lives and in general with workers living in the western states, with mine workers' struggles and with the various sections of the U.M.W.A. During the war and during the period immediately following the war, it became the target of attacks by mine owners and by the police, who did not hesitate to massacre workers as they did in Ludlow in 1914.

IL RISVEGLIO ITALIANO   Q Montreal   1926

Title trans.:	The Italian Awakening	*First issue:*	1926
Subtitle:		*Last issue:*	
Add. lang.:		*Vols. (nos.):*	
First editor:	Antonio Spada	*Frequency:*	w
First publ.:		*Preservation:*	7
Related pubs.:		*Supplements:*	
Circulation:		*Category:*	antifascist

Depositories:

This paper was founded by the Montreal antifascist Antonio Spada and was supported by the "Giacomo Matteotti Club," but after only four months it was silenced by the Canadian authorities. Yielding to pressure from the Italian Consul General in Montreal the Department of Immigration suppressed the paper and placed its editor under order of deportation. Eventually Spada avoided this fate as a result of a petition signed by several thousand people; nonetheless the paper had to stop publication.

Sources: Spada, p. 114; Principe, p. 120; Bruti Liberati, p. 66-67.

LA RIVOLTA		WI Madison	1913-1914

Title trans.:	The Revolt	*First issue:*	5 Ag 1913
Subtitle:		*Last issue:*	5 Je 1914
Add. lang.:		*Vols. (nos.):*	I(1)-II(6)
First editor:		*Frequency:*	ir
First publ.:		*Preservation:*	4
Related pubs.:		*Supplements:*	
Circulation:		*Category:*	anarchist

Depositories: Nl-IISG (4); Usa-MnU-I (4,m)

This was a publication connected with the extreme individualist wing of Italian anarchism and it was particularly active in the campaign for the defense of the Italian anarchist Augusto Masetti, who was persecuted by the Italian authorities and imprisoned in a criminal lunatic asylum.

LA RIVOLTA DEGLI ANGELI		NY New York	1923-1926

Title trans.:	The Rebellion of Angels	*First issue:*	? D 1923
Subtitle:	Giornale degli anormali, esce quando piace a noi	*Last issue:*	15 My 1926
Add. lang.:		*Vols. (nos.):*	(1)-(5)
First editor:	Cesare Stami	*Frequency:*	ir
First publ.:		*Preservation:*	1
Related pubs.:		*Supplements:*	
Circulation:		*Category:*	anarchist

Depositories: Nl-IISG (1,o); I-INSML (1,m)

Subtitle translation: Journal of the Anomalous, It Comes Out When We Like It

This paper pretended ironically to be edited by "la ghenga del fil di ferro" [the gang of iron wire] and to be administered by "-000-." This well represents the attitude of the paper which was fiercely individualist and antiorganizational. It denounced over and over again unionists (Antonini) and libertarians (Tresca, Zonchelli). It published theoretical articles on the family, anarchism etc. Among its contributors was Angiolina Algeri, who was initially favorable to intervention in war, as she thought that World War One was "a fierce war against German imperialism and, above all, against all imperialism," but who in 1924 criticized her previous positions. The paper which was as irregular as denounced in the subtitle, suspended publication between March 1924 and May 1926.

LA SCOPA	NJ Paterson	1925-1928

Title trans.:	The Broom	*First issue:*	Ag 1925
Subtitle:	Dinamico d'igiene pubblica edito a cura della lega antifascista di Paterson	*Last issue:*	15 S 1928
Add. lang.:		*Vols. (nos.):*	I(1)-IV, n.s.(13)
First editor:	Francesco Pitea	*Frequency:*	w
First publ.:		*Preservation:*	6
Related pubs.:		*Supplements:*	
Circulation:		*Category:*	antifascist/ anarchist

Depositories: Nl-IISG (6:[1926-27]); Usa-MnU-I (6:[1926-27],m)

Subtitle translation: A Dynamic Review of Public Health Edited by the Antifascist League of Paterson

This was an antifascist review published by Francesco Pitea who was also known as Libero Arseno in literary cirlces. With the use of strong and decisive antifascist propaganda, the review became an important link between antifascist activities.

SECOLO NUOVO	CA San Francisco	1894-1906 ?

Title trans.:	New Century	*First issue:*	1894
Subtitle:		*Last issue:*	1906 ?
Add. lang.:	English	*Vols. (nos.):*	
First editor:	Cesare Crespi	*Frequency:*	bm, w
First publ.:	Secolo Nuovo Publishing Co.	*Preservation:*	5
Related pubs.:		*Supplements:*	
Circulation:		*Category:*	anarchist

Depositories: I-ISSOCO (5:[1903],o); Usa-MnU-I (5:[1903],m)

The few available issues of this paper cover local news and contain contributions to the debate going on in the anarchist movement in which it opposed Giuseppe Ciancabilla, the editor of *L'Aurora* who was against any form of organization.

IL SEME	NY Brooklyn	1937-1938 ?

Title trans.:	The Seed	*First issue:*	1 My 1937
Subtitle:		*Last issue:*	Je 1938 ?
Add. lang.:		*Vols. (nos.):*	I(1)
First editor:		*Frequency:*	ir
First publ.:		*Preservation:*	1
Related pubs.:		*Supplements:*	
Circulation:		*Category:*	reform ?

Depositories: Nl-IISG (3:[1937]); I-INSML (3:[1937],mp); Usa-NN (1)

Written in a popular style (dialogues, short plays) 'the seed comes out to speak to those who are low, in the shadow...'

LA SENTINELLA	MI Calumet	(1906)

Title trans.:	The Sentry	*First issue:*	1896
Subtitle:	Giornale Socialista	*Last issue:*	6 F 1906
Add. lang.:		*Vols. (nos.):*	XI
First editor:	Teofilo Petriella	*Frequency:*	w
First publ.:		*Preservation:*	5
Related pubs.:	*L'Avanti*	*Supplements:*	
Circulation:		*Category:*	socialist-SP

Depositories: Usa-ICHi (5:[1906],mp); Usa-MnU-I (5:[1906])

Subtitle translation: A Socialist Newspaper

In 1906 the socialist paper *L'Avanti* [Forward] bought out the bourgeois journal *La Sentinella*, added the subtitle "A Socialist Newspaper" and appeared for one issue. The editor, Teofilo Petriella, was an organizer for the Italian section of the Socialist Party.

LA SENTINELLA	NJ Hoboken	1903-1907

Title trans.:	The Sentry	*First issue:*	20 Je 1903
Subtitle:		*Last issue:*	20 Je 1907
Add. lang.:		*Vols. (nos.):*	
First editor:	Giovanni Gallina	*Frequency:*	w
First publ.:	Giovanni Gallina	*Preservation:*	5
Related pubs.:		*Supplements:*	
Circulation:		*Category:*	radical

Depositories: I-ISSOCO (5:[1907]); Usa-MnU-I (5:[1907],m)

The few existing issues provide local news coverage "in order to solve the urgent problems and needs of the Italians."

LA SFERZA	NJ Westfield	1924-1925

Title trans.:	The Lash	*First issue:*	7 N 1924
Subtitle:	Pubblicazione periodica	*Last issue:*	1 D 1925
Add. lang.:		*Vols. (nos.):*	I(1)-II(3)
First editor:	Nicola Piesco, Luigi Vella, Carmelo Briguglio	*Frequency:*	ir
First publ.:		*Preservation:*	2
Related pubs.:		*Supplements:*	
Circulation:		*Category:*	anarchist

Depositories: I-INSML (2,mp); Nl-IISG (2,o)

Subtitle translation: A Periodical Publication

This paper was published by the anarchist groups in Westfield and Philadelphia (where the paper was in fact edited and printed) to criticize the management of *L'Adunata dei Refrattari* [The Call of the Refractaires], the anarchist antiorganizational paper, and particularly its editor, Costantino Zonchello. *La Sferza* was intended to be used for internal debate inside the anarchist movement; other groups in the United States followed the example of those in Philadelphia and the polemics against *L'Adunata* spread and developed on the pages of many anarchist papers.

Source: Bettini, *Bibliografia dell'anarchismo*, p. 217.

IL SOLCO	NY New York	1927-1928 ?

Title trans.:	The Furrow	*First issue:*	Ja 1927
Subtitle:	An Italian Monthly Magazine of Popular Culture Published by Vincenzo Vacirca	*Last issue:*	Je 1928 ?
Add. lang.:		*Vols. (nos.):*	I(1)-II(6)
First editor:		*Frequency:*	m
First publ.:	Vincenzo Vacirca	*Preservation:*	3
Related pubs.:		*Supplements:*	
Circulation:		*Category:*	antifascist/ reform

Depositories: I-FF (3:[1927-28]); I-ISTAM (4:[1927-28]); Usa-MnU-I (4:[1927-28])

This paper featured theoretical articles on fascism, bolshevism, democracy, news on international politics and on Italy, besides serializing educational stories and publishing poems.

SOLIDARIETA ANTIFASCISTA		NY New York	1946
Title trans.:	Antifascist Solidarity	*First issue:*	Ja 1946
Subtitle:	Bollettino dell'Ufficio italiano dell'International Rescue and Relief Committee	*Last issue:*	
Add. lang.:		*Vols. (nos.):*	I(1)
First editor:	Bruno Pierleoni	*Frequency:*	
First publ.:		*Preservation:*	5
Related pubs.:		*Supplements:*	
Circulation:		*Category:*	antifascist

Depositories: I-IG (5,o)

Subtitle translation: The Bulletin of the Italian Bureau of the IRRC

This bulletin was designed to provide information on the activities of the IRRC, a committee organized in order to help the reintegration of Italian antifascists returning from concentration camps or prisons in foreign countries and to lend a helping hand to the families of the dead. The chairman of the IRRC was L. Hollingsworth Wood, while Charles A. Beard was its honorary chairman. Many personalities belonged to the national committee of the IRRC; among them there were unionists (Abraham Bluestein, Victor Reuther, Samuel Wolchok and Luigi Antonini) as well as politicians and intellectuals (John Dewey, John dos Passos, Upton Sinclair).

SORGIAMO!		NY New York	1908-1909
Title trans.:	Let Us Arise!	*First issue:*	My 1908
Subtitle:	Foglio di critica e di propaganda anarchica	*Last issue:*	Mr 1909
Add. lang.:		*Vols. (nos.):*	I(1)-II(2)
First editor:	Ugo Di Somma, Luigi Florio	*Frequency:*	ir
First publ.:		*Preservation:*	7
Related pubs.:		*Supplements:*	
Circulation:		*Category:*	anarchist

Depositories:

Subtitle translation: A Leaflet of Anarchist Criticism and Propaganda

An individualistic propaganda leaflet containing theoretical articles with clear educational intentions, it was favorably accepted by the anarchist press at first. It soon changed its style, becoming more and more polemic and arousing bitter criticism within the anarchist movement itself.

Source: Bettini, *Bibliografia dell'anarchismo*, pp. 184-185.

LA STAMPA LIBERA   NY New York   1931-1938

Title trans.:	The Free Press	*First issue:*	21 O 1931
Subtitle:	Quotidiano dei lavoratori italiani d'America	*Last issue:*	30 Mr 1938
Add. lang.:		*Vols. (nos.):*	I(1)-VIII(73)
First editor:	Girolamo Valenti	*Frequency:*	d
First publ.:		*Preservation:*	1
Related pubs.:	c *Il Nuovo Mondo*	*Supplements:*	
Circulation:		*Category:*	antifascist

Depositories: I-ISTAM (1,m); Usa-Cu (1); Usa-MnU-I (1); Usa-NN (1,m)

Subtitle translation: The Daily of the Italian Workers of America

This paper was a continuation of *Il Mondo* which was forced to close because it was ravaged by the various antifascist trends. Directed by Girolamo Valenti, it counted among its contributors Serafino Romualdi, Oscar Mazzitelli and Fort Velona. It dealt with international news, Italy's internal situation, the workers' struggles in the United States and Italian-American labor unions. It paid particular attention to the activities of the Italian Trade Union of New York and had a column called "News of Greater New York and the suburbs." The paper was active in denouncing the fascist infiltration of Italian-American cultural organizations like the Casa Italiana [Italian House] and of the lodges of the Order of the Sons of Italy. It never ceased opposing fascism and supporting the masses who emigrated to the United States.

LO STATO OPERAIO   NY New York   1940-1943

Title trans.:	The Workers' State	*First issue:*	15 Mr 1940
Subtitle:	Rassegna di politica proletaria	*Last issue:*	D 1943
Add. lang.:		*Vols. (nos.):*	I(1)-III(4)
First editor:	Giuseppe Berti, Ambrogio Donini	*Frequency:*	ir
First publ.:	Nuove Edizioni Italiane	*Preservation:*	1
Related pubs.:		*Supplements:*	
Circulation:		*Category:*	communist

Depositories: I-INSML (1); I-FF (1); Usa-NN (1); Usa-CSt-H (1)

Subtitle translation: A Survey of Proletarian Politics

Published by the Italian Communist Party (PCI), this paper was issued in Paris from 1927 to 1939. In Paris it was the (unofficial) organ of the Party and, besides fulfilling a theoretical and cultural task, it functioned as a constant source of information on national and international politics. Suppressed by the French government at the outbreak of war, it started publication in New York in 1940. The American phase is the least interesting in the life of the review: too far from the "Centro interno" [Internal Center] of the Party to represent its political line. In the United States *Lo Stato Operaio* became a publication for the Italian emigrants under the control of the American Communist Party. It had a limited circulation in the United States and only a few copies were sent clandestinely to Italy. It published articles on Italian emigration to the United States and on the Italian political and economic situation, giving a great deal of space to problems with the Soviet Union. Besides contributions from its editors, Berti and Donini, the review published writings of the Italian communist leader Palmiro Togliatti (Ercoli) and of Mario Montagnana and Vittorio Vidali, the Italian communist exiles in Mexico. With the clandestine publication of *L'Unità* (the organ of the Party) in Italy in 1942, it became even less significant and it was discontinued by the Party in 1943 with the promise of "meeting again in Italy," a promise which was never kept.

LA STRADA
NY New York   1937-1938

Title trans.:	The Street	*First issue:*	Je 1937
Subtitle:	Rivista mensile di cultura popolare diretta da V. Vacirca	*Last issue:*	D 1938
Add. lang.:		*Vols. (nos.):*	I(1)-II(11)
First editor:	Vincenzo Vacirca	*Frequency:*	m
First publ.:	La Strada Publishing Co.	*Preservation:*	5
Related pubs.:		*Supplements:*	
Circulation:		*Category:*	socialist

Depositories: I-ISTAM (5); Usa-MnU-I (5)

Subtitle translation: A Monthly Review of Popular Culture Edited by Vincenzo Vacirca

"An eclectic and varied review, which will deal with everything and everybody, with no set tracks, no preconceived ideas and no theoretical bondage of any kind. Politics, science, literature, theater - everything is and will be the subject of curiosity and exploration," declared the first issue. Of socialist inspiration, the review dealt with labor unionism, health and hygiene, political and international affairs and counted among its contributors such personalities as Felice Gadagnati, Arturo Giovannitti and Raimondo Fazio. It published Carla Vacirca's novel "Cupid mong the Black Shirts" in instalments.

LA TERRA
CA Stockton   1906-1910 ?

Title trans.:	The Earth	*First issue:*	26 My 1906
Subtitle:	Organo del Popolo	*Last issue:*	1910 ?
Add. lang.:		*Vols. (nos.):*	
First editor:	Enrico Travaglio	*Frequency:*	w
First publ.:		*Preservation:*	6
Related pubs.:		*Supplements:*	
Circulation:		*Category:*	socialist

Depositories: Usa-MnU-I (6:[1907],mf)

Subtitle translation: The Organ of the People

This was a radical newspaper critical of the AFL bureaucracy for taking positions in the interests of the capitalist class. The general conditions of workers, including those in Mexico, were presented in addition to more specific news about strikes. Both antimilitarism and anticlericalism were discussed as well as the role of women in society and the destruction of the working-class family. The paper also serialized *The Mother* by Gorki.

IL TESSITORE LIBERO	NY New York	1920

Title trans.:	The Free Textile Worker	*First issue:*	1920
Subtitle:		*Last issue:*	
Add. lang.:		*Vols. (nos.):*	
First editor:	Anthony Capraro	*Frequency:*	
First publ.:		*Preservation:*	7
Related pubs.:		*Supplements:*	
Circulation:		*Category:*	labor union

Depositories:

This was the official organ of the ATWA (Amalgamated Textile Workers of America) affiliated with the ACWA (Amalgamated Clothing Workers of America). Source: Vecoli, "Anthony Capraro," p. 19.

IL TRADITORE	NY New York	1942-1943

Title trans.:	The Traitor	*First issue:*	10 Je 1942
Subtitle:	Benito Mussolini and His 'Conquest' of Power	*Last issue:*	1 My 1943
Add. lang.:		*Vols. (nos.):*	I(1)-I(8)
First editor:	Angelica Balabanoff	*Frequency:*	m
First publ.:	Giuseppe Popolizio	*Preservation:*	1
Related pubs.:		*Supplements:*	
Circulation:		*Category:*	antifascist

Depositories: I-INSML (1,o); Usa-CSt-H (1); Usa-DLC (1); Usa-NjP (1); Usa-NN (1)

As pointed out in the first issue of this publication, its aim was to educate "those who do not know." It was the task of those who knew, and particularly of the editor who had lived through many of the episodes related in the publication, to inform on the rise of fascism. *The Traitor* was a popular serialized story of the origins and development of fascism, so that "the readers may be able to face recent and future events."

LA TRIBUNA ITALIANA   Q Montreal   1963-1979

Title trans.:	The Italian Tribune	*First issue:*	15 O 1963
Subtitle:		*Last issue:*	1979
Add. lang.:		*Vols. (nos.):*	XV
First editor:	Camillo Carli	*Frequency:*	w, m
First publ.:	Camillo Carli	*Preservation:*	2
Related pubs.:		*Supplements:*	
Circulation:	3000	*Category:*	socialist

Depositories: Cdn-OONL (2:[1963-78],o)

This was the most prestigious Italian-Canadian periodical in Montreal. Under the direction of Camillo Carli it took the responsibility of fighting against the isolation and marginalization of the Italian immigrants from the social contest. Its attacks on the so-called "leaders of the Italian Canadians" were remarkable. In Carli's opinion and not only his, there was an attempt, unfortunately successful, to keep the immigrants in a position of ignorance and dependence on the media and the economic elite so that they could maneuver them at their will. After Carli went back to Italy, the paper declined until it closed down three years later.

IL TRIBUNO   NJ Newark   1908-1913

Title trans.:	The Tribune	*First issue:*	12 D 1908
Subtitle:	Published every Saturday	*Last issue:*	1913
Add. lang.:		*Vols. (nos.):*	
First editor:	Olindo Marzulli	*Frequency:*	w
First publ.:	Il Tribuno Publishing Co.	*Preservation:*	5
Related pubs.:		*Supplements:*	
Circulation:		*Category:*	radical

Depositories: I-ISSOCO (5:[1908],o); Usa-MnU-I (5:[1908],m)

The only existing issue provides coverage of international as well as local events; it claims to look after the immigrants' interests.

UMANITA NOVA	NY Brooklyn	1924-1925

		First issue:	1 N 1924
Title trans.:	New Humanity	*Last issue:*	1 My 1925
Subtitle:	Periodico libertario	*Vols. (nos.):*	I(1)-II(10)
Add. lang.:		*Frequency:*	w
First editor:	Maris Baldini (pseud. Siram Nibaldi)	*Preservation:*	1?
First publ.:		*Supplements:*	
Related pubs.:		*Category:*	anarchist
Circulation:			

Depositories: NI-IISG (1,?); I-FF (5:[1925],o)

Subtitle translation: A Libertarian Periodical

The complete collection, supposedly held in IISG, could not be found. The only available issue contains theoretical articles, besides news from the anarchist committee in favor of Italian political victims "Pro vittime politiche d'Italia."

L'UNIONE	CO Pueblo	1897-1926

		First issue:	19 N 1897
Title trans.:	Union	*Last issue:*	28 N 1926
Subtitle:	Giornale protettore degli interessi della classe operaia	*Vols. (nos.):*	I(1)-XXIX(2806)
Add. lang.:		*Frequency:*	d, w, m
First editor:	Ettore Chiariglione	*Preservation:*	2
First publ.:	Abruzzo-Molise Publishing Co.	*Supplements:*	
Related pubs.:	s *Abruzzo e Molise*, s *Il Risveglio*, s *Marsica Nuova*		
Circulation:		*Category:*	labor

Depositories: I-ISTAM (2,m); Usa-CoP (2)

Subtitle translation: A Paper Protecting Working-Class Interests

This periodical was directed by Ettore Chiariglione, then by Vincenzo Massari. It had ties with the Columbian Federation of Italian-American Societies, a patriotic and masonic association founded in Chicago in 1893 which supported workers' interests and solidarity among workers.

The organization was never connected with fascism; on the contrary, it was strengthened by the collaboration of socialists and communists and later even that of Count Carlo Sforza. The periodical was a channel of communication between the sections of the Columbian Federation and other associations (for mutual aid and workers' associations) as well as among Italian Americans living in states across the country, especially in Colorado. During the period of fascist rule, it harshly attacked Giovanni Di Silvestro, Respectful Venerable of the Order of the Sons of Italy, who had made that organization nationalist and fascist. The numbering of the issues continues with *Abruzzi e Molise*, 1924-26. The periodical continues with *Il Risveglio* [The Awakening].

L'UNITA	NY New York	1954-1961

Title trans.:	Unity	*First issue:*	D 1954
Subtitle:	Mensile progressista Italo-americano	*Last issue:*	1961
Add. lang.:		*Vols. (nos.):*	
First editor:	John Ribelli	*Frequency:*	m, sm
First publ.:		*Preservation:*	3
Related pubs.:	c *L'Unità del Popolo*	*Supplements:*	
Circulation:		*Category:*	communist

Depositories: Usa-CMS (3); I-IG (3)

Subtitle translation: A Progressive Italian-American Monthly

This was the continuation of *L'Unità del Popolo* edited by Gino Bardi, which ceased publication in June 1954. It provided information on North American and international politics, publishing correspondence from Spain (Dolores Ibarruri), Italy (Pietro Ingrao, Palmino Togliatti) and so on. Among its contributors were its editor (John Ribelli), Diogene Ghibellino and Luigi Costa. It aimed at propagating the activity of the American Committee for the Protection of the Foreign Born and the activities of the AFL and CIO. It published comprehensive abstracts of and comments on the Italian and North American conferences of the Communist Party and of the Socialist Party.

L'UNITA DEL POPOLO	NY New York	1939-1951

Title trans.:	Unity of the People	*First issue:*	25 My 1939
Subtitle:	Settimanale delle forze progressive italo-americane	*Last issue:*	11 Ag 1951
Add. lang.:		*Vols. (nos.):*	I(1)-XIII(29)
First editor:	Gino Bardi	*Frequency:*	w, m
First publ.:	L'Unità del Popolo Publishing Co.	*Preservation:*	2
Related pubs.:	s *L'Unità*	*Supplements:*	
Circulation:	30,000	*Category:*	communist

Depositories: Usa-DLC (2:[1939-51],m); Usa-ICRL (2:[1939-51], m); Usa-MnU-I (2:[1939-51],m); I-INSML (3:[1941-44],o); I-FF (3:[1939-40],o)

Subtitle translation: An Italian-American Progressive Weekly

In 1939, at the outbreak of war in Europe, this paper was the only official publication of the Italian Communist Party (PCI) in the world. It was the faithful interpreter of the line followed by the Communist Party after the Nazi-Soviet pact of Munich which meant fighting on two opposite sides, putting Nazis and European democratic countries on the same level. This attitude did not change until Hitler's attack on the USSR. In contrast to the non-communist antifascist exiles who were not favorable to antifascist unity, *L'Unità del Popolo* had the function of establishing a link between the Communist Party and the less integrated section of the Italian-American community, while the role of ideological guide was played by *Lo Stato Operaio* [The Workers' State]. In accordance with this line, *L'Unità del Popolo* provided general international (especially Italian) and local news as well as news from the labor unions. Among its contributors were the most significant communist exiles, such as Giuseppe Berti and Ambrogio Donini (who were also its editors) and Vittorio Vidali and Mario Montagnana from Mexico.

L'UNITA OPERAIA   NY New York   1932-1938

Title trans.:	Working-Class Unity	*First issue:*	17 D 1932
Subtitle:	Settimanale di Battaglia dei Lavoratori Italiani d'America. Giornale del Partito Comunista d'Italia.	*Last issue:*	S-O 1938
Add. lang.:		*Vols. (nos.):*	I-V; (60)
First editor:	Tito Nunzio	*Frequency:*	w, m, sm
First publ.:	L'Unità Publishing Association	*Preservation:*	3
Related pubs.:		*Supplements:*	
Circulation:	7000	*Category:*	communist

Depositories: Usa-NN (3:[1932-34, 1936-38],m)

Subtitle translation: The Weekly Paper of the Struggles of Italian Workers in America. The Journal of the Italian Communist Party

Officially the offspring of the Italian Communist Party, this paper began publication as a bulwark of the United Front and strongly criticized those forces in the center and on the left that resisted it. *L'Unità Operaia* focused its attention on several issues. First, it strove to keep Italians in the United States abreast of the latest crimes of the Italian fascist government. Second, it promoted the participation of Italians in the development of the American communist movement and in the active organization of industrial unions. Furthermore, Tom De Fazio, following an orthodox Stalinist line, wrote carefully about the political and social life in the Soviet Union. In 1936, Giuseppe Altieri became the official editor. It had regular columns called 'Union Struggles,' 'International News' and one that dealt with American events. The paper's editorials on American politics were generally in agreement with the positions of the American Communist Party.

UNITED MINE WORKERS' JOURNAL   IN Indianapolis   (1914-1933)

Title trans.:		*First issue:*	?25 Ag 1892
Subtitle:		*Last issue:*	1958
Add. lang.:	Slovak, English	*Vols. (nos.):*	
First editor:		*Frequency:*	w, sm
First publ.:	National Executive Board of the United Mine Workers of America	*Preservation:*	1
Related pubs.:		*Supplements:*	
Circulation:		*Category:*	labor union- U.M.W. of A.

Depositories: Usa-NN (1,m); Usa-WHi (1,m)

The United Mine Workers' Union responded to the pressures of its constituency on 3 December 1914 when it added sections in Slovak and Italian to its official English-language publication. The *United Mine Workers' Journal* was founded in 1892. Three editors - Edgar Wallace, Joseph Poggiani and Michael Halapy - were appointed for the English, Italian and Slovak sections respectively. In the Italian section many articles were signed by Armando Pellizzari, who sometimes contributed to the English section too. Some were translated from the English section, especially the ones concerning major issues of union policy. Others were reproductions of articles that had appeared in the Italian labor press currently published in Italy, such as *La Confederazione del Lavoro*, *La Cooperazione Italiana* and *La Guerrin Meschino*. Many Italian workers reacted positively to this initiative, writing to the paper about their activities in the locals, their strike efforts (especially in Colorado and Ohio) and their struggles with American institutions. After some time a column in the Italian section was devoted to the reports on the attempts to organize consumers' cooperatives that appear to have been on the agenda of several Italian locals, especially in Illinois. Another column gave brief news about events in the United States. While specific partisan politics were carefully shunned, issues such as the war, both in Italy and in the United States, or the relationship with the rival IWW union were often monitored in the Italian-language section. In 1918 Joseph Poggiani was dismissed from his position as editor. Michael Halapy met with the same fate. The foreign-language sections were then transformed into mere translations of the articles published in the English section, while direct correspondence from foreign locals ceased to be published. In 1933 the United Mine Workers' Journal discontinued its foreign-language sections. (The journal itself survived until 1958).

L'UOMO NUOVO	NY New York	1916-1917

Title trans.:	The New Man	*First issue:*	1 D 1916
Subtitle:	Periodico anarchico	*Last issue:*	30 Ja 1917
Add. lang.:		*Vols. (nos.):*	I(1)-II(3)
First editor:		*Frequency:*	bm
First publ.:		*Preservation:*	4
Related pubs.:		*Supplements:*	
Circulation:		*Category:*	anarchist

Depositories: I-ISRT (4); Usa-MnU-I (4,m); Nl-IISG (4,o)

Subtitle translation: An Anarchist Periodical

This leaflet defined itself as "an anarchist leaflet without adjectives," but in fact it was highly individualist and antiestablishment, disseminating antimilitary and anticlerical propaganda.

IL VELTRO		NY New York	1924-1925

Title trans.:	The Greyhound	*First issue:*	1 Mr 1924
Subtitle:		*Last issue:*	F 1925
Add. lang.:		*Vols. (nos.):*	II
First editor:	Arturo Giovannitti	*Frequency:*	bw, m
First publ.:	Italian Chamber of Labor	*Preservation:*	4
Related pubs.:		*Supplements:*	
Circulation:		*Category:*	antifascist/ socialist

Depositories: Usa-MnU-I (4:[1924-25],oub); I-ISTAM (3:[1924-25],m)

This unofficial antifascist journal was critical of socialists in the Italian parliament and included a long letter by Amadeo Bordiga on the development of Italian fascism. On 15 July 1924 it published a special edition on Giacomo Matteotti, including a notice on a protest meeting held in Carnegie Hall. It had educational articles on the Russian Revolution and it supported Trotsky against charges of bonapartism. The paper also contained a number of Italian translations of Giovannitti's poetry.

LA VERA REDENZIONE		CT Bridgeport	1916-1917

Title trans.:	The True Redemption	*First issue:*	1916
Subtitle:	Fortnightly Newspaper of Mazzinian Republican Propaganda	*Last issue:*	1917 ?
Add. lang.:		*Vols. (nos.):*	I-II
First editor:		*Frequency:*	bw
First publ.:		*Preservation:*	5
Related pubs.:		*Supplements:*	
Circulation:		*Category:*	anarchist

Depositories: Usa-MnU-I (5:[1916],m); I-BMN (5:[1916],o)

The only available issue of this paper was mainly devoted to asking for solidarity on behalf of Carlo Tresca who had been arrested during the strikes in Minnesota. In the same issue the newspaper condemned American democracy and its political parties as false and defined both as reactionary and the enemies of proletarians. In Bridgeport the supporter of the publication was the "Circolo Studi Sociali" [Circle for Social Studies]; this circle held conferences on the European war and bourgeois reaction in the United States, promoted dances to finance *La Vera Redenzione* and supported anarchist, socialist and republican propaganda.

VITA NUOVA	WY Rock Springs	1908-1911

Title trans.:	New Life	*First issue:*	7 F 1908
Subtitle:		*Last issue:*	1911
Add. lang.:		*Vols. (nos.):*	
First editor:	Giulio Nigro	*Frequency:*	w
First publ.:	F. DiGiacomo	*Preservation:*	5
Related pubs.:		*Supplements:*	
Circulation:		*Category:*	labor

Depositories: Usa-MnU-I (5:[1908-09],oub)

The goal of this newspaper was the "defense of the interests of the workers" and it wanted to accomplish this through education. It included information on Freemasonry and socialism in art. In January 1909 Vincenzo De Gregoriis became the editor.

LA VITTORIA	O Toronto	1942-1943

Title trans.:	Victory	*First issue:*	18 Ap 1942
Subtitle:	Rassegna settimanale di pensiero e di azione	*Last issue:*	16 O 1943
Add. lang.:		*Vols. (nos.):*	I-II
First editor:	Augusto Bersani	*Frequency:*	w
First publ.:	La Vittoria Publishing Co.	*Preservation:*	2
Related pubs.:		*Supplements:*	
Circulation:		*Category:*	antifascist

Depositories: Cdn-OONL (2)

Subtitle translation: A Weekly Review of Thought and Action

This paper was founded by Rev. Augusto Bersani, a Montreal antifascist, with the aim of spreading democratic ideals among Italian Canadians and supporting the Allied war effort. At the beginning the paper was a sort of mouthpiece of the Mazzini Society of Canada (founded in 1941). But in September 1942 Bersani left his position and the Italian communist Ennio Gnudi became the new editor. Under Gnudi's leadership *La Vittoria* fought against American and Canadian moderate antifascists maintaining that a true antifascist alliance could not exclude the communists.

LA VOCE DEGLI ITALO-CANADESI	O Toronto	1938-1940

Title trans.:	The Voice of Italian Canadians	*First issue:*	1 O 1938
Subtitle:	Giornale d'opinione e di educazione popolari	*Last issue:*	30 Ap 1940
Add. lang.:		*Vols. (nos.):*	I(1)-II(12)
First editor:	Remo Sandrini	*Frequency:*	bw
First publ.:		*Preservation:*	1
Related pubs.:		*Supplements:*	
Circulation:		*Category:*	antifascist

Depositories: Cdn-OONL (1,m)

Subtitle translation: A Journal of Popular Opinion and Education

This paper tried to create a new broad alliance among antifascists; for the first time in a Canadian antifascist paper the interests of small business, merchants and professional people were explicitly defended. The line of the paper changed after the Nazi-Soviet pact of August 1939 and the outbreak of the war. *La Voce* aligned itself with the communist position of non-intervention and therefore most non-communists withdrew their support. The paper was forced to stop publication in the spring of 1940 when the Canadian Communist Party was outlawed.

LA VOCE DEL TIPOGRAFO	NY New York	1934-1940

Title trans.:	The Typographer's Voice	*First issue:*	1934
Subtitle:		*Last issue:*	1940
Add. lang.:		*Vols. (nos.):*	
First editor:	Primo Calcaterra	*Frequency:*	m
First publ.:		*Preservation:*	6
Related pubs.:		*Supplements:*	
Circulation:		*Category:*	labor union

Depositories: Usa-MnU-I (6:[1936-38],oub)

This paper was the official organ of the New York Italian Typographical Union, No. 261. It contained mainly union news and general news about the economy and the New Deal. It also fought against the 1938 attempt by the House of Representatives' committee on un-American activities to suppress Italian-American newspapers. In 1938 its editor was Ovidio Fusco.

LA VOCE DELLO SCHIAVO	FL Tampa	1900-1901

Title trans.:	The Slave's Voice	*First issue:*	Ag 1900
Subtitle:		*Last issue:*	21 Mr 1901
Add. lang.:	Spanish	*Vols. (nos.):*	I(1)-II(12)
First editor:	Pietro Calcagno	*Frequency:*	ir
First publ.:		*Preservation:*	3
Related pubs.:		*Supplements:*	
Circulation:		*Category:*	anarchist

Depositories: Nl-IISG (3)); Usa-MnU-I (3,m)

This was an anarchist review connected with the Spanish-Italian-Cuban community in Ybor City. Besides dealing with anarchist propaganda, it also dealt with the working conditions of Italian and Spanish-speaking immigrants.

LA VOCE INDIPENDENTE	PA Philadelphia	1938-1942

Title trans.:	The Independent Voice	*First issue:*	1938
Subtitle:		*Last issue:*	1942
Add. lang.:		*Vols. (nos.):*	
First editor:	Roberto D'Antonio	*Frequency:*	
First publ.:		*Preservation:*	6
Related pubs.:		*Supplements:*	
Circulation:		*Category:*	labor union

Depositories: Usa-MnU-I (6:[1938],oub)

The Board of Directors of this paper included representatives of a number of union locals in the Philadelphia area including the Carpenters Union and the American Commercial Workers as well as representatives of independent labor groups. The paper was published in the interest of "social progress and the good of the people." It also contained articles on fascism by Pietro Nenni.

LA VOCE OPERAIA	O Toronto	1933-1935

Title trans.:	The Worker's Voice	*First issue:*	Jl 1933
Subtitle:	Periodico Antifascista	*Last issue:*	? 1935
Add. lang.:		*Vols. (nos.):*	
First editor:		*Frequency:*	ir
First publ.:		*Preservation:*	6
Related pubs.:		*Supplements:*	
Circulation:		*Category:*	antifascist

Depositories: Cdn-OONL (6:[1933]); I-ACS (6:[1933]); I-INSML (6:[1933])

Subtitle translation: An Antifascist Periodical

This paper was edited by the militant workers of the Mazzini Club of Toronto, founded in 1928, and it was also supported by other groups such as Local 253 of the Amalgamated Clothing Workers of America, the Italian section of the Independent Labor Party and the Italian branch of the United Workers of America. The paper attacked fascism in two ways: it published facts and reports about the Italian situation under the dictatorship and it exposed the schemes and frauds of local fascists in Canada. It also fought against the fascist takeover of Italian-Canadian mutual benefit associations.

Source: Principe, p. 119-137.

VOLONTA	NY New York	1919 ?

Title trans.:	Will	*First issue:*	1919 ?
Subtitle:		*Last issue:*	
Add. lang.:		*Vols. (nos.):*	
First editor:		*Frequency:*	
First publ.:		*Preservation:*	7
Related pubs.:		*Supplements:*	
Circulation:		*Category:*	anarchist

Depositories:

No further information could be obtained.

Source: *Revolutionary Radicalism*, pp. 2003-06.

IL VOMERO	PA Philadelphia	1940-1942

Title trans.:	The Ploughshare	*First issue:*	Mr 1940
Subtitle:		*Last issue:*	O 1942 ?
Add. lang.:		*Vols. (nos.):*	I(1)-II(3)
First editor:		*Frequency:*	ir
First publ.:		*Preservation:*	1
Related pubs.:		*Supplements:*	
Circulation:		*Category:*	anarchist

Depositories: NI-IISG (1,o); I-INSML (1,mp)

This paper was intended to spread information on international news and North American labor. Even if it devoted less space to the polemics that spread inside the anarchist movement than other papers did, it was definite and sharp in its rejection of "alleged radicals" such as Carlo Tresca, Max Sartin, Auro d'Arcola and Virgilio Gozzoli who were condemned as corrupt dictators. Its main contributors were Ezio Taddei, Celestino Lalli (with the pseudonym L'Udito delicato [Delicate Hearing]) and Edmondo Rajola (with the pseudonym Manga Nello). The Canadian authorities prevented its delivery in Canada.

WORLD LABOR FORUM	NY New York	1948-1949

Title trans.:	Panorama del Lavoro nel Mondo	*First issue:*	N 1948
Subtitle:	Monthly Review of Labor, Science, Art, Literature and International Events	*Last issue:*	Ag 1949
Add. lang.:		*Vols. (nos.):*	
First editor:	Frank Bellanca	*Frequency:*	m
First publ.:	Italian People's Union	*Preservation:*	1
Related pubs.:		*Supplements:*	
Circulation:		*Category:*	labor/reform

Depositories: Usa-NN (1,o); Usa-CSt-H (1); Usa-CtY (1); Usa-DLC (1); Usa-MH (1)

Although this magazine had been planned and supported by a group of Italian labor leaders, its main purpose was to raise the political awareness of its readership. Thus one of its major topics was criticism of the Republican Party and its programs. The paper did not abstain from criticizing the church hierarchy when its actions damaged the workers. Besides articles by its editor Frank Bellanca and Amerigo Ruggiero as well as poems by Arturo Giovannitti, there were also contributions by Norman Thomas and the Supreme Court judge Francis X. Giaccone. Postwar conditions in Italy were analyzed and the paper often emphasized the need for industrial development in the Italian South. It also upheld the idea that the economic attitude of the United States toward the peninsula should have been similar to the one held toward England and France.

Title Index

Abruzzo e Molise
  See also *Marsica Nuova, L'Unione.*
Adunata dei refrattari, L'
Agitazione, L'
  See also *La Protesta Umana* (Boston).
Al popolo italiano
  See *La Questione Sociale* (Paterson).
Alba
Alba nuova, L'
  See also *Il Lavoratore* (Chicago).
Alba sociale, L'
Allarme, L'
Anarchia, L'
Anarchico, L'
Appello, L'
Ascensa del proletariato, L'
Asino, L'
Aurora, L' (Boston)
Aurora, L' (West Hoboken)
Aurora socialista
Avanti! (Chicago)
  See also *Fiaccola* (Chicago), *La Parola del Popolo.*
Avanti, L' (Newark)
  See also *La Sentinella* (Calumet).
Avanti! (Philadelphia)
  See also *Il Proletario.*
Avvenire, L' (New York)
Avvenire, L' (New Kensington)
Avvenire, L' (Steubenville)
Azione, L' (Barre)
Azione, L' (New York)
Balilla, Il
Barbiere moderno, Il
Bohemien, Il
Bollettino (Chicago, I)
Bollettino (Chicago, II)
Bollettino de l'era nuova, Il
  See also *L'Era Nuova*
Bollettino del comitato promotore de IL popolo
  See also *Il populo*
Bollettino dello sciopero dei sarti
Bollettino mesile della Federazione Giustizia e liberta del Nord America
Campana, La
Chanteclair
Ci vaiu
Cogito, ergo sum
Coltura popolare
Comune, La
Conquista, La

In memoria di Ettore Tresca
  See *Il Martello.*
Internacional, El
Internazionale, L' (Boston)
Internazionale, L' (Philadelphia)
Intesa libertaria
Italia d'oggi, L'
Italia libera, L'
  See *Legione dell'Italia del popolo, La*
Italian American
  See *Il Lavoratore Italiano.*
Italiana, L'
Italiano, L'
Jacquerie, La
Justice
  See *Ladies' Garment Worker.*
Ladies' Garment Worker
Lavoratore, Il (Chicago)
  See also *Alba Nuova.*
Lavoratore, Il (New York)
Lavoratore, Il (Toronto)
Lavoratore, Il (Montreal)
Lavoratore italiano, Il
Lavoro, Il (New York, I)
Lavoro, Il (New York, II)
Leydis garment voyrker, Der
  See Jewisch Migrants Section, volume 2.
Legione dell'Italia del popolo, La
Liberatore, Il
Libertà, La
Lotta, La (New York)
Lotta, La (State of NY)
Lotta di classe (New York, I)
  See also *L'Operaia, La Giustizia.*
Lotta di classe (New York, II)
Lotta operaia
Man!
  See *Emancipazione, L'.*
Manet immata fides
  See *Il Martello.*
Manifesto ai compagni degli Stati Uniti
  See *La realtà dei problemi sociali contemporanei.*
Marsica nuova
  See also *Abruzzo e Molise, L'Unione, Il Risveglio.*
Martello, Il
Mastro Paolo
Mazzini News
  See *Nazioni Unite.*
Minatore, Il (Chicago)
Minatore, Il (Pueblo)
Minatore, Il (Salt Lake City)
Minatore italiano, Il
Mondo, Il (New York, I)
  See also *Il Mondo* (New York, II)

Place Index

East Boston
Movimento anarchico

Lynn
Balilla

MICHIGAN
Calumet
Sentinella

Detroit
Realta'" dei problemi sociali contemporanei

MINNESOTA
Duluth
Minatore italiano

Minneapolis
Campana

NEW JERSEY
Hoboken
Sentinella

Newark
Avanti
Tribuno

Paterson
Bollettino de l'era nuova
Era nuova
Jacquerie
Nuovi tempi
Pensiero operaio
Questione sociale
Scopa

West Hoboken
Aurora
Giovane Italia

Westfield
Sferza

NEW YORK
Bronx
Chanteclair
Eresia di oggi e di domani

Brooklyn
Ci vaiu
Domani
Parola dei dressmakers
Riscossa

Ordine nuovo
Palcoscenico
Parola del medico
Pensiero
Popolo
Proletariato
Proletario
Questione sociale
Ribelle
Risorgere
Rivolta degli angeli
Solco
Solidarieta''' antifascista
Sorgiamo!
Stampa libera
Stato operaio
Strada
Tessitore libero
Traditore
Unita'''
Unita''' del popolo
Unita''' operaia
Uomo nuovo
Veltro
Voce del tipografo
Volonta'''
World Labor Forum

Rochester
  Domenica
  Italiana

State of New York
  Lotta

Utica
  Lotta operaia

OHIO
Cleveland
  Appello
  Gioventu''' libertaria

Steubenville
  Avvenire

PENNSYLVANIA
Altoona
  Operaio italiano

New Kensington
  Avvenire
Philadelphia
  Avanti!

Chronological Index

1880 1890 1900 1910 1920 1930 1940 1950 1960 1970 1980
01234567890123456789012345678901234567890123456789012345678901234567890123456789012345

??
??
??

Minatore, Il	CO Pueblo
Liberatore, Il	Unknown
Grido antifascista	IL Chicago
Anarchico, L'	NY New York
Grido degli oppressi	NY New York
Pensiero operaio, Il	NJ Paterson
Secolo nuovo	CA San Francisco
Qestione sociale, La	NJ Paterson
Mastro Paolo	PA Philadelphia
Avanti	PA Philadelphia
Proletario, Il	NY New York
Unione, L'	CO Pueblo
Critica, La	CA San Francisco
Giovane Italia, La	NJ West Hoboken
Aurora, L'	NJ West Hoboken
Voce dello schiavo,	FL Tampa
Protesta umana, La	CA San Francisco
Operaio, L'	NY New York
Alba sociale, L'	FL Tampa
Protesta umana, La	IL Chicago
Liberta, La	NY New York
Lavoratore italiano,	CO Trinidad
Sentinella, La	NJ Hoboken
Cronaca sovversiva	VT Barre
Internacional, El	FL Tampa
Avanti, L'	NJ Newark
Terra, La	CA Stockton
Sentinella, La	MI Calumet
Risveglio, Il	CO Pueblo
Plebe, La	PA Philadelphia

144

1880   1890   1900   1910   1920   1930   1940   1950   1960   1970   1980
01234567890123456789012345678901234567890123456789012345678901234567890123456789012345

Grido del popolo, Il	CO Denver
Corriere di Chicago,	IL Chicago
Vita nuova, La	WY Rock Springs
Tribuno, Il	NJ Newark
Sorgiamo!	NY New York
Propaganda, La	IL Chicago
Parola dei socialist	IL Chicago
Minatore, Il	UT Salt Lake City
Era nuova	NJ Patterson
Cogito, ergo sum	CA San Francisco
Asino, L'	NY New York
Ascensa del proletar	PA Wilkes Barre
Ragione nuova, La	RI Providence
Nihil	CA San Francisco
Lotta, La	NY New York
Internazionale, L'	PA Philadelphia
Gogna, La	IL Kensington
Fiaccola, La	NY Buffalo
Avvenire, L'	OH Steubenville
Operaio italiano, L'	PA Altoona
Novatore, Il	NY New York
Ladies' Garment Work	NY New York
Corriere del popolo,	CA San Francisco
Comune, La	PA Philadelphia
Bollettino dello sci	IL Chicago
Avvenire, L'	PA New Kensington
Cooperazione, La	VT Barre
Contropelo, Il	VT Barre
Lotta di classe (I)	NY New York
Italiano, L'	CO Denver

1880   1890   1900   1910   1920   1930   1940   1950   1960   1970   1980
012345678901234567890123456789012345678901234567890123456789012345678901234567890123456789012345

Domenica, La	NY	Rochester
Balilla, Il	MA	Lynn
Rivolta, La	WI	Madison
Movimento anarchico,	MA	East Boston
Lotta operaia	NY	Utica
Lavoratore, Il	NY	New York
Germinal! (I)	IL	Chicago
Azione, L'	VT	Barre
Aurora socialista	UT	Salt Lake City
United Mine Workers'	IN	Indianapolis
Riscatto, Il	IL	Chicago
Qestione sociale, La	NY	New York
Lavoro, Il (I)	NY	New York
Gioventu libertaria,	OH	Cleveland
Corriere libertario	VT	Barre
Barbiere moderno, Il	NY	New York
Pensiero, Il	NY	Buffalo
Operaia, L'	NY	New York
Conquista, La	PA	Philadelphia
Allarme, L'	IL	Chicago
Vera redenzione, La	CT	Bridgeport
Uomo nuovo, L'	NY	New York
Riscossa, La	NY	Brooklyn
Parola proletaria, L	IL	Chicago
Parola del medico, L	NY	New York
Martello, Il	NY	New York
Grido del popolo, Il	NY	New York
Appello, L'	OH	Cleveland
Internazionale, L'	MA	Boston
Giornale dell'unione	IN	Indianapolis

146

1880   1890   1900   1910   1920   1930   1940   1950   1960   1970   1980
01234567890123456789012345678901234567890123456789012345678901234567890123456789012345

Campana, La	MN	Minneapolis
Nuovo proletario, Il	IL	Chicago
Nuovi tempi	NJ	Paterson
Minatore italiano, I	MN	Duluth
Marsica nuova	CO	Pueblo
Lotta, La	NY	New York
Fiaccola, La	IL	Chicago
Difesa, La	IL	Chicago
Cooperatore, Il	CO	Pueblo
Contro-Veleno	PA	Philadelphia
Avanti!	IL	Chicago
Anarchia, L'	NY	New York
Volonta	NY	New York
Proletariato, Il	NY	New York
Ordine, L'	NY	New York
Minatore, Il	IL	Chicago
Jacquerie, La	NJ	Paterson
Guardia rossa, La	NY	New York
Giustizia, La	NY	New York
Domani	NY	Brooklyn
Bollettino de l'era	NJ	Patterson
Tessitore livero, Il	NY	New York
Organizzatore, L'	FL	Tampa
Inevitabile, L'	NY	New York
Agitazione, L'	MA	Boston
Parola del popolo, L	IL	Chicago
Alba nuova, L'	NY	New York
Frusta dei cloakmake	NY	New York
Adunata dei refratta	NY	New York
Rivolta degli angeli	NY	New York

1880   1890   1900   1910   1920   1930   1940   1950   1960   1970   1980
01234567890123456789012345678901234567890123456789012345678901234567890123456789012345

Idea, L'   NY New York
Difesa, La   NY New York
Diana, La   NY New York
Veltro, Il   NY New York
Umanita nuvo   NY Brooklyn
Sferza, La   NJ Westfield
Lavoratore, Il   IL Chicago
Abruzzo e Molise   CO Pueblo
Scopa, La   NJ Paterson
Nuovo mondo, Il   NY New York
Bohemien, Il   NY New York
Risveglio italiano,   Q Montreal
Protesta umana   MA Boston
Germinal (II)   IL Chicago
Bollettino (I)   IL Chicago
Solco, Il   NY New York
Lotta di classe (II)   NY New York
Emancipazione, L'   CA San Francisco
Aurora, L'   MA Boston
Eresia di oggi e di   NY Bronx
Contravveleno, Il   NY New York
Ci vaiu   NY Brooklyn
Alba   PA Pittsburgh
Stampa libera La   NY New York
Risorgere   NY New York
Difesa de Il lavorat   NY New York
Bollettino (II)   IL Chicago
Unita operaia, L'   NY New York
Realta dei problemi   MI Detroit
Ordine nuovo, L'   NY New York

148

		1880	1890	1900	1910	1920	1930	1940	1950	1960	1970	1980

```
1880      1890      1900      1910      1920      1930      1940      1950      1960      1970      1980
01234567890123456789012345678901234567890123456789012345678901234567890123456789012345
```

Voce operaia, La	O Toronto
Voce del tipografo,	NY New York
Palcoscenico, Il	NY New York
Lavoratore, Il	O Toronto
Riscossa, La	FL Tampa
Strada, La	NY New York
Seme, Il	NY Brooklyn
Parola dei dressmake	NY Brooklyn
Parola, La	IL Chicago
Coltura popolare	CA San Francisco
Voce indipendente, L	PA Philadelphia
Voce degli italo-can	O Toronto
Popolo, Il	NY New York
Pensiero, Il	NY New York
Paese, Il	PA Philadelphia
Mondo, Il (I)	NY New York
Italiana, L'	NY Rochester
Controcorrente, La	MA Boston
Bollettino del comit	NY New York
Unita del popolo	NY New York
Ribelle, Il	NY New York
Intesa libertaria	PA Philadelphia
Vomero, Il	PA Philadelphia
Stato operaio, Lo	NY New York
Mondo, Il (II)	NY New York
Azione, L'	NY New York
Vittoria, La	O Toronto
Traditore, Il	NY New York
Quaderni italiani	MA Boston
Nazioni unite	NY New York

1880   1890   1900   1910   1920   1930   1940   1950   1960   1970   1980
01234567890123456789012345678901234567890123456789012345678901234567890123456789012345

Legione	NY New York
Chanteclair	NY Bronx
Avvenire, L'	NY New York
Italia d'oggi, L'	NY New York
Solidarieta antifasc	NY New York
Notiziario internazi	NY New York
World Labor Forum	NY New York
Unita, L'	NY New York
Lavoro, Il (II)	NY New York
Tribuna italiana, La	Q Montreal
Lavoratore, Il	Q Montreal
Forze nuove	O Toronto
Parola, La	O Toronto

Spaniards

Language

Spanish

Area Covered

Spain

Compiled by

·H. Rafael Chabrán

Whittier College, Whittier, CA

Acknowledgements

The following people and institutions have supported me in my work: Gail
Echternacht Chabrán, Louisiana State University; Richard Chabrán, Chicano
Studies Research Library, University of California, Los Angeles; Vivian Fisher,
University of California, Berkeley; Bettie Eriksen, University of California,
Berkeley; Thea Duijker, International Instituut voor Sociale Geschiedenis,
Amsterdam; Nélida Perez, Centro de Estudios Puertorriquenos, New York;
Laura Gutiérrez-Witt, Benson Latin American Collection, University of Texas,
Austin; Professor Lily Litvak, University of Texas, Austin; Professor W. Dirk
Raat, State University of New York; Professor James D. Cockcroft, University
of New Brunswick; César Caballero, University of Texas, El Paso; James P.
Danky, State Historical Society of Wisconsin, Madison; Marisa Zanatta, Univer-
sidad Estadual de Campinas, Sao Paulo, Brazil; The New York Public Library,
The Economic and Public Affairs Division

Depositories

Brazil:

Br-Camp   Universidad Estadual de Campinas,
Arquivo Edgard, Lewenroth, Sao
Paulo.

Netherlands:

Nl-IISG   International Instituut voor Soci-
ale Geschiedenis [International
Institute of Social Sciences],
Amsterdam.

United States:

Usa-CU	University of California, Berkeley, CA.
Usa-DL	United States Department of Labor Library, Washington, DC.
Usa-DLC	United States Library of Congress, Washington, DC.
Usa-IU	University of Illinois, Urbana, IL.
Usa-MH	Harvard University, Cambridge, MA.
Usa-MH-PA	Harvard University, Littauer Library of the Kennedy School of Government, Cambridge, MA.
Usa-NIC	Cornell University, Ithaca, NY.
Usa-NN	New York Public Library, New York, NY.
Usa-NNC	Columbia University, New York, NY.
Usa-NNHuC-CEP	Hunter College of the City University of New York, The Center for Puerto Rican Studies (Centro de Estudios Puertorriquenos), New York, NY.
Usa-WHi	State Historical Society of Wisconsin, Madison, WI.

Introduction

Newspapers are important sources for understanding the history of the Spanish-speaking working class of the United State. Often the press of Spanish immigrants, Puerto Ricans and Chicanos has offered the only documentation of the lives and struggles of these workers. Through this essay and bibliography, we hope to demonstrate that the Spanish-speaking workers were well aware of their history and documented it in their press. It is the primary intention of this essay to give a brief introduction to the nature and history of Spanish-language labor and radical newspapers, which were published in the United States from 1890 until 1972. Some of the more specific objectives of the bibliography are: (1) to shed light on previously unstudied titles of Spanish-language labor and radical newspapers in the United States and (2) to provide a record of the publishing activity of this press, by presenting a chronological account of the establishment of such newspapers. It is only through a careful examination of these journals that historians and Hispanists will arrive at a more complete vision of the political, economic and social milieu of the Spanish-speaking working class of the United States.

Studies of the Spanish-language press of the United States as a subject of historical research are of recent origin. Research on the radical and labor press is even more recent. While there are some studies on the Mexican-Chicano radical press, to the best of our knowledge there are no complete studies dealing with the press of Spanish immigrants and Puerto Ricans.

As has been stated, we have set the chronological limits of this study and bibliography from 1890 to 1972. The earliest papers which we have found are *La Correspondencia de Puerto Rico* a general newspaper published in Puerto Rico in 1890 which was firmly committed to reporting information on Puerto Rican workers and *El Despertar* an anarchist paper published in New York City by Spanish immigrants.

The greatest number of radical newspapers existed from the end of the nineteenth to the beginnings of the twentieth century. During the 1920s and 1930s there was a sizable decline in the numbers of these newspapers. This decrease can be explained by the fact that the radical and labor press was especially effected by the ups and downs of the economy. A great number of Spanish-language newspapers (not only the radical press) were extremely sensitive to the economic crisis of the 1930s. In addition, there was a decrease in the migration of workers to the United States because of the Great Depression and the coming of the World War. Furthermore it must not be forgotten that in the 1930s more than half a million Mexicans (many of them American citizens) were deported or repatriated to Mexico. All of these factors contributed to the decline of the Spanish-language labor and radical press during the 1930s.

However, the 1960s and 1970s witnessed a significant increase in this press. The student movement, the protest movement against the war in Vietnam and the Civil Rights Movement, along with the rise of Cesar Chavez, the noted Chicano activist, and the United Farmworkers Union, which he helped found stimulated the radical and labor press in Spanish. One such newspaper was *El Malcriado* (1964-75), the official organ of Chavez's union. During these years numerous radical and labor newspapers appeared in Mexican communities throughout the United States. Many newspapers were associated with Chicano student organizations and were published at local high schools, colleges and universities. Frequently student organizations such as the Movimento Estudiantil de Aztlan [Student Movement of Aztlan] published their own newspapers. In addition, the farmworkers' struggle stimulated an outgrowth of many farmworkers union papers such as *El Cuhamil* (San Juan, TX, 1975) and *Espuelazo* (Springfield, MA, 1975). We have not attempted to include these papers in our bibliography because of the large numbers, short runs and the difficulty in locating them. Neither have we included the press of Mexican mutual aid societies or papers associated with such organizations as the League of United Latin American Citizens (LULAC). While many of these organizations had newspapers which defended the interst of the Spanish- speaking people, it is often difficult to identify a radical political or labor perspective behind their editorials. Unfortunately limitations of time and space also prevented us from including newspapers such as *Sin Fronteras* (Los Angeles, 1974), a paper whose primary intention was the defense and organization of undocumented workers.

The Spanish-language labor press must necessarily be studied in relation to the general Spanish-language press of the United States. Both were closely linked to the immigration of Spanish-speaking workers.[1] As the Spanish-speaking population increased, so did the demand for Spanish-language newspapers. However, the Spanish labor newspapers appeared well after the establishment of the general Spanish-language press. The first Spanish-language newspaper published in what is now the United States was *El Misisipi* (New Orleans, LA, 1808).[2] Other important early newspapers which arose were *El Mexicano* (1813) and *El Crepúsculo* (1834).[3] As is the case for all newspapers, these journals were primarily vehicles for the dissemination of information, news and opinion. Through the articles in their pages they sought to mirror the particular political and cultural forces of their times and communities. The majority of these general newspapers were closely affiliated with particular business or commercial interests. Nonetheless they aided in raising the emerging ethnic consciousness of Spanish-speaking communities. Radical and labor newspapers, on the other hand, were what Park has negatively termed the "propagandist type"[4] which is to say that they were the official organs of particular political or labor groups. These papers concentrated on news that was directly relevant to the membership to which were they addressed. Often these newspapers reflected a particular political program (anarchist or socialist for example) and saw themselves as important organizing tools.

In his 1960 discussion of the nature of the Spanish-language press of the United States, Edward Hunter remarked that there was "no, strictly speaking, Spanish press, but only a Puerto Rican press, a Mexican press and a Latin American press."[5] While we do not agree with many of his conclusions, (are not Mexicans and Puerto Ricans Latin Americans ?) it is clear that Hunter was aware of the problems involved in identifying a Spanish-language press in the United States. A similar problem is encountered today with the use of the term "Hispanic Press." Such terms more often than not only confuse the issue by attempting to blur the cultural traditions and unique historical and political aspects of particular Spanish-speaking communities. In general, journalism historians have largely ignored the history of the Spanish-language press in the United States. Traditional histories of the press include small chapters on Spanish-language newspapers. More often, however, Spanish-language newspapers are grouped into chapters on "foreign-language newspapers," which receive little critical attention.[6] It is with no doubt for this reason, among many others, that some narrow-minded historians came to believe that the Spanish-speaking people of the United States, especially the working class, had no history or that they had not recorded it.

We have dealt with newspapers from three groups of Spanish speakers: Spanish immigrants, Puerto Ricans and Mexican-Chicanos.[7] Each of these groups published their own newspapers; but they also collaborated frequently. This was the case especially with Spaniards and Puerto Ricans in New York and Tampa, Florida. As these groups worked together, they also suffered together. They suffered greatly under espionage laws, during times of restricted immigration and economic depression.[8] Before we continue we must define the members of the particular groups whose press is under investigation. We take Spanish immigrants to be those Spanish-speaking people who were born in Spain and came to the United States. Mexicans and Chicanos (Mexican Americans) are those people of Mexican descent who were born in the United States or migrated there from Mexico. The case of Puerto Ricans is more complex since Puerto Rico did not become a territory of the United States until 1898. However, we have included Puerto Rican newspapers published before 1898 in our bibliography, because we believe that they are important for understanding subsequent migrations of workers to the United States. Also we have included newspapers published by Puerto Ricans on both the United States mainland and the island of Puerto Rico.

Labor press is defined as those newspapers published by a labor union or organized body of workers. By radical newspapers we are speaking of those newspapers which defined themselves as being of or for the working class. In this category, we include communist, socialist, syndicalist and anarchist newspapers. In a third category, we include those newspapers which, like exile Spanish Republican papers published in the United States after the Spanish Civil War (1936-39) and *La Correspondencia de Puerto Rico*, a general newspaper, were firmly on the side of the working class.[9]

Spanish Immigrants and Their Press

Large numbers of Spanish immigrants came to the United States during the last part of the nineteenth century and the beginnings of the twentieth. From 1890 to 1930, around 130,000 immigrants arrived from Spain.[10] The largest number, around 69.000 came between 1911 and 1920.[11] Thus they were part of the so-called new immigration wave of southern and eastern Europeans.

Most Spaniards, the majority of them single males, literate and skilled, left their country because of social, economic and political problems. From 1868 to 1878, Spain had experienced political turmoil.[12] First there were the problems caused by the Carlist Wars (1830s through 1870s), those dynastic wars between the urban liberals, the followers of Queen Isabel II and the rural traditionalists, the followers of Don Carlos. Then came the Revolution of 1868 which brought the fall of Isabel II. This event was followed by the coming of the First Republic of 1873 and finally the Restoration of the Borbon monarchy in 1875.[13] In addition to these political events, Spain was also troubled by the Cuban Wars of Independence (1868-78) and the Cantonal insurrections and revolts in the areas of Cartegena, Alcoy and Malaga (1873-74).

The Restoration (1875-1917) was a complex and difficult time for Spaniards. The return of the Borbon dynasty was a re-establishment of the values and interests of the nobility, the landed classes and the Church. Canovas del Castillo, the architect of the political programs of the Restoration sought to establish a stable political "order" in the face of the "disorder" and agitation brought on by the rising working-class movements. According to Canovas' program voting and the participation in government were limited to the wealthy and land-owning class. An oligarchy, which by some accounts was made up of less then 3 percent of the population, ruled the country. The rights of the individual, especially the rights of organized workers as well as regional and provincial laws (fueros) were neglected or violated. During this time Spain witnessed both internal and external migrations of population. One of the major factors for these migrations was rural poverty of the south of Spain (Andalucia) where large concentrations of land were in the hands of a small and very powerful elite. The rural poor had two options: internal migration to large urban centers, which most often meant Madrid in the center of the country or external migration to the United States or Latin America.[14]

Immigration from Spain to the United States, 1820-1976	
Years	Figures
1820	139
1821-1830	2,477
1831-1840	2,125
1841-1850	2,209
1851-1860	9,298
1861-1870	6,697
1871-1880	5,266
1881-1890	4,419
1891-1900	8,731
1901-1910	27,935
1911-1920	68,611
1921-1930	28,958
1931-1940	3,258
1941-1950	2,898
1951-1960	7,894
1961-1970	44,659
1971	3,661
1972	4,284
1973	5,538
1974	4,704
1975	2,573
1976	2,758
Total	249,092

Source: U.S. Immigration and Naturalization Service, *Annual Report*, 1976 (Washington, DC, 1977), pp. 88-91.

New York was the main port of entry to the United States. The first immigrants to New York City were quickly attracted to the "Barrio Latino" or Latin Quarters later known as Spanish Harlem. This area was to become the heart of the city's Hispanic community. The neighborhood was home to many Spanish-speaking groups: Spanish immigrants, Spanish Jews, Cubans and Puerto Ricans. Among these, there were many anarchists, socialists and other radicals deeply committed to defending the cause of the working class. It was also not uncommon for workers from different ethnic groups, such as Spaniards and Italians to band together to defend their rights. In addition to the groups already mentioned, New York City was also home to political exiles and intellectuals associated with the Cuban Republican Party. This group was headed by the noted Cuban patriot and poet, José Marti.[15]

From 1891 to 1912, several important labor and radical newspapers were founded in the New York City area. These were *El Despertar* (1891-1912), *Cultura Proletaria* (1910-1959) and *Brazo y Cerebro* (1912). These were primarily anarchist journals which carried articles by some of the most noted Spanish anarchists of the day, including Federico Urales and Anselmo Lorenzo.[16] These newspapers were staffed by Spanish anarchists, a great number of whom were Catalans, as well as Puerto Rican and Cuban immigrants. Much of this anarchist press was aimed at Spanish-speaking readers who worked in the cigar industry in New York. *El Despertar* was a biweekly anarchist paper which published labor news and anarchist tracts by such writers as J.C. Campos and Manuel Gonzales.[17] The paper was edited and run by Luis Barcia and Abello. *Brazo y Cerebro*, another New York Spanish anarchist newspaper, edited by Juan Martinez published essays on anarchism, communism and feminism. It frequently carried articles on politics, the arts and social issues such as marriage. *Cultura Proletaria* was one of the most important and longest running Spanish anarchist newspapers. The noted Spanish anarchist writer and editor Pedro Esteves worked on this newspaper. In later years the newspaper was staffed by Puerto Ricans and Cubans.

The Spanish Civil War and the subsequent fall of the Second Republic was another impetus for the immigration of Spaniards to the United States. Exiled Spanish Republicans, among them a great number of intellectuals, artists and those who had been very active in radical and left oriented politics came to New York. Many of these exiles worked on radical newspapers. Several important republican (anti-Franco, antifascist) newspapers appeared between 1931 and 1950. Among them were *Espana Republicana* (1931-35), *Espana Libre* (1939-77) edited by José Castro in Brooklyn, *Pueblos Hispanos* (1943-44), a Marxist oriented paper edited by Juan Antonio Cretiza and *Liberacion* (1946-49) edited by Carmen Mean and Aurelio Perez. This journal began as a Spanish Republican newspaper and later became associated with Puerto Ricans. By 1946 it came to represent the voices of the Hispanic working class in New York. The noted Puerto Rican writer José Luis Gonzales collaborated on this newspaper. Once again we have an example of Spanish immigrants joining ranks with working-class Puerto Ricans and other Hispanics in New York. *Liberacion* became what its subtitle proclaimed: "The Defender of the Spanish, Puerto Rican and Latin American Workers of the United States."

Spanish immigrants were attracted to other cities in the United States, cities where there were other Spaniards and where the cigar industry flourished, e.g. Key West, Tampa and Ybor City, Florida. In 1935, there were 7,000 Cubans and 5,000 Spaniards in Ybor City [18] most of them working in the cigar industry. Cubans and Spaniards often congregated around the city's "Spanish Clubs," which provided social contacts and activities for the Spanish-speaking residents of Ybor City.

The history of labor unions in the Tampa/Ybor City area is intimately connected with the rise of the cigar industry. In Tampa and Ybor City, Spanish immigrants worked side by side with Cubans and Puerto Ricans, just as they did in New York. Anarchists were active in organizing workers and in establishing working-class newspapers. As in New York City, Spanish-speaking workers also worked with Italians in organizing unions. The most important of these unions were the "Sociedad de Torcedores de Tabaco" and "La Federacion."[19] Florida's first labor newspaper *El Internacional* (1906) was the official organ of the cigar workers' union of Tampa. Other labor and radical Spanish-language newspapers to be published in the Tampa/Ybor City area were *El Esclavo* (1894) and *La Voz del Esclavo* (1900). These two newspapers were anarchist publications. *La Voz* was published with the help of Italian workers in Tampa.

Puerto Rican Immigrants and Their Press

Puerto Ricans also have a well developed labor and radical press in the United States. Any discussion of the social history of Puerto Rican workers to the United States must necessarily begin with the year 1898 when Spain was forced to cede Puerto Rico to the United States as a consequence of the Spanish American War. It is from this date that the political and economic domination of Puerto Rico begins. Puerto Rico remained under direct military rule of the United States until 1900, when the United States Congress set up an administration with a governor and an executive council appointed by the President of the United States (Foraken Act). In 1917, United States citizenship was imposed on all Puerto Ricans (Jones Act). Finally, in 1952, Puerto Rico changed status from a United States territory to become the Commonwealth of Puerto Rico, known in Spanish as *Estado Libre Asociado* [Free Associated State].

Net Migration of Puerto Ricans to the United States, 1900-1969			
Years	Figures	Annual Average	Rate
1900-09	2,000	200	0.0
1910-19	11,000	1,100	0.1
1920-29	42,000	4,200	0.3
1930-39	18,000	1,800	0.1
1940-49	151,000	15,100	0.7
1950-59	430,000	4,300	1.9
1960-69	253,000	25,300	1.0

Sources: For 1900-1950: José L. Vázquez Calzada. "Las causas y efectos de la emigración puertorriquena," mimeo. (San Juan: Escuela de Medicina, Universidad de Puerto Rico, 1968). For 1960-69 estimates by José Hernández Alvarez, Sociology Department, University of Arizona, mimeo.

Throughout its history, the island has seen many strong nationalist movements, which have demanded the independence of Puerto Rico from the United States. Likewise there have been other groups which have opted for the status quo (commonwealth status) or others which have sought statehood. But aside from the question of political status one of the most significant issues in political and scholarly debate is the subject of population movement.

The earliest migration of Puerto Ricans to the United States took place in the 1860s.[20] This involved the immigration of a "criollo" elite, who came to New York after 1868, many of them as political exiles. Often they had participated in the Lares insurrection against the Spanish in 1868. Since the revolt failed many were deported or voluntarily left the island. This group of Puerto Ricans joined with the existing group in New York in the 1890s, especially after 1895, the year of the second Spanish-Cuban war. During this time, pro-Independence Puerto Ricans joined forces with Cuban revolutionaries and collaborated on such radical papers as *La Revolucion* and *El Provenir*.

Movement of People Entering and Leaving Puerto Rico, 1909 to 1940				
Year ending June 30	Incoming	Outgoing	Gain	Loss
1909	5,085	1,974	3,111	-
1910	5,693	2,193	3,500	-
1911	5,953	4,478	1,475	-
1912	5,028	4,833	195	-
1913	3,895	3,873	22	-
1914	6,806	7,394	-	588
1915	6,221	6,560	-	339
1916	7,293	7,260	33	-
1917	8,458	10,812	-	2,354
1918	11,122	15,334	-	4,212
1919	22,472	25,784	-	3,312
1920	15,003	19,142	-	4,139
1921	17,749	17,137	612	-
1922	14,154	13,521	633	-
1923	13,194	14,950	-	1,756
1924	14,057	17,777	-	3,720
1925	15,356	17,493	-	2,137
1926	16,389	22,010	-	5,621
1927	18,626	27,355	-	8,729
1928	21,772	27,916	-	6,144
1929	20,791	25,428	-	4,637
1930	20,434	26,010	-	5,576
1931	20,462	18,524	1,938	-
1932	18,932	16,224	2,708	-
1933	16,215	15,133	1,082	-
1934	16,687	13,721	2,966	-
1935	18,927	19,944	-	1,017
1936	20,697	24,145	-	3,448
1937	22,793	27,311	-	4,518
1938	23,522	25,884	-	2,362
1939	21,165	25,653	-	4,488
1940	30,002	31,906	-	1,904

Source: Harvey Perloff, *Puerto Rico's Economic Future* (Chicago: University of Chicago Press, 1950).

We can distinguish three distinct periods of out-migration from the island of Puerto Rico from 1909 to 1940.[21] The first period lasted until the end of World War One. During this early period the expedition of contracted Puerto Rican workers to Hawaii from 1900 to 1901 constituted the first important migration.[22] This year, the Hawaiian Sugar Producers Association organized eleven expeditions of 450 Puerto Rican workers to labor on sugar plantations. The Puerto Rican newspaper, *La Correspondencia de Puerto Rico* carefully chronicled and documented this labor migration. The majority of these workers had previously been employed in the sugar cane industry or in the production of coffee and cigars. Most came from rural areas. From 1910 to 1920, the Puerto Rican population in the United States grew from 1,500 to 12,000.[23] The second period of migration occurs in the 1920s. At this time the Island witnessed crises in coffee and tobacco cultivation. Workers made their way from the country to the cities, such as San Juan. However, the cities could not support the social and economic problems brought on by these population movements. Emigration to the United States was suggested as a solution.

By 1930, the Puerto Rican population of New York City was 34,000.[24] There was limited migration in the 1930s because of the Depression and during World War Two migration almost ceased. In 1940 the population of Puerto Ricans had grown to 61-63,000, already making up a substantial portion of the city's population. An intense wave of migration began after 1945 and reached a peak in the 1950s. Between 1960 and 1965 migration of Puerto Ricans to the United States declined and between 1969 and 1970 significant return migration occurred.[25] By 1970 there were more than 800,000 Puerto Ricans in the state of New York, most of them living in New York City.

The first labor organizations in Puerto Rico date from the last third of the nineteenth century. Artisans and typesetters were first to organize. One of the most active groups, both in Puerto Rico and the United States was Federacion Libre de Trabajadores [Free Federation of Workers] founded in 1899.[26] After 1901, the Federacion became an affiliate of the American Federation of Labor. This organization published several newspapers in Puerto Rico and throughout the United States. Another important group which was active in organizing Puerto Rican workers was the Partido Socialista [Socialist Party], founded in Puerto Rico in 1915. Tabaqueros or cigar-makers played an important role in the Partido Socialista of New York and Florida.

Aside from working together with Spanish immigrants on their labor newspaper, Puerto Ricans also established their own press such as *La Misera* (1901), *Union Obrera* (1902) and *Vida Obrera* (1930-1932). Frequently, radical Puerto Rican newspapers followed socialist and pro-Independence lines such as in the newspapers *Nueva Lucha* (1934) and *Claridad* (1959). At other times, they followed established labor lines as was the case with *Boletin del Trabajo* (1934) and *Salario* (1969).

As we have indicated, one of the most important sources for studying the early migration of Puerto Rican workers was the general newspaper *La Correspondencia de Puerto Rico* (1890-1943).[27] This newspaper was one of the oldest and most popular newspapers in Puerto Rican history. A great deal of its success was based on the fact that it was a daily and that it sold for one cent. Its readership was diverse. According to some accounts: "Everyone read it. The rich and the poor, the city and the farmworkers, the intellectuals and the businessmen."[28] We can delineate three clear political positions in the history of this paper. First, a "Republican" period during 1899, second a "Unionist" period in 1902 and finally a pro-Independence position in 1912.[29] Nevertheless, the newspaper declared itself to be "absolutely impartial." During the beginning of this century the newspaper was deeply committed to labor news. From 1900 to 1929 it offered its readers a great deal of information on the migration of Puerto Rican workers. It reported on expeditions to Hawaii, to Cuba, Santo Domingo and Venezuela.[30]

Mexican Americans and Their Press

The largest number of Spanish-language labor and radical newspapers were published in the Southwest of the United States, mainly Texas, New Mexico, Colorado, Arizona and California. The growth of this press demonstrates that Mexicanos and Chicanos were forging a new socio-political identity in the Southwest. The press sought to document the problems and special needs of Mexican workers. The rise of this press must be contextualized within the history of the Southwest and especially with the incorporation of the Southwest into the U.S. national economy at the end of the nineteenth century. We must recall that from 1836 to 1848 this area was part of Mexico. These lands changed character dramatically from 1836 to 1853, as a result of the claims of the Texas Republic (1836) and the Mexican American War of 1845-1848. Two states, Texas and California and four territories: Nevada, Utah, Colorado and New Mexico were formed in part or entirely from the Mexican Cession of 1848. Any discussion of the population of the Southwest must take into account those Mexicans who were descendants of the original settlers of these areas and not view the Mexican population of this region only in terms of migration.

Mexican Immigrants to the United States (1900-1977)					
Years	Figures	Years	Figures	Years	Figures
1900	237	1927	67,721	1953	17,183
1901	347	1928	59,016	1954	30,645
1902	709	1929	40,154	1955	43,702
1903	528	1930	12,703	1956	61,320
1904	1,009	1931	3,333	1957	49,321
1905	2,637	1932	2,171	1958	26,791
1906	1,997	1933	1,936	1959	22,909
1907	1,406	1934	1,801	1960	32,708
1908	6,067	1935	1,560	1961	41,476
1909	16,251	1936	1,716	1962	55,805
1910	18,691	1937	2,347	1963	55,986
1911	19,889	1938	2,502	1964	34,448
1912	23,238	1939	2,640	1965	37,969
1913	11,926	1940	2,313	1966	45,163
1914	14,614	1941	2,824	1967	42,371
1915	12,340	1942	2,378	1968	43,563
1916	18,425	1943	4,172	1969	44,623
1917	17,869	1944	6,598	1970	44,469
1918	18,524	1945	6,702	1971	50,103
1919	29,818	1946	7,146	1972	64,040
1920	52,361	1947	7,558	1973	70,141
1921	30,758	1948	8,384	1974	71,586
1922	19,551	1949	8,083	1975	62,205
1923	63,768	1950	6,744	1976	57,863
1924	89,336	1951	6,153	1977	44,079
1925	32,964	1952	9,079		
1926	43,316				

Source: The statistics from 1900 to 1964 are from Bureau of the Census, *Historical Statistics of the United States*, Washington, DC, 1976. The statistics from 1965 to 1977 are from the Immigration and Naturalization Service, *Annual Report* for those years. Immigration data to 1907 refer only to seaport arrivals.

Mexican migration to the United States is generally described as occurring in three waves. The smallest was the first which took place at the turn of the century. The deteriorating economic situation in Mexico brought Mexicans to the Southwest. The second wave came from the time of the Mexican Revolution to the beginnings of World War One. The violence and political turmoil of the Mexican Revolution coupled with the demand for cheap agricultural and industrial labor in the United States brought many Mexicans across the border.

From 1911 to 1924, the number of legal immigrants is said to have totalled 470,000.[31] From 1932 to 1939 there was a marked decrease in migration because of the Depression and coming World War. During this time Mexicans in the United States felt the effects of racism and xenophobia. From 1931 on there were many governmental efforts to remove Mexicans from the United States in order to help alleviate the pressures of the Depression.[32] At this time more than half a million Mexicans, many of them U.S. citizens, were deported to Mexico. The third wave of Mexican migration took place after World War Two, especially after 1950 when large numbers of Mexican immigrants, *braceros* and undocumented workers came to meet the needs of U.S. agriculture and industry. The Bracero Program was established and between 1942 and 1964 more than four million "visiting temporary" Mexican workers were contracted to labor in agriculture and on the railroads in the United States.

"Illegal" migration of undocumented workers has continued throughout the century and accurate statistics are difficult to obtain.

Deportable Aliens Found			
Years	Mexicans	Others	Total
1968	151,705	60,352	212,057
1969	201,636	81,921	283,557
1970	277,377	67,976	345,353
1971	348,178	71,948	420,126
1972	430,213	75,736	505,949
1973	576,823	79,145	655,968
1974	709,959	78,186	788,145
1975	680,392	86,208	766,600
1976	781,474	94,441	875,915
1977	954,778	87,437	1,042,215
1978	976,667	81,310	1,057,977
1979	998,830	77,588	1,076,418

Source: U.S. Immigration and Naturalization Service, *Annual Reports*.

Radical and labor groups sought to organize Mexican and Chicano workers throughout the Southwest. From 1900 to 1918, several organizations were active, including the Partido Liberal Mexicano [Mexican Liberal Party, PLM] founded by Flores Magon (1873-1922).[33] Also active in the Mexican communities were the Industrial Workers of the World, the Socialist Party and the American Federation of Labor.[34] During the 1920s and 1930s, the Christian Workers Union and the Congress of Industrial Workers further contributed to the unionizing of Mexican laborers.

The increasing number of Spanish-speaking people in the Southwest implied a need for a large Spanish-language press. The exact number of Spanish-language newspapers published is not known. In 1938, the San Antonio newspaper, *La Prensa* identified a total of 451 Spanish-language newspapers published throughout the United States.[35] The majority of these newspapers (360) were published in the southwestern states, others were published in New York, Florida, Illinois, Missouri, Pennsylvania and Louisiana. The figures in the *La Prensa* article were for the years 1813-1937. The cities with the largest number of papers were San Antonio and El Paso.

The exact number of radical and labor newspapers in the Southwest is also difficult to arrive at. According to some estimates, there were between 30 to 100 such papers.[36] The majority of these papers were aimed at Mexican and Chicano workers. The particular character and nature of these papers varied with the political and labor organizations which they represented. What they had in common was that they were "institutions of activism" which sought to document the major problems confronting Mexican workers.[37]

The Mexican Revolution was an important stimulus for the Mexican-American press of the Southwest. Political exiles published newspapers in the United States representing the various political factions of the Mexican Revolution whether they were pro-Diaz, anti-Diaz or pro-Madero. Among the most impor- t⌐·.t anti-Diaz radical newspapers were those founded by Ricardo Flores Magon and his followers. These papers were the organs of the Partido Liberal Mexicano. They were very popular and appeared in the barrios of San Antonio, El Paso and Los Angeles.

Without a doubt, the most important of these radical newspapers was *Regeneracion* which was founded in Mexico by the journalist and political leader Ricardo Flores Magon in 1900.[38] Because of its strong attacks on the govern- ment of President Porfirio Diaz, *Regeneracion* was forced to leave Mexican soil. In 1904 it was published in San Antonio, TX. Besides Magon, it was edited by Juan Sarabia, Librado Rivera and Antonio Villarreal.[39] Subsequently, the paper moved to St. Louis, MO and finally to Los Angeles, CA. As the political organ of the PLM *Regeneracion*, which lasted for more than eighteen years, espoused a revolutionary point of view and supported the international working-class movement. After 1906, Flores Magon and his followers became more and more anarchist in their political views. The reading public of *Regen- eracion* was composed of Chicano and Mexican workers. At one point, the newspaper had a circulation of 20,000.[40] It was read on both sides of the border. Not only was the paper an important informational and organizing tool for Mexican workers, it also set the tone for other papers which followed the cause of Flores Magon such as *Revolucion*, *El Liberal* and *Resurreccion*.[41] As a result of its activities, *Regeneracion* was suspended several times, its offices were ransacked and its editors were jailed.

Los Angeles was the main center for the publication of Spanish-language newspapers. From 1850 to 1900 sixteen Spanish-language newspapers were published in this city.[42] Among these were such important papers as *El Clamor Publico* (1855-59) and *La Cronica* (1872-92).[43] These newspapers made Mexicans and Chicanos aware of issues concerning widespread discrimination in the Los Angeles area. They also condemned lynchings and the general mis- treatment of Mexicans. Francisco P. Ramires, editor of *El Clamor Publico* often decried the theft of Californian lands from Mexicans.[44]

In more recent times Los Angeles became a base of operations for Chicano and Mexican immigrant and agricultural workers.[45] Since the city was the center for expansion of the railroads, numerous Mexicans came here to find work with the Southern Pacific and the Santa Fe railroad companies. Between 1913 and 1918 a "Brown Scare" [46] gripped Southern California and Los Angeles in particular. From 1910 to 1921 the entire United States wit- nessed a rise of strong nativist sentiments brought on by the influx of foreign immigration and the rise of radical labor movements just before World War One.[47] Throughout the Southwest, and especially in California this xenophobia was directed against Mexican immigrants and radicals. Nativists feared the spread of the Mexican Revolution into the Southwest and suspected colla- boration between Mexicans and Germans. Throughout the United States immigrants and aliens were quickly associated with radicalism. These fears brought police actions against Mexican radicals such as the followers of Flores Magon and his PLM. Before World War One, such instruments as the Selective Service Act and the Espionage Act were used against Mexican political radicals and labor leaders.[48] Mexican immigrants who had not been naturalized were forced to join the military or they were deported.

This was a difficult time for the Mexican radical and labor press. Any form of labor radicalism was seen as anti-American and in favor of the enemies of the United States. Often newspapers were excluded from the U.S. mail. Frequently they were shut down because their publications were judged to be seditious. Nevertheless, several newspapers continued to meet the needs of the Los Angeles Mexican community. They were *El Heraldo de Mexico* (1915)[49], *La Prensa* (1912), *La Gaceta de Los Angeles*, as well as the radical and labor press: *Huelga General*, *Pluma Roja*, *El Rebelde* and of course, *Regeneracion*.

In spite of many predictions to the contrary, the Spanish-language press of the United States is flourishing today. Since the 1970s, there has been a sharp rise in the number of Spanish-language publications in the United States.[50] This is due, no doubt, in large part to the growth of the Hispanic population, which numbered an estimated 17.6 million in 1984 and which will total around 3o million by the year 2000.[51] At present (1985) the United States has six general Spanish-language dailies with a combined circulation of 325,000.[52] Two of the nation's largest general Spanish-language papers are *El Diario/La Prensa* of New York and *La Opinion* of Los Angeles.

As our bibliography demonstrates Spanish-speaking people, whether they are Spanish immigrants, Puerto Ricans or Mexicans, were and in many cases still are very active in developing a radical and labor press from the 1890s until the present. These newspapers appeared throughout the United States especially in the New York area, in Florida and in the Southwest. This study has also shown that Spanish-speaking workers, while they often came from different countries, frequently worked together on labor and radical newspapers. This is especially true of Spanish immigrants, Puerto Ricans and Cubans in New York City and Tampa, Florida. A careful study of the newspapers found in the bibliography will reveal the complex social history of the Spanish-speaking workers in the United States.

Spanish-Language Labor and Radical Newspapers by Founding Year

Spanish and Latin-American:

El Internacional. Ybor City, FL, 1906-1926. Spanish and Cuban.

Justicia. New York, NY, 1914-1981. Spanish, Puerto Rican, Cuban.

Solidaridad. Chicago, IL; Brooklyn, NY; New York, NY, 1918-1930. Spanish, Puerto Rican, Cuban and other Latin Americans.

El Obrero. New York, NY, 1931-1932. Spanish and Puerto Rican.

Noticias de la UCAPAWA (Local 300). New York, NY, 1939-1940.

Noticiario Obrero Norteamericano. Washington, DC, 1944-(?) 1979. Spanish, Puerto Rican and Cuban.

Boletin Latino Americano de CIO. New York, NY, 1945-1955. Spanish, Puerto Rican and Cuban.

Obrero de la Carne. Chicago, IL, 1946-1948.

Spanish:

El Despertar. New York, NY, 1891-1902.

El Esclavo. Tampa, FL, 1894-1898.

La Voz del Esclavo. Tampa, FL, 1900.

Doctrina Anarquista-Socialista. Paterson, NJ, 1905 (?).

Cultura Proletaria. New York, NY, 1910-1959.

Cultura Obrera. Brooklyn, NY, 1911-1923.

Brazo y Cerebro. New York, NY, 1912-1914.

El Obrero Industrial. Tampa, FL, 1914.

Espana Nueva. New York, NY, 1923-1942.

Espana Republicana. New York, NY, 1931-1935.

Frente Popular. Brooklyn, NY, 1937-1939.

Espana Libre. Brooklyn, NY, 1939-1973.

Pueblos Hispanos. New York, NY, 1943-1944.

Liberación. New York, NY, 1946(?)-1949.

Puerto Rican:

La Correspondencia de Puerto Rico. San Juan, 1890-1943.

El Problema. Ponce, 1901.

La Miseria. San Juan, 1901.

Unión Obrera. Ponce, Mayaguez, San Juan, 1902.

Obrero Libre. 1902.

Vida Obrera. New York, NY, 1930-1932.

Nueva Lucha. New York, NY, 1934.

Boletin del Trabajo. San Juan, 1934-1935.

Claridad. San Juan, 1959-1982.

Salario. San Juan, 1969-1972.

Mexican-Chicano:

La Reforma Social. El Paso, TX, 1900-1905.

El Clarín del Norte. El Paso, TX, 1903.

Regeneración. San Antonio, TX, (1904); St. Louis, MO, (1905-1906); Los Angeles, CA, (1910-1918).

El Liberal. Del Rio, TX, 1905-1911.
Revolución. Los Angeles, CA, 1907-1908.
Resurrección. San Antonio, TX, 1907.
La Voz de la Mujer. El Paso, TX, 1907.
Reforma. Libertad y Justicia. Austin, TX, 1908.
Pluma Roja. Los Angeles, CA, 1913-1914.
Huelga General. Los Angeles, CA, 1913-1914.
El Rebelde. Los Angels, CA, 1915-1917.
El Unionista. San Antonio, TX, 1919.
El Malcriado. Delano, CA, 1964-1975.

Notes

1. R.E. Park, *The Immigrant Press and its Control* (New York and London: Harper and Brothers, 1922). See Chapter IX, "The Class War," pp. 214-247.

2. R.R. MacCurdy, *A History and Bibliography of Spanish-Language Newspapers and Magazines in Louisiana, 1808-1949* (Albuquerque: The University of New Mexico Press, 1951).

3. Félix Gutiérrez, "Spanish Language Media in America: Background, Resources, History," *Journalism History* 4, (Summer 1977), pp. 37-38.

4. Park, *The Immigrant Press*, pp. 214-247

5. Edward Hunter, *In Many Voices* (Norman Park, GA: Norman College, 1960), p. 56.

6. See "Foreign Language Newspapers," in Frank Mott, *American Journalism* (New York: The Macmillan Co., 1941); F. Gutiérrez, "Spanish Language Media," p. 34.

7. Since the Labor Newspaper Preservation Project covers only periodicals by labor immigrants from Europe, the annotated bibliography contains mainly newspapers published by and directed at migrants from Spain. However, we are aware that becaue of the close cooperation among the Spanish-speaking working class sometimes this distinction might seem rather artificial we have included two detailed appendices containing information on Puerto Rican and Mexican-Chicano labor newspapers.

8. One of the Spanish-language radical newspapers to suffer the most was *Regeneración*. Its property was confiscated and its editors jailed. See J. Gomez-Quinones, *Sembradores* (Los Angeles: Chicano Studies Publications, University of California, 1977) and W. Dirk Raat, *Revolotosos* (College Station: Texas A&M University Press, 1981).

9. Rafael Chabrán, "La Correspondencia de Puerto Rico: A Chronicle of Puerto Rican Migration, 1900-1901," unpublished manuscript.

10. "Immigration from Spain to the United States, 1820-1976," U.S. Immigration and Naturalization Service, *Annual Report*, 1976 (Washington, DC, 1977), pp. 88-91.

11. Ibid.

12 See Raymond Carr, *Spain 1808-1975* (Oxford: Clarendon Press, 1982).

13. Ibid., see chapter IX, "The Restoration and Disaster, 1874-1898."

14. R. Carr, *Modern Spain, 1875-1980* (Oxford: Oxford University Press, 1980), see chapter 3, "Society in Transition 1875-1914."

15. History Task Force, Centro de Estudios Puertorriquenos, *Labor Migration Under Capitalism* (New York: Monthly Review Press, 1979), pp. 83-84.

16. For studies on Spanish anarchists see Jose Alvarez Junco, *La ideologia politica del anarchismo espanol (1868-1910)* (Madrid: Siglo XXI, 1976).

17. For more information on *El Despertar* see Lily Litvak, *Musal libertaria* (Barcelona: Antoni Bosch, 1981).

18. Ralph Steele Boggs, "Spanish Folklore from Tampa, Florida," *Southern Folklore Quarterly* I (September 1937), p. 2; *The WPA Guide to Florida* (New York: Pantheon, 1984), pp. 90-91 and 290-293, and Gary R. Mormino and George E. Pozzetta, "Spanish Anarchism in Tampa, Florida, 1886-1931," in *Struggle a Hard Battle: Essays on Working-Class Immigrants* edited by Dirk Hoerder (DeKalb: Northern Illinois University Press, 1986), pp.170-198.

19. D. Long, "La Resistencia: Tampa's Immigrant Labor Union," *Labor History* VI (Fall 1965), pp. 193-213 and G.E. Pozzetta, "Immigrations and Radicals in Tampa, Florida," *Florida Historical Quarterly* 57 (1979), pp. 337-348.

20. History Task Force, *Labor Migration Under Capitalism*, pp. 83-84.

21. Ibid., pp. 108-109, 223-224.

22. Ibid., pp. 108.

23. Jose L. Vazquez Calzada, "Demographic Aspects of Migration," in History Task Force, *Labor Migration Under Capitalism*, pp. 223-225.

24. History Task Force, Centro de Estudios Puertorriquenos, *Sources for the Study of Puerto Rican Migration 1879-1980*, (New York: Research Foundation of CUNY, 1982), see "Introduction," p. 3.

25. History Task Force, *Labor Migration under Capitalism*, p. 141.

26. G. Garcia, "La primera decada de la Federacion Libre de Trabajadores de Puerto Rico," (San Juan: CEREP, 1924) and History Task Force, *Labor Migration under Capitalism*, p. 101.

27. For information on *La Correspondencia de Puerto Rico* see Paul Nelson Chiles, *The Puerto Rican Press Reaction to the United States (1888-1894)* (New York: ARNO, 1975) and Antonio S. Pedreira, *El periodismo en Puerto Rico* (La Habana: Imprenta Ucar, Garcia y Cia., 1941).

28. Chiles, *The Puerto Rican Press*, p.6.

29. Luis Antonio Velez Aquino, "Puerto Rican Press reaction to the shift from Spanish to United States Sovereignity: 1898- 1917," (Ed.D. Dissertation, Columbia University, 1968), p. 9.

30. History Task Force, *Labor Migration under Capitalism*, p. 83.

31. "Mexican Immigrants to the United States (1900-1977)," in Bureau of the Census, *Historical Statistics of the United States* (Washington, DC, 1976).

32. See "Repatriation, 1930s," in Matt S. Meier and Feliciano Rivera, *Dictionary of Mexican American History* (Westport, CT: Greenwood Press, 1981), pp. 300-302; see also Abraham Hoffman, "Mexican Repatriation During the Great Depression: A Reappraisal," in *Immigrants and Immigrants: Perspectives on Mexican Labor Migration to the United States*, edited by A.F. Corwin (Westport, CT: Greenwood Press, 1978).

33. On Flores Magon see J. Gómez-Quinones, *Sembradores, Ricardo Flores Magon y el Partido Liberal Mexicano: A Eulogy and Critique* (excerpts from *Regeneración* (1900-1923) (Los Angeles: Aztlan Publications, University of California, 1973) and W. Dirk Raat, *Revoltosos*.

34. For the history of the Chicano Labor Movement, see Juan Gómez-Quinones, *Origens del movimiento obrero chicano* (Mexico, 1978); see also "Labor Organization," in M. Meier and F. Rivera, *Dictionary of Mexican American History*, pp. 179-183.

35. Jose Carlos Valadez, "Mas de cuatrocientos periodicos en espanol se han editado en los Estados Unidos," *La Prensa* (San Antonio, TX), 25th Anniversary Issue, 13 February 1938, p. 8.

36. Raat, *Revoltosos*, pp. 37-38.

37. Gutiérrez, "Spanish Language Media," p. 41.

38. On *Regeneración* see Armando Bartra, ed. and comp., *Regeneración 1900-1918* (Mexico City: HADISE, S.A., 1972).

39. For information on the editors and writers of *Regeneración* and related newspapers see Gómez-Quinones, *Sembradores* and Raat, *Revoltosos*.

40. John M. Hart, *Anarchism and the Mexican Working Class, 1860-1931* (Austin: University of Texas Press, 1978), pp. 89-90.

41. Raat, *Revoltosos*, pp. 37-38.

42. "Spanish Language Newspapers in Los Angeles 1850-1900," in Richard Griswold del Castillo, *The Los Angeles Barrio, 1850-1890: A Social History* (Berkeley and Los Angeles: University of California Press, 1982), p. 126.

43. Ibid., pp. 125-128.

44. On Francisco P. Ramirez see Griswold del Castillo, *Los Angeles Barrio*, pp. 127-128 and Leonard Pitt, *The Decline of the Californios: A Social History of the Spanish-Speaking Californians, 1846-1890.* (Berkeley and Los Angeles: University of California Press, 1970), chapter 9.

45. Ricardo Romo, *East Los Angeles: History of a Barrio* (Austin: University of Texas Press, 1983), p.32-22.

46. Ibid., chapter 5.

47. Ibid., pp. 89-94.

48. Ibid., p. 107.

49. R.D. Chacón, "The Chicano Immigrant Press in Los Angeles: A case of El Heraldo de Mexico 1917-1920." *Journalism History* 4 (Summer 1977), p. 48ff.

50. Gutiérrez, "Spanish Language Media," p. 34.

51. George J. Church, "A Melting of Cultures," *Time* (8 July 1985), p. 36.

52. James Kelly, "In the Hand of Free Speach," *Time* (8 July 1985), p. 95.

Bibliography

Alvarez Junco, José.
   La Ideología Política Del Anarquismo Espanol (1868-1910). Madrid: Siglo XXI, 1976.

Avrich, P.
   An American Anarchist: The Life of Voltairine de Cleyre. Princeton: Princeton University Press, 1978.

Bartra, Armando, ed. and comp.
   Regeneración (1900-1918). Mexico City: HADISE, S.A., 1972.

Benson Latin American Collection.
   University of Texas at Austin. Listing of "Serial Titles Filmed Preservation Microfilming Project." Benson Latin American Collection Serials List.

Boggs, R.S.
   "Spanish Folklore From Tampa, Florida." *Southern Folklore Quarterly* I (September 1937), pp. 1-12.

Centro de Estudios Puertorriquenos.
   Hunter College (CUNY) "Library Materials on Microfilm." N.d.

Centro de Estudios Puertorriquenos.
   "Listing of Newspapers." N.d.

Chabrán, Richard.
   "Listings of 143 Chicano Publications on Microfilm." Chicano Studies Library, University of California at Berkeley.

Chacón, Ramon D.
   "The Chicano Immigrant Press in Los Angeles: The Case of 'EL Heraldo de México,' 1917-1920." *Journalism History* 4 (Summer 1977), pp. 48 ff.

Chicano Studies Research Library.
   "Chicano Studies Serial Holdings." University of California, Los Angeles, n.d.

Chicano Studies Research Library.
   "Listing of Spanish Language Newspapers 1876-1937." University of California, Los Angeles, n.d.

Cockcroft, James D.
   Intellectual Precursors of the Mexican Revolution. Austin, 1968.

Cumberland, Charles.
   "Precursors of the Mexican Revolution, 1910." *Hispanic American Historical Review* XXII (May 1942), pp. 344-356.

Gómez-Quinones, J.
   Sembradores. Ricardo Flores Magon y el Partido Liberal Mexicano: A Eulogy and Critique (excerpts from *Regeneración* 1900-1923). Los Angeles: Aztlan Publications, University of California, Los Angeles, 1973.

Origenes del Movimiento Obrero Chicano. Mexico, 1978.

Griswold del Castillo, Richard.

"The Mexican Revolutionary Press in the Borderlands." *Journalism History* 4 (Summer 1977), pp. 42-47.

Gutiérrez, Felix.

"Spanish Language Media in America: Background, Resources, History." *Journalism History* 4 (Summer 1977), p. 34 ff.

Hart, J.M.

Anarchism and the Mexican Working Class 1860-1931. Austin: University of Texas Press, 1978.

History Task Force.

Centro de Estudios Puertorriquenos. *Labor Migration Under Capitalism: The Puerto Rican Experience*. New York: Monthly Review Press, 1979.

History Task Force.

Centro de Estudios Puertorriquenos. *Sources of the Study of Puerto Rican Migration, 1879-1930*. New York: Research Foundation, CUNY, 1982.

Hunter, Edward.

In Many Voices: Our Fabulous Foreign Language Press. Norman Park, GA, Norman College, 1960.

Ireland, Robert E.

"The Radical Community, Mexican and American Radicalism, 1900-1910." *Journal of Mexican-American History* II, 1 (Fall 1971), pp. 22-32.

Litvak, Lily.

Musa libertaria. Barcelona: Antoni Bosch, 1981.

Long, D.

"La Resistencia: Tampa's Immigrant Labor Union." *Labor History* VI (Fall 1965), pp. 193-213.

Meier, M. and Rivera, F.

Dictionary of Mexican-American History. Westport, CO: Greenwood Press, 1981.

Mott, Frank.

American Journalism. New York: The Macmillan Co., 1941.

Naas, Bernard G. and Sakr, C.S.

American Labor Union Periodicals: A Guide to their Locations. Ithaca, NY, 1956.

Park, Robert E.

The Immigrant Press and Its Control. New York: Harper, 1922.

Pozzetta, G.E.

"An Immigrant Library: The Tampa Italian Club Collection." *Ex Libris* I (Spring 1978), pp. 10-12.

Pozzetta, G.E.

"Immigrants and Radicals in Tampa, Florida." *Florida Historical Quarterly* 57 (1979), pp. 337-348.

Raat, W. Dirk.

Revoltosos: Mexico's Rebels in the United States, 1903-1923. College Station: Texas A and M University Press, 1981.

Ríos, C. Hermino and Castillo, L.

"Toward a True Chicano Bibliography: Mexican American Newspapers: 1848-." El Grito 3, 4 (Summer 1970), pp. 17-24.

"Toward a True Chicano Bibliography: Mexican American Newspapers: 1848-." Part II (includes editorial note) El Grito 5, 4 (Summer 1972), pp. 38-47.

Thernstrom, Stephan and Orlov, Ann, eds.

Harvard Encyclopedia of Americna Ethnic Groups. Cambridge, MA: Harvard University Press, 1980.

Valades, Jose C.

"Mas de cuatrocientos periodicos en espanol se han editado en Los Estados Unidos." La Prensa, San Antonio Texas, 13 February 1938.

Wisconsin State Historical Society.

Labor Papers on Microfilm. A Combined List. Madison WI, 1965; Supp. 1971.

Woodcock, George.

El anarquismo. Barcelona, 1978.

The WPA Guide to Florida.

The Federal Writers Project Guide. 1930s Florida. 1939. Reprint New York: Pantheon Books, 1984.

Annotated Bibliography

BOLETIN LATINOAMERICANO DE CIO		NY New York	1945-1955

Title trans.:	Latin American CIO Bulletin	*First issue:*	F 1945
Subtitle:		*Last issue:*	N 1955
Add. lang.:		*Vols. (nos.):*	
First editor:		*Frequency:*	q
First publ.:		*Preservation:*	2
Related pubs.:		*Supplements:*	
Circulation:		*Category:*	labor

Depositories: Usa-CU (2:[O 1948-N 1955]); Usa-DL (1945); Usa-IU; Usa-NIC; Usa-MH-PA

The paper was published by the CIO committee on Latin American affairs.

BRAZO Y CEREBRO		NY New York	1912-1914

Title trans.:	Arms and Brains	*First issue:*	22 Je 1912
Subtitle:		*Last issue:*	1914
Add. lang.:		*Vols. (nos.):*	
First editor:	Juan Martinez	*Frequency:*	ir
First publ.:		*Preservation:*	5
Related pubs.:		*Supplements:*	
Circulation:		*Category:*	anarchist

Depositories: Nl-IISG [1912,nos.1-2]

The paper contained essays by and about anarchists and anarchism, communism (theoretical) and feminism as well as news, politics, social issues (marriage, treatment of women), articles on arts and sciences and poetry. Some articles were written by women. It printed many cartoons and some photos. The paper was free or given for donations. No. 2 (22 October 1912) printed a list of contributors from all over the United States and Cuba. It seems to have been written for and by Spanish immigrants, Puerto Ricans and Cubans.

CULTURA OBRERA	NY Brooklyn	1911-1927

Title trans.:	Workers' Culture	*First issue:*	1911
Subtitle:	Educación, organización, emancipacion - periodico obrero + de doctrina y de combate.	*Last issue:*	1927
Add. lang.:		*Vols. (nos.):*	
First editor:		*Frequency:*	w
First publ.:		*Preservation:*	2
Related pubs.:		*Supplements:*	
Circulation:		*Category:*	anarchist

Depositories: Nl-IISG (2:[1911-12,1914-17,1922-27]); Usa-NNC (6:[1912,1913]); Br-Camp (2:[1923,1925-27])

Subtitle translation: Education, Organization, Emancipation - Workers' Organ for Doctrine and Struggle.

This was the Organo de la Union de Fogoneros del Atlantico [Organ of the Firemen and Ship Stockers Union]. It published information about Spain, Mexico and the Mexican Revolution and contained a number of references to the Partido Liberal Mexicano [Mexican Liberal Party]. Some articles were written by Ricardo Flores Magon and J. Vidal.

CULTURA PROLETARIA	NY New York	1910-1959

Title trans.:	Proletarian Culture	*First issue:*	1910
Subtitle:	Portavoz de la Federación de grupos anarquistas de la lengua castellana en los EEUU	*Last issue:*	1959
Add. lang.:		*Vols. (nos.):*	
First editor:	Marcelino Garcia	*Frequency:*	bw
First publ.:		*Preservation:*	3
Related pubs.:		*Supplements:*	
Circulation:		*Category:*	anarchist

Depositories: Usa-NNHuC-CEP (3:[1927-59]); Br-Camp (3:[1927,1932-41, 1945-50],1951-53)

According to the subtitle this was "The Voice of the Federation of (Spanish-speaking) anarchists in the United States." The noted Spanish anarchist Pedro Esteve as well as Puerto Ricans and Cubans worked for this paper.

EL DESPERTAR

			NY New York		1891-1902

Title trans.:	The Awakening		*First issue:*	1891
Subtitle:	Periodico anarquista		*Last issue:*	1902
Add. lang.:			*Vols. (nos.):*	
First editor:	J.C. Campos		*Frequency:*	bw
First publ.:			*Preservation:*	2
Related pubs.:			*Supplements:*	
Circulation:			*Category:*	anarchist

Depositories: NI-IISG [1891-1902]

This "anarchist newspaper" contained articles by noted Spanish anarchists such as Lorenzo, Pral, Mella, Urales and Azorin. It also covered social issues such as "To a prostitute" by Manuel Gonzales in No. 16. M.M. Abello functioned as administrator and the office was situated at 105 Fulton St.

For more information on the Spanish Anarchist Press see: L. Litvak, *Musa libertaria*; G. Woodcock, *El anarquismo* ; J. Alvarez Junco, *La Ideología Política del Anarquismo Espanol.*

DOCTRINA ANARQUISTA SOCIALISTA

			NJ Paterson		1905-?

Title trans.:	Socialist, Anarchist Doctrine		*First issue:*	1905
Subtitle:			*Last issue:*	
Add. lang.:			*Vols. (nos.):*	
First editor:	Pedro Esteve		*Frequency:*	
First publ.:			*Preservation:*	4
Related pubs.:			*Supplements:*	
Circulation:			*Category:*	anarchist

Depositories: NI-IISG [1905,no.1-7]

The paper contained long articles from an anarchist perspective as well as short stories. The price was 5 cents. For more information on Pedro Esteve see Woodcock, *El anarchismo.*

EL ESCLAVO

			FL Tampa		1894-1898

Title trans.:	The Slave		*First issue:*	9 Je 1894
Subtitle:	Periodico Obrero Semanal		*Last issue:*	1898
Add. lang.:			*Vols. (nos.):*	
First editor:			*Frequency:*	w
First publ.:			*Preservation:*	2
Related pubs.:			*Supplements:*	
Circulation:			*Category:*	anarchist

Depositories: NI-IISG [1896-98]

This was a "weekly workers' paper", which contained editorials and news from an anarchist perspective, informing about the anarchist movements in Paris, Jerez and Barcelona (Spain) and Sicily. Some articles were written by Maximino Goicoitia. It mainly addressed Spanish immigrants, Cubans and Puerto Ricans working in the cigar industry of Tampa. The price was for "each according to his means."

ESPANA LIBRE	NY Brooklyn	1939-1977

Title trans.:	Free Spain	*First issue:*	1 N 1939
Subtitle:	Comite antifascista espanol de los Estados Unidos	*Last issue:*	1977
Add. lang.:		*Vols. (nos.):*	
First editor:	José Castro	*Frequency:*	bm, m, w
First publ.:		*Preservation:*	2
Related pubs.:	c *Frente Popular*	*Supplements:*	
Circulation:		*Category:*	republican/ antifascist

Depositories: Usa-NN (2:[1939-77])

According to one of the subtitles the paper represented the "Spanish Antifascist Committee." It was founded by Spanish immigrants for the Spanish Republican community in New York. It was a weekly from 1939-54, a bimonthly from 1955-62 and a monthly from 1963-77.

ESPANA NUEVA	NY New York	1923-1942

Title trans.:	New Spain	*First issue:*	Mr 1923
Subtitle:		*Last issue:*	N 1942
Add. lang.:		*Vols. (nos.):*	
First editor:	A.F. Arguelles	*Frequency:*	m
First publ.:		*Preservation:*	4
Related pubs.:		*Supplements:*	
Circulation:		*Category:*	republican/ antifascist

Depositories: Usa-DLC; Usa-NN [1923-42]

This was a Spanish anti-Franco newspaper for the Spanish immigrant community of New York.

ESPANA REPUBLICANA   NY New York   1931-1935

Title trans.:	Republican Spain	*First issue:*	Ap 1931
Subtitle:		*Last issue:*	S 1935
Add. lang.:		*Vols. (nos.):*	
First editor:		*Frequency:*	m, sm
First publ.:		*Preservation:*	5
Related pubs.:		*Supplements:*	
Circulation:		*Category:*	republican/ socialist/ antifascist

Depositories: Usa-NN [1931-35]

The paper was founded by Spanish immigrants for the Spanish Republican community of New York. It was the organ of the Alianza republicon a espanola and its contents were mainly antifascist.

FRENTE POPULAR   NY Brooklyn   1937-1939

Title trans.:	Popular Front	*First issue:*	My 1937
Subtitle:	Organo del comite antifascista espanola de los Estado Unidos de Norte America	*Last issue:*	O 1939
Add. lang.:		*Vols. (nos.):*	1-3 no. 43
First editor:		*Frequency:*	w
First publ.:		*Preservation:*	3
Related pubs.:	s *Espana Libre*	*Supplements:*	
Circulation:		*Category:*	republican/ antifascist

Depositories: Usa-NN [1937-39]

According to the subtitle this was the "Organ of the Spanish antifascist committee of the United States of North America."

EL INTERNACIONAL   FL Ybor City   1906-1926

Title trans.:	The International	*First issue:*	1906
Subtitle:	Organo local de la Union Internacional de tabaqueros de America	*Last issue:*	1926
Add. lang.:	English	*Vols. (nos.):*	
First editor:		*Frequency:*	w
First publ.:		*Preservation:*	2
Related pubs.:		*Supplements:*	
Circulation:		*Category:*	labor union

Depositories: Usa-DL (1914-26)

This was the bilingual official Organ of Local 462 of the Cigar Maker International Union (AFL). It was first published as a monthly, than as a bimonthly and later as a weekly.

La Federación (16 February, 2, 9 March 1900), El Resistente (Key West 1900-1901?), Yara (Key West, 1872 - Cayo Hueso 1892), The Tobacco Worker (1897-1924), Verdad (New Orleans) were publications representing similar or related organizations. "La Sociedad de Torcedores de Tabaco de Tampa" was a related organization. Other related newspapers include El Esclavo and La Voz del Esclavo.

JUSTICIA		NY New York	1914-1918
Title trans.:	Justice	First issue:	O 1914
Subtitle:		Last issue:	1918?
Add. lang.:		Vols. (nos.):	
First editor:		Frequency:	
First publ.:	ILGWU	Preservation:	4
Related pubs.:		Supplements:	
Circulation:		Category:	labor union

Depositories: Usa-NN [1914-26]

The paper was the official organ of the International Ladies Garment Workers Union. It published comments on national and local issues, on political and economic rights and responsibilities and involvement in community affairs.

The Spanish paper stopped publishing when the ILGWU began to publish the English Justice in 1919. In 1933 La Justicia appeared again as the monthly organ of ILGWU and its editor was Anthony Lespier.

LIBERACION		NY New York	1946-1949
Title trans.:	Liberation	First issue:	1946
Subtitle:	"por la libertad de Espana, Puerto Rico y los demás paises oprimidos"	Last issue:	My 1949
Add. lang.:		Vols. (nos.):	
First editor:	Carmen Meano	Frequency:	w
First publ.:	Aurelio Perez	Preservation:	2
Related pubs.:	c Pueblos Hispanos, Republica Espanola (Mexico)	Supplements:	
Circulation:	1947: 4000	Category:	socialist

Depositories: Usa-NNHuC-CEP [1946-49]; Usa-NN [1946-49]

According to the subtitle the paper fought for "the liberty of Spain, Puerto Rico and the other oppressed countries." It represented the Spanish Republican Committee and its coordinator was Pro-República Espanola. Starting out as a paper by Spanish immigrants (Pueblos Hispanos [Hispanic People]) it later closely associated with the Puerto Rican community. By 1946, it represented the voice of Hispanos in New York; especially the voice of the working class. Rafael López Rosas and José Luis González worked on this paper.

NOTICIARIO OBRERO NORTEAMERICANO   DC Washington   1944-1979

Title trans.:	North American Labor News	*First issue:*	1944
Subtitle:		*Last issue:*	1979
Add. lang.:		*Vols. (nos.):*	
First editor:		*Frequency:*	sm
First publ.:		*Preservation:*	3
Related pubs.:		*Supplements:*	
Circulation:	10,500	*Category:*	labor union

Depositories: Usa-CU [1956-79]

This was an AFL-CIO publication addressing Spanish-speaking workers covering mainly American labor news. It was distributed free of charge.

NOTICIAS DE LA UCAPAWA   NY New York   1939-1940

Title trans.:	News of the UCAPAWA	*First issue:*	1939
Subtitle:		*Last issue:*	1940
Add. lang.:		*Vols. (nos.):*	
First editor:		*Frequency:*	
First publ.:		*Preservation:*	2
Related pubs.:		*Supplements:*	
Circulation:		*Category:*	labor union

Depositories: Usa-CU [1939-40]

This was the official organ of Local 300 of the United Cannery Agriculture, Packing and Allied Workers of America. This organization was chartered in mid 1937 by the CIO (Congress of Industrial Labor) as an international organ for agricultural workers and was regarded as competition to the AFL. In 1944, UCAPAWA became the Food, Tobacco and Agricultural Workers International. Subsequently it was ousted from the CIO because of communist influence.

Source: Meier/Rivera, *Dictionary of Mexican-American History*, pp. 180, 354.

EL OBRERO   NY New York   1931-1932

Title trans.:	Worker	*First issue:*	24 Jl 1931
Subtitle:		*Last issue:*	26 Jl 1932
Add. lang.:		*Vols. (nos.):*	
First editor:		*Frequency:*	w
First publ.:	Centro Obrero de Nueva York	*Preservation:*	2
Related pubs.:		*Supplements:*	
Circulation:		*Category:*	labor

Depositories: Usa-NN [1931-32]

This was published by the "New York Workers' Center" also known as "Centro Obrero de habla espanola" [Center of Spanish-speaking workers]. It was issued during the suspension of the Puerto Rican paper *Vida Obrera* [Workers' Life].

OBRERO DE LA CARNE		Il Chicago	1946-1948
Title trans.:	Meat Worker	*First issue:*	1946
Subtitle:		*Last issue:*	1948 ?
Add. lang.:	English, Portuguese	*Vols. (nos.):*	
First editor:		*Frequency:*	
First publ.:		*Preservation:*	4
Related pubs.:		*Supplements:*	
Circulation:		*Category:*	labor

Depositories: Usa-DL [1946-1948]

This was the official organ of the Pan American Committee of Meat Workers.

EL OBRERO INDUSTRIAL		FL Tampa	1914
Title trans.:	The Industrial Worker	*First issue:*	1914
Subtitle:	Semenario Sindicalista	*Last issue:*	
Add. lang.:		*Vols. (nos.):*	
First editor:	Herminio Gonzales	*Frequency:*	
First publ.:		*Preservation:*	4
Related pubs.:		*Supplements:*	
Circulation:		*Category:*	syndicalist-IWW

Depositories: Nl-IISG [1914]

The paper was closely associated with the IWW.

PUEBLOS HISPANOS		NY New York	1943-1944
Title trans.:	Hispanic Peoples	*First issue:*	20 F 1943
Subtitle:		*Last issue:*	O 1944
Add. lang.:		*Vols. (nos.):*	1-2 no. 87
First editor:	Juan Antonio Cretiza	*Frequency:*	
First publ.:		*Preservation:*	2
Related pubs.:	s *Liberación*	*Supplements:*	
Circulation:		*Category:*	communist

Depositories: Usa-NN [1943-44]

The paper seems to have been initiated by Spanish immigrants (Republicans), but was later staffed by Puerto Ricans and Cubans.

SOLIDARIDAD	IL Chicago	1918-1930

Title trans.:	Solidarity	*First issue:*	28 Ap 1918
Subtitle:	El Periodico de los Trabajadores	*Last issue:*	21 My 1930
Add. lang.:		*Vols. (nos.):*	
First editor:	Adolfo Garcia	*Frequency:*	bw
First publ.:		*Preservation:*	2
Related pubs.:		*Supplements:*	
Circulation:		*Category:*	syndicalist-IWW

Depositories: Usa-WHi (2:[1919-30],m); Usa-NN (?); Usa-DLC (?); Usa-MH (1918,1920-30); Nl-IISG (1923-24,1928-29)

According to the subtitle it was a "Workers' Newspaper." No. 1 - 22 were published as *La Nueva Solidaridad*. In August 1926 publication moved to New York.

LA VOZ DEL ESCLAVO	FL Tampa	1900

Title trans.:	The Voice of the Slave	*First issue:*	1900
Subtitle:		*Last issue:*	
Add. lang.:	Italian	*Vols. (nos.):*	
First editor:		*Frequency:*	
First publ.:		*Preservation:*	4
Related pubs.:		*Supplements:*	
Circulation:		*Category:*	anarchist

Depositories: Nl-IISG [1900]

This paper was published by Spanish immigrants, Puerto Ricans, Italians and Cubans addressing the workers in the cigar industry of Tampa and Ybor City. It contained many articles in Italian which were not translated into Spanish. Besides news and editorials from an anarchist perspective it also published poetry.

Appendixes

Appendix 1: Mexican Labor Periodicals appearing in the United States

Title: EL CLARIN DEL NORTE
Place: TX El Paso
Period: 1903-1907
Title Trans.: The Clarion of the North
Depositories: Usa-Cu-Chics
Category: anarchist

Title: HUELGA GENERAL
Place: CA Los Angeles
Period: 1913-1914
Title Trans.: General Strike
Depositories: Usa-DL; Nl-IISG
Category: syndicalist-IWW

Title: EL LIBERAL
Place: TX Del Rio
Period: 1905-1911
Title Trans.: The Liberal
Depositories: Nl-IISG; Usa-DNA
Category: anarchist

Title: EL MALCRIADO
Place: CA Delano
Period: 1964-1975
Title Trans.: The Spoiled Brat
Depositories: Usa-CU-BANC
Category: labor union-UFW/AFL-CIO

Title: PLUMA ROJA
Place: CA Los Angeles
Period: 1913-1915
Title Trans.: Red Pen
Depositories: Nl-IISG
Category: anarchist

Title: EL REBELDE
Place: CA Los Angeles
Period: 1915-1917
Title Trans.: The Rebel
Depositories: Usa-DL
Category: syndicalist-IWW

Title: REFORMA, LIBERTAD Y JUSTICIA
Place: TX Austin
Period: 1908
Title Trans.: Reform, Liberty and Justice
Depositories: Nl-IISG
Category: anarchist

Title:	LA REFORMA SOCIAL
Place:	TX El Paso
Period:	1900-1905
Title Trans.:	The Social Reform
Depositories:	Usa-CU-BANC; Nl-IISG
Category:	anarchist

Title:	REGENERACION
Place:	TX San Antonio
Period:	1904-1918
Title Trans.:	Regeneration
Depositories:	Usa-NNC
Category:	anarchist

Title:	RESURRECCION
Place:	TX San Antonio
Period:	1907
Title Trans.:	Resurrection
Depositories:	Nl-IISG
Category:	anarchist

Title:	REVOLUCION
Place:	CA Los Angeles
Period:	1907-1908
Title Trans.:	Revolution
Depositories:	Usa-CU-BANC; Nl-IISG
Category:	anarchist

Title:	EL UNIONISTA
Place:	TX San Antonio
Period:	1919-1922
Title Trans.:	The Unionist
Depositories:	Usa-CU
Category:	labor union

Title:	LA VOZ DE LA MUJER
Place:	TX El Paso
Period:	1907
Title Trans.:	Woman's Voice
Depositories:	Usa-CU-BANC; Nl-IISG
Category:	anarchist/women

Appendix 2: Puerto Rican Labor Periodicals appearing in the United States

Title: BOLETIN DEL TRABAJO
Place: PR San Juan
Period: 1934-1935
Title Trans.:   Work Bulletin
Depositories: Usa-DL; Usa-MH-PA; Usa-NN
Category: labor

Title: CLARIDAD
Place: PR San Juan
Period: 1959 +
Title Trans.:   Clarity
Depositories: Usa-CEPR
Category: socialist

Title: LA CORRESPONDENCIA DE PUERTO RICO
Place: PR San Juan
Period: 1890-1943
Title Trans.:   The Correspondence of Puerto Rico
Depositories: Usa-NNCEP
Category: general/labor

Title: LA MISERIA
Place: PR San Juan
Period: 1901-1902
Title Trans.:   Misery
Depositories: Usa-CEPR
Category: labor

Title: NUEVA LUCHA
Place: NY New York City
Period: 1934
Title Trans.:   New Struggle
Depositories: Usa-NN
Category: socialist

Title: EL PROBLEMA
Place: PR Ponce
Period: 1901
Title Trans.:   The Problem
Depositories: Usa-NNCEP
Category: labor recruiting

Title: SALARIO
Place: PR San Juan
Period: 1969-1972
Title Trans.:   Salary
Depositories: Usa-CU
Category: labor union

Title: UNION OBRERA
Place: PR Ponce, Mayaguez, San Juan
Period: 1902-?

Title Trans.:	Workers' Union
Depositories:	Usa-NNCEP
Category:	labor

Title:	VIDA OBRERA
Place:	NY New York
Period:	1930-1932 ?
Depositories:	Usa-NNCEP; Usa-NN
Category:	labor

Title Index

Place Index

United States

FLORIDA
Tampa
  Esclavo, El
  Obrero Industrial, El
  Voz del Esclavo, La

Ybor City
  Internacional, El

ILLINOIS
Chicago
  Obrero de la Carne
  Solidaridad

NEW JERSEY
Paterson
  Doctrina Anarquista Socialista

NEW YORK
Brooklyn
  Cultura Obrera
  Espana libre
  Frente Popular

New York
  Boletin Latinoamericano de CIO
  Brazo y Cerebro
  Cultura Proletaria
  Despertar, El
  Espana Nueva
  Espana Republicana
  Justicia
  Liveracion
  Noticias de la UCAPAWA
  Obrero, El
  Pueblos Hispanos

WASHINGTON DC
  Noticiario Obrero Norteamericano

Chronological Index

1890   1900   1910   1920   1930   1940   1950   1960   1970
01234567890123456789012345678901234567890123456789012345678901234567890123456789

Desperta, El	NY New York
Esclavo, El	FL Tampa
La Voz del Esclavo	FL Tampa
Doctrina Anarquista	NJ Paterson
Internacional, El	FL Ybor City
Cultura Proletaria	NY New York
Cultura Obrera	NY Brooklyn
Brazo y Cerebro	NY New York
Obrero industial, El	FL Tampa
Justicia	NY New York
Solidaridad	IL Chicago
Espana Nueva	NY New York
Obrero, El	NY New York
Espana Republicana	NY Brooklyn
Frente Popular	NY New York
Noticias de la UCAPA	NY New York
Espana Libre	NY Brooklyn
Pueblos Hispanos	NY New York
Noticiario Obrero No	DC Washington
Boletin Latinoameric	NY New York
Obrero de la Carne	IL Chicago
Liberacion	NY New York

Portuguese

Language:

Portuguese

Area covered:

Portugal and Cape Verde Islands

Compiled by:

Eduardo Mayone Dias

University of California
Dept. of Spanish and Portugese, Los Angeles, CA

Introduction

The Portuguese-Language Press in North America and Hawaii

1. Portuguese Immigration in North America and Hawaii: General Characteristics

1.1. Early Immigration

Although some Portuguese exploration of North American shores, mainly the Labrador coast, took place in the sixteenth century, settlement or immigration did not start until a much later date. The first Portuguese to settle in North America may have been Matias de Sousa, possibly a "new Christian" or converted Jew, who arrived in Maryland in 1643. In 1654 a group of 23 Portuguese Jews from Brazil established residence in what was then called New Amsterdam, the present-day New York.[1] Another group of Portuguese Jews may have arrived in 1658, and settled in Newport. It was also in Newport that in the second half of the eighteenth century, the American whaling industry seems to have been started, by another Portuguese Jew, Aaron Lopez.

In the long run it was this very same whaling industry which accounted for the first sizable Portuguese immigration wave to North America. Due to the very harsh conditions aboard whaling ships sailing out of New England ports, it was difficult to recruit local seamen for these long voyages. As a result, many whalers left with a skeleton crew only and later complemented it with men hired in the Azores and Cape Verde Islands. Due to the feeble economy of these Atlantic archipelagoes, islanders were happy to accept what to U.S. sailors looked like particularly meager "lays", or payment for a share of the oil collected aboard after a trip which often lasted two or three years. The Portuguese crew members were prized for their docility and eagerness to work hard. However, after becoming more familiar with living conditions in the New England harbor towns, many jumped ship and settled ashore, mainly as offshore cod fishermen. When the U.S. whaling fleet began operating in the Pacific a similar pattern took place, although in a more limited degree. Thus small numbers of Portuguese began to appear in or around whaling ports such as San Francisco, Honolulu and Lahina.

1.2. Increasing Levels of Immigration Since the Late Nineteenth Century

Massive immigration from Portugal, especially from the Azores, was due, however, to rapidly changing economic conditions in the United States. When whaling began to decline, owing to the scarcity of animals to be captured and the discovery of oil in Pennsylvania, many New England investors shifted their capital to the textile industry. Cheap labor was now demanded by the cotton mills and these needs were filled with the importation of immigrants from Europe, including many Portuguese. To this day the Portuguese population of the Eastern region of the United States [2] still consists by and large of unskilled industrial workers, plus a number of fishermen, especially in Gloucester and New Bedford, small business owners and occasional white collar workers. Approximately 60 percent of these hail from the Azores. The remaining 40 percent are mainly composed of people from Northern Portugal and Cape Verdeans.[3]

| Portuguese Immigration to the United States ||
Years	Figures
1820-30	179
1831-40	829
1841-50	550
1851-60	1,055
1861-70	2,658
1871-80	14,082
1881-90	16,978
1891-00	27,508
1901-10	69,149
1911-20	89,732
1921-30	29,994
1931-40	3,329
1941-50	7,423
1951-60	19,588
1961-70	76,065
1971-77	75,717

Source: Stephan Thernstrom and Ann Orlov, *Harvard Encyclopedia of American Ethnic Groups*, (Cambridge, MA: Harvard University Press, 1980), p. 814.

In California it was mainly the Gold Rush that attracted early Portuguese immigration, although a number of the first settlers came over as crew members on whaling ships.[4] Having attained little success as miners, the Portuguese started to engage in support activities. Thus they raised poultry and grew vegetables in the San Francisco Bay area, and opened restaurants and hotels. Later many went into sheep raising in the arid San Joaquin Valley. When irrigation canals were established here in the 1920s the vast holdings they had acquired at low prices suddenly became highly profitable, as dairy farming and the cultivation of alfalfa took the place of sheep raising. To the present day, dairy farmers of Portuguese ancestry still constitute up to 70 percent of the total in some areas of the San Joaquin Valley. Portuguese dairy farms were also established in areas east of Los Angeles, mainly Chino and Artesia.

In San Diego a Portuguese presence was felt since the late nineteenth century. Whaling and offshore fishing constituted the first occupations. In the 1920s tuna fishing developed in that area. Today the Portuguese own and man approximately 70 percent of the San Diego based U.S. tuna fleet [5], now operating in several oceans.

Before 1878 only some four hundred Portuguese had settled in Hawaii, most of them deserters from whaling ships. In that year organized Portuguese immigration began.

Manpower was desperately needed for the rapidly developing sugar cane industry, and the Kingdom of Hawaii decided to look for European laborers to offset any possible "Orientalization" of the labor force. The only Europeans they could find willing to work for the low wages then offered were Azorean and Madeiran islanders. After arriving in the cane fields as common laborers, many Portuguese rose to semi-skilled positions such as mechanic, machine operator, team driver or "luna" (foreman), particularly as unskilled Oriental workers began to arrive on the islands. Other Portuguese moved to the larger towns and became tradesmen or opened small businesses. Portuguese immigration practically stopped after the first quarter of the century. Second and third generation Portuguese intermarried with other ethnic groups, and nowadays very little of the language and culture is preserved, although Hawaiians of Portuguese descent form approximately 10 percent of the islands' population.[6]

Portuguese immigration to Canada began only in the 1950s. The first immigrants were employed in railroad track maintenance or farming in isolated areas under extremely harsh climatic conditions. It was thus no surprise that most of them moved to large cities as soon as they could. Toronto, Montreal, Quebec and Vancouver now boast of large Portuguese concentrations.[7] Whether settling in English or French-speaking areas, they became mainly industrial and maintenance workers. However, a rather impressive number of Portuguese owned restaurants; cafes, stores and travel agencies cropped up in such neighborhoods as Augusta Avenue in Toronto or Boulevard Saint-Laurent in Montreal. In its major features, the character of the Portuguese immigration in Canada presents striking similarities with that of the east coast of the United States.

1.3. The Profile of the Portuguese Community in North America and Hawaii

The four main areas of Portuguese settlement in Canada and the United States present a common cultural denominator alongside with sociological differences resulting from economic and geographic conditions found in each of them. Thus it can be said that the Portuguese immigrant in Canada and the east coast of the United States is basically an urban dweller engaging in low paid occupations, and residing in heavily "Portuguese" neighborhoods.[8] To this type one must add a sprinkling of fishermen, store keepers and white collar workers. The relative proximity to their places of origin (with the exception of the Vancouver community) has made contact with the home country easier than in California or Hawaii, and allowed for a higher number of permanent returns to Portugal or at least frequent visits of variable duration. Contrarily to this the Portuguese immigrant in California, especially up to recent times, has enjoyed better opportunities to become an entrepreneur, mainly by entering developing fields. Intensive saving and a spartan life style made it possible for many to rise from milker to dairy farmer, and from fisherman to tuna boat skipper and/or owner.[9] However, pouches of industrial workers have recently developed associated with the electronics industry of the so-called Silicone Valley (San Jose/Santa Clara/Mountain View) and metal work and food processing in Artesia and San Pedro, not to speak of an older urban community in the Bay Area (Oakland, San Leandro, Hayward, etc.)[10]

In rural areas isolation prevailed, and opportunities for socializing came mainly during special events such as the Holy Ghost festivals. Even in the cities geographic dispersion is much higher than in the east coast or Canada, as no true "Portuguese" neighborhoods ever took shape.

In Hawaii social mobility came rapidly and the change from the cane field to an urban setting took place in a couple of decades. Here, too, geographic dispersion was a factor to be taken into account when the preservation of group unity and cultural values is to be considered.

It could be safely asserted without danger of stereotypification that the Portuguese immigrant in North America and Hawaii comes from a rural habitat (often an isolated village in the Azores or Madeira) and possesses a limited (e.g. fourth grade or less) education.[11] His behavior is strongly conditioned by a strict adherence to traditional patterns and to the tenets of the Roman Catholic religion. The improvement of his economic level becomes almost an

obsession, and he will go to extreme lengths to achieve it in the shortest possible time. Unfamiliar as he is with modern ways, he nevertheless adapts
rather easily to an infinitely more advanced technology than the one he was
accustomed to, while keeping away from social contacts with the host community or other ethnic groups and almost completely ignoring the political,
intellectual and artistic life around him. Under these circumstances
economic success, usually representing ascent from a peasant to a lower middle class level, often materializes during the first decade of residence in the
host country. At the same time his interests rarely go beyond his own family
circle or the Portuguese community in which he functions. Reminiscing about
life in the old country is another very prevalent form his conservatism takes.

2. The Portuguese Press in North America and Hawaii

2.1. General Considerations

Soon after massive immigration began, the Portuguese in North America and
Hawaii felt the need to establish some sort of a written communication
mechanism in their native language. Thus the first newspapers, as well as
fraternal organization bulletins, came into existence. Their role was obviously
that of any immigrant publication, namely to report and comment on current
affairs in the home and host countries and on local community events. The
vast number of Portuguese language publications which appeared since the
last quarter of the nineteenth century is indeed surprising, mainly if one con-
siders the high rate of illiteracy among the Portuguese community at the
time, and the general indifference toward national and international issues.

All along this trajectory, up to the present time, most newspapers were
launched and directed by individuals with no prior journalistic experience.
Several of the editors have been priests or former printers. In many cases the
newspaper has been little more than a one man operation. This lack of pro-
fessionalism is still very much felt at the present time. Alberto S. Lemos, editor of the California based *Jornal Portugues* commented on this problem during an interview granted to a Lisbon reporter:

> Remember that, besides my being a small editor, staff writer, photogra-
> pher, janitor, porter, sales manager and subscriptions agent, I also have to
> be a manager, administrator, treasurer and bookkeeper and a careful one
> at that, otherwise the newspaper will go bankrupt...[12]

An exhaustive analysis of the contents and philosophies of many of these
newspapers is made almost impossible by the unavailability of complete collections. In addition, quite a number of the periodicals had an ephemeral
existence, often lasting less than one year, thus allowing little time for the
assertion of a continued editorial policy.

Most publications have appeared on a weekly basis. In principle this might
have tended to emphasize the editorial facet rather than the periodical's
newsworthiness. The results were, however, different, presumably due to the
fact that editorial talent did not abound and the unsophisticated readers
were more interested in raw information than in interpretation.

2.2. Basic Attitudes

In spite of an occasional case when a liberal editor took over, Portuguese-language newspapers normally conformed to the generalized conservative attitude which prevailed among the Portuguese community they served. Several of them, like *O Amigo dos Católicos* in California or *A Luta* in New York, were Catholic publications, and even those which were not, usually revealed a deep respect for the Church.[13] There were, however, some signs of anticlericalism in early California newspapers, although the basis for these positions may have been personal differences with the priests who ran rival periodicals, rather than philosophical principles.

Patriotism has always been a predominant feature, up to the point of unconditional homage being rendered to figures like Peter Francisco or Cabrillo, whose Portuguese origin is nebulous at best, or to such unscientific interpretations as the thesis that an early sixteenth century Portuguese navigator left a Latin inscription on Dighton Rock, in Massachusetts.

Support for the most rightist regimes that have ruled Portugal has been frequent. It is almost ironical, for instance, that in 1923-1924, more than a decade after the Portuguese monarchy had been deposed by a coup, a royalist newspaper, *Talassa*, flourished in New Bedford. In more recent times, other publications such as *Voz de Portugal* in Montreal or *Jornal Portugues* in California showed complete allegiance to the dictatorship which existed in Portugal from 1926 to 1974.

Strongly racist attitudes in the Portuguese press of Hawaii are pinpointed by Edgar Knowlton in an article appearing in *Social Progress in Hawaii*. The following is an excerpt the author translated from *O Luso-Havaiano* of 25 October 1885:

> foreigners, white or Chinese. It is too bad that this takes place, because for hygienic reasons known to us all, in no wise do we advise Portuguese to marry native women... On this account we deem it suitable that Portuguese not marry native women, so as not to compromise their posterity.[14]

In California also *Voz Portuguesa* and *Progresso Californiense* echoed violent anti-Oriental sentiments then prevailing in the West Coast. In the aftermath of anti-Chinese riots in several California communities, the *Progresso wrote:*

> The demonstrations against the Chinamen continue. In several parts of this State already there is not a single Chinaman, and it is to be hoped that soon in the larger localities fewer will be seen than now... Take all work away from them and give it to whites, and in a short time we will see ourselves completely free of this plague.[15]

Even a liberal editor like Bettencourt da Camara had this to say, a few years later:

> The general crisis that assails the working classes in this State, and no one doubts it, is due exclusively to.. the Chinese workman and laborer and is not the inevitable consequence of the general economic crisis.[16]

It is only fair to note, however, that by this time the Portuguese press in California protested anti-Semitic incidents in San Francisco and the lynchings of blacks and of Italian immigrants.

Geoffrey L. Gomes comments on the attitudes of two above mentioned early California newspapers toward labor conflicts. He points out that both *Uniao Portuguesa* and *Progresso Californiense* had this to say in regard to a strike by San Francisco streetcar operators in 1886:

> When... the streetcar workers... went on strike with the objective of obtaining from their respective companies a reduction in hours of work and a wage increase there was not a conscientious person who did not sympathize with them.

Their request was just and their cause appealing; thus, when it was learned that the companies obstinately refused to reach an agreement with the strikers the general sentiment showed itself in their favor...

> When the first disturbance took place there was a decided tendency to absolve them of any and all involvement... in the bloodshed that occurred then, everything being attributed to a certain class of people who take advantage of such occasions to attack and destroy the property of others. However, the events of the morning of the 27th, rock throwing, employees beaten, dynamite placed on the rails, cars set loose, thus placing at risk the lives of peaceful citizens the events of that day came to prove that the strikers are not as innocent as they would have us believe.[17]

In the aftermath of the Pullman strike in 1894, the *Uniao Portuguesa* considered the walkout staged by the American Railway Union and led by Eugene V. Debs "a great calamity", which only served the purpose of contributing to the economic depression the country was then going through.

In the second decade of the twentieth century *O Lavrador Portugues* also expressed sympathetic feelings toward strikers. Here is what Gomes has to say about the paper's position on this issue:

> Its owner and editor, Arthur V. Avila, made conflict between labor and capital a regular feature and consistently supported the efforts of organized labor. This pro-union posture, however, was not characteristic of California progressives, who tended to view labor unions, at best, as necessary evils in an industrial society.[18]

3. Conclusion

Despite some dissonant platforms defended by a limited number of liberal journalists, the Portuguese press in North America and Hawaii had necessarily to conform to the idiosyncrasies of its readership. Considering the traditionalistic and submissive nature of the Portuguese community it is thus no wonder that no labor newspapers rose from within. There were, to be sure, a few instances of Portuguese-language labor newspapers sponsored by national organizations, but everything leads to believe that their impact among Portuguese workers was minimal. Editorial policies, the immigrant literature and direct observation make it more than clear that this community was definitely no fertile breeding ground for progressive ideas.

Notes

1. The reconquest of Northern Brazil from the Dutch by the Portuguese in that same year displaced many Jews, who had enjoyed considerably more freedom under the Dutch.

2. Areas of Portuguese settlement in the United States are almost exclusively the States of Massachusetts, Rhode Island, New York, New Jersey, Connecticut, Pennsylvania, California and Hawaii. Small numbers live in Florida and Nevada.

3. It was probably due to the presence of the Cape Verdeans that the derogatory expression "black portagee" developed to cover all Portuguese immigrants in that area.

4. A number of shore whaling stations, manned mainly by Azoreans, cropped up along the California coast in the late nineteenth century.

5. The only other area where U.S. commercial tuna boats are based is Puerto Rico.

6. In the second decade of the present century many Portuguese migrated from Hawaii to California, due to declining wages at the sugar cane plantations.

7. An estimated 100,000 have settled in the province of Ontario alone.

8. With the partial exception of East Santa Clara Street in San Jose, nowhere in California or Hawaii are "Portuguese" streets to be seen, such as Ferry Street in Newark, Columbia Street in Fall River or Asushnet Avenue in New Bedford.

9. Even at the lower of these levels, present-day earnings for a milker or tuna fisherman may reach respectively close to $30,000 or up to $80,000 a year.

10. Portuguese workers in this area may however earn up to $14 an hour.

11. At the turn of the century illiteracy among Portuguese immigrants probably hovered around 80.

12. Helder Pinho, *Portugueses na California* (Lisbon, 1978), p.75 (translated by E. M. Dias).

13. It is interesting to note that in 1983 the San Pablo *Jornal Portugues* even displayed an ultra-Catholic attitude when it became highly critical of an ecclesiastical commission which found no grounds for attributing a miraculous character to the alleged self-displacement of an image of Our Lady of Fatima in a heavily Portuguese attended church in Thornton, California.

14. Edgar Knowlton, "The Portuguese Language Press in Hawaii," *Social Progress in Hawaii* 24 (1960), p. 96.

15. Geofrey L. Gomes, "The Portuguese Language Press in California, 1880-1928," unpublished MA thesis (California State University, Hayward, 1983), p. 12. The quote was translated from the 14 January 1886 issue.

16. Gomes, p. 13. The quote was translated from the 19 October 1983 issue of *A Uniao Portuguesa*.

17. Ibid., pp. 15-16. The quote was translated from the 1 January 1887 issue of *O Progresso Californiense*.

18. Ibid, p. 29.

Bibliography

Cardozo, Manoel daSilveira, comp.

The Portuguese in America 590 B.C. - 1974. A Chronology and Fact Book. Dobbs Ferry, NY: Oceana, 1976.

Fothergill-Payne, Peter A.

"Portuguese-Canadian Perodical Publication: A Preliminary Check List." *Canadian Ethnic Studies* 2(1) (June 1970), pp.169-70, supplement by Grace M. Anderson and David C. Higgs 5 (1-2) (1973), pp. 243-244.

Knowlton, Edgar C., Jr.

"The Portuguese Language Press of Hawaii." *Social Process in Hawaii* 26 (1960), pp.89-99.

Lang, Henry R.

"The Portuguese Element in New England." *Journal of American Folklore* 5 (1892), pp. 9-18.

Pap, Leo.

The Portuguese in the United States: A Bibliography. Beverly Hills, CA, 1974.

Rogers, Francis M.

American of Portuguese Descent: A Lesson in Differentiation. Beverly Hills, CA, 1974.

Appendix

Periodicals in Portuguese or dealing with Portuguese and Brazilian topics published in North America and Hawaii

A Abelha, San Francisco and Oakland, CA, ca. 1924 to ?.

A Alvorada, New Bedford, MA, ca. 1912 to ca. 1927.

American Portuguese Cultural Society Journal, New York, NY, 1966 to ? present.

O Amigo dos Catolicos, Irvington, Pleasanton and Oakland, CA, 1888 to 1896.

O Arauto, Hayward and Oakland, CA, 1896 to 1917.

Aurora Brasileira, New York, NY, ca. 1876 to ca. 1878.

Aurora Havaiana, Honolulu, HI, 1889 to 1891.

Azorean Times, ?Providence, RI, 1976 to ? present.

As Boas Novas, ?, HI, 1896 to 1908.

Boletim da I.D.E.S., Hayward, CA, 1898 to present.

Boletim da S.P.R.S.I., Oakland, CA, 1901 to ? present.

Boletim da Uniao Pan-Americana, Washington, DC, ca. 1913 to ? 1930

Boletim da U.P.E.C. / U.P.E.C. Life, San Leandro, CA, 1898 to present.

Boletim da U.P.P.E.C., Oakland, CA, ? 1910 to ?.

Brasil e os Estados Unidos, New York, NY, ca. 1898 to ca. 1905.

Brazil News, New York, NY, 1969 to ?.

Brazil Exchange, New York, NY, 1977 to ?.

Brazil Post, New York, NY, 1976 to ?.

Brazialian American Bulletin, New York, NY?, ca. 1972 to ?.

A Califórnia Alegre, Oakland, Lemoore, Tulare and Hanford, CA, 1914 to ? 1940.

Cape Verdean, Lynn, MA, ? to ?.

Civilizacao, Boston, MA, ca. 1883 to ?.

O Clarim, Oakland, CA, 1934 to ? 1936.

A Colonia Portuguesa, Oakland and Alameda, CA, 1924 to 1932.

O Colônial, Fall River, MA, ca. 1913 to ?..

Comércio, Toronto, O, 1976 to ?.

O Companheiro da Alegria, Hayward, CA, 1961 to ?.

Comunidade, Hull, Q, Jan. 1974 to ? Oct. 1974.

Comunidade, Toronto, O, 1975 to ?.

Correio Operário Norte-Americano, Washington, DC, 1963 to ?.

Correio Portugues, New Bedford, MA, ca. 1897 to ca. 1913.

Correio Portugues, Toronto, O, 1963 to ?.

O Cosmopolitano, Fairhaven, MA, 1922 to 1925.

A Crónica, San Francisco, CA, 1895 to 1896.

Cronica Portuguesa, San Leandro, CA, 1926 to ? 1927.

O Despertar, Edmonton, A, 1972 to ?.

Diário de Notícias, New Bedford, MA, 1919 to 1973.
O Directo, Honolulu, HI, 1896 to 1898.
Ecos de Portugal, Oakland, CA, 1934 to ?.
O Elo de Portugal, Vancouver, BC, ca. 1976 to ?.
O Emigrante, Montreal, Q, 1977 to ?.
O Engenheiro e o Empreiteiro, New York, NY, ca. 1920 to ?.
Era Nova, Fall River, MA, ca. 1925 to ?.
Estádio, ? Providence, RI, 1979 to ? present.
Exportador Americano, New York, NY, ca. 1915 to ?.
O Facho, Hilo, HI, 1906 to 1927.
Factos & Gente, Newark, NJ, Jan. 1976 to July 1976.
Família Portuguesa, Toronto, O, 1979 to ?.
Friends of the Foundation, Oakland, CA, 1970 to present.
Gávea/Brown, Providence, RI, 1980 to present.
A Gazeta Portuguesa, San Jose, CA, 1926 to ?.
O Heraldo, Oakland, CA, 1936 to ?.
Independente, New Bedford, MA, 1904 to 1945.
Impacto, Danbury, CT, ? to ?.
O Imparcial, Sacramento, CA, 1913 to 1932.
Jornal Acoriano, Toronto, O, 1975 to ?.
Jornal de Fall River, Fall River, MA, 1975 to present.
Jornal de Notícias, Erie, PA, 1877 to 1890.
Jornal de Notícias, San Francisco and Alameda, CA, 1917 to 1932.
Jornal Portugues, Oakland and San Pablo, CA, 1932 to present.
O Jornal Portugues, Toronto, O, 1968 to 1975.
O Lavrador Portugues, Lemoore, Hanford, Tulare and Oakland, CA, 1912 to ? 1928.
A Liberdade, Honolulu, HI, 1900 to 1910.
A Liberdade, Sacramento and Oakland, CA, 1900 to 1937.
Lusitano, Montreal, Q, 1964 to ?.
Lusitano, Toronto, O, 1964 to ? 1974.
O Lusitano, Cambridge, O, 1978 to ?.
O Luso, Honolulu, HI, 1896 to 1924.
Luso-Americano, ? Boston / ? New Bedford, MA, ca. 1881 to ?.
Luso-Americano, Newark, NJ, 1928 to 1932 and 1939 to present.
Luso-Canadiano, Montreal, Q, ? 1953 / ? 1971 to ?.
Luso-Havaiano, Honolulu, HI, 1885 to 1891.
A Luta, New York, NY, 1935 to 1970.
O Mensageiro, Vancouver, BC, 1968 to ?.
Micaelense, Fall River, MA, ca. 1916 to ca. 1920.
O Mundial, Winnipeg, M, ca. 1972 to ?.
O Mundo, ?, CA, ? 1915 to ?.
Nosso Jornal, Vancouver, BC, 1969 to ?.

Noticiá rio do Sindicalismo Livre, Washington, DC, 1945 to ?.

As Novidades, Newman, CA, 192? to ?.

Novidades, Fall River, MA, 1908 to ?1930.

Novo Mundo, New York, NY, ca. 1871 to ca. 1879.

Novo Mundo, Toronto, O, 1970 to ca. 1973.

O Novo Mundo, New Bedford, MA, 1890 to ?.

Novos Rumos, Newark, NJ, 1960 to ?.

Operário de Carne, Chicago, IL, 1946 to 1948.

Our Lady of Fatima Magazine, New York, NY, 1932 to ?.

Paróquia Portuguesa, Toronto, O, ? 1966 to 1979.

A Pátria, Oakland, CA, ? 1892 to 1897.

Paz, Lowell, MA, ? ca. 1914 to ?.

O Popular, Honolulu, HI, 1911 to 1913.

O Popular, Providence, RI, 1914 to 1940.

O Popular, Toronto, O, 1975 to ?.

Popular, New Bedford, MA, ? ca. 1914 to ? ca. 1930.

Portu-Info, Stanford, CA, 1961 to ?.

Portugal, New Bedford, MA, ? ca. 1916 to ? ca. 1930.

Portugal, Newark, NJ, 1928 to ?.

O Portugal, Oakland, CA, 1930 to ?.

Portugal-América, Fresno, CA, 1905 to ?.

Portugal no Mundo, Bridgeport, CT, ca. 1980 to ?.

Portugal Press, Newark, NJ, 1980 to ?.

Portugália, Oakland, CA, ca. 1933 to ?.

Portuguese News, Newark, NJ, 1978 to ?.

Portuguese Times, Newark, NJ and New Bedford, MA, 1971 to present.

The Portuguese Tribune, San Jose, CA, 1979 to present.

O Progresso, Sacramento, CA, 1933 to ?.

O Progresso Californiense, San Franciso, CA, 1884 to 1887.

O Reporter, Oakland, CA, 1897 to 1916.

A Revista Portuguesa, Hayward, CA, 1915 to 1924.

Revista Dental Internacional, Pittsburg, PA, ca. 1918 to ?.

Revista Industrial, New York, NY, ca. 1880 to ?.

Revista Internacional de Dun, New York, NY, ca. 1920 to ? ca. 1930.

A Sentinela, Honolulu, HI, 1892 to 1896.

A Seta, Hilo, HI, 1903 to 1921.

Talassa, New Bedford, MA, 1923-1924.

Tribuna Portuguesa, Montreal, Q, 1972 to 1975.

A Uniao Lusitana-Havaiana, Honolulu, HI, 1892 to 1896.

A Uniao Portuguesa, San Francisco and Oakland, CA, 1887 to 1942.

A Verdade, Toronto, O, ? 1964 to ? 1965.

Vigilante, Fall River, MA, ca. 1917 to ? ca. 1929.

A Voz da Colónia, Bristol, RI, 1926 to 1928.

A Voz da Verdade, Oakland, CA, 1908 to ? 1909.
Voz de Portugal, Hayward, CA, 1960 to present.
Voz de Portugal, Montreal, Q, 1960 to ?.
Voz de Portugal, Halifax, NS, 1961 to ?.
A Voz Portuguesa, San Francisco, CA, 1880 to 1887.
A Voz Portuguesa, Oakville, O, 1970 to ?.
A Voz Pública, Hilo, HI, 1899 to 1904.

MIGRANTS FROM
WESTERN EUROPE

The Press of Labor Migrants From Western and Central Europe: Introduction

by Dirk Hoerder

The West European emigration areas are politically speaking those parts of Europe where nation states were first formed and soon achieved durability. (This is in many ways comparable with the situation in the Nordic countries, but there alliances and the dominating positions of Sweden and Denmark played an important role.) Because of their similarities with the northern and western migration areas, we have included the central European German-language provinces and empires in this section. Hence the countries dealt with in this volume are Great Britain with its constituent parts of England, Scotland and Wales; its colony Ireland; France; Belgium (independent since 1830), the Netherlands and Luxemburg; Germany, Switzerland and the German-speaking parts of Austria. (See Figure 1)

Linguistically this area includes publications in English, French, Dutch and German as well as some in Welsh. In Great Britain English is the main language spoken, but it is also the home of five of the six Celtic languages, the sixth being Breton, the language of Brittany in France. It appears that the Welsh were the only Celtic nationality to develop a press of their own in North America. French migration to North America was limited, since France had itself become an immigration country by the middle of the nineteenth century. Accordingly the size of the North American French-language immigrant press was limited, too. Dutch and Flemish (which is as similar to Dutch as American is to British English) produced only a very small labor press in North America since the migration from these areas did not achieve the volume and social characteristics necessary for the development of a large number of separate working-class periodicals. Under the German language we have subsumed high and low German as well as the Swiss, Austrian and Alsatian dialects. German and Austrian socialists in North America cooperated relatively closely, and therefore a separate classification of their publications is - with few exceptions - almost impossible. Emigration from Switzerland's Italian, Rhaeto-Romanic and French-speaking parts does not need separate mention in the context of the LNPP since no labor periodicals were published by emigrants from these areas.

Within western and west central Europe labor migration had a long and varied tradition.[1] Before the beginning of industrialization there were three types of migration involving (1) skilled artisan journeymen (Handwerksgesellen), (2) seasonal agrarian labor and (3) mainly female domestics. In addition there was a continuous flow of population toward urban centers and circulation between cities and market towns. Finally a number of governmental measures and changes in the balance of power increased (forced) population mobility: these included shifts in the borders between the four central and east European empires; encouragement of immigration for mercantilist purposes and expulsion of religious dissenters. Labor migration in the modern sense began in the first half of the nineteenth century, when its target was the Netherlands and England. These two areas (including Belgium until 1830) attracted German workers because of the high degree of urbanization and their role as centers of commercial activities.

By the middle of the nineteenth century up to 50 percent of the population of cities in Germany and western Europe consisted of in-migrants. The majority of them came from the same linguistic group as the native inhabitants. The

Figure 1   West European Languages and German

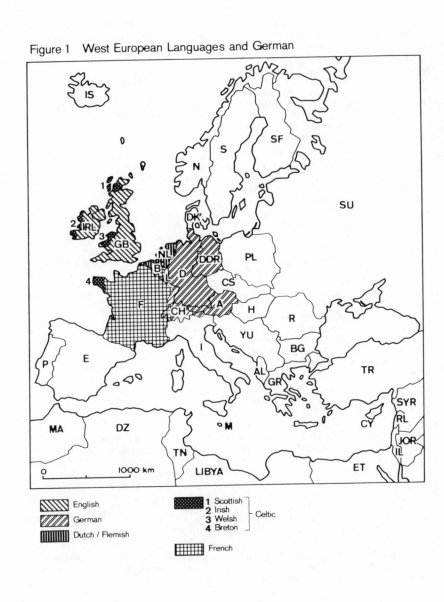

English		1 Scottish	
German		2 Irish	Celtic
Dutch / Flemish		3 Welsh	
		4 Breton	
		French	

percentage of in-migrants was higher in newly created industrial towns and planned cities, lower in stagnating middle-sized provincial towns.

Internal migration was common in Germany, Great Britain and especially in France where it became a way of life for about one fifth of the population. In Great Britain restrictions existed on the emigration of skilled workers till 1824. According to mercantilist theory the purpose of these measures was to prevent the export of their skills to other nations. Early immigrants to England (since the sixteenth century) included Flemish clothmakers, Walloon weavers and French Huguenots, who were involved in the manufacture of silk and linen. Welsh laborers migrated to English industrial areas in increasing numbers after the completion of a railroad link in 1850. Scottish towns absorbed the migration from the Scottish Highlands, but some labor migrants continued to England. Great Britain passed a law restricting immigration in 1905 to prevent the entry of East European, particularly Jewish workers. Irish migration, which had begun long before the famine years, was originally mainly directed toward Britain.

In the Netherlands, Belgium and Luxemburg internal migrants went to industrializing areas and to the urban centers and there was some seasonal migration to neighboring ·countries. Thus Walloon (=French-speaking) workers migrated to rural areas in France to be able to stay in their occupations. In government statistics this migration to a culturally similar area shows up as international migration, while the migration from the Flemish countryside to the culturally different Wallonia was hardly counted, though in addition to changing culture these migrants usually also changed from agrarian to industrial work.

In France many regions provided labor for specific trades in the whole or large sections of the country, particularly Paris, where ethnic organizations sprang up just as in North America and among the Poles in the Ruhr district.[2] Lumberjacks and charcoal burners came from the Auvergne, masons from the Creuse, longsawyers from the Haute-Loire, vineyard workers from the Cevennes etc. Paris, like London and Swiss towns also attracted political refugees from many countries. For centuries Switzerland was a source of mercenaries - it is estimated to have supplied up to two million between the sixteenth and nineteenth centuries - and dairymen spread Swiss dairying customs to Germany and elsewhere. But by the second half of the nineteenth century, Switzerland also had to import labor. In Germany, too, dozens if not hundreds of regional patterns of seasonal, annual or multiannual migration may be discerned.

What had been a limited flow of international migration in the first half of the nineteenth century became a broad stream in the second half. In these countries internationalized labor markets in the lowest job categories developed and assumed considerable magnitude. In addition skilled workers and artisans migrated in order to improve either their skills or their wages or both. For artisans German was the *lingua franca* throughout central and eastern Europe, and because of the presence of political exiles also in parts of western Europe, especially in the journeymen's quarters of large cities like Paris and London. With the exception of Luxemburg and the Netherlands all of these countries became labor-importing countries. Britain - or rather England - recruited its labor from its Irish colony. France did so from all of its neighbors - the French- speaking parts of Belgium, Germany and Spain - as well as from Italy. By the 1880s East European Jews were coming by the tens of thousands and before and after World War One systematic recruitment of Polish workers began. Germany relied mainly on Italian and Polish in-migration. One of its war aims in 1914 was to assure a permanent flow of cheap, if necessary forced, labor from the east European territories. While France encouraged permanent immigration, Germany pursued a policy of rotating the foreign labor force by administrative and legal devices to prevent acculturation. (Poles and Italians were Catholics and Poles were considered culturally and socially inferior. Poles were also a threat to Germanization policies in the occupied part of Poland) Switzerland like France relied on the neighboring countries, especially Germany and later Italy. The percentage of foreign workers among its population achieved North American proportions, while for the other countries it remained considerably lower. Labor exporting countries were situated on the periphery: Ireland for England, Italy for Switzerland, Germany and France, Poland for Germany and later France.

These labor migrants developed a press of their own just as immigrant workers in North America did. There was an Italian press in Switzerland and France. In Germany both the Catholic church and the German bricklayers' union put out publications for them.[3] A kind of labor exchange and emigrants' aid center backed by Italian socialists was opened in Milan to inform migrants about their rights, to put them into contact with unions in the countries of arrival and to prevent them from acting as strikebreakers.[4] Poles were addressed through a special paper published with the support of the federation of German trade unions, but more important were their own papers. Again the church was behind this effort but since the press addressed a working-class community it could not avoid questions of work and wages. In France there were separate Italian, Polish and Jewish presses addressing the migrants.[5] To this labor and ethnic press have to be added the many periodicals issued in Switzerland, France, Belgium or London by exiled social democrats, socialists and anarchists. Much of the exile press was written for the whole of Europe, some of it for individual countries. Thus periodicals of the German Social Democratic Party had to be printed abroad and smuggled into Germany for the period of the Anti-Socialist Law and many publications destined for Russia had to be printed elsewhere. A detailed study of this press will reveal many links with the North American labor press, links which in the LNPP can only be hinted at through the international careers (or wanderings) of some editors, through party connections, through union ties. It is not yet possible to make a systematic assessment.

The rate of emigration from Great Britain, Ireland, Germany and Austria to the United States and Canada was high.[6] Some British trade unions encouraged emigration to reduce the surplus of labor in the British labor market or to open up (agrarian) opportunities to members of declining crafts.[7] British immigrants in the United States, particularly Welsh and Cornish miners were in the forefront of struggles for mine safety.[8] Irish emigration increased after the famine years. It was caused less by the potato blight than by the changes in agrarian structures resulting from the penetration of British capital into Ireland. The Irish struggles for freedom from English domination, for land and for a republican government merged with labor struggles in North America.[9] French emigration needs no special mention here. As for German migration, it should be remembered that it took fifty years after 1820 for 2.9 million Germans to come, most of them farmers but also artisans and workers, and only fifteen years after 1878 for another two million to arrive, mainly skilled and unskilled workers. Among these were large numbers of migrants escaping from the miserable living conditions in the agrarian regions east of the Elbe. They were replaced by Polish workers on the larger agricultural estates.[10] The German migrants took a tradition of bourgeois-democratic and Jacobin radicalism with them after 1848, of social-democratic and socialist thought from the 1870s onward.[11] As they were among the early arrivals their separate working-class culture had already become part of the English-speaking mainstream by the turn of the century. This fact - which contradicts the customary picture of the demise of German ethnic culture as a whole having occurred as late as World War One - was first established by the Munich-project on the acculturation of German workers in Chicago and it is dramatically confirmed by the pattern of establishment of labor periodicals after 1902 (see below).[12]

Of the west European labor migrants the English, Scots, Welsh and Irish did not establish separate labor presses, though large numbers of workers migrated. That of Flemish/Dutch and of French migrants remained small, that of the German-North American working class was the only to achieve a considerable size.

The process of acculturation of the British peoples and the Irish reveals some similarities but also important differences. They shared the language of the culture of arrival - even if for some Gaelic-speakers it was a second language - and thus they could join the English-language United States or Canadian labor movements and read their publications. Accordingly all four groups only established a small-sized ethnic press compared to that of other groups. The absence of a labor press is also explained by the backward linkage to the old culture. British labor migrants remained members of their British unions, frequently expected to move back to Britain, and simply had their "home" union periodicals forwarded. Some British unions even established branches in North America. The backward linkage of the Irish, on the other hand, was not to union traditions but to anti-colonial and republican struggles. They supported the land leagues and adapted their "home" rhetoric to North American conditions. Internationalist-minded labor leaders from Ireland (often with British industrial experience), from Scotland and England, edited labor journals in conjunction with the North American native white workers' labor movement. Like internationalists of other ethnic groups they often moved back to their original cultures.

The position of labor migrants from these four ethnic groups in the new society differed according to skill and prior work experience. Skilled workers of many trades came from England, miners from Wales, miners, carpetweavers and others from Scotland, unskilled workers from Ireland. Accordingly the Irish presence in the Knights of Labor was considerably larger than that of the other ethnicities, who would tend to join craft unions or establish locals of the British craft unions. No common British consciousness developed. (The exception was a few attempts to publish British periodicals - partly in reaction to Irish organizational and political successes.) Therefore no parallels can be drawn to the Scandinavianism or Yugoslavism of north and southeast European ethnic groups.

The press of the four ethnic groups does, however, reveal a similarity to that of east European immigrants in one respect: general middle-class and denominational periodicals often addressed a working-class readership. Thus some periodicals may be defined as pro-labor, or sympathetic to socialist demands. But their number was limited. (For details see the introductions to the relevant sections.)

According to the information available no separate Cornish press was published, though up to 100,000 Cornish migrants reached North American shores. Many were displaced miners who gathered in United States mining towns.

The Welsh press, addressed largely to miners, is the only Celtic-language press that was published in North America. Its character was mainly denominational and "general." While Welshmen were active in trade unions, historians have paid more attention to their impact on mining techniques, safety regulations and work processes than to their militancy or lack of it.

The - unsuccessful - search for a labor press of the Irish and British migrant workers teaches us that for these groups (and to a lesser degree for other groups) questions about the labor movement should not focus on a labor militancy as traditionally defined, but rather on the internationalism of a leadership that felt at home on both sides of the Atlantic, and the role it played in transferring the movement's and the ethnic groups' ideas back and forth. Secondly it should focus on the consciousness of the internationally mobile rank and file workers, who were seemingly able to adapt the specific forms of expression of their original cultures to fit the new culture - and in the case of return or multiple migration - to take up their discourse in the old culture again. While such questions have been explored for the Chartists [13] answers are still needed for the period up to World War One.[14] A neglected source for a comparative study of working conditions and the societal and economic framework which shaped migrants' experiences and their consciousnesses are reports by governmental institutions, and delegations of entrepreneurs comparing work and production costs on both sides of the Atlantic.[15]

The Dutch press, including the Flemish variant, was mainly hostile to the unionization of labor. This was due to the agrarian and urban as well as religious characteristics of the immigration. Thus only a few labor periodicals came into existence. Furthermore, Dutch socialists and labor militants easily merged with German or English-language groups.

As explained in the introduction to the whole bibliography the French-language press addressed several different groups of migrants and the French-Canadian population. The Franco-Canadians are not dealt with in this bibliography. Their radical literature and press is listed in the comprehensive bibliography by Weinrich and Beaulieu.[16] A second French-speaking group in North America, already resident on the continent before their territory fell to the United States, are the Louisiana "Creoles." French-language migrants to the United States (or to the British colonies) include five distinct groups: the Acadians, migrants from French possessions in the Caribbean, the Franco-Canadians and the European French and French-speaking Belgians.

The first "migration" of French-speaking settlers from formerly French to British colonies occurred in the eighteenth century. French families from Acadia, i.e. the territory of the present-day maritime provinces of Canada which had come under British rule in 1713, were expelled in 1755 and established settlements in Louisiana ("Cajuns") and northern Maine. They were largely illiterate and at that time no press existed in Louisiana. A second migration, relatively small in number, brought Caribbean migrants to Louisiana, augmenting the local French-speaking social aristocracy. The press of this group was also read by the literate Acadian migrants. No labor press in the strict sense of the term emerged, but some periodicals advocating a radical black republicanism were addressed to the black and white working classes in the second half of the nineteenth century. Since 1916 compulsory education in the English-language school system has further reduced French-language publications.

A third migration, mainly in the period from 1845 to 1895 but continuing to the present, brought French-Canadians to the New England states and upstate New York, as well as to the Middle West. Many of them came on a seasonal or multiannual basis.[17] Their extensive press - with one or two possible exceptions - did not include labor periodicals although many of them worked as agricultural workers on New England farms and as spinners and weavers in the textile mills.

Because of the small number of immigrants from France and Wallonia to North America during the nineteenth and twentieth centuries - particularly after the middle of the nineteenth century when France became a labor-importing country - there were no working-class publications which appeared continually. In the 1840s and 50s a few periodicals advocated early socialism. To these must be added the Icarian publications. In the 1860s and early 70s a small number of "republican/labor" newspapers were published in the tradition of an egalitarian French-inspired revolutionary republicanism. Two shortlived labor periodicals also appeared before the onset of the Long Depression. After an intermission of fifteen years, the labor press reappeared in the Pennsylvania coalfields in 1888. In addition a syndicalist, a socialist and three anarchist papers were published for some years after 1899. The syndicalist paper was published by the "Federation Franco-Belge I.W.W." for French and Flemish-speaking workers. The French-language labor and radical press for and by immigrants finally ceased to exist in 1927.

Since the west European and German labor presses in North America do not form a unified group it is impossible to generalize about places and continuity of publication. All five Dutch/ Flemish reformist and labor periodicals were issued in two Michigan towns, Grand Rapids and Holland. French radical publishing was concentrated in Louisiana and in the Pennsylvania/ Chicago/ New England triangle. Only the Icarian papers were published elsewhere: Illinois, Missouri, Iowa, Kansas and finally California. In the early period of French radical publishing (1845-73) the periodicals espousing black radical republicanism (3), early socialism (2) and labor (1) were published in New Orleans or nearby. In this period only four periodicals appeared in the North, two in Chicago and two in New York. During the second period, 1888 to 1927 only an ephemeral black republican and a populist paper appeared in the South, the rest (except one shortlived paper in San Francisco) appeared in Illinois (2), Pennsylvania (4), Paterson, NJ (1) and Rhode Island (1). Thus over the years a clear shift of French labor periodicals from the South to the North may be discerned.

Of the Dutch/ Flemish periodicals only the reformist, church-affiliated *Stemmen uit de Vrije Gemeende* achieved continuity of publication (1880-1920). Of the two Christian trade-union publications of the early 1890s and the two socialist publications of the pre-World War One period (1908-15) none lasted more than three years. Of the French-language periodicals, the first two in 1846 and 1852 lasted for only a year each. The periodicals published between 1857 and 1873 survived for two to eight years, the average being about four years. The second period of publication (1888-1927) is even more difficult to quantify: the Pennsylvania miners' paper changed its title and numbering four times, but it was published practically consecutively for 29 years, the populist paper for 20 years, while the syndicalist, socialist and anarchist papers lasted from two to six years, the anarchist *Germinal* living on for four years as a section of an Italian-American anarchist publication of the same title.

The German-language reform, labor and radical press from 1845 to 1945 may be divided into four periods and an aftermath post-1945. (See Figures 2 and 3)

Figure 2   Number of German-North American Periodicals Founded by Decade, 1844 – 1974

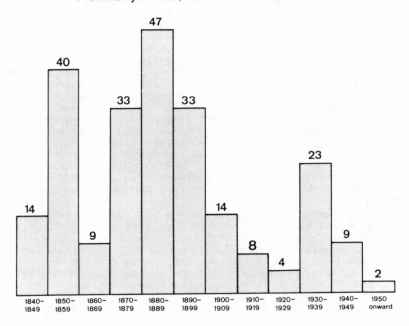

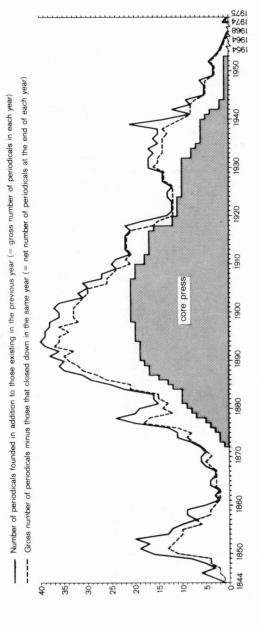

Figure 3   German-North American Periodicals Founded and Closed Down by Years 1844 - 1974

——— Number of periodicals founded in addition to those existing in the previous year (= gross number of periodicals in each year)

– – – Gross number of periodicals minus those that closed down in the same year (= net number of periodicals at the end of each year)

core press

40
35
30
25
20
15
10
5

1844 1850 1860 1870 1880 1890 1900 1910 1920 1930 1940 1950 1954 1964 1968 1974 1975

217

Phase 1 extends for approximately a quarter of a century from 1845 to 1869. Radical Fortyeighter, reform and early socialist periodicals characterize the beginning of an organizationally heterogeneous movement.[18]

Phase 2 covers the movement's apogee, the three decades from 1870 to 1902. While a slight decline in the number of periodicals published begins in 1895, the large quantity of new publications appearing each year testifies to the vitality of the German-language elements in the German-American labor movement. In this period the "core press" was founded (see below).

Phase 3 (1903-29) covers a period of stabilization as well as decline, including the changes wrought by the years of war and repression, but continuing through the 1920s.

Phase 4 (1930-45) was the period of change from a labor to an exile and antiwar press, though the "hard-core press" still accounts for about two fifths of the total number of publications appearing each year.

During the initial phase a broad variety of often shortlived periodicals were founded. Many were publications of radical Fortyeighters both sympathetic and genuinely committed to working-class interests. A large number belonged to the category of "early socialist" and local "workers' club" papers. A few reform, general labor and utopian communist publications complete the list. The five years after 1848 saw the founding of 34 new periodicals but after 1854 fewer newspapers were founded and existing ones closed down. Throughout the sixties (the Civil War) publishing activities remained as low as in the late forties (see Figure 1). Of the 63 periodicals founded in the initial phase, more than half (32) lasted only one year or less.[19] This reflects both undercapitalization of new ventures, lack of experience of political exiles in the new culture and the absence of an organizational basis of labor activists. About one third[20] lasted from two to four years, eleven survived longer (see Table).

Length of Publication								
Years	Phase 1 1845-1869		Phase 2 1870-1902		Phase 3 1903-1929		Phase 4 1930-1945	
	no.	%	no.	%	no.	%	no.	%
1 year or less	32	50.8	35	28.4	6	37.5	10	33.4
2-4 years	20	31.7	36	29.3	3	18.8	14	46.6
5-19 years	9	14.3	31	25.2	5	31.2	5	16.6
20 or more years	2	3.2	21	17.1	2	12.5	1	3.4
Total	63	100.0	123	100.0	16	100.0	30	100.0
Average length of publ. in years	-	3.43	-	10.8	-	8.2	-	3.6

The five periodicals achieving continuity beyond ten years had a social-democratic viewpoint (*New Yorker Abendzeitung*, 1850-1874), relied on the organizational basis of the "Turner"-movement (*Turnzeitung*, New York, 1850-1861), or were rooted in the Fortyeighter movement (*Pionier*, Boston, 1854-1879), (*Beobachter am Ohio*, Louisville, 1844-1856) and the labor movement (*Arbeiterfreund*, WV Wheeling, 1865-1876). By the middle of the seventies when periodicals published by a broad organized labor movement began to appear, they had ceased to exist.

Phase 2 from 1870 to 1902 marked the high period of German labor activism in the United States. The founding of the Socialist Party in 1901 also completed the realignment of the left parties, groups and clubs in which German-American workers were active. The temporary shift toward anarchism at a time when neither bourgeois-democratic nor socialist approaches seemed to improve the situation of workers had already come to an end. In these three decades 123 periodicals were founded, i.e. on the average almost four per year. (During the next phase up to 1929, an average of only one periodical was founded every two years). Periodicals of the high period had more stability than those of the initial and later phases. About one quarter closed down within one year, another quarter existed from two to four years (average 2.75 years), and a further quarter from five to nineteen years (average 9.7 years). The remaining group of 21 periodicals survived from 21 to 79 years (average 45.9 years), the last until 1953. The establishment of this "core" of periodicals was the main achievement of this phase. It reflected the whole spectrum of labor activities: freethinkers (1), general labor (3), labor union (6), social-democratic (2), socialist-"Turner" (gymnast movement) (1), socialist (7), anarchist (1). Throughout the period this hard core accounted for approximately half of the periodicals available. They continued publication into Phase 3 during which they even accounted for about three-quarters of the publications available. What seems surprising at first glance is that these established journals suffered heavy losses during the two world wars and the first years of the Great Depression. However, they were faced with a declining readership, probably with ageing editors, and with an increasing integration of their potential audience into the English-language labor movement. Furthermore, the occupational composition of the German-American working-class community was changing. Thus anti-German hostility during the wars, repression during and after World War One and the financial problems of the depression years seriously affected a press whose longevity was paralleled by a decline in importance. Compared to the German press as a whole, World War One and "Red Scare" losses were somewhat less marked: (21). On the one hand, the process of merging with the English-language labor movement had been under way since the 1890s and early 1900s, on the other hand, commitment was not only to ethnicity but also to class and thus it served as an impetus to continue, adverse conditions notwithstanding.

Phase 3, the quarter century from 1903 to 1929, covers the end of the German-American labor movement. While more than a dozen "core" labor periodicals from the previous phase continued publication, the number of newly established journals and the totals decreased till 1912, then remained stable at half the early 1890s level till 1917, and finally dropped sharply under the impact of the war and the Department of Justice persecution to twelve periodicals annually with few new additions. The thirties and particularly the beginning of World War Two (Phase 4) witnessed a flurry of publishing activity, but most of the new periodicals were shortlived. During both phases the average length of publication of periodicals became shorter (see Table 1) - one-third closed down within a year and one-third of those existing from three to five years had an average life-span even of only two and a half years. The number of places of publication had fallen to eight by the twenties; to two, New York and Chicago, during Phase 4. The period after 1945 needs no separate classification - it formed the aftermath of a once important press.

German-language periodicals were also established in Canada during the first half of the twentieth century, but as most of Canada's labor migrants came from Eastern Europe, the six publications appearing in Toronto, Winnipeg and Edmonton remained ephemeral with the exception of the *Arbeiterzeitung*

(Winnipeg, 1930-37).

This extended description of the German-North American press revises some common notions about the German-American labor movement. (We will not consider the German influence in Canada, because it seems to have been negligible] Contrary to the assumption that World War One and the "Red Scare" dealt a death blow to the German labor press, the most important change occurred from the middle of the 1890s to 1912 because of accultura-tion and entry into English-language movements, whether parties or unions; because of the end of mass migration from Germany in 1893 and because of a consolidation of the press with a hard-core group of union and socialist publi-cations achieving continuity and wide circulation. From 1870 to 1902 twenty-two journals lasting over twenty years were established; only three more were added to this group after 1903. The number of trade-union and local labor periodicals published in this period also indicates that the historiographical emphasis on the "sectarianism" of German-American labor leaders is mis-placed. Their contribution to the American labor movement and working-class culture can only be assessed when seen in conjunction with that of other immigrant groups. While their role was important during the 1870s, 80s and 90s, they concentrated more on forming organizations than strike activity. Just as in other countries and cities, older more settled elements supported the organizations and thus provided the movement with continuity; newco-mers, on the other hand, were more militant in action and thus provided the spearhead and ventured in new directions.[21] This was the role of the south and east European immigrants.

For German migrant workers, just as for those from the Nordic countries, Bel-gium and the Netherlands as well as the British Isles, the craft-union struc-tures and the immigrants' work experience provided points of entry into the upper echelons of work-place hierarchies and into the U.S. native white labor movement. The Irish and the Finns, being mostly unskilled, followed a some-what different path, though both groups were active in the labor movement. The former also relied on the political leverage of urban machines,[22] while the latter formed their own partly separate cooperative movement. Like these two groups, east European migrants came - for the most part - without skills and with peasant notions of community and mutual aid. Thus with the excep-tion of urbanized east European Jewish migrant workers (shtetl culture) they took a different course when approaching North American institutions and movements. They found access only to those AFL unions that were organized on an industrial basis, like the mine workers. In other branches they had to wait for the coming of the CIO. In the meantime, they devoted their attention to the establishment of independent republican nations or multiethnic states in eastern and southeastern Europe, a concern that had provided the initial impetus for German radicalism and the emigration of German radicals but which for the Germans had been settled by the early 1870s.[23]

Notes

1. For a survey see D. Hoerder, "An Introduction to Labor Migration in the Atlantic Economies, 1815-1914" in idem, ed., *Labor Migration in the Atlantic Economies: The European and North American Working Classes during the Period of Industrialization* (Westport, CT, 1985). References to specialized studies on specific countries and ethnic groups are listed in the notes to the Introduction and in a bibliographic essay, ibid.

2. Isabelle Bertaux-Wiame, "The Life History Approach to the Study of Internal Migration: How Men and Women Came to Paris between the Wars" in P. Thompson and N. Burchardt, eds., *Our Common History: The Transformation of Europe* (London, 1982), pp. 186-200; Krystyna Murzynowska, *Polskie wychodzstwo zarobkowe w Zaglebiu Ruhry 1880-1914* (Wroclaw, 1972), German transl. under the title *Die polnischen Erwerbsauswanderer im Ruhrgebiet während der Jahre 1880-1914* (Dortmund, 1979).

3. This press has not yet been studied in detail. For a bibliography of Italian-language publications in France see the research note by Michel Dreyfus in C. Harzig and D. Hoerder, eds., *The Press of Labor Migrants in Europe and North America, 1880s-1930s* (Bremen, 1985); for the Polish press in Germany and France see the essays by K. Murzynowska and C. Kleßmann, ibid., pp. 129-156 and by A. Paczkowsky, ibid., pp. 157-170; for a study of a periodical of Scandinavian labor migrants in Europe the essay by C. Riegler, ibid., pp. 205-219.

4. Maurizio Punzo, "La Societá umanitaria e l'emigrazione. Dagli inizi del secolo alla prima guerra mondiale," pp. 119-144 in B. Bezza, ed., *Gli Italiani fuori d'Italia* (Milan, 1983).

5. See note 3 and N. L. Green, *Der Idisher Arbayter*, and W. J. Fishman, "Morris Winchevsky and the *Poilishe Yidl*: First Chronicle of the East London Immigrant Ghetto" in Harzig/ Hoerder, eds., *The Press of Labor Migrants*, pp. 89-128.

6. Since numerous bibliographies on migration to North America exist, only authors' names and details of lesser-known specialized studies will be cited here.

7. See the studies by Rowland Berthoff, Charlotte Erickson and Clifton K. Yearley, John H.M. Laslett, *Nature's Nobelmen: The Fortunes of the Independent Collier in Scotland and the American Midwest, 1855-1889* (Los Angeles, 1983).

8. On the Cornish see the studies by Arthur C. Todd, Alfred L. Rowse and John Rowe; on the Welsh Edward G. Hartmann and Alan Conway, as well as the studies on the British by Berthoff and Erickson.

9. See the studies by Lynn Hollen Lees, *Exiles of Erin: Irish Migrants in Victorian London*, (Ithaca, 1979), Hasia Diner, *Erin's Daughters in America: Irish Immigrant Women in the 19th Century* (Baltimore, 1983) and others as well as David Brundage "Irish Workers and Western Populism: A Catholic Newspaper in the 1890s," in Harzig/ Hoerder, eds., *The Press of Labor Migrants*, pp. 369-384.

10. See the studies by Mack Walker and Peter Marschalck,

11. Bruce Levine, "'In the spirit of 1848': German-Americans and the Fight over Slavery's Expansion," (Ph.D. diss., University of Rochester, 1980).

12. Hartmut Keil, "German Working-Class Radicalism in the United States from the 1870s to World War One" in D. Hoerder, ed., *"Struggle a Hard Battle" - Essays on Working-Class Immigrants* (DeKalb, IL, 1986), pp. 71-94.

13. Ray Boston, *British Chartists in America, 1839-1900* (Totowa, NJ, 1971).

14. A research project on these questions is presently being planned at the University of Bremen.

15. But see Peter R. Shergold *Working-Class Life: The "American Standard" in Comparative Perspective, 1899-1913* (Pittsburgh, 1982) on comparative wage rates in Birmingham and Pittsburgh, and D. Hoerder's edition of the report of German diplomats and agents in the U.S. labor movement: *Plutocrats and Socialists: Reports by German Diplomats and Agents on the American Labor Movement, 1878-1917* (München, New York, 1981).

16. Peter Weinrich, *Social Protest from the Left in Canada, 1870-1970. A Select Bibliography* (Toronto, 1982); see also André Beaulieu and Jean Hamlin, *Les journaux du Quebec de 1764 à 1964* (Quebec, 1965).

17. Robert Rumilly, *Histoire des Franco-Américains* (Montreal, 1958). See also notes to the introduction of the French section for specialized literature and Gerard J. Brault, "Etat présent des études sur les centres Franco-Americains de la Nouvelle-Angleterre" in Claire Quintal and André Vachon, eds., *Situation de la recherche sur la franco-américanie* (Quebec, 1980), and Ralf Vicero, "Immigration of French Canadians to New England, 1840-1900," (Ph.D. diss., University of Wisconsin, 1968).

18. No new periodicals were founded in 1866 and 1867, thus an incision might be made here. However, the few periodicals founded in 1868 and 1869 lasted for no more than three years, while those published after 1870 lasted longer on the average. Thus we have made the break in 1869/70.

19. Years for which there is no definite evidence of publication are not counted. Years in which publication began and those in which it ended are counted as a full year each.

20. In 1920 the radical press stood at 54.5 percent of its 1910 level while the total German-language press had declined to 43.5 percent of its 1910 level.

21. See e.g. William H. Sewell,Jr., "The Working Class of Marseille Under the Second Republic: Social Structure and Political Behavior" pp. 75-116, in Peter N. Stearns and Daniel J. Walkowitz, eds., *Workers in the Industrial Revolution: Recent Studies of Labor in the United States and Europe* (New Brunswick, NJ, 1974).

22. From progressive reformers' points of view urban machines equalled corruption. It is suggested here that machines provided access to political institutions for lower-class immigrants. The middle-classes had institutional access via regular political and administrative channels. The upper classes sought to influence politics and society - aside from direct pressure or bribery - through philanthropy.

23. David Montgomery, "Nationalism, American Patriotism, and Class Consciousness among Immigrant Workers in the United States in the Epoch of World War One" in D. Hoerder, ed. *"Struggle a Hard Battle,"* pp. 327-351.

English and Scots

Language

English

Area Covered

England and Scotland

Compiled by

Charlotte Erickson

University of Cambridge, England

Introduction

The purpose of this essay is to examine in some depth why English and Scottish immigrants in North America did not produce a labor or radical press directed specifically to British immigrant readers. They created other ethnic institutions, many of which were exclusively or predominantly working class in membership, but not a press.

There are no accurate statistics of the British emigration to the United States and Canada until well into the twentieth century, after the migration subsided. Until 1912 British official figures were concerned with passengers, not distinguishing those intending to settle overseas. Before 1853 they recorded outward-bound passengers according to the port from which they sailed. From that date onwards English and Welsh, Scots and Irish passengers were distinguished by nationality. Apart from the fact that the British never have recorded the cross channel passengers in these statistics and therefore may have omitted emigrants who departed *via* continental ports, the British passenger statistics from 1853 to 1912 exaggerated the actual flow of permanent migrants. (See Table 1)

Table 1: Outward Movement of Passengers, by Nationality, from England and Wales, and from Scotland to the United States and Canada, 1853-1980				
	To *United States*		To *Canada*	
	England & Wales	Scotland	England & Wales	Scotland
1853-1860	195,684	35,065	30,326	28,402
1861-1870	365,114	76,667	65,893	24,338
1871-1880	549,756	88,067	126,381	25,812
1881-1890	909,189	178,160	222,222	35,195
1891-1900	600,232	118,371	159,747	16,581
1901-1910	649,721	187,563	623,583	169,640
1911-1920[1]	280,051	90,928	653,592	169,310
1921-1930	153,733	157,374	345,124	161,587
1931-1938[2]	10,082	3,506	18,102	5,795
1946-1950[3]	68,585	6,077	72,022	12,573
1951-1960[4]	(126.9)		(310.9)	
1961-1970	(218.4)		(338.5)	
1971-1980	193.8 (224.4)		178.3 (230.8)	

1. After the first quarter of 1912 figures include only passengers declaring an intention to take up residence in these countries.

2. Similar returns not published for 1939.

3. No returns published for 1940-1945.

4. From 1950 the returns cover Commonwealth citizens declaring their intention of remaining one or more years in these countries. The returns are given in thousands. Figures for Commonwealth citizens are in parenthesis. English and Welsh passengers given separately 1971-1980.

Sources: 1853-1950: N.H. Carrier and J.R. Jeffery, *External Migration, A Study of the Available Statistics, 1815-1950*, Studies on Medical and Population Subjects, No. 6, G.P.O. H.M. S.O., 1953, pp. 95-6. 1951-1963: U.K. Central Statistical Office. Emigrants from the U.K. Abstract of Statistics. Board of Trade Figures. 1964-1980: U.K. Office of Population Censuses and Surveys,

International Migrations.

Nor are the Canadian figures reliable before the 1920s. It is generally agreed that, at least before 1900, they included many who intended to settle in the United States, or who very soon decided to do so. Early Canadian immigration legislation did not provide for adequate measurement, and statistics came to be compiled from ships' manifests at Quebec from 1865, Halifax from 1881, St. Johns, New Brunswick from 1900, and other seaports thereafter. Until 1962 the Canadian authorities distinguished immigrants by ethnic origin, and thus included British arrivals from the United States and elsewhere among English and Scottish immigrants. In 1950 a separate series was begun which classified immigrants according to country of last permanent residence. It is obviously impossible to get a consistent and reliable series on British immigrants to Canada. (See Table 2)

Table 2: English and Scottish Immigrants in Canada, 1841-1978			
Years	from England	from Scotland	not stated
1841-50[1]	100,854	35,173	-
1851-60	97,059	37,777	-
1861-70	123,259	27,727	-
1871-80	154,545	27,900	-
1881-90	(250,773)[2]		
1891-1900	(146,450)[2]		
1901-10[3]	488,040	135,093	17,425
1911-20	463,136	140,745	14,014
1921-30[4]	297,229	162,176	9,710
1931-40	47,016	17,085	-
1941-50[5]	156,297	38,961	-
1951-60	296,930	89,893	-
1961-70	254,500	75,428	-
1971-78	140,155	26,591	-

1. Cabin and other passengers through ports of Montreal and Quebec.
2. Immigrants by country of last residence, i.e. from British Isles including Ireland. Thus given in parentheses.
3. British (by ethnic origin) immigrants arriving from overseas reported from 1901-25.
4. British (by ethnic origin) immigrants arriving form overseas and United States reported from 1926-45.
5. From 1946 onwards immigrants are reported according to place of last permanent residence. For most postwar years figures are also available for immigrants by birthplace and by ethnic origin.

Sources: 1841-80: Imre Ferenczi and Walter Wilcox, ed., *International Migrations, 1931*, vol. 1, p. 360. Figures supplied by Canadian government and not elsewhere published; 1881-1900: *Canada Yearbook*, 1936, p. 186; 1901-45: M.C. Urquhart, ed., *Historical Statistics of Canada*, (Toronto, 1965), p. 27; 1945-77: *Canada Yearbooks* (annual).

Those responsible for producing the official counts of immigrants to the United States recorded levels much lower than those supplied in the British passenger statistics. The American estimates also have serious limitations, however. The method used to distinguish immigrants from other arrivals of aliens was simply to include only steerage or third class passengers in the statistics, though after 1892 information about intended future permanent residence was recorded. In 1906, when a distinction was finally made between immigrant and non-immigrant aliens, returning immigrants ceased to be counted each time they arrived in the States. Needless to say, figures of immigration to the United States *via* Canada have never been satisfactory. Immigrants who entered from Canadian ports began to appear in the published statistics from 1894 onwards, but those simply crossing the land border have never been fully recorded. The frequent changes from fiscal year to calendar year and back again further complicate comparisons between British and American series. (See Table 3)

Table 3: Immigration from England and Wales, and Scotland to the U.S., 1851-1977			
Years	from England & Wales	from Scotland	G.B. not specified[1]
1851-60	247,125	38,331	132,999
1861-70[2]	222,277	38,769	341,537
1871-80	437,706	87,564	16,142
1881-90	644,680	149,869	168
1891-1900	216,726	44,188	67
1901-10[3]	388,017	120,469	-
1911-20	249,944	78,357	-
1921-30	157,420	159,781	-
1931-40	31,756	6,887	-
1941-50	112,252	16,131	-
1951-60	156,171	32,854	3,884
1961-70	174,452	29,849	3,675
1971-77[4]	79,510	6,500	3,168

1. 1951-77 not specified includes "other Europe" not specified.

2. Before 1868 and 1895-97 returns covered immigrant aliens arriving. From 1868-91 and 1898 onwards they covered aliens declaring their intention to reside permanently in the United States. Up to 1903 the term "immigrant" applied only to steerage or third-class passengers. From 1868 onwards American Citiziens and Foreigners not intending to reside in the United States were excluded from figures.

3. From 1907 onwards "Arriving alienes whose permanent domicile has been outside the United States who intend to reside permanently in the United States were classed as *immigrant aliens.*" See Brinley Thomas, *Migration and Economic Growth*, (Cambridge, 1954), pp. 42-43.

4. No similar returns were published after 1977.

Sources: U.S. Immigration and Naturalization Service, *Annual Report*, 1974, pp. 56-58, and subsequent reports.

Thus the official British statistics exaggerated the flow of *bona fide* emigrants to the United States and Canada more than do those of the receiving countries. That even the more restrictive counts made by the North Americans also produced overestimates is indicated by the disparity between their figures and those suggested by the census returns of the net increase of British inhabitants from one decade to the next. These can be regarded as ten-yearly net balances of additions to the foreign-born population. They will underestimate the actual inflow of people by failing to record those who died, those who arrived and departed again within the ten-year period, and those who were temporarily out of the country on census day. (See Table 4.)

Table 4: Place of Birth of Inhabitants According to Decennial Census of Canada				
Years	England	Scotland	British Isles	total population
1871	-	-	496,595	3,605,011
1881	-	-	470,906	4,324,810
1891	-	-	477,735	4,833,239
1901	201,285	83,631	-	5,371,315
1911	510,674	169,391	-	7,226,643
1921	686,663	226,481	-	8,787,849
1931	723,864	279,765	-	10,376,786
	Census of U.S.		United Kingdom	
1850	278,675	70,550	-	23,191,876
1860	433,494	108,518	-	31,443,321
1870	555,046	140,835	-	39,818,449
1880	664,160	170,136	-	50,155,783
1890	909,092	242,231	62,947,714	
1900	840,513	233,524	-	75,994,575
1910	877,719	261,076	-	91,972,266
1920	813,853	254,570	-	105,710,620
1930	809,563	354,323	-	122,775,046
1940	n.a.	n.a.	-	n.a.
1950	n.a.	n.a.	846,570	150,697,361
1960	528,205	213,219	-	179,323,175
1970	458,114	170,134	-	203,235,298

Sources: Canada, *Fifth Census*, 1911, II, p. 444; *Seventh Census*, 1931, *Population*, I, pp. 540 ff, U.S. Department of Commerce, Bureau of the Census, *Historical Statistics of the United States from Colonial Times to 1970*, (Washington, DC, 1975) Part 1, pp. 117-18.

No source is definitive. Yet taken together they demonstrate some of the main features of the British migrant flow. The outflow was not reversed by maturing industrialization in Great Britain, but continued to increase secularly during the last half of the nineteenth century and the first decade and a half of the twentieth, both in absolute numbers and in the incidence in the sending population. The outflow from England and Wales never attained the levels of a mass movement such as Ireland and parts of the continent experienced. At the peaks in the 1880s and 1900s, net emigration represented no more than 23/10,000 of population. The rates from Scotland's much smaller population rose as high as 58/10,000 in those decades.

Throughout the nineteenth century English emigrants favored the United States over Canada as a destination. Emigrants from Scotland did not begin to show a preference for the States as a first destination until the great surge of emigration which began in the late 1840s; but, once begun, that pull of the American economy, supported now by cheaper travel facilities, prevailed for the rest of the century.

As Canada experienced her great decade of economic growth after the turn of the century, both English and Scots emigrants began to leave in greater numbers for Canada than the United States from 1905 to 1914. That preference, reinforced by the American Quota Act of 1924, continued even after emigration revived at the conclusion of World War One. The level of estimated net emigration from England and Wales never again reached the peak of the 1880s, the last major movement to the United States. Scottish emigration revived in the 1920s to reach higher rates of incidence than previously attained. By the end of that decade, the movement to Canada was again exceeding that to the United States. Emigration fell away sharply in the Great Depression of the 1930s, and since World War Two has been both lower in numbers and different in character from the relatively free and unregulated international migration of the period 1845 to 1914 when manual workers dominated the migration.

The emigrants in the nineteenth century from the world's most industrialized nation consisted more largely of skilled industrial workers than did those from most other European centers of emigration. While farmers were overrepresented in the emigration from Britain, because they formed so small a share of the British labor force, industrial workers and unskilled laborers far outnumbered them among emigrants to the United States. Although we do not have systematic data on the geographical origins within the country of British emigrants, there is evidence that the Scots were leaving from the more industrialized lowlands in the late nineteenth century rather than from the highlands, and that, at least by the late 1880s, workers in towns of 20,000 or more inhabitants outnumbered emigrants from smaller towns and rural villages by four to one.

The industrial workers from Britain carried with them a diversified array of empirical skills. Those who possessed essentially pre-industrial skills, not changed much by the technological innovations of the first industrial revolution - miners, building trades workers, blacksmiths, and tailors, for example - far outnumbered the emigrants from the newer branches of industry such as textile workers, iron workers, engineers and potters. Before the American Civil War many industrial workers left for America in hope of acquiring land of their own in the short or longer run. The increasing attraction of industrial and urban employment and decreasing accessibility of land are reflected in a distinct shift in the distribution of postwar immigrants towards the more industrialized New England and mid-Atlantic states. The prospect of higher wages and employment opportunities in expanding industries clearly drew some migrants to the United States in the late nineteenth century, just as they did to Canada as her railway network and engineering shops expanded in the decade before World War One.

Beyond these broad inducements which help explain the timing of British emigration in conformity with that from other parts of Europe, in distinct waves which correlated with the American business cycle and upswings in long-term investment, particular factors operated among specific groups of workers at particular times. One of the most difficult of these to document was the erosion of opportunities for craftsmen making a variety of consumer goods and farming implements for local consumption. Many of these trades faced competition from factory-made goods as railways penetrated the countryside; their prospects might also dim as population fell or ceased to expand in so many rural parishes especially in southern and eastern England. Some of these people chose to emigrate.

Changing technology sent other British industrial workers overseas more directly. The best-known example perhaps was that of the handloomweavers of Lancashire and Yorkshire. The introduction of power looms in cotton, and subsequently in woollen and worsted manufacture, was reflected in temporary bulges in the emigration of weavers, though only a small proportion of those affected chose, or were able to meet their difficulties in this way. In Cornwall and the North Riding of Yorkshire the exhaustion of tin, lead and copper mines, along with their inability to be operated "beneficially" in the face of overseas competition, uprooted miners who went not only to Wisconsin, Michigan and the Rocky Mountain States but to many other parts of the world as well. British miners were over-represented in the American labor force far more than they were in any other major category of employment, though this was not true of the emigration to Canada. Cornwall had the highest emigration rates of any county in England. The raising of American tariff rates, especially the McKinley Tariff of 1890, had disastrous effects on employment for Welsh tinplate workers and Bradford worsted manufacturers; and they left for the States in significant numbers. The reverse, Britain's free trade treaty with France in 1860, combined with a backward technology, sent thousands of silk workers from Macclesfield and Coventry to Paterson, NJ.

Less important, in terms of the numbers of emigrants involved, were the instances when emigration was encouraged because of trade disputes, trade-union assistance, or victimization of individuals. Ray Boston traced more than sixty Chartists, important enough as leaders to have left biographical details, who fled to the United States, often to escape arrest. Over half of them eventually returned to Britain. The many trade unions which experimented with emigration schemes found workers who had been assisted to emigrate returning home so frequently that few of these schemes lasted over a long period. Trade disputes, such as the long lockout in the iron trade of the North of England in 1866, also precipitated, on occasion, temporary and not very successful emigration schemes.

A backward flow of returned migrants seemed to have been a feature of the migration throughout the period of European emigration to America in the nineteenth century, so much so that Ravenstein announced this as one of the laws of migration in the 1880s. The British government did not begin to measure the return flow of passengers from North America until 1877, and to distinguish among the different British nationalities until 1894. The Americans did not start to record the counterflow until 1908. Yet in the mid-nineteenth century, when modern estimates place the return flow as low as 1,5 - 2 percent, newspapers reported emigrants returning to Britain, or going elsewhere, whenever business conditions slackened in the United States.

British artisans, in certain trades that had a tramping tradition and tramping benefit, sometimes regarded emigration as an extension of the tramp, for experience, a better berth, or because of loss of a job. After the Civil War, with the victory of steam navigation in the Atlantic passenger trade, transatlantic seasonal migration emerged, with English and Scots workers spending part of a year in the States. Coal-mining employment had a pronounced seasonal aspect in America, as bituminous mining began its great expansion from the 1870s onwards, because the harsher winters augmented the demand for domestic fuel. In the building trades the seasonal expansion came during spring and summer months. At least some British miners and building trades workers recognized that, with the floating dollar after the war, their American earnings might appreciate in terms of sterling, and British sterling buy more dollars than before the United States left the gold standard. The resumption of specie payments in 1879 did not end these seasonal flows. Indeed the seeming preponderance of building trades workers and miners on the passenger lists of the 1880s may in part be accounted for by such multiple arrivals. In 1885 the unions estimated that 15 percent of the building workers in the state of New York consisted of immigrant workers from Britain, out for the season.

Furthermore, throughout the period of greatest emigration many English and Scottish workers cherished the thought that they might eventually return to the old country. Naturalization rates among them lagged behind those for most other nationalities. How many actually fulfilled this ambition we will never know.

The Quota Acts of the 1920s coincided with a significant decline in the rate of return migration which had been measured since 1908. As fewer British immigrants gained entry, a smaller proportion returned home, at least until the Great Depression.

In the United States British immigrants tended to be concentrated in manufacturing industry to a greater extent than the foreign-born as a whole or the labor force as a whole. This was demonstrated in the censuses of 1870, 1880 and 1890 which reported the occupation of workers by nativity. When these returns are manipulated to show the percentage of British workers in specified occupations, in comparison with the percentage of all white male gainful workers, some trades stood out with exceptionally high concentrations of British-born workers - chiefly in textiles, mining, iron and steel and engineering. (See Table 5.)

Table 5: Industries With Highest Concentrations of British-born Workers in the United States 1890	
Industry	Concentration Ratio
Coal mining	627
Other mining	442
Bleachers and dyers	459
Carpet makers	404
Cotton mill operatives	340
Glovemakers	316
Print-works operatives	386
Silk mill operatives	386
Woollen mill operatives	422
Hosiery workers	271
Pattern makers	309
Iron and steel workers	278
Steam boiler makers	287
Tool and cutlery makers	274
Marble and stonecutters	357
Potters	399

Source: E.P. Hutchinson, *Immigrants and Their Children, 1850-1950,* (New York, 1956), pp. 124-131.

After the British emigration shifted towards Canada in the 1900s these high concentration ratios were eroded. The children of British immigrants tended to be more concentrated in professions, trade and transport than in mining and manufacturing. (See Table 6.)

Table 6: Occupational Distribution of English and Welsh-born and
Scottish-born Males, 10 Years and Older in the U.S. Labor Force, 1890

English and Welsh

Occupation	Figures	%	CR/FB*	CR/MLF*
Agriculture & fisheries	100,346	20.6	83	49
Mining & quarrying	56,745	11.6	264	552
Manufacturing & mechanical industries	173,562	35.6	114	165
Trade and transport	76,284	15.6	101	96
Domestic & Personal Service	63,310	13.0	59	91
Professions	17,198	3.6	163	105
All occupations	487,445	100.0	-	-

Scottish

Occupation	Figures	%	CR/FB*	CR/MLF*
Agriculture & fisheries	22,548	19.3	78	46
Mining & quarrying	11,794	10.0	227	500
Manufacturing & mechanical industries	46,349	39.2	126	181
Trade and transport	19,603	16.6	107	101
Domestic & Personal Service	13,929	11.8	54	83
Professions	3,706	3.1	148	91
All occupations	118,171	100.0	-	-

*CR/FB = Concentration ratio/foreign born
CR/MLF= Concentration ratio/male labor force

Source: U.S. *Eleventh Census*, 1890, *Population*, Part II, Table 109, pp. 484 ff
and Table 77.

Similar occupational returns by nativity are not available for Canada until
1930, by which time the shift both of the labor force as a whole, and of British
immigrants in particular, towards tertiary and clerical employments had
already diluted the very large input of industrial workers of the pre-war
years. At least by 1930 the British showed less excessive concentration in
industrial occupations in Canada than they had in the United States in 1890.
(See Table 7.)

Table 7: Occupational Distribution of English and Scottish-born Males, 10 Years and Older in Canadian Labor Force					
Occupation	English	%	CR/MLF*	Scottish	CR/MLF*
Agriculture	86,325	22.9	67	31,580	21.8	64
Mining	6,722	1.8	81	3,458	2,4	108
Other primary	2,590	0.7	23	1,232	0.1	29
Building & Construction	33,586	8.9	114	12,238	8.4	108
Manufacturing	58,805	15.6	97	22,797	15.7	98
Transport & communication	32,320	8.6	99	12,848	8.9	102
Trade & warehousing	38,182	10.1	109	15,048	10.4	112
Other services	11,974	3.1	121	4,921	3.4	130
Personal service	21,287	5.6	103	7,271	5.0	92
Laborers	39,593	10.5	61	15,028	10.4	61
Clerical	20,758	5.5	110	8,583	5.9	119
Professional & public administration	25,186	6.7	109	9,872	6.8	111
Unspecified	250	-	-	66	-
Total	377,588	100.0	-	144,994	100.1

*CR/MLF = Concentration ratio/male labor force

Source: *Census of Canada*, 1931, Table 254, pp. 372 ff and Table 40, pp. 62 ff.

After that last great influx to the States in the 1880s, the greatest absolute numbers of British immigrants were to be found in the largest northern cities. Even so, in places like New York, Chicago, Boston and Philadelphia, the British constituted only between 2.6 and 3.7 percent of the population in 1890. In such cities the working-class presence of the British may not have been sufficiently concentrated to enable them to create institutions of their own. The Knights of St. George, established in all these cities, tended to be elitist organizations of professional and mercantile men.

It was in these large cities, whose immigrants represented a wide range of the social spectrum, from unskilled laborers to merchants in foreign trade, that newspapers addressed to British immigrants first appeared. The first British immigrant newspaper to be published in America, *Albion, or the British Colonial and Foreign Gazette*, began publication in 1822 and endured until 1876. It was addressed to educated merchants and professional people. In 1830 the *Old Countryman* was launched to appeal to a working-class readership. Critical of *Albion* it merged with *The Emigrant* in 1835 or 1836, but expired before the end of the forties. More newspapers were started after 1850. Both Scottish and Welsh papers in English managed to survive whereas no newspaper directed specifically at English immigrants lasted long. The *Scottish American Journal* (1857-1919), the *Scotsman* (New York, 1869-86) and the *Boston Scotsman* (1906-14) did better than the New York *English American* (1885) which lasted no more than a year and an *Anglo-American* launched in Lawrence, Massachusetts, in the 1870s and in Boston in 1899 also collapsed very soon.

Several displays of Irish immigrant hostility to celebrations in these large cities of the Queen's Jubilee in 1887 appear to have inspired the launching of a number of newspapers addressed to British, rather than Scottish, Welsh or English readers, in a fruitless attempt to weld the British into a united political force, and to encourage naturalization. The *British-American Citizen* appeared in Boston, (1887-1913), the *Western British-American* in Chicago (1888-1922), the *British-American* in New York and Philadelphia, (1887-1919), and a monthly, *The British Californian*, in San Francisco, (1897-1931). Most of these were eight-page weeklies that combined some news from the old country with items about British-American immigrants and immigrant communities. By 1935 there was not a single English, Scottish or British-American journal still in existence in the United States.

The British and English-language Scottish press in Canada was on the whole even more ephemeral than that in the States. The first decade of decided net immigration to Canada, the 1850s witnessed the appearance of the first of these. In view of the fact that this was the only decade in the last half of the century when Canada managed to retain more emigrants than left, it is not surprising that the *Old Countryman*, launched in Toronto in 1853 to carry British news for British immigrants, did not last beyond 1861, in spite of a merger. However, the *British Canadian*, published in Simcoe, Ontario, from 1860 did continue until perhaps 1927, the longest-lasting of any of these Canadian papers. The first paper in English directed at Scottish immigrants, started in 1868, the *Canadian Scotsman*, collapsed within five years.

The great emigration of the early twentieth century produced a few more attempts: *The British Canadian*, Winnipeg (1929-31?); *British News in Canada*, Toronto (1911?); the *Canadian Scotsman*, Winnipeg (1905-18?); *Canada Scotsman*, Toronto (1908-09?); *Alberta Scottish Review*, Edmonton, (1910?). It is perhaps worth noting that two papers begun in the 1960s for Scottish people in Canada, the *North American Scotsman*, 1969+ and the *Scottish Banner*, 1978+ may perhaps still be in existence. Do they reflect the resurgence of ethnic consciousness in North America from that time?

If the immigrant press was concentrated in a few large cities, it was in some of the smaller industrial towns, particularly those with textile industries or nearby mines, that the British working-class immigrants succeeded in establishing, or leading in the establishment of organizations, and in which a dense array of formal and informal institutions was created in some places. Fall River, MA, was a cotton town which still employed mule spinners. With 11,000 English-born inhabitants in 1890, 29 percent of its foreign-born population and 15 percent of the entire population was British-born. It was perhaps the outstanding example in the United States of a place which had a sufficient English presence to enable them to form trade unions, consumer cooperatives, friendly societies such as the Old Fellows and Foresters, clubs, pubs and reading rooms. Fall River had 25 soccer clubs to Philadelphia's seven, and Ashton wakes were held. Its Lancashire operatives even organized an English-American Club in 1876 to try to secure more influence in local government.

Fall River was perhaps not typical. Yet there were many communities in the States which did contain, at least for a few decades during the peak period of British immigration, from 1850 to 1890, an English, Scots or British working-class community, conscious of its identity and recreating its institutions across the Atlantic. Other examples would be the silk workers of Paterson, NJ, cotton and woollen workers in New Bedford, Lawrence and Lowell, MA, the potters of East Liverpool, OH, and Trenton, NJ, and iron workers of Troy, NY. Above all, the British left their mark on many mining communities. Their identity was most focussed in some of the Illinois mining towns such as Braidswood where Scottish miners clustered. In Illinois, the British not only organized trade unions but also were largely responsible for putting protective legislation on the statute books of the state, as well as serving as inspectors of mines.

Trade unions were the most enduring of these institutions, but, like other working-class institutions stimulated by British immigrants, they tended over time to lose any peculiarly British flavor and to be assimilated into the host society. Clearly British precedents and British immigrants had considerable influence upon the infant American trade-union movement. Many British immigrants became leaders of unions, especially in textiles, mining and the building trades.

One reason why trade unions did not have a British allegiance was that in many industrial and mining towns, the Irish outnumbered the British. Successful organization, even of skilled workers, could not be achieved without co-operating with Irish workers. As Daniel Walkowitz writes of Troy, New York, the English and Irish worked together, combining English experience of trade unions with the Irish tradition of resistance. Lots of Irish immigrants in industrial America had spent some time working in industrial Britain. And indeed such men were often prominent as union leaders in the States, Robert Howard of the Fall River mule spinners and John Siney, head of the Miners and Laborers Benevolent Association in the sixties and seventies, are but two of many examples that might be cited.

While American unions did not have the elaborate and generous benefit schemes of British trade unions, the craft unions in the AFL were close to British unions of this period in organization and purpose. The Miners National Association of the United States copied the constitution of Alexander MacDonald's Scottish union when launched on its short life in 1873. Some immigrants were loathe to give up the trade-union benefits they had enjoyed. This made it possible for two British unions, the Amalgamated Society of Engineers and the Amalgamated Society of Carpenters and Joiners, to establish branches in the United States and Canada, the Engineers in 1861 and the Carpenters in 1867. By 1913 the Carpenters and 1920 the Engineers had been absorbed by American unions.

The British leaders in the American trade-union movement were largely heirs of the Chartist tradition and Methodism as well as craft unionism. The great influx of English and Scots workers to Canada's industrial labor force came at a time when socialist parties, other than Christian Socialist, were being born. Thus in Canada, in addition to work in organizing trade unions, British immigrants were more conspicuous in socialist and syndicalist organization than they were in the States. James Pritchard and Samuel Mottishaw, who founded the socialist movement in the Island coalfields of British Columbia had been Independet Labour Party (ILP) members in Lancashire before they emigrated; and Ernest Burns, a leader in the Vancouver movement, had been a member of the Social Democratic Federation (SDF). Influences from the United States were at least equally strong, however.

The small and exclusive Socialist Party of Canada, founded in 1903, was not only led by British immigrants, but they also comprised the bulk of the membership. Nine-tenths of the readers of its journal, *Clarion*, were said to have been recently arrived from England. This exclusive body dismissed the British Labour Party, with its trade-union and liberal connections, and found it difficult to work with non-English-speaking groups in Winnipeg.

In his study of western Canadian radicalism, Ross McCormack emphasizes that many of the British, who were emigrating in such large numbers just before World War One, had been exposed to agitation for syndicalism and industrial unionism. Yet one of the most prominent in western Canada, Bob Russell, who emigrated from Glasgow in 1911, held that the ballot box was a better means of destroying capitalism than the general strike. In contrast to the United States during these years of the "new immigration," in Canada immigrants from the United Kingdom formed the majority of members in urban radical parties.

While Scottish and British-American newspapers and literary magazines did succeed for a while, British-American labor leaders did not found a British labor press in either the United States or Canada, any more than they did a specifically British trade-union movement. The most obvious explanation is, of course, the fact that most working class immigrants spoke and read the same language as the host society. The common language enabled British-born labor leaders to influence the natives and their institutions. But the matter cannot simply be left there.

To begin with one or two somewhat speculative points, it might be suggested that some of the working-class leaders from Britain exhibited a somewhat internationalist outlook. Samuel Gompers, himself reared in London, certainly did so; but it is not his Marxian-influenced internationalism to which I refer. It has already been pointed out that in some working-class communities the British and Irish cooperated in union organization, whereas in other places mutual hostilities survived emigration. Clifton Yearley emphasized the Christian missionary zeal of many of these labor leaders who arrived from Britain in the third quarter of the nineteenth century, as well as of British organizers who visited the United States. This outlook led them to think in terms of shouldering the workingman's burden, rather than in nationalistic terms. As Yearley wrote, "when these Englishmen, and their comrades from other parts of the United Kingdom, struck hands with American labor leadership, which was among the most religious in the world, positive action resulted." Chartists in America clearly saw themselves as missionaries with a "responsibility to God to liberate workingmen everywhere." As Daniel Weaver, ex-Chartist founder of the American Miners Association said, "Let there be no English, no Irish, Germans, Scotch or Welsh. We are just all workers together."

There is yet another less exalted way of considering the question of why the British did not found ethnic working-class institutions in the United States. English and Scottish skilled workers had been welcomed, and even recruited, by American employers in the early years of American industrialization. By the last half of the nineteenth century, employers no longer valued or relied upon British immigrants. In fact, the British acquired a bad reputation in comparison with other immigrants, not only because they were likely to organize unions and strikes, but because they were sticklers for high wages, set in their attitudes to working methods, and prone to drink. They were criticized as slow workers in both the United States and Canada. In the States, British workers had little reason to stress their British identity in negotiations with employers either individually or in a body. In contrast, Ross McCormack has maintained that British skilled workers arriving in Canada in the decade after 1900 found that they gained advantages in the labor market precisely by asserting their cultural identity. Canada's industrialization was as yet in its infancy, and British skills at a premium. Many an unskilled worker secured a job for which he was not trained by asserting his ethnic identity, particularly when a British-born foreman or supervisor was in charge of hiring.

Although British immigrants did not initiate ethnically oriented labor papers, they did in fact found or edit a number of labor newspapers in America. Most, but not all, of these editors were either journalists or printers by training. That such opportunities were afforded them outside the ethnic community goes far to explain why they did not have to realize their ambitions within it.

The *Workingman's Advocate* of Chicago was edited by a printer from Berwick, son of a Chartist printer, Andrew Carr Cameron (1834-1890), who emigrated to Chicago in 1854 at the age of 20. Active in the Typographical Union in Chicago, Cameron left a job on the Chicago *Times* to edit the *Workingman's Advocate* when it was initiated during a printer's strike in 1864. He continued in that position until 1880, when it was discontinued, after which he edited the *Inland Printer*, a journal for the print trade, until his death. A friend of Alexander MacDonald, Cameron was a "pillar" of the National Labor Union of the late 1860s, of the Chicago Trades Assembly and the state Labor Assembly.

Perhaps equally well-known, with a circulation beyond the center of its publication, New York City, was *John Swinton's Paper* published from 14 October 1883 to 7 August 1887. John Swinton (1829-1901) was never a manual worker, though he edited a labor paper and helped to organize the great textile strike in Fall River in 1875. Swinton was born in Salton, near Edinburgh, emigrated as a boy with his family in 1843 to Montreal where he was apprenticed in the office of the Montreal *Witness*. He worked as a reporter for the Lawrence (Kansas) *Republican* in the years just before the Civil War, and went to New York in 1860 to study medicine. Instead, his medical journalism gained him the post of chief of the editorial staff of the New York *Times* and later that of principal assistant to Charles Dana on the *Sun*. There he developed an interest in unions and eventually began his own newspaper from disgust with the major dailies. His paper was far more than local in its coverage of labor news. He had to suspend publication in 1887 because it was boycotted by the New York District Assembly No. 49 of the Knights of Labor for its coverage of news concerning craft unions. Swinton was able to secure work as an editorial writer for the New York *Sun* until blindness forced his retirement.

The other such papers that have been identified emanated largely from British immigrants in textile or mining unions. John Hinchcliffe (1822-78) had progressed from factory hand to master tailor in his native Bradford and become a Chartist, before he emigrated in 1847. Arriving in Belleville, Illinois, in 1857, he was admitted to the Illinois Bar and assumed the editorship of the Belleville *Democrat and Daily Despatch* in 1860. Hinchcliffe became lawyer for miners struggling to organize a union under the leadership of Staffordshire-born Chartist Daniel Weaver and the Welshman Thomas Lloyd. In 1861 Hinchcliffe joined the union, when it was formally organized, and served as its president before the end of the Civil War until its demise in 1868. He founded and edited its official newspaper, the *Weekly Miner* from 1863 to 1865. Also active in the National Labor Union, he was eventually sent to the Illinois legislature by his mining constituency.

Another English editor of a miners' journal was John Kane, an Ohio miner, who edited the *United Mine Workers Journal* after the federation was founded in 1890.

In Fall River, there were at least two shortlived labor journals edited by English immigrants. Henry Sevey, Shropshire-born, edited the Fall River *Labor Journal* from 1874 to 1878. George Gunton, a cotton weaver in Stockport, Cheshire, emigrated in 1874, became involved in the strike of 1875, and was blacklisted. He then became editor of the *Labor Standard*, a socialist journal, from 1876 to 1881. Gunton later wrote a number of pamphlets for the AFL. In March 1891, he was able to secure backing to found his own journal, the *Social Economist* which, while sympathetic to labor, was solidly Republican, protectionist, and pro-gold standard in its views. His journal contained industrial labor news and was run in conjunction with an adult education College of Social Economics which he founded in Union Square in 1892. The *Social Economist* was succeeded by Gunton's *Magazine of American Economics and Political Science* (New York, 1896-1904).

In Lawrence, Massachusetts, where in 1890 there were nearly five thousand English-born inhabitants constituting 25 percent of the foreign-born and 11 percent of the entire population, two English immigrants "kept the labor cause alive" with their Lawrence *Journal* from 1868 to 1891. Robert Bower, a Lancashire weaver and physical force Chartist, emigrated in 1848 to Lawrence. Philip Foner judged him to have been the "most important labor leader in Lawrence just before and after the Civil War." By the early seventies Bower had been elected to the Massachusetts Senate. His coeditor, Richard Hinchcliffe, brother of John q.v., also a Chartist weaver, emigrated to Boston and then Lawrence in 1847.

In another industry in which the British were hugely represented, James Duncan (1857-1928), who had been apprenticed as a granitecutter in Aberdeen, emigrated in 1880 and straightaway joined the Granite Cutters National Union in New York, was active in the organization of the AFL in 1886, and edited the *Granite Cutters Journal* from 1895 to 1928.

British-born labor leaders were also able to gain access to the columns of American labor journals and newspapers. One of the earliest of these was Robert MacFarlane (1815-83), a Scottish dyer who organized the Mechanics Mutual Protection Association in Buffalo in the 1840s, a secret organization which admitted both masters and men. It was devoted to securing 10-hour legislation, education, the abolition of prison labor. It claimed 38 locals in New York, Ohio, Michigan, Pennsylvania and Wisconsin by 1847. From Buffalo, MacFarlane moved to Albany in 1848 and for 17 years edited at various times the *State Mechanic*, the *Mechanics Mirror*, and finally *Scientific American*, before retiring to his old trade of dyeing.

Richard Trevellick (1830-1895), born in the Scilly Isles, worked as a joiner and ships carpenter in Southampton, a Chartist and active trade unionist. In 1852 he emigrated to Australia and arrived in the United States in 1856 or 1857 by way of New Orleans, where he quickly came to head a local ships carpenters and caulkers union. Moving to Brooklyn after the outbreak of the Civil War, he worked for The Marine Railway Company. Trevellick wrote articles on labor conditions in the shipyards for the famous Philadelphia labor newspaper *Finchers' Trades Review*, edited by Jonathan Fincher, Secretary of the Mechanics and Blacksmiths Union, a man convinced that British and American workingmen faced "a common enemy and common problems." Later Trevellick moved to Detroit where he soon became president of the local branch of the International Union of Ships Carpenters and Caulkers and President of the National Labor Union on Sylvis' death in 1869 until its collapse in 1873: he was one of the most widely travelled and influential men in the American labor movement of his day.

Thomas Phillips (1833-1916), a Yorkshire-born shoemaker who had been apprenticed to his brother-in-law, an active Chartist, also contributed to Jonathan Fincher's newspaper as well as to its successor the *National Trades Review*. Phillips went on to organize a Philadelphia Assembly for the Knights of Labor and demonstrated that this generation of British immigrant labor leaders could also gain access to the non-labor press in America. William Swain, owner of the Philadelphia *Record*, gave a column of 1770 words a day for 14 months to Knights of Labor activities, and Phillips wrote the copy.

Eventually he broke with Powderly and turned to pure and simple unionism in helping to found the International Boot and Shoeworkers Union.

The Amalgamated Society of Engineers (ASE) and the Amalgamated Society of Carpenters and Joiners (ASCJ) did not need to publish journals in the United States - journals which might have served an all-British membership, because American labor papers opened their columns to them and published, for example, their annual reports. In any case these unions were closely controlled from London, the U.S. branches not being allowed any autonomy, one reason for the stagnation of membership from 1890 to 1920.

Finally, labor publications from Great Britain, newspapers, tracts and pamphlets followed their emigrating subscribers overseas both to the United States and Canada, further reducing the need for a separate press in America.

British immigrants were not so active in socialist organizations in America as they were in trade unions, the co-operative movement, temperance, Greenback and labor parties, and 8 and 10-hour movements. For the most part they were moderates who favored cooperation between capital and labor and the avoidance of strikes, especially in depression. Nonetheless they were often blacklisted by American employers. There were no English-speaking branches of the SDP in America in 1901. Immigrants who were to the left of the trade unionists and cooperationists were also able to get their views in print without relying upon ethnic outlets. Richard Hinton, a Lancashire weaver and Chartist who emigrated in 1848 to Boston, was still a trade unionist and cooperationist when he made his career as a labor journalist as labor correspondent for the Boston *Weekly Voice*. His articles appeared not only in trade organs and labor newspapers but also in *Galaxy*, *Atlantic Monthly*, *Old and New*, and the *North American Review*. Hinton became a socialist.

Cornwall-born John Spargo became one of the leaders of the American Socialist Party. A prolific writer he published in the *Independent*, a paper founded in 1848 to oppose slavery, which survived as a popular religious journal with wide-ranging reformist interests "making common cause with struggling negroes, disfranchised women, hunted Indians and opprest Chinamen." Spargo also wrote feature articles on developments in socialism and labor for the shortlived *Social Crusader*, later *Socialist Spirit* (1898-1903), a Christian Socialist/Fabian publication backed by Rev. George D. Herron who joined the SDP in 1899.

Mathew Mark Trumbull, born in 1826 in Westminster, London, tramped as a bricklayer's laborer all over London and the home counties and became a Chartist before emigrating in 1846. Still tramping for a time in the United States, by 1858 he was admitted to the Bar in Iowa, but later moved to Chicago to practice law. Trumbull became a socialist, a good friend of George Schilling, Henry Demerest Lloyd and Thomas Morgan (1847-1912). The latter came from a poor nailer family in Birmingham. Emigrating in 1869, he worked for the Illinois Central Railway Car Works and became president of the Chicago Machinists and Blacksmiths Union by 1873. This Union became the International Machinists Union, established by Socialist Labor Party members under Morgan's leadership. It had an overtly Marxist preamble to its constitution, but was recognized by the AFL in 1890 because the International Association of Machinists (IAM) discriminated against negros in its constitution. When the AFL finally recognized the IAM as the larger and stronger union, Morgan, like Trumbull, also became a lawyer by the time he mounted the famous socialist challenge to Samuel Gompers at the AFL convention in 1894. Trumbull had become an assistant editor of *Open Court*, a longlived journal founded in 1887 and dedicated to "establishing ethics and religion upon a scientific basis." This journal was originally the mouthpiece of Edward C. Hegeler for propagating Monism. From the outset it contained some labor writings by Trumbull, and others, written under the *nom de plume* of Wheelbarrow, may have come from Morgan. At least, Thomas Morgan edited and published *The Provoker* from 1909 to 1912.

Still another example of a radical newspaper founded by British immigrants, though not directed to a British audience, was the *American Non-Conformist and Kansas Industrial Liberator* of Winfield, Kansas. This journal founded by English-born James Vincent, a Congregational minister, was edited by his two sons in Winfield from 1886 to 1891. These young men were prominent in the southern populist movement, and their paper was anti-monarchy, anti-English, anti-monopoly, against clerical interference in politics and described as a "powerful reform voice."

In Canada the only British-born radical editor identified was Arthur Puttee, who, like several of those in the States, was a printer by trade. Puttee settled in Winnipeg in 1891 and was instrumental in founding the Trades Council, the Labor Party and a journal, *The Voice*. By 1899 he was its editor, and in 1900 the first Labor member elected to the Canadian House of Commons. Puttee wanted a broadly based labor party and held up the British party as an example, printing detailed reports of the British party and of the activities of its members at Westminster. "British in personnel, preconceptions and prejudices," the Labour Party failed to retain the vote of Eastern European immigrants and was weakened by socialist defection in 1902 and the liberals' drift into opposition to them by 1904. *The Voice* regularly reprinted material from Robert Blatchford's *Clarion*.

Bibliography

Berthoff, Roland T.

British Immigrants in Industrial America, 1790-1950. Cambridge, MA: Harvard University Press, 1953.

Boston Ray.

British Chartists in America, 1839-1900. Manchester: Manchester University Press, 1971.

Cumbler, John T.

Working-class Community in Industrial America: Work, Leisure and Struggle in Two Industrial Cities, 1880-1930. Westport, CT: Greenwood Press, 1979.

"Transatlantic Working-class Institutions." *Journal of Historical Geography* 6,3 (1980), pp. 275-290.

Erickson, Charlotte.

"Who were the English and Scots Emigrants to the United States in the Late Nineteenth Century?" In David Glass and Roger Revelle, eds., *Population and Social Change.* London: Edward Arnold, 1972.

American Industry and the European Immigrant. 1860-1885. Cambridge, MA: Harvard University Press, 1957.

"The Encouragement of Emigration by British Trade Unions, 1850-1900." *Population Studies* 1,3 (1949), pp. 248-273.

Fink, Gary M. ed.

Biographical Dictionary of American Labor. Westport, CT: Greenwood Press, 1974.

Gottlieb, Amy Zahl.

"Immigration of British Coal Miners in the Civil War Decade." *International Review of Social History* 23 (1978), pp. 257-75.

"British Coal Miners: a Demographic Study of Braidwood and Streator, Illinois." *Journal of the Illinois State Historical Society* 73,3 (1979), pp. 179-92.

Jefferys, James B.

The Story of the Engineers, 1800-1945. London: Lawrence and Wishart, 1945.

Jones, Huw R.

"Modern Emigration from Scotland to Canada." *Scottish Geographical Magazine* 95,1 (1979), pp. 4-12.

Jones, Maldwyn A.

"The Background to Emigration from Great Britain in the Nineteenth Century." *Perspectives in American History* 7 (1973), pp. 3-92.

McCormack, A. Ross.

"Cloth Caps and Jobs: the Ethnicity of English Immigrants in Canada, 1900-1914." In Jorgen Dahlie and Tissa Fernando, eds., *Ethnicity, Power and Politics in Canada*. London, etc.: Methuen, 1981.

Reformers, Rebels, and Revolutionaries: the Western Canadian Radical Movement, 1899-1919. Toronto: University of Toronto Press, 1977.

Reuter, Frank T.

"John Swinton's Paper." *Labor History* 1 (1960), pp. 298-307.

Reynolds, Lloyd G.

The British Immigrant: His Social and Economic Adjustment in Canada. Toronto: Oxford University Press, 1935.

Walkowitz, Daniel J.

Worker City, Company Town, Iron and Cotton-worker Protest in Troy and Cohoes, New York, 1955-1984. Urbana, etc.: University of Illinois Press, 1978.

Yearley, Clifton K. Jr.

Britons in American Labor: A History of the Influence of the United Kingdom Immigrants on American Labor, 1820-1914. Baltimore: The Johns Hopkins Press, 1957.

Welsh

Language

Welsh and other Gaelic languages

Area covered

Wales and other Gaelic language areas

Compiled by

Deian Rhys Hopkin

University College of Wales, Aberystwyth

Introduction

The Celtic languages have been in a state of crisis, more or less, for the best part of four centuries. The Celtic languages have probably been spoken in the British Isles for more than three thousand years and consisted of two groups of languages, reflecting the chronology of early migration. The earliest group, Goedelic, survived in recent times in Ireland, the Highlands and Islands of Scotland and the Isle of Man, while the later Brythonic languages survived in Wales, Cornwall and Britanny. The Anglo-Saxons, who began to arrive in Britain from the fifth century, gradually drove the various Celtic people to the peripheries of the islands, and increasing political and economic pressure marginalised the languages themselves, especially after the establishment of the Norman State. English became, in time, the language of official transactions, of politics, religion and economy, and this led to a rapid decline in the perceived value and usage of most Celtic languages. Indeed ,in the period before the advent of direct government support by the Irish and British governments, the decline was accentuated by the social and educational stigma associated with these languages to which no formal political or economic institutions were attached. By the twentieth century only the Welsh language survives with any considerable vigor, and that for special reasons.

The great migrations to North America from Ireland and, to a lesser extent from Wales and Scotland, took place at a time when the linguistic stigma was at its greatest. In a sense, many of the emigrants who had been forced to leave their homes for economic and social reasons sought to eradicate their Celtic origins once they reached America. The index of their success was the degree to which they could abandon language and culture and the Irish in particular were encouraged in this by the Catholic Church which had always forbidden the use of the vernacular in its activities. Moreover, the political movement for Irish independence, which developed in the late nineteenth century did not make the Gaelic language the fulcrum of political identity.

The situation among the Welsh was rather different. Religious nonconformity acted as a bulwark of the language, identifying the Welsh language with political dissent and although strenuous efforts were made, especially after the Educational Commissioners' report of 1847 to extirpate the language, the chapels and informal cultural institutions, such as the Eisteddfod, provided effective defenses. Welsh emigrants took these institutions with them to America and hence the language survived longer, and in a more robust way, than any other Celtic language. Only the Welsh, of all the Celts, sustained a publishing industry entirely in their own language largely because of the central importance of the Welsh language in religion. Nevertheless the language failed to permeate the modern economic and political institutions of America such as the trade unions, and no periodical press was developed in the Welsh language to represent the aspirations of the Welsh as workers.

For their part, the Cornish and the Scots have always had an ambivalent relationship with the English. The Cornish were more quickly assimilated into the English state than any other part of Celtic Britain and the language survived only in the smallest pockets. For many other inhabitants of Britain, indeed, Cornwall was largely indistinguishable from the other regions of England; notions of "Cornishness" did not seriously challenge loyalty to the British state. The Scots, on the other hand, differed from all the other Celts in that they were able to maintain separate legal and educational institutions as part of the terms of the Union with England. Perhaps for this reason there was less reason for sustaining a separate language as well. Certainly, with little help from England, many of the Scots allowed their language to be replaced by English for all formal activities and it was only in the highlands and islands of Scotland that Gaelic remained by the end of the nineteenth century. Emigrants from Cornwall and Scotland took little or nothing of their language with them except for limited domestic purposes.

The Welsh

There were three major phases of Welsh emigration to the United States and Canada, each of which reflected the particular economic and/or social pressures which induced them. In each phase, moreover, there was a distinct pattern of settlement. Religious and cultural oppression encouraged an indeterminate number of Welsh families to join the larger English migration from the late sixteenth century onwards. The spread of non-conformity in Wales in the 17th century, moreover, stimulated this migration especially after the restoration of the Stuarts; Welsh Baptists and Quakers were among the founders of Pennsylvania. The early Welsh immigrants were quickly assimilated, leaving only their surnames as evidence of their distinctiveness.

The second phase of Welsh emigration, which began from around 1795, was prompted by a combination of political dissent and economic necessity,the impoverishment of the small tenant farmers by economic depressions and the political repression which was introduced by William Pitt in the wake of the Jacobin phase of the French Revolution. In Oneida County, New York, for example, they founded one of the most flourishing and persistent Welsh communities which, in the late nineteenth century, became the center of Welsh-language publishing. Throughout the first half of the nineteenth century and especially during the post-Napoleonic depression and the "hungry forties," a steady stream of emigrants arrived from Wales.

Even as the agricultural phase was developing, the first trickle of Welsh industrial migration was beginning. Wales had been industrialized early. The iron and coal industries were rapidly developing in South Wales and in the northeast corner of Wales from 1750 onwards, where in 1789 John Wilkinson founded his famous ironworks in Bersham, North East Wales. Welsh expertise soon found its way to America. In 1817 Thomas Cotton Lewis erected the first American mill for puddling and rolling bar iron, and in 1839 a Pennsylvania company hired David Thomas, a Welsh ironworks superintendent, to set up the first hot-blast furnace in the United States. By the 1830s, however, Welsh industry was suffering from severe cyclical depression and from time to time this acted as a spur to skilled Welsh workers to emigrate in numbers. Welsh industrial emigration to America began in earnest from around 1830 when a group of twenty families arrived in Carbondale, Pennsylvania. Where the English had sent woollen workers and weavers, and Scotland its carpet weavers, the Welsh sent miners to the coalmines of the Schuylkill, Susquehanna and Wyoming Valleys in Pennsylvania, anthracite districts which so resembled their own homes. The depression of the 1860s and the late 1870s brought fresh waves, though there was constant emigration from Wales throughout the century. After the coal miners came the steel workers, and from Pennsylvania they spread out as American industry itself expanded; to Johnstown, Ohio, Richmond, Virginia, Pittsburgh and Knoxville, Tennessee (where there were Welsh-owned rolling mills). In the 1890s there was a new wave when the McKinley tariff all but destroyed the Welsh sheet iron industry which had hitherto provided most of the world's supplies; by 1900 most native Welsh mills had gone, and the 40 mills in the United States had a high proportion of Welsh skilled workers. The relative familiarity of most Welsh people, notably the industrial workers, with the dominant Anglo-Saxon culture of America, the high skills and the express desire to establish themselves as full citizens in their new State all aided the process of acculturation. These produced, respectively, the erosion of the Welsh language, an intergenerational upward social mobility and the development of political conservatism. Paradoxically, the Welsh religious establishment encouraged the process of assimilation while asserting the value of cultural independence. In practice, a new form of American-Welshness developed which was sui generis.

The bulk of the early settlers and the agricultural emigrants were monoglot Welsh speakers but they had been exposed to English forms of speech and English practices of administration and this aided the process of acculturation. In general, as in Wales itself, the Welsh quickly became bilingual and, within a generation, monoglot English. Nevertheless, the continuing flow of emigration from Wales ensured a steady supply of Welsh speakers, sufficient to sustain existing Welsh chapels at least to the end of the century. In 1846 there were 46 Welsh churches in America, and this rose to 384 by 1872. Once the emigration had dwindled, as it did in the interwar years, the erosion of the Welsh language was very rapid indeed. If the language declined, other manifestation of Welsh identity remained surprisingly resilient. Of the 606 churches founded by Welsh immigrants, 177 survived to the 1980s.

Largely because they had an identifiable culture, history and religious practice, the Welsh sustained a thriving denominational press and a number of general journals in the United States for three quarters of a century. In all some 72 periodicals were published by the Welsh from 1832 onwards, some of which are no longer extant; only one, Y Drych [The Mirror] was published continuously to the present day. There were two kinds of Welsh-American periodicals, general newspapers and religious periodicals. The first general newspaper, Y Cymro Americanaidd [The Welsh American] was launched in 1832 and between that time and the 1930s a further twenty newspapers were published at one time or another. All but two were published either in New York State or Pennsylvania; the exceptions were Haul Gorllewinol [Western Sun] of Milwaukee and Colomen Columbia [The Columbia Pigeon] which was published first in Kansas and later in Chicago before merging with Y Drych , the only paper to survive the entire period.

The bulk of the remaining Welsh periodicals were denominational magazines, produced either by one of the three main religious denominations or as an interdenominational effort, such as Cyfaill o'r Hen Wlad yn America [A Friend from the Old World in America], which was the first Welsh magazine published in the United States in 1838. Again, the majority of these periodicals were printed and published in either Utica, New York, or in the mining areas of Pennsylvania, with an occasional exception published in Ohio, such as the Baptist magazine, Y Glorian [The Balance]. Given that the majority of Welsh readers in these areas were miners or iron and steel workers, it is clear that there was substantial working-class readership for all these papers, yet there is little evidence that the papers made any particular concessions to this.

A general examination of the Welsh periodical press reveals four features. Firstly, the geographical distribution of the Welsh press does not reflect the actual distribution of the Welsh in the United States. Instead, the press reflects the strength of particular communities, Utica, New York and the district around Scranton, Pennsylvania. Utica became, from the mid-nineteenth century, the center of Welsh-language publishing, mostly of a religious kind, and there was a symbiotic relationship between book and periodical publishing. Scranton was the center of a particularly dense concentration of Welsh. It has been estimated that some 20 percent of all the Welsh in America could be found in the coal fields in the Wyoming and Lackawanna Valleys. It is perhaps significant that the Utica press was the most durable, reflecting the importance for the Welsh-language press of thriving religious institutions. Most communities which had a large number of Welsh immigrants did not develop their own distinctive press. There were a number of Welsh columns in conventional local newspapers but on the whole the Welsh communities relied on papers from Utica and Scranton.

Secondly the Welsh periodicals mostly contained material of ubiquitous interest, suggesting that they did not regard themselves as parochial. Their very titles suggest a wider ambition than their specific geographical location might suggest such as *Cymro-America* [The Welsh American], *Baner America* [The American Flag], *Haul Gorllewinol* [The Western Sun], and *The Cambrian*. In practice, they often reflected the interests of the particular communities where they were published. From early on, for example, *Y Drych* carried news of Welsh communities as far afield as California and Orgeon and by the turn of the century, it was only the title page which suggested that it was produced in Utica. *Y Cylchgrawn Cenedlaethol* [The National Periodical] was clearly addressed to the widest possible audience as, indeed, were most of the denominational journals.

Thirdly, the Welsh press on the whole tended to be politically neutral, even though most Welsh communities appear to have been overwhelmingly Republican. It appears that some titles were published in the Democratic interest between 1845 and 1962, but none of the issues have survived and evidence about them is extremely sketchy. Most Welsh periodicals, including the religious papers, had something to say about politics, even if only a passing reference. Slavery and temperance were topics of particular interest. *Y Dyngarwr* [The Philanthropist], published in Remsen, New York, in 1843 was entirely devoted to antislavery and temperance , but its standpoint was more moral than political, while *Y Gwron Democrataidd* [The Democratic Hero] made a brave attempt in its twelve month existence from 1856-57 to support James Buchanan in the antislavery cause. For this reason the Welsh press took particular pride in Abraham Lincoln's election and stand. A few papers were openly Republican. *Y Seren Orllewinol* [The Western Star], a Methodist paper, urged its readers to vote Republican, while *Y Drych* was consistently and strongly pro-Republican, regarding the Democratic Party as "corrupt, dishonest and unruly." At the same time, the paper claimed to be politically quite objective.

There appears to have been no Welsh-language labor press, nor indeed any kind of labor paper produced for the Welsh working class. It is possible that some of the non-extant papers were intended for such a readership, though the only evidence for this lies in the titles such as *Baner y Gweithiwr* [The Worker's Banner], published briefly in Hyde Park, Pennsylvania, in the heart of the coal mining district. There is little evidence, moreover, of any serious interest in socialism or working-class politics among Welsh periodicals generally, even though there is some evidence that Welsh miners, for example, took a keen interest in the Greenback-Labor ticket in the 1870s. *Y Cymro Americanaidd* [The Welsh American] edited and published from 1855 to 1860 by John M. Jones of New York City featured, for a brief period, a column by the renowned Chartist, John Frost, but the column disappeared after Frost's return to Britain. In the 1900s the *Cambrian* published a few articles on socialism and socialist thinkers, one by a well-known member of the British Independent Labour Party, Julia Dawson, but their inclusion was more a reflection of the paper's eclecticism than any sudden enthusiasm for the subject.

There is no reliable evidence for the actual readership of the Welsh press beyond the occasional claims for circulation figures and these have to be treated skeptically. On average Welsh papers claimed to have between two and three thousand readers but it is impossible to judge what the institutional readership might have been. Moreover, it is impossible to establish the geography of the circulation since, for some of the time at least, most Welsh papers were read on a denominational rather than a community basis.

Yet, the character of the Welsh press in America did change during the nineteenth century. At the beginning the periodicals were overwhelmingly religious in character and even in the 1860s and 1870s, denominational periodicals tended to outlive their secular contemporaries. But as the century developed, and as the churches themselves began to feel the cold winds of an increasingly secular society, religion played a diminishing role in the Welsh periodical press. The Welsh publishing industry, however, died with the Welsh religious press. There were at one time or another in the nineteenth century 62 publishing houses producing books in Welsh and virtually all of these were either run by religious denominations or run on their behalf. Notable among them were the houses of Evan Roberts and Thomas J.Griffiths of Utica, both of whom were leaders in their religious community, and Robert R. Meredith of Rome, New York. A general bibliography prepared by an eminent bibliophile, Henry Blackwell of New York, reveals that with very rare exceptions indeed these books were either Bibles, testaments and hymnals or sermons, commentaries on sermons and memoirs of leading clergymen. This preoccupation tended to surface in nearly all the periodicals as well and it is not surprising, therefore, that the Utica papers were not only more numerous but more durable than any others. It was not so much the size of the population as its character which determined the survival of its press. When that character became secular the press itself dwindled and changed.

Welsh identity, the Welsh language, and what persisted of the Welsh way of life was sustained more than anything else by the chapels and religious institutions; the press was often simply a reflection of that reality. The lack of a distinctly working-class press is itself a reflection of the absence of Welsh working-class institutions in the United States while the wide dispersal of the Welsh made it difficult if not impossible to publish community newspapers. Above all, the upward social mobility of the Welsh, which has been observed by many historians, severed the roots which tied many of them to the class and culture from which they arose.

The Irish

Migration from Ireland to the United States began as early, almost, as the States themselves but it is important to distinguish two main forms. Early migrants in the seventeenth and eighteenth century were largely Ulster Protestants, usually known in North American parlance as the "Scotch Irish." On the whole these first immigrants, who shared the major language and religion of their hosts, assimilated well and prospered. Even in this early phase, however, there was some Catholic migration, largely from the South; indeed they came in such numbers and settled in such density that restrictive legislation was passed against them in several States. Philadelphia, in particular, became a haven for Irish immigrants in the late eighteenth century. It is these later migrants which are conventionally understood to be Irish.

In the first half of the nineteenth century, however, the stream became a torrent as economic distress compounded the religious and political disadvantages experienced by Catholics in Ireland. A third of all immigrants to the United States between 1820 and 1840 came from Ireland and after the potato blight this proportion rose to 45 percent. The great Irish famine of the 1840s impelled one of the most long-lasting and remarkable examples of serial migration in the history of modern Europe. Within a century of the end of the Napoleonic Wars, some 4.7 million Irish arrived in the United States, or over half of the population of Ireland as measured in 1841.

Though largely literate, these later Irish immigrants were mostly peasants and were obliged, in the main, to accept low-paid, unskilled work. In the canal-building era, the Irish accounted for a large proportion of the construction gangs. Irish navvies were prominent in the building of the National Road and so numerous were the Irishmen employed in the construction of railroads that a popular saying arose that there was "an Irishman buried under every tie." In the coalmining industry and in the steelworks, the Catholic Irish formed the lowest tier of employment in marked contrast to their Welsh, Scottish, Scotch-Irish and English fellow-immigrants. This is not to say that every Irishman was a laborer. There were large numbers of Irish craftsmen in New York, notably shoemakers, carpenters and skilled building workers and individual Irish men and women entered higher echelons of American society.

Though from rural peasant stock, the Irish tended to settle in urban areas. Over 80 percent of Irish immigrants in 1850 settled in urban areas, concentrating largely in the cities of the east coast, and by 1920 90 percent of all Irish Americans lived in urban areas. Generally, however, the Irish were slow to adapt to urban life in America and upward social mobility among first generation Irish immigrants was smaller than virtually any other ethnic group apart from the blacks. In the 1860 census two-thirds of the 1.6 million Irish in America were listed as unskilled. Their sense of consanguinity and the social cohesion wrought by their religious practices rendered the Irish more identifiable as a group within American society than other British immigrants and this, in a sense, acted as a brake on individual social mobility. The Irish, moreover, sought to assimilate themselves by abandoning the most obvious outward signs of their Irishness, their language, but social and religious ties ensured that their group identity was strong. The solidarity enforced by economic deprivation, furthermore, proved to be a powerful nexus for economic opportunism. Irish trade-union activity was a natural corollary to ethnically determined patterns of employment and this, in turn, led to the emergence of an Irish political block of almost incomparable power within the Democratic Party in many parts of urban America between 1860 and 1930. Indeed there was received wisdom that the priesthood, trade-union leadership and politics were the main routes for the advancement of individual Irishmen.

The Irish-American press developed as an outcrop of many of these activities and reflected the character and aspirations of the Irish ethnic group as a whole. Three characteristics of this press are striking. Firstly, although Gaelic was the mother tongue of the vast majority of Irish immigrants to the United States, no Gaelic-language newspapers or periodicals were established though there was a limited amount of Irish from 1857 in the Irish-American and in monthly papers such as the *Brooklyn Gael* or the *Boston Gaelic Journal*, the overwhelming bulk of the Irish-American press was written in English, the language of their hosts. In part, however, this was a continuation of a long-standing historical process for religious, political and economic institutions devalued the Gaelic language no less in Ireland than in America. The "hedge schools," through which it survived as a medium of education, could hardly be transposed to urban America. In the United States as in Ireland, English took the place of Irish in the curriculum and, consequently, in social intercourse. There was no market for an Irish-language press in the United States.

Secondly, the bulk of the press was concentrated in New York and Boston, with a small number of papers in Milwaukee, Minneapolis, St Louis, Cincinnati, Pittsburgh and San Francisco. The circulations of the East Coast papers, however, far outstripped those further afield and increased steadily to the point at which some New York Irish papers were near to becoming national papers for the Irish in America. In 1876, when the *San Francisco Irish News* had 500 subscribers, the *Irish-American* and *Irish-World*, both New York papers, could boast more than 30,000 subscribers, while the weekly *Boston Pilot* had an audited circulation of 50,187. By 1896, *the Pilot's* circulation exceeded 75,000. However, the *Irish World* in the same year reached 125,000, making it the most successful of all *Irish American* papers; indeed, in that year, a special edition of 1,650,000 copies was published which was claimed to be "the largest single edition of any paper published since the invention of printing."

Finally, there was a strong political tendency in the Irish-American press. The daily *Irishman* was a Democratic Party organ as early as 1835 while the *Irish World* originally had an additional longer title, *And American Industrial Liberator* and was until the 1880s a strong advocate of social and political reforms. On the other hand, many Irish papers directed their attention to the politics of Ireland, notably *The Citizen* and Fenian papers such as *The American Gael* and the *Sunday Citizen*.

The survival rate of Irish papers was reasonably high. A number lasted well into the twentieth century and in the period up to the World War Two, papers such as the *Irish World*, *The Gaelic-American* and, above all, *The Irish Echo*, maintained high circulations. By the 1930s, however, the *Irish World* had become distinctly less progressive and the general political outlook of Irish papers followed suit.

Conclusion

By the time the mass migration to the United States of British Celts had begun, the Celtic languages were no longer viable political symbols; even the Welsh language, the most vigorous by the late nineteenth century and the only one to be imported into the United States in any strength, was a weak focus for political activity. It is not surprising, then, that the language of political dissent, of socialism and radicalism, among the Celts was English. Added to this, the upward social mobility of many Welsh and Scots took them quickly out of the arena of working-class politics, leaving the Irish as the only identifiable working-class force. The revival of the Welsh language, and the official sponsorship of the Irish language by the government of Eire, came too late for the millions of Celts who had long ago left for America. The haste with which they abandoned all vestiges of their Celtic identity makes an ironic contrast to the strenuous efforts of many of their descendants now to recapture it.

Bibliography

Bertoff, R.T.

"Welsh." In *The Harvard Encyclopaedia of American Ethnic Groups*, edited by S. Thernstrom and A. Orlov. Cambridge, MA: Harward University Press, 1980.

Dodd, A.H.

The Character of Early Welsh Emigration to the United States. Cardiff: University of Wales Press, 1953.

Hartmann, Edward G.

Americans from Wales. Boston, MA: Christopher Publishing House, 1967.

Jones, Emrys.

"Some Aspects of Cultural Change in an American Welsh Community." In *Transactions of the Honourable Society of Cymmrodorion, 1949-51*. London, 1954, pp. 15-41.

Jones, Gareth.

Modern Wales. Cambridge: Cambridge University Press, 1985.

Thomas, R.D.

Hanes Cymry America: A History of the Welsh in America. Utica, 1872, transl. Phillips G. Davies; New York: University Press of America, 1983.

Williams, David

A History of Modern Wales. London: Murray, 1950.

Williams, Gwyn A.

The Search for Beulah Land. The Welsh and the Atlantic Revolution. London: Cromm Helm, 1980.

When was Wales. London: Black Raven Press, 1985.

Irish

Language

English

Area covered

Ireland

Comiled by

David Brundage

University of California, Santa Cruz, CA

Acknowledgements

I would like to thank Joshua B. Freeman, American Social History Project, City University of New York and Michael Musuraca, Labor Studies Department, Rutgers University for their help.

Introduction

Until the advent of massive eastern and southern European migrations in the late nineteenth century, the Irish were (with the Germans) one of the two largest immigrant groups within the American working class. Even as their numerical weight receded after 1890, they continued to put their imprint on the American labor movement. Their role in the Knights of Labor, the American Federation of Labor, and the Congress of Industrial Organizations is well known. From Terence V. Powderly to George Meany, the Irish and their descendants have provided American labor with some of its most famous leaders.

While acknowledging their importance in the labor movement, however, scholars have sometimes denied the existence of a distinctly Irish-American "labor philosophy."[1] Yet two intellectual currents, catholicism and nationalism, have exerted a tremendous influence within the Irish-American working-class community. At certain key moments in the history of the American working class, these currents have been associated with militant trade unionism, social reform, or socialism. At those moments, the distinctive Irish contribution to the American labor movement can be seen.

Survey of Irish Emigration to the United States and Canada

Emigration has been a central fact of Irish life since the middle of the nineteenth century. Between 1851 and 1900, nearly 4 million Irish emigrated to the United States, while another 250,000 emigrated to Canada. More than 1.75 million people left Ireland between 1846 and 1854, in response to three successive years of potato blight (1846-48). But emigration from Ireland began before, and continued long after, the 1840s and 1850s. The potato famine added intensity to a process already in motion.[2]

Some 1.75 million people left Ireland between 1780 and 1845. Although the majority of these early migrants went to Great Britain, between 1815 and 1845 as many as 33,000 people a year on average may have emigrated to the United States or Canada. Unemployment created by the spread of capitalist agriculture was the major cause of the movement. The lack of industrial employment in Ireland itself, combined with improvements in transportation, led to emigration abroad. Migration in these years was mainly from the northern and eastern areas of Ireland (Ulster and Leinster), where change was occurring most rapidly and where people had the economic resources and knowledge to emigrate. Emigration was far less important in the poorer and more isolated southern and western regions of the country (Munster and Connaught), where social and economic structures remained intact and where poverty provided a large obstacle to movement.[3]

This pattern underwent only slight change during the years of the potato famine. The largest number of trans-Atlantic migrants now came from central and eastern counties. Poorer emigrants from the west made their way towards closer destinations, often walking to eastern ports to board ships for England. Only in the later 1850s did large numbers of people from the west begin to emigrate. Improving economic conditions (and growing remittances from America) finally enabled the poor to pay for the trans-Atlantic passage.

This pattern of emigration explains the near-absence of the Irish language in the United States. Although Irish was still spoken in some areas of the south and west as late as 1850, by the time emigration from these areas began, the

English language had made considerable headway. Indeed, the spread of
English itself contributed to emigration. Because emigration was mainly
economic in motivation, it increased as the spread of literacy and English
increased awareness of opportunities in other areas of the English-speaking
world.

Like other migrations from Europe, Irish immigration to the United States in
the later nineteenth century was dominated by the young and unmarried.
Between 1850 and 1887, more than 66 percent of emigrants were between 15
and 35 in age, and in the remaining years of the century, the proportion
rarely fell below 80 percent. Except for the early famine years, when the emigration of families was more common, the proportion of unmarried migrants
was typically higher than 84 percent. Unlike the other European migrations,
however, that from Ireland was marked by a relatively high proportion of
women. Of the nearly 4 million people emigrating to the United States
between 1851 and 1900, men outnumbered women by only 170,000.[4]

Immigration from Ireland to the United States and Canada, 1820-1970.			
Year	U.S. Figures	Irish Figures	To Canada (Irish Figures)
1820-1830	54,338		
1831-1840	207,381		
1841-1850	780,719		
1851-1860	914,119	989,880	118,118
1861-1870	435,778	690,845	40,479
1871-1880	436,871	449,549	25,783
1881-1890	655,482	626,604	44,505
1891-1900	388,416	427,301	10,648
1901-1910	339,065		
1911-1920	146,181		
1921-1930	220,591		
1931-1940	13,167		
1941-1950	26,967		
1951-1960	57,332		
1961-1970	37,461		

Sources: United States, Immigration and Naturalization Service, *Annual
Report*, 1975, (Washington, DC, 1976), pp. 62-64. Eire, Commission on Emigration and Other Population Problems 1948-1954, *Report*, (Dublin, 1954), p. 119,
in Schrier, p. 159.

Also providing a contrast with other immigrants was the absence of
significant remigration among the Irish. According to Schrier, "the outstanding fact" about the return tide of migrants was "its minuteness." Unlike
Italian immigrants of the early twentieth century, many of whom returned to
their home villages (at least temporarily), few Irish men or women did so.
Although precise statistics are unavailable, Schrier estimates that by the end
of the century, no more than six Irish Americans returned to each Irish town-
land yearly, even for the purpose of visits.[5]

In the United States, the Irish were heavily concentrated along the North
Atlantic seaboard during the late nineteenth century, moving only gradually
westward. As late as 1900, 75 percent of the Irish-born population resided in
seven states: Massachusetts, Connecticut, New York, New Jersey, Pennsylvania, Ohio, and Illinois. These were the most heavily urbanized states in the

nation. In Canada, too, the bulk of the Irish immigrants arriving during and after the famine were urban dwellers.[6]

The Irish Immigrant Working Class

Mass emigration preceded the industrialization of Ireland itself. The immigrants to America, thus, became the first urbanized, working-class Irish. As the nineteenth century progressed, emigrants were drawn from less prosperous social groups. By 1900, they were no longer "strong and active farmers," but were more commonly landless and poor. An important continuity, however, was the rural origin of Irish emigrants. Throughout these years, they were drawn overwhelmingly from the countryside.[7]

One should not conclude from this that those arriving in America were totally "pre-industrial" in outlook. Many, particularly those from the west, had originally settled in Manchester or Liverpool or had obtained some industrial experience through seasonal labor in Britain. Early Irish activists in the American labor movement were especially likely to have spent some time in Britain.[8]

The Irish in the United States were originally concentrated in unskilled jobs. As late as 1870, four out of ten Irish immigrants worked as common laborers or domestic servants. Young Irish women worked in textile and shoe factories in New England mill towns or as domestic servants in the larger cities. Irishmen, the builders of America's pre-Civil War transportation network, commonly labored on the railroads, at building sites, in mines, or on the docks.[9]

By 1900, the Irish had improved their position dramatically. An estimated 5-6 percent of Irish Americans were by that date manufacturers, professionals, bankers, or other members of the upper middle class, while another 16-17 percent could be classified as lower middle class. "Irish America," David Doyle notes, "had attained class-structure parity with native stock Protestant America."[10]

Most Irish immigrants and their children remained in the working class. But unskilled labor had declined sharply among them. By 1900, only 15 percent of all working Irish Americans were unskilled manual laborers. Irishmen were now highly represented in a number of skilled trades. Though making up only one-thirteenth of the total American work force, Irish Americans constituted one-sixth of all metal workers, one-fifth of all stone cutters, and one-third of all plumbers. Although the Irish formed a national majority in no occupations, they did leave an imprint on specific occupations in specific cities. As late as the 1930s, for example, first-generation Irish immigrants dominated the ranks of New York City's transit workers.[11]

Prior to 1870, Irish workers remained generally outside the ranks of the North American labor movement. But the 1870s and 1880s marked a turning point. Irish workers in both the United States and Canada were prominent in the Knights of Labor, despite the efforts of French-Canadian bishops to prohibit catholic membership in the Order. By the early twentieth century, the Irish could be found throughout the labor movement, dominating the leadership of a number of AFL unions for example.

Irish-American workers have been somewhat less prominent in reform and radical organizations. They did play a central role in the "great upheaval" of the mid-1880s, providing critical support for land reformer Henry George's New York City mayoralty campaign in 1886, for example. The American Land League also drew thousands of Irish-American workers to its ranks, cultivating among them a "producer's ideology" which was a central ingredient in late nineteenth-century labor radicalism.

Irish Americans also dominated the leadership of the Western Federation of Miners, a constituent union of the Industrial Workers of the World, and helped give socialism its first local victories in Haverhill and Brockton, Massachusetts, in the 1890s. But they were not a significant force in either the Socialist or Socialist Labor Party. A recent scholar calls the Irish "the missing factor in the New York Socialist movement," for example, showing that they made up less than one percent of that city's Socialist Party. The efforts of the Irish revolutionary leader, James Connolly, to organize an Irish Socialist Federation in America proved, on the whole, a failure.[12]

Though the Communist Party boasted a number of famous Irish-American leaders, it had no more success in sinking deep roots in the Irish working-class community. The closest links between Irish workers and communism were forged in the rise of the Transport Workers Union in New York during the 1930s. But it is significant that the key organizers of this union were not long-time Irish Americans, but rather recent Irish immigrants, a number of them veterans of the Irish Republican Army.[13]

The Irish-American Press

Although the potato famine of the 1840s may not have been the root cause of emigration, it had a tremendous impact on the outlook of Irish emigrants, intensifying the power of both catholicism and Irish nationalism. Not surprisingly, Irish-American newspapers tended to identify with one or both of these currents. Beginning in the 1870s, some of these newspapers were also drawn into the orbit of the labor movement. Nevertheless the class tensions each newspaper exhibited makes it difficult to consider any of them labor papers. Only *The Harp* fits that description.

The Boston *Pilot*, founded in 1836, was for many years the most influential of Irish-American newspapers. It became the official organ of the Archdiocese of Boston in 1876. Under John Boyle O'Reilly, who edited it from 1876 to 1890, the *Pilot* was a strong reform paper, supporting black and American-Indian rights and expressing outrage at the poverty of many Irish Americans. Although a majority of its 50,000 readers in 1876 were workingmen, the paper did not at first devote much attention to labor issues. But the growth of the Knights of Labor had a profound effect on the *Pilot*. "Phineas," the paper's labor correspondent during the 1880s, argued that labor and capital had fundamentally antagonistic interests and O'Reilly occasionally endorsed strikes. But the 1886 Henry George campaign marked a turning point. The Catholic church's condemnation of George convinced O'Reilly to follow suit. Under O'Reilly's successor, James Jeffrey Roche, the paper continued to maintain a moderately pro-labor stance. But after Pope Leo XIII's *Rerum Novarum* in 1891, it ended its flirtation with labor radicalism.[14]

Lesser known catholic papers were occasionally more oriented towards the labor movement or political radicalism. During the 1890s, the *Colorado Catholic*, edited in Denver by Father Thomas Malone, took a firm pro-union stance and eventually gave a strong endorsement to the Colorado Populist movement. Less reform-oriented, but more thoroughly rooted in Irish working-class life, was the San Francisco *Leader*, edited by Father Peter Yorke. A key advisor to P.H. McCarthy, leader of the San Francisco Building Trades Council, Yorke made his paper a strong supporter of the city's labor movement.

Second only to the catholic press in importance was the nationalist press. Many nationalist papers were obscure, taken seriously only by frightened British diplomats. The New York papers edited by John Devoy (The *Irish Nation*, 1881-1885, and the *Gaelic-American*, founded in 1903) were in a different category, Devoy being one of the most important nationalist writers on either side of the Atlantic. In Toronto, the center of Ontario's Irish immigrant community, nationalism provided the intellectual underpinning for the *Irish Canadian* (1863-92).

But of the nationalist newspapers, Patrick Ford's *Irish World*, published in New York, was far and away the most attuned to the struggles of the working class. Combining Irish nationalism with a deep belief in America's republican political values, Ford endorsed the Greenback-Labor Party in the 1870s and Henry George's land reform programs in the early 1880s to rescue the nation from monopoly and political corruption. More important, the *Irish World and Industrial Liberator* (as it was known after 1878), with a circulation of 60,000 in 1882 and readers in both the United States and Ireland, served as the organ for a radical, working-class tendency within the American Land League, a tendency which in some areas of the nation practically merged with the Knights of Labor. Yet, as early as 1884, Ford was moving away from labor radicalism. He played little role in George's 1886 campaign and thereafter moved towards support of the Republican Party. By 1900, the *Irish World* had a circulation of 125,000--but also an antipathy to socialism, anarchism, and labor radicalism in general.[15]

Among the organizations Ford specifically denounced was the Irish Socialist Federation, established in New York City in 1907 by a group of Irish-American socialists "to develop the spirit of revolutionary class-consciousness among the Irish working class of America." Its most important figure from the start was the Edinburgh-born Irishman James Connolly, an Irish nationalist and socialist who had come to the United States in 1903, as a member of the Socialist Labor Party. Though nominally still a member, Connolly had broken with the SLP's leadership by 1907.[16]

The Harp, official organ of the ISF, first appeared in December 1907 as a 12-page monthly. It was published by J.E.C. Donnelly, an immigrant from Donegal, who apparently covered most of the costs out of his pocket. Taking as his subtitle the Jesuit maxim, "in things essential, unity; in things doubtful, diversity; in all things charity," Connolly used the paper to denounce the sectarianism of the SLP and to call for unity between within the socialist movement. An organizer for the Industrial Workers of the World, Connolly also repeatedly denounced the American Federation of Labor's craft unionism and called for the establishment of strong industrial unions.

At first *The Harp* was hawked on corners and at meetings by Connolly and other ISF members in New York. By the end of 1908, however, the paper was finding subscribers in other areas of the country and among socialists in Ireland as well. Connolly's writing fell clearly within the Irish nationalist and catholic traditions. In one editorial he compared the IWW to the Land League, and in nearly every issue he tried to counteract the anti-catholicism of much of the socialist left. He also responded enthusiastically to the growth of Arthur Griffith's Sinn Fein League, advised Irish-American socialists not to "abjure all ties of kinship or tradition," and even began to learn Irish himself.

In June 1909 Connolly, who had endorsed the Socialist Party of America in the 1908 elections, took up an appointment as a national organizer for the party and began a trip through the midwest. This caused problems for *The Harp*, and Donnelly decided not to issue it in June. In July the paper changed format, going to 8 pages. This issue also contained an appeal for money, which was apparently successful enough to keep it in business for another year. Connolly shaped *The Harp*'s general editorial policy and sent in editorials, but the remaining issues were taken up mainly by a serialized version of his important work, *Labour in Irish History*.

The rapid growth of both the socialist and nationalist movements in Ireland soon attracted Connolly, who moved to Dublin, taking *The Harp* with him. Though it did not appear in December 1909, it appeared the following month in Dublin, managed by the Irish labor leader James Larkin, Connolly acting as a titular editor. The last issue appeared in June 1910, the paper's collapse resulting mainly from libel suits against Larkin. Connolly himself would die in the Easter Week Uprising of 1916.

Though later revered as a nationalist martyr, Connolly had little impact among the Irish workers of America. Although subscription figures are not available, it seems clear that *The Harp*'s readership was quite small. His greatest impact may have come through the later Irish immigrants who helped organize the Transport Workers Union in the 1930s. A number of these men had been members of the Irish Republican Army in Ireland. While not a socialist organization, the IRA had encouraged a respect among its members for Connolly's brand of militant industrial unionism. But even communists among these newer Irish workers had no immigrant radical press of their own, reading instead the newspaper of the Communist Party of Ireland.[17]

Notes

1. See Wilentz, "Industrializing America," pp. 587-88, for a discussion.

2. Lees, *Exiles of Erin*, p. 39.

3. Lyons, *Irland Since the Famine*. p. 38; see, generally, Lees, *Exiles of Erin*, pp. 22-41.

4. Schrier, *Ireland and the Amrican Emigration*, p. 4.

5. Ibid, p. 130.

6. Ibid, p. 6; Nicolson, "Peasants in an Urban Society," p. 49.

7. See Doyle, "The Irish and American Labor," pp. 42-43; Lees, *Exiles of Erin*, pp. 37-38.

8. Wilentz, "Industrializing America," p. 586; Montgomery, "The Irish Influence, p. 2.

9. Doyle, "The Irish and American Labor," pp. 42-43; Montgomery, "The Irish Influence," p. 4.

10. Doyle, "The Irish and American Labor,"p. 43; See also Montgomery, "The Irish Influence," p. 10.

11. Doyle, "The Irish and American Labor," p. 43; Montgomery, "The Irish Influence," p. 12.

12. Leinenweber, "The Class and Ethnic Basis," p. 47.

13. See Freeman, "Catholics, Communists, and Republicans," pp. 256-83.

14. Abell, *American Catholicism and Social Action*, pp. 55-58.

15. Foner, "Class, Ethnicity and Radicalism," pp. 157-76; Rodchenko, "An Irish-American Journalist," pp. 524-40.

16. See Greaves, *The Life and Times of James Connolly*, pp. 214-40; Edwards, *James Connolly*, pp. 55-65.

17. Freeman, "Catholics, Communists, and Republicans," pp. 264-65.

Bibliography

Abell, Aaron I.
   American Catholicism and Social Action: A Search for Social Justice,
   1865-1950. Notre Dame, IN, 1963.
Doyle, David.
   "The Irish and American Labor 1880-1929," *Saothar: Journal of the*
   Irish Labor History Society 1 (1975), pp. 42-53.
Edwards, Ruth Dudley.
   James Connolly. Dublin, 1981.
Foner, Eric.
   "Class, Ethnicity, and Radicalism in the Gilded Age: The Land League
   and Irish-America." In his *Politics and Ideology in the Age of the Civil*
   War, pp. 150-200. New York, 1980.
Freeman, Joshua B.
   "Catholics, Communists, and Republicans: Irish Workers and the
   Organization the Transport Workers Union," in *Working-Class Amer-*
   ica, edited by Michael H. Frisch and Daniel J. Walkowitz, pp. 256-83.
   Urbana, IL, 1983.
Greaves, C. Desmond.
   The Life and Times of James Connolly. London, 1961.
Kealey, Gregory S.
   "Labour and Working-Class History in Canada: Prospects in the
   1980s." *Labour/Le Travailleur* 7 (1981), pp. 67-94.
Lees, Lynn Hollen.
   Exiles of Erin: Irish Migrants in Victorian London. Ithaca, NY, 1979.
Leinenweber, Charles.
   "The Class and Ethnic Bases of New York City Socialism, 1904-1915."
   Labor History 22 (1981), pp. 31-56.
Lyons, F.S.L.
   Ireland Since the Famine. London, 1971.
Montgomery, David.
   "The Irish Influence in the American Labor Movement." Hibernian
   Lecture, Cushwa Center for the Study of American Catholicism,
   Notre Dame, IN, 1984.
Nicolson, Murray W.
   "Peasants in an Urban Society: The Irish Catholics in Victorian
   Toronto." In *Gathering Place: Peoples and Neighbourhoods of*
   Toronto, edited by Robert F. Harney, pp. 47-74. Toronto, 1985.
Rodechko, James P.
   "An Irish-American Journalist and Catholicism: Patrick Ford of the
   Irish World." *Church History* 49 (1970), pp. 524-40.
Schrier, Arnold.
   Ireland and the American Emigration, 1850-1900. 1958; reprint, New
   York, 1970.
Wilentz, Robert Sean.
   "Industrializing America and the Irish: Towards the New Departure."
   Labor History 20 (1979), pp. 578-95.

Dutch-Speaking Peoples

Language

Dutch

Area Covered

The Netherlands and Belgium (Flanders)

Compiled by

Pieter R.D. Stokvis, Leiden

Depositories

Netherlands:

Nl-KB	Koninklijke Bibliotheek [Royal Library], The Hague.
Nl-UBl	Rijksuniversiteit te Leiden, Bibliotheek [University Library], Leiden.
Nl-UBUvA	Universiteitsbibliotheek [University Library], Universiteit van Amsterdam, Amsterdam.

United States:

<Usa-MiHoN	Netherlands Museum, Holland, MI.
Usa-WHi	Wisconsin State Historical Society, Madison, WI.

Introduction

The Dutch and Flemish Press in the United States

The Dutch and Flemish immigration into the United States remained comparatively small. Until 1920 some 250,000 Dutchmen and 138,000 Belgians of whom at least three fifth were Flemish, arrived on American shores.[1] Many more Dutch and Belgians did take part in international migration, as tables 1 and 2 show, their preferred determination were the neighboring countries.

The Dutch presence abroad as deduced from census figures rose steadily in proportion to the population at home. In 1909 it reached an all time high of 6 percent Netherlanders. Of these only 2 percent were counted in the United States. Germany took the main share, followed by Belgium. In-migration to the Netherlands, on the other hand, decreased and stabilized below 2 percent until World War One. In general emigration surpassed immigration. This was even more the case in Belgium, although the timing and direction was somewhat different. Around 1880 and 1890 almost one tenth of the Belgian people resided abroad, mainly in France. Since then the development reversed. The relative number of Belgians abroad declined, while the foreign share in the Belgian population rose markedly; immigration was overtaking emigration. From 1900 onwards the United States share of Belgians abroad made a sharp upturn partly due to the downturn of the French share and partly due to a real increase in overseas emigration. In the period of the so-called New Immigration both Dutch and Belgian immigration was still accelerating.

Census Figures Concerning Foreigners Residing in the Netherlands (in thousands)				
Year	1849	1859	1869	1879
Germans	41.2	36.6	33.8	42.0
Belgians	21.6	19.4	19.1	18.8
Others	8.1	5.9	6.2	7.0
All foreign nationals	-	-	-	-
All foreign born	70.9	61.9	59.1	67.8
per 100 inhabitants	2.3	1.9	1.6	1.7
Year	1889	1899	1909	1920
Germans	28.8	31.9	37.5	56.4
Belgians	13.7	14.9	18.3	30.4
Others	5.4	6.2	14.2	25.3
All foreign nationals	47.9	53.0	70.0	112.1
All foreign born	76.0	79.7	95.3	169.4
per 100 inhabitants	1.7	1.5	1.6	2.5

Census Figures Concerning Netherlanders Abroad (in thousands) [2]				
Year	1849	1859	1869	1879
Germany	18.0	18.0	20.0	17.6
Belgium	31.2	33.0	33.9	41.4
England	6.0	6.7	6.3	5.4
France	3.5	3.8	4.8	5.7
U.S.A.	9.8	28.3	46.8	58.1
Canada	-	-	-	-
Australia	-	-	-	-
New Zealand	-	-	-	-
South Africa	-	-	-	-
Total	68.5	89.8	111.8	128.2
per 100 Netherlanders	2.2	2.7	3.1	3.2
Year	1889	1899	1909	1920
Germany	37.0	88.0	144.2	82.3
Belgium	47.5	54.5	64.7	47.2
England	6.0	6.9	7.3	6.3
France	9.9	6.9	6.4	7.0
U.S.A.	81.9	95.0	120.0	131.8
Canada	-	0.4	3.8	5.8
Australia	-	-	0.7	1.4
New Zealand	-	-	-	0.1
South Africa	0.9	1.9	5.4	5.3
Total	183.2	253.6	352.5	287.2
per 100 Netherlanders	4.0	4.9	6.0	4.2

Census Figures Concerning Belgians Abroad (in thousands)								
Year	1850	1860	1870	1880	1890	1900	1910	1920
F	128.1	204.7	347.6	432.3	465.9	323.4	287.1	349
NL	21.6	19.4	19.1	18.8	13.7	14.9	18.3	30.3
D	(3.0)	3.2	3.7	4.6	7.3	12.1	13.5	6.9
E	(2.4)	2.5	2.5	2.5	3.9	4.3	4.4	9.1
U.S.A.	1.3	9.1	12.6	15.5	22.6	29.8	49.4	62.7
Total	156.4	238.9	385.5	473.7	513.4	384.5	372.7	458
Belgians	3.5	5.1	7.6	8.6	8.5	5.7	5	6.2

Census Figures Concerning Foreigners Residing in Belgium (in thousands)								
Year	1850	1860	1870	1880	1890	1900	1910	1920
French	34.6	31.4	32	51.1	64.8	85.7	119.1	115.6
Dutch	31.2	33	33.9	41.4	47.5	54.5	64.7	47.2
German	12.9	15.2	20.7	34.2	38.4	43	50.4	13.1
All foreign b.	92.8	94.8	98.1	143.3	171.5	212.5	277.9	216.9
inhabitants	2.1	2	1.9	2.6	2.8	3.2	3.7	2.9

Like the Scandinavians the Dutch tended to concentrate in a few states and there again in rural communities with less than 25,000 inhabitants. In 1920 43 percent of first generation Dutch immigrants were living in rural communities. The Belgian percentage was only 33 percent.[3]

The Dutch were mainly concentrated in the agrarian Mid- and Far West, while the Belgians were relatively numerous in urban New England, Middle and South Atlantic states. These settlement patterns reflect the demographic and occupational composition of both immigrant groups. The male/female ratio was much higher for Belgian than for Dutch immigrants, although both showed a shift from family migration in the 1880s to single and male migration in the pre-war period.[4] Almost 90 percent of all registered overseas emigrants (71,338) were U.S. bound. The rural-agrarian preponderance in the Dutch America trek is confirmed by the occupational distribution of the 23,248 economically active heads of families and singles who departed overseas in 1880-99. Of every 100 economically active persons 9 were farmers, 17 resident farmhands, 36 daylaborers, 17 craftsmen and 21 had an occupation in commerce, communication or services. Farmhands and daylaborers were clearly overrepresented.[5] A 10 percent sample of those Belgian emigrants that departed via Antwerp in the period 1901-12, reveals some characteristics. One fifth were remigrants. Of those that departed for the first time 59 percent were familyheads or singles, 20 percent dependent persons and 21 percent seeking family reunion. Of the actual emigrants half were between 18 and 35 years old and a quarter under 18. The occupational distribution varied for emigrants travelling alone, those travelling with their family and remigrants. The percentages active in agriculture were 50, 39 and 23 for the respective categories. The equivalent percentages active in industry were 29, 46 and 57. So unaccompanied emigrants had the highest agrarian score, returning emigrants the highest industrial score, while accompanied emigrants were in the middle. Compared with their Dutch counterparts in the foregoing decades industry seems to have been more prominent among these Belgian emigrants of whom 68 percent spoke Flemish.[6]

The Dillingham report reveals the occupational structure of Dutch and Flemish immigrants combined during the first decade of the twentieth century, because they were lumped together as a Germanic ethnic group. In 1899-1910 87,658 immigrants from the Low Countries were counted of which approximately three fifth came from the Netherlands. The next table summarizes the occupational distribution of Dutch and Flemish immigrants and remigrants compared with all immigrants.

The Occupational Distribution of Dutch and Flemish Immigrants 1899-1912 in percent [7]					
Year	1899-1910	1899-1909	1912	Remigr.	1899-1910
Farmers		7	7	6	
Farmhands	20	17	26	1	23
Unskilled Labor	23	25	13	46	36
Skilled Labor	31	31	31	28	20
Professionals	4	4	4	6	1
Commerce, Communication, Services	22	15	19	13	19
ec. active	49,852	42,103	6,239	2,092	7,049,953
% active	57	56	57	71	74

The agrarian sector was fairly represented. Most unskilled labor also belonged to this sector. The proportion and advance over time of skilled labor was however significant. In spite of this tendency the census of 1920 and even 1950 revealed to what extent especially the Netherlands born preferred traditional, non-industrial occupations. Compared with all immigrants Dutch and Flemish immigrants were better educated, more literate and well-to-do. All these characteristics explain in part why a Dutch or Flemish labor press did hardly emerge. The main reason, though, was the peculiar interplay between religion and ethnic background especially in the Dutch case.

Ethnicity, Church, Politics and Press [8]

The immigrant Dutch who resided since the 1840s in Mid-western settlements, ethnic urban clusters or scattered among other immigrants and native Americans, were divided or united along denominational and regional lines. Dutch Catholics easily submerged in a church which from its transnational nature aimed to obliterate national or ethnic differences. In practice Dutch Catholics mostly fraternized with their linguistically and culturally congenial Flemish and German coreligionists. Dutch Calvinists, on the other hand, adhered sternly to religious principles, which they considered Dutch and which were largely incorporated in the Reformed Church and its more orthodox and more Dutch split-off, the Christian Reformed Church. Both churches fostered an ethno-religious solidarity and identity that pushed Dutchmen of other persuasions to a relatively marginal position.

Early Dutch immigrants favored the Democrats over the Whigs, because the Democrats were supposed to represent the interests of the agricultural West, the common man and the immigrant. During the 1850s most Protestant Dutch shifted their allegiance to the new political formation of "Republicans" attracted by such issues as free soil, federal unity and containment of slavery. Civil War enthusiasm for the Union inaugurated a pronounced Republican tradition in Dutch-American politics and press. Whether they lived in towns or on the countryside, Dutch Calvinists were politically conservative. They clung to the values of individualism, self help and free competition. Making it on your own by working hard and saving was held in high esteem. They distrusted any sort of secular collectivism, government interference or trade unionism. Working-class organizations were eschewed, because they ran counter to individual bargaining and the God-ordained subordination or cooperation between employers and employees. The principle of Christian cooperation and class harmony was elaborated upon by some Dutch-American neo-Calvinists who, inspired by the political activism of Abraham Kuyper in the Netherlands, sought to establish Christian working-class organizations. Dutch-American Kuyperians endeavored to impose Dutch polarization patterns in uniting and mobilizing the Christian Reformed and Reformed populace for ecclesiastical, educational, social and political ends from 1890 onwards.

Departing from the principle of "sovereignty in own circle" and the antithesis of "Christian" and "pagan" in western society, the Kuyperians set out to Christianize society or at least to gather their own flock in Christian organizations and institutions. From 1892 until 1894 an "American Christian Workmen's Union: Patrimonium" which published *De Christen Werkman* [The Christian Workman], existed in Grand Rapids, Michigan. Attempts to start a political party along these lines resulted in 1921 in a Chicago based newspaper "The Daily Standard" and in 1931 in the founding of the Grand Rapids based "Christian Labor Association" which publishes the periodical *Christian Labor Herald* since 1947. Looking for guidance in Gods Word the association preaches prayerful cooperation between capital and labor to foster a Christian society and rejects atheistic ideologies and organizations, strikes and violence. This association is a peculiarly Dutch contribution to the world of American labor.

With regard to politics proper one should note that the Dutch Americans never formed a solid block. Due to the anticatholic and antiforeign element in the Republican Party the Dutch-Catholic settlements of Wisconsin voted continuously Democratic and so did even some Protestant settlements. The pattern of political and denominational disunion was reflected in the Dutch-language press. In order to survive, newspapers with a political message had to please their audience, that is to say, they had to cover news from the Netherlands, news from the Dutch settlements and Reformed and Christian Reformed congregations and personal items. They had to compete with many local and national church-affiliated periodicals, which had a steady market. The potential of labor periodicals was on the contrary rather shaky. The Dutch-American settlements and clusters were bound together by a value system that was unsympathetic towards trade unions, the labor movement in general let alone socialism or worse. Still the larger or more industrial centers occasionally produced reform, labor or socialist periodicals. Socialist immigrants rather aired their views in newspapers and periodicals at home.

In the course of time at least a hundred Dutch-language periodicals appeared in the United States since 1894. Between 1880 and 1930 Ayer mentions already 56 periodicals.[9] Of those 28 appeared in Michigan, 8 in Iowa, 7 in Illinois, 4 in New Jersey, 2 each in New York and South Dakota and 1 each in Utah and California. As to politics 8 were Republican and 6 Democratic, 2 changed loyalties, 1 was prohibitionist, 1 populist, 1 socialist, 14 religious and 23 independent with religious undertones.

The number of periodicals published simultaneously doubled during the third wave of immigration in the 1880s and 1890s and remained close to 20 declining somewhat in the 1920s. The average circulation climbed from about 1,000 to 2,000 and 3,000 or more in the first decades of the twentieth century. This was, however, mainly due to the huge circulation figures of church periodicals. The highest circulation figures of secular periodicals were 9,009 in 1928 for the *Gazette van Detroit*, 7,506 in 1924 for the *Gazette van Moline*, 7,400 in 1905 for the *Grondwet*, 6,500 in 1920 for the *Hollandsche Amerikaan* and 5,780 in 1928 for *De Volksvriend*.

Continuity of publication was not lacking: 7 periodicals of 1880 were still going strong in 1930 and 27 appeared for more than ten years at least. The publication of new periodicals reached a peak in the decades before and after 1900, when immigration was highest and the communities not yet shaken by the Americanization agitation of World War One. In 1880-89 according to Ayer's registration 7 new periodicals appeared, both in 1890-99 and 1900-09 12, in 1910-19 10 and in the 1920s only 4.

As the total number of Dutch-language newspapers and periodicals of minor importance or ephemeral existence is large, I shall introduce but a few of the most influential or lasting ones.[10] Just after the Dutch had settled on arable lands around Lake Michigan, Jacob Quintus ventured the first Dutch-language newspaper from Sheboygan, WI in 1849. His weekly *De Sheboygan Nieuwsbode* [The Sheboygan Newsmessenger] initially reflected the Democratic leanings of the newcomers. Before it merged with the German-language *Sheboygan Zeitung* [Sheboygan Newspaper] in 1860 it had changed from Democratic to Republican. The weekly *De Hollander* (1850-94) of Holland, Michigan defended for a long time the Democratic stands against the Republican *De Grondwet* [The Constitution] (1860-1938) of Holland, Michigan and the Calvinist *De Standaard* (1872-1944) of Grand Rapids. Another widely read journal in Michigan was *De Hollandsche Amerikaan* (1890-1945) of Kalamazoo. In Iowa the Democratic *Pella's Weekblad* [Pella's Weekly] lasted from 1861 till 1942. A wider circulation had *De Volksvriend* [People's Friend] published in Pella's daughter colony Orange City, Iowa from 1874 till 1951. In the Catholic settlements of Wisconsin Dutch newspapers appeared since 1878 of which *De Volksstem* [The People's Voice] (1890-1919) of De Pere was the most successful. In 1919 it merged with the Flemish Catholic *Gazette van Moline* (1907-40), which in turn was taken over by the *Gazette van Detroit*. This *Gazette van Detroit*, which started in 1914, had already absorbed *De Detroitenaar* in 1921. So by 1940 it was the only Dutch-language newspaper for Flemish and Dutch Catholics.

Reformist, labor and radical periodicals were few. Of some only the names survive. *De Christen Werkman*, which appeared in Grand Rapids from 1892 till 1894, propagated the ideas of the American Christian Workmen's Union: Patrimonium. Likewise in Grand Rapids in 1892 *Het Volksblad* [The People's Paper] circulated under the auspices of The Dutch Cabinetmakers Union. It was "devoted to the interests of working classes," but no more is known. A genuine reformist periodical was the modernist Protestant *Stemmen uit de Vrije Hollandsche Gemeente de Grand Rapids* [Voices from the Free Congregation] (1880-1920). Socialist periodicals were rare and shortlived. In the election year 1908 a socialist weekly *De Volksstem* [The People's Voice] circulated in Grand Rapids and in 1914 *Voorwaarts* was published in Holland, MI. There seems to have been a socialist paper *Nieuw Nederland* [New Netherlands] (1911-12) in the industrial city of Paterson, NJ.

Dutch Socialists and Trade Unionists in America

Only two socialist Dutch-language papers could be traced, none with a Flemish background or in the Frisian language. This does not mean that Dutch socialists did not emigrate or were not active in America. Indeed, they did hardly raise their voices within the Dutch-American community dominated by church and affiliated institutions. Dutch individuals, however, played an important part in American labor, socialist and pacifist movements. From the 1890s onwards many, mainly Frisian socialist laborers emigrated to the United States. They formed circles that kept in touch with the socialist movement at home. Many joined American or German organizations, while others disengaged from political activism.

The founder and leader of the American Federation of Labor (1886) Samuel Gompers (1850-1924) was of Dutch-Jewish descent.[11] His father, a cigarmaker, had moved from Amsterdam to London, where Samuel was born. In 1863 the family settled in New York. Samuel joined the Cigarmakers Union the following year which inaugurated a long career as a moderate trade unionist. In his autobiography he refers to his knowledge of the Dutch language and to Dutch customs. "With thorough going Dutch cleanliness" the children were regularly scrubbed in the tub. Housekeeping in general bore the mark of Dutch traditions: "My parents were both Hollanders born in Amsterdam. Our home preserved many of the customs of the Dutch community from which mother and father came. In our big room was a large fire place, in which mother had a Dutch oven... All mother's cooking utensils were of the squat, substantial Dutch make, necessary for the old-fashioned Dutch cooking that nourished us youngsters three times a day. We had plenty of dishes - an unusual possession in our neighborhood. These mother brought to this country."[12]

One of his more radical opponents was the Sephardic Dutch Jew Daniel DeLeon (1852-1914). He was born on Curacao where his father was an army surgeon. After some secondary education in Hildesheim and Amsterdam, De Leon settled in New York in 1874 where he got a low degree in 1878. In 1888 he joined the Knights of Labor and in 1899 the Socialist Labor Party, which dated from 1877. Since 1892 editor of the weekly *The People*, he rose to prominence as a revolutionary theorist. In practical politics he achieved little because his doctrinaire authoritarian leadership and failure to cooperate with organized labor kept the party small, if not sectarian.[13]

The life story of A.J. Muste (1885-1967) illustrates the impact of Dutch Calvinism on the Dutch-American community and in spite of his non-conformism also on Muste's personal choices. In 1891 his family moved from Zierikzee to Grand Rapids. As a minister in New York he preached the "social gospel" and joined the pacifist "Fellowship of Reconciliation." After World War One he became involved with Trotskyism and unionism until he found a way back to religiously inspired pacifism in 1936, which he professed until his death.[14] According to Muste's autobiography Dutch immigrants were much appreciated because of their sober, religious way of life, their industry and antiunion sentiments. "The church, especially in the first years, when our life was mainly lived within the Dutch community was the center of social life and culture, as well as of worship and religious training... The Hollanders settled in the Middle West in the decades before World War One, formed a fairly numerous group in Grand Rapids... With the rarest of exceptions every Dutch family belonged to a church, the Reformed or Christian Reformed, to which it had belonged in the old country. The services and the preaching were all in Dutch. In the larger population in Grand Rapids the Dutch constituted a lower stratum."[15]

A good many were of rural and especially Frisian background. Other Frisians settled in cities like Chicago and Paterson, New Jersey. When about 1890 land laborers were striking in Het Bildt, emigrated comrades in Chicago constituted an association called Hulpbetoon [Assistance] to collect money. Afterwards many disappointed strikers like the social-democratic strike leader Jan Stap left for the United States.[16] Another militant, Tjeerd Stienstra, left the same year (1896), but for personal reasons. To escape continuous quarreling with his wife, Tjeerd joined his older brother Tjibbe in Paterson, NJ. Both in Paterson and in Grand Rapids Dutch or rather Frisian socialists like Jan Stap had organized chapters of the antiparliamentary Socialisten Bond [Socialists' League]. Besides they were active in American trade unions and socialist parties. For a time Tjeerd Stienstra was a member of the Socialist Labor Party of Daniel DeLeon, but after 1900 he turned away from revolutionary socialism and became involved in land nationalization schemes.[17] His younger brother Klaas who had literary inclinations, came in 1900 to Paterson accompanied by his mother. He worked first as a tailor like his brother Tjeerd, but soon opened a shop. Married within the Frisian community of Paterson, he actively supported a Frisian cultural circle: Untspanning troch Ynspanning [Recreation through exertion], but refrained from politics. The tendency to forget about socialism and settle for material gains and respectable community life seems to have been quite general. Often it also had to do with the life course: once married and settled revolutionary laborers became less ardent. A socialist militant had tried to establish a socialist association and later a benevolent Domela Nieuwenhuis-club in Rochester met only with disappointment after a while, because the Dutch and Frisian laborers fared so well in material respect that they had lost interest in ideology. A Dutch militant who visited his old comrades in 1923, found that they had lost their ideals and had become terribly bourgeois. They told him their socialist ideals had materialized as a job, a house, a car and a good education for their children.[18]

There were, however, also immigrants who remained radicals or became so in the United States. The anarchist H.J. van Steenis (1862-1939) spent the late 1890s in the United States. In New York he took part in editorial meetings of the German-language periodical *Der Anarchist: Anarchistisch-Communistisches Organ,* which was also read by congenial Dutch immigrants in Grand Rapids and Chicago. He was disappointed with the anarchists in America who just like all other immigrants aspired to be rich as soon as possible and have a share in the American pie. On the other hand, he had to admire the technical and organizational progress that even benefitted the workers eventually.[19]

The Frisian communist militant Gerrit Roorda who was born in 1890, became politically involved in the United States where he initially joined his older brother in 1910. In the Dutch communities of Iowa he found work as a carpenter. He was advised not to walk about town on Sundays if he cared about a good reputation. Although the minister preached against trade unions and Freemasons, he became a Freemason in 1917 and a member of the Industrial Workers of the World in 1918. He sided with pacifists and socialists who were considered pro-German. After a forced stay in the American military he returned to the Netherlands in 1919 as a staunch supporter of the Russian Revolution.[20]

In general those Dutch immigrants who were active in trade unions or socialist parties operated outside the Dutch-American communities. They joined either American or German organizations so they had no need for a press of their own. One can assume that Dutch contributors may very well be met in the German immigrant press as the Dutch labor and socialist movement closely resembled and partly followed the German example.

Notes

1. A more detailed account of facts and sources is given in P.R.D. Stokvis, "Nederland en de internationale migratie 1815-1960," in F.L. van Holthoon, ed., *De Nederlandse samenleving sinds 1815* (Assen, 1985).

2. Bureau of the Census, *Abstract of the Fourteenth Census of the U.S. 1920* (Washington, DC, 1923), p. 306.

3. N. Carpenter, *Immigrants and Their Children, 1920* (Washington, DC, 1927), pp. 84-86, 107, 132, 340.

4. *Abstracts of Reports of the Immigration Commission (Dillingham)* (Washington, DC, 1911, dl. 1), pp. 82-96.

5. Computed from H. de Vries, "The Labormarket in Dutch Agriculture and Emigration to the U.S.," in Robert P. Swierenga, ed., *The Dutch in America; Immigration, Settlement and Cultural Change* (Brunswick, NJ: Rutgers Un. Press, 1985).

6. G. Kurgan and E. Spelkens, *Two studies on emigration through Antwerp to the New World* (Brussels, 1976), pp. 9-49.

7. *Abstracts of Reports of the Immigration Commission (Dillingham)* (Washington, DC. 1911, dl. 1), pp. 97-118, 172; J.W. Jenks and W.J. Lauch, *The Immigration Problem. A Study of American Immigration Conditions and Needs* (New York, 1913), pp. 80, 448, 522.

8. The major studies are: J. van Hinte, *Nederlanders in Amerika*, 2 vols., (Groningen, 1928), H.J. Lucas, *Netherlanders in America* (Ann Arbor, MI, 1955) and G.F. de Jong, *The Dutch in America 1609-1974* (Boston, 1975).

9. N.W. Ayer and Son's Directory, *Newspapers and Periodicals* (Philadelphia, 1880-1930).

10. The most recent historical and bibliographical survey is C. Bult, "Research Concerning Dutch-American Newspapers: The State of the Art," in: R.P. Swierenga, ed., *The Dutch in America*.

11. *Dictionary of American Biography* (New York, 1946, dl. VII), pp. 369-373.

12. S. Gompers, *Seventy Years of Life and Labor* (New York, 1957), pp. 46-48.

13. *Dictionary of American Biography* (New York, 1946, dl. V), pp. 222-224.

14. J.A. Ooiman Robinson, *Abraham went out: a biography of A.J. Muste* (Philadelphia, 1981).

15. N. Hentoff, *The essays of A.J. Muste* (New York, 1970), pp. 5, 27-28.

16. J. Frieswijk, "De beweging van Broedertrouw op het Bildt (1889-1892)," *Jaarboek Arbeidersbeweging* (1978), pp. 83-139.

17. J. Frieswijk, "Een socialistisch propagandist in revolutionaire jaren; biografie van Tjeerd Stienstra (1859-1935)," *Tijdsch. voor Soc. Gesch.* 6 (1976), pp. 219-256.

18. J. van Hinte, *Nederlanders in Amerika* (Groningen, 1928, dl. 2), pp. 466-467.

19. J.M. Welcker, *Heren en arbeiders in de vroege Nederlandse arbeidersbeweging 1870-1914* (Amsterdam, 1978), pp. 455-466.

20. K. Huisman, *Id libben fan Gerrit Roorda* (Alternatijf De Tille, 1957), pp. 1-113.

Annotated Bibliography

DE CHRISTEN WERKMAN. ...		MI Grand Rapids	1892-1894

Title trans.:	The Christian Workman. Organ of Patrimonium	*First issue:*	1892 ?
Subtitle:		*Last issue:*	1894 ?
Add. lang.:		*Vols. (nos.):*	
First editor:	Ate Dijkstra ?	*Frequency:*	
First publ.:		*Preservation:*	7 ?
Related pubs.:		*Supplements:*	
Circulation:		*Category:*	Christian trade union

Depositories:

The complete title of the paper was: *De Christen Werkman. Orgaan van Patrimonium.*

Several writers quoting the same sources mention this periodical which supposedly propounded neo-Calvinist views and advocated Christian trade unionism. It may have been linked to another periodical, of which too, only the name survives: *Het Volksblad. Orgaan van de Hollandsche Meubelbewerkers - Vereeniging* (Grand Rapids, MI, 1892) [The People's Paper. Organ of the Dutch Cabinetmakers Union].

Sources: J. van Hinte, *Nederlanders in Amerika* (Groningen, 1928); H. J. Lucas, *Netherlanders in America* (Ann Arbor, MI, 1955); G. F. de Jong, *The Dutch in America 1609-1974* (Boston, 1975).

STEMMEN ...		MI Grand Rapids	1880-1920

Title trans.:	Voices from the Independent (Dutch) Congregation	*First issue:*	1880
Subtitle:		*Last issue:*	1920
Add. lang.:		*Vols. (nos.):*	
First editor:	F. W. N. Hugenholtz	*Frequency:*	m
First publ.:	P. Th. Hugenholtz	*Preservation:*	3
Related pubs.:		*Supplements:*	
Circulation:		*Category:*	reformist

Depositories: Nl-UBUvA [1886-88]; Nl-KB [1886-87]; Nl-UBL [1887-89]

The complete title of the paper is: *Stemmen uit de vrije (hollandsche) gemeente te Grand Rapids.*

This periodical was published by two independent Unitarian ministers who held modernist views in theology and preached the so-called social gospel. They were reformist in politics and devoted much attention to working conditions, industrial disputes and the like.

HET VOLKSBLAD. ...   MI Grand Rapids   1892

Title trans.:	The People's Paper. Organ of the Dutch	*First issue:*	1892
	Cabinetmakers Union.		
Subtitle:		*Last issue:*	
Add. lang.:		*Vols. (nos.):*	
First editor:		*Frequency:*	
First publ.:		*Preservation:*	
Related pubs.:		*Supplements:*	
Circulation:		*Category:*	Christian trade union

Depositories:

The complete title of the paper is: *Het volksblad. Orgaan van de hollandsche meublebewerkers vereeniging.*

No further information could be obtained.

DE VOLKSSTEM   MI Holland   1908-1909

Title trans.:	The People's Voice	*First issue:*	My 1908
Subtitle:		*Last issue:*	My 1909
Add. lang.:		*Vols. (nos.):*	1-2
First editor:	John G. Blok	*Frequency:*	m
First publ.:	A. Van Doesburg	*Preservation:*	2
Related pubs.:		*Supplements:*	
Circulation:	1333	*Category:*	socialist

Depositories: Usa-WHi [1908-09]; <Usa-MiHoN [Jl 1908]

This paper was started by a local branch of the Socialist Party to campaign for Eugen V. Debs, but according to one participant it failed because of incompatibility between Americanized social-democratic oriented party organizers and recent Dutch immigrants with more radical anarcho-syndicalist leanings.

Source: Hendrik G. Meyer, *Thrifty Years. The Life of Hendrik Meyer* (Grand Rapids, MI: Eerdmans, 1984), p. 45.

VOORWAARTS	MI Holland	1914-1915

Title trans.:	Forward	*First issue:*	1914
Subtitle:		*Last issue:*	Ja 1915
Add. lang.:		*Vols. (nos.):*	
First editor:		*Frequency:*	bw
First publ.:		*Preservation:*	7
Related pubs.:		*Supplements:*	
Circulation:		*Category:*	socialist

Depositories: ?

This periodical is first referred to by a contemporary writer on Dutch journalism in the United States as a socialist biweekly journal starting in 1914 and succumbing to an early death in 1915. In all probability it was a socialist campaign paper with as little success as the previous campaign paper *De Volksstem* [The People's Voice] of 1908-09.

Source: H. Beets, *Neerlandia* (1915), pp. 253-256.

Title Index

Place Index

Chronological Index

```
1880      1890      1900      1910      1920
01234567890123456789012345678901234567890
-----------------------------------------
        --
        ---        --            --
```

Stemmen uit de vrije	MI Grand Rapids
Het Volksblad	MI Grand Rapids
De Christen Werkman	MI Grand Rapids
De Volksstem	MI Holland
Voorwaarts	MI Holland

French-Speaking Peoples

Language

French

Area covered

France

On the Franco-Canadian labor press see the introduction

Compiled by

Jeffrey Kaplow, Paris

Depositories

Italy:

I-ISSOCO	Istituto per lo Studio della Societá contemporanea, Rome.

United States:

Usa-CSdS	San Diego State University, San Diego, CA.
Usa-CU	University of California, Berkeley, CA.
Usa-ICN	Newberry Library, Chicago, IL.
Usa-IHi	Illinois State Historical Library, Springfield, IL.
Usa-InU	Indiana University, Bloomington, IN.
Usa-LNT	Howard Memorial Library, Tulane University, New Orleans, LA.
Usa-LU	Louisiana State University, Baton Rouge, LA.
Usa-MWA	American Antiquarian Society, Worcester, MA.
Usa-NHi	New York Historical Society, New York, NY.
Usa-NN	New York Public Library, New York, NY.
Usa-NNC	Columbia University, New York, NY.
<Usa-PPBI	The Emily C. Balch Institute for Ethnic Studies, Philadelphia, PA.
Usa-WHi	State Historical Society of Wisconsin, Madison, WI.

Introduction

French immigration to the United States in the nineteenth and twentieth centuries was always extremely limited. In 1850, the French-born population living in the United States was 54,000, in 1860, 109,000 and in 1870, 116,000.[1] Unaffected by the massive new immigration of the period 1880-1910, this number remained stable, or even declined slightly in the next fifty years. Among these immigrants were several hundred utopian experimenters, mainly followers of Etienne Cabet (who himself arrived at the end of 1848), and a small group of political refugees fleeing the repression that reigned in Second Empire France after the defeat of the Revolution of 1848, and, of course, the Paris Commune twenty years later. Their small numbers account for the undeveloped state of labor and working-class French-language journalism in the new world.

If the "français de France," as the Québécois call them, were not numerous, there were large communities of French-Canadians or Franco-Americans in New England, in the area around the Great Lakes, and in the upper Mississippi Valley. Starting out as small farmers, the majority were increasingly integrated into the industrial working class, especially in the New England and upstate New York textile mills, in the last third of the nineteenth century.[2]

This French-speaking working class did not produce any labor newspaper, with the possible exception of L'Emancipation. The Massachusetts-based Le Travailleur was not a labor paper.[3] A variety of reasons may explain this absence of a class-conscious, or even politically independent, press: the influence of the Catholic Church, continuing ties to peasant communities on both sides of the United States-Canadian border, the sense of ethnic difference in regard to, and isolation from new immigrants such as the Italians and the Slavs, the paternalism of large employers. Whatever the reasons, the French-language press in these communities tended to be catholic and anti-assimilationist, mainly concerned with the maintenance of a French, or more properly, Franco-American cultural identity than with anything else, a question they continued to debate until the late 1930s.[4]

What was true of New England appears also to have been true of the Middle West, where Joyaux found traces of at least 60 French-language newspapers, seven of them published before the Civil War, 33 between 1865 and 1890, and 30 after that date. The leading figure here, the equivalent of Ferdinand Gagnon and the Belisle brothers in New England, was Louis Bachand-Vertefeuille, like them Canadian-born, with a catholic, traditionalist and nationalist orientation. His papers included Le Courrier de l'Ouest (1903), Le Courrier Canadian (1904), and Le Courrier Franco-américain (1905).[5]

In contrast to the French-Canadians, the French-speaking community of Louisiana (Acadians, French immigrants, Caribbean migrants) supported a press of which four newspapers are included here, though they were not, strictly speaking, a French-language labor press (L'Union, La Tribune, L'Echo, Crusader). All four, published in and around New Orleans, were edited by Blacks in their struggle for equal rights and, as such, form part of the radical tradition in the United States, dealing with questions vital to the interests of the white, as well as of the black, working class. That they appeared partially in French was due to the existence of a Creole community in Louisiana.[6] (Category: Black Republican)

In the Middle West and South a few newspapers were published by French immigrants whose point of view was staunchly Republican. In so far as the period 1848-71 was marked in French politics by an alliance between bourgeois Republicans and an emerging working-class movement, or, to put it another way, by the very gradual development of an autonomous working-class movement within the Republican coalition,this made it appropriate to include these titles here. Two examples published in Chicago are *Le Journal de l'Illinois* (1857-64) and *L'Amérique* (1869-70). In the South, Charles Testut's various publications (see below and bibliography under *La Commune*) displayed a similar orientation, and their editor was, for a time, involved with the New Orleans Section No. 15 of the First International, another instance of republican enthusiasm sometimes blending in with labor revolutionary agitation.

"L'Union Républicaine de Langue Francaise," publisher of the *Bulletin*, with its sections in Chicago, St. Louis, Newark, New York, San Francisco, among others, seems to have belonged to the same political current. It was an organization in the French Republican tradition of 1792 to 1794 and 1848. According to a brochure published by the French Republicans of St. Louis in 1869 [7] this association pursued three main goals in the establishment of their "La République": Establishment of a general system of education free from any religious influence, achievement of a permanent peace including the abolition of all standing armies, improvements of the situation of the laboring classes including a total change of the tax system and a satisfactory resolution of the relations between capital and work. The organization demanded a universal franchise, freedom of the press, freedom of speech and freedom of assembly. Once universal franchise was achieved, the era of violent revolutions would come to an end, so would civil wars and class wars as well as wars between nations. While the brochure of the "Union Républicaine" spoke derisively of the bourgeoisie, it did not follow the slogan that the emancipation of the working classes must be achieved by the working classes themselves. Rather it demanded "that the educators of the people, those who have the good fortune to study the question of social economy, should pay their debt to the Proletariat by teaching those truths which alone should govern the world."[8] In the 1870s "L'Union Républicaine" cooperated with the English-language American labor movement (Category: "republican/labor"). In a similar vein *Le Clarion*, which has been designated "populist," may have been published.

Since the 1850s, Etienne Cabet and his followers published a number of periodicals, much of them taken up with the chronicle of the factional strife within the successive communities of Nauvoo, Illinois, and Adams County, Iowa. (See Appendix "Icarian Newspapers.")

As representative of the pre-1848 socialist movement, *Le Grelot* has to be named. The apparently shortlived *Le Réveil des Peuples*, New Orleans, 1852, was published in the interests of political exiles after the failure of the Revolution of 1848. *Le Libertaire*, the one-man enterprise of Joseph Déjacque, belongs to the same period. It was communist-anarchist in orientation and ceased publication in 1861, just at the outbreak of the Civil War. (Category: early socialist).

Following the "early socialist" press and chronologically parallel to the "republican/labor" and "Icarian" press, two labor periodicals were published during the years from 1869 to 1873. *La Commune*, an official organ of certain American sections of the First International, had an ephemeral existence between 1871 and 1873, and it seems to have had a sister paper, *Le Socialist*, published in New York at the same time. With the coming of the Long Depression in 1873 the French-language labor press ceased to exist for a decade and a half.

Working-class interests were taken up again by Louis Goaziou in four successive publications between 1888 and 1916, beginning with *Le Reveil des Masses*, published in the Pennsylvania coal fields but apparently circulating at least as far west as Kansas. The above named populist-minded paper appeared at the same time in Louisiana.

In the period from 1911 to 1927 a syndicalist (*L'Emancipation*), a socialist (*Le Socialiste*), and an anarchist periodical (*Germinal*, 1899-1902, *L'Effort*, 1922-27), the latter in conjunction with the Italian *Germinal*, were published.

Aside from the activity of a very few, mainly anarchist and/or syndicalist, militants, the working class of French origin in the United States, small in number and scattered over a wide area, seems to have made no separate impact on the development of either the labor press or the labor movement.

Beyond noting their small numbers, one can only speculate on the reason for this. Perhaps it was due to the cosmopolitan, internationalist orientation of the French workers themselves, who felt no need to work exclusively within their own, very limited community. Perhaps, too, the fact that they were "white" in the full sense of the word as then used in the United States, i.e., that they were western Europeans marked by no particular characteristic (not even catholicism, which almost all had long since abandoned) that would impede their integration into the native working class made it unnecessary for them to affirm a particular national or cultural identity and seek to preserve it.

Notes

1. Ben J. Wattenberg, ed., *The Statistical History of the United States from Colonial Times to the Present* (New York, 1976), Series C, 228-295, pp. 117-118.

2. See, for example, Tamara K. Hareven, *Amoskeag* (New York, 1978); Daniel J. Walkowitz, *Worker City, Company Town. Iron and Cotton-Worker Protest in Troy and Cohoes, New York, 1855-84* (Urbana, IL, 1978); Bruno Ramirez, "French Canadian Immigrants in the New England Cotton Industry: A Socioeconomic Profile," *Labour/Le Travailleur* 11 (1983), pp 125-142.

3. Letter of Prof. Bruno Ramirez of the Université de Montreal to D. Hoerder, 5 June 1984.

4. The history of the French-Canadian press in the United States may be studied in the books by Belisle and Tetrault, as well as in the articles by Ham, Joyaux and Cormier, all listed in the bibliography. The American Antiquarian Society at Worcester, MA, has a considerable collection of these newspapers. Others can be found in the public libraries of the cities concerned, mainly in Massachusetts and Vermont.

5. See the articles by Joyaux and Cormier.

6. See the bibliographies of the French press in Louisiana, by Tinker and McMurtrie.

7. *77e Anniversaire du 22 septembre 1792 célébré par les Républicains de langue française de St. Louis, Mo., Etats-Unis d'Amérique* (St. Louis, 1869), copy in New York Public Library.

8. *The Socialist*, 3 June 1876.

Bibliography

Belisle, Alexandre.

    Histoire de la Presse Franco-canadienne aux Etats-Unis. Worcester, MA, 1911.

Cormier, L.-Ph.

    "La Presse française de l'Illinois." *Revue d'Histoire de l'Amérique Française* XI (December 1957), pp. 380-92.

Daggett, M.D.

    "Vermont's French Newpapers." *Vermont History* XXVII (January 1959), pp. 69-75.

Ham, Edward B.

    "Journalism and French Survival in New England." *New England Quarterly* XI (March 1938), pp. 89-107.

Joyaux, Georges J.

    "French Press in Michigan." *Michigan History* XXXVI (September 1952), pp. 260-78.

    "The French Language Press in the Upper Mississippi and Great Lakes Areas." *Mid-America* XLIII (October 1961), pp. 242-59.

McMurtrie, Douglas C.

    "The French Press in Louisiana -- Notes in Supplement to Tinker's 'Bibliography.'" *Louisiana Historical Quarterly* XVIII (1935), pp. 947-65.

Tétrault, Maximilienne.

    Le Role de la presse dans l'évolution du peuple franco-américain dans la Nouvelle Angleterre. Marseille, 1935.

Tinker, Edward L.

    "Bibliography of French Newspapers and Periodicals of Louisiana." *Proceedings of the American Antiquarian Society.* New series. XLII (1933), pp. 247-370.

Annotated Bibliography

L'AMERIQUE		IL Chicago	1869-1870
Title trans.:	America	*First issue:*	1869
Subtitle:		*Last issue:*	1870
Add. lang.:		*Vols. (nos.):*	
First editor:	Guéroult and Pintu	*Frequency:*	bw
First publ.:		*Preservation:*	3
Related pubs.:		*Supplements:*	
Circulation:		*Category:*	republican/labor

Depositories: Usa-ICN [1869-70]

This newspaper was apparently of classical French-republican orientation. Its offices at 162, Madison Street were the meeting place for the Chicago section of L'Union Républicaine de Langue Française. (See Introduction.)

L'AMI DES OUVRIERS		PA Hastings	1894-1896
Title trans.:	The Friend of the Workers	*First issue:*	1 Ag 1894
Subtitle:	Organe des Travailleurs de Langue Française des Etats-Unis	*Last issue:*	1896
Add. lang.:		*Vols. (nos.):*	
First editor:	Louis Goaziou	*Frequency:*	m
First publ.:		*Preservation:*	5
Related pubs.:	c *Le Réveil des Mineurs*, s *L'Union des Travailleurs*	*Supplements:*	
Circulation:		*Category:*	communist-anarchist

Depositories: Usa-NNC [1894-95]

The paper, which was "The Organ of French-speaking workers in the United States," announced meetings of anarchist groups in places like Kiokotte, Kansas, Weir City, Kansas, and noted commemorations of 11 November 1887 (execution of the Haymarket martyrs) in Cincinnati, Pittsburgh, New York, and Litchfield, Kansas.

The political line of the paper was defined in issue no. 2: "The bourgeoisie reacts to the workers' arguments with Winchester rifles, without mercy; without weakness the workers will respond with guns. The triumph of revolution and anarchism is here." And in no. 5 they point out that there are many honest and well-meaning men among the populists and socialists, however, they need to be told time and again that only communist anarchism will bring change to society. The newspaper cost 50 "sous" per year and its "office" was at Box 82, Hastings, Cambria CO., PA.

BULLETIN DE L'UNION ...		NY New York	1869-1871

Title trans.:	French Language Bulletin of the Republican Union	*First issue:*	1869
Subtitle:		*Last issue:*	1871?
Add. lang.:		*Vols. (nos.):*	
First editor:		*Frequency:*	
First publ.:	Union Républicaine	*Preservation:*	4
Related pubs.:		*Supplements:*	
Circulation:		*Category:*	republican/ labor

Depositories: Usa-WHi [1869-71]

The complete title of the paper was: *Bulletin de l'union républicaine de langue francaise.*

Although these republicans who supported Union Républicaine did not constitute a labor or working-class movement properly so-called, they paid close attention to social questions, e.g., the condition of workers and of blacks, the resolution of which went hand in hand with the adoption of the new form of the state.

How long the Union Républicaine continued to exist and to publish its *Bulletin* we do not know, but it appears that they were still active (and perhaps radicalized by the experience of the Commune) in 1876. On June 3 of that year, the *Socialist*, the organ of the Social Democratic Workingmen's Party of North America (soon to become *The Labor Standard*) quoted in translation the *Bulletin*'s positive appreciation of itself:

"Here we have another defender of our grand principle of Solidarity which enters the field with a masterly hand. Courage friends, we hope that the people of the United States will second your efforts and that before four years have passed the Bourgeoisie will be compelled to measure itself with us."

For further information on Union Républicaine see Introduction.

LE CLARION		LA Opelousas	1890-1909

Title trans.:	The Clarion	*First issue:*	1890
Subtitle:		*Last issue:*	1909
Add. lang.:	English	*Vols. (nos.):*	
First editor:		*Frequency:*	w
First publ.:		*Preservation:*	2
Related pubs.:		*Supplements:*	
Circulation:		*Category:*	populist

Depositories: Usa-LU [1890-1903,1905-09]

This paper, which was also called *St. Landry Clarion*, had, according to Ayers' Directory in 1891, a populist affiliation. It appeared weekly on Saturdays.

LA COMMUNE		LA New Orleans	1871-1873

Title trans.:	The Commune	*First issue:*	12 Je 1871
Subtitle:	Bulletin mensuel du Club International	*Last issue:*	20 S 1878
	Républicain et d'Assistance Mutuelle		
Add. lang.:		*Vols. (nos.):*	
First editor:		*Frequency:*	m
First publ.:		*Preservation:*	
Related pubs.:		*Supplements:*	
Circulation:		*Category:*	labor

Depositories: Usa-LNT; I-ISSOCO [1871-73]

La Commune started life as the official organ of the *Club Républicain et d'Assistance Mutuelle*, which soon became Section No. 15 de l'Association Internationale des Travailleurs (IWA), as announced in number 4 of 3 September 1871. The group met at the Salle Cosmopolite, New Orleans. As was often the case in the American sections of the A.I.T., there was a struggle over leadership, in this case between Dr. Charles Testut (c. 1818-1892), among other things an inveterate publisher of newspapers, novelist and partisan of spiritism, and Charles Caron, the director of a commercial school, who is listed as *secrétaire de la rédaction* from no. 5 (24 September 1871). It appears that Caron won this battle for influence, spiritism being rejected by the A.I.T. Testut, who had started to publish another paper, *L'Equité. Journal du Progrès Universel* on 9 April 1871, founded a rival organization, l'Association Fraternelle des Travailleurs, whose existence was announced in its edition dated 3 September. In all, 25 numbers of *L'Equité* were published, the last on 24 September 1871. Tinker, who gives it the label "radical republican," notes that the first three issues were printed on the press of *Le Propagateur Catholique*, which then refused to print further issues, because the paper's espousal of the cause of spiritism and conciliation between whites and blacks made it intensely unpopular. A run of the paper is in the Howard Memorial Library, Tulane University, New Orleans. The Tamiment Institute of New York owns a microfilm of a single copy, issue of 7 May 1871.

Testut went on to publish a number of other shortlived papers, among them:

La Lanterne, weekly on Sundays (1873), *Le Journal des Familles*, weekly (1879-1880), and *Le Journal du Peuple*, weekly (1880).

Tinker was unable to locate copies of any of them.

For Testut, see Dumas Malone (ed.), *Dictionary of American Biography* (New York and London, 1936), vol. XVIII, p. 383.

THE CRUSADER	LA New Orleans	1890-1896

Title trans.:		*First issue:*	1890
Subtitle:		*Last issue:*	1896
Add. lang.:	English	*Vols. (nos.):*	
First editor:	Louis A. Martinent	*Frequency:*	
First publ.:	Louis A. Martinent	*Preservation:*	
Related pubs.:		*Supplements:*	
Circulation:		*Category:*	black republican

Depositories: Usa-WHi (19 Jl 1890); Usa-CSdS (1890)

From 1895 on the paper was called *The Daily Crusader*. It was a bilingual paper founded by Louis A. Martinent, a Mulatto and former member of the Reconstruction State Legislature of Louisiana.

Tinker labels it "very radical" and says that its influence was "negligible, because it was not founded until after the Negro cause had been completely lost."

Source: Tinker, p. 267.

L'ECHO	LS St. Martinville	1865-1874

Title trans.:	The Echo	*First issue:*	1865?
Subtitle:		*Last issue:*	1874?
Add. lang.:	English	*Vols. (nos.):*	
First editor:		*Frequency:*	w
First publ.:		*Preservation:*	6
Related pubs.:		*Supplements:*	
Circulation:		*Category:*	black republican

Depositories: Usa-NHi (15 Mr 1873)

This was a bilingual paper published weekly on Saturdays. The only trace of it is found in Tinker's bibliography, where it is listed as having been founded by J.F. Penne, a Black man, sometime between 1865 and 1874. He quotes a local paper, *La Sentinelle des Attakapas*, published at Pont-Breaux, St. Martin Parish, describing it on 11 June 1874 as the official journal of the parish and of Black Republicanism.

Tinker could find no copies of this paper, but there is, according to the Union List of Serials, a single copy in the Library of the New York Historical Society, New York City.

Source: Tinker.

L'EMANCIPATION   1) MA Lawrence 2) RI Olneyville   1911-1912

Title trans.:	Emancipation	First issue:	1911
Subtitle:	Bulletin Mensuel de la Fédération	Last issue:	1912
	Franco-Belge, des Syndicats Adherents		
	aux Ouvriers Industriels de l'Univers		
Add. lang.:		Vols. (nos.):	
First editor:		Frequency:	m
First publ.:		Preservation:	6
Related pubs.:		Supplements:	
Circulation:		Category:	syndicalist

Depositories: Usa-WHi (S 1911)

Dubofsky notes the existence in Lawrence, MA, of Local 20 of the National Industrial Union of Textile Workers, and says that in May, 1911 the French-speaking branches of the NIUTW "met at Lawrence's IWW headquarters, where they planned to establish the French paper L'Emancipation upon a firmer foundation and to increase agitation among French-speaking workers."

The single existing copy of September 1911 (vol. 2, no. 16) bears the subtitle "monthly bulletin of the Franco-Belgian Federation of the IWW."

The statutes of the "Fédération Franco-Belge I.W.W.," as published in this number call the group an organization of French- and Flemish-speaking workers. The 4-page issue is completely in French. It contains an essay on the international association of textile manufacturers and its machinations, on the IWW, on Louisiana woodworkers' strikes, on the international trade-union conference at Budapest and news of locals.

Source: Melvin Dubofsky, We Shall Be All: A History of the Industrial Workers of the World, (Chicago, 1969) p. 234.

GERMINAL   IL Chicago   1922-1923

Title trans.:		First issue:	1922
Subtitle:	see below	Last issue:	1923?
Add. lang.:		Vols. (nos.):	
First editor:	A. Champion	Frequency:	
First publ.:	Fédération Socialiste de Langue	Preservation:	
	Française des Etats-Unis		
Related pubs.:	c Le Socialist (Johnson City)	Supplements:	
Circulation:		Category:	socialist/
			anarchist

Depositories: Usa-NN(?)

According to the subtitle it was an "Organ of workers' education and for the emancipation of the French workers in the United States, published on the 10th of each month by the French-Speaking Socialist Federation of the United States."

Germinal is supposed to have succeeded Le Socialist, and it survived for several years in the form of French-language pages inserted in the Italian

Germinal is supposed to have succeeded *Le Socialist*, and it survived for several years in the form of French-language pages inserted in the Italian *Germinal*, *Quindicinale Anarchico*, (see Italian section).

LE GRELOT		LA New Orleans	1846
Title trans.:	The Bell	*First issue:*	Jl 1846
Subtitle:	Journal Politique et Littéraire	*Last issue:*	1846
Add. lang.:		*Vols. (nos.):*	
First editor:		*Frequency:*	
First publ.:		*Preservation:*	sw
Related pubs.:		*Supplements:*	
Circulation:		*Category:*	early socialist

Depositories: Usa-LNT (3 Jl 1846)

The paper appeared semiweekly on Thursday and Saturday. According to Tinker, from whom the above information is taken, it was founded in July 1846 and published by an association of workers, probably printers.
Source: Tinker.

LE JOURNAL DE L'ILLINOIS		IL Chicago	1857-1864
Title trans.:	Illinois Journal	*First issue:*	1857
Subtitle:		*Last issue:*	1864
Add. lang.:		*Vols. (nos.):*	
First editor:	Claude Petit	*Frequency:*	
First publ.:	Alexandre Grandpré	*Preservation:*	7
Related pubs.:		*Supplements:*	
Circulation:		*Category:*	republican/ labor

Depositories:

Claude Petit was a political exile from France whose editorials were anticlerical in tone and denounced the regime of Louis-Napoleon, even going so far as to approve Orsini's attempt on the Emperor's life.

LE LIBERTAIRE	NY New York	1858-1861

Title trans.:	The Libertarian	*First issue:*	5 Je 1858
Subtitle:	Journal du Mouvement Social	*Last issue:*	4 F 1861
Add. lang.:		*Vols. (nos.):*	
First editor:	Joseph Déjacque	*Frequency:*	ir, m
First publ.:	Joseph Déjacque	*Preservation:*	2
Related pubs.:		*Supplements:*	
Circulation:		*Category:*	early socialist

Depositories: Usa-NN ([1858], 1859-61)

Déjacque (1822-64) was converted to communist anarchism after the Revolution of 1848. Banished and transported briefly after the June days, he fled to London in 1851 to avoid serving a prison sentence provoked by the publication of his poems, *Les Lazaréennes*. Maitron, *Dictionnaire Biographique du Mouvement Ouvrier Français*, first series, 1789-1864, volume 2, pp. 38-39, makes no mention of his activity in the United States, but see M. Prévost et al., (eds), *Dictionnaire de Biographie Française*, X (1965), p. 574.

He coined the neologism "libertaire," and stated his creed in the third issue of his newspaper (the earliest number we have seen): against the family, property, government and religion, all of them considered to be the products of the childhood of humanity, and for anarchy. He was, of course, an abolitionist, who, at the beginning of the Secession Crisis, wrote that it would be better to let the Union perish, if it could not stand the liberation of the blacks and the equality of man. (No. 27, p. 3). At the same time, he insisted on the necessity of black-white solidarity, whose expression, he said, the bourgeoisie sought to inhibit, in order to divide and conquer.

Déjacque attributed the failure of 1848 (and no doubt his own personal failure as well, for he had taken up arms in the June days much against his will) to a lack of principled struggle and at the same time he expressed many of the habitual themes of 1848: hatred of the Jesuits, belief in conspiracies, romanticizing of *le révolté* (in the person of the bandit of the 1750s, Mandrin). Less commonly, he was a feminist who denounced the Icarians as reactionaries on the twin grounds of their cult of authority and of their refusal to accept the equality of women. (No. 12)

Déjacque several times announced his intention to cease publication of *Le Libertaire*, and finally did so with number 27, not wishing, as he said, to enter into competition with the "nouvel organe révolutionnaire" *Le Revendicateur* (38 Wooster St., New York City), the publication of whose first two numbers he announced at that time. Unfortunately, we have found no trace of this publication.

Déjacque returned to Europe, first to London, then to Paris, where he died in 1864.

Source: J. Déjacque, *La Question Révolutionnaire* (Paris, 1970), ed. Valentin Pélosse; V. Pélosse, "Joseph Déjacque et la creation du neologisme 'libertaire' en 1857," *Cahiers de l'Institut de Science Economique Appliquée*, Série S, no. 19 (1972), p. 2313; Nicole Riffault Perrot, *Le Libertaire* (Memoire de maitrise, under the direction of Prof. J. Droz, Université de Paris-I).

LE REVEIL DES MASSES	PA Newfoundland	1888-1890

Title trans.:	The Awakening of the Masses	*First issue:*	1888
Subtitle:	Bulletin International Mensuel	*Last issue:*	1890
Add. lang.:		*Vols. (nos.):*	
First editor:	Louis Goaziou	*Frequency:*	
First publ.:		*Preservation:*	3
Related pubs.:	s *Le Réveil des Mineurs*	*Supplements:*	
Circulation:		*Category:*	communist-anarchist

Depositories: Usa-NNC [1889-90]

The price of the paper was one cent an issue, twenty cents a year and the correspondence was to be addressed to Edward E. David, P.O. Box 93, Newfoundland, Wayne Co., PA.

No. 5 announced that *le groupe communiste-anarchiste* of Houtzdale, PA. met the second and last Sundays of every month *chez Lazare.*

In no. 7, Goaziou called for the anarchist revolution, which, he wrote, could only take place by force, since the bourgeoisie would not accept revolutionary election results and would always find "an endless number of ignorants and poor wretches who will defend their privileges."

The editorial of no. 10 was devoted to combatting anti-immigrant sentiment and noted that ethnic antagonisms were used to divide the proletariat. The irony of the cry "America for Americans" is underlined by a reference to the native American "who, for this cry, has paid with his live through your weapons."

Another issue of *Le Réveil des Masses. Organe Communiste Anarchiste* dated: 2nd year, no. 1 (June 1890) is in the same collection. It gives the place of publication as 27 South Fifth Avenue, New York, and looks to be, in fact, the same publication. It, too, spoke of insurrection and violence as the only way to revolutionary change, "la fin justifie les moyens" [the end justifies the means].

LE REVEIL DES MINEURS	PA Hastings	1890-1893

Title trans.:	The Awakening of the Miners	*First issue:*	1890
Subtitle:	Organe des Travailleurs de Langue Française de l'Amérique	*Last issue:*	1893
Add. lang.:		*Vols. (nos.):*	
First editor:	Louis Goaziou	*Frequency:*	
First publ.:		*Preservation:*	3
Related pubs.:	c *Le Réveil des Masses* s *L'Ami des Ouvriers*	*Supplements:*	
Circulation:		*Category:*	

Depositories: Usa-NNC [1890-93]

According to the subtitle it was "The organ of French- speaking workers in America." Volume I, no. 2 bore the subtitle: We demand the right to a life free from want." No. 4 of the second year contained a dual injunction on the mast-head: "From each according to his abilities, to each according to his needs. Well-being for all." And "Freedom will be but a vain word as long as the minor-ity will have to conform to the wishes of the majority."

LE REVEIL DES PEUPLES	LA New Orleans	1852

Title trans.:	The Awakening of the Peoples	*First issue:*	1852
Subtitle:	Organe des Emigrants et de la Democratie Sociale et Universelle	*Last issue:*	1852
Add. lang.:		*Vols. (nos.):*	
First editor:		*Frequency:*	w
First publ.:	L. Caboche, G. Vidal	*Preservation:*	7 ?
Related pubs.:		*Supplements:*	
Circulation:		*Category:*	early socialist

Depositories:

According to the subtitle it was the "Organ of emigrants and of social and universal democracy." Tinker claims that the paper was published in "the interests of political exiles from France."

Neither Caboche nor Vidal is mentioned in Maitron, *Dictionnaire Biographique.*

A Louis-Claude-Firmin Caboche (1791-1863) is mentioned as a refugee of the Revolution of 1830 in M. Prévost et al., *Dictionnaire de Biographie Française*, VII (Paris, 1956), p. 767. He was associated with the general daily newspaper *L'Abeille* of New Orleans for a number of years. We are unable to ascertain if this is the same person who edited *Le Réveil.*

LE SOCIALISTE	NY New York	1869-1873

Title trans.:	The Socialist	*First issue:*	15 N 1869
Subtitle:		*Last issue:*	11 Mr 1873
Add. lang.:		*Vols. (nos.):*	1-4(31)
First editor:	Les Sociétés revolutionnaires et internationales	*Frequency:*	
First publ.:		*Preservation:*	1
Related pubs.:		*Supplements:*	
Circulation:		*Category:*	labor

Depositories: Usa-WHi (1,m)

So far no further information could be obtained.

LE SOCIALISTE	IL Johnson City	1916-1921

		First issue:	1916
Title trans.:		*First issue:*	1916
Subtitle:		*Last issue:*	1921
Add. lang.:		*Vols. (nos.):*	
First editor:		*Frequency:*	
First publ..		*Preservation:*	
Related pubs.:	s *Germinal*	*Supplements:*	
Circulation:		*Category:*	

Depositories: Usa-WHi (?)

So far no further information could be obtained.

LA TRIBUNE DE LA NOUVELLE ORLEANS	LA New Orleans	1864-1870

Title trans.:	Tribune of New Orleans	*First issue:*	21 Jl 1864
Subtitle:		*Last issue:*	1870
Add. lang..	English	*Vols. (nos.):*	
First editor:	Charles J. Dalloz	*Frequency:*	tr, w
First publ..		*Preservation:*	
Related pubs.:	c *L'Union*	*Supplements:*	
Circulation:		*Category:*	black republican

Depositories:

This was a bilingual paper published three times a week for the first 32 issues (21 July-14 October 1864), then daily until May 1869, when it became a weekly, published on Saturdays.

Edited by Charles J. Dalloz (pseud. Jean Charles Honzeau, exiled Belgian republican and astronomer), with the assistance of Paul Trevigne.

The paper was the official organ of the Republican Party in Louisiana, and adopted as its slogan: "Universal Suffrage, Equal Rights before the Law."

L'UNION	LA New Orleans	1862-1864

Title trans.:		*First issue:*	1862
Subtitle:	Journal Politique, Littéraire, et Progressiste	*Last issue:*	1864
Add. lang.:	English	*Vols. (nos.):*	
First editor:	Paul Trévigne, Frank F. Barclay	*Frequency:*	sw
First publ.:		*Preservation:*	4
Related pubs.:	s *La Tibune de la Nouvelle Orléans*	*Supplements:*	
Circulation:		*Category:*	black republican

Depositories: Usa-WHi [1862-64]; Usa-MWA (14 Jl 1863); Usa-LNT [1863]

The paper was founded by Dr. Louis C. Roudanez, a medical doctor originally from Guadeloupe, and edited by Paul Trevigne, although the name of a white man, Frank F. Barclay, was given as editor for, says Tinker, "diplomatic reasons." The paper was the organ of black, radical republicanism.

When certain of his associates whithdrew because of threats to kill the editor and burn the press, Roudanez purchased the equipment and founded a new paper, *La Tribune de la Nouvelle Orléans*.

L'UNION DES TRAVAILLEURS	PA Charleroi	1901-1916

Title trans.:	The Union of the Workers	*First issue:*	Mr 1901
Subtitle:		*Last issue:*	S 1916
Add. lang.:		*Vols. (nos.):*	
First editor:	Louis Goaziou	*Frequency:*	
First publ.:		*Preservation:*	1
Related pubs.:		*Supplements:*	
Circulation:		*Category:*	labor

Depositories: Usa-WHi (1,m)

So far no further information could be obtained.

Appendix: Icarian Newspapers

Colonie Icarienne
IL Nauvoo, 19 July-27 December 1854

The paper was published as a weekly, its price was $ 1.50 per year. It was edited by M. E. Cabet and was the official organ of the community founded at Nauvoo in 1850.

Depositories: Usa-WHi (1); Usa-IHi; Usa-NN

La Revue Icarienne
IL Nauvoo, 1855-1856.

A split developed among the settlers in the Nauvoo community, a majority of whom rejected Cabet's authority in 1856. Cabet removed to St. Louis, where he died shortly afterwards. A group of his disciples then published:

La Nouvelle Revue Icarienne
MO St. Louis, 1857- ?

Depositories: Usa-InU (nos. 1-31, 33-43)

The settlers at Nauvoo gave up their colony in 1856 and went to Adams Co., Iowa, to join a vanguard group that had moved there in 1853. This group published

La Revue Icarienne
IO Corning, 1878 ?

The dating of this publication is somewhat confusing. The Union List of Serials puts vol. X, no. 2 in 1878. But the New York Public Library and the Balch Institute for Ethnic Studies, Philadelphia, both of which have runs for 1878- 1888, list 1878 as volume I.

Depositories: Usa-NN (1878-88); <Usa-PPBI (1878-88)

But all manner of divisions continued to plague the Icarians, each one giving rise to a new publication. Among them were:

La Jeune Icarie. Organe du Communisme Progressif
IO Corning, 1878-1883

Depositories: Usa-NN (1)

and

Le Communiste Libertaire
IO Corning, 1880-1882
Editor: Emile Péron

Depositories: Usa-NN (1)

To the above may be added:

L'Observateur, feuille communiste non-séparatiste
Editor: J.-B. Géerard.

The paper was probably published during the crisis of 1855-56, which caused Cabet to leave the colony he had founded at Nauvoo. J.-B. Gérard left the colony in 1862. No trace of this paper has been found in public collections.

L'Etoile du Kansas

Founded in Kansas in 1867 by Jules Leroux père, brother of Pierre Leroux and former deputy (1849). No copies found.

Superceded by:

L'Etoile du Kansas et de l'Iowa
IO Corning, 1873-1880, 51 numbers

Edited by Jules Leroux fils, who continued his father's work, but left the Iowa colony in 1878.

Depositories: Usa-NHi [1876-80]

Superceded by:

L'Etoile des Pauvres et des Souffrants
CA St. Helena, January 1881-October 1883, 23 numbers

Depositories: Usa-CU [1883]; Usa-WHi [1881-83]

For more information about the Icarian publications, see A.J.M. Prévos, "Histoire et Ethnographie d'un groupe de communistes utopistes français dans l'Etat d'Iowa au dix-neuvième siècle. Le Cas des Icariens du Comté d'Adams dans la seconde moitié du siécle: 1858-1898," unpubl. dissertation for the doctorat 'du troisième cycle' (forthcoming, Université de Paris-VIII Vincennes/ St. Denis, 1986).

Title Index

Le Réveil des Peuples
La Revue Icarienne (Nauvoo)
　See Appendix.
La Revue Icarienne (Corning)
　See Appendix.
Le Revendicateur
　See *Le Libertaire*.
St. Landry Clarion
　See *Le Clarion*.
Le Socialiste (New York)
Le Socialiste (Johnson City)
　See also *Germinal*.
La Tribune de la Nouvelle Orléans
　See also *L'Union*.
L'Union
　See also *La Tribune de la Nouvelle Orléans*.
L'Union des Travailleurs

Place Index

United States

ILLINOIS
Chicago
  L'Amérique
  Germinal
  Le Journal de l'Illinois

Johnson City
  Le Socialiste

LOUISIANA
New Orleans
  The Crusader
  Le Grelot
  Le Réveil des Peuples
  La Tribune de la Nouvelle Orléans
  L'Union

Opelousas
  Le Clarion

St. Martinville
  L'Echo

MASSACHUSSETS
Lawrence
  L'Emancipation

NEW YORK
New York
  Bulletin de L'Union Républicaine de Langue Française
  Le Libertaire
  Le Socialiste

PENNSYLVANIA
Charleroi
  L'Union des Travailleurs

Hastings
  L'Ami des Ouvriers
  Le Réveil des Mineurs

Newfoundland
  Le Réveil des Masses

Chronological Index

1840   1850   1860   1870   1880   1890   1900   1910   1920
0123456789012345678901234567890123456789012345678901234567890123

Le Grelot	LA New Orleans
Le Reveil des Peuple	LA New Orleans
Le Journal de l'Illi	IL Chicago
Le Libertaire	NY New York
L'Union	LA New Orleans
La Tribune	LA New Orleans
L'Echo	LA St. Martinville
Le Socialist	NY New York
Bulletin de L'Union	NY New York
L'Amerique	IL Chicago
La Commune	LA New Orleans
Le Reveil des Masses	PA Newfoundland
Le Reveil des Mineur	PA Hastings
The Crusader	LA New Orleans
Le Clarion	LA Opelousas
L'Ami des Ouvriers	PA Hastings
L'Union des Travaill	PA Charleroi
L'Emancipation	MA Lawrence
Le Socialist	IL Johnson City
Germinal	IL Chicago

308

German-Speaking Peoples

Language

German

Area covered

Germany, Austria and German-speaking areas

Compiled by

Anne Spier

University of Bremen

Prefatory Remarks and Acknowledgements

This bibliography is based mainly on earlier bibliographies by Arndt/Olson, Eberlein and Knoche together with much additional information gleaned from the *Buchdrucker-Zeitung*, the organ of the German-American printers' union. While many periodicals of the years before the Civil War have been lost, information about the Fortyeighters is available in abundance. Considerably less is known about trade-union, socialist and anarchist editors of the post-Civil War period. A cursory reading of some of this period's newspapers has yielded a considerable amount of bibliographic data. As yet no systematic analysis of this press has been possible because of the widely dispersed archival holdings, but the library of the John F. Kennedy Institute for North American Studies (Freie Universität Berlin, West Berlin) has recently begun to build up a comprehensive microfilm collection of all German-language labor periodicals that are still available. (For information write to the Chief Librarian, John F. Kennedy Institute, Freie Universität Berlin, Lansstr. 5-9, D-1000 Berlin-West 33.)

Because of their role in helping us to understand the development of the German-American labor press additional information about the German-American printers' union (Deutsch-Amerikanische Typographia) and Fortyeighter and working-class editors has been included in Appendices 1 and 2. These editors are marked with an asterisk in the descriptions. Four appendices list titles which have been omitted from the bibliography: newspapers and broadsheets of the Deutsch-Amerikanische Typographia (App. 3) - these were usually issued irregularly, particularly on the occasion of labor disputes; periodicals which temporarily adopted a pro-labor viewpoint (App. 4); English-language anti-Nazi publications by German exiles (App. 5); periodicals with German or German-sounding titles assumed to be German-American labor periodicals, but which were either not labor or not written in German (App. 6). A detailed title index will help the reader to find his/her way through the various cross references. Because of the superficial similarity of the English and German languages we have provided translations only where this is absolutely necessary.

A number of institutions and individuals have assisted me in the preparation of this volume. The preparatory work was done at the University of Bremen by Dirk Hoerder and Thomas Weber. The considerate assistance of the staff of the Library of the John F. Kennedy Institute in Berlin, especially Dr. Hans Kolligs, Mrs. Ilse Repplinger and Mr. John Muirhead expedited my use of the sources under their care. I am also deeply indebted to the technical staff of the John F. Kennedy Institute, Mr. Karge and his colleagues, for their untiring support and friendliness. Thanks must also go to Mr. Friedemann and the staff of the Institut für Geschichte der Arbeiterbewegung in Bochum and to the staff of the Deutsche Bibliothek in Frankfurt/Main. Hans-Joachim Kämmer has made an important contribution by designing and drawing the diagrams and charts. Ronald Creagh, Bruce C. Nelson, Sally Miller, Hartmut Keil, Ralf Wagner and especially Carol Poore offered advice at different stages of the work and R. Cazden even shared his research with me. For the newspapers which appeared between 1933 and 1945 I benefitted greatly from the competent advice of Dr. Liselotte Maas. For her efficient and patient help with the technical side of the preparation I owe thanks to Dorothea Westphal. Special thanks go to Annelie Edelmann, Bettina Goldberg and Christiane Harzig for their friendly and critical advice. For his scholarly help and his encouragement in every way during the last two years I would like to thank in particular Lester J. Mazor.

Depositories

Austria

AuN	Österreichische Nationalbibliothek [Austrian National Library], Vienna.

Canada

Cdn-OONL	National Library, Bibliotheque National, Ottawa, O.
Cdn-MWUC	University of Winnipeg, M.
Cdn-OTP	Toronto Public Library, Toronto, O.

Federal Republic of Germany

D-12	Bayerische Staatsbibliothek, München.
D-16	Universitätsbibliothek, Heidelberg.
D-19/1501	Universitätsbibliothek, Amerika Institut, München.
D-46	Staats- und Universitätsbibliothek, Bremen.
D-188/144	John F. Kennedy Institut, Freie Universität, Berlin.
D-212	Institut für Auslandsbeziehungen [Institute for Foreign Relations], Stuttgart.
D-292	Deutsche Bibliothek, Frankfurt.
<D-A	Internationales Zeitungsmuseum [International Newspaper Museum] der Stadt Aachen.
D-B 815	Institut für Publizistik [Institut for Journalism], Freie Universität, Berlin.
D-Bm 41/IGA	Institut der Geschichte der Arbeiterbewegung [Institute for the History of the Labor Movement] Ruhruniversität, Bochum.
D-N1	Germanisches Nationalmuseum, Bibliothek [Germanic National Museum, Library], Nürnberg.

German Democratic Republic

DDR-LDB	Deutsche Bibliothek, Leipzig.
DDR-ULB	Universitäts- und Landesbibliothek, Halle.
DDR-IML	Institut für Marxismus-Leninismus, Berlin.

Great Britain

Gb-BM	British Museum, London.

Netherlands

Nl-IISG	Internationaal Institut voor Soziale Geschiedenis [International Institute für Social History], Amsterdam.

United States

Usa-CFlS	California State University, Library, Fullerton, CA.
Usa-CSt	Stanford University, Libraries, Stanford, CA.
Usa-CU	University of Californiy, Berkeley, CA.
Usa-Ct	Connecticut State Library, Hartford, CT.
Usa-CtY	Yale University, Library, New Haven, CT.
Usa-DL	U.S. Department of Labor, Library, Washington, DC.
Usa-DLC	United States Library of Congress, Washington, DC.
Usa-HU	University of Hawaii, Honolulu, HI.
Usa-ICHi	Chicago Historical Society, Chicago, IL.
Usa-ICJ	John Crerar Library, Chicago, IL.
Usa-ICMW	Midwestern Interlibrary Center, Chicago, IL.
Usa-ICN	Newberry Library, Chicago, IL.
Usa-ICRL	Center for Research Libraries, Chicago, IL.
Usa-ICU	University of Chicago, Chicago, IL.
Usa-IHi	Illinois State Historical Library, Springfield, IL.
Usa-IU	University of Illinois, Library, Urbana-Champaign, IL.
Usa-InI	County Public Library, Indianapolis-Marion, IN.
Usa-InU	Indiana University, Bloomington, IN.
Usa-KHi	Kansas State Historical Society, Topeka, KS.
<§Usa-KyLC	Robert Cazden, University of Kentucky, College of Library Science, Lexington, KY, private collection.
Usa-KyU	University of Kentucky, Lexington, KY.
Usa-MB	Boston Public Library, Boston, MA.
Usa-MH-PA	Harvard University, Littauer Library of the Kennedy School of Government, Cambridge, MA.
Usa-MWA	American Antiquarian Society, Worcester, MA.
<§Usa-MWKJA	Karl J.R. Arndt, Clark University, Worcester, MA. Private collection, U.S. part donated to Usa-MWA.
Usa-MdBJ	Johns Hopkins University, Library, Baltimore, MD.
Usa-MdBZ	Archives of Zion's Church, Baltimore, MD.
Usa-MiU	University of Michigan, Libraries, Ann Arbor, MI.
Usa-MnHi	Minnesota Historical Society, St.Paul, MI.
Usa-MoS	St.Louis Public Library, St.Louis, MO.
<§Usa-MoSHo	G.A. Hoehn, St. Louis. Privat collection, see MoS.
<§Usa-NFBA	Private Collection of F.B. Adams,(according to Obermann) New York, NY.
Usa-NIC	Cornell University, Libraries, Ithaca, NY.
Usa-NHi	New York Historical Society, New York, NY.
Usa-NN	New York Public Library, New York, NY.
Usa-NNC	Columbia University, Libraries, New York, NY.
Usa-NNRa	Rand School of Social Science, New York, NY.
Usa-NbHi	Nebraska State Historical Society, Lincoln, NB.

Usa-OC	Public Library of Cincinnati and Hamilton County, Cincinnati, OH.
Usa-OCAJ	American Jewish Periodical Center, Jewish Institute of Religion, Hebrew Union College, Cincinnati, OH.
Usa-OCHi	Historical and Philosophical Society of Ohio, Library, Cincinnati, OH.
Usa-OClWHi	Western Reserve Historical Society, Cleveland, OH.
Usa-OHi	Ohio State Historical Society, Columbus, OH.
<Usa-PPBI	Emily C.Balch Insitute for Ethnic Studies, Philadelphia, PA.
Usa-PPG	German Society of Pennsylvania, Philadelphia, PA.
Usa-PPiU	University of Pittsburgh, Pittsburgh, PA.
Usa-Tx	Texas State Library and Historical Commission, Austin, TX.
Usa-TxU	University of Texas, Libraries, Austin, TX.
Usa-WHi	State Historical Society of Wisconsin, Madison, WI.
Usa-WM	Milwaukee Public Library, Milwaukee, WI.
Usa-WMCHi	Milwaukee County Historical Society, Milwaukee, WI.
Usa-WU	University of Wisconsin, Madison, WI.

Introduction

German Immigration to North America

Next to the Irish the Germans constitute the largest immigrant group in the United States.[1] Throughout the nineteenth century, because of their sheer number, their presence was felt in every aspect of economic and social life. Many of them settled in rural areas and became farmers but the great majority, including millions of artisans and workers, began a new life in the cities. Here they found employment in industry and commerce, built up class-differentiated ethnic communities and developed an equally class-differentiated German-American culture. The German-American labor press is one of the most vibrant expressions of this culture.

The history of German emigration to the United States extends over three centuries. Immigration by Germans in colonial times involved an estimated total of 65,000 to 100,000 people. From the mid-1830s to the mid-1840s the number of immigrants increased to a yearly average of 20,000 (see Figure 1). The economic crisis of 1846/47 and the failed Revolution of 1848 triggered the first wave of mass emigration. At its peak in 1854 almost 220,000 Germans left their country. Though many came with the intention of returning, in this phase the migration was primarily one involving peasants and small, self-employed artisans from southern Germany who wanted to settle. After a decline, probably caused by the Civil War the second wave of emigration in 1866-73 brought more than a million Germans to America. During the years 1873-1879, the first and most violent phase of the Long Depression (1873-95), which hit the German and American economies alike, the emigration figures decreased drastically. But in 1878/79 the third and largest wave of emigration began. It reached its peak in 1882 with more than 250,000 immigrants and continued until the beginning of the 'panic of 1893.' The second and third emigration waves are characterized by an increased participation of landless peasants from northeastern Germany, who came as individuals and tended to seek work in the trades of industry. At the turn of the century indigenous German industry had developed to such a degree that surplus labor could be absorbed within Germany itself. Overseas emigration lost importance in comparison with internal migration. After the break caused by World War One the immigration figures climbed significantly again in 1924, a time of political and economic instability in Germany, only to fall again precipitously during the Great Depression.

At the beginning of the 1930s German immigration declined almost to zero level, but then reached a new peak with the immigration of political exiles and Jewish refugees in 1939. After World War Two immigration figures rose again sharply, but since 1970 less than 10,000 Germans have come to the United States per year.[2] Only after the 1920s can we talk about a significant mass migration of Germans to Canada when its proportion of the total immigration reached about 10 percent. During the war years it came to an almost complete halt with only 600 Germans entering the country in 1945. However from 1951 to 1956 an average of about 30,000 people (about 20 percent) left war-torn Germany behind them to seek their fortune in Canada. Most of them settled in the larger cities of the East.[3] Thus we cannot speak of a sizable German-Canadian population until the 1950s.

Figure 1   German Migration to the United States (U.S. gross figures)

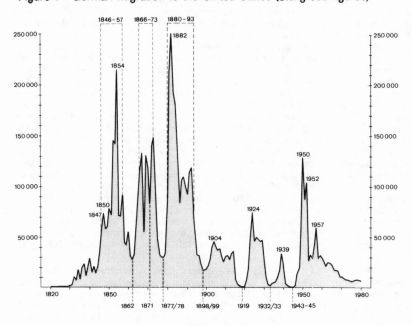

Development and Structure of the German-Language Labor Press

The German-language press is the oldest and, with a total of approximately 5000 newspapers also the largest foreign-language press in the United States. Its history began with the *Philadelphische Zeitung* [Philadelphia Journal] published in 1732 by Benjamin Franklin. In the following century the majority of German-language publications were of a religious nature. In ante-bellum times the number of German-American newspapers increased rapidly from about 40 in 1840 to about 250 in 1860. The flowering of the German-American press began around 1870 and it reached its peak in 1892-94 with more than 790 publications. In accordance with the heterogeneous social, political, religious and regional origins and convictions of the German immigrants, their press was very varied in its nature. Along with bourgeois dailies, religious, socialist and labor newspapers, there were organs of diverse clubs and occupational groups, humorous, literary and historical magazines as well as newspapers with local news from particular regions of Germany. With the end of mass immigration after 1893 a slow, but steady decline of the German-American press set in, (1900: 750 publications, 1905: 702, 1910: 634, 1915: 533) which was accelerated by the anti-German attitudes during World War One. In 1970 about 40 German-language newspapers still existed in the United States.[4]

The development of the German-American labor press is closely related to political emigration to the United States. Three groups can be distinguished: a) the refugees of the failed Revolution of 1848; b) the socialists and anarchists expelled from Germany under the antisocialist law between 1878 and 1890; c) the emigré opponents of Nazism between 1933 and 1945. Although the political emigrants made up a numerically insignificant proportion of the total emigration, they played the decisive role in the development of the socialist and the labor press, since many, if not most of its publishers and editors came from their ranks. Fortyeighters and early socialists gave a distinctive character to the early labor and radical press (phase 1: 1844-69). Socialist, anarchist and union publications mark phase 2, from 1870 to 1902. Phase 3, 1903-29, is characterized by the consolidation of the existing press but also by the decline in the number of new immigrants and new periodicals. Finally phase 4, 1930-45, involves the rise of a radical antifascist and antiwar press (See Figure 2).

From the beginning the labor press was concentrated in centers of industrial development and German immigration. They were to remain the centers of labor and left German publishing activities in the United States. (See Figure 3). In the 1840s nine out of thirteen periodicals were published in four middle Atlantic seaboard cities (New York, Newark, Philadelphia, Baltimore) and during the 1850s and 60s these cities maintained their dominance. Following the settlement pattern of German immigrants a second important publishing area began to emerge in the Northeast Central states: ten cities and settlements from Milwaukee to St. Louis in the Midwest and from Pittsburgh to Cleveland in the East accounted for another nineteen publications. During phase 2, only seven out of 123 new periodicals were published outside the two main areas,[5] which practically merged, since publications also appeared in Syracuse, Erie and McKeesport. To the west, outposts of publishing included Omaha and Kansas City. The German-American labor movement remained tied to the commercial and industrial areas of the Middle Atlantic and East North Central areas. In phase 3 this trend toward concentration continued. By the twenties newspapers were published in three Eastern, three North Central and two Southern cities. During phase 4, only Chicago and New York were left.

Figure 2   Number of German-American Labor Periodicals Founded by Years

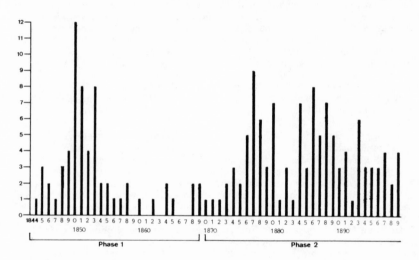

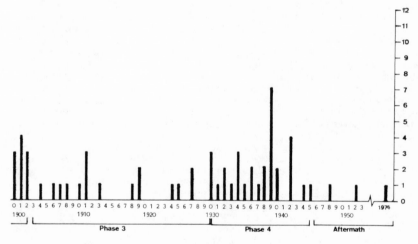

Figure 3   Places of Publication of German-American Labor Periodicals

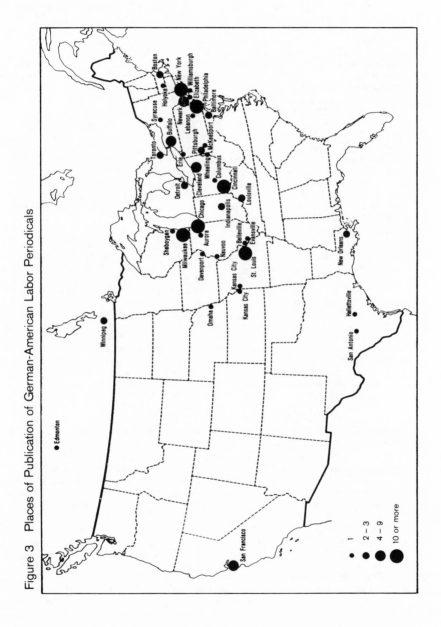

Phase 1 included the publications of radical artisans, the Fortyeighters, the first Marxists arriving in the United States and a number of local workingmen's organizations. Active participation in the Civil War by many politically active Germans resulted in a decrease in the number of periodical publications during the 1860s. From 1844 to 1869 a total of sixty-three periodicals are listed here. This includes the press of Fortyeighters and Freethinkers (18), advocates of utopian communism (3), and middle-class reformers (2) addressed to workers. The rest[6] were issued by workers' clubs (16), advocated early socialist, social-democratic, socialist (including freethought sympathies, gymnastics club affiliation or IWA support) and general labor principles (24). A number of the Fortyeighter publications fall into the category of "personal journalism," papers reflecting the views and personalities of their editors.

Many of the artisans who emigrated in the 1840s and 50s had already been organized in workers' clubs in Germany.[7] Some of them supported social ideas originating in utopian communism (Charles Fourier, Robert Owen, Etienne Cabet).[8] Others were influenced by the Jacobin tradition of the French Revolution.[9] The first German-American labor newspaper was George Dietz's *Der Adoptivbürger* [The Adoptive Citizen] which appeared in 1845. The most important exponents of the early German-American labor movement were Hermann Kriege (*Der Volkstribun* [The People's Tribune], 1850) and Wilhelm Weitling (*Republik der Arbeiter* [The Republic of Workers], 1850-55).[10] (Categories: "labor," "workers' club," "utopian communist").

After the failure first of the 1830 uprisings and more importantly of the 1848 Revolution in several German states many intellectuals, predominantly of bourgeois background emigrated to the United States as political refugees. A number of them had already published and/or edited newspapers in their home country. The so-called Fortyeighters were not a homogeneous group, neither in respect of their political views brought from Germany nor in respect of the development they underwent in America. Generally it can be said that they supported the abolition of feudal and clerical power structures, and demanded political equality and religious freedom for all. Although the newspapers they published in America had a progressive tendency, most of them were concerned with liberal reforms rather than with the working class. Prominent editors of this group were: Fritz and Mathilde Anneke (*Newarker Zeitung* [Newark Journal], 1849, and others), Ludwig Fenner von Fenneberg (*Die Arbeiterzeitung* [Labor News], 1851-52, and others), Gustav Struve (*Die Sociale Republik*, 1858-60), Gottfried Theodor Kellner (*Die Reform*, 1853-54) and Karl Heinzen (*Der Pionier*, 1854-79).[11] Only the more radical periodicals, the first dating from 1844, are included here. (Categories: "radical Fortyeighter," "reform," "freethought").

Some of the German immigrants were labor leaders who had been active in Germany, some of whom shared the ideas of Marx and Engels. Among them was Joseph Weydemeyer (*Die Revolution*, 1852), who in the 1850s became the foremost theorist and propagandist of the Marxist socialist movement among the German workers in America.[12] (Categories: "early socialist," "social-democratic," "socialist").

Another important group for the spreading of socialist ideas especially during the 1850s were the German Turnvereine (gymnastics clubs) which traced their ideas back to Friedrich Ludwig Jahn (1778-1852). Up to the prohibition of the Gymnasts Movement in Germany in 1819 (Karlsbad decrees) its members came mainly from the nationally oriented well-educated (progressive) middle class. By the time of the Revolution of 1848 skilled journeymen and master artisans made up the core of the movement. In the United States a large number of local clubs were formed after 1848 under the leadership of refugees and a decided shift to the moderate left had taken place by 1851 when the national organization was renamed "Sozialistischer Turnverein." After that date a number of splits occurred, some of them over the question of slavery, most of them, however, due to intrigues and misunderstandings. Thus the socialist *Turnzeitung* [Gymnasts News], and the *Turn-Blatt* [Gymnasts Journal], the organ of the opposing eastern faction had no major differences in their platforms. In 1865 differences were set .aside and the "Nordamerikanischer Turnerbund" became the unifying organization. During the 1870s and 1880s "Lehr- und Wehrvereine" [Education and Defense Associations] began to emerge when the repression of the labor movement induced a section of the working classes to opt for armed resistance. But the movement as a whole tended more and more toward conservatism.[13] (Category: "socialist gymnasts").

German-American socialists and liberals and their newspapers were ardent supporters of the Abolition movement in the ante-bellum period - with the exception of the New York paper *Der Arbeiter* [The Worker] - and during the Civil War they sided with the North. Many Fortyeighters, socialists and members of the Turnvereine, some of whom had functioned as editors, became soldiers in the Union army. This was one reason why during the war many newspapers were discontinued and hardly any new ones appeared.

Phase 2, the most prolific period of the German-American labor press, began in the 1870s and lasted into the early years of the new century. 123 new periodicals were established during the three decades. Of these, one - the *Amerikanische Turnzeitung* [American Gymnasts' News] - was a radical democratic, almost socialist periodical and another - the *Freidenker* [Freethinker] - freethought in nature. The two papers were closely related. Local and general labor periodicals accounted for 17 publications, socialist (16), Workingmen's Party (6) and Socialist Labor Party publications (15) for another 37 publications. Later during this phase the social-democratic, municipal socialism and Socialist Party press made its debut with 7 publications. Temporarily the anarchist press (21) was influential, and throughout the period the trade-union periodicals (30) achieved impact and continuity.[14] The different political and organizational leanings of the press will be discussed below.

The influence of early socialism and utopian communism was on the wane. Workers' clubs on a city basis were replaced by organizations of more continuity and broader influence. Socialist ideas began to play a larger role,[15] especially among German immigrant workers, and, to a lesser extent, also among the immigrant workers of other nationalities (e.g. French and Czech)[16] as well as among those born in the United States. Some local groups joined the First International (or IWA - International Workingmen's Association), which had been founded in London by Karl Marx and others in 1864. In 1872 about 30 sections existed in the United States with a total of about 5000 members. When in the same year the followers of Marx (socialists) and Bakunin (anarchists) split, the seat of the General Council of the IWA was transferred to New York. Here, Friedrich Sorge, a loyal follower of Marx, had built up a strong local section mainly composed of German socialists since the end of the 1860s. The IWA had German-language organs in San Francisco, New York, and Milwaukee.[17]

Table 1: Periodicals related to the International Workingmen's Association		
Abendpost	CA San Francisco	1868-?
Arbeiter-Union	NY New York	1868-1870
Arbeiter-Zeitung	NY New York	1873-1875
Der Socialist	WI Milwaukee	1875-1818

The San Francisco *Abendpost* [Evening Post] linked the development of international socialists with the internationalism of the bourgeois Revolutionaries of 1848. Former Fortyeighters headed the San Francisco branch of the IWA. The *Arbeiter-Union* [Workers' Union] developed from a German-American workers' club paper to IWA-support under the influence of another Fortyeighter, Adolf Douai. The *Socialist* was published under continuing financial difficulties by Section 1, Milwaukee IWA and printed by various cooperative printing associations, but it existed for less than three years. Like many other German-American socialist institutions, the *Arbeiter-Zeitung* [Labor News] was plagued by splits into rival factions. However, it should be noted that the emphasis on German socialist sectarianism in the United States is misplaced. It stems from the undue attention paid to questions of theory and organizational details among labor historians (see "core press" below). During the next decade part of the German-American working class moved toward armed resistance (Lehr- und Wehrvereine) and anarchism. Under the leadership of Johann Most "Section 1," which retained its name even after the dissolution of the IWA, joined the anarchist International Working People's Association (IWPA).

The controversy about whether the labor movement should organize in trade unions as well as in political parties (Marx) or if it should concentrate exclusively on the political struggle (Lassalle) was also carried on in the United States and resulted in the establishment of political parties. The immediate successor to the remnants of the IWA and of numerous other local and regional labor organizations was the Workingmen's Party of the United States (WMPUS), founded in 1876 as a united labor party. In the same year it amalgamated with other socialist organizations and was renamed the Socialist Labor Party (SLP). Even though Lassalleans were influential in this party, the Marxist position of combining trade-union and political action was the accepted doctrine of the SLP. It had about 14 German-language organs, which were published by the relatively autonomous local sections of the party or by publishing societies. In this respect it differed from the contemporary social-democratic press in Germany, which was highly centralized. Many editors and publishers came from the ranks of journalistically experienced socialists who had to leave Germany after the enactment of the antisocialist law in 1878,[18] whereas others left for personal and economic reasons. Until 1890 when the antisocialist law was repealed the importing of foreign socialist newspapers into Germany was prohibited.[19] In this period the German police sent or hired agents to report on emigrants' political activities in the United States.[20]

Table 2: Periodicals of Social-Democratic and Socialist Leanings, 1874-1902 by Date and Place of Publication		
a) Workingmen's Party		
Arbeiter-Stimme	NY New York	1874-1878
Tribüne	NY Buffalo	1876-1878
Chicagoer Sozialist	IL Chicago	1876-1879
Emanzipator	WI Milwaukee	1877
Neue Zeit	KY Louisville	1877-1878
Vorwärts	NJ Newark	1877-1879
b) Socialist Labor Party		
Ohio Volkszeitung	OH Cincinnati	1876-1878
Arbeiter von Ohio	OH Cincinnati	1877-1879
Freiheitsbanner	OH Cincinnati	1878-1879
Illinois Volkszeitung	?	1884-1885
Volks-Anwalt(later SDP)	OH Cincinnati	1889-1898
Tageblatt	OH Cincinnati	1895-1896
Volksstimme des Westens	MO St. Louis	1877-1880
New Yorker Volkszeitung	NY New York	1878-1932
Bull. Social Labor Movem.	NY New York	1880
Sozialist	NY New York	1885-1892
Vorwärts	NY New York	1892-1894
Clevelander Volksfreund	OH Cleveland	1886-1918
Socialist. Arbeiter-Ztg.	OH Cleveland	1900-1908
Illinoiser Volkszeitung	IL Chicago	1893
Tageblatt	CA San Francisco	1893-1906
c) socialist, not (permanently) affiliated		
Arbeiterfreund	IL Chicago	1874
Chicagoer Arbeiter-Ztg.	IL Chicago	1876-1924
Volkszeitung	IL Chicago	1877
Hammer	LA New Orleans	1876
Tageblatt	PA Philadelphia	1877-1944
Vorwärts	WI Wilwaukee	1878-1879
Arbeiter-Zeitung	WI Milwaukee	1879
Milwaukee Journal	WI Milwaukee	1880-1881
Volkszeitung	WI Milwaukee	1890-1892
Wisconsin Vorwärts	WI Milwaukee	1893-1898
Laterne	NY Buffalo	1880
Buffaloer Arbeiter-Ztg.	NY Buffalo	1887-1918
Buffalo Herold	NY Buffalo	1897-1898
Herold	MI Detroit	1884-1918
Tageblatt	MO St. Louis	1888-1897
Volksblatt	WI Sheboygan	1895-1905
d) social-democratic		
Vorwärts	WI Milwaukee	1887-1932
Wahrheit	WI Milwaukee	1889-1910
Stimme des Volkes	WI Milwaukee	1900-
New Yorker Arbeiter-Ztg.	NY New York	1890-1902
Arbeiter-Zeitung	MO St. Louis	1898-1935
Neues Leben	IL Chicago	1902-1910
Habt Acht*	TX Hallettsville	1913-1919

*See als Volks-Anwalt (OH Cincinnati) which changed from SLP to SDP and SP sympathies. *Habt Acht* was the only specifically social-democratic newspaper which appeared after 1902.

The first publication of phase 2 was *Arbeiter-Stimme* [Workers' Voice, 1874], the organ of the Sozial-demokratische Arbeiterpartei von Nordamerika [Social-Democratic Workingmen's Party of North America], which became one of the founding organizations of the Workingmen's Party of the United States in 1876. Other city sections of the WMPUS also established papers, partly in response to the strikes of 1877. *Der Emanzipator* was the German-language edition of the official party organ, *The Emancipator*.

Many papers of the Socialist Labor Party were shortlived. Some reflect the views of different wings of the party. The *New Yorker Volkszeitung* [New York People's Journal], which existed for 54 years, is one of the most important sources for the history of the German-American labor movement.[21] The *Bulletin, Socialist, Vorwärts* [Forward] *and Clevelander Volksfreund* [Cleveland Friend of the People] were official organs of the party's headquarters. Most of these newspapers paid more attention to women's rights than the labor press in general. Some papers kept ties with the freethought movement (*Tageblatt*, San Francisco). On the one hand some Freethinkers moved to the left, cf. the connection between the *Amerikanische Turnzeitung* [American Gymnasts' News] and *Freidenker*. On the other hand the reform/social-democratic/socialist movements were a broad spectrum of progressive forces rather than distinct and clearly separable units.[22]

Among the non-affiliated socialist papers two are comparable with the *New Yorker Volkszeitung*: the *Chicagoer Arbeiter-Zeitung* [Chicago Labor News] and the Philadelphia *Tageblatt* [Daily News] were of similar importance for these two cities, the first illustrating the political shift of a considerable section of the German-American working class from the WMPUS to socialism and via anarchism back to social democracy. The *Buffaloer Arbeiter-Zeitung* and the Detroit *Herold* were equally important locally but of less national impact than the first three. In Milwaukee the socialist and social-democratic press as well as the organs of the city's federated trade unions are difficult to classify. Several of them had links with each other editorially and through their publishing offices (See Figure 4). In addition to their role at the national level ("Victor Berger for Congress"), from the 1890s on they were the best examples of advocacy of "municipal socialism." Their columns also reflect the cooperation between the Polish and German ethnic working-class communities. The *New Yorker Arbeiter-Zeitung* was the organ of the Social Democratic Party, which was founded in 1898 and merged into the Socialist Party in 1901.

During phase 3 of the German-American labor press from the turn of the century to the Great Depression only one social-democratic periodical was published. The social-democratic Socialist Party never established a major German-language periodical with the exception of the Milwaukee papers. By the time of the rivalry between the SP and the SLP after 1901, the majority of German immigrant workers had been integrated into the mainstream labor movement. During phase 4 the *Neue Volkszeitung* [New People's Journal] continued this strain of thought. The other two socialist publications of this period, *Sozialdemokratischer Informationsbrief* and *Austrian Labor Information* were exile publications.

In response to the governmental action against the working class after the 1877 strike and to the deteriorating social conditions in the industrial centers some SLP members advocated the immediate revolutionary reorganization of society, and defended the use of violence. In the 1870s the anarchist Social Revolutionary Clubs were founded, first in Chicago, then in Boston,

Figure 4: Genealogy of Milwaukee's Labor Periodicals

1875–1878	*Der Socialist* with *Milwaukee'r Leuchtkugeln* as Sunday supplement *Rothe Laterne* as annual supplement title variant, 1876–78 *Milwaukee's Socialist*	*Emanzipator* 1877 (WMP US)
	followed by	
1878–1879	*Vorwärts* (Milwaukee'r Socialist) continued by the non–labor *Milwaukeer Freie Presse*, 1879–90 (which even follows *Der Socialist*'s volume numbering)	
	followed indirectly by	
1879	(Biron's) *Arbeiterzeitung* renamed	
1880–1881	*Milwaukee Journal* bought by the non–labor *Milwaukeer Freie Presse* and published temporarily as supplement	
		Wisconsin 1880
	followed indirectly by	*Advocate*
1882–1889	*Milwaukee'r Arbeiter–Zeitung*	
		Volksblatt 1882
	related with	related with ?
	Biron's *Arminia*	*Volksblatt* 1882–90
	(through subscribers' list)	has the same editor as
		Reformer 1880–90
	merged with	which becomes
	Täglicher Reformer	*Täglicher Reformer*
	to form	while the weekly edition
1890–1892	(Milwaukee) *Volkszeitung*	*National Reformer* continued independently
	continued by	
1893–1898	*Wisconsin Vorwärts*	
	Sunday edition of the last three: *Vorwärts* becomes independent publication	
1898–1932	*Vorwärts*	
	Weekly edition of the same three: *Wahrheit* becomes independent publication	
1898–1910	*Wahrheit*	
1900–1910	*Stimme des Volkes/ Voice of the People/ Naprazod* published periodically by the SP during election campaigns	

Note: During this period the *Freidenker* (1872–1942) and the closely related *Amerikanische Turnzeitung* (1878–1942) were also published in Milwaukee.

Philadelphia and Milwaukee. A strong anarchist movement, however, did not develop until the arrival of Johann Most in New York in 1882. Exiled under the antisocialist law, Most had started to publish his newspaper *Freiheit* [Liberty] in London. In America this paper became the longest-living and most influential organ of the anarchist movement. At a congress of anarchist groups in Pittsburgh in 1883 a declaration of principles was adopted which served as a basis for the formation of the "black" International, the International Working People's Association (IWPA). The IWPA had organs in Philadelphia, St. Louis, Chicago and New York. The anarchist press was characterized by an extremely short duration of publication. All except *Die Freiheit* had closed down by 1902.

Table 3: Anarchist Periodicals, 1879-1911, by Founding Year		
Freiheit(IWPA)	NY New York	1879-1910
Zukunft(IWPA)	PA Philadelphia	1884-1885
Parole(IWPA)	MO St. Louis	1884-1891
Der Arme Teufel	MI Detroit	1884-1900
Amerikan. Arbeiter-Zeitung	NY New York	1886
Anarchist(IWPA)	IL Chicago	1886
New Yorker Arbeiter-Zeitung	NY New York	1886
Libertas	MA Boston	1888
Tramp	NY New York	1888
Anarchist(IWPA)	MO St. Louis	1889-1891
Anarchist(IWPA)	NY New York	1891-1895
Brandfackel	NY New York	1893-1895
Freie Wacht	PA Philadelphia	1894-1895
Sturmglocke	IL Chicago	1896
Kämpfer	MO St. Louis	1896
Sturmvogel	NY New York	1897-1899
Wolfsaugen	MO St. Louis	1900-1901
Zeitgeist	NY New York	1901
Mephisto	MO St. Louis	1901-1902
Tramp	NY New York	1901-1902
Zigeuner	IL Chicago	1902
Freie Wort	NY New York	1907
Strom	NY New York	1910
Anti-Autoritär	NY New York	1911
Einziger	O Toronto	1918

Only the IWPA-affiliated periodicals and the Detroit-based *Der Arme Teufel* [The Poor Devil], edited by Robert Reitzel, were published for more than three years. Anarchist periodicals appearing around the turn of the century, such as *Der Tramp*, *Mephisto* and *Der Zigeuner* [The Gypsy], were either more of a literary and satirical nature, or dominated by individual anarchism, like the three New York papers edited by Hans Koch and the only German-Canadian anarchist publication. New York, with nine publications and St. Louis with five accounted for more than half of the papers published. It should be kept in mind, however, that some major newspapers like the *Chicagoer Arbeiter-Zeitung* temporarily leaned toward anarchism. Behind the seeming diversity of publications was a certain continuity of editors: Max Baginski edited *Der Arme Teufel* after Reitzel's death, *Wolfsaugen* [Wolf's Eyes], 1900-01, *Mephisto*, 1901-02, *Der Zigeuner*, 1902; George Biedenkapp, associated with *Der Arme*

Teufel since 1898, had edited *Der Tramp* in 1901-02, which for a time was the supplement to Großmann's *Der Zeitgeist* [Spirit of the Age]; Claus Timmermann was the editor of *Der Anarchist* 1888-91, *Die Brandfackel* [The Torch of War] 1893-94, *Sturmvogel* [The Petrel] 1897-99; Otto Rinke edited *Der Anarchist*, New York 1891-95 and *Der Kämpfer* [The Combatant] 1896. The most direct link between American and German-American anarchism was *Libertas*, a German edition of Tucker's *Liberty*. In summary, it might be said that the IWPA-affiliated periodicals represented anarchism as a movement, while many of the shortlived publications represented the anarchist sequel to the "personal journalism" of the pre-Civil War period. Anarchism, ranging from collective anarchism through mutual-aid anarchism to individualist anarchism, from advocates of violent action to pacifists (for a relatively short period of time from the 1880s to 1910), added to the spectrum of alternative models of a free American society.[23]

A final group of periodicals were published by local labor organizations or national labor unions. Many of the publications of local labor organizations were shortlived and none of them were published in English. While the *Arbeiter-Zeitung* (IL Belleville) achieved a publication period of 28 years, several of the shortlived papers were related to other papers in the same city, preceding or following them, with or without avowed or indirect connections (see place of publication-index; see Figure 5 for an example). In other cases - Milwaukee and Cincinnati are examples - several labor papers competed with each other and with a middle-class press, thus providing a board spectrum of opinion but competing for subscribers.

A number of periodicals were published in German by the Knights of Labor, but few of them have survived. The labor union periodicals of national (or at least regional) craft unions differ from the rest of the press because of their bi or multilingualism and their longevity. Only a few SLP publications and one issued by the Knights of Labor contained English sections, but almost all trade-union periodicals were in English and German. Some were founded in English and later added a German section, others were bilingual from the beginning, and in a number of cases German-language union periodicals merged with English ones.

Other foreign-language sections of these periodicals were in Czech, Italian, Swedish and French. In many cases the union periodicals do not constitute an ethnic press, but the press of a labor organization with translations of articles into the languages of different ethnic groups and sometimes news specific to a particular ethnic group. Many of these periodicals existed for several decades (see below: "core press").[24] The *Cigar Makers Official Journal* published reprints and translations from German trade-union publications. For the other periodicals international connections require further research. A special case is the *Deutsch-Amerikanische Buchdrucker-Zeitung* [German-American Printers' Journal], which kept to German as its only language during the whole of its existence.[25]

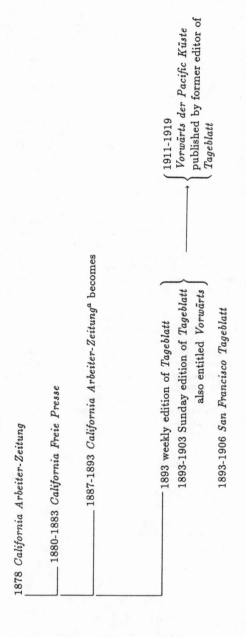

Figure 5: California Labor Periodicals Published in San Francisco

1878 *California Arbeiter-Zeitung*

1880-1883 *California Freie Presse*

1887-1893 *California Arbeiter-Zeitung*[a] becomes

1893 weekly edition of *Tageblatt*

1893-1903 Sunday edition of *Tageblatt* also entitled *Vorwärts*

1893-1906 *San Francisco Tageblatt*

1911-1919 *Vorwärts der Pacific Küste* published by former editor of *Tageblatt*

[a]Title variants *San Francisco Arbeiterzeitung, Californier Arbeiterzeitung*

Table 4: Periodicals of Labor Unions and Local Labor Organization, by First Year of Appearance

a) labor union periodicals*

Coopers 'Journal	coopers	OH Cleveland	1870-1875
Dt.-Am. Buchdrucker-Ztg	printers	IN Indianapolis	1873-1940
Cigar Makers 'Off. J.	cigarmkrs.	NY New York	1875-1953
Wisconsin Advocate	K of L	WI Milwaukee	1880
Familien-Journal	K of L	IA Davenport	1880-1898
Carpenter	carpenters	IN Indianapolis	1881-1917
Progress	cigarmkrs	NY New York	1882-1885
Hammer	metalwkrs	PA Philadel.	1882-1889
Möbel-Arb.-Journal	furniture wrks	NY New York	1883-1891
Protection	K of L	NJ Newark	1884
Dt.-Am. Bäcker-Ztg.	bakers	NY New York	1885-1941
Brauer-Zeitung	brewers	OH Cincinnati	1886-1934
Küfer-Zeitung	coopers	NY New York	1887
Tailor	tailors	NY New York	1887-1891
Metallarbeiter	metalwkr	NY New York	1888
Chicagoer Bäcker-Ztg	bakers	IL Chicago	1888-1889
Coopers 'Int. J.	coopers	KS Kansas C.	1890-1918
General Woodworkers 'J	furniture wkrs	NY Brooklyn	1891-1896
Sattler und Wagenbauer	carriage wkrs	IL Chicago	1891-1904
Painter	painters	NY New York	1893-1900
Int. Wood Worker	furniture wkrs	IL Chicago	1896-1906
Carriage and Wagon W. 's J.	carriage wkrs	ILChicago	1899-1906
Butchers 'Journal	butchers	NY Syracuse	1899-1908
Piano and Organ Wkrs Off.J.	piano wkrs	IL Chicago	1899-1911

b) local labor organisations*

Arbeiter	PA Lebanon	1871-1880
Chicagoer Volkszeitung	IL Chicago	1877-1879
Arbeiterstimme am Erie	NY Buffalo	1878
Gewerkschafts-Zeitung	NY New York	1879-1881
California Freie Press	CA San Francisco	1880-1883
Reformer (K of L?)	WI Milwaukee	1880-1906
Volksblatt(K of L/*?)	WI Milwaukee	1882
Illinois Volkszeitung	IL ?	1884-1885
Arbeiter-Zeitung	IL Belleville	1884-1912
Neue Zeit *	IL Evansville	1885
New Jersey Arbeiter-Ztg. *	NJ Newark	1886-1889
Milwaukee 'r Arbeiter-Ztg. *	WI Milwaukee	1886-1889
Cincinnatier Zeitung	OH Cincinnati	1886-1901
Arbeiter-Zeitung	MO St. Louis	1888
Michigan Arbeiterzeitung	MI Detroit	1888-1892
Arbeiter-Stimme *	IL Chicago	1889
Volkszeitung der Pacific-Küste	CA San Franc.	1891-1894
Arbeiter-Zeitung	PA Erie	1891-1899
Agitator	NJ Elizabeth	1893
Biene	MA Holyoke	1894-1920
Freie Presse	IL Aurora	1895-1896
Industrial News *	NY New York	1897
Gross-New Yorker Arbeiter-Ztg.	NY New York	1898
Nebraska Arbeiterzeitung	NE Omaha	1899
Arbeiter-Zeitung	OH Cincinnati	1902-1903

* These are organs of city-wide labor organizations of German-American or all workers such as the Central Labor Union or the United Trades Council.

In addition to the variety and number of periodicals published[26] the most significant achievement in phase 2 was the creation of a "core press:" twenty-one periodicals, founded mainly in the 1870s and 1880s[27] which lasted for more than twenty years (see Figure 2 in the Introduction to this volume and Table 5). This press accounted for about half of the periodicals available during this phase, for about three quarters of the press in phase 3 (1903-29) and for about one third in phase 4 (1930-45).

Table 5: The "Core Press" Established 1872-1898 with Dates of Affiliation and Ending			
Freidenker	freethought	WI Milwaukee	1872-1942
Buckdrucker-Zeitung	labor union	IN Indianapolis	1873-1940
Cigar Makers' Off. J.	labor union	NY New York	1875-1953
Chicagoer Arbeiter-Ztg.	socialist	IL Chicago	1876-1924
Tageblatt	socialist	PA Philadelphia	1877-1944
New Yorker Volkszeitung	socialist	NY New York	1878-1932
Turnzeitung	Gymnast's soc.	WI Milwaukee	1878-1942
Freiheit	anarchist	NY New York	1879-1910
Reformer	labor	WI Milwaukee	1880-1906
Carpenter[1]	labor union	IN Indianapolis	1881-1917
Arbeiter-Zeitung	labor	IL Belleville	1884-1912
Herold	socialist	MI Detroit	1884-1918
Dt.-Am. Bäcker-Ztg.	labor union	NY New York	1885-1941
Volksfreund	socialist	OH Cleveland	1886-1918
Brauer-Zeitung	labor union	OH Cincinnati	1886-1934
Buffaloer Arbeiter-Ztg.	socialist	NY Buffalo	1887-1918
Vorwärts[2]	social-dem.	WI Milwukee	1887-1932
Wahrheit[2]	social-dem.	WI Milwaukee	1889-1910
Coopers' Journal[3]	trade union	KS Kansas City	1890-1918
Biene	labor	MA Holyoke	1894-1920
Arbeiter-Zeitung	socialist	MO St. Louis	1898-1935

1. Bilingual publication from the beginning.
2. Preceded by a sequence of related periodicals of other titles.
3. Preceded by other coopers' periodicals.

It represented the whole spectrum of the German-American labor press with one freethought, gymnasts' and anarchist publication each, twelve labor, social-democratic and socialist publications of particular parties and cities (with influence beyond the city limits) and six labor union periodicals. While the periodicals lasting less than twenty years show the vivacity of the German-American reform, labor and left press and reflect personal journalism as well as doctrinal differentiation and the many attempts to establish periodicals in small towns, the core of the labor movement is represented by longlived periodicals. To those listed in Table 5, however, must be added sequences of shortlived periodicals from cities not represented among the places of publication of the "core press."

Phase 3 is not only characterized by the continuity of the "core press" and the incision of the World War One years. On the one hand seven other publications continued into this phase, on the other a dramatic decline in the founding of new periodicals can be registered as well as a decline in the total number of periodicals published. Both developments are foreshadowed in the nineties, when the German-American labor movement passed its apogee as an ethnic movement and began to integrate into the English-language multiethnic organizations.

Table 6: Periodicals Founded 1902-1929 with Affiliation by Year			
Dt.-Am. Fleischer Ztg.	labor union	NY Brooklyn	1904
Solidarität	socialist	NY New York	1906-1954
Freie Wort	anarchist	NY New York	1907
Strom	anarchist	NY New York	1910
Anti-Autoritär	anarchist	NY New York	1911
Vorwärts der Pacific K.	socialist-SP	CA San Franc.	1911-1919
Echo	socialist-SP	OH Cleveland	1911-1920
Habt Acht	social-dem.	TY Hallettsville	1913-1919
Einziger	anarchist	O Toronto	1918
Klassen-Kampf	syndicalist	IL Chicago	1919-1920
Arbeiter-Freund	Catholic labor	IL Chicago	1919-1921
Sänger-Zeitung	socialist	NY New York	1924-1944
Volks-Stimme	socialist-SP	PA Philadelphia	1925
Arbeiter-Sport	socialist	NY Brooklyn	1927-1933
Arbeiter	communist-CP	NY New York	1927-1937

The phase of stabilization marked by the establishment of the "core press" is replaced by a phase of stagnation and decline. Of the 15 periodicals founded in these years one was a Catholic labor union paper, one syndicalist-oriented (IWW) and one published by the Communist Party. The low representation of syndicalist and communist periodicals also indicates the integration of German-American - by now often second-generation - workers into the mainstream, as well as their underrepresentation among unskilled workers. The three new anarchist publications remained without great or lasting influence. Only one new labor union publication demonstrates once again that German-American workers no longer saw their role in separate organizations. The social-democratic and socialist organs became less and less easy to distinguish on doctrinal grounds and three of them were affiliated with the Socialist Party. No new SLP-periodicals in German were founded. Geographically the stagnation of German-American ethnicity is indicated by the fact that eight of the new papers were published in New York and Brooklyn and the geographical expansion of places of publication noted during Phase 2 was replaced by strong contraction. The founding of the socialist *Solidarität* (1906-54) and of the *Sänger-Zeitung* [Singers' Journal] (1924-44) both in New York represented the only additions to the "core press." Of the others only two SP, one CP, one unaffiliated social- democratic and two cultural publications achieved medium continuity. The latter two merit attention: the publication of the socialist singing clubs lasted for twenty-one years and the proletarian athletic clubs of the twenties with their publication *Arbeiter-Sport in Amerika* [Proletarian Sports in America] (1927-33) presented a challenge to the staid socialist *Turnzeitung*. The cultural and socializing function was also a mainstay of two of the new socialist periodicals. Both the New York *Solidarität* and the Cleveland *Echo* were organs of numerous working-class clubs, especially the sick and death benefit societies. The press of the period represents the last phase of an ethnic community in which the period of integration as reflected by bilingual publications is past. Only two new bilingual publications appeared (*Solidarität* and *Arbeiter-Sport*). For the most part, readers obtained their daily news from the English-language press or from the surviving core periodicals of a general nature (New York, Philadelphia, Chicago (till 1924), St. Louis, Milwaukee).[28]

World War One meant a serious break in continuity. In the fall of 1917 much of the foreign-language press was suppressed and the German socialist press was particularly affected by this, both because of its pacifist standpoint and as an "enemy alien" press. Mailing privileges were denied and newspapers lost their entire circulation outside their cities of publication. The *New Yorker Volkszeitung* and other affected organs did not regain the mailing privilege until the summer of 1921.

During Phase 4 the "core press" declined to six publications in the late 1930s[29] plus *Solidarität* which had been founded in 1906. In 1945 only one paper was left. (See Table 7.)

Of the new periodicals only the social-democratic *Neue Volkszeitung* [New People's Journal] and the communist *German-American*[30] (from 1942), which addressed German immigrants, achieved continuity. The newspapers of the early thirties mark the change in the German-American press to reports about cultural clubs (*Chicagoer Arbeiter-Zeitung*, 1931) and the brief emergence of a Canadian-German labor movement (*Kampf* [The Struggle], *Deutsche Arbeiterzeitung* [German Labor News], Edmonton and Winnipeg). The *Kampfsignal* [Battle Signal] provides the transition from culturally left periodicals to antifascist periodicals. From then on the German-American social-democratic, socialist, communist and non-aligned left periodicals followed an antifascist line and were of fundamentally different character compared to the immigration labor press. (Note that given the scope of this bibliography only German-language labor and left antifascist periodicals have been described here. English-language publications produced by German exiles are listed in Appendix 3. For a survey of the exile literature as a whole cf. the studies by Maas and Cazden.)[31] Since many of the antifascist publications were addressed to fellow exiles in North America or Europe and to the German resistance movement most of them were published in German only.[32] The variety of antifascist publications on the one hand reflects difficulties in raising funds and clandestine operations in Europe. (Cf. the sequence of publications produced by the resistance movement Neu Beginnen: *Sozialdemokratischer Informationsbrief*, *Sozialistische Informationsbriefe*, *I.B. Berichte*). On the other hand this diversity also reflects the splits in the resistance movement on ideological and personal grounds, tensions between immigrants and exiles as well as insecurity about support for the war. After 1941 many publications were concerned intensively with plans for post-war Germany.

Table 7: Periodicals Published 1930-1944, 1945 and in the Postwar Decades (by First Year of Publication)			
Kampf	labor	M Winnipeg	1930
Dt. Arbeiter-Ztg.	labor	A Edmonton	1930-1931
Dt. Arbeiter-Ztg.	labor	M Winnipeg	
Chicagoer Arbeiter-Ztg.	socialist	IL Chicago	1931
Kampfsignal	socialist	NY New York	1932-1943
Neue Volks-Zeitung	soc. dem.	NY New York	1932-1949
Stimme	communist	PA Philadelphia	1933
antifascist perodicals mainly published by exiles			
Einheitsfront	com./soc.	NY New York	1934
Dt.-Am. Arbeiterklubs	communist	NY New York	1934-1938
Volksfront	communist	IL Chicago	1934-1939
Mitteilungsblatt	communist	NY New York	1935-1936
Dt. Zentralbücherei	communist	NY New York	1936
Schiffahrt	com./lab.union	NY New York	1936-1939
Deutsches Volksecho	communist	NY New York	1937-1939
Gegen den Strom	socialist	NY New York	1938-1939
Anti-Faschist	socialist	NY New York	1938-1939
Neue Leben	communist	NY New York	1939
Soz.-dem. Informationsbrief	soc. dem.	NY New York	1939
Socialist. Informationsbriefe	socialist	NY New York	1939
Youth Outlook	communist	NY New York	1939
I.B. Berichte	socialist	NY New York	1939-1940
Int. Arbeiterfront	?	NY New York	1939-1940
Mitteilungsblatt	?	NY New York	1939-1940
Unser Wort	Trotzkyite	NY New York	1940-1941
Unsere Zeit	communist	NY New York	1940-1942
German American Conference	communist	NY New York	1942
Austrian Labor Information	soc. dem.	NY New York	1942-1945
Österreichische Rundschau	?	NY New York	1942-1945
German American	communist	NY New York	1942-1968
Volksstimme	antifascist	O Toronto	1944-1949
AFL "labor" publication			
Int. Freigewerkschl. Nachrichten	"labor"	DC Washington	1945-?
postwar publications			
Vorwärts	soc. dem.	O Toronto	1948
Bulletin der SLP	socialist	NY New York	1952-1964
Spartacists	Trotzkyite	NY New York	1974

After World War Two one trade-union periodical continued for a few years, the communist *German-American* appeared till 1964 and the German-language *Bulletin* of the SLP from 1952 to 1964. In addition two minor publications appeared briefly (Toronto *Vorwärts* [Forward], New York *Spartacist*). At the end of the war a "labor" publication issued by the AFL-CIO Department for International Affairs (also known as the Free Trade Union Committee) and called *Internationale Freigewerkschaftliche Nachrichten* [International Free Labor Union News] appeared in German, English, French and Italian.[33] This publication was an anticommunist sheet with many photos of its editors advocating U.S. domination or influence in many parts of the world. It may be classified as "imperialist." While issued by a labor organization, it is neither left nor reform.[34] The publications from 1945 onward provide a somewhat undistinguished ending to a once important element of the North American ethnic labor press.

The Socialist Newspapers: Content, Production and Distribution

In this part a brief survey of the content, publication data and distribution network of the German-American labor press will be given, particularly of the socialist press between 1870 and World War One. Anarchist newspapers and the union press here are considered here only marginally.[35]

The News: The heading "American and European News" was a standard component of every American newspaper and likewise of every German-American labor newspaper. Before the Civil War news from Europe had to be transmitted by ship and in the 1850s even steamers needed more than two weeks for the route Liverpool/New York. In 1866 the first permanent telegraph connection, the transatlantic cable, was installed and thereafter many newspapers contained short cable dispatches dated the previous day from Europe and other parts of the world.[36]

Another important feature was sensational reports about gruesome accidents, suicides, natural catastrophes, etc. The accounts of local events in the German-speaking areas of Europe were similar in character. The labor press had this type of reporting in common with the bourgeois press.

What is characteristic of the labor press is the different ideological alignment in the selection of and commentary upon political news, the strong accent on news of the labor movement and about progress of socialism throughout the world. A prominent place was given to events such as major strikes in America, victories of the Social Democrats in Germany or the October Revolution in Russia. During national, state and local elections, the corruption and election swindles of the Democrats and Republicans were commented upon bitingly. In time of war the question was often asked who paid with his life and who made a profit. When anarchists or socialists were prosecuted (e.g. the Haymarket Martyrs, Emma Goldman), the labor press took the side of the defendants, thereby exposing itself to reprisals. Frequently, cases of police brutality as well as class discrimination in the courts were highlighted. The speaking tours of U.S. or European socialists (Paul Grottkau, the Avelings) were reported in detail and the texts of their speeches reproduced. Considerable space was also given to reports about celebrations of 1 May, the anniversary of the Paris Commune, and funerals of prominent socialists, which were often attended by thousands.

Reports from correspondents in Germany were numerous. The close personal relationship between the German-American and the German labor press is an important chapter in the still unwritten history of the interaction between the labor movements of the two countries.[37]

The Literary Section: Most newspapers contained an extensive literary section consisting of serialized novels, short stories and poetry. This is especially true of weekly and Sunday editions, whose news sections were usually restricted to a summary of the previous week's events. Primarily, contemporary German literature was reprinted. Since no legal protection was given to foreign authors in the United States at that time, their writings could be reprinted without remitting royalties.[38] Often editors themselves wrote literary contributions, as was the case with Adolf Douai, A. Otto-Walster and Otto Sattler.[39] Among the authors whose work was published there was a relatively high proportion of female writers. Frequently the same serialized novels or humorous pieces appeared in different newspapers because of the utilization of prefabricated printing plates.

The numerous articles on scientific, historical, medical, technical, economic, political and social topics demonstrate on the one hand the great hunger of the working classes for knowledge, and on the other hand the aim of the labor editors and party leaders to raise the level of education of their readership. Above all, this reflected the widespread belief within the labor movement of that period that the world could be understood scientifically.

Women and the Labor Press: Up to now only a few women have been discovered who served as publishers and editors: Mathilde Franziska Anneke, one of the Fortyeighters, was prominent as a publisher, editor and journalist; and the women's pages of the *New Yorker Volkszeitung* and *Solidarität* were edited by women. It has not yet been determined whether this practice was also followed in other socialist newspapers. Women were often the authors of short stories and novels, e.g. Nataly von Eschstruth, Minna Kautsky, Julie Romm and Lily Braun. Women's pages or sections were frequently limited to the traditional areas of child raising, health information, household advice such as recipes, and, in the twentieth century, fashion. The women's pages of the *New Yorker Volkszeitung* and the *Stimme des Volkes* had a somewhat wider horizon, reporting also about women in the labor movement, the suffrage campaign or the situation of women in other countries.[40]

Advertisements: For labor newspapers, which were generally not profit-oriented, as for other newspapers, advertisements were the most important source of revenue, since subscriptions could not even cover the price of paper, let alone the production costs.[41] Dependence on advertisements was precarious, however. Particularly during labor conflicts firms withdrew advertisements when their striking workers received support in the editorial columns. "Naturally" there were no advertisements in the socialist newspapers from the housing and real estate industry, no balance sheets for stockholders, no stock market reports, and rarely 'help wanted' or job seeking advertisements, all of which took up a large amount of space in a newspaper like the bourgeois *New Yorker Staatszeitung*. The majority of advertisers came from German-American small businesses, saloons, doctors, etc. The disappearance of these small businesses may have been a factor in the decline of the labor press at the turn of the century. Anarchist newspapers usually included few advertisements, and what there were came mostly from sympathizers. In contrast, the union newspapers received advertisements from national producers of specialized products, for example, advertisements for yeast in the *Bäckerzeitung* or tools in the *Carpenter*.

Announcements: One of the most important functions of the labor press was to provide publicity for party and union meetings, lectures, boycotts, anniversaries and benefits, picnics, etc. Announcements also covered the events of politically aligned labor, athletic or singing groups and mutual benefit associations. In addition, newly published pamphlets or books received mention. In fact, they were often written and published by newspaper editors and their printing companies.

Anniversary issues provide personal and graphic accounts of the history of the newspaper and of the local German labor movement and unions. Noteworthy are the anniversary issues of the *New Yorker Volkszeitung*,[42] the *Brauerzeitung* and *Freiheit*, because of their broad scope and their value for historians. The *Buchdrucker-Zeitung* published a review of developments within the German-American printer's union (Typographia) every ten years. Anniversary issues were often embellished with a grandiosely illustrated title page which in various ways symbolically represented the victory of socialism.[43] Socialism was often symbolized by a female angel.

Publishing companies: Socialist newspapers were rarely owned by a single person who could impose his opinion upon the content of the newspaper. Their organization and structure usually reflected the ideas of socialism. Often a paper was owned by a cooperative which was either identical with the local party section or one could become a member by purchasing a share. A meeting which included the owners, the printers of the cooperatively run printing office as well as delegates from various unions elected a board of supervisors and the editor-in-chief was responsible to the members of the cooperative publishing company. A large number of papers functioned according to variations of this model. Party sections, unions or the publishing company itself organized fund-raising events such as fairs, concerts and excursions - in 1879 the boat excursion of the *New Yorker Volkszeitung* publishing company drew a crowd of 5000 people - or, as was the case in Chicago, the democratically organized printing office of the *Vorbote* helped to consolidate the party finances. Thus, the organization and production of the socialist press was often closely related with the local working-class movement.[44]

Circulation: Circulation figures are known for only about 50 of the 236 newspapers which were published. The sources of these figures are the Arndt/Olson bibliography or the newspaper directories for advertisers published by Ayer and von Rowell.[45] Practically no information is available for the newspapers which appeared before the Civil War. During phase 2 the core periodicals achieved a relatively high circulation, though they never reached the levels of the major bourgeois papers.

Table 8: Circulation Figures of Selected Major Labor Newspapers							
Name	1880	1890	1900	1915	1918	1925	1935
Phil. Tageblatt (1877-1944)	8,000	5,200	41,000	30,000	26,000	2451	
Chic. Arb.-Ztg. (1876-1924?)	3,000	4,600	10,000	15,000	18,000	n.p.	
N.Y. Volksztg. (1878-1932)	10,200	19,680	18,000	18,000	18,000	20,942	n.p.
Wisc. Vorwärts (1892-1932)	n.p.	34,000	8,708	38,000	4,314	n.p.	n.p.

for comparison the circulation figures of two bourgeois periodicals:

Phil. Gazette-Demokrat (1890-1954)	n.p.	-	-	35,000	35,000	51,612	50,160
N.Y. Staatsztg. (1834-1924)	50,000	60,000	56,000	20,000	55,945 (1924)	n.p.	

n.p.: not yet/ no longer published

Sources: Ayer, Arndt/Olsen.

Newspapers which had a circulation of between 1000 and 3000 were the most common. Those with a circulation of under 1000 did not usually survive very long. The circulation figures for most anarchist newspapers are not known. Among the union papers, the circulation is known for the *Bäckerzeitung* (22,000), the *Tailor* (8000) and the metal workers' *Hammer* (800).

Sales and Subscriptions: Newspapers were distributed by street vendors and delivery people or mailed to subscribers. Street vendors sold about 1,500 copies daily of the *New Yorker Volkszeitung* and 4000 copies went to subscribers. Mail delivery was made possible by reduced rates according to a law of March 1878. Mailing privileges, if granted, were noted in a paper's publication data. During World War One postal privileges were withdrawn as a means of reprisal against the German-language press and the foreign-language socialist press in general.

A well-documented subscription drive was that of the *New Yorker Volkszeitung* during the four to six weeks before it began publication. 278 "volunteers" recruited from the New York section of the Socialist Labor Party were each allotted a district, primarily in the German workers' neighborhoods to solicit subscriptions. Each district comprised four to ten adjacent apartment buildings. After working hours the volunteers distributed handbills the first time round, and then in a second round compiled a subscription list of 4,000 persons. On the eve of the first edition on 28 January 1878, a corps of delivery men and women made up of unemployed people was organized. This was necessary because the bourgeois *New Yorker Staatszeitung*, which dominated the New York German-language market at that time, had forbidden its delivery people to distribute the new paper.[46]

Duration and Frequency of Publication: Figure 6 demonstrates how shortlived most of the labor periodicals were. In the labor press itself there was some discussion of the reasons for this.[47] (1) The newspapers suffered from a lack of funds from the moment they were founded. Their financial means were rarely sufficient to obtain even the most meager supplies and equipment for the editorial staff and the printing department and also pay the personnel. Their capital was raised either by loans or by the pooling of private resources. Many newspapers could only keep their heads above water through donations and contributions from unions, often of tiny amounts. Even such a longlived and relatively high-circulation newspaper as the *Chicagoer Arbeiterzeitung* had to struggle with these problems. Additional money was raised by festivities, e.g., a successful commemoration of the Commune on 21 March 1879. On this occasion $4400 net profit enabled the newspaper not only to change to daily appearance, but also to establish a Sunday edition. Some years later an association of various unions, sick-benefit associations, and gymnasts' and singing groups was organized to support the papers, under the name of the *Chicago Arbeiterzeitung Conferenz*. In October 1907, for instance, the *Conferenz* agreed to impose a levy on its members. Typographia No. 9 granted $5 on that occasion.[48] (2) The founders of the newspapers were, as a rule, idealists who, though they had a great deal of willingness, lacked knowledge in the sales, technical, organizational and editorial areas. This had negative consequences for both quality and sales volume. (3) Political and/or personal controversies occasionally led to crises (*Chicagoer Arbeiterzeitung*) or to the closing of a newspaper (*New York Arbeiterzeitung*). (4) Outside of the large cities with a well-organized German working class, such as New York or Chicago, it was difficult to find the necessary amount of subscriptions. (5)

Figure 6 Total Number of Issues Printed by the
German-American Labor Press (per year)

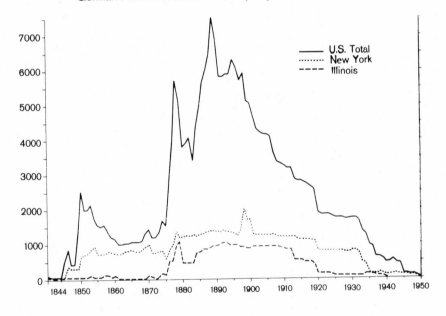

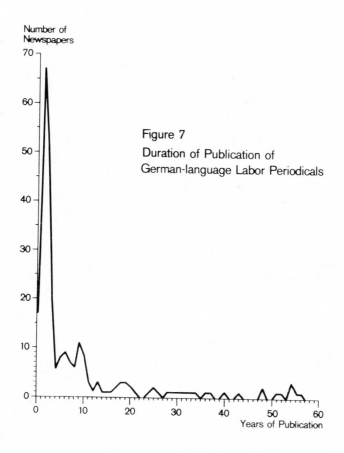

Figure 7
Duration of Publication of
German-language Labor Periodicals

Occasionally the complaint was heard that German-American workers preferred to read the bourgeois newspapers. Contemporaries wondered whether the labor papers were too difficult to understand or did not sufficiently meet the needs of the workers for diversion and entertainment.[49] (6) When their papers had to suspend publication, some editors bitterly complained about lack of support from their readership. They charged the German working class with spending money on elaborately planned one-evening meetings for traveling speakers rather than on a labor press providing continuity. They chastised workers for having so little intellectual interest that they preferred to spend their money on tobacco and alcohol and under "the hypnotic effect of the dollar" allowed themselves to be turned into traitors to the cause of the workers.[50]

Saloons (Kneipen), Reading Rooms and the Labor Press

The connection between the labor press and saloons can be seen at several levels. First, saloons were important advertisers in the labor newspapers. Second, editors of labor newspapers occasionally changed their trade and became saloon owners (e.g. Ernst Kurzenknabe of the *Brauer-Zeitung*; Wilhelm Hasselmann; Carl Klings). Third, these saloons were not only meeting places but also information centers at which labor newspapers were available.[51] Thus, saloons became an important factor in multiplying the distribution of the labor press.[52]

One of the best known anarchist meeting places was Justus H. Schwab's "Internationale Bierhöhle - Pechvogel's Hauptquartier" [International Den for Beer Drinkers - Headquarters of the Unlucky] on New York's First Street. The "Grobe Michel" [the "Rough German" - "Michel" is a stereotype German] on Fifth Street was a gathering place for New York's radical labor groups, where discussion meetings took place every Saturday. All of the international communist-anarchist and revolutionary newspapers and pamphlets could be obtained there. Such meeting places existed in every city with a substantial German population. Thus, in Philadelphia at the end of the 1870s there were over 3000 German saloons. However a Supreme Court decision in 1887 permitting a considerable increase in license fees and the prohibition of sales of alcoholic beverages on Sunday, and to an even greater extent the Prohibition Enforcement Act of 1920 endangered their existence.

Labor newspapers were also on display in so-called "Reading Rooms." Leopold Stiger's "politico-literary establishment" already existed in Cleveland at the beginning of the 1850s (see the Cleveland *Kommunist* 1852-53). Other examples are the "Labor Lyceum" in New York, in which labor newspapers from all over the world could be read,[53] the "Internationales Arbeiter Lesezimmer" at 400 East 76th Street, and the "Radical Reading Room" at 180 Forsyth Street, where anarchist and socialist newspapers in every language were kept.[54] It should also be noted that the St. Louis section of the anarchist international maintained a literary club whose principal function was the support of their newspaper *Parole*.

As we have seen, the German-American labor press closely reflects the structure of German emigration to North America as a whole. Its development on the one hand followed the rise and fall of German mass migration and its character was formed and dominated by the political exponents and leaders of the various waves of immigrants. On the other hand, over a period of almost a whole century, the German-American working class was able to maintain a large number of permanent newspapers ("core press") which reflected and supported the German-American working-class community and culture in a dialectical process, each giving the other stability and vitality at the same time. The press was an integral part of the labor movement, its influence often exceeding the ethnic community and thus it was subject to change when the German-American working class became part of the rising and strengthening American labor movement. Because of this close relationship between the working-class community and the press and because of the developments it mirrored, the German-American labor press is one of the most important sources of working-class history and of the history of the Germans in the United States.

Notes

1. The German mass emigration of the nineteenth and early twentieth centuries was mainly, but not exclusively directed toward the United States. Of about 4.5 million Germans who emigrated overseas between 1847 and 1914 almost 4 million (89 percent) went to the United States and about 86,500 (1.9 percent) to Canada. Other receiving countries were Australia (1.3 percent) and Brazil (2 percent). During the 1920s the importance of South American destinations increased and the share of the United States sank to 71 percent. (Bade, pp. 270, 273).

2. On German immigration to North America, see *Harvard Encyclopedia of American Ethnic Groups*. Ed. by Stephan Thernstrom (Cambridge, MA/London, 1980). (s.v. Austrian, German, Luxembourger and Swiss.); Bade; Marschalck; Rippley.

3. *Historical Statistics of Canada*, M.C. Urquhart, ed., (Cambridge: The University of Toronto Press, 1965), pp.27- 28; see also Rudolf A. Helling, ed., *A Socio-Economic History of German-Canadians: They, too, Founded Canada* (Wiesbaden: Skiner Verlag, 1984).

4. On the German-American Press, see Arndt/Olson, Wittke, *Press;* Faust, Albert Bernhard, *The German Element in the United States* (New York, 1927) pp. 360-376; *Das Buch der Deutschen in Amerika [The Book of Germans in America]*, herausgegeben unter den Auspicien des Deutsch-Amerikanischen National-Bundes, (Philadelphia, 1909), pp. 473-594 contains a detailed account of the German-American bourgeois press, a history of its daily newspapers and biographies of its publishers and editors; Felix L. Senff, "Die Deutsche Presse in Amerika," *New Yorker Staatszeitung*, 24 April 1910, (jubilee edition). Figures from Robert E. Park, *The Immigrant Press and Its Control* (New York, 1922), Table XVIII.

5. New England (2), New Orleans (1), San Francisco (4).

6. Some lost periodicals are not included in this classification because their political and organizational leanings could not be determined definitely. Note that the classifications overlap and that numerous periodicals would fit into more than one category.

7. Cf. P.H. Noyes, *Organization and Revolution: Working-Class Associations in the German Revolutions of 1848-1849* (Princeton, NJ, 1966).

8. Cf. French Section, Appendix "Icarian Newspapers".

9. Cf. Levine.

10. On pre-civil war socialist literature, see Cazden, *Book Trade*; Harnack; Schlüter, *Anfänge*; Wittke, *Wilhelm Weitling*.

11. On the Fortyeighters, see Levine; Dobert; Mueller; Wittke, *Refugees*; Zucker.

12. Cf. Obermann, *Weydemeyer*.

13. On the gymnasts' movement, see Metzner; Ueberhorst.

14. Nine periodicals cannot be classified. Note that the categories overlap.

15. On socialism in America and on German-American socialist literature in general, see Foner, *History*; Herreshoff; Hillquit; Kamman; Poore; Sorge; Waltershausen.

16. Richard Schneirov, "Free Thought and Socialism in the Czech Community in Chicago, 1875-1887," in *"Struggle a Hard Battle"* - *Working-Class Immigrants*, edited by Dirk Hoerder (DeKalb, 1986), pp. 121-42.

17. On the First International in America, see Bernstein; Schlüter, *Internationale*; Sorge, *Labor Movement in the United States*.

18. On socialists who emigrated to the United States after being expelled from territories in Germany see Heinzpeter Thümmler, *Sozialistengesetz § 28. Ausweisungen und Ausgewiesene 1878-1890* [Anti-Socialist Law § 28. Deportations and the Deported] (Berlin/GDR, 1979) and Hartmut Keil, "Deutsche sozialistische Einwanderer in den USA im letzten Drittel des 19. Jahrhunderts: Lebensweise und Organisation im Spannungsfeld von Tradition und Integration" [German Socialist Immigrants to the U.S. During the Last Third of the 19th Century: Organization and Everyday Life between Tradition and Integration] (unpubl. manuscript, Munich, 1985). Thümmler mentions 146 persons, e.g. about 18 percent of all people expelled who emigrated to the U.S. whereas Keil found 191 persons = 24 percent (pp.146-50).

19. Cf. Auer. Affected were the *Bäckerzeitung, California Arbeiterzeitung, Chicagoer Arbeiterzeitung* and its weekly and Sunday editions, *Philadelphia Tageblatt*, the New York *Sozialist*, the *Amerikanische Turnzeitung* and probably others.

20. Cf. D. Hoerder, ed., *Plutocrats*.

21. Cf. Dirk Hoerder and Thomas Weber, eds., "Die Jubiläumsnummern der *New Yorker Volkszeitung* 1888, 1903, 1928," *Glimpses of the German-American Radical Press* (Bremen, 1985).

22. The Buffalo *Laterne* represented a link with a further reform movement, Greenbackism.

23. On anarchism in the United States, see Creagh; Rocker.

24. Several of the periodicals listed in the bibliography existed beyond the closing date: in all cases the end of publication of the German section is given as the closing date. (Continuation in English is noted in the "Description.")

25. For the discussion about a bilingual edition, see *Buchdrucker-Zeitung* 16 June 1913.

26. Not identified as to their affiliation among the periodicals of the period 1870-1902 are: *Newarker Post* (NJ Newark, 1874-75), *Arbeiterblatt* (OH Cincinnati, 1877-87), *California Arbeiter-Zeitung* (CA San Francisco, 1878), *Arbeiter-Freund* (PA McKeesport, 1884-85), *Arbeiter-Freund* (PA Philadelphia, 1887), *Arbeiter-Zeitung* (PA Pittsburgh, 1889-90), *Arbeiter-Zeitung* (MO Kansas City, 1894), *Tageblatt-Abendpost* (MO St. Louis, 1897-98), *Wahrheit* (PA Philadelphia, 1901).

27. There were only three additions to this group in the 1890s.

28. In addition to the labor union papers, a freethought and a gymnasts' periodical survived.

29. *Cigar Makers' Official Journal* (published up to 1953), Philadelphia *Tageblatt* (up to 1944), *Freidenker* and *Turnzeitung* (both up to 1942), *Bäcker-Zeitung* (up to 1941) *Buchdrucker-Zeitung* (up to 1940).

30. The *German American* was preceded by *Deutsch-Amerikanische Arbeiterklubs: Mitteilungsblatt* (1934- 38), *Unsere Zeit* (1940-42), *German-American Emergency Conference Bulletin* (1942).

31. On the period 1933-1945, see Cazden, *Exile Literature*; Diamond; Maas; Radkau; Ragg.

32. Of thirty periodicals published less than one third were bilingual.

33. *International Free Trade Union News, Nouvelles Internationales du Mouvement Syndical Libre, Notiziario Internazionale del Movimento Sindicale Libero*, later also in other languages; the date of first publication was probably 1945, but it seems to differ for the various language editions.

34. Editor's note: The cooperating language specialists for the other languages used in this publication decided to exclude it as non-labor. For the role of the AFL and the CIO in the split of the World Federation of Trade Unions see Horst Lademacher et al, "Der Weltgewerkschaftsbund im Spannungsfeld des Ost-West-Konflikts. Zur Gründung, Tätigkeit und Spaltung der Gewerkschaftsinternationale" [The World Federation of Labor Within the East-West Conflicts: Foundation, Activities and Division of the Trade Union International],*Archiv für Sozialgeschichte* 18 (1978), pp. 119-215.

35. For a detailed analysis of Chicago periodicals see Renate Kiesewetter, "Die Institution der deutsch-amerikanischen Arbeiterpresse in Chicago. Zur Geschichte des *Vorboten* und der *Chicagoer Arbeiterzeitung*, 1874-1886" (M.A. thesis, University of Munich, 1982); Elisabeth Pitzer, "Bürgerliche Presse und Arbeiterpresse im Wandel. Deutsch- amerikanische Tageszeitungen am Ende des 19. Jahrhunderts, dargestellt am Beispiel von *Illinois Staatszeitung* und *Chicagoer Arbeiterzeitung*" [The Development of the Bourgeois and the Labor Press. German-American Daily Newspapers at the End of the 19th Century. *Illinois Staatszeitung* and *Chicagoer Arbeiter-Zeitung*, a Case Study] (M.A. thesis, University of Munich, 1980), and Anneliese Edelmann.

36. For the cable service of the bourgeois German-American daily *New Yorker Staatszeitung*, see "Im Silberkranz" in its jubilee edition of 24 April 1910.

37. In 1920 a special labor news service called "The Federated Press" was founded. Among others, the *New Yorker Volkszeitung* was linked up with it. The "Federated Press" had offices in New York, Washington and Chicago, from where it supplied altogether 58 newspapers, among them AFL, socialist and communist organs. It was directed by Carl Haessler and among its staff were Scott Nearing and Harvey O'Connor. See Carl Haessler, "Kritik eines Fachmanns," in *New Yorker Volkszeitung* 29 January 1928; "Federated Press," in *Buchdrucker-Zeitung* February 1928.

38. See the chapter on "Der deutsche Autor und der amerikanische Autoren-schutz" in Münsterberg.

39. See the excellent content analyses of the literary section of labor newspa-pers in Poore, pp. 178-183.

40. See also: Buhle.

41. See: "Schwierigkeiten einer Arbeiterzeitung" in Cleveland *Echo*, 20 May 1916.

42. D. Hoerder and Thomas Weber, eds., *Glimpses of the German-American Radical Press: Die Jubiläumsnummern der New Yorker Volkszeitung 1888, 1903, 1928* (Bremen,1985).

43. See e.g. New York *Vorwärts* (18 Mr 1893); New York *Der Anarchist* (10 F 1894); Cincinnati *Volksanwalt* (15 Mr 1898); *New Yorker Volkszeitung* (21 F 1903); *Brauer-Zeitung* (1 S 1906); *Solidarität* (O 1919); Detroit *Herold* (23 Je 1911).

44. Kiesewetter, p. 190.

45. The question has been raised of how reliable their figures were. The *Buchdrucker-Zeitung* of 1 October 1888 reported that Rowell had prom-ised a reward of $100 to anyone who could prove a circulation figure to be fraudulent. The *Buchdrucker-Zeitung* estimated that about half of all newspapers listed gave inflated circulation figures . In Ayer, circulation figures were not included before 1880.

46. See Alexander Jonas, "Wie die New Yorker Volkszeitung entstand" in *New Yorker Volkszeitung* 21 February 1903.

47. See "Das Philadelphia Tageblatt 1877-1927" in Philadelphia *Tageblatt* (18 N 1927); "Die Arbeiterzeitung und die Typographia" in *Buchdrucker-Zeitung* (16 D 1888); "Die Sozialistische Presse" in *Neues Leben* (16 My 1903). Figure 6 was prepared by Nora Ferne.

48. See *Buchdrucker-Zeitung* 16 December 1907.

49. See Adolf Roeckner's letter to the editor in *Chicagoer Arbeiterzeitung* (23 November 1900).

50. E.g. New York *Der Anarchist* 22 June 1895; Cleveland *Echo* 17 April 1920.

51. Advertisements for saloons frequently included references to which papers were available.

52. See also Klaus Ensslen "Die deutsch-amerikanische Arbeiterkneipe in Chi-cago: Ihre soziale Funktion im Spannungsfeld ethnischer und klassenspezifischer Kultur" [The German-American Working-class Saloon in Chicago: Its Social Function Between Ethnic and Working-class Cul-ture], in *Amerikastudien*, vol. 29, no. 2, (1984), pp.183-198.

53. See advertisement in *Vorwärts* (weekly of *New Yorker Volkszeitung*) e.g. in issue of 19 November 1892.

54. See advertisements in *Freiheit* 1902/1903.

Bibliography

American Labor Press Directory
Publ. by The Labor Research Department of the Rand School of Social Sciences, Director: Solon DeLeon. 1925, repr. London, 1977.

Arndt, Karl J.R. and Olson, May E.
Deutsch-Amerikanische Zeitungen und Zeitschriften, 1732-1955. Geschichte und Bibliographie [German-American Newspapers and Periodicals, 1732-1955. History and Bibliography]. 2 Vols. 1955, repr. New York, 1965, vol. 2: München, 1973.

Auer, Ignaz.
Nach zehn Jahren. Material und Glossen zur Geschichte des Sozialistengesetzes [*After Ten Years. Material and Notes on the History of the Anti-Socialist Law*]. Nürnberg, 1913.

Ayer, N.W. and Son, Inc.
Directory of Newspapers and Periodicals. Philadelphia, 1869ff.

Bade, Klaus J., ed.
Auswanderer - Wanderarbeiter - Gastarbeiter. Bevölkerung, Arbeitsmarkt und Wanderung in Deutschland seit der Mitte des 19. Jahrhunderts [Emigrants - Migrants- Guestworkers. Population, Labor Market and Migration in Germany since the Middle of the 19th Century]. 2 vols. Ostfildern, 1984.

Bianco, Rene, Creagh, Ronald and Riffaut-Perrot, Nicole.
Quand Le Coq Rouge Chantera. Anarchistes Français et Italiens aux Etats-Unis d'Amérique. Bibliographie [When the Red Rooster Sings. French and Italian Anarchists in the U.S.A. A Bibliography]. Montpellier-Cedex, 1985.

Bernstein, Samuel.
The First International in America. New York, 1965.

Broadbent, T.L.
"The German-Language Press in California: Record of a German Immigration." *Journal of the West* 10 (1971), pp. 637-61.

Canadian Ethnic Studies.
Bulletin of the Research Center for Canadian Ethnic Studies. Published by University of Calgary. Calgary, 1970.

Cazden, Robert E.
German Exile Literature in America, 1933-1950. Chicago, 1970.

Cazden, Robert E.
A History of the German Book Trade in America to the Civil War. Columbia, SC, forthcoming. Pages are quoted in brackets since only draft was available.

Checklist of Canadian Ethnic Series.
Published by National Library of Canada. Ottawa, 1981.

Commons, John R. and Associates.

> *History of Labor in the United States.* 2 vols. 1918, repr. New York, 1960.

Creagh, Ronald.

> *L'Anarchisme aux Etats-Unis* [Anarchism in the United States]. 2 vols. Berne, Frankfurt, New York, Nancy, 1983.

Cunz, Dieter.

> *The Maryland Germans.* Princeton, NJ, 1948.

Deiler, John Hanno.

> "Geschichte der New Orleanser Deutschen Presse." In Arndt, Karl J.R. and Olsen, May E., *The German Language Press of the Americas.* München, New York, London, Paris, 1980, vol. 3, pp. 619-659.

DeLeon, Solon, ed.

> *The American Labor Who's Who.* New York, 1925.

Diamond, Sander A.

> *The Nazi Movement in the United States, 1924-1941.* Ithaca, NY, 1974.

Dobert, Eitel W.

> *Deutsche Demokraten in Amerika. Die Achtundvierziger und ihre Schriften* [German Democrats in America. The Fortyeighters and Their Writings]. Göttingen, 1958.

Eberlein, Alfred, ed.

> *Die Presse der Arbeiterklasse und der sozialen Bewegungen, 1830-1967* [The Press of the Working Class and the Social Movements]. Incl. Union List of depositories, D, A, CH. Supplement: *Deutschsprachige Presse in anderen Ländern* [German-Language Press in Other Countries].

Edelmann, Anneliese.

> "Das Verhältnis der Deutschamerikaner zum Deutschen Reich (vom deutsch-französischen Krieg bis zur Samoa-Krise, 1870-1900), anhand ausgewählter Beispiele aus der deutschamerikanischen Presse." [The Relationship of the German Americans to the German Reich (from the Franco-Prussian War to the Samoa Crisis, 1870-1900) based on Selected Readings of the German-American Press]. Unpublished Manuscript, J.F. Kennedy Institut, Freie Universität Berlin, 1982.

Ely, Richard Theodore.

> *The Labor Movement in America.* 1886, New York, 1969.

Ernst, Robert.

> *Immigrant Life in New York City, 1825-1863.* New York, 1969.

Exil in den USA.

> [Exile in the U.S.A.]. By Middell, Eike, Dreifuss, Alfred u.a. Leipzig, 1979.

Fink, Gary M.

> *Biographical Dictionary of American Labor Leaders.* Westport, CO, 1974.

Fink, Gary M., ed.
    Labor Unions. Westport, CO, 1977.
Foner, Philip S.
    Autobiographies of the Haymarket Martyrs. New York, 1969.
    History of the Labor Movement in the United States. 4 vols. New York, 1962.
Foner, Philip S. and Chamberlin, eds.
    Friedrich A. Sorge's Labor Movement in the United States. New York, 1977.
Fränkel, Ludwig.
    Allgemeine Deutsche Biographie [General German Biography]. Leipzig, 1907.
Geschichte der deutschen Arbeiterbewegung.
    Biographisches Lexikon [History of the German Labor Movement. Biographical Dictionary]. Edited by Institut für Marxismus-Leninismus. Berlin, DDR, 1970.
Goldman, Emma.
    Living My Life. 1934, repr. New York, 1970.
Harnack, Arvid.
    Die vormarxistische Arbeiterbewegung in den Vereinigten Staaten [The Pre-Marxist Labor Movement in the U.S.]. Jena, 1931.
Herreshoff, David.
    American Disciples of Marx: From the Age of Jackson to the Progressive Era. Detroit, 1967.
Hillquit, Morris.
    History of Socialism in the United States. 1903, repr. of the 5th revised and enlarged edition of 1910, New York, 1971.
History of Foreign Journalism in San Francisco.
    Monograph I from *History of Journalism,* W.P.A. Project 10008. San Francisco, 1939.
Hoerder, Dirk, ed.
    Plutokraten und Sozialisten. Berichte deutscher Diplomaten über die amerikanische Arbeiterbewegung, 1878-1917 [Plutocrats and Socialists. Reports of German Diplomats about the American Labor Movement]. München, London, Paris, 1981.
Hoerder, Dirk and Weber, Thomas, eds.
    "Die Jubiläumsnummern der *New Yorker Volkszeitung* 1888, 1903, 1928." [Jubilee Editions]. In *Glimpses of the German-American Radical Press.* Published by Labor Newspaper Preservation Project, dir. Dirk Hoerder, Universityof Bremen, 1985.
Kamman, William Frederic.
    Socialism in German-American Literature. Philadelphia, 1917.
Kiesewetter, Renate.
    "Die Institution der deutsch-amerikanischen Arbeiterpresse in Chicago: Zur Geschichte des *Vorboten* und der *Chicagoer Arbeiterzeitung,* 1874-1886" [The Institution of the German- American Labor Press in Chicago: The History of *Vorbote* and *Chicagoer*

Arbeiterzeitung]. In *Glimpses of the German-American Radical Press*. Published by Labor Newspaper Preservation Project, dir. Dirk Hoerder, University of Bremen, 1985.

Kleim, Kurt.

"Der sozialistische Widerstand gegen das Dritte Reich dargestellt an der Gruppe "Neu Beginnen" [Socialist Resistance against the Third Reich with Special Emphasis on the Group "New Beginning"]. Ph. Diss, University of Marburg, 1957.

Knoche, Carl Heinz.

The German Immigrant Press in Milwaukee. 1969, New York, 1980.

Koerner, Gustav.

Das deutsche Element in den Vereinigten Staaten von Amerika, 1818-1848 [The German Element in the U.S.A.]. Cincinnati, OH, 1880.

Kosch, Wilhelm, ed.

Deutsches Literatur-Lexikon [German Encyclopedia on Literature]. Bern, München, 1971.

Krueger, Lillian.

"Madame Matilde Franziska Anneke, an Early Wisonsin Journalist." *Wisconsin Magazine of History* 21, 2 (Dec. 1937), pp. 160-167.

Levine, Bruce C.

"In the Heat of Two Revolutions: The Forging of German- American Radicalism." In *"Struggle a Hard Battle" - Working Class Immigrants*, edited by Dirk Hoerder. DeKalb, 1986, pp. 19-45.

Leyh, Eduard.

Baltimore. Seine Vergangenheit und Gegenwart mit besonderer Berücksichtigung des deutschen Elements [Baltimore. Its Past and Present, with Special Emphasis on the German Element]. Baltimore, 1887.

Maas, Lieselotte.

Handbuch der deutschen Exilpresse, 1933-1945 [Handbook of German Exile Press]. 4 vols. München, 1976.

Marschalk, Peter.

Deutsche Überseewanderung im 19. Jahrhundert [German Migration Overseas in the 19th Century]. Stuttgart, 1973.

Marx, Karl and Engels, Friedrich.

Werke [Works] 38 vols. Berlin/DDR.

Metzner, Henry, ed.

Jahrbücher der deutsch-amerikanischen Turnerei [Yearbook of the German-American Gymnasts' Movement]. 3 vols. New York, 1891-94.

Miller, Sally M.

The Radical Immigrant. New York, 1974.

Mueller, Jacob.

Erinnerungen eines Achtundvierzigers. Skizzen aus den deutsch-amerikanischen Sturm- und Drangperioden der 50er Jahre [Memoirs of a Forty-Eighter. Scetches of the German-American Storm and Stress Period of the 1850s] Cleveland, OH, 1896.

Naas, Berhard G. and Saakr, Carmelita S.
American Labor Union Periodicals. A Guide to their Location. Ithaca, NY, 1971.

Nan, John Frederick.
The German People of New Orleans, 1850-1900. Leiden, NL, 1958.

Obermann, Karl.
Joseph Weydemeyer. Ein Lebensbild 1818-1866. Berlin, 1968.

Joseph Weydemeyer, Pioneer of American Socialism. New York, 1947.

"Weydemeyer in Amerika: Neues zur Biographie von Joseph Weydemeyer, 1854-1860" [Novelties on the Biography of J. Weydemeyer]. *International Review of Social History* (Part 2, 1980), pp. 176-208.

Osterroth, Franz.
Biographisches Lexikon des Sozialismus. Bd. 1: *Verstorbene Persönlichkeiten* [Biographical Encyclopedia of Socialism. Vol. 1: Deceased Personalities]. Hannover, 1960.

Poore, Carol Jean.
"German-American Socialist Literature in the Late 19th Century." Ph.Diss. University of Wisconsin, Madison, 1979.

Radkan, Joachim.
Die deutsche Emigration in den USA. Ihr Einfluß auf die amerikanische Europapolitik 1933-1945 [The German Emigration in the U.S.A. Its Influence on American Politics Concerning Europe]. Düsseldorf, 1971.

Ragg, Albrecht.
"The German Socialist Emigration in the United States, 1933- 1945." Ph.Diss, Loyola University of Chicago, 1977.

Raltermann, Heinrich A.
"Die deutsche Presse in den Vereinigten Staaten" [The German Press in the U.S.]. *Der Deutsche Pionier* [The German Pioneer] 7 (1876), p. 463-66, (8 Oct.1876), pp. 289-320.

Rippley, La Vera J.
The German-Americans. Boston, 1976.

Rocker, Rudolf.
Johann Most. Das Leben eines Rebellen [John Most. The Life of a Rebel]. Berlin, 1924.

Rocker, Rudolf.
Memoiren eines deutschen Anarchisten. Frankfurt a. Main, 1974.

Schem, Alexander.
Deutsch-Amerikanisches Conversations-Lexicon, mit spezieller Berücksichtigung auf die Bedürfnisse der in Amerika lebenden Deutschen [German-American Encyclopedia with Special Emphasis on the Concerns of Germans who Live in America]. New York, 1969-74.

Schlicher, J.J.

"Bernhard Domschke: 1) A Life of Hardship, 2) The Editor and the Man." *Wisconsin Magazine of History* 29 (1946), pp. 319-332, 435-456.

Schlüter, Hermann.

Die Anfänge der deutschen Arbeiterbewegung in Amerika [The Beginnings of the German Labor Movement in America]. Stuttgart, 1907.

"Die Anfänge der deutschen Arbeiterbewegung in New York und ihre Presse" [The Beginnings of the German Labor Movement in New York and Its Press]. In *New Yorker Volkszeitung* (Jubilee Edition for 25th Anniversary) 21 F 1903, p. 8-12.

Die Internationale in Amerika [The International in America]. Chicago, 1918.

Schultz, Arthur R.

German-American Relations and German Culture in America: A Subject Bibliography, 1941-1980. 2 vols. New York, 1984.

Sorge, Friedrich A.

Labor Movement in the United States. A History of the American Working Class from Colonial Times to 1890. Edited by Philip S. Foner and Brewster Chamberlin. Westport, CO, 1977.

Thümmler, Heinzpeter.

Sozialistengesetz §28. Ausweisungen und Ausgewiesene 1878- 1890 [Anti-Socialist Law § 28. Expulsion and the Expelled]. Vaduz, 1979.

Ueberhorst, Horst.

Turner und Sozialdemokraten in Milwaukee: 5 Jahrzehnte der Kooperation (1910-1960) [Gymnasts and Social Democrats in Milwaukee: 5 Decades of Cooperation] Bonn, 1980.

Union List.

Union List of Canadian Newspapers Held by Canadian Libraries/ Liste collective des journaux canadiens disponibles dans les bibliotheques Canadiennes. Published by National Library of Canada. Ottawa, 1977.

Waltershausen, Sartorius von.

Der moderne Socialismus in den Vereinigten Staaten von America [Modern Socialism in the U.S.A.]. Berlin, 1890.

Ward, Norman J.

The Labor Movement in the United States, 1860-1895. A Study in Democracy. 1929; New York, 1964.

Weinrich, Peter.

Social Protest from the Left in Canada 1870-1970. "Checklist of Serials." Toronto, 1982, pp. 383-461.

Wittke, Carl F.

Against the Current. The Life of Karl Heinzen. Chicago, 1945.

The German-Language Press in America. Lexington, KY, 1957.

Refugees of Revolution. The German Forty-Eighters in America. Philadelphia, 1952.

The Utopian Communist. The Life of Wilhelm Weitling, Nineteenth Century Reformer. Baton Rouge, LA, 1950.

Zucker, Adolf Eduard.

The Forty-Eighters. Political Refugees of the German Revolution of 1848. New York, 1967.

Annotated Bibliography

ABENDPOST	CA San Francisco	1868-?

Title trans.:	Evening Post	*First issue:*		
Subtitle:		*Last issue:*		
Add. lang.:		*Vols. (nos.):*		
First editor:		*Frequency:*		
First publ.:		*Preservation:*	7	
Related pubs.:		*Supplements:*		
Circulation:		*Category:*	socialist-IWA	

Depositories:

This paper was the organ of the San Francisco branch of the First International. This branch had been founded by a man from Baden, Germany. Two fighters of the 1848 Revolution, Reiter and Cohnheim, were at the head of the movement there.

Source: Waltershausen, p. 48.

DER ADOPTIV-BÜRGER	PA Philadelphia	1845?-1846

Title trans.:	The Adopted Citizen	*First issue:*	Ja 1845?
Subtitle:		*Last issue:*	1846
Add. lang.:		*Vols. (nos.):*	
First editor:	George Dietz	*Frequency:*	d
First publ.:	George Dietz	*Preservation:*	7
Related pubs.:		*Supplements:*	
Circulation:		*Category:*	labor

Depositories:

This paper was referred to by Schlüter as the first labor paper printed in the German language. George Dietz had previously published the *Pittsburger Beobachter*. The paper was an exponent of Wilhelm Weitling's "Handwerker-Kommunismus." It was discontinued in January 1846 but a few issues appeared later.

Sources: Arndt/Olson; Eberlein 22621; Kamman, p. 37; Wittke, *Press*, p. 111; Schlüter, *Anfänge*, p. 19.

AGITATOR	NJ Elizabeth	1893-?

Title trans.:	Agitator	*First issue:*	15 Je 1893
Subtitle:	Den Interessen der Arbeiterklasse des Staates New Jersey gewidmet.	*Last issue:*	?
Add. lang.:		*Vols. (nos.):*	1(1)-?
First editor:		*Frequency:*	m
First publ.:	Arbeiter Publishing Association	*Preservation:*	6
Related pubs.:		*Supplements:*	
Circulation:		*Category:*	labor

Depositories: Usa-NN (15 Je 1893)

According to the subtitle this labor monthly was "dedicated to the interests of the working class of the state of New Jersey." It was printed by the Elizabethport Printing Co. and appeared as a 12-page Octavo.

Sources: Arndt/Olson; Eberlein 22623.

AMERIKANISCHE ARBEITER-ZEITUNG (I)	NY New York	1848-?

Title trans.:	American Labor News	*First issue:*	1848?
Subtitle:		*Last issue:*	?
Add. lang.:	English	*Vols. (nos.):*	
First editor:	Wilhelm Beschke	*Frequency:*	
First publ.:		*Preservation:*	7
Related pubs.:		*Supplements:*	
Circulation:		*Category:*	

Depositories:

No further information could be obtained.

Source: Cazden, *Book Trade* (p. 643), whose source was: *Deutsch-Amerikanische Didaskalia.*

AMERIKANISCHE ARBEITERZEITUNG (II)	NY New York	1886

Title trans.:	American Labor News	*First issue:*	2 Ja 1886
Subtitle:		*Last issue:*	Je 1886
Add. lang.:		*Vols. (nos.):*	
First editor:	Wilhelm Hasselmann	*Frequency:*	
First publ.:		*Preservation:*	4
Related pubs.:		*Supplements:*	
Circulation:		*Category:*	anarchist

Depositories: Nl-IISG [1886]

This was an anarchist paper, founded and edited by Wilhelm Hasselmann* in opposition to Johann Most's *Freiheit.* The paper failed after six months, having "devoured" a subsidy of $500-600.

Sources: Arndt/Olson; Eberlein 22665; Rocker, p. 298. On Hasselmann, see Kamman, p. 48; *Geschichte der deutschen Arbeiterbewegung*, pp. 189-190; Waltershausen, pp. 170, 363-364; Hoerder, *Plutokraten*, p. 329.

AMERIKANISCHE TURNZEITUNG	WI Milwaukee	1878-1942

Title trans.:	American Gymnasts' News	*First issue:*	Jl 1878
Subtitle:		*Last issue:*	1942
Add. lang.:		*Vols. (nos.):*	
First editor:		*Frequency:*	
First publ.:	Freidenker Publishing Co.	*Preservation:*	3
Related pubs.:	*Freidenker*	*Supplements:*	
Circulation:		*Category:*	freethought/ Gymnasts

Depositories: Usa-WHi (1878-1914?); D-19/1501 (1885-1909,m)

At their national convention in Cleveland, 1878, the Gymnasts' national organ, *Die Zukunft* [The Future] (Indianapolis) lost its official status. In spite of some opposition the *Freidenker* [Freethinker] (Milwaukee, 1872-1942) was chosen as the movement's official organ and according to the convention's stipulation it began to publish a three-page weekly supplement entitled *Turnzeitung* [Gymnasts' News], which appeared from July 1878 till December 1884. The main section of the *Freidenker* also increased its coverage of Gymnast events until conservative groups among the Gymnasts began to attack the freethought faction. From January 1885 the two publications appeared separately. The *Turnzeitung* was now published under the title of *Amerikanische Turnzeitung. Turnerische Ausgabe des Freidenkers*. After January 1888? the subtitle, which translates as "the supplement of the *Freethinker* concerning Gymnasts' events" disappeared. Both *Freidenker* and *Amerikanische Turnzeitung* had the same editors and their general pages were identical. The paper was first published in Milwaukee, later in New Ulm, MN.

Sources: Arndt/Olson; Eberlein 22814.

DER ANARCHIST	IL Chicago	1886

Title trans.:	The Anarchist	*First issue:*	Ja 1886
Subtitle:		*Last issue:*	My 1886
Add. lang.:		*Vols. (nos.):*	(1)-(4)
First editor:		*Frequency:*	m
First publ.:		*Preservation:*	6
Related pubs.:	s *Der Anarchist* (St. Louis/New York)	*Supplements:*	
Circulation:	300	*Category:*	anarchist-IWPA

Depositories: Usa-Julius S. Grinnell Collection (Ja 1886, Ap 1886)

This paper was the organ of the "Autonome Gruppen der Internationalen Arbeiter-Association" [Autonomous Groups of the International Working People's Association]. It was edited by George Engel, A. Fischer und

"Genossen" [Comrades] and accused the *Chicagoer Arbeiter-Zeitung* and the English-language anarchist paper *Alarm* of corruption. After the Haymarket Riot it was suppressed but continued as *Der Anarchist* (St. Louis/New York)

Sources: Arndt/Olson (who give 1884-1894? as the dates of appearance); Eberlein 22625; Waltershausen, p. 311; Rocker, pp. 146-149 (reprint of the platform of the IWPA written by Most and adopted by the international socialist congress in Pittsburgh on 16 October 1883); Michael Schaak, *Anarchy and Anarchists: A History of the Red Terror and the Social Revolution in America and Europe* (Chicago, 1889), p. 358; John Kebabian, ed., *The Haymarket Affair and the Trial of the Chicago Anarchists* (New York, 1970), item 29, p. 20 and item 33, p. 23.

DER ANARCHIST		MO St. Louis/NY New York	1889-1895

Title trans.:	The Anarchist	*First issue:*	1 Ag 1889
Subtitle:	Anarchistisch-Communistisches Organ	*Last issue:*	22 Je 1895
Add. lang.:		*Vols. (nos.):*	1-7(9)
First editor:	Claus Timmermann	*Frequency:*	bw, w, bw
First publ.:	Claus Timmermann	*Preservation:*	5
Related pubs.:	*Der Anarchist*, Chicago	*Supplements:*	
Circulation:		*Category:*	anarchist-WPA

Depositories: Usa-WHi [1892,1894]; Usa-NN [1892]; Nl-IISG [1889-1892]; D-188/144 (22 Je 1895)

This 4-page paper was first published as a biweekly, from 23 January 1892 to 27 October? 1894 as a weekly and then as a biweekly again. According to the subtitle it was an "anarchist-communist organ" and its motto was: "Die Zeit wird kommen, wenn unser Schweigen mächtiger sein wird, als die Stimme, die Ihr heute erdrosselt" (A. Spies) [The time will come when our silence will be more powerful than the voices which you strangle today].

First it was edited, published and printed in St. Louis by Claus Timmermann (see also *Die Brandfackel* and *Sturmvogel*). After 19 September 1891 it was published in New York by the Autonomous Groups of America, successor of the *Anarchist*, which was founded by Lingg, Fischer, Engel and comrades and suppressed by reactionary forces (see *Der Anarchist*, Chicago, 1886). By then it was edited by Nic. Mauer. The St. Louis paper, "in debt up to its ears" (Rocker), was bought in 1891 from Timmermann through Otto Rinke and served thereafter as the organ of the autonomous groups of New York and vicinity, a faction of the anarchist movement, which was influenced by Josef Peukert, an opponent of Johann Most. It contained news from the anarchist movement in America, Germany and France; criticism of social-democratic thought and trade unionism, articles on topics such as authority, property and the founding of colonies, reports from the diverse autonomous groups, quotations from the international anarchist press, book reviews, e.g. of Henry Mackay's "Die Anarchisten," advertisements and announcements exclusively for anarchist publications and meetings. Contributions came from Paul Berwig, Matzinger, Charles Diether, Peter Kropotkin, Saverio Merlino, "Satan," "Mephisto," "Anarchist." *Der Anarchist* was suspended because "the comrades had considered it as unimportant," leaving the publishers with a debt of $400.

Sources: Arndt/Olson; Rocker, pp. 341, 354; Goldman, pp. 74-75; Creagh. On Peukert, see Rocker, *Most* pp. 216-283; Bianco.

DER ANTI-AUTORITÄR	NY New York	1911

Title trans.:	The Antiauthoritarian	*First issue:*		15 Mr 1911
Subtitle:		*Last issue:*		29 Jl 1911
Add. lang.:		*Vols. (nos.):*		
First editor:	G. Rahmlow, Hans Koch	*Frequency:*		m
First publ.:		*Preservation:*		1
Related pubs.:		*Supplements:*		
Circulation:		*Category:*		anarchist

Depositories: D-Bm 41/IGA [1911]; Usa-MiU, Labadie Collection; Usa-NNC, special collection B 335.8/7926

This was a monthly anarchist-communist organ published by the "Anti-Autoritär" Group.

Source: *Der Strom*, issue of Mr 1911; Bianco.

DER ANTI-FASCHIST	NY New York	1938-1939?

Title trans.:	The Antifascist	*First issue:*	Ja 1938
Subtitle:		*Last issue:*	N 1939?
Add. lang.:		*Vols. (nos.):*	1(1)-?
First editor:	Karl Maison	*Frequency:*	m
First publ.:	German-American Anti-Fascist Club	*Preservation:*	6
Related pubs.:		*Supplements:*	
Circulation:		*Category:*	socialist

Depositories: D-292 [F 1938]

This paper was published as the official organ of the Club Deutscher Antifaschisten [Club of German Antifascists], which was a group of dissident members of the Deutscher Arbeiter Klub [German Workers' Club] who had left that communist-controlled organization. As an independent socialist anti-Nazi publication it aimed at non-communist German-American workers. The only preserved issue has 16 pages; it contains satirical articles directed against Fritz Kuhn and against antisemitism, announcements of the Club Deutscher Antifaschisten and of anti-Nazi sports clubs. It was illustrated with photographs and cartoons and contained contributions by Flegel and Haller.

Sources: Cazden, *Exile Literature*, pp. 184-185; Maas I, p. 72; Maas IV; Arndt/Olson. See also: *Gegen den Strom*, Mr 1938 and N 1939.

DER ARBEITER		WI Milwaukee	1854-?
Title trans.:	The Worker	*First issue:*	21 My 1854
Subtitle:		*Last issue:*	?
Add. lang.:		*Vols. (nos.):*	
First editor:	Heinrich Loose	*Frequency:*	w
First publ.:		*Preservation:*	7
Related pubs.:		*Supplements:*	
Circulation:		*Category:*	workers' club

Depositories:

According to Knoche, only one issue of this paper has been found and it states "herausgegeben und redigiert von einer Gesellschaft Arbeiter" [published and edited by an association of workers]. According to Knoche and Arndt/Olson the editor was Heinrich Loose, who had published the freethought weekly *Der Humanist*, 1851-53, "ein Organ für die Freien Gemeinden und Freien Schulen" [an Organ for the Free Congregations and Free Schools]. Loose was the chairman of the "Sozialer Turnverein," founded in Milwaukee in 1853. He was a Fortyeighter refugee and is said to have been a follower of Weitling's ideas. In an article entitled "Unser Programm" [Our Program] the paper claimed that it was not interested in political parties and intended to serve only the worker. It did not exist very long.

Sources: Arndt/Olson; Eberlein 22633; Knoche, p. 80.

DER ARBEITER (I)		NY New York	1858
Title trans.:	The Worker	*First issue:*	27 Mr 1858
Subtitle:		*Last issue:*	8 My 1858//
Add. lang.:		*Vols. (nos.):*	1(1-7)
First editor:	W. Benque	*Frequency:*	w
First publ.:	Allgemeiner Arbeiterbund in New York	*Preservation:*	1
Related pubs.:		*Supplements:*	
Circulation:		*Category:*	workers' club

Depositories: Usa-WHi; D-188/144 [1858,m]

When the Arbeiterbund of New York [Workingmen's League of New York] split in April 1858, its organ, *Der Arbeiter*, remained in the hands of W. Benque (spelled incorrectly Banque by Schlüter and Arndt/ Olson). Benque belonged to the minority faction and appears to have been the sole owner as well as its editor. See also *Die sociale Republik*.

The first six issues consist of six editorial pages and two pages of advertisements. The editorial part contains news of the Arbeiterbund, reports about the political situation (mostly in America), articles on slavery and taxation, invectives against Marxist communism and other, often not well defined enemies, local news and a feuilleton. In its last, one-page issue, Benque announced the founding of a successor, the *New Yorker Morgenzeitung* [New

York Morning Paper]. This appears to be lost. According to Schlüter the *New Yorker Morgenzeitung* was the only German newspaper openly in favor of slavery. *Der Arbeiter* had favored the idea that slaves should be set free and be shipped to Africa and South America in order to civilize these continents. *Der Arbeiter* has been criticized as confused, vague and even corrupt.

Sources: Arndt/Olson; Arndt/Olson 2, p. 438; Eberlein 22634; Schlüter, *Anfänge*, p. 169.

DER ARBEITER		PA Lebanon	1871-1880

Title trans.:	The Worker	*First issue:*	My 1871
Subtitle:	A Weekly Paper for English and German Readers	*Last issue:*	N 1880
Add. lang.:	English	*Vols. (nos.):*	
First editor:	John Shupe	*Frequency:*	w
First publ.:	John Shupe	*Preservation:*	6
Related pubs.:		*Supplements:*	
Circulation:	1876: 600 (est]; 1880: 580	*Category:*	labor

Depositories: Usa-MWA, Rowell Collection (20 Jl 1876)

This was a labor paper, which supported President Hayes. Pages 1 and 4 were written in English with the title *The Laborer*. According to Arndt/Olson, the paper merged with the *Pittsburger Volkszeitung* but the *Pittsburger Volkszeitung* did not exist before 1891.

Sources: Arndt/Olson; Arndt/Olson 2, p. 525; Eberlein 22632.

DER ARBEITER (II)	NY New York	1905?-1906?

Title trans.:	The Worker	*First issue:*	1905
Subtitle:		*Last issue:*	1906
Add. lang.:		*Vols. (nos.):*	
First editor:		*Frequency:*	
First publ.:		*Preservation:*	?
Related pubs.:		*Supplements:*	
Circulation:		*Category:*	

Depositories: Nl-IISG (1905-06)

No further information is available.

DER ARBEITER (III)	NY New York	1927-1937

Title trans.:	The Worker	*First issue:*	15 S 1927
Subtitle:	see below	*Last issue:*	13 F 1937
Add. lang.:		*Vols. (nos.):*	1-11(7)
First editor:	Carl Gertig	*Frequency:*	m,bw,w
First publ.:		*Preservation:*	2
Related pubs.:	s *Deutsches Volksecho*	*Supplements:*	
Circulation:		*Category:*	communist-CP

Depositories: Usa-NN ([1927-30]-1937); D-188/144 ([1927-30]-1937, m)

This was the organ of the Communist Party and it appeared as a monthly (15 September 1927 - 15 March 1928) (not semimonthly, as erroneously mentioned by Arndt/Olson), as a biweekly (1 April 1928 - December 1929) and as a weekly (1 January 1930 - 13 February 1927). It had 2 pages in 1927, 4, 6 or 8 pages in 1928-29, 4 pages after 1930. The title varied: 1) *Mitteilungsblatt* (15 September - 15 December 1927); 2) *Kommunistisches Mitteilungsblatt* (January - 15 June 1928); 3) *Der Arbeiter* (1 July 1928 - 13 February 1937), as did the subtitle: 1) Offizielles Organ der Deutschen Sprachfraktion der Workers' (Communist) Party of America (after 8 January 1929) [Official Organ of the German-language section of the WCP]; 2) Offizielles Deutsches Organ der Communist Party, U.S.A. [Official German Organ of the CP] (after 1 May 1930); 3) Antifaschistische Kampfzeitung [Paper of the Antifascist Struggle] (after 6 January 1935). Its emblem also changed: 1) a hammer and sickle in the masthead (15 September - 15 December 1927 and after 31 March 1931); 2) a disc-shaped emblem with the inscription "Antifaschistische Aktion" (2 May 1933 - 13 February 1937). The motto was: "Arbeiter aller Länder, vereinigt Euch!" [Workers of all countries, unite!]. Gertig was only mentioned as the editor in the first issue. He was a candidate for the office of general secretary and treasury of the Amalgamated Food Workers Union in 1928. No other editor was mentioned. The paper was published 1) by the Deutsche Sprachfraktion der Workers' (Communist) Party, German Language Bureau; 2) the Deutsche Sprachfraktion, the Workers' (Communist) Party; 3) the German Language Bureau der Workers' Communist Party N.Y., i.e. der Arbeiter Publishing Co. (after 1 July 1928). It was superseded by *Deutsches Volksecho*. The paper intended to "rouse German-speaking workers to participate in the class-struggle," to "fight against imperialism and the danger of war," to "help to create a mass-party of the American proletariat," and to promote "the organization of councils for the protection of foreign-born workers." It wanted to inform German workers about the revolutionary movements and to give a "Leninist interpretation of events of the day, which are most important for the worker." (Quotations translated from the first issue). It strongly opposed the *New Yorker Volkszeitung*. Originally it contained mostly news from the American and German communist movement and polemics against Ludwig Lore. Later it increasingly covered international news from the communist movement, especially from the Soviet Union and China; it also contained traveller's reports, book reviews, columns on proletarian culture and sports, a women's and a youth section, serialized novels, the cash reports of the "Antifaschistische Aktion", announcements of labor organizations such as the "Naturfreunde," singing societies, diverse unions, of the Workmen's Sick and

Death Benefit Fund, of the Prolet-Bühne (a theater), of diverse labor defense associations, e.g. Rote Hilfe [Red Help]. Advertisements became increasingly frequent and included those of local doctors, funeral homes, saloons, union bakeries, workers' homes. After 1928 it printed photographs and cartoons. Contributions came from Israel Kassvan, Willi Bredel, Karl Radek, Henry Barbusse, Theodor Plivier, Egon Erwin Kisch, Willi Münzenberg, Alfred Kurell, William Z. Foster, Heinrich Mann, Stefan Heym, Ilja Ehrenburg, Erich Weinert, Alfons Goldschmidt and many others. Lenin, Marx and Liebknecht were frequently quoted. The jubilee issue appeared on 29 February 1936. It also published irregular supplements, e.g. "Literaturbeilage" [Literary Supplement] in 1933, "Mitteilungsblatt der Deutschen Arbeiterklubs" [Newsletter of the German-American Workers' Clubs] around 1935; (see also: *Deutsch-Amerikanische Arbeiterklubs. Mitteilungsblatt*); "Mitteilungen der Deutschen Zentralbücherei" in March 1936 (see *Deutsche Zentralbücherei: Mitteilungsblatt* [German Central Library: Newsletter]). There were special issues on 1 May and a special issue devoted to the "Sängerfest" [Choral Festival] in 1929.

Sources: Arndt/Olson; Eberlein 22635, 22754; Cazden, *Exile Literature*, pp. 39-41, 187; Ragg, p. 35.

ARBEITER ABENDZEITUNG	OH Cincinnati	1850?-1852?

Title trans.:	Workers' Evening News	*First issue:*	1850?
Subtitle:		*Last issue:*	1852?
Add. lang.:		*Vols. (nos.):*	
First editor:	Johannes Peyer	*Frequency:*	d
First publ.:	Arbeiterverein von Cincinnati	*Preservation:*	7
Related pubs.:	*Arbeiter-Union*	*Supplements:*	
Circulation:		*Category:*	workers' club

Depositories:

Die *Arbeiter Abendzeitung* and the *Arbeiter-Union* were two of the four German papers Cincinnati had in 1850. The *Cincinnati Arbeiter Abendzeitung* was the "Organ des Arbeitervereins von Cincinnati" [Organ of the Workers' Club of Cincinnati]. Its editor, Johannes Peyer, was a Fortyeighter who had been trained for a career in medicine.

Sources: Arndt/Olson; Eberlein 22618, 22638; Wittke, *Press*, pp. 88, 171.

DAS ARBEITERBLATT   LA New Orleans   1851-?

Title trans.:	The Workers' Gazette	*First issue:*	26 Ja 1851
Subtitle:		*Last issue:*	?
Add. lang.:		*Vols. (nos.):*	
First editor:	August Kathmann	*Frequency:*	w
First publ.:	Allgemeiner Arbeiterverein	*Preservation:*	7
Related pubs.:		*Supplements:*	
Circulation:		*Category:*	workers' club

Depositories:

According to Deiler, on 14 October 1850, a workers' meeting took place at Sacramento House, the oldest German club-house in New Orleans. At this meeting the Allgemeiner Arbeiterverein was founded by joiners, tailors, shoemakers, cartwrights and metalworkers. It was also resolved to publish an organ under the editorship of August Kathmann (Arndt/ Olson: "Kattmann"). The paper should appear "for the present" as a weekly and then later as a daily. A first number appeared on Sunday, 26 January 1851 (*Tägliche Deutsche Zeitung*, 28 January 1851).

Sources: Arndt/Olson; Arndt/Olson 2, p. 387; Eberlein 22640; Cazden, *Book Trade*, note 123; Deiler; Nau, p. 57 (On Allgemeiner Arbeiterverein, see Nau, p. 57]

ARBEITERBLATT (Cincinnati Arbeiterblatt)   OH Cincinnati   1877-1887?

Title trans.:	Cincinnati Workers' Gazette	*First issue:*	? S 1877
Subtitle:		*Last issue:*	?
Add. lang.:		*Vols. (nos.):*	
First editor:	Cincinnatier Freie Presse Kompagnie	*Frequency:*	d
First publ.:	Cincinnatier Freie Presse Kompagnie	*Preservation:*	4
Related pubs.:		*Supplements:*	
Circulation:		*Category:*	

Depositories: Usa-OCHi [1877]

This was a daily evening paper. It did not appear on Sunday. Its reported successor (Arndt/Olson), the *Tägliche Abend-Presse*, claimed to be an independent paper. The connection between the two papers remains unclear.

Sources: Arndt/Olson; Eberlein 22641.

DER ARBEITERFREUND	NY New York	1855-?

Title trans.:	The Workers' Friend	*First issue:*	My 1855
Subtitle:		*Last issue:*	?
Add. lang.:		*Vols. (nos.):*	
First editor:	Heerbrandt	*Frequency:*	
First publ.:		*Preservation:*	7
Related pubs.:		*Supplements:*	
Circulation:		*Category:*	workers' club

Depositories:

The only information about this paper is that Heerbrandt offered to let the Arbeiterbund [Workers' League] make it its official organ, but his offer was declined.
Sources: Arndt/Olson; Eberlein 22646; Schlüter, *Anfänge*, p. 156; Kammann, p. 43; Cazden, *Book Trade*, p. (666).

DER ARBEITERFREUND	IL Chicago	1874

Title trans.:	The Workers' Friend	*First issue:*	? 1874
Subtitle:		*Last issue:*	? 1874
Add. lang.:		*Vols. (nos.):*	
First editor:	Rudolph Ruhbaum	*Frequency:*	w
First publ.:	Rudolph Ruhbaum	*Preservation:*	7
Related pubs.:		*Supplements:*	
Circulation:		*Category:*	socialist

Depositories:

No further information could be obtained.
Sources: Arndt/Olson; Eberlein 22643.

DER ARBEITER-FREUND	OH Cincinnati	1849-?

Title trans.:	The Workers' Friend	*First issue:*	1849?
Subtitle:		*Last issue:*	?
Add. lang.:		*Vols. (nos.):*	
First editor:	Dr. Ciolini	*Frequency:*	?
First publ.:	Dr. Ciolini	*Preservation:*	7
Related pubs.:		*Supplements:*	
Circulation:		*Category:*	labor

Depositories:

Ciolini is also mentioned as "Cialdini."

Sources: Arndt/Olson; Eberlein 22645.

DER ARBEITER-FREUND		WV Wheeling	1865?-1876

Title trans.:	The Workers' Friend	*First issue:*	1865?
Subtitle:		*Last issue:*	1876?
Add. lang.:		*Vols. (nos.):*	
First editor:	Troll and Carl Neuhauser	*Frequency:*	w
First publ.:	Carl Neuhauser	*Preservation:*	6
Related pubs.:		*Supplements:*	
Circulation:	1871: 800; 1876: 1200 [est]	*Category:*	labor

Depositories: Usa-MWA, Rowell Collection (22 Ja 1876)

The paper was published in the interest of labor and labor reform. Neuhauser is also mentioned as 'Neuhausen.'

Sources: Arndt/Olson; Eberlein 22648; Schem XI, pp. 485 and 492 (mentions 1866 as year of beginning).

DER ARBEITER-FREUND		PA McKeesport	1884?-1885?

Title trans.:	The Workers' Friend	*First issue:*	1884?
Subtitle:		*Last issue:*	1885?
Add. lang.:		*Vols. (nos.):*	
First editor:	Häfelyn and Joos	*Frequency:*	w
First publ.:	Häfelyn and Joos	*Preservation:*	7
Related pubs.:		*Supplements:*	
Circulation:		*Category:*	labor

Depositories:

No further information could be obtained.
Source: Arndt/Olson.

DER ARBEITER-FREUND		PA Philadelphia	1887-?

Title trans.:	The Workers' Friend	*First issue:*	Mr 1887
Subtitle:		*Last issue:*	?
Add. lang.:		*Vols. (nos.):*	
First editor:	Kaupp & Co.	*Frequency:*	w
First publ.:	Kaupp & Co.	*Preservation:*	7
Related pubs.:	c *Vorwärts* (Philadelphia)	*Supplements:*	
Circulation:	1887: 1200	*Category:*	labor

Depositories:

On 2 March 1887 the Philadelphia *Vorwärts* (see Appendix I) was bought by G. Kaupp (Arndt/Olson: J.M. Kaupp & Co] from Typographia No. 1 of Philadelphia and began its second volume under the new title of *Arbeiter-Freund*.

Sources: Arndt/Olson; Eberlein 22647; *Buchdrucker-Zeitung (BZ)* 16 M 1887.

ARBEITER-FREUND	IL Chicago	1919-1921?

Title trans.:	Workers' Friend	*First issue:*	Ap 1919
Subtitle:		*Last issue:*	1921
Add. lang.:		*Vols. (nos.):*	
First editor:		*Frequency:*	m
First publ.:		*Preservation:*	7
Related pubs.:		*Supplements:*	
Circulation:		*Category:*	catholic labor

Depositories:

This paper was established by the Chicago branch of the Kolping Society, the German Roman Catholic Association for journeymen artisans and workers. It existed for about two years.

Sources: Arndt/Olson; Eberlein 22644.

ARBEITER-SPORT IN AMERIKA	NY Brooklyn	1927-1933

Title trans.:	Proletarian Sports in America	*First issue:*	Ja? 1927
Subtitle:		*Last issue:*	D? 1933
Add. lang.:	English	*Vols. (nos.):*	1-7
First editor:	L. Daiber	*Frequency:*	m
First publ.:	Arbeiter Turn- und Sport-Bund	*Preservation:*	3
Related pubs.:		*Supplements:*	
Circulation:		*Category:*	socialist

Depositories: Usa-NN [1930-33]

This was a monthly published in English and German. Volume 7 had a German title but the text was in English; with volume 8, no. 1, the title changed to *Proletarian Sports*. It was the Organ of the Workers' Gymnastic and Sport Alliance of America (Arbeiter Turn- und Sportbund), 1927-1929; of the Workers' Sports League of America, 1930-33. It was an octavo of 8 pages and contained illustrations.

Sources: Arndt/Olson; Eberlein 22650.

ARBEITER-STIMME   NY New York   1874-1878

Title trans.:	Workers' Voice	*First issue:*	28 N 1874
Subtitle:	see below	*Last issue:*	2 Je 1878//
Add. lang.:		*Vols. (nos.):*	1(1)-4(23)
First editor:	Gustav Lyser	*Frequency:*	w
First publ.:	Sozial-demokratische Arbeiterpartei	*Preservation:*	1
Related pubs.:		*Supplements:*	
Circulation:	1875: 1500; 1878: 1300	*Category:*	social democrat

Depositories: Usa-WHi; D-188/144 (1,m)

From 1(1) to 2(32) this weekly was called *Social-Demokrat* with the subtitle: Organ und Eigenthum der sozial-demokratischen Arbeiterpartei von N. Amerika [Organ and Property of the Social-Democratic Workers' Party of North America] and from 2(33) to 4(23) *Arbeiter-Stimme* with the subtitle: Organ und Eigentum der Arbeiterpartei der Ver. Staaten [Organ and Property of the Workers' Party of the United States]. It was printed by the Social-demokratische Genossenschafts-Druckerei.

Editors after Lyser* were: A. Vossberg (1875-76), August Otto-Walster* (1876-77), Georg Winter (1877), Alexander Jonas* (1877-78). The first issue contained the fourteen articles of the Social-Democratic Party platform. The paper contained news from America and Europe, reports from correspondents in other American cities and towns, labor news, articles on economic, educational and housing problems and on women's problems. There were serialized novels and some poems. The title was changed in 1876 when the Sozial-demokratische Arbeiterpartei and three other workingmen's organizations formed the Arbeiterpartei. The last issue announced that it was to be discontinued because the *Arbeiterstimme* as a weekly had lost more than half of its subscribers to the newly founded daily *New Yorker Volkszeitung*. The *National Socialist* was recommended to its readers.

Among the contributors were Georg Stiebeling, Minna Kautsky, Adolf Douai, Johann Most, Ferdinand Freiligrath, Heinrich Heine, Robert Schweichel.

Sources: Arndt/Olson; Eberlein 22652, 22791; Schlüter, *Internationale*, pp. 392-393; "Presse;" Hillquit, p. 191; Sorge, pp. 28, 199-200. On Lyser, see *Die Fackel*; on Jonas, see *New Yorker Volkszeitung*; on Otto-Walster, see *Geschichte der deutschen Arbeiterbewegung* pp. 360-361 and Friedrich, Wolfgang, *August Otto-Walster. Leben und Werk. Eine DDR Auswahl mit unveröffentlichten Briefen an Karl* (Berlin, 1966).

ARBEITER-STIMME		IL Chicago	1889

Title trans.:	Workers' Voice	*First issue:*	? 1889
Subtitle:		*Last issue:*	? 1889
Add. lang.:		*Vols. (nos.):*	
First editor:		*Frequency:*	w
First publ.:	Central Labor Union	*Preservation:*	7
Related pubs.:		*Supplements:*	
Circulation:		*Category:*	labor union-CLU

Depositories:

No further information could be obtained.
Sources: Arndt/Olson; Eberlein 22651.

DIE ARBEITERSTIMME AM ERIE		NY Buffalo	1878

Title trans.:	The Workers' Voice at the Erie	*First issue:*	My 1878?
Subtitle:		*Last issue:*	N 1878?
Add. lang.:		*Vols. (nos.):*	
First editor:	Paul Koberstein	*Frequency:*	w
First publ.:	Paul Koberstein	*Preservation:*	7
Related pubs.:		*Supplements:*	
Circulation:		*Category:*	labor

Depositories:

According to Arndt/Olson this was a "radical labor weekly." Its editor, Paul Koberstein, had edited the *Buffalo Tribüne*, 1876-78.
Source: Arndt/Olson.

ARBEITER-UNION		OH Cincinnati	1849?-1852?

Title trans.:	Workers' Union	*First issue:*	1849?
Subtitle:		*Last issue:*	1852?
Add. lang.:		*Vols. (nos.):*	
First editor:	Dr. William Peyer	*Frequency:*	
First publ.:	Dr. William Peyer	*Preservation:*	7
Related pubs.:		*Supplements:*	
Circulation:		*Category:*	

Depositories:

This paper was one of the four German newspapers published in Cincinnati in 1850. It was superseded by the *Union*, which was according to Rattermann a "frei-protestantische Zeitschrift" [a free-protestant periodical].

Sources: Arndt/Olson; Eberlein 22655; Rattermann.

ARBEITER-UNION		NY New York	1868-1870

Title trans.:	Workers' Union	*First issue:*	13 Je 1868
Subtitle:	see below	*Last issue:*	17 S 1870//
Add. lang.:		*Vols. (nos.):*	1(1)-2(101)
First editor:	Dr. Landsberg	*Frequency:*	w, d
First publ.:	Association Vereinigter Arbeiter	*Preservation:*	1
Related pubs.:		*Supplements:*	
Circulation:		*Category:*	workers' club/ socialist-IWA

Depositories: Usa-NN; D-188/144 (1,m)

The paper was a weekly from 13 June 1868 to 15 May 1869 (volume 1, no. 1-49) and a daily from 22 May 1869 to 17 September 1870 (volume 2, no. 1-101). Until 16 May 1869 the subtitle was: Volkswirtschaftliches und Sociales Organ der Arbeiter [Economic and Social Organ of the Workers]; from 20 May 1869 the subtitle changed to Organ der Nationalen Arbeiter-Verbindung [Organ of the National Workers' Union]. After Dr. Landsberg it was edited by Adolf Douai* from October 1868.

The Arbeiter-Union [Workers' Union] was an organization founded in 1866 by German-speaking associations of carvers, cigarmakers and other trades in New York. In the spring of 1868 delegates of the Arbeiter-Union set up the "Association Vereinigter Arbeiter" [Association of United Workers] whose purpose was to establish a newspaper. As this newspaper depended on subscriptions, it had to publish not only labor matters but also educational and entertaining articles. Its readers were mainly workers, but by no means all socialists. Besides news from the Arbeiter-Union and from the American and European labor movement, it contained local news, articles on the eight-hour day, political news, serialized novels, riddles and jokes. A serialized version of Karl Marx's "Kapital" was reprinted in the weekly editions from No. 21.

When Douai became editor the paper came more under the influence of the First International (IWA}. At the beginning of the Franco-Prussian war it strongly favored internationalism. The horrors of war and the sufferings it brings for the workers who are forced to be soldiers are vividly described. Because of this "unpatriotic" attitude the *Arbeiter-Union* lost many subscribers and advertisers and it was finally forced to suspend publication.

Contributors were Karl Schrader, Friedrich Gerstäcker, A. Bernstein, Moritz Hartmann, Julius Grosse, Georg Hiltl, Friedrich Spielhagen, Julius Rodenberg, E. Marlitt, Ernst Pitawall.

Sources: Arndt/Olson; Eberlein 22656; Schlüter, *Internationale*, pp. 94-98; Kamman, p. 44; Waltershausen, pp. 41-43. On Douai, see *San Antonio Zeitung*.

DIE ARBEITER VON OHIO   OH Cincinnati   1877-1879?

Title trans.:	The Workers of Ohio	*First issue:*	? 1877
Subtitle:	Organ und Eigenthum der Arbeiter-	*Last issue:*	1879 ?
	Partei von Cincinnati		
Add. lang.:		*Vols. (nos.):*	
First editor:	Heinrich Ende	*Frequency:*	w
First publ.:		*Preservation:*	5
Related pubs.:		*Supplements:*	
Circulation:		*Category:*	socialist-WP / SLP

Depositories: Usa-NN [1877]

Subtitle translation: Organ and Property of the Workingmen's Party of Cincinnati; after 1878 ? Organ of the Socialist Labor Party.

According to the *Milwaukee Socialist*, the Cincinnati as well as the Milwaukee section of the Arbeiterpartei der Vereinigten Staaten was urging political action, whereas other sections were in favor of cooperation with the trade unions.

Variants of title: *Der Arbeiter von Ohio (Buchdrucker-Zeitung) Arbeiter vom Ohio* (Schlüter 394) *Arbeiter am Ohio* (Kamman)

Sources: Arndt/Olson; Eberlein 22637; Schlüter, *Internationale*, p. 394; Kamman, p. 46; *BZ* 1 Mr 1877.

ARBEITERZEITUNG (Belleville Arbeiterzeitung)   IL Belleville   1884-1912?

Title trans.:	Labor News	*First issue:*	? 1884
Subtitle:		*Last issue:*	1912?
Add. lang.:		*Vols. (nos.):*	
First editor:	Robert Steiner	*Frequency:*	d
First publ.:	Hans Schwarz	*Preservation:*	4
Related pubs.:		*Supplements:*	see below
Circulation:	1890: 550; 1901: 878	*Category:*	labor

Depositories: Usa-NNC (1903-1910); D-188/144 (Ja 1903-D 1910,m)

This was a daily labor paper, which appeared in the evening except on Sundays. Its title changed: *Arbeiterzeitung und Tageblatt* (1893) and *Tageblatt und Arbeiterzeitung* (1899?-1912). In 1880 the paper had been banned in Germany under the antisocialist laws.

In 1889 Hans Schwarz, the publisher was excommunicated from the Catholic Church because he had criticized the clergy in his paper. Bishop Jansen of the diocese of Southern Illinois threatened in a sermon to excommunicate all Catholics who read, distributed or advertised in the *Arbeiterzeitung* because its doctrines were "hostile towards the church" and its language "inappropriate for the family." (*BZ* 16 My 1890). Schwarz was the founding member and secretary of Typographia No. 18 of Belleville. Being both "boss" and union-member he was accused of intimidating his employees in union meetings and there were complaints that his printing shop was not run in accordance with union rules. In May 1899 Typographia No. 18 was expelled from the Local Trades and Labor Assembly because it would not or could not exclude Schwartz. At the same time the Trades and Labor Assembly imposed a boycott on the *Arbeiterzeitung* because it did not endorse their candidates for a local election. In 1901 the staff consisted of one foreman, four typesetters and one apprentice, all of them union members who worked nine hours daily.

Eberlein gives 1884-1899 as the dates of appearance.

Sources: Arndt/Olson; Eberlein 22657, 22801; *BZ* 16 Mr 1889, 16 My 1890, 16 F 1893, 1 N 1894, 1 My 1899, 16 My 1899, 1 Je 1899, 16 Ja 1901.

The *St. Clair County Volksblatt* (1889?-1915?) appeared as a weekly edition of the *Tageblatt und Arbeiterzeitung* 1889-1912 and as a semiweekly in 1919. Then it became an independent weekly. Its title varies: *Wöchentliche Arbeiter-Zeitung*. The circulation was: 1890: 775; 1901: 1400; 1909: 1000. The paper was published by the St. Clair Printing & News Co. 1913-1915.

Source: Arndt/Olson.

The *Sonntagsblatt der Arbeiter-Zeitung* (1890-1898?) was the Sunday edition of the *Arbeiterzeitung*. Depository: Usa-IHi [1903-1910].

Source: Arndt/Olson.

DIE ARBEITERZEITUNG (I)	NY New York	1851-1852?

Title trans.:	Labor News	*First issue:*	? 1851
Subtitle:		*Last issue:*	1852?
Add. lang.:		*Vols. (nos.):*	
First editor:	Ludwig Ferdinand Fenner von Fenneberg	*Frequency:*	
First publ.:		*Preservation:*	7
Related pubs.:		*Supplements:*	
Circulation:		*Category:*	radical fortyeighter

Depositories:

In August 1851 Engels mentions in a letter to Marx that Joseph Weydemeyer* wanted to go to America to try to take over the *Arbeiterzeitung*, which was edited at that time by Fenner von Fenneberg*.

Sources: Arndt/Olson; Eberlein 22661; Schlüter, *Anfänge*, p. 130; Marx/Engels, *Werke* XXVII, p. 294-295; Cazden, *Book Trade*, p. (645); Wittke, *Press*, p. 88.

ARBEITERZEITUNG	PA Philadelphia	1869?-?

Title trans.:	Labor News	*First issue:*	1869?
Subtitle:		*Last issue:*	?
Add. lang.:		*Vols. (nos.):*	
First editor:	Carl Daut, Peter Haß	*Frequency:*	
First publ.:		*Preservation:*	7
Related pubs.:		*Supplements:*	
Circulation:		*Category:*	workers' club

Depositories:

Schlüter mentions that the German workers in Philadelphia at the beginning of the 1870s were influenced by the *Arbeiterzeitung*. He says that the German labor movement had its own platform, which differed in its aims from the English one and was more radical in several points. Essentials were the eight-hour day for public workers, abolition of contract labor and compulsory education. According to Schlüter, there was no clear notion of class struggle behind these demands.

Source: Schlüter, *Internationale*, p. 326.

ARBEITERZEITUNG (II)	NY New York	1873-1875

Title trans.:	Labor News	*First issue:*	8 F 1873
Subtitle:		*Last issue:*	13 Mr 1875
Add. lang.:		*Vols. (nos.):*	1(1)-3(11)
First editor:	Conrad Carl, R. Starke	*Frequency:*	w
First publ.:		*Preservation:*	1
Related pubs.:		*Supplements:*	
Circulation:	1873: 3000+; 1875: 960	*Category:*	socialist-IWA

Depositories: Usa-WHi; D-188/144 (1,m)

The title was *Arbeiterzeitung* up to 2(36); from 2(37) (17 October 1874) it was called *Nothblatt* [Emergency News] and from 2(38) (24 October 1874) the title was changed to *Neue Arbeiterzeitung*.

The *Arbeiterzeitung* was established as the organ of the German-speaking sections of the (First) International in New York. Its aims were organization and unification of all American workers, development of class consciousness among them, criticism of capitalism and the abolition of wage labor. The paper had a promising start and won readers in most major cities. It contained news from the labor movement in America and Europe, reports of correspondents, poems and serialized novels. Among its contributors were F.A. Sorge, Julius Hoffmann, Dr. Georg Stiebeling and A. Otto-Walster*.

In 1874 a controversy arose over the editorial management between F.A. Sorge and C. Carl. The dispute ended with a scuffle in the editor's office (described vividly in the *Nothblatt*) and the expulsion of C. Carl and Section 1 from the International. Carl and his adherents from Section 1, who had always considered the paper as their property, continued to publish it under the name *Neue Arbeiterzeitung*. Besides articles on living conditions in tenement houses, strikes and other news of the labor movement, its issues contain mostly furious polemics against F.A. Sorge and G. Stiebeling. The last available issue contains no indication of the paper's discontinuation.

Sources: Arndt/Olson; Arndt/Olson 2, p. 461; Eberlein 22675, 22662; Kamman, p. 45; Waltershausen, pp. 84, 93-94; Schlüter, *Internationale*, pp. 213-214, 333-336; Hillquit, p. 186; Sorge, pp. 25, 159-160; Protokoll des Verwaltungsrathes der *Arbeiterzeitung* [Minutes of the Board of Trustees of *Arbeiterzeitung*] are contained in *Socialist Collections in the Tamiment Library, 1872-1956*, ed. by Thomas C. Prado, (Sanford, NC, 1979).

ARBEITER-ZEITUNG   WI Milwaukee   1879

Title trans.:	Labor News	*First issue:*	1 O 1879
Subtitle:		*Last issue:*	31 D 1879?
Add. lang.:		*Vols. (nos.):*	
First editor:	Michael Biron	*Frequency:*	d
First publ.:	Michael Biron	*Preservation:*	7
Related pubs.:	s *Milwaukee Journal*	*Supplements:*	
Circulation:		*Category:*	socialist

Depositories:

After the *Milwaukee Freie Presse*, formerly called *Vorwärts (Milwaukee'r Socialist)* abandoned its socialist connections, Biron invested $1700 of his own money in the daily *Arbeiter-Zeitung*. For a time the paper was apparently successful, since Biron enlarged it and improved its appearance several times. On 1 June 1880 it was renamed the *Milwaukee Journal*.

Source: Knoche, p. 193.

ARBEITER-ZEITUNG (I)   MO St. Louis   1888-?

Title trans.:	Labor News	*First issue:*	1 My 1888
Subtitle:		*Last issue:*	?
Add. lang.:		*Vols. (nos.):*	
First editor:		*Frequency:*	
First publ.:		*Preservation:*	7
Related pubs.:		*Supplements:*	
Circulation:		*Category:*	labor

Depositories:

No further information is available.

Source: *BZ* 1 My 1888 and 16 My 1888.

ARBEITER-ZEITUNG   PA Pittsburgh   1889?-1890?

Title trans.:	Labor News	*First issue:*	1889?
Subtitle:		*Last issue:*	1890?
Add. lang.:		*Vols. (nos.):*	
First editor:		*Frequency:*	
First publ.:	Deutsche Arbeiter-Verlagsgesellschaft	*Preservation:*	7
Related pubs.:		*Supplements:*	
Circulation:		*Category:*	

Depositories:

This daily evening paper had the "union cut," which meant that only members of the Deutsch-Amerikanische Typographia worked in the office of the Deutsche Arbeiter-Verlagsgesellschaft [German Publishing Co.]. (*BZ* 16 S 1889) At a meeting of Typographia No. 9 of Pittsburgh in November 1889, a delegate of this publishing company gave a positive report on the condition of the *Arbeiter-Zeitung* (*BZ* 16 N 1889), but in March of the following year the typographers of the *Arbeiter-Zeitung* called a meeting where they asked for financial help from Typographia No. 9. When they were asked to give a report, it showed a "hair-raising deficit," which made the Typographia decide that any financial help would be futile. They recommended publishing a weekly (*BZ* 16 Ap 1890).

Sources: Arndt/Olson; *BZ*.

ARBEITER-ZEITUNG   PA Erie   1891-1899?

Title trans.:	Labor News	*First issue:*	? Ag 1891
Subtitle:		*Last issue:*	1899?
Add. lang.:		*Vols. (nos.):*	
First editor:	Samuel Weiss	*Frequency:*	w
First publ.:	Erie Arbeiter-Zeitung Publishing Company	*Preservation:*	7
Related pubs.:		*Supplements:*	
Circulation:	1897: 1300	*Category:*	labor

Depositories:

Editors after Weiss* were Charles Backofen (1892) and M.P. Jahn from spring of 1893 until early 1895. The paper was published by Carl Brandt, Sr., & G. Jahn, 1897?-1899.

Sources: Arndt/Olson; Eberlein 22659. Obituary on Weiss in *BZ* 16 D 1897.

ARBEITER-ZEITUNG   KS Kansas City   1894-?

Title trans.:	Labor News	*First issue:*	1894
Subtitle:		*Last issue:*	?
Add. lang.:		*Vols. (nos.):*	
First editor:		*Frequency:*	?
First publ.:	Deutscher Arbeiter-Freund	*Preservation:*	6
Related pubs.:		*Supplements:*	
Circulation:		*Category:*	

Depositories: Usa-NN (17 F 1894)

No further information could be obtained.
Sources: Arndt/Olson; Eberlein 22660.

ARBEITER-ZEITUNG (II)   MO St. Louis   1898-1935?

Title trans.:	Labor News	*First issue:*	27 Ag 1898
Subtitle:		*Last issue:*	1935?
Add. lang.:		*Vols. (nos.):*	
First editor:	G.A. Höhn	*Frequency:*	w
First publ.:	Co-operative Commonwealth Association	*Preservation:*	1(?)
Related pubs.:	s *Abendpost und Tageblatt* (St. Louis), *Volks-Anwalt* (Cincinnati)	*Supplements:*	
Circulation:	1914: 3000	*Category:*	socialist-SDP/ SP

Depositories: Usa-WHi (Ag 1898-N 1916); D-188/144 (Ag 1898-N 1916, m); Usa-MoS (1917-28); §Usa-MoSHo

The paper was established through the merger of the St. Louis *Tageblatt und Abendpost* with the Cincinnati *Volks-Anwalt*. Its mottoes and subtitles changed. It was supported by the Social-Democratic Party and later by the Socialist Party. The title varied: *Arbeiter-Zeitung und Volks-Anwalt* (27 August 1898-1910) and it was edited by G.A. Höhn until May 1910 with the assistance of Robert Steiner in 1899 and perhaps longer; it is probable that Höhn continued to edit the paper until 1931. Later it was published by the Arbeiter-Zeitung Gesellschaft and then by the Labor Publishing Co. (?-1935).

It contained political news from America and from foreign countries, news and platforms of the party, news from labor unions and organizations, such as the AFL, the Central Trades and Labor Union, the International of Workers, many reports from Germany, e.g. on the trials against socialists, articles on scientific and historical subjects, on health, advice on farming and housekeeping, photographs of socialist candidates and after 1912 (?) a political cartoon on the first page, jokes, reviews of plays and advertisements, frequently for union products. In 1913 it published a report of Philip Scheidemann's lecture tour through the United States. It strongly opposed World War One.

The *Arbeiter-Zeitung* was one of the few newspapers, which put a great emphasis on women's and children's concerns, not only on its women's page but throughout the whole paper. It dealt with educational questions, child labor, the idea of a child-bearing strike, children's sufferings in World War One. It proclaimed a national holiday for the children of strikers on 28 December 1913. Many articles dealt with the organization of women in general and of female workers in particular as well as with women's right to vote. It had an unusually high proportion of female contributors. It reprinted articles from *Vorwärts* (Berlin/Germany), the *Philadelphia Tageblatt*, the *New Yorker Volkszeitung*, the *Freidenker* and others.

Contributors were Arnold Dodel, Clara Zetkin, Joseph Dietzgen, Hedwig Heurich-Wilhelmi, Paul Heyse, Philip Rapaport, Emile Zola, Mathilde Sorge, Eleonore Marx-Aveling, Anna Julia Wolff, Julie Romm, August Bebel, Otto Ludwig, Karl Kautsky, Maxim Gorki, L. von Berlepsch, Max Norden, Carl Legien and many others.

Sources: Arndt/Olson; *BZ*, see 1 O 1910, 1 Mr 1912, My 1929 (on the paper's 30th anniversary).

ARBEITER-ZEITUNG (Cincinnati Arbeiter-Zeitung)   OH Cincinnati   1902-1903

Title trans.:	Cincinnati Labor News	*First issue:*	6 Ja 1902
Subtitle:		*Last issue:*	11 Ap 1903
Add. lang.:		*Vols. (nos.):*	
First editor:		*Frequency:*	d
First publ.:	Cincinnati Arbeiter-Zeitungsverein	*Preservation:*	7
Related pubs.:	c *Cincinnatier Zeitung*	*Supplements:*	
Circulation:		*Category:*	labor

Depositories:

This paper appeared daily in the afternoon and on Sunday mornings. A specimen number appeared on 21 December 1901. It replaced the *Cincinnatier Zeitung* as the organ of union labor. The Socialistische Verein of Cincinnati and several unions were involved in publishing the new paper, particularly because they had been dissatisfied with the quality of its predecessor. The paper received initial financial assistance from unions, e.g. $50 from Typographia No. 7 of New York and $25 from St. Louis, as well as from the treasury of the Deutsch-Amerikanische Typographia.

Source: *BZ* 16 D 1901, 1 Ja and 16 Ja 1902.

ARBEITER-ZEITUNG		WI Sheboygan	1908?-1909?

Title trans.:	Labor News	*First issue:*	1908?
Subtitle:		*Last issue:*	1909?
Add. lang.:		*Vols. (nos.):*	
First editor:		*Frequency:*	w
First publ.:	Sheboygan Arbeiter Zeitungs Publ. Company	*Preservation:*	7
Related pubs.:		*Supplements:*	
Circulation:		*Category:*	socialist

Depositories:

No further information could be obtained.
Sources: Arndt/Olson; Eberlein 22664.

DER ARME TEUFEL		MI Detroit	1884-1900

Title trans.:	The Poor Devil	*First issue:*	6 D 1884
Subtitle:		*Last issue:*	6 S 1900
Add. lang.:		*Vols. (nos.):*	1-16(822)
First editor:	Robert Reitzel	*Frequency:*	w
First publ.:	Robert Reitzel	*Preservation:*	1
Related pubs.:	s *Wolfsaugen*	*Supplements:*	
Circulation:	1890: 3000; 1898: 2700; 1900: 3525	*Category:*	anarchist

Depositories: Usa-Cty [1884-1900]; Usa-InU; Usa-DLC (1884-98); D-Bm 41/IGA
[1888-1900]; D-188/144 (17 Ja 1899)

This was a radical 8-page weekly edited and published by Reitzel* until his death on 30 March 1898; thereafter it was edited by Martin Drescher* and published by Reitzel's widow Anna Reitzel. Cofounder and technical manager until his death in 1897 was George P. Goettmann (see obituary in *BZ* 16 S 1897); George Biedenkapp* was the paper's "General-Consul for New York and Vicinity" in 1898.

Der Arme Teufel expressed the radical ideas of its editor and it was individualistic without any party affiliations. Reitzel wrote many of the articles himself. The paper gave space to freethinker, socialist, anarchist and other dissenting authors and attacked authority in all its manifestations: prohibition, oppression by capital, marriage law, puritanism, Bismarck, German nationalism. It denounced the shocking conditions in orphanages and schools, of railroad management and of poor relief. It criticized classical medical treatment and recommended natural remedies. It published articles on the development of psychology and on scientific subjects as well as reviews of musical and artistic events. After the Haymarket Massacre its tone became even more poignant. It published reprints from and contributions by Knut Hamsun, Fanny Gräfin zu Reventlow, August Strindberg, Ludwig Thoma, Theodor Storm, Robert Seidel, Karl Henckell, John Henry Mackay, Theodor Curti, Eduard Dorsch, Leopold von Sacher-Masoch, Hedwig Heinrich-Wilhelmi, Gottfried Keller, Hanns Heinz Ewers, Edna Fern, Carmen Sylva, Bruno Wille,

Bret Harte, Friedrich Theodor Vischer, Gabriele d'Annunzio, Hermann Bahr, Johannes Schlaf, Rudyard Kipling, Edgar Allan Poe, Georg Biedenkapp, W.L. Rosenberg. Its last page contained advertisements for local shops and saloons. After two years as editor, Drescher suspended the paper and went to St. Louis, where he founded *Wolfsaugen.*

Der Arme Teufel became so influential that it instigated the establishment of "Arme Teufel Clubs" in Toledo, Pittsburgh, Cincinnati, St. Louis and other cities.

Sources: Arndt/Olson; Eberlein 22808; Kamman, p. 49-50; Creagh, 1113-1114; Rocker, pp. 380-381; Ritter, Erwin F., "Robert Reitzel, A.T. (1849-1898)," *German-American Studies* V (1972), pp. 12-16; Zucker, A.E., "Robert Reitzel as Poet," *German American Annals* N.S., XIII (1915), pp. 58ff. On Reitzel, see Kammann, pp. 111-112; Kosch, p. 2207; Fränkel, vol. 53, pp. 296-300. Obituary on Reitzel, e.g. in *New Yorker Volkszeitung,* 2 Ap 1898. On Drescher, see *Wolfsaugen.*

AUSTRIAN LABOR INFORMATION　　　　　NY New York　　　　1942-1945

Title trans.:		*First issue:*	20 Ap 1942
Subtitle:	Anti-Hitler Magazine	*Last issue:*	1 My 1945
Add. lang.:	English	*Vols. (nos.):*	nos. 1-37
First editor:	Otto Leichter	*Frequency:*	m
First publ.:	The Austrian Labor Committee	*Preservation:*	1
Related pubs.:	*Austrian Labor News*	*Supplements:*	*Freie Tribüne des Internationalen Sozialismus*
Circulation:		*Category:*	social democrat/ antifascist

Depositories: Usa-CU; Usa-DL; Usa-NN; D-Bm 41/IGA [1942-45]

This was a 16-page illustrated monthly with slight irregularities. As the organ of the Austrian Labor Committee (Austrian Social Democrats in exile) it was the German edition of the English-language *Austrian Labor News,* which was published "from time to time" and is bound with the German edition. It contained information on the situation, problems and tasks of labor in Austria and other Nazi-occupied countries, articles on the Warsaw Ghetto, on the future after Hitler's overthrow, lists of executed Austrian antifascists, obituaries of executed labor leaders, e.g. Albert Sever, Robert Danneberg, Heinrich Steinitz, Heinz Berendt, reprints from antifascist newspapers, book reviews, news and announcements from local Austrian social-democratic groups of exiles in New York, San Francisco and London. Contributors were Karl Czernetz, Carl Furtmueller, Julius Deutsch, Oskar Jaszi, Hans Schmidt, Hugo Breitner, Arnold Eisler. It also reprinted a poem by Walt Whitman on a defeated revolutionary.

Sources: Arndt/Olson; Arndt/Olson 2, p. 442; Cazden, *Exile Literature,* p. 183.

The *Freie Tribüne des Internationalen Sozialismus* was the monthly supplement. It appeared from May 1944 to May 1945 and Wilhelm Ellenbogen was its editor. The content was similar to *Austrian Labor Information* but it contained more articles on the political situation in Spain, Germany, the Soviet

Union, France and England. It also published articles on the reconstruction of the International and reprints from illegal foreign newspapers. Contributions came from Hugo Fernandez Artucio, Desider Benau, Theodor Dan, Paul Hertz, Paul Keri, Siegfried Taub.

Sources: Arndt/Olson 2, p. 453; Cazden, *Exile Literature*, pp. 68, 183.

DER BALTIMORE HEROLD		MD Baltimore	1849-?

Title trans.:	The Baltimore Herald	*First issue:*	? 1849
Subtitle:		*Last issue:*	?
Add. lang.:		*Vols. (nos.):*	
First editor:	Moritz Wiener	*Frequency:*	d
First publ.:	C.W. Schneidereith & T. Kroh	*Preservation:*	7
Related pubs.:		*Supplements:*	
Circulation:		*Category:*	radical freethought

Depositories:

This was a radical daily founded as a counterweight to the Baltimore *Deutscher Correspondent*, which refused to give space to freethinker views. Carl W. Schneidereith and Theodor Kroh had emigrated to America in the thirties and established their printing shop in 1849. Schneidereith later published the family paper *Glocke am Sonntag* [The Bell on Sunday] (1863). The paper seems to have appeared only for a few weeks. That same year the editorship changed hands to Karl Heinrich Schnauffer, who then changed the name to *Baltimore Wecker* [Baltimore Reveille], which became a successful Republican liberal daily.

Sources: Arndt/Olson; Leyh, p. 303; Wittke, *Press*, p. 86; Körner, p. 398. On Schnauffer, see Schem X, p. 7 and Cunz, pp. 259, 276-281.

BEOBACHTER AM OHIO		KY Louisville	1844-1856

Title trans.:	Observer on the Ohio	*First issue:*	16 Mr 1844
Subtitle:		*Last issue:*	? 1856
Add. lang.:		*Vols. (nos.):*	1-12
First editor:	Heinrich Beutel	*Frequency:*	
First publ.:		*Preservation:*	6
Related pubs.:		*Supplements:*	
Circulation:		*Category:*	radical fortyeighter

Depositories: Usa-MWA [1853]; Usa-ICU [1852]

After Beutel Anton Eickhoff (1851) and Ludwig N. Dembitz (1853) became editors. According to Wittke this paper was "launched in 1844 by Heinrich Beutel, once a press foreman for the *Cincinnati Volksblatt* [Cincinnati People's Gazette] in response to a demand of a mass meeting of Germans who wanted a more liberal paper." (p. 53) It changed ownership several times before 1850 and, "though edited in a liberal spirit, did not fill the needs of the radical newcomers by 1849." (p. 86) Elsewhere Wittke mentions that this "radical sheet" "attacked all private property and urged that capitalists and priests be hanged together, according to the 'philosophy of the guillotine and the gallows'." (p. 167) *The Beobachter am Ohio* published the German translation of Harriet Beecher-Stowe's "Uncle Tom's Cabin."

Sources: Arndt/Olson 2, p. 396; Eberlein 22685; Wittke, *Press*, pp. 53, 86, 171, 228; *Refugees* p. 167; Weisert, John J., "Lewis N. Dembitz and 'Uncle Tom's Cabin,'" *The German-American Review* XIX, 3 (1953), pp. 7/8.

DIE BIENE		MA Holyoke	1894-1920
Title trans.:	The Bee	*First issue:*	9 Ag 1894
Subtitle:	Herausgegeben im Interesse des Arbeiters und seiner Familie	*Last issue:*	30 S 1920
Add. lang.:		*Vols. (nos.):*	1-27
First editor:	August Lehmann	*Frequency:*	w, q
First publ.:	August Lehmann	*Preservation:*	3
Related pubs.:		*Supplements:*	
Circulation:	1905: 1275; 1910: 1000; 1915: 2880	*Category:*	labor

Depositories: Usa-ICJ (1897-1902); Usa-WHi (1904-20)

Subtitle translation: Published in the Interest of the Worker and his Family.

The paper appeared as a weekly from 1894 to 1902 and as a quarterly from 1903 to the end. The title varies: *Die Biene und Springfield Vorwärts* [The Bee and Springfield Forward] from 13 February to 30 September 1919. From 1894 to 1918 it was edited and published by August Lehmann, then by the Lehmann Publishing Company.

Sources: Arndt/Olson; Eberlein 22689; Ayer, 1904-21.

DIE BRANDFACKEL		NY New York	1893-1895?
Title trans.:	The Torch of War	*First issue:*	Jl 1893
Subtitle:	Anarchistische Monatsschrift	*Last issue:*	Ja 1895?
Add. lang.:		*Vols. (nos.):*	1(1)-3
First editor:	Claus Timmermann	*Frequency:*	m
First publ.:	Claus Timmermann	*Preservation:*	1
Related pubs.:		*Supplements:*	
Circulation:		*Category:*	anarchist

Depositories: Usa-CtY

According to the subtitle this paper was an "anarchist monthly." Timmermann was previously editor of the St. Louis *Der Anarchist*, 1889-1891. From 1897 to 1899 he edited *Sturmvogel* in New York. The first issue which contained 18 pages was dedicated to Alexander Berkman, who had made an unsuccessful attempt to assassinate Henry Clay Frick. The issue of November 1893 published the plea which Emma Goldman had been prevented from delivering in court in a trial for seditious speech in October 1883.

Sources: Arndt/Olson, Eberlein 22690; Bianco. On Timmermann, see *Sturmvogel*.

BRAUER-ZEITUNG   OH Cincinnati   1886-1934

Title trans.:	Brewer's Journal	*First issue:*	2 0 1886
Subtitle:		*Last issue:*	3 Mr 1934
Add. lang.:	English	*Vols. (nos.):*	1(1)-49(5)
First editor:	Louis Herbrand	*Frequency:*	w, bw
First publ.:		*Preservation:*	1
Related pubs.:		*Supplements:*	
Circulation:		*Category:*	labor union

Depositories: Usa-WHi; D-188/144 (1886-1973,m); D-19/1501 (1886-1925,m)

This labor union journal appeared as a weekly (1886-1919) and then as a biweekly (1920-1934). It was established as a journal entirely in German but from 30 May 1891 some material was published in English. The amount of English increased and the last issues contained only one page in German; with the issue of 3 March 1934, the publishers state that "The German language will be abolished;" it continued as *The Brewery Worker*, in English only, up to the present.

Title changes: 1. Die Brauer Zeitung, October 1886 - October 1910; 2. Brauerei Arbeiter Zeitung, November 1910 - 4 January 1918; 3. Brewery & Soft Drink Worker's Journal, 5 January 1918 - November 1918; 4. Brewery, Flour, Cereal & Soft Drink Worker's Journal, December 1918 - April 1934 (with this change the German subtitle was dropped, although one or two pages were printed until March 1934, when it became known as 5. The Brewery Worker, March 1934 to present. Subtitle: 1. Fachblatt des National-Verbandes der Brauer der Vereinigten Staaten; 2. Brauerei Arbeiter Zeitung, Brewery Worker Journal; 3. Brauerei- und Mineralwasser-Arbeiter-Zeitung; 4. Brauerei-und Sodawssser-Arbeiter-Zeitung. It was the organ of 1. National Union of Brewers of the U.S., 1886; 2. Brewers National Union, 1887; 3. National Union of the United Brewery Workmen of the U.S., 1887-1903; 4. International Union of the United Brewery Workmen of America, 1903-17; 5. International Union of United Brewery and Soft Drink Workers of America, 1917; 6. International Union of United Brewery, Flour, Cereal and Soft Drink Workers of America, 1918-34.

The emblem of the first issues represented Gambrinus, the legendary king of beer; thereafter it showed two sturdy brewers shaking hands in solidarity over a beer barrel; both emblems bear the motto: "Hopfen und Malz - Gott erhalt's!" [Hops and malt - God preserve them]. The motto in 1926 was: "Workingmen of all countries, unite!" The place of publication changed frequently: New York (2 October 1886 June? 1892); St. Louis (July 1892 - May 1899); Cincinnati (May 1899 - March 1934). Each issue had 4 - 8 pages. It was edited by: 1. Louis Herbrand from 2 October 1886 - 7 July 1888 when he was dismissed. The substitute editor for Herbrand whose name still appeared in the imprint, was Ernst Böhm (April 21 - July 1888). 2. Ernst Kurzenknabe (28 July 1888 - 10 October 1896). In May 1897 Böhm sued Kurzenknabe successfully for slander. The latter had maintained that Böhm, as secretary of the Socialist Trade and Labor Alliance, had embezzled union money for years (*BZ* 1 Je 1897). By 1908 Kurzenknabe was the proprietor of the "Central Beer Saloon" in St. Louis, the motto of which was: He who loves his freedom may come to me; here he can listen to liberal words but - he must pay for his beer! (translated). 3. Jacob L. Franz (16 October 1886 - September 1900); 4. William

Trautmann (October 1900 - April 1905), a member of the SLP and advocate of syndicalism who helped to found Industrial Workers of the World in 1905. This was the reason for his dismissal (*BZ* 1 My 1905). 5. John P. Weigel (May 1905 - August 1906); his obituary appeared in the issue of 25 August 1906. 6. August Mostlar (August 1906 - March 1917); 7. Julius Zorn (April 1917 - January 1926); his obituary appeared in the issue of 13 February 1926. Most of the time the paper was published by the union; by Ernst Kurzenknabe during part of his editorship and Franz' editorship. In 1893 a conflict arose between Kurzenknabe and the typographers of the *Brauer-Zeitung* (Typographia No. 3, St. Louis) because they refused to work more than 8 hours a day, unless they were paid time and a half (*BZ* 9 F, 16 O, 1 N 1893).

The *Brauer-Zeitung* contained union news such as reports of the National Executive, of union locals and of the American Federation of Labor, articles on the eight-hour campaign, appeals for contributions, official announcements and communications; lists of breweries which did not employ union members and recommendations of strict union breweries; articles on Prohibition, on the treatment of industrial accidents, on the chemistry of brewing, on the harvesting of hops. The paper supported Henry George in 1886. The jubilee edition on the twentieth anniversary of the paper on 1 September 1906, vol. XXI, no. 35, had 32 pages and contained articles on the history of the *Brauer-Zeitung*, of the union and of its locals; on the brewery workers' movement in Germany, on the union label. It had a colored front page with elaborate symbolic representation of the trade. The Golden Anniversary Edition of the English *The Brewery Worker* had 10 pages and appeared on 29 August 1936, vol. LI, no. 35.

Among the contributors were Minna Kautsky (a serialized version of "Ein Proletarierkind" [A Proletarian Child]), Max Vogler, Morris Hillquit, Adolf Hepner.

In 1910 the Brewers' Union allocated money for some socialist and labor journals; among the German papers the *New Yorker Volkszeitung* got $ 200 and the *Philadelphia Tageblatt*, the *Buffaloer Arbeiterzeitung*, the *Chicagoer Arbeiterzeitung* and the *Arbeiter-Zeitung* of St. Louis $100 each.

Sources: Arndt/Olson; Naas/Sakr, p. 21; *BZ*; Fink, *Labor Unions* pp. 39-42 (on the history of the union); Fink, *Biographical Dictionary*, pp. 358-359 (on Trautmann); Schlüter, Hermann, *The Brewing Industry and the Brewery Workers' Movement in America*, (1910), repr. New York, 1970; McGann Drescher, Nuala, "Organized Labor and the 18th Amendment," *Labor History* 8, 3 (Fall 1967), pp. 280ff; "Die Prohibition und die Brauerei-Arbeit," *New Yorker Volkszeitung*, 29 Ja 1928; Laslett, John, *Labor and the Left. A Study of the Socialist and Radical Influences in the American Labor Movement, 1881-1924* (New York/London, 1970), see Chapter 2: "Marxist Socialism and the German Brewery Workers of the Midwest," pp. 9-53.

DER BUFFALO HEROLD	NY Buffalo	1897-1898

Title trans.:	The Buffalo Herald	*First issue:*	17 Mr 1897
Subtitle:		*Last issue:*	30 O 1898
Add. lang.:		*Vols. (nos.):*	
First editor:	Joseph Mostler	*Frequency:*	w
First publ.:		*Preservation:*	5
Related pubs.:	m *Buffaloer Arbeiter-Zeitung*	*Supplements:*	
Circulation:		*Category:*	socialist

Depositories: Usa-WHi (18 Je 1898)

This paper began as a weekly founded in 1897 by Joseph Mostler, a former editor of the *Buffaloer Arbeiter-Zeitung* [Buffalo Labor News], who had quit because of a wage dispute. The paper was an opponent of the *Buffaloer Arbeiter-Zeitung*. On 19 July 1898 it was bought by the *Buffaloer Arbeiter-Zeitung* and amalgamated with its *Sonntags-Ausgabe* [Sunday Edition], which was from then on subtitled *Buffalo Herold* until the issue of 30 October 1898. Mostler remained its editor. It contained political news, a "plattdeutsche Ecke" [column in Low German], news of general interest, jokes, humorous short stories, anecdotes, poems, advertisements and announcements of meetings and social events.

Sources: Arndt/Olson; "Blätter aus der Geschichte der *Buffaloer Arbeiter-Zeitung*," *Buffaloer Arbeiter-Zeitung*, 5 O 1912.

BUFFALOER ARBEITER-ZEITUNG	NY Buffalo	1887-1918?

Title trans.:	Buffalo Labor News	*First issue:*	3 S 1887
Subtitle:	see below	*Last issue:*	2 F 1918?
Add. lang.:		*Vols. (nos.):*	
First editor:	George M. Price	*Frequency:*	w, d, w
First publ.:	Arbeiter-Zeitung Publishing Co.	*Preservation:*	2(?)
Related pubs.:	m *Buffalo Herold; Freiheit*	*Supplements:*	see below
Circulation:	1891: 1800; 1910: 3250; 1915: 7700	*Category:*	socialist

Depositories: Usa-WHi (Ap 1898-S 1917); D-188/144 (Ap 1898-S 1917,m)

From 1887 to 1897 this paper was mainly a weekly (except for 6 weeks in 1888 when it appeared as a daily); from September 1897 to January 1899 it became a daily and appeard as a weekly again till its end. In May 1899? a *Fair-Zeitung. Officielles Organ des allgemeinen Fair-Comites* was published to advertise a fair to be held in May to raise funds for further daily editions. The title varies: *Buffaloer Arbeiter-Zeitung und Buffalo Herold* (11 September - October 1898); *Arbeiter-Zeitung* (6 November 1898 - 1918). It absorbed *Buffalo Herold* in July 1898. Johann Most's *Freiheit* was published as "Wochenbeilage" (weekly supplement) from 18 September 1897 to July 1898. Subtitles: Gewidmet dem Fortschritt, der Unterhaltung und Belehrung und dem Allgemeinen deutschen Vereinsleben [Dedicated to Progress, Entertainment and Instruction and German Club Life in General] (September 1887?-1897); Officielles Organ der Vereinigten Deutschen Gewerkschaften von Erie County

[Official Organ of the United German Labor Union Movement] (15 January 1899-?); Officielles Organ der United Trades and Labor Councils und der Vereinigten Deutschen Gewerkschaften von Erie Co. [Official Organ of the United Trades and Labor Councils and of the United German Labor Unions of Erie County] (September? 1897 - January? 1898); Das officielle Organ des Central Labor Council of Buffalo; "Die einzige deutsche Zeitung im Westlichen New York, welche Eigenthum der Organisierten Arbeiter ist und von ihnen kontrolliert wird" ["The only German newspaper in the west of New York that is the property of and controlled by organized labor"] (1898?- 1918).

Place of publication varied: Rochester, NY (1890-95); Erie, PA (1890-95). Subsequent editors were Charles Hoffmann (November 1887 - May 1888), Ernst Walter (June 1888-?), Samuel Weiss* (?-1891), Charles Hoffmann (October - December 1891), Adolph Drexler (1892-1893), Joseph Mostler (9 September - February 1897), Richard Baginski (February 1897 - September 1897), Johann Most* (September 1897 - 29 July 1898), Joseph Mostler (July 1898 - 5 August 1899), Max Forker (August 1889 - March 1900), Robert Steiner (17 March 1900 - May 1916). Assistant editor: Julius Hecht (1892-?). It was published by the Buffalo Labor New Publishing Association (September 1897 - September 1900?) and by the Buffalo Printing Co. (October 1900 - 1918).

It cooperated closely with the brewers' union and contained political news, news from the labor movement, especially reports of strikes, reports on accidents, tragic events and people; it also published poems, serialized novels, illustrations (later photos), advertisements, announcements of union and club meetings.

In 1888 and 1899 the paper had difficulties with Typographia No. 4 of Buffalo (see introduction). In 1900 the Brewers' Union subscribed to the paper and made it obligatory for all its members (*BZ* 1 Ap 1900). In 1902 Bishop J.E. Quigley issued a pastoral letter in which he threatened to excommunicate those parishioners who adhered to social democracy and read the *Buffaloer Arbeiter-Zeitung*.

The jubilee edition for the twenty-fifth anniversary on 5 October 1912 contained a detailed history of the paper entitled "Blätter aus der Geschichte der *Buffaloer Arbeiter-Zeitung*" [Pages from the History of the *Buffalo Workers' Journal*]

Sources: Arndt/Olson; *BZ* 1 S 1888; 1 Jl 1889; 1 N 1893; 16 Ja 1899. For the *Freiheit* as weekly supplement, see Rocker, pp. 386-388.

Sonntags-Ausgabe (September 1897 - 8 January 1899) This was the Sunday editon of the *Buffaloer Arbeiter-Zeitung* which merged with the *Buffalo Herold* on 19 July 1898. It contained mostly entertaining features, such as serialized novels, short stories, jokes and cartoons.

Depositories: Usa-WHi (bound with daily edition); D-188/144 (bound with daily edition)

Source: Arndt/Olson.

BULLETIN OF THE SOCIAL LABOR MOVEMENT	NY New York	1880-?

Title trans.:		*First issue:*	My? 1880
Subtitle:		*Last issue:*	1882?
Add. lang.:	English	*Vols. (nos.):*	
First editor:	Philip van Patten	*Frequency:*	w
First publ.:	National Executive Committe of the Socialist Labor Party (Sozialistische Arbeiter-Partei)	*Preservation:*	4
Related pubs.:		*Supplements:*	
Circulation:		*Category:*	socialist-SLP

Depositories: Usa-NN [1880-82]; D-188/144 (My 1882,m)

Van Patten was the National Secretary of the SLP. The paper consisted of 8 pages, 4 of them in English, 4 in German (translation of the English text, set in Gothic letters.) It contained news from the different sections of the SLP, advertisements of socialist pamphlets and tracts by such authors as George C. Stiebeling, Karl Marx and Ferdinand Lassalle, which could be bought from the National Executive Committee.

Sources: Hillquit, pp. 217, 291-292. On Van Patten, see Hoerder, *Plutokraten*, pp. 337-338; Waltershausen, p. 169; Rocker, pp. 150-151.

BULLETIN ...	NY New York	1952-1964

Title trans.:	Bulletin of the SLP	*First issue:*	Jl 1952/53
Subtitle:		*Last issue:*	N 1964
Add. lang.:		*Vols. (nos.):*	1-12 (1-44)
First editor:		*Frequency:*	ir
First publ.:		*Preservation:*	2
Related pubs.:		*Supplements:*	
Circulation:		*Category:*	socialist-SLP

Depositories: D-Bm 41/IGA (Ap 1954-N 1964)

The complete title of the paper was: *Bulletin der Sozialistischen Arbeiter-Partei (U.S.A.)*

This was an organ of the SLP (DeLeonites) which appeared irregularly. The DeLeonite socialists favored a new form of government, called "Industrial Government," in which every worker had the "industrial right to vote" for the "Socialist Congress of Industrial Nations." The subtitle after July 1955 can be translated as follows: "The SLP of America, which was founded as early as 1890, has in regard to its principles and organization no connection with either the international communist movement of any direction or tendency, or with the so-called socialist parties, whether in America or abroad." It had a disc-shaped emblem with a strong arm holding a hammer. Published by the German Committee of the SLP, it contained mostly theoretical articles, e.g. on "Freedom and Socialism," on the political impact of strikes, on "nationalization versus the free market economy," on the use of violence, against "Soviet Despotism," on the economic development of Germany and other European countries after World War Two, on space research and on atomic war.

Resolutions of the SLP concerning automation, race relations and the internal political situation were published in the issue of November 1964. A mimeographed circular of January 1965 announced that the bulletin had been discontinued mainly because of a 100 percent rise in the cost of paper. Almost all contributions were unsigned; some came from Arnold Petersen; there were also reprints of Daniel DeLeon and Karl Marx.

BUTCHERS' JOURNAL		NY Syracuse	1899-1908

Title trans.:		*First issue:*	O 1899
Subtitle:		*Last issue:*	S 1908
Add. lang.:	English	*Vols. (nos.):*	1-9 (7)
First editor:	Homer D. Call	*Frequency:*	m (bm)
First publ.:		*Preservation:*	1
Related pubs.:		*Supplements:*	
Circulation:		*Category:*	labor union

Depositories: Usa-NNC; Usa-DL (1900-08)

This was a 4-page monthly journal which occasionally appeared bimonthly in English and German. The title changed to *Official Journal, A.M.C. and B.W. of N.A.* (Amalgamated Meat Cutters and Butcher Workmen of North America) after November 1906. This union included "all wage earners in any way connected with the wholesale and retail markets, slaughtering and packing establishment, sausage makers, poultry, egg and creamery workers, sheep shearers and livestock handlers and those handling fish in wholesale and retail establishments." (Fink)

It printed mostly short articles and notices on matters of interest to union members, e.g. on Labor Day parades, on the eight-hour movement, on the organization of the food trades, circular letters and reports of AFL elections.

Sources: Arndt/Olson (see there for errors concerning place, frequency and volume); Naas/Sakr, p. 72; Fink, *Labor Union*, pp. 216-218 (on the history of the A.M.C. and B.W. of N.A]; Brody, David, *The Butcher Workmen: A Study in Unionization* (Cambridge, MA, 1964); "Butcher Union No. 211 von Brooklyn," *New Yorker Volkszeitung* 21 F 1903;

CALIFORNIA ARBEITER-ZEITUNG (I)	CA San Francisco	1878

Title trans.:	California Labor News	*First issue:*	? 1878
Subtitle:		*Last issue:*	? 1878
Add. lang.:		*Vols. (nos.):*	
First editor:	F. Werner	*Frequency:*	w
First publ.:	F. Werner	*Preservation:*	7
Related pubs.:		*Supplements:*	
Circulation:		*Category:*	labor

Depositories:

This lost weekly had four pages and was sold at a subscription price of $2. It closed down the same year.

Sources: Arnd/Olson; Eberlein 22667; *History of Foreign Journalism in San Francisco*, p. 32.

CALIFORNIA ARBEITER-ZEITUNG (II)	CA San Francisco	1887-1893

Title trans.:	California Labor News	*First issue:*	? 1887
Subtitle:		*Last issue:*	? 1893
Add. lang.:		*Vols. (nos.):*	
First editor:	G. Backstein	*Frequency:*	w
First publ.:	G. Backstein	*Preservation:*	3
Related pubs.:	m San Francisco *Tageblatt*	*Supplements:*	
Circulation:	1892: 2500	*Category:*	socialist

Depositories: Usa-KHi [1888]; Usa-NN [1892]; Usa-WHi (24 O 1891); Nl-IISG [1887-91]

This was a socialist weekly and the official organ of the German Unions and Workers' Associations. The original title was San Francisco *Arbeiterzeitung*; it was edited by Albert Currlin until March 1891, then by Paul Grottkau. Later it was published by the Arbeiter-Zeitung Publishing Co., also known as the San Francisco Arbeiter-Zeitung Verlags-Gesellschaft. According to Kamman, the paper was "excluded in Europe (sic!) in 1879 by antisocialist laws." In 1893 it merged with San Francisco *Tageblatt*. Title variant: *Californier Arbeiter-Zeitung*.

Sources: Arndt/Olson; Eberlein 22668; Auer, p. 337; *History of Foreign Journalism in San Francisco*, p. 32; *BZ* 16 Mr 1891, 1 Ag 1892.

CALIFORNIA FREIE PRESSE   CA San Francisco   1880?-1883

Title trans.:	California Free Press	*First issue:*	1880 ?
Subtitle:		*Last issue:*	? 1883
Add. lang.:		*Vols. (nos.):*	
First editor:	H. Brandt & Otto Müller	*Frequency:*	w
First publ.:	H. Brandt & Otto Müller	*Preservation:*	?
Related pubs.:		*Supplements:*	
Circulation:	1881: 1500; 1882: 1300	*Category:*	labor

Depositories: Usa-NHi(?)

This labor weekly was founded by H. Brandt and Otto Müller and edited by W. Sozing after 1881. It became non-labor in 1882.

Sources: Arndt/Olson (who date its beginning as 1879); Eberlein 22765; Ayer, 1880-83; *History of Foreign Journalism in San Francisco*, p. 30.

THE CARPENTER   IN Indianapolis   1881-1917

Title trans.:		*First issue:*	My 1881
Subtitle:		*Last issue:*	Jl 1917
Add. lang.:	English, French	*Vols. (nos.):*	
First editor:	James Peter McGuire	*Frequency:*	m
First publ.:		*Preservation:*	1
Related pubs.:		*Supplements:*	
Circulation:		*Category:*	labor union

Depositories: Usa-WHi; D-188/144 (1911-17,m)

This monthly labor union journal was published in English with a section in German entitled *Der Carpenter*, which begins with vol. 1, no. 2. Until 1903 *Der Carpenter* consisted of half a page or more, after January 1904 there were almost three pages in German and one in French; from April 1904 the section was called 'Für unsere deutschen Leser'[For our German readers]; the last issue with a German section appeared in 1917. Thereafter it was a publication in English only.

The subtitle varied: 1. Monthly Journal for Carpenters and Joiners, May 1881-?; 2. A Monthly Journal for Carpenters, Stair Builders, Machine Wood Workers, Planing Mill Men and Kindred Industries. The place of publication also changed: St Louis (1881-1882); New York (1883-?); Philadelphia, PA; Indianapolis (1904 ?- 1917). Until September 1901 the editor was P.J. McGuire, an organizer of the SLP 1874-79, union secretary and first vice president of the AFL who was removed from office because he embezzled union money. From 1901-17 it was edited by Frank Duffy, secretary of the union and second vice president of the AFL. The paper was owned and published by the union as its official organ: 1. the Carpenters' and Joiners' National Union; 2. the Brotherhood of Carpenters and Joiners; 3. the United Brotherhood of Carpenters and Joiners of America. In 1887 the union had 306 locals, 25 of them German. The German pages of *The Carpenter* contained official reports of meetings of the General Executive Board, labor news from Germany and other European countries and articles on child and women's labor. After 1916 only official reports were published. Sources: Arndt/Olson; Naas/Sakr, pp. 24-25; DeLeon, *American Labor Who's Who*, p. 63 (on Duffy); Fink, *Biographical Dictionary*, pp. 222-223 (on McGuire), p. 85 (on Duffy); Fink, *Labor Unions*, pp. 49-51 (on the history of the United Brotherhood of Carpenters and Joiners in America); Christie, Robert A., *Empire in Wood. A History of the Carpenters' Union* (Ithaca, NY, 1956); *New Yorker Volkszeitung* 21 F 1903, on the "United Brotherhood of Carpenters" and 29 Ja 1928, on "Deutsche Carpenter-Union;" *BZ* 1 N 1886, 16 S 1887; Schlüter, *Anfänge*, p. 176; Ware, pp. 231-236; Galenson, Walter, *The United Brotherhood of Carpenters: The First 100 Years* (Cambridge, MA and London, 1983).

CARRIAGE AND WAGON WORKER'S JOURNAL	IL Chicago	1899-1906

Title trans.:		*First issue:*	Je 1899
Subtitle:		*Last issue:*	Je 1906
Add. lang.:	mainly English	*Vols. (nos.):*	1-8(12)
First editor:	Peter Damm	*Frequency:*	m
First publ.:		*Preservation:*	1
Related pubs.:	s *Sattler und Wagenbauer*	*Supplements:*	
Circulation:		*Category:*	labor union

Depositories: Usa-DLC; Usa-NN; D-188/144 (1,m)

According to Arndt/Olson this journal was a continuation of *Sattler und Wagenbauer*, which ceased to exist in 1904?. It had 16 pages, mostly in English but with 2-3 pages in German and continued 1906-1908 in English only. It was the organ of the Carriage and Wagon Workers' International Union of North America and the first editor of the German section was Peter Damm; in 1904 he was succeeded by Charles Schneider.

The place of publication varied: Chicago (June 1899 - January 1901); Cleveland (February 1901 - January 1904); New York (February - December 1904), Chicago (January 1905 - 1908).

It contained union news, articles on wage labor, child labor; reprints from other union journals, poems, short didactic dialogues. In 1900 the union called upon members to vote for the SLP and favored the party's organization, the 'Socialist Trades and Labor Alliance,' which was opposed to pure and simple trade unionism. The union's constitution was published in the issue of 1 July 1905. Contributions came from Karl Marx, Gustav Falke, Hoffmann von Fallersleben, Georg Biedenkapp, Paul Lafargue, A. Otto-Walster, Henry George.

Sources: Arndt/Olson; Eberlein 22735; Naas/Sakr, p. 25; "United Carriage and Waggon Workers' Union of Greater New York," *New Yorker Volkszeitung* 21 F 1903.

CHICAGOER ARBEITER-ZEITUNG (I)   IL Chicago   1876-1924?

Title trans.:	Chicago Labor News	*First issue:*	1 Je 1876
Subtitle:		*Last issue:*	1924?
Add. lang.:		*Vols. (nos.):*	1-43 (138)
First editor:	Conrad Conzett	*Frequency:*	3/w, d, w
First publ.:	Conrad Conzett	*Preservation:*	2
Related pubs.:		*Supplements:*	Vorbote, Die Fackel
Circulation:	1880: 3000; 1886: 5780; 1895: 15,000; 1910: 15,000; 1920: 15,000	*Category:*	socialist

Depositories: Usa-ICN [1879,3 issues missing]; Usa-ICMW (1886-Ap 1920); D-19/1501 (1886-89,m); D-188/144 ([1885-86]-1910,m)

This radically socialist paper turned anarchist in the 1880s - 1910(?), thereafter it became social democratic. The subtitle varied: Organ der internationalen Vereinigung des arbeitenden Volkes [International Association of the Working People]; Organ of the Workingmen's Party of the United States; after 1879 of the Socialist Labor Party. It appeared three times a week from 1 June 1876 to April 1879; daily, evenings except Sunday from 1 May 1879 to 13 October 1919; thereafter weekly. It was excluded from Germany under the antisocialist laws in 1879 (Auer). Suppressed by the Chicago police on 5 May 1886, it was then censored but permitted to resume on 8 May 1886; the entire staff of typesetters and editors was arrested at the time of the Haymarket Affair on 4 May 1886. Difficulties again arose during World War One and the shop was raided in September 1917.

It absorbed the *Volks-Zeitung* (see there), see *Vorbote* for the weekly edition and *Fackel* for the Sunday edition. It was edited by Conrad Conzett* (1 June 1876 - 13 June 1880); Paul Grottkau* (July 1879 - fall 1880), with Gustav Lyser* as his assistant; Dr. Liebig (fall 1880 - fall 1881); Paul Grottkau* (fall 1881 - 16 September 1884); August Spies* (September 1884 - 5 May 1886) with Michael Schwab*; Joseph Dietzgen* (May 1886 - April 1888) with Moritz Schulze* after April 1887; Jens L. Christensen* (April 1888 - November? 1889); Simon Hickler (December 1889 - 1890); Moritz Schulze (November 1890 - 1894) with Robert Steiner and G.A. Hoehn; Max Baginski* (1894-1907?); Heinrich Bartel* (1907-1911); Albert Currlin; Adolf Dreifuß (?-April 1924?). Other members of the staff were Adolf Fischer*, the foreman and William Urban*, the managing director 1892-1915.

The paper was published by Conrad Conzett; by the Socialist Publishing Co. (Deutschsprechende Sektion der SAP) (13 July 1878 - 1892?); by the Chicagoer Arbeiter-Zeitung Publishing Co. (1892-1924?). It contained political news from America and abroad, frequently combined with editorial comments; local news; news from unions and from the SP; reports of workers' meetings and strikes; cultural events for workers; news from the international labor movement; a women's page; serialized novels; short stories; educational articles on socio-political subjects; advertisements and announcements on the last page, especially of Gymnasts' clubs and socialist singing groups; there were also "want" ads and after 1920 photographic illustrations. It published contributions by Karl Marx (a reprint of the "Communist Manifesto" in 1888), Charles Sealsfield (a serialized version of "Nationale Charakteristiken"), A. Von Der Elbe, Robert Steiner, Ivan Turgeniev, Gustav Frenssen, Noel Chretien,

A. Rosenberg, Erwin Hoernle.

For fund-raising for *Chicagoer Arbeiter-Zeitung*, see introduction. It is unclear at what date the paper was discontinued. Arndt/Olson suggest 13 October 1919, but thereafter it was continued as a weekly. Eberlein gives 1931, which is the year of the establishment of its successor, also entitled *Chicagoer Arbeiter-Zeitung* (see there), but lists holdings only until 1924. Possibly the *Chicagoer Arbeiter-Zeitung* closed down together with *Vorbote* on 30 April 1924.

Sources: Arndt/Olson; see also the jubilee edition of *Chicagoer Arbeiter-Zeitung* of 5 S 1897; Eberlein 22670 (who mentions that it existed until 1931); Sorge, pp. 159-160 et passim; Edelmann, pp. 27-42; Kiesewetter; on Fischer, see *BZ* 16 N 1887 and Waltershausen, pp. 315-316. Obituary on William Urban in *BZ* 1 Ag 1915. On the editors, see *Vorbote*.

CHICAGOER ARBEITER-ZEITUNG (II)	IL Chicago	1931-?

Title trans.:	Chicago Labor News	*First issue:*	F 1931
Subtitle:		*Last issue:*	?
Add. lang.:		*Vols. (nos.):*	
First editor:		*Frequency:*	m
First publ.:		*Preservation:*	?
Related pubs.:		*Supplements:*	
Circulation:		*Category:*	socialist

Depositories: D-Bm 41/IGA [1931]; DDR-LDB (1931)

This 4-page monthly was published by the Arbeiterkultur- und Sportkartell, Chicago, which was an association of 15 local workers' organizations concerned with sport, singing, benefit and education and was founded with the purpose of establishing a workers' home and this monthly. Officials of the Kartell were Jos. Schlesinger, Rud. Weier, Paul Mattick. It contained news from the American and international labor movement, political news, e.g. on the Nazi movement in Chicago and on the League of Nations; commemorative articles in March 1931 for the Paris Commune and in November 1931 for the Haymarket victims and for the Russian Revolution of 1917; a reprint of Rosa Luxemburg's "Märzstürme" [March Winds]. It opposed the communist *Der Arbeiter*. The paper probably did not exist for a long time: in October 1931 one member of the Kartell, the Naturfreunde [Nature's Friends], which had been opposed to the establishment of the paper from the beginning, was expelled and another member, the Chicago Kickers, resigned membership and joined the 'Plattdeutsche Gilde' [Low-German League], "which has to be considered as hostile to workers' concerns" (issue of October 1931).

Source: Arndt/Olson.

CHICAGOER BAECKER-ZEITUNG		IL Chicago	1888-1890

Title trans.:	Chicago Bakers' Journal	*First issue:*	1888
Subtitle:	Für Wahrheit, Fortschritt und	*Last issue:*	1890
	Brüderlichkeit		
Add. lang.:		*Vols. (nos.):*	
First editor:		*Frequency:*	bw
First publ.:		*Preservation:*	3
Related pubs.:		*Supplements:*	
Circulation:		*Category:*	labor union

Depositories: NI-IISG [1888-1889]

Subtitle translation: For Truth, Progress and Fraternity.

This paper was founded by the Unabhängige Bäckerunion [Independent Bakers' Union] No. 1 (Chicago) and remained its property and official organ.

CHICAGOER SOZIALIST		IL Chicago	1876-1879?

Title trans.:	Chicago Socialist	*First issue:*	1 N 1876
Subtitle:		*Last issue:*	1879?
Add. lang.:		*Vols. (nos.):*	
First editor:	Johann Joseph Brucker	*Frequency:*	d
First publ.:		*Preservation:*	7
Related pubs.:		*Supplements:*	
Circulation:		*Category:*	socialist-WP

Depositories:

This morning daily (except Sundays) was published by the Arbeiterpartei der Vereinigten Staaten [Workingmen's Party of the United States] and printed by the Socialist Printing Association. Joseph Brucker was previously editor of several papers in Milwaukee (see *Freidenker, Milwaukee Socialist* and *Blitzstrahlen* established in February 1875, of which nothing but the title has survived). Typographia No. 10 of Milwaukee welcomed the new socialist paper at which all members who had been out of work because of a strike found employment again. (*BZ* 15 N 1876). According to Schlüter the *Sozialist* was founded by a petty bourgeois ("kleinbürgerliche") faction of the socialist movement. Variant: Arndt/Olson name Robert List as editor and the Socialist Printing Association as publisher.

Sources: Arndt/Olson; Schlüter, *Internationale*, p. 394; Eberlein 22794; *BZ* 15 N 1876.

CHICAGOER VOLKS-ZEITUNG		IL Chicago	1877-1879?

Title trans.:	Chicago People's News	*First issue:*	18 F 1877
Subtitle:	Unabhängiges Organ für die Interessen	*Last issue:*	1879 ?
	des Volkes		
Add. lang.:		*Vols. (nos.):*	
First editor:		*Frequency:*	d
First publ.:	Chicago Press Society	*Preservation:*	5
Related pubs.:		*Supplements:*	see below
Circulation:		*Category:*	labor

Depositories: Usa-ICN [1877]

This paper appeared daily in the morning, except Sundays and was "an independent organ representing the interests of the people." From 13 April 1877 it was published by the Genossenschaftsdruckerei der Volkszeitung."

Die Neue Zeit was the Sunday edition of *Chicagoer Volks-Zeitung*. In 1878 it had an estimated circulation of 1500. The *Wöchentliche Chicagoer Volks-Zeitung* was its weekly edition. It probably appeared from 1877 to 1879 and was mentioned in the daily edition.

Sources: Arndt/Olson; Eberlein 22867.

CIGAR MAKERS' OFFICIAL JOURNAL		NY New York	1875-1953?

Title trans.:		*First issue:*	N 1875
Subtitle:		*Last issue:*	1953
Add. lang.:	mainly English, Bohemian	*Vols. (nos.):*	
First editor:	George Hurst	*Frequency:*	m
First publ.:		*Preservation:*	1
Related pubs.:	*Progress*	*Supplements:*	
Circulation:		*Category:*	labor union

Depositories: Usa-WHi; D-188/144 (Mr 1876-Je 1895,m)

This was the organ of the Cigar Makers' International Union, which was founded in 1864 as one of the earliest national unions. Initially it had 4 pages, from September 1880 8 pages and in 1886 12 pages. The first issues were only in English; in June and July 1876 one column, thereafter a whole page was printed in German; after February 1883 it had a regular column in Czech. It could not be established if and when the German page was given up. After October 1877 it was edited by Adolph Strasser. The place of publication varied: Suffield, CO (November 1875 - September 1877); New York (October 1877 - ?); Chicago. The paper contained union news, accounts of the union treasury, proceedings of union sessions, names of new as well as of expelled members, fines imposed because of behavior injurious to the union. The column "State of Trade" was important to traveling cigarmakers, because it enabled them to know in which towns there might be vacancies. Locals experiencing poor working conditions or enforcing boycotts or strikes placed warnings in the *Journal*. Traveling cigarmakers used the *Journal* as a means of communication: local unions accepted mail for members and letters not

delivered were listed in the "Letter Box" column. Articles dealing with the cigarmaking industry in Germany were often translated from the German labor union press. Other subjects were the cooperative movement, the eight-hour campaign and the abolition of tenement house factories.
Sources: Arndt/Olson; Naas/Sakr p. 24; Fink, *Labor Unions*, pp. 55-57; Ware, pp. 258-279; Cooper, Patricia A., "The Travelling Fraternity: Union Cigar Makers and Geographic Mobility 1900-1919," *Journal of Social History* (1983), pp. 127-138; *BZ* 1 S 1886 "Die Internationale Union der Cigaretten-Arbeiter;" *BZ* 1 F 1887 "Das Cigar Makers' Official Journal und das *Philadelphia Tageblatt;*" *BZ* 1 O 1887 (on the union); *BZ* 1 Ap 1895 (on the "horribly mutilated" German language in the journal); *New Yorker Volkszeitung* 1 F 1908 "Die Cigarrenarbeiter. Die Lage des Gewerkes während der letzten 20 Jahre" [Cigarmakers. The State of the Trade over the Last 20 Years]. On Strasser see Fink, *Biographical Dictionary*, pp. 340-341; Cooper, Patricia A. "Whatever happened to Adolph Strasser?" *Labor History* XX, 3 (Summer 1979), pp. 414-419. See also *Progress*, organ of the Cigarmakers' Progressive Union.

CINCINNATIER ZEITUNG		OH Cincinnati	1886-1901

Title trans.:	Cincinnati News	*First issue:*	7 Je 1886
Subtitle:		*Last issue:*	21 O 1901
Add. lang.:		*Vols. (nos.):*	
First editor:	Ernst A. Meier	*Frequency:*	d
First publ.:	Zeitung Publishing Co.	*Preservation:*	2
Related pubs.:	s Cincinnati *Arbeiter-Zeitung*	*Supplements:*	
Circulation:	1886: 2000; 1890: 7500; 1900: 6000	*Category:*	labor

Depositories: Usa-ICHi [1901]; Usa-ICJ [1901]; Usa-OC [1887-1901]

This paper appeared daily, except on Sundays. The editor after Weier was F. Detmers and from 1890 to 1895 it was edited and published by Jacob Willig. From 1895 to 1901 Emil Paetow was the publisher. Title variant: *Cincinnati Zeitung* (Arndt/Olson).

The paper was founded during a strike by a cooperative of German typesetters who had become unemployed. It was intended to serve as an organ for union workers. One of the founders was Friedrich Schiele*. In 1887 and 1888 picnics and a ball were organized for the benefit of the paper. It was frequently attacked by the socialist *Cincinnati Tageblatt*, which even called for a boycott of the *Zeitung* in June 1896. In February 1893 the paper's typesetters, all organized in the Typographia No. 2 of Cincinnati, protested against publisher Willig because the composing room was insufficiently heated and lighted. Disputes between Willig and the typesetters continued until Willig resigned in May 1895. The organized workers of Cincinnati wanted to keep the paper as their organ but they were not able to raise enough money to buy it. It was bought for a song ("für ein Butterbrot") at an auction by Emil Paetow, owner of the *Cincinnati Anzeiger*. In 1900 both *Anzeiger* and *Zeitung* were composed by hand by nine typesetters and one apprentice who worked 8 hours daily. Both papers were discontinued on the same day. According to the *Buchdrucker-Zeitung*, the reasons were a decline in advertisements, a decline in quality after the dismissal of editor Weier and the introduction of printing plates as well as the fact that there were too many, i.e. six, German dailies in Cincinnati at that time (while there were only four English ones).

Sources: Arndt/Olson; *BZ* e.g. 16 Je 1892, 16 F, 16 Mr 1893, 16 F, 16 My, 1 Je, 16 Jl, 16 S 1895, 1 N 1901. Obituary on Schiele in *BZ* 16 O 1908.

Sonntagsblatt der Cincinnatier Zeitung 1887?-1901. This was the Sunday edition of the *Cincinnatier Zeitung.* Circulation: 1890: 8000; 1900: 7500. Sources: Arndt/Olson; Ayer 1887-1901.

CLEVELANDER VOLKSFREUND		OH Cleveland	1886-1918?

Title trans.:	Cleveland Friend of the People	*First issue:*	? 1886
Subtitle:	see below	*Last issue:*	26 Ja 1919?
Add. lang.:		*Vols. (nos.):*	1(1)-33(4)
First editor:	August Keitel	*Frequency:*	3/w, w, d, w
First publ.:		*Preservation:*	4
Related pubs.:	m *Socialistische Arbeiterzeitung* (Cleveland)	*Supplements:*	*Wochenblatt* (Cleveland)
Circulation:	1890: 3200; 1900: 2800; 1908: 2850; 1910: 4867; 1915: 8500; 1918: 8500	*Category:*	socialist-SLP

Depositories: Usa-WHi (Jl 1908-Ja 1918); D-Bm 41/IGA (29 Ap 1911)

This paper appeared three times a week (1886-89); weekly (1890 - September 1894); daily for 7 weeks (September - October 1894); weekly (October 1894 - 1918). The title changed after it merged with *Socialistische Arbeiterzeitung* (see there for difficulties of dating) either on 1 August 1901 or on 18 July 1908, the title was *Volksfreund und Arbeiter-Zeitung* until 1918.

Subtitles were: 1. Den Interessen des arbeitenden Volkes gewidmet. Herausgegeben von der Volksfreund Publication Association: Offizielles Organ der Sektion Cleveland, S.A.P. [Dedicated to the Interests of the Working People. Published by the Volksfreund Publication Association. Official Organ of the Cleveland Branch of the SLP]; 2. Den Interessen der Arbeiterklasse gewidmet. Officielles deutsches Organ der Socialistischen Arbeiter-Partei, 25 July 1908 - 1918.

Editors were August Keitel* (1886-1892); Karl Ibsen (1893-?) and Richard Koppel (1908?-1918). Its publisher, the Volksfreund Publication Association, consisted of local assemblies of the Knights of Labor and diverse German unions and it was supported by the Cleveland section of the SLP. When *Socialistische Arbeiter-Zeitung* and *Volksfreund* merged, the Publication Association was dissolved and the paper became the property of the SLP.

The paper contained American and foreign news, party news, short stories, poems and advertisements mostly for local business. Among the contributors were Fritz Jacobi, Heinrich Berg, Rudolf Katz, Karl Dannenberg, A. Bogdanow. The jubilee edition for the 25th anniversary on 29 April 1911 contains details of the paper's history and an article commemorating Keitel.

Sources: Arndt/Olson; Eberlein 22824, 22827.

Wochenblatt des Clevelander Volksfreund: 1886?-1889?. This was the weekly edition of the *Clevelander Volksfreund.*

Source: Arndt/Olson.

DER COMMUNIST		MO St. Louis	1845?-1846?

Title trans.:	The Communist	*First issue:*	1845?
Subtitle:		*Last issue:*	1846?
Add. lang.:		*Vols. (nos.):*	
First editor:	Heinrich Koch	*Frequency:*	w
First publ.:	Heinrich Koch	*Preservation:*	7
Related pubs.:		*Supplements:*	
Circulation:		*Category:*	

Depositories:

No further information could be obtained.

Sources: Arndt/Olson; Eberlein 22700; Kamman, p. 35; Schlüter, *Anfänge*, pp. 19, 46. On Koch, see *Der Reformer* (MO St. Louis, 1847).

DER COMMUNIST		LA New Orleans	1853-?

Title trans.:	The Communist	*First issue:*	? 1853
Subtitle:		*Last issue:*	?
Add. lang.:		*Vols. (nos.):*	
First editor:	Etienne Cabet (?)	*Frequency:*	w
First publ.:		*Preservation:*	7
Related pubs.:		*Supplements:*	
Circulation:		*Category:*	utopian communist

Depositories:

This paper was founded early in 1853 as the organ of the New Orleans Communisten-Verein, a communist club which had been founded after Wilhelm Weitling's visit to the city. Samuel Stamm was the club's president and Georg Rehkopf its secretary. In respect to E. Cabet's editorship of *Der Communist* Cazden has reservations, since Cabet's biographer, Prudhommeaux, does not mention any German Icarian paper in New Orleans.

Sources: Arndt/Olson; Eberlein 22699; Wittke, *Press*, p. 111; Deiler, p. 12; Cazden, *Book Trade*, pp. (664-665).

COOPER'S INTERNATIONAL JOURNAL　　　　KS Kansas City　　　　1890-1918

Title trans.:		*First issue:*	N? 1890
Subtitle:		*Last issue:*	My 1918
Add. lang.:		*Vols. (nos.):*	1-28 (5)
First editor:	James A. Cable	*Frequency:*	
First publ.:		*Preservation:*	3
Related pubs.:	c *Coopers' Journal*; *Küfer-Zeitung* (?)	*Supplements:*	
Circulation:	1910: 8480	*Category:*	labor union

Depositories: Usa-DLC (1898-1918); Usa-KHi (1899-1918)

This labor union monthly was published in English and German; each issue had 40-70 pages. It was the official organ of the Coopers' International Union of North America. Various errors in numbering occurred.

The German section, entitled "Die Internationale Küfer-Zeitung," was last published in the issue of May 1918. The place of publication varied: Cleveland, Boston. It was edited and published by William R. Deal after 1914.

Sources: Arndt/Olson; Eberlein 22787; Naas/Sakr, p. 33.

COOPERS' JOURNAL　　　　　　　　　　OH Cleveland　　　　1870-1875

Title trans.:		*First issue:*	Jl 1870
Subtitle:		*Last issue:*	Je 1875//
Add. lang.:	English	*Vols. (nos.):*	
First editor:	Robert Schilling	*Frequency:*	m
First publ.:		*Preservation:*	4-5
Related pubs.:	*Küfer-Zeitung* (?); s *Coopers'*	*Supplements:*	
	International Journal		
Circulation:		*Category:*	labor union

Depositories: Usa-MdBJ [1870-73]

This monthly labor union journal published in English and German was the organ of the Coopers' International Union. The president of the union, which was founded in 1870, was Martin Ambrose Foran, who also edited the English part of the paper from 1870 to 1874. According to the union's proceedings in 1871, there were over 20 German unions or lodges under its jurisdiction. The German journal's translation from English was considered defective, especially as far as technical and trade terms were concerned. In 1873 the cost of printing, binding and shipping of the English and German journals was approximately $12,000. Robert Schilling* was later also the editor of several papers in Milwaukee.

Sources: Naas/Sakr, p. 33; Fink, *Labor Unions*, pp. 74-75 (on the history of the Coopers' International Union); Commons, *History of Labor II*, pp. 74-76; Fink, *Biographical Dictionary*, pp. 109 and 319 (on Schilling and on Foran); Coopers' International Union Proceedings, *Proceedings of the Second Annual Session of the Coopers' International Union of North America held in the City of New York, October 1871*, Cleveland, OH, 1871; *Proceedings of the Fourth Convention of the Coopers' International Union in St. Louis, October 1873,*

Cleveland, OH, 1873.

DEMOKRAT	MD Baltimore	1850?

Title trans.:	The Democrat	*First issue:*	1850?
Subtitle:		*Last issue:*	1850?
Add. lang.:		*Vols. (nos.):*	
First editor:		*Frequency:*	
First publ.:		*Preservation:*	7
Related pubs.:		*Supplements:*	
Circulation:		*Category:*	labor ?

Depositories:

This paper encouraged the establishment of "Gewerbevereine" [Workers' Clubs organized by the crafts].
Source: Schlüter, *Anfänge*, p. 128.

DEUTSCH-AMERIKANISCHE ARBEITERKLUBS ...	NY New York	1934-1938?

Title trans.:	Newsletter of the German-American Workers' Clubs, U.S.A.	*First issue:*	My 1934
Subtitle:		*Last issue:*	1938?
Add. lang.:		*Vols. (nos.):*	
First editor:		*Frequency:*	ir(?)
First publ.:		*Preservation:*	5?
Related pubs.:	s *Unsere Zeit*	*Supplements:*	
Circulation:		*Category:*	communist

Depositories: D-292 (Mr 1937,S 1937); <§Usa-KyLC (?)

The complete title of the paper was: *Deutsch Amerikanische Arbeiterklubs U.S.A: Mitteilungsblatt*

This was the organ of the Föderation der Deutsch- Amerikanischen Arbeiter-Klubs U.S.A., communist workers' clubs, which existed in New York, Chicago, Milwaukee, Newark and Philadelphia. It probably appeared irregularly and the volume and issue numbering are very confused. The title varied: *Deutsche Arbeiter-Klubs. Mitteilungsblatt* (May 1934 - April 1935); *Deutsch-Amerikanische Arbeiter-Klubs. Mitteilungsblatt* (May 1935 - March 1937). From May 1935 until January 1937 the *Mitteilungsblatt* was published as a supplement to *Der Arbeiter*, New York. The first issues were mimeographed; after December 1934 it was printed. It contained resolutions, open letters, e.g. from Heinrich Mann in September 1937 and announcements of locals. Contributions came from Joseph Deck, Erika Mann, Heinrich Mann, Thomas Mann, Erich von Schroeter, G. Tieland. It was continued in 1940 by *Unsere Zeit*. The *German-American Emergency Conference Bulletin* and the *German American* are probably also related to this paper.

Sources: Cazden, *Exile Literature*, pp. 187, 48; Maas II, p. 371; Maas IV.

DEUTSCH-AMERIKANISCHE BÄCKER-ZEITUNG   NY New York   1885-1941

Title trans.:	German-American Bakers' Journal	*First issue:*	2 My 1885
Subtitle:		*Last issue:*	? Ap 1941
Add. lang.:	English	*Vols. (nos.):*	1-56
First editor:	George G. Block	*Frequency:*	w, bw, w
First publ.:	Bäcker-Arbeiter-Union von New York	*Preservation:*	1
Related pubs.:	m *Bakers' Journal* (English)	*Supplements:*	
Circulation:	1890: 9000; 1900: 5500; 1905: 23,000;	*Category:*	labor union
	1920: 18,800		

Depositories: Usa-WHi (1885-95); Usa-NN; D-188/144 [1886-95,m]; D-19/1501
(1888-1925,m)

This was the official organ of the Bakers' union and it appeared as a weekly (2 May 1885 - June 1897), as a biweekly (July 1897 - August 1899) and again as a weekly (September 1899 - April 1941). In the issue of 26 January 1887 an English page was introduced. The title changed: after merging with the *Bakers' Journal* it became *The Bakers' Journal and Deutsch-Amerikanische Bäcker-Zeitung* (11 September 1895 - 30 January 1937), and then *Bakers' Journal* (6 February 1937 - April 1941). After April 1941 it appeared in English only. The place of publication varied: New York (1885 - 1894); Brooklyn (December 1894 - August 1899?); Cleveland (September 1899? - 1904); Chicago (1904 - 1941?).

Editors were George G. Block (May 1885 - 1 May 1889); Robert Degen (see *New Yorker Volkszeitung*, May - October 1889), Karl Ibsen (October 1889 - March 1891), Henry Weismann (March 1891 - 1 November 1897), John Schudel (November 1897 - 21 August 1903), Joseph Schmidt (5 September 1903 - 8 May 1908) and Charles F. Hohmann (16 May 1908 - ?). It was published by the National-Verband der Bäckergehülfen der Ver. Staaten; by the Journeymen Bakers' National Union of U.S. until April 1887; by the Journeymen Bakers' and Confectioners' International Union of America.

It had an elaborate title emblem with the motto: "Vereint sind wir alles, vereinzelt aber nichts" [United we are everything, but separately we are nothing] on a streamer binding a sheaf of wheat. After 1888 all union members automatically received a subscription. It contained news from the unions locals, articles on matters relating to the bakers' trade, e.g. on the system of guilds, on diverse types of bread, on the history of breadmaking, on baking in foreign countries, on diseases frequently occurring in the trade, on socialist cooperative bakeries, appeals to boycott, e.g. "Fleischmann's Yeast" in 1890. Regular features were a letterbox, short stories, serialized novels, poems, proverbs, advertisements, frequently of products particular to the trade. Contributions came from Minna Kautsky (a serialized version of "Stephan vom Grillenhof"), Ulrich Frank, A. von Winterfeld, Johann Jacoby, Peter Rosegger, Ludwig Anzengruber, Ferdinand Lassalle. The Silver Anniversary issue was printed on 14 January 1911.

Sources:Arndt/Olson; Naas/Sakr, p. 17; Fink *Labor Unions*, pp. 26-28; Jentz, John B. "Bread and Labor: Chicago's German Bakers Organize," *Chicago History* XII, 2 (Summer 1983), pp. 24-35; *BZ* 16 My 1888, 16 Mr, 16 Ap 1889, 1 Ja 1895, 1 Ag 1897; *Möbelarbeiter-Journal* 13 Ap 1889.

DEUTSCH-AMERIKANISCHE BUCHDRUCKER-ZEITUNG IN Indianapolis   1873-1940

Title trans.:	German-American Printers' Journal	*First issue:*	1 Jl 1873
Subtitle:	Officielles Organ der Deutsch-Amerikanischen Typographia	*Last issue:*	Jl 1940 //
Add. lang.:		*Vols. (nos.):*	1(1)-67(13)
First editor:	Charles G. Bachmann	*Frequency:*	m, sm
First publ.:	Deutsch-Amerikanische Typographia	*Preservation:*	2
Related pubs.:	see below	*Supplements:*	
Circulation:	1878: 600; 1885: 1150; 1895: 1800; 1910: 1250	*Category:*	labor union

Depositories: D-188/144 (1876-1917,1927-40,m); D-19/1501 (1876-88,m); Usa-NN; Usa-MdBJ (1873-74,1888-98); Usa-DLC (1898-1907); Usa-ICJ (1899-1932?)

This was the oldest German-American labor union journal; and the "official organ of the German-American Typographical Union" (Typographia). It appeared as follows: monthly (1 July 1873 - 1874), semimonthly (1875 - 1 December 1918), monthly (16 December 1918 - 16 March 1920), semimonthly (1 April 1920 - 16 June 1926), monthly (July 1926 - July 1940). It contained 8 pages (1873 - May 1876), 4 pages (June 1876 - March 1882), 8 pages (April 1882 - 1884), 4 pages (January 1885 - 1940). After June 1876 every union member automatically received a subscription. It was set in Roman type instead of Gothic after June 1876, a rarity at that time. The title changed: *Deutsch-Amerikanisches Journal für Buchdruckerkunst, Schriftgießerei und die verwandten Fächer* [German-American Journal for Typography, Type-Foundry and Related Trades] (1 July 1873 - May 1876), *Buchdrucker-Zeitung* [Printers' Journal] (June 1876 - March 1881), *Deutsch-Amerikanische Buchdrucker-Zeitung* (1 April 1881 - July 1940). It was edited by Charles G. Bachmann, the secretary of the union (July 1873 - 30 June 1876), Jean Weil (July 1876 - June 1883), Friedrich Milke (July 1883 - June 1886), Hugo Miller (July 1886 - January 1926 - Miller died on 19 February 1926 but his name remained as editor until 16 April), Henry Rutz (January - June 1926), Ferdinand Foernsler (16 June 1926 - May 1928), Julius Theil (June 1928 - July 1940). The place of publication changed: Philadelphia (July 1873 - July 1876), New York (July 1876 - October 1894), Indianapolis (November 1894 - June 1926), NY Brooklyn (July 1926 - 1928), Chicago (1928 - 1940).

The *Buchdrucker-Zeitung* is a rich source for the history of the German-American labor movement as well as for the technical development of the printing trade. The first three volumes contain mostly technical treatises. After 1876 it included reports from the local branches of the German-American Typographia, financial reports, motion statistics, obituaries of deceased members and articles on strikes, the eight-hour campaign of the 1880s, the union-cut and the printers' misuse of traveling money; it published lists of companies boycotted by the AFL and took an ambivalent, if not hostile attitude toward women in the trade. The *Buchdrucker-Zeitung* contained a wealth of information on the development of the German-American, American and international press, the monopolization of the press, technical developments in newspaper production and their effect on job security. It also contained articles on occupational diseases, e.g. tuberculosis and failing eyesight, reports on exhibitions, museums etc. related to the press, oddities and funny misprints, artificial languages. In World War One the *Buchdrucker-Zetung* published lists of German printers killed in action; it appealed to its readers to collect money for destitute German, Austrian and Hungarian printers. From the late 1920s it contained detailed analyses of the devastating effect of fascism on the German and Italian press; in the 1930s it discussed the position of German Americans, criticizing tendencies among them to accept Nazism; it fought against armament and war.

On 1 July 1940 the Deutsch-Amerikanische Typographia was dissolved. The trade was becoming extinct: due to rationalization, printers' had become less and less in demand, the German-American press had declined steadily, and the old, active members were literally dying out. See also: Appendix 'Newspapers and Broadsheets of the German-American Typographia.'

Sources: Arndt/Olson; *BZ* 16 Je 1913 (articles on 40th anniversary), *New Yorker Volkszeitung* 21 F 1903 (on Typographia No. 7 of New York).

DEUTSCH-AMERIKANISCHE FLEISCHER-ZEITUNG	NY Brooklyn	1904

Title trans.:	German-American Butchers' Journal	*First issue:*	1 Ag 1904
Subtitle:		*Last issue:*	N 1904
Add. lang.:		*Vols. (nos.):*	
First editor:	Max Ferle	*Frequency:*	bw, w?
First publ.:		*Preservation:*	7
Related pubs.:		*Supplements:*	
Circulation:		*Category:*	labor union

Depositories:

This labor union journal of a "progressive tendency," was dedicated to the concerns of butchers. It was published biweekly until October, after that it was to appear weekly. It was discontinued after three months.

Sources: *BZ* 16 Ag and 1 D 1904. See also *Butchers' Journal*.

DER DEUTSCHE ARBEITER	IL Chicago	1869-1870

Title trans.:	The German Worker	*First issue:*	Mr 1869
Subtitle:	Organ zur Förderung eines	*Last issue:*	1 Ag 1870//
	Verständnisses der immer mehr in den		
	Vordergrund tretenden "Sozialen Frage."		
Add. lang.:		*Vols. (nos.):*	1(1)-2(20)
First editor:	Carl Klings	*Frequency:*	w
First publ.:		*Preservation:*	2
Related pubs.:		*Supplements:*	
Circulation:		*Category:*	workers' club

Depositories: D-188/144 [1869-70],m); D-46 (Ag 1869-Ag 1870,m)

Subtitle translation: Organ to Support a Better Understanding of the Growing Urgency of the "Social Question."

This paper was the organ of the Deutscher Arbeiter- Central- Schutz und Unterstützungs-Verein of Chicago [Central German Workers' Support and

Protection Association]. This organization was formed in early 1869 by several German trade associations in Chicago. The paper was started three months later at the beginning of March 1869 . Karl Klings*, its "leading spirit" (Schlüter, p 309) had collaborated with Ferdinand Lassalle in Germany. The paper urged its readers to organize and it reported about strikes, other workers' struggles and the proceedings of the First International. It also paid attention to the organization of Black workers. It was suspended because the weekly $25 subsidy from the Verein was to be spent on agitation among European workers against their participation in the FrancoPrussian war. Future announcements of the Verein were to be published in the *Arbeiter-Union* of New York. Contributors included J.B. v. Schweitzer, J.P. Becker, Dr. Kossak.

Sources: Arndt/Olson 2, p. 371; Schlüter, *Internationale*, pp. 308-309. On Klings, see *Geschichte der deutschen Arbeiterbewegung*, pp. 241-242.

DEUTSCHE ARBEITERZEITUNG	A Edmonton	1930?-1931?

Title trans.:	German Labor News	*First issue:*	N 1930?
Subtitle:		*Last issue:*	1931?
Add. lang.:		*Vols. (nos.):*	
First editor:		*Frequency:*	m
First publ.:		*Preservation:*	6
Related pubs.:		*Supplements:*	
Circulation:		*Category:*	labor

Depositories: Cdn-OONL (Ja 1931)

No further information could be obtained.

Sources: *Checklist*, p. 115; *Union List*, p. 10.

DEUTSCHE ARBEITER ZEITUNG	M Winnipeg	1930-1937

Title trans.:	German Labor News	*First issue:*	Je? 1930
Subtitle:	Zentralorgan des Verbandes deutschsprechender Arbeiter	*Last issue:*	14 Jl 1937
Add. lang.:		*Vols. (nos.):*	
First editor:		*Frequency:*	m, bw, w
First publ.:	German Workers' and Farmers' Association	*Preservation:*	1
Related pubs.:		*Supplements:*	
Circulation:	2500	*Category:*	labor

Depositories: Cdn-MWUC; Cdn-OONL (O 1930-Jl 1937)

Subtitle translation: Organ of the German Workers' and Farmers' Association.

This paper was published monthly (to February 1932), biweekly (1 March 1932 - 15 November 1934), weekly (November 1934 - July 1937).

Sources: Arndt/Olson; *Checklist*, p. 115; *Canadian Ethnic Studies* 1 (1), p. 17; *Union List*, p. 75.

DEUTSCHE FRAUEN-ZEITUNG   WI Milwaukee   1852-1854?

Title trans.:	German Women's Journal	*First issue:*	Mr? 1852
Subtitle:	Central-Organ der Vereine zur	*Last issue:*	1854?
	Verbesserung der Lage der Frauen		
Add. lang.:		*Vols. (nos.):*	1-3?
First editor:	Mathilde Franziska Anneke*	*Frequency:*	m, sm, w
First publ.:	Mathilde Franziska Anneke	*Preservation:*	6
Related pubs.:		*Supplements:*	
Circulation:		*Category:*	radical fortyeighter

Depositories: Usa-MWA (15 O 1852)

Subtitle translation: Central Organ of the Associations for the Improvement of the Situation of Women.

This paper appeared monthly from 1852-1853; semimonthly 1853; and again weekly from 1853-1854. The title was changed to: *Neue Frauenzeitung*. The place of publication varied: Milwaukee (March - September 1852), New York (15 October 1852 - 1853), Jersey City (1853 - 1854). Each issue contained 8 pages.
Sources: Arndt/Olson; Kamman, p. 42; Miller, pp. 60-61; Krueger, pp. 163-167. See *Newarker Zeitung* for references on Anneke. For information on the German career of Anneke see: Martin Henkel and Rolf Taubert, *Das Weib im Conflict mit den Socialen Verhältnissen. Mathilde Franziska Anneke und die erste deutsche Frauenzeitung* (Bochum, 1976).

DER DEUTSCHE REPUBLIKANER   OH Cincinnati   (1858-1861)

Title trans.:	The German Republican	*First issue:*	28 S 1842
Subtitle:	Ein Tageblatt für Politik, Gewerbe und	*Last issue:*	23 Mr 1861
	Wirtschaft		
Add. lang.:		*Vols. (nos.):*	
First editor:	J.H. Schroeder	*Frequency:*	d
First publ.:	J.H. Schroeder	*Preservation:*	
Related pubs.:		*Supplements:*	Weekly edition: *Der Deutsche Republikaner*
Circulation:		*Category:*	

Depositories: Usa-DLC (O 1850-Jl 1851,1852-54,[1855],1858); Usa-IU [1858-61]

Subtitle translation: A Daily for Politics, Trade and Economics. Later the subtitle changed to: "Organ of the Workers."
This paper started out as a Whig paper and turned toward Labor in December 1858. In January 1856 the title changed to *Cincinnati Republicaner*. Later editors were: C.F. Schmidt (1843-44), Wilhelm J.L. Kiderlen (1844-48), Heinrich Geider (1848-49), Emil Klauprecht (1849-51), Ludwig F. von Fenneberg* (1851-52), Emil Klauprecht again (1852-56). From 1858 to 1861 it was

published by the Socialer Arbeiterverein.

DEUTSCHE SCHNELLPOST		NY New York	(1848)-1851
Title trans.:	German Express Mail	*First issue:*	4 Ja 1843
Subtitle:	Ein Organ der Zustände und Interessen der alten und neuen Heimat	*Last issue:*	1 S 1851
Add. lang.:		*Vols. (nos.):*	1-9(1-196)
First editor:	(Wilhelm Eichthal)	*Frequency:*	d
First publ.:	(Wilhelm Eichthal)	*Preservation:*	2
Related pubs.:		*Supplements:*	Sonntagsblatt (New York)
Circulation:		*Category:*	radical fortyeighter

Depositories: Usa-NN ([1848],1851); D-188/144 ([1848]-1851,m)

Subtitle translation: An Organ on the Situation and Interests in the Old and New Home Countries.

The editors after 1848 were Rudolph Dowiat (January - February ? 1848), Karl Heinzen and Ivan Tyssowski (February - March 1848), Ivan Tyssowski (March 1848 - ?), Karl Heinzen (January - September 1851). The publishers after 1848 were Wilhelm Wagenitz (January - February 1848), Karl Heinzen and Ivan Tyssowski (February - March 1848), A.Ch. Fromm (January - February 1851).

This paper was founded in 1843 by Wilhelm von Eichthal as a democratic semiweekly paper. Under Dowiat's and Heinzen's editorship it became a radical paper in 1848. The *Schnellpost* and its *Sonntagsblatt* contained poetry, serialized stories, European correspondence, literary criticism and scientific articles. It advocated equality for women and opposed temperance legislation. When the *Deutsche Schnellpost* was discontinued, it was sold at a sheriff's sale and the money was used to start a new paper, the *New Yorker Deutsche Zeitung.*

Sources: Arndt/Olson; Wittke, *Against the Current*, pp. 85-86. On Heinzen, see *Pionier.*

DEUTSCHE ZENTRALBÜCHEREI: MITTEILUNGSBLATT	NY New York	1936
Title trans.: German Central Library: Newsletter	*First issue:*	F 1936?
Subtitle:	*Last issue:*	
Add. lang.:	*Vols. (nos.):*	
First editor:	*Frequency:*	bm
First publ.:	*Preservation:*	7
Related pubs.:	*Supplements:*	
Circulation:	*Category:*	communist

Depositories:

The publication of this bimonthly was proposed by an antifascist book-club established in September 1935 by the Deutsche Zentralbuchhandlung [Central Book Store]. The latter existed from 1935 - 1941 and was a publishing house as well as a wholesale and retail enterprise for the distribution of antifascist publications and publications on the Soviet Union. The proposal to issue the *Mitteilungsblatt* as a separate publication was probably never carried out, for in the issue of 21 March 1936 of *Der Arbeiter* a column appeared with the title "Mitteilungen der Deutschen Zentralbücherei."

Sources: Cazden, *Exile Literature*, pp. 117, 176, 187-188; *Der Arbeiter*, 15 S 1935 and 21 Mr 1936.

DEUTSCHES VOLKSECHO	NY New York	1937-1939

Title trans.:	German People's Echo	*First issue:*	20 F 1937
Subtitle:		*Last issue:*	16 S 1939
Add. lang.:	English	*Vols. (nos.):*	1-3(37)
First editor:	Stephan Heym	*Frequency:*	w
First publ.:		*Preservation:*	1
Related pubs.:	m *Volksfront*; c *Der Arbeiter* (New York, III)	*Supplements:*	
Circulation:		*Category:*	communist

Depositories: Usa-NN; D-292

This was the official German-language weekly of the Communist Party in continuation of *Der Arbeiter*, the numbering of which it continued. Some articles were written in English. The title changed: *Deutsches Volksecho und Deutsch-Kanadische Volks-Zeitung* (issues of 1 and 8 January 1938, which contained a special page titled "Deutsch-Kanadische Nachrichten.") The subtitle also varied: Das Blatt für die Deutsch-Amerikanische Familie (20 February 25 December 1937) [The Paper for the German-American Family]; German People's Echo (1 January 1938 - 16 September 1939). Also printed in the masthead was: Die freie deutsch-amerikanische Wochenzeitung, reich illustriert [The free German-American weekly, richly illustrated]. The editor-in-chief for the duration of the paper's existence was Stephan Heym* and the editor was Martin Hall. The publishers were Deutsches Volksecho Publishing Company, Alfons Goldschmidt after 25 July 1938, the Pastorius Publishing Company (president: Alfons Goldschmidt) after 16 July 1938. It contained articles on communist Volksfront policy, news from Nazi Germany, occupied Austria and Spain under Franco, news from Canada after 1938, reports on German-American antifascist organizations, the reception of emigrants in various countries, Nazism in America; among regular features there were a medical advice column, reviews of cultural events, a women's column, a calendar of meeting-places and dates of beneficial and cultural workers' organizations and of unions. It also contained advertisements, e.g. for lawyers who helped with naturalization and serialized reports, e.g. Kurt Kesten's "Deutsche in Amerikas Freiheitskämpfen" [Germans in America's Struggles for Independence]. Contributions came from Alexander Abusch (pen-name: Ernst Bayer), Albert Norden, Walter A. Berendson, Harry Binder, Franz Boas, Bertolt Brecht, Rudolf Breda, Ilja Ehrenburg, Hanns Eisler, Albert Einstein, Lion Feuchtwanger, Alfons Goldschmidt, Oskar Maria Graf, Heinrich Mann, Kurt Rosenfeld, Otto Sattler, Gustav Regler, Paul Tillich, Paul Weber, Franz Carl Weiskopf, Franz Werfel, Arnold Zweig and many others.

Sources: Arndt/Olson; Eberlein2283; Cazden, *Exile Literature*, pp. 42-45, 188; Maas I, pp. 195-200; Maas IV; Ragg, pp. 62-70; *Exil in den USA*, pp. 144-145; Reinhard Conrad Zachau, "Stephan Heym in Amerika: Eine Untersuchung zu

Stephan Heyms Entwicklung im amerikanischen Exil 1935-1952," Ph. Diss., University of Pittsburgh, 1978.

ECHO		OH Cleveland	1911-1920
Title trans.:	Echo	*First issue:*	29 Ap 1911
Subtitle:	Wochenblatt der deutschen Sozialisten (S.P.) des Staates Ohio	*Last issue:*	17 Ap 1920
Add. lang.:		*Vols. (nos.):*	1-9 (52)
First editor:	W.L. Rosenberg	*Frequency:*	w
First publ.:	Vereinigte Deutsche Socialisten der S.P. Clevelands	*Preservation:*	1
Related pubs.:		*Supplements:*	
Circulation:		*Category:*	socialist-SP

Depositories: Usa-OHi [1919-20]; D-188/144 (Ap 1911-Ap 1917,D 1918-Ap 1920,m)

Subtitle translation: Weekly of the German Socialists (SP) of the State of Ohio. This paper began as the official organ of several Cleveland labor organizations, i.e. a worker's sick fund, a cremation society, the carpenters' and bakers' union; it was also the official organ of the Socialist Party of Ohio and after 1919 the official organ of the Socialist Party of Ohio and Indiana. Editors after Rosenberg* were Joseph Jodlbauer (16 March 1912 - 1918), Fritz Frebe (1918 - October 1919), Carl Altenbernd (8 November - 6 December 1919) and Hermann G. Haupt (13 December 1919 - 17 April 1920). It was published by the United German Socialists of the SP of Cleveland (1911 - 1918?), the Deutsches Staatsagitations-Komitee (S.P] für Ohio (1918?-1919), the Deutsches Staats- Agitations-Komitee der fortschrittlichen Arbeiterorganisationen für Ohio und Indiana [German Committee for Agitation of the Progressive Labor Organizations of the States of Ohio and Indiana] (1920).

It contained news of the American and German socialist movements and local news. Other articles dealt with topics such as prohibition, cremation, health insurance, educational questions, women's right to vote and the elections in Germany. Regular features were a women's page after 13 May 1911, the reports of the National Committee of the German branches of the Socialist Party, short stories and serialized novels. The paper strongly opposed World War One. After 1918 it also printed poems, jokes and cartoons. Contributors included Robert Schweichel, Julie Romm, Fritz Mauthner, Hermann Sudermann (a serialized version of "Frau Sorge" [Mrs. Care]), Leopold von Sacher-Masoch, Kurt Eisner, Karl Kautsky, Luise Westkirch and many others. The "farewell"-editorial in the last issue was a detailed and bitter comment on the state of the German-language labor press after World War One.

Sources: Arndt/Olson; Eberlein 22704.

DIE EINHEITSFRONT		NY New York	1934

Title trans.:	The United Front	*First issue:*	Ag 1934
Subtitle:	Kampforgan gegen den Faschismus	*Last issue:*	Ag 1934
Add. lang.:		*Vols. (nos.):*	1(1)
First editor:	Otto Durick	*Frequency:*	m
First publ.:	Antifaschistische Aktion	*Preservation:*	1
Related pubs.:		*Supplements:*	
Circulation:		*Category:*	communist/ socialist/ antifascist

Depositories: Usa-NN; D-292; D-188/144 (1,m)

Subtitle translation: Weapon in the Fight against Fascism.

This was the organ of the "Antifaschistische Aktion" [Antifascist Action], an alliance of communist and socialist German-American workers' organizations, founded in March 1933. At the time when *Die Einheitsfront* was published, the non-communist members had already left the alliance.

The paper was to be published monthly, but only one issue appeared. Other members of the board of editors were Christian Blohm, Ernst Huettig and Fritz Herder. It was supported by the Communist Party and contained an appeal to liberate Ernst Thälmann. It published articles on the economic involvement of American firms and banks with Nazi Germany, the profits of the armament industry, resistance in Germany, women and war, fascist organizations and antisemitism in America, the "pimp" Horst Wessel and Hanns Heinz Ewers. There were drawings by William Gropper. Contributors were Josef Stahl, Bertholt Brecht, Gertrud Luby, Milton Howard, Otto Sattler, Ilja Ehrenburg, Fritz Herder.

Sources: Arndt/Olson 2, p. 357; Cazden, *Exile Literature*, p. 188; Maas I, p. 216; Maas IV; *BZ* Jl 1934.

DER EINZIGER		O Toronto	1918

Title trans.:	The Only One	*First issue:*	? 1918
Subtitle:		*Last issue:*	? 1918
Add. lang.:		*Vols. (nos.):*	
First editor:	Marcus Graham	*Frequency:*	
First publ.:		*Preservation:*	7
Related pubs.:		*Supplements:*	
Circulation:		*Category:*	anarchist

Depositories:

On Graham, see Graham, Marcus ed., *An Anthology of Anarchist Ideas, Essays, Poetry and Commentaries* (London, 1974), VIII- XXI.

Source: Weinrich 5209.

DER EMANZIPATOR	WI Milwaukee	1877

Title trans.:	The Emancipator	*First issue:*	13 Ja 1877
Subtitle:		*Last issue:*	8 S 1877?
Add. lang.:	English	*Vols. (nos.):*	1(1-29)
First editor:		*Frequency:*	w
First publ.:	Socialist Printing Co.	*Preservation:*	7
Related pubs.:	*The Emancipator*	*Supplements:*	
Circulation:		*Category:*	socialist-WP

Depositories:

This weekly was the German edition of the English *The Emancipator*, the motto of which was "No political liberty without commercial independence." It was the organ of the Arbeiterpartei der Vereinigten Staaten [Workingmen's Party of the United States.), which was formed in 1876 as a successor to the First International and which, like the latter, had many German sections. The Milwaukee Typographia reported in May 1877 that the English *Emancipator* was merging with the *Social Democrat* thus gaining 400-500 subscribers. William Haller was to become editor of the English paper. (*BZ* 1 My 1877).

Sources: Arndt/Olson; *BZ.*

DIE FACKEL	IL Chicago	1879-1919

Title trans.:	The Torch	*First issue:*	11 My 1879
Subtitle:	Unabhängiges Organ zur Belehrung, Unterhaltung und Erheiterung	*Last issue:*	12 0 1919
Add. lang.:		*Vols. (nos.):*	1-41(24)
First editor:	Gustav Lyser	*Frequency:*	w
First publ.:	Socialistic Publishing Comany	*Preservation:*	3
Related pubs..:		*Supplements:*	
Circulation:	1880: 5000; 1890: 16,000; 1895: 25,000; 1900: 15,000; 1910: 24,000; 1915: 14,000; 1919: 24,000	*Category:*	socialist

Depositories: Usa-IHi (My 1894-1910); Usa-WHi (Ap 1903-0 1919); D-188/144 (bound with Chicagoer Arbeiter-Zeitung,m)

Subtitle translation: Independent Organ for Instruction, Entertainment and Amusement.

This was the Sunday edition of the *Chicagoer Arbeiter-Zeitung*. Its motto was: "Dem Ernst und Scherz sein Recht belassend - und nichts als das Gemeine hassend" [Leaving Earnestness and Fun in its Place - hating nothing but the Vile]. This paper was banned from Germany under the antisocialist laws in 1889. It was edited by Gustav Lyser* until 1880, Wilhelm Ludwig Rosenberg*, Jens L. Christensen* (April 1888-1889), Heinrich C. Bechtold (1889-1895) and R. Grossmann (November 1902-?). It was first published by the Socialist Printing Company and then by the Chicagoer Arbeiter-Zeitung Publishing Company after 1892. It contained mostly leisure reading material; large parts of the paper were taken up by reprints of serialized novels, some news with a full page of local news from Germany, in the 1890s lengthy essays and treatises, e.g. on socialism and on scientific problems, reports of strange fatal accidents. Contributors included M. Eiton, Franz Mehring, Luise Westkirch, Marie Stahl, Ludwig Fulda, Emile Zola (a serialized version of *Le ventre de Paris*). The jubilee edition was published on 5 September 1897.

Sources: Arndt/Olson; Eberlein 22707; Auer p. 337; On Lyser see Heinz Ickstadt and Hartmut Keil, "A Forgotten Piece of Working-Class Literature: Gustav Lyser's Satire of the Hewitt Hearing of 1878," *Labor History* 20, 1 (Winter 1979), pp. 127-140. On Rosenberg, see *Der Tramp*; on Christensen, see *Vorbote*.

FAMILIEN-JOURNAL		IA Davenport	1880?-1898?

Title trans.:	Family Journal	*First issue:*	1880?
Subtitle:		*Last issue:*	1898?
Add. lang.:		*Vols. (nos.):*	
First editor:	Emil Geisler	*Frequency:*	m
First publ.:	H. Pfabe	*Preservation:*	7
Related pubs.:		*Supplements:*	
Circulation:	1885: 1400; 1890: 1200; 1897: 800	*Category:*	labor union-K of L

Depositories:

This lost monthly was the organ of the Ancient Order of United Workingmen. The editor after Geisler was H. Pfabe (1882-1898).

Source: Arndt/Olson.

FREIDENKER		WI Milwaukee	1872-1942

Title trans.:	Freethinker	*First issue:*	1 Ap 1872
Subtitle:		*Last issue:*	25 O 1942
Add. lang.:		*Vols. (nos.):*	1(1)-71(44)
First editor:	Michael Biron	*Frequency:*	bw, w
First publ.:	Michael Biron	*Preservation:*	1
Related pubs.:	m *Der Pionier*	*Supplements:*	*Turnzeitung*
Circulation:	1876: 3534; 1885: 5250; 1915: 1500; 1925: 1000; 1931:810	*Category:*	freethought

Depositories: Usa-WMCHi; Usa-WHi (1872-1909;1914-1942); D-19/1501 (1872-1920,m)

This paper was a fortnightly till 1873, when it became a weekly. No issues were published from 17 November to 29 December and from 5 to 26 January 1919 because of "loss of mailing privileges." See Arndt/Olson for other irregularities. It was banned from Germany and Austria under the antisocialist laws in 1879. The title changed: *Milwaukee Freidenker* (1872 - March 1874), *Biron and Bruckers Sonntagsblatt... vormals Milwaukee Freidenker* (5 April - December 1874), *Freidenker* (after 3 January 1875). The subtitle also varied: Zeitschrift für freies Menschenthum [Periodical for Free Humanity] (1872), Sonntagsblatt für freies Menschenthum [Sunday Newspaper for Free Humanity] (January 1873 - March 1874), Freiheit, Bildung und Wohlstand für Alle! [Freedom,

Education, and Prosperity for All!] (after 5 April 1874). From August 1874 it was the official organ of the Bund Freier Gemeinden von Nordamerika and the Verband Freier Gemeinden von Wisconsin, from 3 January 1875 of the Freidenker von Nordamerika, from 1877 to 1879 of the Freidenker von Nordamerika and the Nordamerikanischer Turnerbund, then of the Freidenker von Amerika and finally the Official Organ of the Free Thought League of North America (formerly Freidenkerbund von Nordamerika) in 1933-42.

It was edited by Michael Biron (1872-73), Biron and Joseph Brucker (1874), Brucker (after 3 January 1875), Carl Hermann Boppe (28 January 1877 - January 1899), Maximilian Großmann, assistant editor (May 1883 - October 1884), by Heinrich Huhn (April 1899 - February 1908), J. Berandun (30 August 1908 - 6 February 1913), Martin L.D. Bunge (23 February 1913 - 9 December 1917), Albert Steinhauser (16 December 1917 - 25 October 1942). Other assistant editors were Heinrich von Ende and Karl Heinzen* (4 January - 28 November 1880). The paper was published by Michael Biron (1872-73), Biron and Joseph Brucker (in 1874), Brucker (3 January 1875 - November 1876), Carl Hermann Dörflinger (November 1876 - 1879), the Dörflinger Book and Publishing Company (1880-83), the Freidenker Publishing Company (1883 - May 1916) and the Turner Publishing Company (May 1916 - 1942). The place of publication changed: Milwaukee (1872 - May 1916), Minneapolis (1916-1918), New Ulm, Minnesota (1918-1942). For supplement, see *Turnzeitung*. It absorbed *Der Pionier* with volume 9, no. 1, 4 January 1880, which appeared with the title: *Freidenker, Der Pionier XXVII Jahrgang*.

The paper contained numerous political articles, critical articles on religion, the church and the Bible, articles propagating a scientific way of thinking as opposed to the "irrational" and "phantastic" thinking of Christianity and other religions, articles on philological and historical subjects; it advocated the complete separation of church and state and contained reprints of short stories and serialized novels, reviews of theatrical and musical events in Milwaukee, many reports of activities of Freethinker, Gymnasts and related organizations as well as announcements of cultural and educational events. There were some commercial advertisements, mostly for publications of the 'Freidenker Publishing Company' and other publishers, some for local businesses and some classified advertisements.

There were contributions by Max Nordau, T. Völkel, Ludwig Büchner, Karl Vogt and reprints of Ivan Turgeniev, Ferdinand Kürnberger, Conrad Ferdinand Meyer, Leopold von Sacher-Masoch, M. Jokai, Bertha von Suttner, August Strindberg, Marie von Ebner-Eschenbach.

Sources: Arndt/Olson; Eberlein 22709, 22711, 22239; Knoche, pp. 162ff; Bettina Goldberg, "Deutsch-amerikanische Freidenker in Milwaukee 1877-1890: Organisation und gesellschaftspolitische Orientierung" [German-American Freethinkers in Milwaukee 1877-1890: Their Organization and Political Orientation], unpublished manuscript (Ruhr-Universität Bochum, 1982), pp. 86-108. See also *BZ* of 16 Mr and 1 Ap 1895 for conflict of Typographia No. 10 of Milwaukee with Freidenker Publishing Company.

DIE FREIE PRESSE	IL Aurora	1895?-1896?

Title trans.:	The Free Press	*First issue:*	1895?
Subtitle:		*Last issue:*	1896?
Add. lang.:		*Vols. (nos.):*	
First editor:	Jacob Hendricks	*Frequency:*	w
First publ.:	Aurora Freie Presse Publishing Company	*Preservation:*	?
Related pubs.:		*Supplements:*	
Circulation:		*Category:*	labor

Depositories: DDR-IML(?); DDR-ULB(?)

No further information is available.

Sources: Arndt/Olson; Eberlein 22766.

FREIE PRESSE	PA Philadelphia	1848-(1856)

Title trans.:	Free Press	*First issue:*	27 My 1848
Subtitle:		*Last issue:*	31 D 1887
Add. lang.:		*Vols. (nos.):*	
First editor:	William Rosenthal	*Frequency:*	sw, d
First publ.:	Frederick W. Thomas	*Preservation:*	1
Related pubs.:		*Supplements:* Sonntagsblatt	
Circulation:	1870: 6000 [est]	*Category:*	workers' club

Depositories: Usa-PPG

This paper appeared in the morning, except on Sundays and was the organ of a "sogenannte Arbeiterpartei" [so-called Workingmen's Party] 1848-56; after 1856 it was a Republican paper. F.W. Thomas had come to America in 1837. In March 1850 Wilhelm Weitling called its editor, W. Rosenthal, "a faithful co-worker."

Sources: Arndt/Olson; Kamman, pp. 37-38.

DAS FREIE WORT	NY New York	1907

Title trans.:	Free Speech	*First issue:*	Jl 1907
Subtitle:		*Last issue:*	D 1907
Add. lang.:		*Vols. (nos.):*	1(1-6)
First editor:	A. Isaak	*Frequency:*	w
First publ.:	Hans Koch	*Preservation:*	1
Related pubs.:		*Supplements:*	
Circulation:		*Category:*	anarchist

Depositories: D-Bm 41/IGA

This was an anarchist monthly. The first issue mentions a predecessor, the anarchist paper *Der Menschenspiegel* [The Mirror of Humans] about which nothing further is known. For Koch, see also *Der Strom* [The Stream]. The paper was published by Georg Stine after September 1907.

It contained news from the American and foreign anarchist and labor movements as well as articles on sex-education, the fate of women, ideal anarchists (e.g. Buddha, Jesus, Tolstoy). It was against marriage. It frequently published polemics against the *New Yorker Volkszeitung* and included regular features such as a letter-box and a list of anarchist publications obtainable from *Das Freie Wort*. Contributors were Jack London, E. Tarbouriech, Anna Riedel, Hans Stromer, E. Westermarck and "Figaro." It ceased publication because of differences among the publishers and a deficit of $ 45.

FREIE WACHT	PA Philadelphia	1894-1895?

Title trans.:	Free Guard!	*First issue:*	F 1894
Subtitle:	Unabhängiges Organ aller	*Last issue:*	1895?
	fortschrittlichen Arbeiter		
Add. lang.:		*Vols. (nos.):*	
First editor:		*Frequency:*	w, bw
First publ.:	Freie Wacht Publication Association	*Preservation:*	6
Related pubs.:		*Supplements:*	
Circulation:		*Category:*	anarchist

Depositories: D-Bm 41/IGA [1895]

This anarchist paper started out as an 8-page weekly. It was planned to publish it biweekly after the issue of 24 August 1895. Its English subtitle was: "Devoted to the interests of the working people" and its motto: "Nieder mit Altar, Thron, Kapital und Arbeitslohn" [Down with altar, throne, capital and wages]. It contained articles concerning religion, against government and on individualism and communism. There were contributions by Peter Kropotkin, Georg Biedenkapp and Louis Weber.

Sources: Arndt/Olson; Rocker, p. 379.

FREIHEIT	NY New York	1879-1910

Title trans.:	Liberty	*First issue:*	4 Ja 1879
Subtitle:		*Last issue:*	13 Ag 1910
Add. lang.:		*Vols. (nos.):*	1-32(17)
First editor:	Johann Joseph Most	*Frequency:*	ir, w, bw
First publ.:	Johann Joseph Most	*Preservation:*	1
Related pubs.:		*Supplements:*	
Circulation:	1892: 4300; 1896: 5000; 1905: 3500; 1910:	*Category:*	anarchist
	4250		

Depositories: Usa-CtY [1879-1931]; Usa-NN [1883-1909,m]; Usa-MiU, Labadie Collection ([1880-81],1883-1910); <D-A [1883-90]; Nl-IISG ([1879-82],1883-1910), D-188/144 [1879-1910,m]

The paper appeared irregularly from 4 January 1879 to December 1880; as a weekly from 1 January 1881 to December 1907; as a biweekly from 4 January 1908 to 13 August 1910. The size varied slightly, each issue having 4-8 pages. Till 1882 the paper was published in London. The title changed to avoid confiscation in Germany where it was banned until 1890 under the antisocialist laws of 1878. Thus the title was changed with every issue from 11 January 1879 onward as a "specimen number" e.g. *Deutschland, Lehmann* (a nickname for Kaiser Wilhelm II), *Frech* [Naughty], *Hunger, Bitter, Bismarck* and others. With the issue of 3 January 1880 the title was established as *Freiheit*. The subtitle changed: 1. Socialdemokratisches Organ (4 January 1879-1882), 2. Organ der Revolutionären Socialisten (9 December 1882 - 1886), 3. Internationales Organ der Anarchisten deutscher Sprache (1 January 1886?-1898). The motto also varied: 1. "Proletarier aller Länder, vereinigt Euch!" [Proletarians of all countries, unite!] (4 January 1879-1881), 2. Gegen die Tyrannen sind alle Mittel gesetzlich [Nothing is against law in the struggle against the tyrants] (9 December 1882-1883), 3. with vol. 5 (32) 11 August 1883 each page had a running-title: a) Gegen die Tyrannen sind alle Mittel gesetzlich!, b) Arbeiter aller Länder, vereinigt Euch!, c) Nieder mit Thron, Altar und Geldsack! [Down with throne, altar and money bags], 4. Agitation, Organisation, Rebellion!

The paper was edited by Johann (John) Most (1879 - March 1906). It had the following assistant editors or substitute editors at times when Most was imprisoned: Justus H. Schwab (November - December 1882), Moritz Schultze, L.T. Krämer, Karl Schneidt, John Müller (a pseudonym for Most, according to Waltershausen p. 363) (1886?-1900). After Most's death it was edited by his widow, Helene Most (March - April 1906) and then by Max Baginski, whose name appears for the first time in the issue of 7 July 1907 - 13 August 1910. It was published by Johann Most (1879-1880), Communistischer Arbeiter-Bildungs-Verein (London) (1881-1882), Johann Most (1882-1906), Helene Most (March - April 1906), Freiheit Publishing Association (1906-1910). The place of publication varied: London (4 January 1879 - September 1882), Berlin (7 October 1882), Exeter (14 October - 18 November 1882), London and New York or London and Hoboken, NJ (1883-1887), Chicago and New York (5 - 12 January 1889), Buffalo (18 September 1897 - 30 July 1898, see also *Buffaloer Arbeiterzeitung*), New York (August 1898 - 13 August 1910). It was printed in New York by Schärrer & Frantz, a small print shop, which was unionized but "probably the most unhealthy print shop in the whole town" (*BZ* 15 Ap 1883).

During its London years *Freiheit* was still aimed mainly at German readers. Its object was to reveal "the crimes of governments, especially the German," (*Freiheit* vol. 1, no. 1). When the place of publication was transferred to New York the emphasis shifted more and more to American issues. It contained discussions of anarchist and socialist theory, it followed the development of anarchism in other countries, especially in Russia, it reported critically on American local politics and elections and attacked the unions for their corruption. Other issues were the use of violence, property, free love (Most was against it), discussion of philosophers such as Friedrich Nietzsche and Max Stirner. It published translations from the anarchist literature of various countries, notices of anarchist and socialist books, pamphlets and newspapers as well as advertisements for hotels, saloons and holiday resorts where anarchists were welcome. The jubilee edition appeared on 26 December 1903.

Among the contributors were Karl Heinzen, Belle of Clark Street (the pen name of Dr. Charles F. Sutterle), Emma Clausen, R. Grossmann, Peter and Sophie Kropotkin, Michail Bakunin, F. Thaumazo, Martin Drescher, Julius Hoffmann, Multatuli (pen name of Eduard Douwes-Dekker), Errico Malatesta,

Elise'''e Reclus, John Neve, Eduard Vaillant, August Reinsdorf, Max Nettlau, M. Leontieff, Robert Reitzel and Georg Biedenkapp.

Note: From 1887-1892 Most published (at first monthly but later irregularly) a collection of anarchist pamphlets entitled *Internationale Bibliothek*. See Rocker, p. 331 for list of titles and dates.

Sources: Arndt/Olson; Rocker (for details on *Freiheit*, see especially chapter XX); Miller, pp. 145-148; Waltershausen, pp. 361-366, 369; Hillquit, pp. 214-217, 211. Obituaries on Most in *Freiheit* of 24 and 31 March 1906 and in many American and European socialist newspapers. On Most, see also *Geschichte der deutschen Arbeiterbewegung*, pp. 334-335; Marx/Engels, *Werke* XXXIV, pp. 639 and 673, XXXV, pp 548 and 575; Goldmann, pp. 3, 29-31 et passim. On Baginski, see *Sturmglocke*.

FREIHEITSBANNER	OH Cincinnati	1878?-1879

Title trans.:	Banner of Freedom	*First issue:*	1878?
Subtitle:		*Last issue:*	1879?
Add. lang.:		*Vols. (nos.):*	
First editor:		*Frequency:*	w
First publ.:		*Preservation:*	7
Related pubs.:		*Supplements:*	
Circulation:		*Category:*	socialist-SLP

Depositories:

This lost weekly is said to have supported the Socialist Labor Party, which was formed in December 1877.

Sources: Arndt/Olson; Eberlein 22714. On the Socialist Labor Party see Hillquit, pp. 188-300.

GEGEN DEN STROM	NY New York	1938-1939

Title trans.:	Against the Current	*First issue:*	Mr 1938
Subtitle:		*Last issue:*	O/N 1939
Add. lang.:		*Vols. (nos.):*	1-2(12)
First editor:	Robert Bek-gran	*Frequency:*	m, ir
First publ.:	Robert Bek-gran	*Preservation:*	1
Related pubs.:		*Supplements:*	
Circulation:		*Category:*	socialist

Depositories: Usa-NN; Usa-DLC; D-292; D-46 [1938-39]

This paper was a socialist monthly not affiliated with any party, after 1(7), 1938 it appeared irregularly. According to Maas it was the organ of the "intransigent left:" the anarchists, the anarcho-syndicalists, the Trotskyites, the oppositional communists and others. It was published by and for pre-1933 emigrants and consisted largely of polemics against individuals and the political organizations of German emigrants. It contained details of communist infiltration in German-American organizations such as the Deutsch-Amerikanischer Kulturverband. There were contributions by Rudolf Brandl,

André   Gide, Ernst W. Mareg, Wilhelm Reich, Rudolf Becker, William S. Schlamm, Max Sievers and Kurt Tucholsky.
Sources: Arndt/Olson; Arndt/Olson 2, p. 454; Eberlein 22716; Cazden, *Exile Literature*, p. 185; Maas I, p. 265; Maas IV; Ragg, p. 36.

GENERAL WOOD WORKERS' JOURNAL	NY Brooklyn	1891-1896

Title trans.:		*First issue:*	15 Je 1891
Subtitle:		*Last issue:*	15 Ja 1896//
Add. lang.:	English	*Vols. (nos.):*	1(1-52)
First editor:		*Frequency:*	m
First publ.:		*Preservation:*	1
Related pubs.:	c *Möbel-Arbeiter-Journal*; c *International*	*Supplements:*	
	Wood Workers		
Circulation:		*Category:*	labor union

Depositories: Usa-WHi; D-188/144 (1,m)

This monthly labor union journal had an irregular numbering. Published by the executive of the International Furniture Workers' Union, it was written in English and German. It had 4 pages; pages 2, 3 and part of 4 entitled "Allgemeines Holzarbeiterjournal. Offizielles Organ der Internationalen Möbelarbeiter-Union von Amerika" [General Wood Workers Journal. Official Organ of the International Furniture Workers' Union of America] were in German. The subtitle of the English part was "An Organ for the Various Branches of the Wood Workers' Trade."

It contained union news and reports from local unions as well as meetings of the American Federation of Labor, financial reports and reprints of articles from other union journals. The issue of 15 November 1893 contained an article of the general condition of woodworkers in America. It had one editorial printed in English and German, but the other articles were mostly different. When the International Furniture Workers' Union amalgamated with the Machine Wood Workers' International Union on 1 January 1896 to form the Amalgamated Wood Workers' International Union of America, its organ was to be the *International Wood Worker*.

Sources: Arndt/Olson; Naas/Sakr, p. 46; Eberlein 22730.

| THE GERMAN AMERICAN | NY New York | 1942-1968 |

Title trans.: Der Deutsch-Amerikaner	*First issue:*	My 1942
Subtitle:	*Last issue:*	My/Je 1968
Add. lang.: English	*Vols. (nos.):*	1(1)-26(3)
First editor: Rudolf Kohler	*Frequency:*	m, bw,m
First publ.: The German American Inc.	*Preservation:*	3
Related pubs.: c *German American Emergency*	*Supplements:*	
Conference. Bulletin		
Circulation:	*Category:*	communist/
		antifascist

Depositories: Usa-NN (My 1942-F 1949); D-292 [1942-45]; D-188/144 [1849,m]

This was a communist newspaper in German and English with 16 pages until 1945 and 8-12 pages from 1945 to 1949. It was published monthly from volume 1, 1942/43 to volume 2, 1943/44, biweekly from volume 3, 1944/45 to volume 7, 1948/49, monthly after volume 8, 1949/50. The subtitle varied: 1. Sponsored by the German-American Emergency Conference (May 1942 - May 1945), 2. Anti-Nazi Monthly (May 1943 - 15 April 1946), 3. Independent Publication (1 May 1946 - ?), 4. Monatsschrift in deutscher Sprache [Monthly in the German Language]. The motto also changed: "Smash the Axis" 1942/43; "Win the War. Buy War Bonds and Stamps," 1944/45 - 1945/46. Originally it was sponsored by the German-American Emergency Conference, which was founded by Kurt Rosenfeld.

It was edited by Rudolf Kohler and Max Schroeder (May 1942 - April? 1945), Gustav Faber (May? 1945 - March 1947), August Kegel (7 April 1947 - ? 1949), Walter Mueller (until? 1949) and George Schmidt (Associate Editors), Margrit Adler (Managing Editor).

It urged German Americans to support the military involvement of the United States in World War Two, published appeals to buy war bonds and initiated fund-raising. It was against strikes during war-time. It contained news from Nazi Germany, a cultural section, a women's section and an English-language youth section. After 1950 it contained increasingly more news from Germany of special interest to German-American communists and very little on America. It was illustrated including portraits and cartoons. There were contributions by Günther Anders, Johannes R. Becher, Felix Boenheim, Willy Brandt, Ilja Ehrenburg, Lion Feuchtwanger, Alfred Kantorowicz, Jürgen Kuczynski, Thomas Mann, Walter Mueller, Albert Norden, Karl Obermann, Ludwig Renn, Otto Sattler, Albert Schreiner, William L. Shirer, Paul Tillich*, Walther Victor, Erich Weinert, Franz Carl Weiskopf, Margarete Weiskopf (pen-name Alex Wedding), Fritz Zorn and many others.

Sources: Arndt/Olson; Maas I, pp. 274-279; Maas IV; Cazden, *Exile Literature*, p. 188.

GERMAN-AMERICAN EMERGENCY CONFERENCE. ...   NY New York   1942

Title trans.:		*First issue:*	Mr 1942
Subtitle:		*Last issue:*	Ap 1942
Add. lang.:		*Vols. (nos.):*	
First editor:		*Frequency:*	m
First publ.:		*Preservation:*	7
Related pubs.:	s *German American*	*Supplements:*	
Circulation:		*Category:*	communist

Depositories:

The complete title of the paper was: *German-Aemrican Emergency Conference. Bulletin*

It is not clear whether this monthly was published in German and/or English.

Sources: Cazden, *Exile Literature*, p. 188; Maas IV. On German-American Emergency Conference, see Cazden, *Exile Literature*, pp. 48-50.

GEWERKSCHAFTSZEITUNG   NY New York   1879-1881

Title trans.:	Union News	*First issue:*	15 Ap 1879
Subtitle:	see below	*Last issue:*	20 Mr 1881?
Add. lang.:		*Vols. (nos.):*	1-2
First editor:	A. Strasser, H. Müller, C. Speyer	*Frequency:*	m
First publ.:		*Preservation:*	1
Related pubs.:		*Supplements:*	
Circulation:		*Category:*	labor

Depositories: D-188/144 (1,m); Usa-NN

The complete subtitle was: Organ für die Förderung der gewerkschaftlichen Bestrebungen. An die deutschsprechenden Arbeiter Amerikas [Organ for the Support of Union Activities. To the German-Speaking Workers of America].

This paper was edited by Adolf Strasser, Hugo Müller, Charles Speyer (15 April - 15 December 1879), A. Strasser, H. Müller, George J. Speyer (15 January - 15 April 1880), A. Strasser, G.J. Speyer (20 May - 20 September 1880), C. Speyer, O. Roepcke, H. Kessler, A. Strasser, G.J. Speyer (20 October 1880 - 20 March 1881). George J. Speyer was President and Hugo Müller (or Miller) was Secretary of Typographia No. 7 of New York. C. Speyer was the Secretary of the International Labor Union of America; A. Strasser was the President of the Cigar Makers' International Union of America.

The editorial of the first issue emphasized that all the editors had been union members for many years and that their aim was to strengthen and unify the labor movement. The *Gewerkschaftszeitung* intended to give a comprehensive and accurate survey of the labor movement in America and elsewhere and to be a place for the exchange of information and opinions. The editors wanted to keep in touch with the English-speaking labor movement. The most urgent problem at the time was the shortening of the work day.

Some contributions were signed with fantasy names, e.g. Veritas, Tabak (perhaps C. Speyer?) or Einer vom Corps. It published serialized contributions by Karl Marx: "Über Strikes and Trade-Unions" and Ira Steward: "Armuth" [Poverty].

In the last preserved issue the editors urged the readers to assist them in their work because they, the editors, were overworked; there is no mention of discontinuation.

Sources: Arndt/Olson; Eberlein 22719. On Strasser see Fink, *Biographical Dictionary*, pp. 340-341.

GRADAUS		PA Philadelphia	1851-1853
Title trans.:	Straight Ahead	*First issue:*	? 1851
Subtitle:		*Last issue:*	? 1853
Add. lang.:		*Vols. (nos.):*	
First editor:	Nikolaus Schmitt, Eduard Graf	*Frequency:*	w
First publ.:	Nikolaus Schmitt, Eduard Graf	*Preservation:*	7
Related pubs.:		*Supplements:*	
Circulation:		*Category:*	workers' club

Depositories:

According to a letter written by Karl Marx to Adolf Cluß in September 1853, Carl Wilhelm Klein, a German worker from Solingen, had founded an "Arbeiterverein" [workers' club] and *Gradaus* had come under the influence of the Arbeiterverein. In the middle of October 1853 Marx informed Cluß that *Gradaus* had been discontinued because it could not pay its contributors. (See also *Der Volksvertreter*)

Sources: Arndt/Olson; Marx/Engels, *Werke* XXVIII, pp. 592, 596, 699; Cazden, *Book Trade*, p. (645). Arndt/Olson give 1852-? as dates and call it a Democratic weekly, dated also at New York.

GROSS-NEW YORKER ARBEITER-ZEITUNG		NY New York	1898-?
Title trans.:	Labor News of Greater New York	*First issue:*	? N 1898
Subtitle:		*Last issue:*	?
Add. lang.:		*Vols. (nos.):*	
First editor:		*Frequency:*	w
First publ.:	Gross-New Yorker Arbeiter-Zeitung Publishing Association	*Preservation:*	7
Related pubs.:		*Supplements:*	
Circulation:		*Category:*	labor

Depositories:

In October 1898 a number of "progressive workers" who did not feel themselves represented by the *New Yorker Volkszeitung* and *The People* (organs of the Socialist Labor Party) considering them to be "sectarian," formed a publishing association (*BZ* 16 O 1899). Their paper supported trade unionism and independent social-democratic organizations (*BZ* 1 D 1898). Typographia No.

7 of New York contributed $25 in support and bought 50 tickets at 10 cents each for a benefit party (*BZ* 16 Ja 1899).
Source: *BZ*.

HABT ACHT		TX Hallettsville	1913-1919
Title trans.:	Watch Out	*First issue:*	Ja 1913
Subtitle:	Sozial-demokratisches Blatt	*Last issue:*	? 1919
Add. lang.:		*Vols. (nos.):*	
First editor:	Zikes Panek	*Frequency:*	w
First publ.:		*Preservation:*	6
Related pubs.:		*Supplements:*	
Circulation:		*Category:*	social democrat

Depositories: Usa-TxU (15 Je 1913)

According to the subtitle this was a "social-democratic weekly." It was inexpensive as it was published at 35 cents a year. It contained 4 pages.
Source: Arndt/Olson.

DER HAHNENRUF		NY New York	1851-?
Title trans.:	The Rooster's Call	*First issue:*	My 1851
Subtitle:		*Last issue:*	?
Add. lang.:		*Vols. (nos.):*	
First editor:	Johann August Försch	*Frequency:*	d
First publ.:	G. Scheibel	*Preservation:*	7
Related pubs.:		*Supplements:*	
Circulation:		*Category:*	labor

Depositories:

This daily was "edited in the interest of the laboring classes."
Sources: Cazden, *Book Trade*, p. (645); Wittke, *Press*, p. 171.

DER HAMMER		LA New Orleans	1876
Title trans.:	The Hammer	*First issue:*	Mr 1876
Subtitle:		*Last issue:*	O 1876
Add. lang.:		*Vols. (nos.):*	
First editor:	Ludwig Geissler, Jakob Müller	*Frequency:*	
First publ.:	Ludwig Geissler, Jakob Müller	*Preservation:*	7
Related pubs.:		*Supplements:*	
Circulation:		*Category:*	socialist

Depositories:

Ludwig Geissler, the founder of this radical socialist labor paper, was a socialist agitator, who later took part in establishing a communist colony, Liberty Settlement at Covington, LA. He wrote plays and staged them in a log-house in the woods. He later wrote a book in English in reply to both Bellamy's "Looking Backward" and Richard Michaelis' "Ein Blick in die Zukunft" [Looking Forward]. Jakob Müller was a shoemaker.

Sources: Arndt/Olson; Eberlein 22723; Deiler, p. 36.

DER HAMMER	PA Philadelphia	1882-1889?

Title trans.:	The Hammer	*First issue:*	1 N 1882
Subtitle:	Officielles Organ der Metall-Arbeiter Union von Nord-Amerika	*Last issue:*	1889?
Add. lang.:	English	*Vols. (nos.):*	1-7(?)
First editor:	Charles Braun	*Frequency:*	m
First publ.:		*Preservation:*	5
Related pubs.:		*Supplements:*	
Circulation:	1883: 800	*Category:*	labor union

Depositories: Usa-NN (1882-[1884-88]); D-188/144 (1882-[1884-88],m)

This was a monthly labor union journal of 4 pages; the first page was in English, pages 2-4 in German, set in Gothic. After 1887 2 pages were in English, 2 in German. After October 1886 the subtitle was in English: Official Organ of the Metal Workers' Union of North America. Its motto was: "Warum denn nicht selbst als Hammer schlagen? Als Amboß mußt du die Schläge tragen" [Why not hit like a hammer yourself? As an anvil you must bear the blows].

The editors after Braun were Louis Tiecke, who was removed from office in January 1886 for embezzling union money; W.M. Schultze (February - September 1886), George W. Appel (after October 1886). After February 1887 the place of publication changed to Baltimore. A copy of the first issue was sent to Police Chief von Madai in Berlin requesting him to ban the paper from Germany, because this would be the best publicity for it in America. (*Der Hammer* 1 December 1882) The letter was signed by Friedrich Wilhelm Fritzsche*. It contained news from the Metal Workers' and other unions, frequent appeals to organize, articles on socialism, cooperative enterprises, economic subjects, the Knights of Labor, the eight-hour day, child and convict labor, piece-wages and technical problems of the trade, e.g. the repair of broken cast-iron parts.

Contributions came from John Jacobi and Adolph Douai. From the start *Der Hammer* was set in non-union shops, which caused complaints from the *Buchdrucker-Zeitung* (1 August 1888, 16 September 1888, 16 March 1889). *Der Hammer* was discontinued from August to November 1888 but existed again in March 1889 (*BZ* 16 S 1888, 16 December 1888, 16 March 1889). It remains unclear how this organ relates to *Der Metallarbeiter*.

Sources: Arndt/Olson; Eberlein 22724; *BZ*, see also 15 N 1882. Polizeipräsidium, Pr. Br. Rep. 30, Berlin C, Tit. 94 Lit. A, Nr. 274: Die gegen Deutschland gerichtete amerikanische Presse 1882-1905 [The American Press Directed against Germany], 3 vols. Vol. 1, pp. 12-13.

HANDWERKER- UND ARBEITER-UNION		OH Cincinnati	1851?-?

Title trans.:	Artisans' and Workers' Union	*First issue:*	1851?
Subtitle:		*Last issue:*	?
Add. lang.:		*Vols. (nos.):*	
First editor:	John Orff	*Frequency:*	
First publ.:	John Orff	*Preservation:*	7
Related pubs.:		*Supplements:*	
Circulation:		*.Category:*	workers' club

Depositories:

Arndt/Olson refer to *Der Hochwächter*, 22 October 1851 as their source. No further information is available.

DER HEROLD		MI Detroit	(1894-1918)

Title trans.:	The Herald	*First issue:*	fall 1884
Subtitle:	Unabhängiges Organ für Freiheit und Recht	*Last issue:*	31 My 1918
Add. lang.:		*Vols. (nos.):*	1-36(22)
First editor:	Adolf Kaufmann	*Frequency:*	w, d, w
First publ.:	Adolf Kaufmann	*Preservation:*	2-3
Related pubs.:		*Supplements:*	Beilage zum Herold
Circulation:		*Category:*	socialist

Depositories: Usa-WHi [1902-1918]; D-188/144 (Ap 1898-My 1918,m)

Contrary to information given by Arndt/Olson this paper was non-partisan only until 1893 or 1894; thereafter it became socialist. It was published weekly (Sunday, 1884 - April 1885), daily (including Sunday, 5 October 1885 - May 1886), weekly (Friday, June 1886 - 31 May 1918). According to the subtitle it was an "Independent Organ for Liberty and Justice." After 1893 or 1894 the subtitle changed to: Für Wahrheit und Recht [For Truth and Justice]. It was: 1. Offizielles Organ der Central Labor Union und Deutschen Gewerkschaften progressiver Richtung [Official Organ of the Central Labor Union and German Progressive Unions], 2. Official Paper of the Central Labor Union and other Progressive Unions (in 1904), 3. Official Paper of the Central Labor Union, Michigan Federation of Labor and other Progressive German Unions. It was edited by Adolf Kaufmann (until October 1889), E. Newald (1893 or 1894 - February 1897), Jacob Fuchs (February - August 1897), Martin Drescher* (August 1897 - April 1898), H. Steichmann (April 1898 - fall 1905); no editor was appointed from 1905 to 1910, then Urban Hartung (January 1911 - ?) and Theodor Dreyer (until 1918?). The paper was published by Adolf Kaufmann (until October 1889), Charles Vollbrecht (October 1889-?), F.A. Draeger (1893 or 1894 - January 1901), H. Steichmann and Theodor Dreyer (February 1901 - fall 1905), Theodor Dreyer (fall 1905 - ?) and the Central Labor Union (?-1918).

It contained political news from America and Europe, regular features: "Vom Felde der Arbeiter" [labor news], a letter-box, local news, announcements by unions and singing societies, serialized novels, "Die Feuchte Ecke" [The Wet Corner], a humorous column, short stories, many reports from Germany, articles on the natural sciences and other educational topics, jokes, illustrations and later also photographs. Contributors included Hermann Modersohn, Gustav Landauer, Horst Bodemer, Margarete Böhme, Emil Peschkau, Jenny Hirsch and Nataly von Eschstruth.

Beilage zum Herold, a supplement, appeared from fall 1884 to 1918, except February - August, when it was suspended because of financial difficulties during Fuchs' editorship. It was a literary supplement of 12 pages and contained serialized novels, short stories, poems, "Meik Habersack's Schreibebrief," a humorous letter to the editor. The jubilee edition on 23 June 1911 gives a historical sketch;a special 8-page supplement was published to mark Labor Day on 5 September 1904.

Sources: Arndt/Olson; Eberlein 22727, 22729.

HEROLD DES WESTENS	KY Louisville	1853

Title trans.:	The Herald of the West	*First issue:*	Ja? 1853
Subtitle:		*Last issue:*	3 D 1853?
Add. lang.:		*Vols. (nos.):*	1(1-102)
First editor:	Ludwig Ferdinand Fenner von Fenneberg	*Frequency:*	d
First publ.:	J.B. Hollocher	*Preservation:*	4
Related pubs.:		*Supplements:*	Halbwöchentl. Herold des Westens
Circulation:		*Category:*	radical fortyeighter

Depositories: Usa-NN (S-D 1853); D-188/144 (S-D 1853,m)

According to Arndt/Olson this paper was edited by Fenneberg* (January - 25 July 1853), Kompe (also known as Konnje (August - 19 September 1853) and Karl Heinzen* (20 September to 3 December 1853). Bernhard Domschke was associate editor from September to December 1853. The publisher was a German coffee-house owner who had made some money in the California gold rush. The *Herold's* front page as well as the last one and a half pages were taken up by advertisements for local businesses, which left only one and a half pages for text.

The few surviving issues deal with questions of the organization of unpolitical workers, current political affairs, brief news from America and abroad, a serialized version of Heinzen's diary of his escape from Germany, notes on the natural science, anticlerical satires. The last preserved number of 3 December 1853 contains an attack on Karl Marx and his influence from Heinzen's point of view. The semiweekly edition, the *Halbwöchentlicher Herold des Westens* advertised in the daily editions, September to December 1853, appears to be lost.

Sources: Arndt/Olson; Wittke, *Press*, pp. 87-88, 99, 123; Wittke, *Against the Current*, pp. 91-92. On Heinzen, see *Pionier*. On Domschke, see Zucker, pp. 287-288; Dobert, pp. 58-60; Schlicher, J.J., "Bernhard Domschke," *Wisconsin Magazine of History* 29 (1946), pp. 319-322 and 435-456.

DER HOCHWÄCHTER   OH Cincinnati   1850-1859?

Title trans.:	The Lookout	*First issue:*	27 S 1850
Subtitle:	Ein Organ für religiöse Aufklärung und sociale Reform	*Last issue:*	1859?
Add. lang.:		*Vols. (nos.):*	1-9
First editor:	Friedrich Hassaurek	*Frequency:*	w
First publ.:	Wilhelm Wachsmuth	*Preservation:*	6
Related pubs.:		*Supplements:*	
Circulation:		*Category:*	radical fortyeighter

Depositories: <D-A (26 N 1856, 19 Ag 1857)

Subtitle translation: Organ for Religious Enlightenment and Social Reform. From 1853-55 it became "Ein Organ des Gesamt-Fortschritts [Organ of Complete Progress].

This paper was edited by Hassaurek (1850-53), Friedrich August Hobelmann and August Becker. It was published by Wilhelm Wachsmuth (1850-52) and Hassaurek (1852-57). Hassaurek, a refugee from the Vienna revolution, came to Cincinnati in 1849. After having worked for the *Ohio Staatszeitung* he founded his own paper, the *Hochwächter*, in 1850 and sold it seven years later. The paper was militantly anticlerical. It was said to have been responsible for the anti-Catholic riot during the visit of the papal nuncio to Cincinnati. It campaigned against immigration agents in American port cities who thrived on the ignorance of new arrivals. In 1855 it supported the Free Soil movement. Hassaurek became active in politics and took part in organizing the Republican party in Cincinnati, a Democratic stronghold. In 1861 he was appointed ambassador to Ecuador by Lincoln. In 1865 he resigned from this post to take on the editorship of the *Cincinnati Volksblatt*.

Sources: Arndt/Olson; Wittke, *Press*, pp. 53, 85, 109, passim; Kamman, p. 37; Zucker, p. 124. On Hassaurek, see Zucker, p. 300; Dobert, pp. 95-96; Schem V, pp. 198-199, Miller, pp. 91-93. On Becker, see Zucker, p. 276; Dobert, pp. 30-31; Schem II, p. 222.

I.B. BERICHTE   NY New York   (1939)-1940

Title trans.:	I.B. Reports	*First issue:*	1939?
Subtitle:		*Last issue:*	1940?
Add. lang.:		*Vols. (nos.):*	
First editor:		*Frequency:*	
First publ.:		*Preservation:*	7
Related pubs.:	Sozialistische Informationsbriefe	*Supplements:*	
Circulation:		*Category:*	socialist

Depositories:

Issued by the Group Neu Beginnen [New Beginning] in London, Oslo and New York, this paper was sometimes referred to as their 'Inlands-Berichte.' Only its last two numbers were issued in New York.

Sources: Cazden, *Exile Literature*, p. 185; Maas IV. On 'Neu Beginnen,' see Klein, Kurt, "Der sozialistische Widerstand gegen das Dritte Reich dargestellt an der Gruppe 'Neu Beginnen,'" Ph. diss., University of Marburg, 1957.

ILLINOIS VOLKSZEITUNG	IL Chicago	1884-1885

Title trans.:	Illinois People's Journal	*First issue:*		Je? 1884
Subtitle:		*Last issue:*		Je? 1885
Add. lang.:		*Vols. (nos.):*		
First editor:	L. Ponstein	*Frequency:*		
First publ.:	Illinoiser Volkszeitung Publishing Association	*Preservation:*		6
Related pubs.:		*Supplements:*		
Circulation:		*Category:*		socialist-SLP

Depositories: Usa-WHi (14 F 1885)

This paper was published by the German section of the Socialist Labor Party, Chicago. The inner pages were apparently prepared by the *New Yorker Volkszeitung* and sent from New York. Julius Vahlteich became its subsequent editor.

Source: Thomas J. Morgan Papers, University of Illinois, Urbana.

ILLINOISER VOLKSZEITUNG	IL Chicago	1893-?

Title trans.:	Illinois People's Journal	*First issue:*		11 Mr 1893
Subtitle:	Den Interessen des arbeitenden Volkes gewidmet	*Last issue:*		?
Add. lang.:	English	*Vols. (nos.):*		
First editor:		*Frequency:*		w
First publ.:	SLP	*Preservation:*		3
Related pubs.:		*Supplements:*		
Circulation:		*Category:*		socialist-SLP

Depositories: Usa-WHi [1893]

Subtitle translation: Dedicated to the Concerns of the Working People.

This was a labor weekly in English and German. From 11 March to 15 April 1893 the title was *Chicago Echo*. It was published by the Sozialistische Arbeiter Partei (SLP).

Sources: Arndt/Olson; Eberlein 22837.

THE INDUSTRIAL NEWS	NY New York		1897-?
Title trans.:	*First issue:*		O 1897
Subtitle:	*Last issue:*		?
Add. lang.: English	*Vols. (nos.):*		
First editor:	*Frequency:*		w
First publ.:	*Preservation:*		7
Related pubs.:	*Supplements:*		
Circulation:	*Category:*	labor union-CLU	

Depositories:

This was the weekly organ of the Greater New York Trades Label League and the New York Central Labor Union. It was printed in English and German and "made-up nicely typographically."

Sourc: *BZ* 16 O 1897.

INTERNATIONAL WOOD WORKER	IL Chicago	1896-1906
Title trans.:	*First issue:*	F 1896
Subtitle:	*Last issue:*	Ap 1906
Add. lang.:	*Vols. (nos.):*	
First editor:	*Frequency:*	bw
First publ.:	*Preservation:*	2
Related pubs.: c *General Wood Worker's Journal*	*Supplements:*	
Circulation:	*Category:*	labor union

Depositories: Usa-MdBJ [1896-1906]; Usa-WHi [1896-1906]

This was the organ of the Amalgamated Wood Workers' International Union of America. It continued the *General Wood Workers' Journal*, which was discontinued in 1896. But according to Naas/Sakr the *International Wood Worker* appeared from 1890 to April 1906, 1-18(4). According to information in the last issue of the *General Wood Workers' Journal* the plan was to publish 6 pages in English and 4 in German.

Sources: Naas/Sakr, p. 130; on the history of the Amalgamated Wood Workers' International Union of America, see Fink, *Labor Unions*, pp. 414-415.

INTERNATIONALE ARBEITERFRONT ...	NY New York	1939-1940

Title trans.:	International Workers' Front against the War	*First issue:*	? 1939
Subtitle:	Informations Bulletin. Deutsche Ausgabe.	*Last issue:*	? 1940
Add. lang.:		*Vols. (nos.):*	
First editor:		*Frequency:*	m
First publ.:		*Preservation:*	5?
Related pubs.:		*Supplements:*	
Circulation:		*Category:*	antifascist

Depositories: D-292 (Ja 1940-F 1940)

The complete title of the paper was: *Internationale Arbeiterfront gegen den Krieg.*

Subtitle translation: Information Bulletin. German Edition.

This was a bulletin published by the Internationale Arbeiterfront gegen den Krieg (I.A.F] - Front Ouvrier International contre la Guerre (F.O.I.). It was probably a mimeographed monthly containing articles on the social, economic and legal situation in Nazi Germany, the military situation, German imperialism in Czechoslovakia and Poland, British workers and the war, the struggle for political independence in India. It published a controversy on the war between the Soviet Union and Finland in the issue of February 1940. Most contributions were unsigned or signed with pseudonyms. It contained quotations of Karl Liebknecht.

Sources: Maas I, p. 305; Arndt/Olson 2, p. 457.

INTERNATIONALE ARBEITER-CHRONIK	NY New York	1914

Title trans.:	International Workers' Chronicle	*First issue:*	1914
Subtitle:	Organ zur Förderung eigener Initiativen, selbständiger Aktionen im Proletariat	*Last issue:*	?
Add. lang.:		*Vols. (nos.):*	
First editor:	Max Baginski	*Frequency:*	
First publ.:		*Preservation:*	
Related pubs.:		*Supplements:*	
Circulation:		*Category:*	anarchist

Depositories: Nl-IISG [1914]

According to the subtitle this was "an organ to encourage independent initiative and action among the proletariat."

INTERNATIONALE ...		NY New York	1945(?)+

Title trans.:	International Free Labor Union News	*First issue:*	Ja 1945?
Subtitle:		*Last issue:*	+
Add. lang.:		*Vols. (nos.):*	
First editor:		*Frequency:*	m
First publ.:	AFL-CIO	*Preservation:*	
Related pubs.:		*Supplements:*	
Circulation:		*Category:*	labor / imperialist

Depositories: D-Bm 41/IGA ([1975-76],1977-79)

The complete title of the paper was: *Internationale freigewerkschaftliche Nachrichten.*

This monthly organ of the AFL/CIO is published separately also in English, Spanish, Portuguese and French editions (in 1977). It has 8 pages and it is issued by the Abteilung der AFL/CIO für internationale Angelegenheiten [Department of International Affairs of the AFL/CIO]. President: George Meany. It is unclear whether this paper was published for distribution among German-language workers in the United States or only for distribution among workers in West Germany after World War Two. It contains international news, reports from the international labor movement, articles against Euro-communism, on dissidents in the Soviet Union; it covered Bukowski's lecture tour of the United States for the AFL/CIO. It favored United States involvement in Vietnam in the late 1960s and was loyal to the government, e.g. an article in the issue of 21 October 1968 entitled "What the Trade Unions can expect from the Nixon Administration" consists of excerpts of Nixon's inauguration speech. Contributions are (badly) translated from English; among the contributors is Lane Kirkland, secretary-treasurer of the AFL/CIO. It contains photographic illustrations, frequently showing George Meany.

Source: Eberlein 22757.

JANUS		NY New York	1852

Title trans.:	Janus	*First issue:*	Ja 1852
Subtitle:		*Last issue:*	D 1852
Add. lang.:		*Vols. (nos.):*	
First editor:	Karl Heinzen	*Frequency:*	w, 3/w
First publ.:	Wilhelm Wagenitz	*Preservation:*	7
Related pubs.:	c *New Yorker Deutsche Zeitung*	*Supplements:*	
Circulation:	Mr 1852: 800; Ag? 1852: 400	*Category:*	radical fortyeighter

Depositories:

This was a weekly except in April when it appeared three times a week. The editor during the spring because of Heinzen's* absence on a lecture tour, was Joseph Fickler. *Janus* acquired a majority of the subscribers from its predecessor, the *New Yorker Deutsche Zeitung* [New York German News]. It was edited in the same general style and contained mostly foreign news with special emphasis on Germany. The editorials were devoted to questions of slavery, women's rights, temperance, penology, religion, education and political and social reform. (Wittke, p. 89). At the end of the year financial troubles led to the paper's discontinuation. Subscriptions had declined and only about a third of the 400 subscribers had paid.

Sources: Arndt/Olson; Wittke, *Against the Current*, pp. 89-90. On Heinzen see *Der Pionier*.

DER KÄMPFER		MO St. Louis	1896
Title trans.:	The Combatant	*First issue:*	25 Jl 1896
Subtitle:		*Last issue:*	29 Ag 1896
Add. lang.:		*Vols. (nos.):*	
First editor:	Otto Rinke	*Frequency:*	w
First publ.:	Debattier Club von St. Louis	*Preservation:*	5
Related pubs.:		*Supplements:*	
Circulation:		*Category:*	anarchist

Depositories: Usa-WHi (22 Ag 1896); Usa-NNC (?); Nl-IISG [1896]

This was a 4-page anarchist weekly published by the Debating Club of St. Louis. It was written in the tradition of Peukert's *Der Anarchist* and contained contributions by workers.

Sources: Arndt/Olson; Eberlein 22740-41; Bianco.

DER KAMPF		M Winnipeg	1930?-?
Title trans.:	The Struggle	*First issue:*	1930?
Subtitle:	Organ des Verbandes deutschsprachiger Arbeiter	*Last issue:*	?
Add. lang.:		*Vols. (nos.):*	
First editor:	Walter Wismer	*Frequency:*	?
First publ.:	Association of German-speaking Workers	*Preservation:*	6?
Related pubs.:		*Supplements:*	
Circulation:		*Category:*	labor

Depositories: DDR-LDB (1930)

No further information could be obtained.

Sources: Arndt/Olson; *Checklist*, p. 125.

KAMPFSIGNAL		NY New York	1932-1934

Title trans.:	Battle Signal	*First issue:*	3 D 1932
Subtitle:		*Last issue:*	15 N 1934
Add. lang.:		*Vols. (nos.):*	1-3
First editor:	Selmar Schocken	*Frequency:*	w, m
First publ.:		*Preservation:*	1
Related pubs.:		*Supplements:*	
Circulation:		*Category:*	socialist

Depositories: Usa-WHi; D-188/144 (1,m)

This was a paper of the left-wing, non-communist socialists with 4 pages. It appeared weekly with irregularities. After 15 August 1934 (vol. 3, nos. 12-16) it became a monthly and was mimeographed. Its motto was "Die Befreiung der Arbeiter kann nur das Werk der Arbeiterklasse sein" [the emancipaiton of the working class must be achieved by the working class itself]. It was edited by Selmar Schocken until May 1933; thereafter by Otto Zander and it was published by the Kampfsignal Publishing Association whose chairman was Hermann Gund. The treasurer was August Burkhardt. Gund and Burkhardt were important officials of the Amalgamated Food Workers, who, with the Arbeiter-Kranken- und Sterbekasse [Workmen's Benefit Fund] were among the chief financial supporters of the paper. It contained news from the American labor movement, appeals to fight fascism, articles on fascism in Germany and America, international arms trade, unjust trials, e.g. against Tom Mooney and Georgi Dimitrov. It supported the Einheitsfront [United Front] and opposed *Der Arbeiter* [The Worker], which satirized its name changing it to "Krampfsignal" ("Kampf" = 'fight'; "Krampf" = 'cramp'). After 28 September 1934 it regularly had a cartoon on the front page. Contributions came from Arthur Holitscher, Paul Mattick, Wendelin Thomas, Rudolf Rocker, Gottlieb Mayer and Joseph Hiess.

Sources: Arndt/Olson; Cazden, *Exile Literature*, pp. 28-46, 186; Radkau, p. 145; Ragg, pp. 34-35.

DER KLASSEN-KAMPF		IL Chicago	1919-1920

Title trans.:	The Class-Struggle	*First issue:*	? 1919
Subtitle:		*Last issue:*	? 1920
Add. lang.:		*Vols. (nos.):*	
First editor:	John Alexander	*Frequency:*	w
First publ.:	IWW	*Preservation:*	?
Related pubs.:		*Supplements:*	
Circulation:		*Category:*	syndicalist-IWW

Depositories:

This lost weekly was the German-language organ of the Industrial Workers of the World (IWW).

Sources: Arndt/Olson; Eberlein 22743.

DER KOMMUNIST	IL Nauvoo	1850?-1856?

		First issue:	1850?
Title trans.:	The Communist		
Subtitle:		Last issue:	1856?
Add. lang.:	English, French	Vols. (nos.):	
First editor:		Frequency:	
First publ.:	Ikarische Gemeinschaften	Preservation:	7
Related pubs.:		Supplements:	
Circulation:		Category:	utopian communist

Depositories:

Following the exodus of the Mormons to Utah in 1847 Nauvoo was settled temporarily by the Icarians, a body of utopian socialists chiefly of French origin led by Etienne Cabet of Dijon. At their peak the Icarians at Nauvoo numbered between 1,200 and 1,800. They cultivated 1000 acres of land, ran a mill, a sawmill and a distillery. They managed a tailor's, a shoemaker's and a carpenter's shop. In order to propagate their ideas they published papers in English, French and German. A crisis developed when Cabet demanded and was refused dictatorial powers over the settlement. Voted from office, he left Nauvoo with 200 loyal followers and went to St. Louis where he died one week later on 8 November 1856. The community never recovered from the split and soon disbanded.

Sources: Arndt/Olson; Eberlein 22693. On Nauvoo see Hillquit, pp. 118-121; Schem II, p. 754 s.v. "Cabet, Etienne."

DER KOMMUNIST	OH Cleveland	1852-1853?

		First issue:	1 Ja 1852
Title trans.:	The Communist		
Subtitle:		Last issue:	1853?
Add. lang.:		Vols. (nos.):	1(1)-?
First editor:	Joseph Leopold Stiger	Frequency:	m
First publ.:	Joseph Leopold Stiger	Preservation:	6
Related pubs.:		Supplements:	
Circulation:		Category:	radical fortyeighter

Depositories: <D-A (1 Ja 1852)

The motto of this paper was "Communism is the extension of the principle of organizing to all existing relations, insofar as the welfare of the individual is enhanced thereby and his individuality is not endangered" (translation). The only surviving issue contains a definition of communism, an open letter to Ludwig Kossuth, the Hungarian revolutionary, a review of contemporary German-American periodicals which supported the Free Soil movement: *New Yorker Demokrat, Republik der Arbeiter, Baltimore Wecker*, Philadelphia *Die Freie Presse, Anzeiger des Westens, Der Hochwächter*, St. Louis *Freie Blätter*, Baltimore *Fackel* and it emphasized the importance of communism for the emancipation of women. Stiger also planned a 'politico-literary establishment' in Cleveland, for the purpose of acquainting the German public with political literature, especially socialist and humanist Free Soil journals.

Sources: Arndt/Olson (they mention it as a weekly); Arndt/Olson 2, p. 496; Eberlein 22744; Wittke, *Refugees*, p. 171; Cazden, *Book Trade*, p. (644), note 120.

KÜFER-ZEITUNG	NY New York	1887-?

Title trans.:	Coopers' News	*First issue:*	Je? 1887
Subtitle:	Organ für das Küfergewerbe	*Last issue:*	?
Add. lang.:		*Vols. (nos.):*	
First editor:	August Schmidt	*Frequency:*	m
First publ.:	August Schmidt	*Preservation:*	7
Related pubs.:	Coopers' *Journal* (?); *Cooper's International Journal*(?)	*Supplements:*	
Circulation:		*Category:*	labor union

Depositories:

Subtitle translation: Organ for the Coopers' Trade.

This monthly, which could also have been a trade journal, contained 16 pages and was edited and published by August Schmidt "unter Mitwirkung practischer Küfer" [assisted by practical coopers]. It intended to "instruct the coopers so that they keep in touch with current social and professional developments" (prospectus, as quoted by the *Buchdrucker-Zeitung*). It is unclear how the *Küfer-Zeitung* was related to the journals of the Coopers' International Union but it was possibly opposed to it. The national association of German coopers ("Küfer") was formed as a permanent organization in Detroit in September 1887. On this occasion the *Küfer-Zeitung* was declared its official organ and August Schmidt was confirmed as editor and elected as secretary of the organization.

Source: *BZ* 16 Je, 1 O 1887.

DIE LATERNE	NY Buffalo	1880

Title trans.:	The Lantern	*First issue:*	F 1880
Subtitle:		*Last issue:*	Jl 1880
Add. lang.:		*Vols. (nos.):*	
First editor:	Emil C. Eckhart	*Frequency:*	w
First publ.:	Emil C. Eckhart	*Preservation:*	7
Related pubs.:	s *Das Banner*	*Supplements:*	
Circulation:		*Category:*	socialist

Depositories:

This socialist paper was continued as *Das Banner* (1880?- February 1883), an organ of the Greenback Party edited by C.H. Stiemke.

Source: Arndt/Olson.

LIBERTAS   MA Boston   1888

Title trans.:	Liberty	*First issue:*	17 Mr 1888
Subtitle:		*Last issue:*	8 S 1888?
Add. lang.:		*Vols. (nos.):*	1(1-8)
First editor:	Benjamin Ricketson Tucker	*Frequency:*	bw
First publ.:	Benjamin Ricketson Tucker	*Preservation:*	1(?)
Related pubs.:	Liberty	*Supplements:*	
Circulation:		*Category:*	anarchist

Depositories: Usa-WHi; D-188/144 (1,m)

According to Arndt/Olson this was the "Organ of 'Rousseau-Anarchy'" and it appeared biweekly until June 1888; it was suspended from July to August 1888 and published irregularly in (and after?) September 1888. It was the German edition of Tucker's English-language *Liberty* (Boston and New York, 1881-1908). Motto: "Freiheit, nicht die Tochter, sondern die Mutter der Ordnung" [Liberty, not the daughter, but the mother of order]. Riley claims that Tucker, a follower of Proudhon, wished to rescue the Germans from Most's communist-anarchism with this German paper.

The assistant editors were Georg Schumm and Emma Heller-Schumm. A regular feature on the first page was "Auf der Wacht" [On Guard], a review of current newspapers such as *Freidenker*, *Der Arme Teufel*, *Alarm*, *Michigan Arbeiter-Zeitung*, Most's *Freiheit* and some European ones. It contained a serialized reprint of a discussion between Henry James, Horace Greeley and Stephen Pearl Andrews on love, marriage and divorce and a serialized version of Felix Pyat's "Der Lumpensammler von Paris" [The Parisian Ragman].

It also published reprints from Karl Heinzen, Ralph Waldo Emerson and contributions by H.C. Bechthold and Paul Berwig. The issue of September 1888 stated that it would continue to be published at "longer or shorter intervals."

Sources: Arndt/Olson; on the controversy Most-Tucker, see Rocker, pp. 298-300, on Tucker, pp. 370-71; Kamman, p. 48.

LUCIFER   NY New York   1850?-1852?

Title trans.:	Lucifer	*First issue:*	1850?
Subtitle:		*Last issue:*	Ja 1852?
Add. lang.:		*Vols. (nos.):*	
First editor:	Ignaz Eduard Koch	*Frequency:*	
First publ.:		*Preservation:*	7
Related pubs.:		*Supplements:*	
Circulation:	1852: 400 subscribers	*Category:*	radical fortyeighter

Depositories:

The spelling of the title varies: *Lucifer* or *Luzifer*. Arndt/Olson give 1850 as the year in which this paper was first issued, Cazden 1851. Arndt/Olson quote the *Leipziger Charivari* of 16 May 1851, which describes *Lucifer's* tendency as "demokratisch." Cazden calls it an anticlerical and labor paper. According to him, the paper was first edited by I.E. Koch, then by Victor Wilhelm Fröhlich. He sold it to Joseph Weydemeyer* who was looking for subscribers to *Die Revolution*.

Sources: Arndt/Olson 2, p. 460; Cazden, *Book Trade*, p. (638).

DIE MENSCHENRECHTE		OH Cincinnati	1853

Title trans.:	Human Rights	*First issue:*	23 Jl 1853
Subtitle:	Ein Organ des Radicalismus	*Last issue:*	5 N 1853?
Add. lang.:		*Vols. (nos.):*	
First editor:	Wilhelm Rothacker	*Frequency:*	w
First publ.:	Wilhelm Rothacker	*Preservation:*	7
Related pubs.:		*Supplements:*	
Circulation:		*Category:*	radical fortyeighter

Depositories:

Subtitle translation: An Organ of Radicalism.

Other publishers were A. Kirsch and F.F. Metschan. This paper may have been a freethought journal (Wittke); Schlüter calls it 'socialist-radical,' while Kamman describes both *Der Unabhängige* and *Die Menschenrechte* as 'obscure communist newspapers.' Rothacker was a disciple of and agent for Karl Heinzen.

Sources: Cazden, *Book Trade*, p. (644) and note 120; Kamman, p. 84; Wittke, *Press*, p. 190; Schlüter, *Anfänge*, p. 131.

MEPHISTO		MO St. Louis	1901-1902?

Title trans.:	Mephisto	*First issue:*	S 1901
Subtitle:		*Last issue:*	1902?
Add. lang.:		*Vols. (nos.):*	
First editor:	Martin Drescher	*Frequency:*	?
First publ.:		*Preservation:*	7
Related pubs.:	s *Der Zigeuner*	*Supplements:*	
Circulation:		*Category:*	anarchist

Depositories:

After the failure of *Der Arme Teufel* [The Poor Devil] and *Wolfsaugen* [Wolf's Eyes] *Mephisto* was Drescher's third attempt to establish a satirical paper. It was succeeded in 1902 by *Der Zigeuner* [The Gypsy].

Source: *BZ* 16 S 1901.

DER METALLARBEITER   NY New York   1888

Title trans.:	The Metal Worker	*First issue:*	My 1888
Subtitle:	Fachblatt der deutschen Metallarbeiter von Nord-Amerika	*Last issue:*	Jl 1888
Add. lang.:		*Vols. (nos.):*	
First editor:	J. Wytzka	*Frequency:*	w
First publ.:		*Preservation:*	7
Related pubs.:		*Supplements:*	
Circulation:		*Category:*	labor union

Depositories:

Subtitle translation: Trade Journal for the German Metalworkers of North America.

This was published by members of the Maschinisten Progressive Union No. 1. It was intended to make metalworkers "acquainted with recent developments and inventions in the metal industry." Concerning politics the paper took the point of view that "the metalworkers were organized in groups which differed widely in their political views and nobody should be forced into a political program" (as quoted by the *Buchdrucker-Zeitung*). The last issue contained an attack on Typographia No. 7 of New York because the typesetters for *Der Metallarbeiter* had demanded union wages.

Sources: Eberlein 22253; *BZ* 1 My 1888, 16 Jl 1888. The relation to *Der Hammer* remains unclear.

MICHIGAN ARBEITERZEITUNG   MI Detroit   1888-1892?

Title trans.:	Michigan Workers' Journal	*First issue:*	1 My 1888
Subtitle:		*Last issue:*	Jl 1889 /-1892?
Add. lang.:		*Vols. (nos.):*	
First editor:	H.C. Bechthold	*Frequency:*	d
First publ.:	German-American Publishing Co.	*Preservation:*	7
Related pubs.:		*Supplements:*	Weekly ed.
Circulation:	1890: 1800	*Category:*	labor

Depositories:

A title variation(?) was: *Detroiter Tageblatt*. This paper was published by the German Co-operative Publishing Association in 1890 and managed by Jacob Hunger who became in 1910 the social-democratic candidate for the Register of Deeds in the congressional elections.

Although a holder of the union cut this paper had considerable difficulties with the German-American Typographical Union. As a result of financial difficulties, it was forced to introduce printing plates after long resistance from the union in April 1889 (*BZ* 16 O 1888; 16 Ap 1889). When it had to cease publication because of continued financial difficulties in July 1889 the typesetters were allowed $40 from the union in order to take legal proceedings for the recovery of wages owed. (*BZ* 1 Ag 1889). As an act of solidarity, the typesetters of Typographia No. 21 of Detroit allowed their unemployed colleagues from the discontinued *Michigan Arbeiter-Zeitung* to replace them for a day's work. (*BZ* 1 O 1889). The paper resumed publication later; the *Buchdrucher-Zeitung* mentions its existence again for December 1891 (1 January 1892). Arndt/Olson list the paper under *Detroiter Tageblatt and Michigan Arbeiter-Zeitung* as a title variant and the name of its weekly edition. According to Eberlein the weekly edition appeared from 3 May 1888 to 1891.

Sources: Arndt/Olson; Eberlein 22803 and 22673; *BZ*.

MILWAUKEE JOURNAL	WI Milwaukee	1880-1881

Title trans.:	Milwaukee Journal	*First issue:*	1 Je 1880
Subtitle:		*Last issue:*	17 S 1881
Add. lang.:		*Vols. (nos.):*	
First editor:	Michael Biron	*Frequency:*	d
First publ.:	Michael Biron	*Preservation:*	1
Related pubs.:		*Supplements:*	
Circulation:		*Category:*	socialist

Depositories: Usa-WHi

An organ of German socialists, this paper was supported entirely from Biron's own funds. "As strife continually eroded the structure of the socialistic workers' parties and their moral support and membership declined, so did the circulation of the *Milwaukee Journal*. It became increasingly difficult to maintain a daily of specialized interest, yet Biron did not wish to change the tendency of the paper to make it acceptable to a large number of readers. He therefore tried to sell the paper to the socialists for the price of his original investment but the group was unable to raise sufficient funds." (Knoche, p. 194). After attempts to sell the paper to *Der Freidenker* [The Freethinker] and to Robert Schilling, it was bought by Richard Günther, owner of the *Milwaukee Freie Presse* and appeared for a short time as page eight of the *Freie Presse*, which was not a labor paper. After the unification of the two papers on 18 September 1881, Biron was no longer connected with the *Milwaukee Journal* and a few months later he started the anticlerical *Lucifer*. Biron died on 7 February 1902. Variant: Arndt/Olson give 1881-1882 as the dates of appearance.

Sources: Arndt/Olson; Knoche, pp. 193-195. Obituary of Biron in *Der Freidenker*, 16 F 1902.

MILWAUKEE'R ARBEITER-ZEITUNG	WI Milwaukee	1886-1889

Title trans.:	Milwaukee Labor News	*First issue:*	4 My 1886
Subtitle:	Officielles Organ der Central Labor Union	*Last issue:*	D 1889
Add. lang.:		*Vols. (nos.):*	
First editor:	Paul Grottkau	*Frequency:*	w, 3/w, d
First publ.:	Milwaukee Arbeiter-Zeitungs Publ.	*Preservation:*	6
	Society		
Related pubs.:	c *Arminia*; s *Milwaukee Volkszeitung*	*Supplements:*	see below
Circulation:		*Category:*	labor
			union-CLU

Depositories: Usa-WHi [1886-87]; Nl-IISG [1888-89]

Subtitle translation: Official Organ of the Central Labor Union.

This paper was published weekly: May 1886; three times a week: May - October 1886; daily: from October 1886. Its motto until 28 January 1887 was "Unser Ruf erschalle: 'Gleiches Recht für Alle!'" [Our call may resound: Equal Rights for all!] It was replaced by a subtitle: Den Interessen des arbeitenden Volkes gewidmet [Dedicated to the Interests of the Working People]. Editors after Grottkau* were Simon Hickler (July - December 1888), Valentin Blatz (December - May 1889), Jacob Hunger (May - December 1889). It was published from July 1888 on by the Socialistic Publishing Society. The predecessor of the *Arbeiter-Zeitung* was apparently Michael Biron's *Arminia*, an anticlerical paper. It seems likely that Biron sold the subscriber list and the right to the numbering of the *Arminia*, but since the Central Labor Union preferred "Arbeiterzeitung" as the title of the new paper, Biron could continue using the name *Arminia*. This is important for the dating of the *Arbeiter-Zeitung*. (See Knoche p. 202. Arndt/Olson give 1882 as the first year).

The *Milwaukee'r Arbeiter-Zeitung* dealt mostly with labor news. There were also a few itmes of local or foreign interest as well as serialized novels, e.g. Heinrich von Kleist's "Michael Kohlhaas" and short stories.

Vorwärts, the Sunday edition, was added in January 1887. *Die Wahrheit* [The Truth], the weekly edition, was added in January 1889. It was continued by the *Milwaukee Volkszeitung* after January 1890 (see there).

Sources: Arndt/Olson; Knoche, pp. 201-205. On Grottkau, see Chicago *Vorbote*.

MITTEILUNGSBLATT ...   NY New York   1935-1936?

Title trans.:	Bulletin of the German-American League for Culture	*First issue:*	1935
Subtitle:		*Last issue:*	1936?
Add. lang.:		*Vols. (nos.):*	
First editor:		*Frequency:*	ir
First publ.:	Deutsch-Amerikanischer Kulturverband	*Preservation:*	7
Related pubs.:	*Mitteilungsblatt des Deutsch-Amerikanischen Kulturverbands (Ostdistrikt)*	*Supplements:*	
Circulation:		*Category:*	communist

Depositories:

The complete title of the paper was *Mitteilungsblatt des deutschamerikanischen Kulturverbandes*

This was the official bulletin of the German-American League for Culture. It was published by the League.

Sources: Cazden, *Exile Literature*, p. 187; *Der Arbeiter*, 6 O 1935.

MITTEILUNGSBLATT ...   NY New York   1939-1940?

Title trans.:	Bulletin of the German-American League for Culture (Eastern District)	*First issue:*	N 1939
Subtitle:		*Last issue:*	1940?
Add. lang.:		*Vols. (nos.):*	1(1)-?
First editor:		*Frequency:*	
First publ.:	Deutsch-Amerikanischer Kulturverband	*Preservation:*	6
Related pubs.:	*Mitteilungsblatt des Deutsch-Amerikanischen Kulturverbandes*	*Supplements:*	
Circulation:		*Category:*	communist

Depositories: D-292 [N 1939]

The complete title of the paper was: *Mitteilungsblatt des deutschamerikanischen Kulturverbands (Ostdistrikt)* This was published by the executive for the Eastern District of the German-American League for Culture. According to Maas, it probably appeared only once; according to Cazden, it may have appeared irregularly until 1940, in New York and Philadelphia. There were contributions by Otto Sattler, Julius Lips and Walter Mueller.

Sources: Maas II, p. 372; Maas IV; Cazden, *Exile Literature*, p. 187.

MÖBEL-ARBEITER-JOURNAL   NY New York   1883-1891

Title trans.:	Furniture Workers' Journal	*First issue:*	1 F 1883
Subtitle:	Offizielles Organ der Internationale	*Last issue:*	14 Ap 1891
	Möbel-Arbeiter-Union von Amerika		
Add. lang.:	English	*Vols. (nos.):*	1(1)-9(4)
First editor:	Henry Emrich	*Frequency:*	bw, m, bw
First publ.:	Executive Committee of the Union	*Preservation:*	1
Related pubs.:	s *General Wood Workers' Journal*; s	*Supplements:*	
	International Wood Worker		
Circulation:		*Category:*	labor union

Depositories: Usa-ICJ [1883-1891]; Usa-WHi (1883-1889); D-188/144 ([1883],1884-91,m)

This labor union journal appeared biweekly except from June 1888 to February 1889 when it was published monthly. From 1884 on the subtitle appeared in English: Official Organ of the International Furniture Workers' Union in America. It had 4 pages, 3 pages in German and 1 page in English, entitled 'Furniture Workers' Journal.' From January 1885 on the title changed to *Furniture Workers' Journal* and thereafter 2 pages were in English and 2 in German. The place of publication varies: Brooklyn, NY; Baltimore. The issue of February 1883 contained a declaration of the union's aims. There were also official reports of union meetings, news of local unions, announcements concerning the union's burial fund and its tool-insurance fund, news from Germany, articles on the eight-hour-campaign, child and convict labor, such subjects as property, usury and wage labor, statistics on the furniture industry and financial reports. It published a serialized report on the history of the Möbel-Arbeiter-Union from 25 April 1884.

Sources: Arndt/Olson; Eberlein 22755; Naas/Sakr, p. 46; Schlüter, *Anfänge*, p. 175. On the union's history, see "Organisierte Möbel-Arbeiter," *New Yorker Volkszeitung* 21 F 1903.

NEBRASKA ARBEITERZEITUNG   NE Omaha   1899

Title trans.:	Nebraska Labor News	*First issue:*	1 Jl 1899
Subtitle:		*Last issue:*	Ag 1899
Add. lang.:		*Vols. (nos.):*	
First editor:	Joseph Tagwerker	*Frequency:*	w
First publ.:		*Preservation:*	7
Related pubs.:		*Supplements:*	
Circulation:		*Category:*	labor

Depositories:

This paper called itself the only German-language labor newspaper west of Chicago. Tagwerker, its founder, publisher and editor, was a member of Typographia No. 20 of Omaha. According to the *Buchdrucker-Zeitung*, "ill fortune had knocked him about in the world and made him as familiar with the sufferings and fights of the working people as anyone." The paper contained

"an abundance of interesting reading material." (1 July 1899)
Tagwerker had to give up his enterprise after only two months because he did not find enough readers in Omaha. He went to Butte, Nebraska and became editor and printer of another new German weekly there. (*BZ* 1 S 1899)
Source: *BZ*

NEU-ENGLAND ZEITUNG		MA Boston	1846-1853
Title trans.:	New England Journal	*First issue:*	1 Jl 1846
Subtitle:		*Last issue:*	S 1853
Add. lang.:		*Vols. (nos.):*	
First editor:	Karl Heinzen, Eduard Schläger (?)	*Frequency:*	w
First publ.:	Boston Free Congregation	*Preservation:*	7
Related pubs.:		*Supplements:*	
Circulation:		*Category:*	radical fortyeighter

Depositories:

Information on this paper is contradictory. Arndt/Olson list its first appearance as 1 July 1846; other sources merely mention its existence in 1852/53. As to the editorship, Arndt/Olson and Schlüter name Heinzen* and Schläger as editors and publishers, while Wittke mentions that Heinzen published *Janus* at that time and that he eagerly noted every sign of abolitionism such as the founding of the *Neu-England Zeitung* in 1852.

Bernard Domschke*, its assistant editor since 1852 and a native of Dresden, had been trained for the ministry and subsequently joined the freethinkers. He came to America in 1850. The *Neu-England Zeitung* was an undertaking of the Boston Freie Gemeinde [Free Congregation]. It was against slavery, it supported the labor movement of the 1850s, was friendly to the aims of the American Workers' League and decidedly anticlerical. It published articles by Marx and Engels, which had been submitted by J. Weydemeier, their "literary agent" in America. Weydemeyer was also a correspondent of this paper. It reported the details of the communist trial in Cologne in 1852.

Sources: Arndt/Olson; Eberlein 22871; Obermann, *Pioneer*, pp. 45, 53, 71; Schlüter, *Anfänge*, pp. 131, 153, 159; Cazden, *Book Trade*, p. (644); Marx/Engels, *Werke* XXVIII, pp. 589-591. On Domschke, see Dobert, pp. 58-61 and Schlicher, p. 324; on Schläger, see Zucker, p. 337; on Heinzen, see *Der Pionier*.

DAS NEUE LEBEN		NY New York	1939
Title trans.:	The New Life	*First issue:*	Je 1939
Subtitle:		*Last issue:*	Ag 1939
Add. lang.:		*Vols. (nos.):*	(1-3)
First editor:		*Frequency:*	m
First publ.:	German Youth Association	*Preservation:*	6
Related pubs.:	s *Youth Outlook*	*Supplements:*	
Circulation:	1939: 1000	*Category:*	communist

Depositories: <§ Usa-MWKJA (Ag 1939); <§ Usa-KyLC(?)

"A German-American newspaper for young people sponsored by the CPA (joined by the Naturfreunde and various sports clubs)... The first issue was printed, the last two mimeographed." (Cazden)

Sources: Cazden, *Exile Literature*, pp. 54, 188-189; *Volksfront* 9 S 1939.

NEUE VOLKSZEITUNG		NY New York	1932-1949
Title trans.:	New People's Journal	*First issue:*	17 D 1932
Subtitle:	Den Interessen des arbeitenden Volkes gewidmet	*Last issue:*	6 Ag 1949
Add. lang.:	English	*Vols. (nos.):*	1-18 (32)
First editor:	Siegfried Jungnitsch	*Frequency:*	w
First publ.:	Progressive Publishing Ass. Inc.	*Preservation:*	1
Related pubs.:	c *New Yorker Volkszeitung*	*Supplements:*	
Circulation:	1934: 21,850; 1944: 21,270; 1946: 9068; 1949: 17,632	*Category:*	social democrat

Depositories: Usa-NN; Usa-WHi; D-Bm 41/IGA [1937-45]; D-188/144 (1,m)

Subtitle translation: Dedicated to the Interests of the Working People.

This was a conservative social-democratic weekly, which was consistently anti-Nazi and anticommunist. Under Seger's editorship it became the American voice of the SPD in exile. "Although the majority of readers were inherited from the defunct *New Yorker Volkszeitung*, ... the paper also appealed to numerous e'"migre'"s" (Cazden, p. 33). The motto changed: "Anti-Nazi Newspaper - Published in U.S.A.," from 1932; "Banned in Germany since 1933," (1941-1942), "Oldest Anti-Nazi Newspaper," (1942-46). The editors-in-chief were Siegfried Jungnitsch (1932-36), Gerhard H. Seger* (May 1936-49), Rudolf Katz*, (substitute editor-in-chief 1936-47), Hilde Walter* (1948-49). Other members of the board of editors were Otto Sattler, Karl Meier, Sergius Ingermann, Ludwig Jablinowski, Karl Schmidt, Walter Wenderich, Bruno Wagner, Fritz Schade, Paul Schueler, Friedrich Stampfer* and Karl Jakob Hirsch. It was published by the Progressive Publishing Association Inc. It contained political news from America and Germany, news from the labor movement, a women's section, articles on the theater, music and art, sports news, gossip, a humorous feature titled "Gaudeamus," local news from America, travel reports, articles on judicial questions, announcements of diverse German labor, singing, sports and beneficial organizations. The jubilee edition

celebrating the paper's 10th anniversary appeared on 12 December 1942. Volume 15, no. 23 of 1945 contained a chronicle of the *Neue Volkszeitung* after 12 years.
There were contributions by Walter A. Berendson, William S. Schlamm, Wilhelm Bernina, Emil Franzel, Wilhelm Sollmann, Franzi Ascher, Max Barth, Siegfried Bernfeld, Willy Brandt, Alfred Braunthal, Robert Breuer, Otto Burgemeister, Arthur Fischer (pen-names: Gaudeamus and Paula Erbswurst), Ernst Fraenkel, Oskar Maria Graf, Fritz Heine, Hans von Hentig, Josef Hofbauer, Fritz Karsen, Kurt Kersten, Eugen Lennhoff, Thomas Mann, Siegfried Marck, Carl Misch, Erich Ollenhauer, Paul Stefan, Dorothy Thomson, Walter Victor, Roda Roda, Victor Schiff, Kurt Schumacher, Eric Seligo, Tony Sender and Carl Zuckmayer.

Sources: Arndt/Olson; Arndt/Olson 2, pp. 461-464; Maas II, pp. 393-409; Maas IV; Eberlein 22839; Cazden, *Exile Literature*, pp. 32-33, 76-78, 186 ff., *Exil in den USA*, pp. 147-148; Radkau, pp. 144-169; Ragg, p. 34; Hirsch, Felix E., "Gerhard Seger: In the Tradition of Carl Schurz," *German-American Review* 33 (1967), p. 26-27.

DIE NEUE ZEIT		NY New York	1855-1858

Title trans.:	New Times	*First issue:*	14 Ap? 1855
Subtitle:		*Last issue:*	3 Ap 1858
Add. lang.:		*Vols. (nos.):*	1-3(52)=1-156
First editor:	Paul Bernhard	*Frequency:*	w
First publ.:	Paul Bernhard	*Preservation:*	4
Related pubs.:		*Supplements:*	
Circulation:		*Category:*	early socialist?

Depositories: < D-A (14 Je 1856); Usa-MoS (Ap 1857-Ap 1858)

This paper had 8 pages. In a letter to Friedrich Engels of 6 September 1855 Karl Marx mentioned that *Die Neue Zeit* was nominally edited by Bernhardt (spelling differs), but actually by Löwe von Calbe. Marx wanted to publish an obituary notice in *Die Neue Zeit* for his friend Roland Daniels who had died "as a victim of the infamy of the Prussian police." It contained political news from America and Europe, articles on historical subjects related to history and science, a serialized novel in June 1856: "Drei Tage aus dem Leben eines deutschen Schullehrers" [Three Days in the Life of a German Teacher], announcements and advertisements. There were contributions by Joseph Weydemeyer.

Sources: Arndt/Olson; Marx/Engels, *Werke* XXVIII.

NEUE ZEIT		MO St. Louis	1862-?

Title trans.:	New Times	First issue:	? 1862
Subtitle:		Last issue:	?
Add. lang.:		Vols. (nos.):	
First editor:		Frequency:	
First publ.:	George Hillgaertner	Preservation:	7
Related pubs.:	George Hillgaertner	Supplements:	
Circulation:		Category:	socialist

Depositories:

This paper was founded in 1862 as an organ to foster the "general emancipation, welfare and education of the people." Joseph Weydemeyer* was a member of the editorial board. Hillgaertner, condemned to death as a participant of the 1848 Revolution, had fled to the United States together with Gottfried Kinkel in 1851/52. In 1854 he was editor of the *Illinois Staatszeitung*, later of the St. Louis *Westliche Post*. Obermann says about the *Neue Zeit*: "The *Neue Zeit* set itself the dual task of struggling against the professional politicians who sought to rule Missouri and of making the will of the people prevail. Both in makeup and content it soon surpassed the other German-American papers. Its editorials gave a clear political line and cogent explanation of both domestic and foreign policy. This publication was Weydemeyer's best instrument in helping to clear up the political dissatisfaction that had arisen among the Republicans and workers generally. ... It was thanks to the *Neue Zeit* that the German Americans, who were originally for Fremont and against Lincoln in the election campaign of 1864, finally supported the latter. ... In 1864 the contest in Missouri took the form of a struggle of the working class for democracy against aristocracy and an economic system of favoritism. German Americans of St. Louis, including Weydemeyer, took a leading part in this struggle."

Sources: Obermann, *Pioneer*, pp. 124-126. On Hillgaertner, see Zucker, p. 305; on Weydemeyer, see *Stimme des Volkes*.

NEUE ZEIT		KY Louisville	1877-1878

Title trans.:	New Times	First issue:	N 1877
Subtitle:		Last issue:	Je? 1878
Add. lang.:		Vols. (nos.):	
First editor:	Gustav Fernitz	Frequency:	d
First publ.:		Preservation:	7
Related pubs.:		Supplements:	Wöchentliche Neue Zeit
Circulation:	1878: 500 (est.)	Category:	socialist-WP

Depositories:

This socialist daily morning-paper was the organ of the Louisville German section no. 1 of the Arbeiterpartei [Workingmen's Party]. The executive committee of the party had refused its permission to establish a daily in Louisville.

Nevertheless, in December 1877 the *Neue Zeit* appeared as an organ of the Louisville section of the Arbeiterpartei. Because some typesetters had found work at the *Neue Zeit*, by November 1877 the Louisville Typographia had 18 members. (*BZ* 15 N 1877). When the paper failed about 8 months later, the Louisville Typographia complained that this had been a hard blow to their weak organization. (*BZ* 15 Jl 1878)

The *Wöchentliche Neue Zeit*, the weekly edition of *Die Neue Zeit*, had an estimated circulation of 800 in 1878. It existed probably from 1877-1878.

Sources: Arndt/Olson; Eberlein 22868, 22870; *BZ.*

DIE NEUE ZEIT	IL Evansville	1885-1886?

Title trans.:	The New Times	*First issue:*	? D 1885
Subtitle:		*Last issue:*	1886?
Add. lang.:		*Vols. (nos.):*	
First editor:		*Frequency:*	
First publ.:		*Preservation:*	7
Related pubs.:		*Supplements:*	
Circulation:		*Category:*	labor union-CLU

Depositories:

This paper was founded by the "Liberale Liga" [Liberal League], a local association of workers and men supporting workers' demands. It was endorsed by the Central Labor Union which was organized at that time and enlarged in February 1886.

Source: *BZ* 15 Ja and 1 Mr 1886.

NEUES LEBEN	IL Chicago	1902-1910

Title trans.:	New Life	*First issue:*	29 N 1902
Subtitle:	Organ der Sozialisten von Illinois	*Last issue:*	2 Jl 1910
Add. lang.:		*Vols. (nos.):*	1-8(391)
First editor:	Ernst Ebel	*Frequency:*	w
First publ.:	Illinois Volksblatt Publishing Association	*Preservation:*	1
Related pubs.:		*Supplements:*	
Circulation:	1906: 2728	*Category:*	social democrat

Depositories: Usa-NN; D-188/144 (1,m)

Subtitle translation: Organ of Illinois Socialists.

The paper was first the organ of the Social Democratic Party and later of the SP. Till 1908 it appeared as a 4-page weekly. Afterwards it contained 12 pages. Its motto was: "Das Alte stürzt, es ändert sich die Zeit, und Neues Leben blüht aus den Ruinen" [Old things decay, times change, and new life blossoms from the ruins]. The editors after Ebel were Robert Saltiel (16 September 1905 - 22 June 1907) and Adolph Dreifuß (6 July 1907 - 2 July 1910).

It published the platform of the Socialist Party, party news, union news and national and international political news as well as articles on questions of socialism. Other topics were health, scientific and medical questions as well as trivia. A regular feature was "Fritz and Hans," a dispute between a socialist (Fritz) and an incorrigible non- socialist (Hans) on current issues. It also published short stories, serialized novels, poems, announcements of unions and clubs and advertisements for local businesses.

There were contributions by Karl Kautsky, Emil Lieβ, Jacob Winnen, Heinrich Lee, William Morris, Emile Zola, Ferdinand Feiligrath, Thomas J. Morgan, Karl Henkell, A. Swientochowski, W.M. Hyndman and Adolf Glasbrenner.

Sources: Arndt/Olson; Eberlein 22748.

NEW JERSEY ARBEITER-ZEITUNG		NJ Newark	1886-1889

Title trans.:	New Jersey Labor News	*First issue:*	25 S 1886
Subtitle:		*Last issue:*	Jl? 1889
Add. lang.:		*Vols. (nos.):*	
First editor:	John Grunzig	*Frequency:*	w, d?
First publ.:	Co-operative Publishing Association	*Preservation:*	7
Related pubs.:	s *New Jersey Freie Presse*	*Supplements:*	
Circulation:		*Category:*	labor

Depositories:

This paper was the organ of the Vereinigte Gewerkschaften [United Trades Assembly] and it appeared weekly, later probably daily. In 1889 it was published by the Volkszeitungs-Publishing Association. In the last two years of its existence the paper did not pay union wages and introduced printing plates. This led to a strike in late 1888, after which the *New Jersey Arbeiter-Zeitung* started to employ scabs. In December Typographia No. 8 organized a boycott against the paper and it was closed to union members. In early 1889 the *New Jersey Arbeiter-Zeitung* appeared as the New Jersey edition of the *New Yorker Volkszeitung*. Alexander Jonas*, editor of the latter, promised in April that the *New Yorker Volkszeitung* would take over completely the publishing of the *New Jersey Arbeiterzeitung* and that they would break any connection with the Newark Co-operative Publishing Associaton. On 1 April 1889 the "scab-paper" *New Jersey Arbeiter-Zeitung* appeared again as a weekly. In July 1889 the *New Jersey Freie Presse* was mentioned as the successor to the *New Jersey Arbeiter-Zeitung* in the *Buchdrucker-Zeitung*.

Variant: According to Arndt/Olson the *New Jersey Arbeiter-Zeitung* appeared 1884?-1890? as a socialist labor daily, edited by Maurice Reinhold von Stern and published by Heinz & Huryos. It is unclear whether this paper is related to the one described above.

Sources: Arndt/Olson; Eberlein 22676; Creagh 1112; *BZ* 16 Ag, 1 O 1886, 16 My, 1 S, 16 S, 16 D 1887, 16 F, 16 My, 16 Ag, 16 O, 16 S, 16 N, 1 D 1888, 1 F, 1 Mr, 16 Jl 1889. On Vereinigte Deutsche Gewerkschaften, see Hillquit, pp. 284-285.

NEW JERSEY ZEITUNG	NJ Newark	1853-1858

Title trans.:	New Jersey News	*First issue:*	9 F 1853
Subtitle:		*Last issue:*	Ap 1858
Add. lang.:		*Vols. (nos.):*	
First editor:	Fritz Anneke*	*Frequency:*	d
First publ.:		*Preservation:*	7
Related pubs.:	*Newarker Zeitung* ?	*Supplements:*	
Circulation:		*Category:*	labor

Depositories:

No further information is available about this labor daily. In 1858 it was bought by Benedict Prieth, who changed the paper's title to *New Jersey Freie Zeitung*, a Republican/ independent paper which existed for almost a hundred years. For additional information see *Newarker Zeitung*.

Sources. Arndt/Olson. Obituary on Prieth in *BZ* 1 N 1879.

NEW YORKER ABEND-ZEITUNG	NY New York	1850-1874?

Title trans.:	New York Evening News	*First issue:*	? 1850
Subtitle:		*Last issue:*	1874 ?
Add. lang.:		*Vols. (nos.):*	
First editor:	Ludwig Ferdinand Fenner von Fenneberg	*Frequency:*	d
First publ.:	Friedrich Rauchfuss	*Preservation:*	6
Related pubs.:		*Supplements:*	see below
Circulation:	1873: 3200 (est.)	*Category:*	radical fortyeighter

Depositories: D-188/144 (24 Je 1852); <D-A (14 Je 1856; 21 D 1861)

This paper was founded by an "Association deutscher Buchdrucker" [Association of German Printers], among them Theodor Barthen. It had various editors and owners, whose names and dates of office could be established neither completely nor with certainty. The editors after Fenneberg* were Friedrich Kapp (until Mr? 1851) and Hermann Raster (1852-67). The publisher was Rauchfuss (1852-74) (Arndt/Olson). According to Cazden, the *Abend-Zeitung* was started in late September or early October 1850 under the editorship of Friedrich Kapp, Franz Zitz and Julius Fröbel. Kapp, a 48 refugee, who had come to America in 1850, was the author of several publications on contemporary American history, especially on German immigration to America. Hermann Raster, a political pamphleteer and journalist in Germany, had escaped to America from pending trials for offenses against the German press laws in 1851. Schem mentions that he had a clear and powerful style of writing, a fact which gained influence and respect for him and his paper. In 1867 he became chief editor of the *Illinois Staatszeitung*.

The only issue at hand, contains one page of political news from Europe and America (a report of a public meeting with Lajos Kossuth, whose exile in America was followed with attention by the German-American radical press), a serialized novel by William H.W. Kingston and many small advertisements.

The paper's weekly, the *Wochenblatt der New Yorker Abend-Zeitung* appeared probably from 1869 to 1887 and had a circulation of 3750 in 1873.
The paper's sunday edition existed from 1850 or 1852 probably until 1879. Its title varied: *Atlantische Blätter und New Yorker Kladderadatsch* (1875?-1879); *New Yorker Kladderadatsch* (1879). The editor and publisher was Friedrich Rauchfuss (1875-79). Its circulation was estimated at 1500 in 1878.
Sources: Arndt/Olson; Arndt/Olson 2, p. 437; Eberlein 22619; Wittke, *Press*, p. 81; Cazden, *Book Trade*, p. (665); Schem IX, p. 244: "Hermann Raster;" Schem VI, p. 79: "Friedrich Kapp;" Zucker, p. 124; Schlüter, *Anfänge*, pp. 88-89. Obituary on Rauchfuss in *BZ* 1 Ap 1878; obituary on Barthen in *BZ* 1 My 1895.

NEW YORKER ARBEITERZEITUNG (I)		NY New York	1864-1865
Title trans.:	New York Labor News	*First issue:*	3 S 1864
Subtitle:	Wochenschrift für Unterhaltung und Belehrung	*Last issue:*	29 D 1865
Add. lang.:		*Vols. (nos.):*	1,2;(1-16)
First editor:	Georg Degen	*Frequency:*	w
First publ.:	Georg Degen	*Preservation:*	1
Related pubs.:		*Supplements:*	
Circulation:		*Category:*	labor

Depositories: Usa-WHi (S 1864-D 1865); D-188/144 (1,m)

Subtitle translation: Weekly for Entertainment and Education

According to Arndt/Olson the editor stated that the paper was not a playground for political parties, but being an organ of workers it had to be neutral. Kamman said that it spread the doctrines of Schulze-Delitzsch, a German advocate of workers' cooperative enterprises but was intended for general reading; it opposed Lassalle.
Sources: Arndt/Olson; Arndt/Olson 2, p. 439; Eberlein 22677.

NEW YORKER ARBEITER-ZEITUNG (II)		NY New York	1886 ?- ?
Title trans.:	New York Labor News	*First issue:*	1886?
Subtitle:		*Last issue:*	
Add. lang.:		*Vols. (nos.):*	
First editor:		*Frequency:*	d
First publ.:		*Preservation:*	7
Related pubs.:		*Supplements:*	
Circulation:		*Category:*	anarchist

Depositories:

The *Freiheit* of 1 May 1886 announced the establishment of an Internationaler Zeitungs-Verein [International Press Association], a stock corporation that issued shares of $1, available at the Verein's printshop and at the meetings of the Internationale Arbeiter-Association. The main object of the Verein was the publication of a daily newspaper with revolutionary-anarchist tendency, "edited by workers for workers." No evidence has yet been found to show whether this plan materialized.

NEW YORKER ARBEITER-ZEITUNG (III)	NY New York	1890?-1902?

Title trans.:	New York Labor News	*First issue:*	1890?
Subtitle:	Kampforgan der gewerkschaftlichen und sozialdemokratischen Bewegung	*Last issue:*	1902?
Add. lang.:		*Vols. (nos.):*	
First editor:		*Frequency:*	?
First publ.:		*Preservation:*	1?
Related pubs.:		*Supplements:*	*Abendblatt?*
Circulation:		*Category:*	social democrat

Depositories: Usa-NN

This was published temporarily by the Social-Democratic Party of the United States of America. According to the subtitle it was an organ of the struggle of the workers' and the social-democratic movement.

Source: Eberlein 22678.

Abendblatt für die Arbeiter-Zeitung

There is no sufficient evidence to prove that the *Abendblatt* was in fact the evening edition of the *New Yorker Arbeiter-Zeitung.*

Depository: Usa-NbHi (28 F 1900).

Source: Arndt/Olson 2, p. 436.

NEW YORKER DEUTSCHE ZEITUNG	NY New York	1851

Title trans.:	New York German News	*First issue:*	2 S 1851
Subtitle:		*Last issue:*	4 D 1851
Add. lang.:		*Vols. (nos.):*	m
First editor:	Karl Heinzen	*Frequency:*	d
First publ.:	Freunde des Fortschritts	*Preservation:*	1
Related pubs.:		*Supplements:*	Sonntagsblatt
Circulation:		*Category:*	radical fortyeighter

Depositories: Usa-NN

Heinzen* started this daily with a capital of $1300 gained from the sale of the *Deutsche Schnellpost.* The paper contained foreign news and correspondence from the leading capitalists in Europe. "It attacked the corrupt politics of New York, exposed the low standards of professional education in the United States, and contained the usual amount of controversial discussion of the Revolution of 1848." (Wittke, p. 87) Because of financial difficulties the *Deutsche Zeitung* had to be suspended and was probably sold at a public auction.

Sources: Arndt/Olson; Wittke, *Against the Current*, pp. 87-88; On Heinzen, see *Der Pionier.*

NEW YORKER VOLKSZEITUNG		NY New York	1878-1932

Title trans.:	New York People's Journal	*First issue:*	28 Ja 1878
Subtitle:	Den Interessen des arbeitenden Volkes gewidmet	*Last issue:*	12 O 1932
Add. lang.:		*Vols. (nos.):*	1 (1)-55(245)
First editor:	Alexander Jonas	*Frequency:*	d
First publ.:	Socialistic Co-operative Publ. Society	*Preservation:*	1
Related pubs.:	s *Neue Volkszeitung, Pionier*	*Supplements:*	see below
Circulation:	see Introduction	*Category:*	socialist

Depositories: Usa-NIC (1878-1900); Usa-KyU (1878-1932); Usa-DLC (Jl 1881-88); D-188/144 (N 1878-1932, m)

Subtitle translation: Dedicated to the Interests of the Working People.

This was the official organ of the SLP and of many socialist groups, trade unions, workers' beneficial organizations and workers' clubs. (See e.g. list of 92 separate organizations in the issue of 21 February 1903). The editors-in-chief were Alexander Jonas* (1878-1889), Sergius Schewitsch* (1890), Julius Grunzig (1890-1891), Hermann Schlüter* (1891-1919), Ludwig Lore* (1919-1931) and Siegfried Lipschitz (1931-1932). On the board of editors at different times were Alexander Jonas* (1878-1912), Sergius Schewitsch (after 1878), Adolf Douai* (1878-1888), Jacob L. Franz* (1882-1896), John Schäfer, Carl Schneppe, Rudolf Gregorovius, Julius von Briesen, Otto Reimer, Georg Winter, Julius Vahlteich* (1901-1908), Robert Degen, John Grunzig (until 1919), Joseph Holler and Ludwig Lore* (1905-1931).

The women's page was edited by Johanna Greie-Kramer, Meta Stern, Julie Romm (until 1919), Lily Lore (see article by Lily Lore in the issue of 29 January 1928). It was published by the Socialistic Co-operative Publishing Association (see article in the issue of 21 February 1903).

The *NY Volkszeitung* contained news of current American and international events, selected and commented upon from a socialist point of view, reports and announcements from the organizations of which it was the official organ, a women's page, human-interest stories, short stories, serialized novels, poems, jokes and advertisements. It was illustrated.

Of great value to the history of socialism and the labor movement are the jubilee editions, especially the 25th and 50th anniversary issues of 21 February 1903 and 29 January 1928. They contain articles on the history of the *NY Volkszeitung*, on the German-American labor press (the most important being Hermann Schlüter's "Anfänge der Arbeiterpresse" [Beginnings of the Labor Press] in the issue of 21 February 1903). Labor unions and socialist organizations, progressive gymnastics and choral societies as well as workers' beneficial organizations contributed articles describing themselves. Other jubilee editions marked the 10th anniversary on 28 January 1888, the 20th on 13 February 1898, the 30th on 23 February 1908 and the 40th on 22 February 1918.

Since it was the organ of so many labor organizations, the history of the *NY Volkszeitung* was a history of conflicts of principles: the socialist principle of attaining political power and social change by means of elections, the anarchist principle, which was in itself divided into the moderate and the bomb-faction and the purely economic demands of trade unionism. The *NY*

Volkszeitung was frequently attacked by the diverse factions because it tried to cover the whole socialist and labor spectrum (with the exception of radical anarchism) and did not affiliate with any faction in particular.

During World War One the paper opposed Germany's imperialistic policy and accused the Kaiser of having started the war, but opposed the American war declaration and refused to let the paper carry advertisements for Liberty Bonds - the only German-American paper to take such a stand. The government never seriously interfered with its publication.

When Lipschitz became editor-in-chief in 1931, the paper was reorganized and endorsed by the Socialist Parties of America and Germany (*New York Times*, 12 October 1932, p. 5).

The following is known about working conditions in the early days of the paper's history: in 1883 the printing shop of the *NY Volkszeitung* was already the second largest in New York, employing 300 typesetters, all union members, who worked 10 hours a day. The staff often voluntarily contributed parts of their wages to support the paper. The office was run according to statutes which were considered a model ("a little republic") in its time: hiring and dismissal were controlled jointly by foremen and staff. However, the sanitary conditions were unsatisfactory: the composing-room was badly ventilated and dirty. (*BZ* 1 F 1883)

Among the authors whose works were published were Friedrich Spielhagen, Marie von Bunsen, Frank Norris, Rudyard Kipling, Georgi Plechanow, Wilhelm Liebknecht, Theodor Storm, Guy de Maupassant, Hermann Sundermann, Käthe Duncker, August Strindberg, Thomas Mann, Robert Reitzel, Ernest Poole, Alfred Polgar, Else Jerusalem, Berhard Shaw, Alfred Kerr, Selma Lagerlöf, Klara Zetkin and Leon Trotzki.

The *NY Volkszeitung* was discontinued in 1932 because of financial difficulties. It was continued the same year by the *Neue Volkszeitung*.

Sources: Arndt/Olson; Arndt/Olson 2, pp. 480-482; Eberlein 22842; Marx/Engels, *Werke* XXXVI, p. 882, XXXVII, p. 629, XXXVIII, p. 677, XXXIX, p. 643; *BZ* 1 F 1883, 16 Jl 1890, 1 Mr and 16 Ag 1893, 16 Ap 1899. See also jubilee editions of *NY Volkszeitung*, esp. of 21 F 1903 and of 29 Ja 1928. On Jonas, see Marx/Engels, *Werke* XXXVI, p. 904 and XXXVII, p. 651; obituary in *NY Volkszeitung* 4 F 1912. On Schewitsch, see obituary in *NY Volkszeitung Sonntagsblatt* of 8 O 1911. On Schlüter, see *Geschichte der deutschen Arbeiterbewegung*, pp. 399-400; Marx/Engels, *Werke* XXXVII, p. 663, XXXVIII, p. 707, XXXIX, p. 678; obituary in *New Yorker Volkszeitung* 27 Ja 1919. On Vahlteich, see *Geschichte der deutschen Arbeiterbewegung*, pp. 464-466; Marx/Engels, *Werke* XXXIV, p. 683; obituaries in St. Louis *Arbeiterzeitung* and Cleveland *Echo* of 6 March 1915. On Lore, see DeLeon, p. 140; obituary in *New York Times* 9 Jl 1942, p. 21. On Douai, see *San Antonio Zeitung*. On Grottkau, see Chicago *Vorbote*. On Franz, see Philadelphia *Tageblatt*.

Sonntagsblatt der New Yorker Volkszeitung [Sunday Edition] 3 February(?) 1878 - 9 October 1932. This was the Sunday edition of the *NY Volkszeitung*. It was set in rotation by the regular staff of the *NY Volkszeitung* (*BZ* 1 F 1883). Circulation: 1880: 7500; 1890: 18,460; 1900: 20,000; 1905: 28,950; 1910: 22,500; 1915: 20,000, 1930: 20,000. It had 12- 20 pages. Initially it had one section, later two sections, Section II in octavo, entitled: "Für Unterhaltung und Wissen" [For Entertainment and Knowledge]. It contained political news, reports from trade unions, socialist organizations and clubs, news from Germany, poems, scientific articles, cartoons, jokes, a young people's page, a women's page, obituaries and advertisements.

Authors published included Ernst von Wolzogen, Ludwig Thoma, Emile Zola, Maurice Maeterlinck, Hanns Heinz Ewers, Schalom Asch, Anatole France; serialized versions of Paul Heyse's "Zwei Gefangene" [Two Prisoners], Leopold Ritter von Sacher-Masoch's "Der neue Hiob" [The New Job], Stephan Zweig's "Die Gouvernante" [The Governess].
Depositories: Usa-ICJ [My 1897-Je 1902]; Usa-NN [1894- 1932] (bound with daily edition).
Source: Arndt/Olson.
Wochenblatt der New Yorker Volkszeitung [Weekly Edition]: See *Vorwärts, Wochenblatt der New Yorker Volkszeitung.*
Pionier: this was the almanac of the *NY Volkszeitung.* It appeared annually from 1881-1933? There were 120 pages in the issue of 1928. The subtitle was: Illustrierter Volkskalender [Illustrated People's Almanac]. It contained a calendar, synoptical tables for weights and measures, postal rates, historical and biographical dates, legal advice and "plenty of interesting and entertaining reading matter appealing to the mind, heart, soul and imagination of the workers" (*BZ* 1 D 1896). It was illustrated. The issue for 1886 contained a biography of Adolf Douai, the issue for 1908 an article on Friedrich Adolph Sorge. Contributors were Julia Romm, Edna Fern, Hermann Schlüter, Arno Holz, Clara Runge and many others. Depositories: Usa-WHi(?); Nl-IISG(?); D-19/1501 (1882-1919, m).
Sources: Advertisements e.g. in *BZ* 1 D 1896 (for issue for 1897); 1 O 1907 (for 1908); 16 N 1909 (for 1910); *New Yorker Volkszeitung* 12 O 1932 (for 1933, with table of contents - last reference found).

NEWARKER POST	NJ Newark	1874-1875

Title trans.:	Newark Post	*First issue:*	? O 1874
Subtitle:		*Last issue:*	? My 1875
Add. lang.:		*Vols. (nos.):*	
First editor:	Charles Hermann Boppe	*Frequency:*	d
First publ.:	Kaufmann & Korn	*Preservation:*	7
Related pubs.:		*Supplements:*	Der Beobachter
Circulation:		*Category:*	

Depositories:

This lost daily which appeared in the morning except Sundays was, according to Arndt/Olson, "radical in character." On 7 December 1874 it was taken over by the German-English Printing Association. *Der Beobachter*, its Sunday edition, appeared from 1874? to 1875?.
Source: Arndt/Olson.

NEWARKER ZEITUNG	NJ Newark	1849?-?

Title trans.:	Newark Journal	*First issue:*	1849?
Subtitle:		*Last issue:*	?
Add. lang.:		*Vols. (nos.):*	
First editor:	Fritz and Mathilde Anneke	*Frequency:*	
First publ.:		*Preservation:*	6
Related pubs.:	*New Jersey Zeitung* ?	*Supplements:*	
Circulation:		*Category:*	workers' club

Depositories: Gb-BM [1858, single issue]

Information concerning the beginning, the political tendency and related publications is incomplete and inconsistent. Arndt/Olson give 1849?-? as date, but mention that vol. 6 appeared in 1858. Eberlein mentions 9 February 1853 as the date of the first issue. Cazden concurs in respect to the date, but says that the *Newarker Zeitung* made its debut on this date as the *New Jersey Zeitung* (see there).

The New York *Die Reform* of 11 May 1853 mentions that the *Newarker Zeitung* had become the organ of the New Jersey Branch of the Deutsch-amerikanischer Arbeiter-Bund. It was edited by Fritz Anneke* and Mathilde Anneke*. Because of lack of prima facie evidence, Fritz Anneke has been associated with almost every conceivable radical position. To quote Cazden: "Wittke groups him with the utopian communists in contrast to the marxists; Obermann states that Anneke supported his old friend Weydemeyer's 'Amerikanischer Arbeiterbund' and even organized a New Jersey branch under the motto "Workers shall become a political power;" Kamman suggests that Anneke's paper supported Wilhelm Weitling; and finally Schlüter lists Anneke as a very active member of the "third" New York 'Arbeiterbund'of 1858."

Sources: Arndt/Olson; Eberlein 22872; Wittke, *Refugees*, p. 171; Obermann, *Lebensbild*, p. 300; Kamman, p. 42; Schlüter, *Anfänge*, p. 168; Cazden, *Book Trade*, pp. (645) and (665), note 126. On Mathilde Anneke, see Schem I, pp. 520-521; Zucker, pp. 272-273; Dobert, pp. 24-25; Maria Wagner, *Mathilde Franziska Anneke in Selbstzeugnissen und Dokumenten* (Frankfurt/Main, 1980); Krueger; On Fritz Anneke, see Schem I, p. 520; Zucker, p. 372; Dobert, pp. 22-23; Miller, pp. 59-62; Bruce Levine, "Immigrant Workers, 'Equal Rights' and Anti-Slavery: The Germans of Newark, New Jersey," *Labor History* 25 (Winter 1984), pp. 23-52.

ÖSTERREICHISCHE RUNDSCHAU	NY New York	1942-1945

Title trans.:	Austrian Review	*First issue:*	F 1942
Subtitle:	Mitteilungsblatt der Austrian Action, angeschlossen dem Österreichischen National-Ausschuß	*Last issue:*	My 1945
Add. lang.:	English	*Vols. (nos.):*	
First editor:		*Frequency:*	m?/ir
First publ.:	Austrian Action	*Preservation:*	5?
Related pubs.:		*Supplements:*	
Circulation:		*Category:*	antifascist

Depositories: D-Bm 41/IGA [1942-43]

Subtitle translation: Bulletin of the Austrian Action, affiliated to the Austrian National Committee.

This was a non-partisan anti-Nazi bulletin and the organ of Austrian Action. It was published in English and German and contained 8-12 pages. The motto of Austrian Action was: "Against Nazi Tyranny and Totalitarian Oppression. For Democracy, Justice, Tolerance, Liberty." It contained news from the Austrian Action and its cultural branch and from the National Committee, articles on legal problems of immigration and naturalization and concentration camps in Austria. Announcements included lists of branches of the Austrian Action in the United States and South America and situations wanted by unemployed Austrians.

Source: Cazden, *Exile Literature*, pp. 67-68.

OHIO STAATSZEITUNG	OH Columbus	1853-?

Title trans.:	Ohio State News	*First issue:*	? 1853
Subtitle:		*Last issue:*	?
Add. lang.:		*Vols. (nos.):*	
First editor:		*Frequency:*	
First publ.:		*Preservation:*	7
Related pubs.:		*Supplements:*	
Circulation:		*Category:*	workers' club

Depositories:

According to Wittke, "in 1853 a newly organized "Arbeiterverein" of Columbus, OH, optimistically assumed that a labor paper, known as the *Ohio Staatszeitung* could be maintained by merely assessing each member ten cents for its support."

Sources: Eberlein 22796; Wittke, *Press*, pp. 171-172.

OHIO VOLKSZEITUNG   OH Cincinnati   1876-1878?

Title trans.:	Ohio People's News	*First issue:*	? 1876
Subtitle:		*Last issue:*	1878 ?
Add. lang.:		*Vols. (nos.):*	
First editor:	Heinrich von Ende	*Frequency:*	d
First publ.:	Heinrich von Ende	*Preservation:*	7
Related pubs.:		*Supplements:*	
Circulation:		*Category:*	socialist-SLP

Depositories:

This morning daily supported the Socialistische Arbeiter Partei [Socialist Labor Party]. In July 1878 its typesetters were criticized because they did not join Typographia No. 2 of Cincinnati.

Sources: Arndt/Olson; *BZ* 15 Jl 1878.

THE PAINTER   NY New York   1893-1900?

Title trans.:		*First issue:*	Je 1893
Subtitle:		*Last issue:*	1900?
Add. lang.:	English	*Vols. (nos.):*	
First editor:		*Frequency:*	bw
First publ.:	German Painters' Union of New York	*Preservation:*	6
Related pubs.:		*Supplements:*	
Circulation:		*Category:*	labor union

Depositories: Usa-WHi [1896-97]; D-188/144 [1896-97,m]

This was a biweeekly labor union journal published largely in German (set in Gothic) with some English text. It had 4 pages. On the left side of the title an oval-shaped emblem showed the painters' insignia: a palette with a bundle of brushes and a paper scroll; at the bottom a spread eagle. The paper contained news of the German Painter's Union and of other unions, articles of general interest, e.g. on genetics, moral issues and political subjects like current elections. The last page contained advertisements and announcements of meetings.

Sources: Arndt/Olson. On the history of the Painters' Union see Fink, *Labor Unions*, pp. 271-274; "Amalgamated Painters and Decorators," *New Yorker Volkszeitung* 21 F 1903.

DIE PAROLE   MO St. Louis   1884-1891?

Title trans.:	The Parole	*First issue:*	(Ja) 1884
Subtitle:	Den Interessen der Lohnarbeiter gewidmet	*Last issue:*	1891 ?
Add. lang.:		*Vols. (nos.):*	1-3?
First editor:	Joseph J. Reifgraber	*Frequency:*	m, w
First publ.:	Internationale Arbeiter Association, Foederation St. Louis	*Preservation:*	4?
Related pubs.:		*Supplements:*	
Circulation:	1884-1885: 2000; 1888: 2200; 1890: 1600	*Category:*	anarchist-IWPA

Lib. code: title translation: Dedicated to the Interests of the Wage kers.
Depositories: Usa-WHi [1884-86]; D-188/144 [1884-86,m)

This paper contained 4 pages and appeared monthly from 1844-85, weekly from 2 January 1886-1891? The motto after August 1884 was "Gleiche Pflichten, gleiche Rechte. Keine Herren, keine Knechte" [Equal Duties, Equal Rights. No Lords, No Serfs].

It was edited by Joseph Reifgraber (Arndt/Olson incorrectly: Reifgräber) until June 1884, E. Lange (July 1884 - April 1885), F.W. Wendt (May 1885 - June 1885), A. Mayer (July 1885 - November 1885), Claus Timmermann (December 1885), J.J. Reifgraber and Claus Timmermann (January 1886-?). Later publishers were the Literarischer Club der Internationalen Arbeiter Association von St. Louis (July 1884-1886) and the Workingmen's Publishing Association (1890-91). It developed from a poorly printed leaflet which contained mostly polemics against other newspapers such as the *New Yorker Volkszeitung* and the *New Jersey Arbeiterzeitung* into a well-edited paper which covered international news and news of local unions. It reprinted serialized novels, e.g. Friedrich Hassaurek's "Hierarchie und Aristokratie" and supported Johann Most, the radical Metal Workers' Union and their organ, *Der Hammer*. It published translations from the French anarchist paper *La Révolte* and the English-language *Alarm*, announcements of IWPA-festivities, meetings of the Central Labor Union, advertisements for national and international anarchist publications and some local businesses. Contributors included Max Nordau and Joseph Mostler (see *Freiheit*).

Sources: Arndt/Olson; Eberlein 22759.

PIANO, ORGAN ...   IL Chicago   1899-1911

Title trans.:		*First issue:*	Ja 1899
Subtitle:		*Last issue:*	D 1911
Add. lang.:	German, Swedish, Italian	*Vols. (nos.):*	
First editor:	Charles Dold	*Frequency:*	m
First publ.:	Piano, Organ and Musical Workers' Union	*Preservation:*	1
Related pubs.:		*Supplements:*	
Circulation:		*Category:*	labor union

Depositories: Usa-MH-PA (1903-11?); Usa-WHi [1901-11]; Usa-IU [1903-11]

The complete title of the paper was: *Piano, Organ and Musical Instrument Workers' Official Journal*

Founded in English only, in 1904 an abortive attempt was made to include foreign-language sections in German and Polish. An Italian section was introduced with the issue of February 1906, a German section with the issue of March 1906 and a Swedish section with the issue of April 1906. These sections were maintained until the paper's suspension in December 1911. They consisted mostly of two pages and contained translations of the most important English articles which were mainly reports of meetings of the Executive Board.

Source: Naas/Sakr, p. 86.

DER PIONIER   MA Boston   1854-1879

Title trans.:	The Pioneer	*First issue:*	3 Ja 1854
Subtitle:		*Last issue:*	1879
Add. lang.:		*Vols. (nos.):*	1-26
First editor:	Karl Heinzen	*Frequency:*	w
First publ.:	Karl Heinzen	*Preservation:*	2-3
Related pubs.:	m *Freidenker*	*Supplements:*	
Circulation:	1870: 1100-1200 (according to *Pionier* 4 Ja 1871)	*Category:*	radical fortyeighter

Depositories: Usa-MB ([1856]-1857,1861-74,1876,1878-79); Usa-NIC ([1867]-1879); Usa-MiU (almost complete)

The place of publication varied: Louisville, KY (January - October 1854), Cincinnati, OH (November 1854 - 18 June 1855), New York City (25 June 1855 - December 1858), from then on, Boston, MA. Deputy editors were Georg Schlumm (July - September 1874) and Heinrich Ende (during Heinzen's absence in Europe).

Like all Heinzen's newspapers, the *Pionier*, his most longlived and successful paper, was filled with highly personal journalism. It contained foreign news and featured all anniversaries related to the revolutionary movement the world over, especially those of Germany and the United States. The most important features were Heinzen's editorials, scientific articles, e.g. on evolution, diet, spiritualism, astronomy, anthropology, biology, geography as well as features, poems, bibliographies of German-American books and periodicals, music criticism and humorous pieces. There were contributions and reprints from Georg Herwegh, Ferdinand Freiligrath, Michelet, Louis Blanc, Harriet Beecher Stowe and classical authors like Johann Wolfgang Goethe, Friedrich Schiller, Charles Dickens and Percy Bysshe Shelley.

It merged with the Milwaukee *Freidenker* in January 1880 under the title: *Der Freidenker: Der Pionier XXVII Jahrgang.*

Sources: Arndt/Olson; Arndt/Olson 2, pp. 403-404; Wittke, *Against the Current*, pp. 107-110; Mueller, p. 191. On Heinzen, see Schem V, pp. 247-249; Wittke, *Against the Current*; Wittke, *Press*, pp. 121-126; Zucker, pp. 302-303; Dobert, pp. 105-116; Friesen, Katherine und Gerhard K. Friesen, "Karl Heinzen's German-American Writings: Some Literary Aspects," in *German-American Studies* VII (1974), pp. 107-129; Creagh 1107-1108; Miller pp.67-72; Hans Huber, *Karl Heinzen (1809-1880). Seine politische Entwicklung und publizistische Wirksamkeit* [Karl Heinzen. His Political Development and Journalistic Activities] (Bern and Leipzig 1932); Karl Marx, "Die moralisierende Kritik und die kritisierende Moral. Beitrag zur deutschen Kulturgeschichte. Gegen Karl Heinzen von Karl Marx" [The Moralizing Criticism and Criticizing Morality. A Contribution to German Cultural History. Against Karl Heinzen by Karl Marx]. Marx/Engels, *Werke* IV, pp. 331-359 (repr. from *Deutsche Brüsseler Zeitung* No. 86, 28 O 1847).

PROGRESS	NY New York	1882-1885

Title trans.:	Progress	*First issue:*	Ag 1882
Subtitle:		*Last issue:*	16 D 1885
Add. lang.:	English, Czech	*Vols. (nos.):*	1(1)-4(5)
First editor:	A. Lange	*Frequency:*	m
First publ.:	A. Lange	*Preservation:*	1
Related pubs.:		*Supplements:*	
Circulation:		*Category:*	labor union

Depositories: Usa-HU; D-188/144(1,m)

This paper initially had 4 pages, after 1884 8 pages. The editor after Lange was Frederic Haller. The motto varied. It was the organ of the Cigarmakers' Progressive Union of America founded on 17 July 1882 by opponents of the leadership of the Cigarmakers' International Union (see *Cigarmakers' Official Journal*). These opponents were mostly German cigarmakers forced out of Germany by the antisocialist laws. Dissatisfied with the bread and butter unionism of the Cigarmakers' International Union, the Progressive Union wanted to abolish the wage system. They lowered the dues and admitted tenement workers.

It contained articles on union alliances such as the Amalgamated Trade and Labor Union, the Central Labor Union and the Knights of Labor. With the latter they cooperated for a time. Other subjects were labor legislation and the introduction of machines in the cigarmaking industry. Regular features were "On the State of Industry," financial reports, obituaries of deceased members, reports of locals, black lists of shops and newspapers to be boycotted by union members. Working conditions in its printing office, Wetzel & Co., were approved by the *Buchdrucker-Zeitung* as being bright, airy and spacious. (*BZ* 15 Ap 1883) The last issue of December 1885 contains no indication of the journal's discontinuation.

Sources: Arndt/Olson. On the Cigarmakers' Progressive Union, see Fink, *Labor Unions*, pp. 56-57; Ware, pp. 271-274; Foner, *History I*, pp. 517-518; *New Yorker Volkszeitung* 21 F 1903; *BZ* 1 and 15 Ag 1883.

DER PROLETARIER		IL Chicago	1853-?

Title trans.:	The Proletarian	*First issue:*	? 1853
Subtitle:		*Last issue:*	?
Add. lang.:		*Vols. (nos.):*	
First editor:	H. Rösch	*Frequency:*	w
First publ.:	H. Rösch	*Preservation:*	7
Related pubs.:		*Supplements:*	
Circulation:		*Category:*	socialist

Depositories:

This lost weekly is said to be one of the earliest socialist papers in Chicago. Another editor was J. Karlen, who had formerly edited *Der Unabhängige* [The Independent] in Bern, Switzerland

Sources: Arndt/Olsen; Arndt/Olsen 2; Eberlein 22768; Cazden, *Book Trade*, p. (644); Wittke, *Press*, p. 111.

PROTECTION		NJ Newark	1884

Title trans.:	Protection	*First issue:*	? 1884
Subtitle:		*Last issue:*	1884?
Add. lang.:		*Vols. (nos.):*	
First editor:		*Frequency:*	bw
First publ.:		*Preservation:*	7
Related pubs.:		*Supplements:*	
Circulation:		*Category:*	labor union-KofL

Depositories:

This lost biweekly was an organ of the Knights of Labor.

Sources: Arndt/Olson

DER RADIKALE	MO St. Louis	1864-?

Title trans.:	The Radical	*First issue:*	1864?
Subtitle:		*Last issue:*	?
Add. lang.:		*Vols. (nos.):*	
First editor:	John Hartman	*Frequency:*	
First publ.:	John Hartman	*Preservation:*	7
Related pubs.:		*Supplements:*	
Circulation:		*Category:*	

Depositories:

No further information could be obtained.
Source: Arndt/Olson.

DIE REFORM	MD Baltimore	1850-?

Title trans.:	Reform	*First issue:*	1 Je 1850
Subtitle:		*Last issue:*	?
Add. lang.:		*Vols. (nos.):*	1(1)-?
First editor:		*Frequency:*	
First publ.:	Arbeiter-Association Baltimores	*Preservation:*	7
Related pubs.:		*Supplements:*	
Circulation:		*Category:*	workers' club

Depositories:

Schlüter and Kamman only mention the existence of this paper. No further details could be found. The jubilee issue of the *New Yorker Volkszeitung*, 21 February 1903, gives a small facsimile of one issue.
Sources: Arndt/Olson; Eberlein 22770; Schlüter, "Presse," p. 9.

DIE REFORM	NY New York	1853-1854

Title trans.:	Reform	*First issue:*	5 Mr 1853
Subtitle:		*Last issue:*	26 Ap 1854//
Add. lang.:		*Vols. (nos.):*	1(1)-2(?)
First editor:	Gottlieb Theodor Kellner	*Frequency:*	w, sw, d
First publ.:	Carl Friedrich	*Preservation:*	3
Related pubs.:		*Supplements:*	Belletristisches Sonntagsblatt
Circulation:		*Category:*	workers' club

Depositories: Usa-WHi [1853]; D-188/144 [1853,m]

The organ of the New Yorker Arbeiterbund appeared weekly from 5 March to 3o April 1853, semiweekly from 4 May to 12 October 1853; from 15 October 1853 to 26 April 1854 it was a daily. After 2 January 1854 the daily editions as well as the supplement *Belletristisches Sonntagsblatt* were not available. It was edited by Kellner*, (5 March - December 1853) and by Joseph Weydemeyer* (1854?) and published by Friedrich, by Friedrich and Kellner (after 15 October 1853) and then by a stock company (10 March - 26 April 1854).

Die Reform has been called the most important among all socialist newspapers founded by German refugees of the 1848 revolution. It dealt with the labor movement and its desirable political influence, economic and political problems and developments in America, Europe (especially England and Germany) and Asia; it contained criticism of social conditions, e.g. series on the seamstresses and on the barbers of New York; other topics were the Gymnasts' movement, American diplomacy, the exhibition at the Crystal Palace in London, serialized novels, e.g. "Auswanderer" [Emigrants] by Talvj (pen-name of Mrs. Robinson) and some poems. Two of its four pages consisted of advertisements, mostly for small or middle-sized local enterprises. Among the contributors were Adolph Cluß, Abraham Jacobi and other friends and pupils of Karl Marx.

Sources: Arndt/Olson; Arndt/Olson 2, p. 466; Schlüter, *Anfänge*, pp. 148-15; Obermann, *Pioneer*, pp. 70-77; Kamman, p. 41; Cazden, *Book Trade*, p. (638). On Kellner, see Schem VI, p. 140; Ernst, p. 119; Zucker, pp. 309-310; Marx/Engels, *Werke* XXVIII, p. 589. On Weydemeyer, see *Stimme des Volkes*.

DER REFORMER	MO St. Louis	1847-?

Title trans.:	The Reformer	*First issue:*	2 Ja 1847
Subtitle:		*Last issue:*	?
Add. lang.:	Heinrich Koch	*Vols. (nos.):*	
First editor:	Heinrich Koch	*Frequency:*	w
First publ.:		*Preservation:*	7
Related pubs.:		*Supplements:*	
Circulation:		*Category:*	reform

Depositories:

Der Reformer, a radical progressive weekly, was the organ of the Communist Club of St. Louis, which backed Herman Kriege's conception of communism and land reform. According to Kamman, the Club lost many of its members because of Koch's domineering attitude. Born in Bayreuth, Germany, Koch, a watchmaker, spent some time in jail for his political views and came to the United States in 1832. Schlüter reports that Koch had been influenced by the ideas of Fourier, that his ideas about communism were vague but his influence among German workers in the West was not inconsiderable. He had previously published the *Antipfaff* [Anti-Priest] in St. Louis (1842-45), which later merged with the socialist *Vorwärts*. According to Körner, he was one of the earliest to espouse communism in St. Louis. He later became a member of the communist cooperative "Communia" in Iowa, which joined Weitling's Arbeiterbund. Koch died in 1879 in Dubuque, Iowa.

Sources: Arndt/Olson; Eberlein 22772; Wittke, *Press*, pp. 107, 111; Kamman, p. 35; Schlüter, *Anfänge*, pp. 19, 46; Koerner, pp. 323, 337; Schlüter, "Presse," p. 9; Cazden, *Book Trade*, pp (622, 636).

DER REFORMER   WI Milwaukee   1880-1906

Title trans.:	The Reformer	*First issue:*	? Ja 1880
Subtitle:		*Last issue:*	1906
Add. lang.:		*Vols. (nos.):*	
First editor:	Robert Schilling	*Frequency:*	w, d
First publ.:	Milwaukee Trades Assembly	*Preservation:*	7
Related pubs.:	m *Milwaukee'r Arbeiterzeitung*, s	*Supplements:*	*Milwaukee*
	Volkszeitung (Milwaukee)		*Volksblatt*
Circulation:	1887: 2064; 1895: 3320; 1900: 1980	*Category:*	labor

Depositories:

This paper started as the weekly *Der National Reformer*, which mostly contained contemporary and labor news. It "often discussed the working man's right to earn a fair wage for his work and, although violence was not condoned, the paper supported the right to strike if mediation and labor talks failed." (Knoche)

In 1886 the Knights of Labor Printing Company was formed, headed by Schilling*. Probably at the same time the *Täglicher Reformer* [The Daily Reformer] was added. In January 1890 Schilling sold the *Täglicher Reformer* to the Socialistic Publishing Society, which amalgamated it with its own *Milwaukee'r Arbeiterzeitung* to form a new daily, the Milwaukee *Volkszeitung*. Schilling retained the *National Reformer* as a weekly. In 1889 the *Reformer* introduced the eight-hour week in its office.

For the Sunday edition, see Milwaukee *Volksblatt*

Sources: Arndt/Olson; *BZ* 1 Ja 1889; Knoche, pp. 211-213.

REPUBLIK DER ARBEITER   NY New York   1850-1855

Title trans.:	Republic of the Workers	*First issue:*	15 Ja 1850
Subtitle:	Centralblatt für die Verbrüderung der	*Last issue:*	21 Je 1855
	Arbeiter		
Add. lang.:		*Vols. (nos.):*	1 (1)-6 (4)
First editor:	Wilhelm Weitling	*Frequency:*	m, w, m
First publ.:	Arbeiterbund	*Preservation:*	1
Related pubs.:		*Supplements:*	
Circulation:	Ja 1850: 950; D 1850: 4000	*Category:*	early
			socialist

Depositories: Usa-NN; Usa-WHi; D-Bm 41/IGA; D-46; D-188/144 (1,m)

The paper appeared monthly from January 1850 to March 1851, weekly from April 1851 to December 1854 and monthly in 1855. On the title page is represented a balance on one tray of which are the words "Pflichten und Arbeiten" [Duties and Tasks], on the other "Rechte und Genüsse" [Rights and Pleasure]. On 18 April 1851 the subtitle "Organ of the Brotherhood of Workers" was added.

The prospectus for the paper was addressed to both employers and workers. "The ultimate goal of the *Republik der Arbeiter* was the bank of exchange, cooperative stores and warehouses, a new currency based on the amount of labor involved in services and production for society, and the founding of a colony where the theories of the philosophical tailor could be demonstrated to the world. Weitling wanted basic revolutionary changes, not mere palliatives." (Wittke, *Press*, p. 118) Many articles were written by Weitling* himself on such topics as "Value," "Capital and Interest," "Property," and "Inheritance." It reprinted extensively from Esselen's *Atlantis* and Fritz Anneke's papers and reported on communitarian colonies in the United States and on reform movements elsewhere.

According to Arndt/Olsen, the paper started with a capital of $1.50. Weitling went from house to house and in 4 days found 400 subscribers. Schlüter mentions that in early 1850 Weitling planned an *Abendzeitung der Republik der Arbeiter* [Evening Paper] edited by a German printers' association as a daily socialist worker's paper. This plan never materialized.

Sources: Arndt/Olson; Eberlein 22776; Schlüter, *Anfänge*, pp. 69-79; Wittke, *Press*, pp. 116-121; Harnack, pp. 153-157; Kamman, p. 39; Foner, *History* I, p. 228. On Weitling, see Ernst, pp. 114-117; Miller, pp. 72-77; Sorge, pp. 88-94; Zucker, p. 353; *Geschichte der deutschen Arbeiterbewegung*, pp. 474-477; Wittke, "Wilhelm Weitling's Literary Efforts," *Monatshefte* 40,2 (1948), pp. 63-68; Wittke, *The Utopian Communist*; Marx/Engels, *Werke* XXXIV p. 685, XXXVII p. 669.

DIE REVOLUTION (I)	NY New York	1852

Title trans.:	The Revolution	*First issue:*		6 Ja 1852
Subtitle:		*Last issue:*		13 Ja 1852
Add. lang.:		*Vols. (nos.):*		1 (1-2)
First editor:	Joseph Weydemeyer	*Frequency:*		w
First publ.:	Joseph Weydemeyer	*Preservation:*		6
Related pubs.:	Die Revolution (monthly)	*Supplements:*		
Circulation:	Ja 1852: 400	*Category:*		socialist

Depositories: Usa-privat collection of F. B. Adams, New York (Obermann)

Joseph Weydemeyer* started this weekly one month after he had come to America. Seven hundred subscribers were needed to cover the costs of a German weekly, but at its start, the *Revolution* had only four hundred who had been taken from the expiring *Lucifer* in January 1852. Die *Revolution* only appeared twice. The response among German immigrants was too small to sustain a Marxist weekly. Weydemeyer wrote to Marx at the end of January: "Most [of the German workers here] are asinine enough to contribute a dollar for this hostile propaganda [i.e. Kinkel and Kossuth] rather than a penny for the expression of their own interests. The American soil has a most corrupting effect on people and at the same time fills them with arrogance, as if they were far superior to their comrades in the Old World." (Herreshoff) An advertisement in the New York *Turn-Zeitung* of New Year's Day, 1852, names K. Marx, F. Engels and F. Freiligrath as contributors. After the weekly had failed, Weydemeyer started a monthly with the same title in the spring of 1852 (see there).

Note: In contrast to the other sources, Schlüter says that the project of the weekly *Revolution* failed and that it never appeared.

Sources: Arndt/Olson: Arndt/Olson 2, p. 466; Eberlein 22778; Herreshoff, p. 59; Obermann, *Pioneer*, pp. 37ff; Cazden, *Book Trade*, p. (638); Schlüter, "Presse," p. 9; Sorge, p. 95. See also Karl Marx' letters to Weydemeyer in 1852, in Marx/Engels, *Werke* XXVIII. On Weydemeyer, see *Stimme des Volkes*.

DIE REVOLUTION (II)		NY New York	1852
Title trans.:	The Revolution	*First issue:*	1 My 1852
Subtitle:	Eine Zeitschrift in zwanglosen Heften	*Last issue:*	June? 1852
Add. lang.:		*Vols. (nos.):*	no 1-2
First editor:	Joseph Weydemeyer	*Frequency:*	m
First publ.:	Joseph Weydemeyer	*Preservation:*	7
Related pubs.:	*Die Revolution* (I)	*Supplements:*	
Circulation:		*Category:*	socialist

Depositories:

Subtitle translation: A Periodical Appearing in Occasional Numbers.

This monthly successor to the weekly *Revolution* also closed down after two issues. The second issue is of special significance because in it the "18. Brumaire des Louis Napoleon" by Karl Marx was first published.

Sources: Arndt/Olson; Eberlein 22779; Schlüter, *Anfänge* p. 159; Cazden, *Book Trade*, p. (645); Ernst, p. 118. On Weydemeyer, see *Stimme des Volkes*.

SÄNGER-ZEITUNG		NY New York	1924?-1944?
Title trans.:	Singers' Journal	*First issue:*	1924 ?
Subtitle:		*Last issue:*	1944 ?
Add. lang.:		*Vols. (nos.):*	
First editor:		*Frequency:*	m?, ir
First publ.:	National Konvention der Arbeiter-Sänger von Amerika	*Preservation:*	5
Related pubs.:		*Supplements:*	
Circulation:		*Category:*	socialist

Depositories: Usa-NN (1931,1942+); Usa-DLC (Ja-D 1942,1943)

This was the organ of the Arbeiter-Sänger von Amerika; it appeared monthly? or irregularly (Cazden). It was edited by emigre'" journalist Walther Victor in 1942 and by G. Schlenker (August 1943-1944?). It was published by the National Convention of Workingmen's Choirs in Chicago later in New York. The workingmen's choirs had a long tradition in the German and German-American labor movement. They sang traditional and revolutionary songs on the occasion of workers' festivities, e.g. jubilees or beneficial festivals of labor organizations.

Sources: Arndt/Olson; Cazden, *Exile Literature*, pp. 23, 186-187.

SAN ANTONIO ZEITUNG	TX San Antonio	1853-1856?

Title trans.:	San Antonio News	*First issue:*	5 Jl 1853
Subtitle:	see below	*Last issue:*	1856?
Add. lang.:	English	*Vols. (nos.):*	1(1-52)-3(1-38)
First editor:	Karl Daniel, Adolf Douai	*Frequency:*	w
First publ.:	"Aktiengesellschaft"	*Preservation:*	2
Related pubs.:		*Supplements:*	
Circulation:		*Category:*	radical fortyeighter

Depositories: Usa-Tx (1853-55,[1856])

The subtitle changed 1) Ein sozial-demokratisches Blatt für die Deutschen in West-Texas, herausgegeben unter Mitwirkung tüchtiger Kräfte von Adolf Douai [A social-democratic paper for the Germans in West Texas published by Adolf Douai and his able assistants] (5 July 1853-June 1854); 2) Ein belehrendes, unterhaltendes und Nachrichten-Blatt [An Educational and Entertaining Newspaper] (January 1856).

At first this paper was published by a stock company and edited by Douai*, then it was purchased by Douai and edited and published by him alone for a year longer; Douai then sold the paper and equipment to the Oswald Brothers.

It was mainly an abolitionist paper. Douai published antislavery editorials in English so that his principles could be read by Americans. This aroused hostility in the whole Texan press. The *Galveston News* of 12 June 1855 commented: "The *San Antonio Zeitung* has made itself notorious of late by attacking slavery. Several of the Texas papers have rapped it pretty hard for its temerity in attacking the institutions of the State, and some of them went so far as to suggest that a coat of tar and feathers would be a fit reward for the editor." Because of threats and riots Douai was forced to abandon his paper and go to the North. In New York he later edited the *Arbeiter-Union* and the *New Yorker Volkszeitung* (see there). Ten years later in 1866, Douai was sent the copy of a newspaper which was owned, edited and printed by Blacks in the same office where he had issued the *San Antonio Zeitung*. The black editors expressed their thanks to him for his fight for their freedom.

Sources: Arndt/Olson; McGrath, "Sister Paul of the Cross, Political Nativism in Texas, 1825-1860," Ph.D. diss., Washington, DC, 1930, pp. 93; Terry G. Jordan, *German Seeds in Texas Soil* (Austin, TX, 1966), pp. 181-82. On Douai, see Schlüter, *Internationale*, pp. 98-102; Hillquit, pp. 170-171; Sorge, pp. 154-155; Dobert, pp. 61-66; Zucker, pp. 288-289; Waltershausen, pp. 43-45; Schem III, pp. 745-746; "Aus dem Leben eines alten Sozialdemokraten" [From the Life of an Old Social Democrat] in *Pionier. Illustrierter Volkskalender für 1886* (publ. by *New Yorker Volkszeitung*); Marx/Engels, *Werke* XXXIV, p.655. Obituaries on Douai in *New Yorker Volkszeitung*, 28 Ja 1888; *BZ* 1 F 1888.

SATTLER UND WAGENBAUER	IL Chicago	1891?-1904?

Title trans.:	The Saddler and Wagon Maker	*First issue:*	1891?
Subtitle:		*Last issue:*	1904?
Add. lang.:		*Vols. (nos.):*	
First editor:	Maurice Weber	*Frequency:*	m
First publ.:	The Trade Publishing Co.	*Preservation:*	5
Related pubs.:	*Carriage and Wagon Workers' Journal*	*Supplements:*	
Circulation:		*Category:*	labor union

Depositories: Usa-DLC (1899-1904, see *Carriage and Wagon Workers' Journal*)

This was the organ of the Carriage and Wagon Workers' International Union of North America. It had 16-32 pages. The title varied: *Sattler Journal*, 1891-92. Sources: Arndt/Olson; Eberlein 22782, 22783.

SCHIFFAHRT	NY New York	1936-1939

Title trans.:	Navigation	*First issue:*	Ja/F 1936
Subtitle:	see below	*Last issue:*	Jl 1939
Add. lang.:		*Vols. (nos.):*	
First editor:		*Frequency:*	m, ir
First publ.:		*Preservation:*	3?
Related pubs.:		*Supplements:*	
Circulation:		*Category:*	communist/ labor union

Depositories: Usa-NN [1937-39]; D-292 [1936-38]

The subtitle changed a) Lesen - weitergeben [Read - Pass on], b) Organ des Gesamtverbandes der Arbeitnehmer der öffentlichen Betriebe. Sektion: Schiffahrt und anverwandte Betriebe [Organ of the Federal Association of Employees of Public Services, Branch: Navigation and Related Services]. This was a clandestine news bulletin aimed at members of the German seamen's trade union. Published for illegal distribution in Nazi Germany it was printed on very thin paper, so that it could be easily smuggled aboard ship. It had 12 pages in 1937, 4 pages in 1938-39. It was intended to appear monthly, but in fact was irregular and after 1937 without numbering. The date-line in 1937 was Hamburg, New York, Bremen. According to Bednarek, the circulation was 1000; *Schiffahrt* of February 1938 states that 4000 copies were read in New York harbor. The paper was for sale at most American harbors. It contained news from the Federal Association, reports from longshoremen and seamen, articles on the political situation in Germany and the Spanish Civil War as well as advice for resistance on board. There were contributions by Fritz Brügel, Heinrich Mann and Max Zimmering.

Sources: Arndt/Olson; Cazden, *Exile Literature*, p. 189; Maas II, p. 521; Horst Bednarek, *Gewerkschafter im Kampf gegen die Todfeinde der Arbeiterklasse und des deutschen Volkes* [Union Members fighting Against the Deadly Enemy of the Working Class and the German People] (Berlin/DDR 1966), p. 66.

DIE SOCIALE REPUBLIK	NY New York	1858-1860

Title trans.:	The Social Republic	*First issue:*	24 Ap 1858
Subtitle:	Organ der freien Arbeiter	*Last issue:*	26 My 1860//
Add. lang.:		*Vols. (nos.):*	1(1) - 3(5)
First editor:	Gustav Struve	*Frequency:*	w
First publ.:	Der Arbeiterbund in New York	*Preservation:*	1
Related pubs.:		*Supplements:*	
Circulation:		*Category:*	workers' club

Depositories: Usa-WHi; D-188/144 (1,m)

Subtitle translation: Organ of the Free Workers. With the issue of 18 February 1860 the subtitle changed to: "Freiheit, Gleichheit, Brüderlichkeit" [Liberty, Equality, Fraternity]

It was edited after Struve by Wilhelm Kopp, (12 February 1859 - 28 May 1860), and the executive committee of the Arbeiterbund [Workingmen's League] P. Rödel, Ph. Koch, D. Steinmetz, (12 February 1859 - 28 April 1860). It was published by the Allgemeiner Arbeiterbund der Vereinigten Staaten (12 February 1859 - 28 April 1860) and the Social-Reform-Club (5 May 1860 - 26 May 1860).

Die sociale Republik was the organ of the majority after the split in the Arbeiterbund in April 1858 (see also *Der Arbeiter*, New York, I). Its first editor, the famous Fortyeighter Gustav Struve, took over the printing machinery from Wilhelm Weitling's *Republik der Arbeiter*, which had been discontinued.

It contained news from the Arbeiterbund, reports from the old and the new world, local news, poems, articles on health and advice on problems of everyday life. The aim of Struve and of the Arbeiterbund was: "Wohlstand, Bildung, Freiheit für Alle" [Welfare, Education and Freedom for All]. The paper has been criticized as being vague and complacent, e.g. by Sorge, who commented: "There is very little in this paper about the position, the needs and efforts of the workers, but much about phrenology, the papacy, jurisprudence, preachers' tricks, Germandom, Alpine pictures and the like."

Occasionally the editor complained about how little echo the paper found among the workers. Time and again he and the publishers had to make financial contributions in order to maintain the newspaper. Financial difficulties made them at last give up *Die sociale Republik*.

There were contributions by Heinrich Heine, E. Cabet, H. Rau, Adolf Douai, T. Bracklow.

Sources: Arndt/Olson; Arndt/Olson 2, p. 470; Eberlein 22777, Sorge, pp. 96-97; Kamman, p. 43; Schlüter, *Anfänge*, pp. 170-71; Obermann, *Pioneer*, pp. 96-97. On Struve, see Schem X, p. 529.

DER SOCIALIST   WI Milwaukee   1875-1878

Title trans.:	The Socialist	*First issue:*	15 N 1875
Subtitle:		*Last issue:*	15 Ag 1878
Add. lang.:		*Vols. (nos.):*	
First editor:	Johann Joseph Brucker	*Frequency:*	d
First publ.:		*Preservation:*	2
Related pubs.:	s *Vorwärts*	*Supplements:*	see below
Circulation:	1878: 500 (est]	*Category:*	socialist-IWA

Depositories: Usa-WHi [1875-78]; D-19/1501 (1875-78,m)

This was the organ of Section 1 of the First International. Its editors were J.J. Brucker (15 November 1875-August 1878); Gustav Lyser (13-26 November 1875) and Hermann Sigel (August 1878). The title varied: it was called the *Milwaukee'r Socialist* from 1 November 1876.

This daily, which appeared in the evening except Sunday, "advocated progress, improvement of living conditions among the working class and the redistribution of private capital" (Knoche, p. 177). The paper was connected with the *Chicagoer Socialist* for a time, one being an evening, the other a morning paper; the set pages were transported to Chicago by train. In December 1876 because of financial difficulties some pages were taken over from the Banner and Volksfreund Printing Co. In January 1877 a cooperative printing association ("Genossenschaftsdruckerei") was founded for the *Socialist* and a social-democratic English-language paper (*BZ* 15 Ja 1877). Less than half a year later the "Genossenschaftsdruckerei" closed down. Its members had been paid so badly that they "did not work very eagerly" and the deficits could not be covered from Brucker's pocket any more. The Socialist Printing Company bought the "Genossenschaftsdruckerei" for $500. (*BZ* 10 Jl and 15 O 1877) One year later, in August 1878, the paper closed down and in September its property and materials were auctioned. It was succeeded by *Vorwärts (Milwaukee'r Socialist)*.

Sources: Arndt/Olson; Eberlein 22747; *BZ*. On Lyser, see Chicago *Fackel*. The description follows Knoche. See Knoche, p. 179 for explanation of Arndt/Olson's errors concerning dating and editorship.

Die Rothe Laterne appeared probably only once on 1 January 1876, vol. 1, no. 1. It was an annual, humorous supplement to *Der Socialist.* "Redacteure: Gustav Lyser und die Nitroglyzerinfabrikanten am Marktplatz." [Editors: Gustav Lyser and the manufacturers of nitroglycerine in the market- place].

Depository: Usa-WHi.

Sources: Arndt/Olson; Eberlein 22747; Knoche, pp. 177-178.

Milwaukee'r Leuchtkugeln [Milwaukee Flares], the Sunday supplement delivered with the Saturday edition of *Der Socialist*, was edited by Gustav Lyser*, who also helped to print it; the first number appeared on 30 April 1876. It had to be suspended when Lyser left for Chicago in November or December 1876. (*BZ* 15 Ja 1877) Subtitle: Ein heiteres Blatt in ernster Zeit [A Cheerful Paper in Serious Times]. It consisted largely of political satires and anecdotes.

Depository: Usa-WHi (30 Ap-4 Je 1876)
Sources: Arndt/Olson; Eberlein 22749; Knoche, p. 178; *BZ.*

SOCIALISTISCHE ARBEITER-ZEITUNG	OH Cleveland	1900-1908?

Title trans.:	Socialist Labor News	*First issue:*	My 1900
Subtitle:	Offizielles Organ der Sozialistischen Arbeiter-Partei der Vereinigten Staaten von Amerika	*Last issue:*	18 Jl 1908?
Add. lang.:		*Vols. (nos.):*	1(1)-9(29)
First editor:		*Frequency:*	w
First publ.:	Socialist Labor Party	*Preservation:*	1
Related pubs.:	*Clevelander Volksfreund*	*Supplements:*	
Circulation:		*Category:*	socialist-SLP

Depositories: Usa-CtY (1900-03); Usa-WHi (1903-08)

Subtitle translation: Official Organ of the Socialist Labor Party of the United States of America.

There is conflicting evidence as to how long this paper existed. Arndt/Olson mention that it was published as a separate publication until 18 July 1908, when it merged with the *Clevelander Volksfreund* to form the *Volksfreund und Arbeiterzeitung,* and list depositories up to this date. The jubilee edition of the latter paper, however, gives August 1901 as the date of merger.

Sources: Arndt/Olson; Eberlein 22679.

SOLIDARITÄT	NY New York	1906-1954

Title trans.:	Solidarity	*First issue:*	Ap 1906
Subtitle:	Offizielles Organ der Arbeiter-Kranken- und Sterbekasse der Vereinigten Staaten von Amerika	*Last issue:*	D 1954
Add. lang.:	English	*Vols. (nos.):*	1-35 (9)
First editor:	Ernst Wegener	*Frequency:*	m
First publ.:	Workmen's Benefit Fund	*Preservation:*	1
Related pubs.:		*Supplements:* Volkskalender	
Circulation:		*Category:*	socialist

Depositories: Usa-NN; D-188/144 (1906-49,m)

From 1932 on the subtitle appeared in English: Official Organ of the Workmen's Sick and Death Benefit Fund. The paper had 24-32 pages and was published with some English text. There were separate German and English editions after October 1940. The title varied: *Solidarität (Solidarity)* (May 1909 - December 1931); *Solidarity (Solidarität)* (January 1932 - June 1936), *Solidarität* (July 1936-December 1954). The place of publication varied: Brooklyn; Stapleton, NY (April 1906 - April 1909); New York (May 1909 - December 1954). It was edited by Ernst Wegener until March 1916, when he had to resign because he had become "too patriotic", Otto Sattler* (June 1916 - 1951) and Selmar Schocken (1952-54). It was printed by the Co-operative

Press after 16 April 1916 (*BZ* 16 Ap 1916).
It contained articles on philosophical, psychological and health questions, e.g. on self-confidence, the importance of gymnastics, correct sleeping and breathing, the dangers of smoking, drinking and snoring, death, modern medical treatment, hygiene at home; there were also articles on economic, political and labor subjects including news from the labor movement, especially in Europe, and on immigration. It published the platform of the Socialist Party; later a women's page was introduced, edited by Maria Gleit. Later issues became increasingly restricted to reports of the National Executive Board, financial reports, specified reports showing the growth and efficiency of branches and other official announcements as well as a readers' forum. The title-page was usually bilingual. Contributors (before 1916) included: Karl Kautsky, Otto Sattler, Paul Göhre, Ernst Preczang, A. Dodel, Theodor Vischer, Kurt Eisner, Alexander Jonas*, Anton Pannekoek, Lily Braun, Wilhelm Liebknecht, Werner Sombart, Paul Lafargue, Karl Henckell, Cäsar Flaischlen, Rosa Luxemburg; reprints of Joseph Dietzgen, Emil Liess and Hermann Schlüter*.
Sources: Arndt/Olson; Cazden, *Exile Literature*, pp. 22-23; *BZ*.
Jubilee editions were published in October 1909 4(7), (the 25th anniversary of the Fund); October 1934, 29(10), (the 50th anniversary of the Fund); April 1956, 51(4), (the 50th anniversary of *Solidarität*).

Volkskalender, deutschamerikanischer

In 1938 and 1939 *Solidariät* published an annual, entitled *Deutschamerikanischer Volkskalender*. According to Cazden, it was an anti-Nazi yearbook, each volume with ca. 200 pages and many articles written by emigre'''s. No copies have been located.
It contained articles on subjects related to popular science, technology, the fine arts, serious and humorous short stories, travelogs, biographies and poems, a "woman's and home" section, a legal guide, a reprint of the American Constitution in German, the most important questions and answers in the examination for naturalization in English and German, anecdotes, jokes and satires. The circulation depended on advance orders.
Sources: Cazden, *Exile Literature*, p. 185; advertisements for the *Volkskalender* in *Solidarität* of N 1937, p.363 and S 1938, p. 307.

SOZIALDEMOKRATISCHER INFORMATIONSBRIEF (SIB)	NY New York	(1939)

Title trans.:	Social-democratic Bulletin	*First issue:*	1936
Subtitle:	Anti-Hitler Paper	*Last issue:*	1939
Add. lang.:		*Vols. (nos.):*	no. 48
First editor:	Karl B. Frank	*Frequency:*	ir
First publ.:	Auslandsbüro "Neu Beginnen"	*Preservation:*	?
Related pubs.:	*Sozialistische Informationsbriefe*	*Supplements:*	
Circulation:		*Category:*	antifascist/ social dem./ socialist

Depositories: D-292 (1939, no 48)

This paper appeared irregularly and the issues were numbered consecutively. From 1936 it was published in Bern(?), Paris and London. Only one issue, no. 48 was published in the United States, in a printed edition.
Source: Maas II, p. 613.

DER SOZIALIST	NY New York	1885-1892

Title trans.:	The Socialist		*First issue:*	3 Ja 1885
Subtitle:	Zentral-Organ der Socialistischen		*Last issue:*	12 N 1892
	Arbeiter-Partei von Nord-Amerika.			
Add. lang.:			*Vols. (nos.):*	
First editor:	Joseph Dietzgen		*Frequency:*	w
First publ.:	National-Exekutiv-Komitee der SAP		*Preservation:*	2
Related pubs.:	s *Vorwärts*		*Supplements:*	
Circulation:	1890:1750; 1892:1750		*Category:*	socialist-SLP

Depositories: Usa-NN (1885-[1888]-1892); D-188/144 (1885-91,m)

Subtitle translation: Central Organ of the Socialist Labor Party of North America.

The English organ was at this time *The Workmen's Advocate*. Till 1890 it was excluded from Germany under the antisocialist laws. Dietzgen* was a loyal follower of Karl Marx and Friedrich Engels. The editor after Dietzgen's resignation at the end of 1885 was W.L. Rosenberg*, who was also corresponding secretary and financial secretary of the paper. It initially had 4 pages, but after 1886 there were 8. Being hostile towards "pure and simple" trade unionism, the *Sozialist* was frequently attacked by union papers such as the *Buchdrucker-Zeitung*. It contained news of social and political events in America and in foreign countries, especially Germany, reports from SLP-sections, book reviews, articles on philosophical and scientific subjects, short stories. A regular feature was a commemorative article on the Paris Commune on 18 March. The political lecture tour of Wilhelm Liebknecht, Edward Aveling and Eleanor Marx-Aveling from 14 September to 26 December 1886 was extensively covered. It published a serialized version of Georg Büchner's "Dantons Tod" [The Death of Danton] in 1886.

There were contributions by Georg C. Stiebeling, Paul Lafargue, Edward Aveling and Johanna Greie (on child labor and capital punishment). On 13 June 1891 the anarchist paper *Die Freiheit* reported that *Der Sozialist* had swallowed huge sums of money and made the SLP bankrupt.

It was continued by the *Vorwärts* after 1892.

Sources: Arndt/Olson; Eberlein 22793; *BZ* 16 Jl 1889, 16 Jl 1890, 16 Ag 1891, 1 and 16 O 1892; Ely, pp. 269-277 (also on SLP); Marx/Engels, *Werke* XXXVI, p. 884, XXXVII, p. 632; Waltershausen, pp. 255-256; Hillquit, pp. 220-221, 233. On Dietzgen, see Chicago *Vorbote*. On Rosenberg, see *Der Tramp*.

SOZIALISTISCHE INFORMATIONSBRIEFE		NY New York	1939

Title trans.:	Socialist Information Bulletins	*First issue:*	? 1939
Subtitle:		*Last issue:*	? 1939
Add. lang.:		*Vols. (nos.):*	
First editor:		*Frequency:*	ir
First publ.:		*Preservation:*	7
Related pubs.:	*Sozialdemokratischer Informationsbrief; I.B. Berichte*	*Supplements:*	
Circulation:		*Category:*	socialist

Depositories:

This was the German-language bulletin of the Group "Neu Beginnen." At first published in Paris and London, the last two issues appeared in the United States and were published by Karl Frank.

Sources: Arndt/Olson 2, p. 470; Cazden, *Exile Literature*, p. 187, on Karl Frank, pp. 34-35; Kleim, p. 256; Maas IV (on the "Gruppe Neu Beginnen").

SPARTACIST		NY New York	1974-?

Title trans.:		*First issue:*	spring 1974
Subtitle:		*Last issue:*	?
Add. lang.:	English, Spanish, French	*Vols. (nos.):*	
First editor:		*Frequency:*	a (ir)
First publ.:	see below	*Preservation:*	?
Related pubs.:		*Supplements:*	
Circulation:		*Category:*	Trotskyite

Depositories: D-Bm 41/IGA (1974-82)

This organ of the Trotskyites has 32 pages. There are editions in English (since 1964), French and Spanish. The German edition was published 1) by the Internationale Abteilung des Zentralen Büros der Spartacist League/U.S. [International Dept. of the Central Bureau] in cooperation with the Austrian Bolsheviki/Leninists; 2) by the Spartacist Interimssekretariat after 1975; 3) by the Internationales Exekutiv-Komitee der internationalen Spartacist Tendenz. It contained statements and reports of conferences of the international Spartacist Tendenz, articles on the political situation in Afghanistan, China, France, Poland, the Soviet Union and West Germany as well as on problems of the labor movement. The issue of winter 1981/82 (no. 10), contained an index of articles published in the first ten issues.

DIE STIMME	PA Philadelphia	1933

Title trans.:	The Voice	*First issue:*	Je 1933
Subtitle:		*Last issue:*	Ag 1933?
Add. lang.:		*Vols. (nos.):*	
First editor:		*Frequency:*	m
First publ.:	Emil Klumpp	*Preservation:*	
Related pubs.:	Emil Klumpp	*Supplements:*	
Circulation:		*Category:*	communist/ freethought

Depositories:

This was the monthly news bulletin of the Philadelphia branch of the Arbeitsgemeinschaft proletarischer Freidenker [Association of Proletarian Freethinkers], the American section of the International Proletarian Freethinkers, who had their headquarters in Basle (Switzerland) and were the communist split-off organization of the freethinkers (see also *Freidenker*). The editor and publisher was probably Emil Klumpp, the secretary of the Philadelphia Arbeitsgemeinschaft. It contained news from the Philadelphia branch and brief news from the "Gottlosenbewegung" [irreligious movement]. It was intended to be published monthly, but according to Cazden it appeared irregularly, and only until August 1933(?).

Source: Cazden, *Exile Literature*, pp. 24, 189; *Der Arbeiter*, 13 Je 1933.

STIMME DES VOLKES	IL Chicago	1860

Title trans.:	Voice of the People	*First issue:*	Ap 1860
Subtitle:		*Last issue:*	D 1860
Add. lang.:		*Vols. (nos.):*	
First editor:	Joseph Weydemeyer, Julius Standau	*Frequency:*	d, w
First publ.:		*Preservation:*	7
Related pubs.:		*Supplements:*	
Circulation:	1000	*Category:*	socialist

Depositories:

No copy of this weekly has yet been found. The following information is taken from Obermann's article "Weydemeyer in America," in which he compiled and evaluated Weydemeyer's hitherto unpublished letters from America.

Early in 1860 Weydemeyer* accepted a call from the "Zentralkomitee des Arbeiterbundes" [Central Committee of the Workers' League] in Chicago to publish a labor daily in order to provide a counter-balance to the predominating *Illinois Staatszeitung*. The prospectus of this new paper proclaimed that it would be independent of all political parties, but partisan to free labor and opposed to slave labor. On 21 April Weydemeyer sent the first copy of this new organ, called the *Stimme des Volkes*, to his wife. As early as June 1860 it was clear that Weydemeyer was having great difficulties with would-be correspondents, whose articles he had refused to publish. Attempts were made to influence Weydemeyer politically, but he remained adamant.

At the beginning the *Stimme des Volkes* had about 1000 subscribers, but in June already half of them had returned to the conservative *Staatszeitung*. Correspondents at that time were Johann Philipp Becker, Eccarius and Liebknecht. On 5 July Weydemeyer wrote to Karl Marx that he had given up publishing the paper daily and that it now appeared weekly. On 11 August he wrote to Marx that he had finally resigned from the paper "without a penny in his pocket." Apparently the paper was continued until the end of the year by Weydemeyer's associate, the printer Ernst Luft. In December 1860 Weydemeyer mentioned in a letter that the *Stimme des Volkes* had "at last peacefully fallen asleep in the Lord."

Sources: Arndt/Olson; Arndt/Olson 2, p. 375; Eberlein 22787; Obermann, "Weydemeyer in America," pp. 196-203, 208; Kamman, p. 43; Schlüter, *Anfänge*, p. 132. On the "Zentralkomitee des Arbeiterbundes," see Schlüter, *Internationale*, p. 307; Cazden, *Book Trade*, p. (639). On Weydemeyer, see Schlüter, *Anfänge*, pp. 157-160; Miller, pp. 77-80; Obermann, *Pioneer*; Obermann, *Lebensbild*; Marx/Engels, *Werke* XXX, p. 834, XXXI, p. 758, XXXII, p. 897, XXXIV, p. 685.

DIE STIMME DES VOLKES / ...	WI Milwaukee	1900-?

Title trans.:	The Voice of the People	*First issue:*	1900
Subtitle:		*Last issue:*	?
Add. lang.:	English, Polish	*Vols. (nos.):*	
First editor:		*Frequency:*	w
First publ.:		*Preservation:*	
Related pubs.:		*Supplements:*	
Circulation:		*Category:*	social democrat-SP

Depositories: Usa-WHi [1910,1918]; D-188/144 [1910,1918,m]

The complete title of the paper was: *Die Stimme des Volkes / The Voice of the People*.

This paper was published in 1910 by the Social-Democratic Party, in 1918 by the Milwaukee County Socialist Party Campaign Committee. It was issued periodically for election campaigns and distributed free of charge. There were 4 pages in English, German and Polish. It endorsed Victor Berger and W. Gaylord. The subtitle of the German page in 1918 was "Gesunder Menschenverstand" [Common Sense]. It contained cartoons. It was founded as the English-language organ of the Social-Democratic Party in 1883 according to Waltershausen. It was the holder of the "Union Label of the Allied Printing Trades Council Milwaukee."

Sources: Arndt/Olson; Eberlein 22798; Waltershausen, p. 169.

DER STROM	NY New York	1910-?

Title trans.:	The Stream	*First issue:*	18 Mr 1910
Subtitle:		*Last issue:*	?
Add. lang.:		*Vols. (nos.):*	
First editor:		*Frequency:*	m
First publ.:	Hans Koch	*Preservation:*	3?
Related pubs.:	Hans Koch	*Supplements:*	
Circulation:		*Category:*	anarchist

Depositories: D-Bm 41/IGA [1910/11-12]; D-188/144 (15 Ap 1910, 18 F 1911)

This was an anarchist monthly individualistic in tendency with 8 pages. It called itself a "free-socialistic organ." Koch had previously published *Das Freie Wort*. The editor after 15 April 1910 was Frau Koch-Riedel. The editor states in the first issue that the paper is the undertaking of an individual and that "everyone who sympathizes with the undertaking and who goes his own ways, may contribute." "The subscription is voluntary; only those who want and are able to, should donate so much as is possible. Those who show interest in the paper shall receive it. Any revenues shall be used for the design of the paper." It contained as a regular feature "Reflexe und Reflexionen," a literary review, articles on subjects such as "Mass or Personality?," self-esteem, free love, the possibility of realizing socialist ideals, as well as many poems. There were contributions by Anna Riedel, Hans Stromer und W.W. Zuericher. The issue of 15 October 1910 commemorated Francisco Ferrer, the Spanish educator and founder of the "Modern School." His principle was to respect the will of the child.

STURMGLOCKE	IL Chicago	1896

Title trans.:	Alarm Bell	*First issue:*	28 Mr 1896
Subtitle:		*Last issue:*	18 Ap 1896
Add. lang.:		*Vols. (nos.):*	1(1-4)
First editor:		*Frequency:*	w
First publ.:	Max Baginski*	*Preservation:*	7
Related pubs.:	Max Baginski	*Supplements:*	
Circulation:		*Category:*	anarchist

Depositories:

This paper is also mentioned as *Sturmglocken* [Alarm Bells] Its motto was "Spieß voran - d'rauf und d'ran!" [Spear forward! At it and onto it!] On 6 April 1896 Typographia No. 9 of Chicago reported in the *Buchdrucker-Zeitung* that the union-cut had been taken away from the "sextons" of the "anarchist leaflet." According to this notice, it was edited (!), printed and set by a Mr. Kuraner, who had previously been expelled from the union because he had not paid his dues. The paper was supported by the *Freiheit*. After Johann Most's death in 1906, Baginski became editor of the *Freiheit*.

Sources: Arndt/Olson; Eberlein 22799; *BZ* 1 and 16 Ap 1896. On Baginski, see Goldman, pp. 216-219, 370-371; Rocker, *Memoiren*, p. 230.

STURMVOGEL	NY New York	1897-1899?

Title trans.:	The Petrel	*First issue:*	1 N 1897
Subtitle:		*Last issue:*	16 My 1899?
Add. lang.:		*Vols. (nos.):*	1-2
First editor:		*Frequency:*	bw
First publ.:	Claus Timmermann	*Preservation:*	3?
Related pubs.:	Claus Timmermann	*Supplements:*	
Circulation:		*Category:*	anarchist

Depositories: D-Bm 41/IGA (1897/98)

The motto of this 4-page paper was: "Lewwer duad ues Slaav." [Rather be dead than a slave] taken from Detlev von Liliencron's poem "Pidder Lueng," written in Low German. For Timmermann, see also the St. Louis *Der Anarchist* and *Die Brandfackel* [The Torch of War] It contained news from the anarchist movement, reports on agitational meetings and the founding of anarchist colonies, articles against socialism, on prostitution, hunger etc. It published "Reise-Briefe" (traveler's reports) by Emma Goldman, articles by Peter Kropotkin and Carl Nold, the secretary of the Alexander Berkmann Defence Association, poems by Friederich Hebbel, Karl Henkell, Martin Drescher, Heinrich Binder, Edna Fern and "Germanus." There were few advertisements, mostly for reading rooms and anarchist books and pamphlets.

Note: Eberlein 22800 lists it (incorrectly) as *Sturmtrommel*.

Sources: Arndt/Olson; Eberlein 22800; Rocker, p. 379. For trials against Timmermann, Nold and other anarchists, see Rocker, chapter XVIII; Goldman, pp. 86, 127, 156.

TAGEBLATT (San Francisco Tageblatt)	CA San Francisco	1893-1906?

Title trans.:	San Francisco Daily News	*First issue:*	F 1893
Subtitle:		*Last issue:*	1906?
Add. lang.:		*Vols. (nos.):*	
First editor:		*Frequency:*	d
First publ.:	Tageblatt Publishing Co.	*Preservation:*	7
Related pubs.:	c *California Arbeiter-Zeitung*; s *Vorwärts der Pacific-Küste*	*Supplements:*	*Wochenblatt*; *Sonntagsblatt*
Circulation:	1895:6000; 1903:4011	*Category:*	socialist-SLP

Depositories:

This daily appeared evenings except Sundays and was the organ of the Socialist Labor Party of North America. It was edited by Emil Ließ (November 1894 - 1899), a well-known freethinker, who gave weekly lectures in San Francisco and published a compilation of them under the title "Was ist Socialismus?" [What is Socialism?] in 1899. In 1911 he became editor of the *Vorwärts der Pacific Küste*. From 1902 to 1906 the *Tageblatt* was edited by E. Ebel. It was published by the Tageblatt Association (1895-96) and the Tageblatt Publishing Society (1897-1906). According to the *Buchdrucker-Zeitung* it was written, typeset and printed by members of the Tageblatt Association, who divided any profits among themselves instead of receiving wages.

Sources: Arndt/Olson; *History of Foreign Journalism in San Francisco*, p. 33; Eberlein 22805; *BZ* 16 F, 16 Mr 1893; 1 D 1894; 16 Ag 1895; 16 Ag 1898; 1 Je 1899; 1 D 1901. See also the reminiscences of a traveling agent for the *Tageblatt:* "Erfahrungen eines Reisenden einer deutschen Zeitung" by Theodor Pfundt, in Cleveland *Volksfreund und Arbeiter-Zeitung* 29 Ap 1911.

Wochenblatt des San Francisco Tageblatt: (February 1893-1910).

This was the weekly edition of the *San Francisco Tageblatt* and the continuation of the *California Arbeiter-Zeitung*, which was possibly the subtitle of the weekly edition. According to Arndt/Olson it was followed by *Vorwärts der Pacific Küste*. Circulation in 1895:4500; 1900:4901; 1906: 2735.

Depositories: Usa-CSt (Ap 1895-1905)

Source: Arndt/Olson.

Sonntagsblatt des San Francisco Tageblatt (February 1893-1903).

This was the Sunday edition of the San Francisco Tageblatt, also entitled *Vorwärts*. Circulation in 1896:7200; 1900:4384.

Sources: Arndt/Olson; Eberlein 22805; *BZ* 16 Mr 1893.

TAGEBLATT (St. Louis Tageblatt)	MO St. Louis	1888-1897

Title trans.:	St. Louis Daily News	*First issue:*	30 Ap 1888
Subtitle:	Den Interessen des arbeitenden Volkes gewidmet	*Last issue:*	?Ag 1897
Add. lang.:		*Vols. (nos.):*	
First editor:	Adolph Hepner	*Frequency:*	d
First publ.:	St. Louis Workingmen's Publishing Association	*Preservation:*	4
Related pubs.:	*Tageblatt-Abendpost*	*Supplements:*	*Sonntagsblatt*
Circulation:	1890:4500	*Category:*	socialist

Depositories: Usa-WHi [1891,1893,1895,1897]

Subtitle translation: Dedicated to the Interests of the Working People.

This was a daily appearing evenings except Sunday. It grew out of a "Bierboykott" of the "Brauer und Mälzer-Union" No. 6. It was edited by Adolph Hepner* (or Heppner) (April 1888-June 1891) until he was "deposed by his enemies" (*BZ* 16 Je 1891) and replaced by Julius Vahlteich*. One month later Heppner was called back to his office. He was described as one of the most able socialist journalists (*BZ* 16 Je 1891), even by his political opponents (see *Freiheit*, 6 Je 1891.) "Well meant, but weak," was Friedrich Engels' judgement in 1889.

In June 1897 the *Tageblatt* amalgamated with the evening edition of the *Anzeiger des Westens* [Western Advertiser] which had been established shortly before. The new paper was entitled *Tageblatt-Abendpost* (*BZ* 1 S 1897).

Sources: Arndt/Olson; *BZ*; *Freiheit*; Marx/Engels, *Werke* XXXVII, p. 133. On Hepner, see Philadelphia *Tageblatt*.

Sonntagsblatt des St. Louis Tageblatt (1888?-1897?)

This was the Sunday edition of the *St. Louis Tageblatt*. Circulation: 1890:4600; 1895:7300.

Source: Arndt/Olson.

TAGEBLATT (Cincinnati Tageblatt)	OH Cincinnati	1895-1896

Title trans.:	Daily News		*First issue:*	22 Jl 1895
Subtitle:	Den Interessen des arbeitenden Volkes gewidmet		*Last issue:*	17 O 1896
Add. lang.:			*Vols. (nos.):*	
First editor:	Wilhelm Ludwig Rosenberg		*Frequency:*	d
First publ.:	Co-operative Labor Press Association		*Preservation:*	1
Related pubs.:			*Supplements:*	
Circulation:			*Category:*	socialist-SLP

Depositories: Usa-OC

Subtitle translation: Dedicated to the Interests of the Working People. "Official Organ of the Deutscher Gewerkschaftsrat [German Union Council]"

Rosenberg* headed the Cincinnati Co-operative Labor Press Association, which was socialistic and opposed to the purely economic aims of the trade unions. This led to conflicts with the Typographia, e.g. in August 1895, when the *Tageblatt* applied for the union-label and it turned out that the paper employed "rats" (non-union typesetters) and did not pay union wages. The arch-enemy of the *Tageblatt* was the *Cincinnatier Zeitung*. According to the *Buchdrucker-Zeitung*, at times the *Tageblatt* contained little else but invectives against the *Cincinnatier Zeitung* and Typographia No. 2 of Cincinnati. The *Tageblatt* closed down because of internal struggles, which caused a continuous change of editors, and also because of strikes and lawsuits brought by its discontented typesetters who had to wait for weeks for their meager wages.

Sources: Arndt/Olson; Eberlein 22802; *BZ* 16 Ag, 16 S 1895, 1 F, 16 F, 16 Je, 1 Ag, 16 N 1896. On Rosenberg, see *Der Tramp* (1888).

TAGEBLATT (Philadelphia Tageblatt)	PA Philadelphia	1877-1944?

Title trans.:	Philadelphia Daily News	*First issue:*	19 N 1877
Subtitle:		*Last issue:*	1944?
Add. lang.:		*Vols. (nos.):*	
First editor:		*Frequency:*	d
First publ.:	Tageblatt Publishing Association	*Preservation:*	3
Related pubs.:	m *Philadelphia Gazette-Demokrat*	*Supplements:*	Sonntagsausgabe
Circulation:	1880:8000; 1890:5200; 1900:41,000; 1910:12,500; 1920:17,500; 1935:2451; 1940:6393;	*Category:*	socialist

Depositories: Usa-PPG [1877-1929]; <Usa-PPBI [1877-1943]; D-188/144 (1927,m); D-212 (1927-30,[1931,1935])

This was a socialist daily appearing in the morning except Sundays; 4 pages; after 24 October 1904, 8 pages. In contradiction to Arndt/Olson's information, this paper was socialist throughout, certainly until the late 1920s. It was founded as the organ of the Socialist Party by a stock corporation of workers with a capital of only $700. The issue of 20 November 1877 lists the names and professions of the 15 members of the elected governing council of the paper. After 1881 it was the organ of the Vereinigte Deutsche Gewerkschaften [United German Unions] which it still was in 1927. It was excluded from Germany under the antisocialist laws in 1879 and merged with the *Philadelphia Gazette-Demokrat*, possibly in 1933. For the conflict with Typographia No. 1 of Philadelphia see introduction. It was edited by Jacob L. Franz*, (1878-1882);other editors were Mitschell, Meyer, Koberstein, Schlesinger, Paul Lossau, Louis Werner (1882?-1918) (Werner was associated with the paper from Ja 1879 until 1926); other editors were Friedrich Wilhelm Frietzche*, H. Kahler, Friedrich Häcker, Martin Darkow, Adolph Hepner*, August F. Herbert (1918-20), E.A. Thomaser (1920-28), Richard Schaffler (1929-33), Hermann Lemke, (1934-40), Louis Mayer (1940-44). Other publishers were Gustav Mayer (1933-38), Herman Lemke (1938-40), the Philadelphia Gazette Publishing Co. (Louis Mayer, pres] (1940-44). It was printed by Julius Weber* (1897-1912). It contained political news and news of general interest, gossip, news of incoming ships, the radio program, sports news, news and announcements of labor organizations such as the Central Labor Union, the Labor Lyceum, the Labor Institute, the Allied Printing Trades Council of Philadelphia, the Arbeiter-Kranken- und Sterbekasse, the Turngemeinde, a serialized novel, jokes, photographic illustrations, classified advertisements and advertisements for local businesses.

A jubilee edition was published to mark the 50th anniversary on 18 November 1927; it contained a lengthy, but rambling history of the paper by Louis Werner and also his account of the trial for high treason against himself and Darkow in 1917.

Sources: Arndt/Olson; Kamman, p. 46; Marx/Engels, *Werke* XXXIV, p. 662, XXXV, p. 566, XXXVI, p. 902; Auer, p. 338. The minutes of the Philadelphia *Tageblatt* are contained in *Socialist Collections in the Tamiment Library, 1872-1956*, ed. by Thomas C. Prado (Sanford NC, 1979). On the conflict with Typographia No. 1, see *BZ*, issues of N 1885 - 1 My 1887. On Franz, see obituary in *BZ* 16 O 1902. On Weber, see obituary in *BZ* 16 N 1912. On Freitzsche, see Hoerder, *Plutokraten*, p. 327. On Hepner, see *Geschichte der deutschen Arbeiterbewegung*, pp. 199-200.

Philadelphia Tageblatt Sonntagsausgabe: 1879-1944? vol. 1-66

The Sunday edition of the *Philadelphia Tageblatt* is bound with the daily edition. Samples of 1927 contained political news and news of general interest, sports news, news from clubs, e.g. singing societies and sports clubs, a column for women and for young people, church news, articles on scientific and medical questions, cooking recipes and advice on good housekeeping, fashion, farming and gardening, reports on towns in Germany, one page of jokes, a humorous letter to the editor, entitled "Offener Schreibbrief des Philipp Sauerampfer", short stories and serialized novels.

Source: Arndt/Olson.

TAGEBLATT-ABENDPOST   MO St. Louis   1897-1898

Title trans.:	Daily News - Evening Post	*First issue:*	? Ag 1897
Subtitle:		*Last issue:*	? Ag 1898
Add. lang.:		*Vols. (nos.):*	
First editor:	G.A. Höhn; Stöhr	*Frequency:*	d (?)
First publ.:	Tageblatt und Abendpost Association	*Preservation:*	6
Related pubs.:	c St. Louis *Tageblatt*; s *Arbeiterzeitung und Volksanwalt*	*Supplements:*	
Circulation:		*Category:*	social democrat

Depositories: Usa-WHi [1891,1893,1895,1897]; Usa-MoS (Ap 1888-Je 1897)

This paper was established through the amalgamation of the St. Louis Tageblatt with the evening edition of the *Anzeiger des Westens* [Western Advertiser]. Two editors of the *Tageblatt*, G.A. Höhn and Stöhr, retained their position. The new paper's print-shop was fully unionized. At a union meeting it was decided which of the typesetters of the two papers should be kept; 4 typesetters of the *Anzeiger* were dismissed because of previous conduct harmful to the union.

Variant: Arndt/Olson give *Abend-Post und Tageblatt* as the title and mention that it existed from 1888 to 1898, as a title variant of the *St. Louis Tageblatt*.

Source: Arndt/Olson; *BZ* 1 S 1897.

THE TAILOR   NY New York   1887-1891

Title trans.:		*First issue:*	O 1887
Subtitle:	Official Organ of the Journeymen Tailors' National Union	*Last issue:*	D 1891
Add. lang.:	English	*Vols. (nos.):*	1(1)-3(5)
First editor:	John Brown Lennon	*Frequency:*	m
First publ.:	Journeymen Tailors' National Union	*Preservation:*	2-3
Related pubs.:		*Supplements:*	
Circulation:	1890: 8000	*Category:*	labor union

Depositories: Usa-ICJ ([1887]-1891); Usa-WHi ([1887]-1891)

Each volume contained no. 1-24, covering a two-year period. This paper was published in English and German until December 1891; thereafter in English only, thus not listed here. The format was large quarto, each issue containing 8 pages; it was illustrated, including portraits and tables.

Sources: Arndt/Olson; Naas/Sakr, p. 114; *American Labor Press Directory*, p. 8. On history of the Journeymen Tailors' Union, see Fink, *Labor Unions*, pp. 365-367; Charles J. Stowell, *The Journeymen Tailors' Union of America: A Study in Trade Union Policy* (Urbana, IL, 1918). On J.B. Lennon, see Fink, *Biographical Dictionary*, p. 199.

DER TRAMP (I)	NY New York	1888

Title trans.:	The Tramp	*First issue:*	? My 1888
Subtitle:		*Last issue:*	11 Ag 1888?
Add. lang.:		*Vols. (nos.):*	
First editor:	Georg Biedenkapp*, W.L. Rosenberg	*Frequency:*	w
First publ.:	G. Biedenkapp, W.L. Rosenberg	*Preservation:*	3
Related pubs.:		*Supplements:*	
Circulation:		*Category:*	

Lib. code: anarchist
Depositories: D-188/144 [1888,m]; Usa-WHi [1888]

This was a satirical weekly of 8 pages, 4 of them taken up by full-page or double-page cartoons on current political issues. The title emblem was a bearded man with a walking stick, resting on a stone; in the background on the left was a factory building the roof of which bore the inscription "No Men Wanted," to the right a statue of liberty surrounded by gravestones. Nos 1 ("Probenummer") and 2 were edited and published by Georg Biedenkapp* and Wilhelm Ludwig Rosenberg*, thereafter by Biedenkapp only. The paper intended to "amuse the reader and give him new perspectives on the rotten-ness of the prevailing state of society." It contained satirical poems and short prose, the targets being Kaiser Wilhelm I, Carl Schurz, the publishers Oswald Ottendörfer (see also *O.O.* Appendix 1), Michael Biron and Hermann Raster, temperance legislation, the church, the Gymnasts' movement. There were also jokes and riddles.

Note: see also Biedenkapp's *Der Tramp* of 1901.

Sources: Arndt/Olson. On Biedenkapp, see Kamman, pp. 108-109; Poore, p. 210. On Rosenberg, see Kamman, pp. 109-111; Poore, p. 214; Schultz I, p. 363; Marx/Engels, *Werke* XXXVI, p. 917, XXXVII, p. 662; Wilhelm Ludwig Rosenberg, "Erinnerungen aus der Frühzeit der sozialistischen Bewegung in den Vereinigten Staaten," [Memories of the Beginnings of the Socialist Movement in the U.S.] *New Yorker Volkszeitung*, 29 Ja 1928, section V, 1-2.

DER TRAMP (II)	NY New York	1901-1902?

Title trans.:	The Tramp	*First issue:*	1 My 1901
Subtitle:		*Last issue:*	1902?
Add. lang.:		*Vols. (nos.):*	
First editor:	Georg Biedenkapp	*Frequency:*	m (ir)
First publ.:	'Der Zeitgeist' Publishing Association	*Preservation:*	?
Related pubs.:	Zeitgeist	*Supplements:*	
Circulation:		*Category:*	anarchist

Depositories: D-188/144 [1901,m]

This was originally a humorous supplement to *Der Zeitgeist* [Spirit of the Age] which bore the same title emblem as Biedenkapp's* *Der Tramp* of 1888. It contained satirical prose articles and poems on diverse topics, e.g. property, British imperialism in Africa, Me and my horse, the expulsion of Adam and Eve from paradise, European monarchs as well as jokes.

From the issue of August 1901 (vol. 1, no. 4), *Der Tramp* appeared as a separate publication, the numbering being continued from *Der Zeitgeist*. It was published by the Tramp Publ. Co. The title emblem was retained. It contained short stories, a serialized novel, book reviews, a letter-box, jokes and poems. The contributions with very few exceptions were all by Biedenkapp. It was illustrated with full-page cartoons. There were few advertisements, mostly for publications.

TRIBÜNE (Buffalo Tribüne)	NY Buffalo	1876-1878

Title trans.:	Buffalo Tribune	*First issue:*	? Ja 1876
Subtitle:	Wochenblatt zur Unterhaltung und Belehrung für das Volk	*Last issue:*	? Ap 1878
Add. lang.:		*Vols. (nos.):*	
First editor:	Charles Blumhardt	*Frequency:*	w, d
First publ.:	Stechholtz & Miller	*Preservation:*	6
Related pubs.:		*Supplements:*	see below
Circulation:	1877:1500	*Category:*	socialist-WP

Depositories: Usa-MWA, Rowell Collection (8 O 1876)

Subtitle translation: Weekly for the Entertainment and Education of the People.

This was the organ of the Workingmen's Party (Summer 1877 - 1878). A title variation was *Tägliche Tribüne* (September 1877 - April 1878). The editor after Blumhardt was Paul Koberstein (1876-78). Koberstein became the editor of the *Arbeiterstimme am Erie* in 1878. Arndt/Olson mention that the *Buffalo Tribüne* was continued as the *Buffalo Täglicher Republikaner*, a republican daily, but the latter began to appear in 1875.

The *Wöchentliche Buffalo Tribüne* which appeared from September 1877 to 1913? was the Sunday edition.

Sources: Arndt/Olson; Eberlein 22809.

TURN-BLATT ...	NY Williamsburgh	1856-1858

Title trans.:	Gymnasts' Journal for the Clubs of the Socialist Gymnasts' Federation of North America	*First issue:*	O 1856
Subtitle:		*Last issue:*	S 1858
Add. lang.:		*Vols. (nos.):*	(1-24)
First editor:		*Frequency:*	m
First publ.:		*Preservation:*	1
Related pubs.:	Turnzeitung	*Supplements:*	
Circulation:		*Category:*	socialist-Gymnasts

Depositories: Usa-NN

The complete title of the paper was: *Turn-Blatt für die Vereine des socialistischen Turnerbundes von Nordamerika*

This monthly organ of the Eastern Gymnasts' Federation was published by the administrative center [Vorort] of the movement in Williamsburgh. The formation of different factions and the decentralization of the gymnasts' movement became apparent with the founding of local gymnasts' journals. The Turn-Blatt was more moderate than the New York *Turnzeitung*. It contained all the official news and some scientific articles. A quarterly report was issued from 1858 to 1859 in Washington DC: *Vierteljahres-Bericht des Socialistischen Turner-Bundes von Nord-Amerika* (vol. 1 (1)-2 (1), 15 December 1858 - October 1859).

Sources: Arndt/Olson; Eberlein 22812; "Turnwesen in den Vereinigten Staaten;" Schem XI, pp. 45-49, Metzner II/4, pp. 175-176.

DIE TURNZEITUNG		NY New York	1851-1861

Title trans.:	The Gymnasts' News	*First issue:*	15 N 1851
Subtitle:	Organ des Sozialistischen Turnerbundes (von Nordamerika)	*Last issue:*	16 Ap 1861//
Add. lang.:		*Vols. (nos.):*	1-10 (22)
First editor:	Sigismund Kaufmann	*Frequency:*	m, w
First publ.:		*Preservation:*	2
Related pubs.:	*Turn-Blatt*	*Supplements:*	Vereins-Organ
Circulation:	1852:1300; 1854:3000	*Category:*	socialist-Gymnasts

Depositories: Usa-NN (1851-15 O 1854); Usa-PPG (N 1854-O 1855); Usa- MnHi (N 1855-O 1859); Usa-MB (O 1857-F 1861)

Subtitle translation: Organ of the Socialist Gymnasts' Federation.

Originally a monthly, this 8-page paper appeared weekly after 11 November 1854. The motto varied e.g. "Wohlstand, Freiheit und Bildung für Alle!" [Prosperity, Liberty and Education for all!]. It was edited by Sigismund Kaufmann and Wilhelm Ehrmann (15 November 1851 - 1853), Wilhelm Rapp (1 November 1853 - October 1855), Gottfrid Becker and Otto Reventlow (6 November 1855 - September 1858), Reventlow (until 14 August 1857), Wilhelm Rothacker (September 1858 - October 1859), Wilhelm Rapp, Georg Edward Wiss and Adolph Wiesner (November 1859 - 16 April 1861) . After November 1859 it was printed in the print-shop of the *Baltimore Wecker* (see Appendix I). The place of publication varied according to the situation of the administrative center ('Vorort') of the Turnerbund: New York (15 November 1851-14 October 1853), Philadelphia (1 November 1853 - 15 October 1856?), Cincinnati (November 1856? - 23 November 1858), Dubuque, IA (December 1858 - 11 October 1859), Baltimore (November 1859 - 16 April 1861). For some years a supplement, seemingly with news of local Turnvereine, was published under the title *Vereins-Organ für die Turnvereine des socialistischen Turnerbundes von Nord-Amerika* as a supplement of the federal organ, published by the 'Vorort.' Besides its main object to further the cause of the Gymnasts' movement, the *Turnzeitung* contained many articles on socialism and the labor movement of its time, especially during the time when it was published in New York. When it became a weekly, advertisements were included and the paper contained more articles on literary and free-religious subjects and political issues such as slavery and nativism. In 1856, besides news from the local Gymnasts' clubs, it contained articles on subjects relating to natural science, physiology and

technology and a serialized version of Georg Büchner's "Dantons Tod." [The Death of Danton] Among the contributors were Gustav Struve, Harro Harring, Joseph Weydemeyer, Victor Wilhelm Fröhlich and Franz Arnold. The paper had to suspend publication in 1861 when Southern rebels assaulted and destroyed its printing office.
Sources: Arndt/Olson; Schlüter, *Anfänge*, pp. 201-214; Kamman, pp. 58-63; Herreshoff, pp.60-62; Wittke, *Press*, pp. 109-110; Obermann, *Pioneer*, pp. 46-52; Cazden, *Book Trade*, pp. (646-648). On Kaufmann see Wittke, *Refugees*, pp. 152-153; Metzner I; 1, pp. 32-35.

DER UNABHÄNGIGE		OH Cincinnati	1850-1853?
Title trans.:	The Independent	*First issue:*	7 N 1850
Subtitle:		*Last issue:*	1853?
Add. lang.:		*Vols. (nos.):*	
First editor:	Karl von Schmidt-Bürgeler	*Frequency:*	w
First publ.:	John Rittig, Wilhelm Rothacker	*Preservation:*	7
Related pubs.:		*Supplements:*	
Circulation:		*Category:*	radical fortyeighter

Depositories:

Rothacker was a disciple of and agent for Karl Heinzen. See also: *Die Menschenrechte* (OH Cincinnati 1853).
Sources: Cazden, *Book Trade*, p. (644, 664 - note 120); Kamman, p. 84.

UNSER WORT		NY New York	(1940)-1941
Title trans.:	Our Word	*First issue:*	O 1940
Subtitle:	Monatszeitung der I.K.D. (Internationale Kommunisten Deutschlands)	*Last issue:*	Jl 1941
Add. lang.:		*Vols. (nos.):*	8 (1) - 9 (3)
First editor:		*Frequency:*	m
First publ.:		*Preservation:*	6
Related pubs.:		*Supplements:*	
Circulation:	3000	*Category:*	Trotskyite

Depositories: D-Bm 41/IGA (D 1940)

Subtitle translation: Monthly Magazine of the International Communists of Germany.
This was the continuation of a Trotskyite monthly of the same name published in Prague in 1933, in Paris in 1933-38 and in Antwerp in 1939. It was intended to be distributed in Europe. It contained news from the anti-Nazi movement in Germany, manifestoes, e.g. on the war and on world revolution, and reports from the Fourth International. There were contributions by Leo Trotzki, L. Baum, James P. Cannon, Oscar Fischer, Walter Held and John G. Wright.

Sources: Cazden, *Exile Literature*, p. 187; Maas II, pp. 565-567.

UNSERE ZEIT		NY New York	1940-1942

Title trans.:	Our Time	*First issue:*	Ja 1940
Subtitle:		*Last issue:*	S 1942
Add. lang.:	English	*Vols. (nos.):*	1-3(9)
First editor:		*Frequency:*	m
First publ.:		*Preservation:*	3
Related pubs.:	c *Deutsch-Amerikanische Arbeiterklubs U.S.A: Mitteilungsblatt*; s *The German American*	*Supplements:*	
Circulation:		*Category:*	communist

Depositories: D-292 (Ap 1940,N 1941); <§Usa-KyLC(?)

This was the monthly bulletin of the Federation of German American Clubs and the successor, after some lapse of time, to the *Mitteilungsblatt der Deutsch-Amerikanischen Klubs*. It contained articles on German Americans, the political situation in Nazi Germany and the occupied countries, legal questions of emigration, frequent polemics against Gerhard Seger*, quotations from the American press in English, a women's section, "Was Scharlie observe tut" an editorial in a curious mixture of German and English. After September 1942 subscriptions to *Unsere Zeit* were transferred to the *German-American*.

Sources: Cazden, *Exile Literature*, pp. 48-49, 54, 189; Maas II, p. 570; Maas IV.

DER VÖLKERBUND		NY New York	1850

Title trans.:	The League of Nations	*First issue:*	N 1850
Subtitle:		*Last issue:*	N 1850
Add. lang.:		*Vols. (nos.):*	1(1)
First editor:	Karl Heinzen	*Frequency:*	w
First publ.:	Karl Heinzen	*Preservation:*	7
Related pubs.:		*Supplements:*	
Circulation:		*Category:*	radical fortyeighter

Depositories:

This paper was intended to be a weekly, but not enough copies of a sample edition were sold to make a second issue worthwhile. Kamman mentions that Heinzen* also published a "Probenummer." [Proof number] In the prospectus Heinzen announced that Ruge and Mazzini would contribute to his new journal, which was to be sold at 8 cents a copy and 20 cents a month.

Sources: Arndt/Olson. On Heinzen, see *Der Pionier*.

VOLKS-ANWALT   OH Cincinnati   1889-1898

Title trans.:	People's Advocate	*First issue:*	25 O 1889
Subtitle:	see below	*Last issue:*	20 Ag 1898
Add. lang.:		*Vols. (nos.):*	1(1) - 9(22)
First editor:	J. Willig	*Frequency:*	w
First publ.:	National-Komitee der S.A.P.	*Preservation:*	4
Related pubs.:	m *Tageblatt-Abendpost*; s *Arbeiterzeitung* (St. Louis)	*Supplements:*	
Circulation:		*Category:*	socialist-SLP / SDP

Depositories: Usa-WHi (1889-[1896-97]); D-188/144 [1896-98]

This was an 8-page weekly. The subtitle changed: 1) Der politischen und öko-
nomischen Befreiung der Arbeiterklasse gewidmet [Dedicated to the Political
and Economic Emancipation of the Working Class] (25 October 1889 - March
1895); 2) Central-Organ der S.A.P. von Nordamerika (1 April 1895-1896?); 3)
Officielles Organ der Social-Demokratischen Federation von Nord-Amerika,
1897?-?; 4) Offizielles Organ der Sozial-Demokratie von Nord-Amerika (1898).
The motto in 1896 was "Wohl an, wer Recht und Wahrheit achtet, zu uns'rer
Fahne steh zu Hauf!" [Onward, those who respect justice and truth, come
gather around our banner!] The paper came into existence after a split in the
SLP and became the organ of the "Orthodox wing of the Socialist Labor
Party," the so-called Cincinnati Wing (Rosenberg, Morgan, Willig). The editors
after Willig were: Gus Müller (June 1891?-1894), Max Silz (editor and manager,
June 1894-1898?), A. Heins-Henryot (1897). The place of publication changed:
Cincinnati (1889-15 April 1893), Baltimore (22 April - 28 October 1893),
Buffalo (18 November 1893-2 June 1894), Cleveland (9 June 1894-1898). At the
beginning the paper was composed mainly of copies from the *Cincinnatier
Zeitung* . It contained official party news, reports from American cities, on
unemployment, women's labor, foreign countries, critical reviews of other
newspapers, serialized novels, short stories and some poems. A regular
humorous feature in 1898 was a letter to the editor, entitled "Höllenbrief"
[letter from hell], signed by "Maulschellenseff" [Joe Box-on-the Ear]. There
were contributions by G.A. Höhn, Adolph Gebelin, Emilio de Marchi, Emile Zola
(a serialized version of "Le Ventre de Paris" [The Bowels of Paris]), Wilhelm
Teschen, Eugen von Jagow, Hermann Sudermann (a serialized version of "Frau
Sorge" [Mrs. Care]), Rudolph Stratz and Robert Oberhuter. The issue of 19
March 1898 commemorated 18 March 1848. It amalgamated with the St. Louis
Tageblatt und Abendpost to form the St. Louis *Arbeiterzeitung*.

Sources: Arndt/Olson; *BZ*.

VOLKSBLATT (I)	WI Milwaukee	1882

Title trans.:	People's News	*First issue:*	1 My 1882
Subtitle:		*Last issue:*	28 N 1882
Add. lang.:		*Vols. (nos.):*	
First editor:		*Frequency:*	d
First publ.:		*Preservation:*	7
Related pubs.:	s Milwaukee *Volksblatt*	*Supplements:*	
Circulation:	1882:700	*Category:*	labor

Depositories:

This daily which appeared every afternoon except Sundays was the organ of the United Labor Unions of Milwaukee. It was founded by 5 members of Deutsch-Amerikanische Typographia No. 10 of Milwaukee, who had pooled their savings. After about a month the initial working capital was exhausted and the local Trades Assembly put $ 12.50 into the paper. The *Volksblatt* never had more than 700 subscribers. In late October 1882 it was bought by Robert Schilling, who immediately tried to reduce the costs of production by using pre-set inner pages.Typographia No. 10 conceded that it had not been edited very well. See *Volksblatt*, WI Milwaukee 1882-1890?

Source: *BZ* 1 S, 1 N, 15 D 1882.

VOLKSBLATT (Milwaukee Volksblatt) (II)	WI Milwaukee	1882-1890?

Title trans.:	Milwaukee People's News	*First issue:*	Ja 1882
Subtitle:	Der Mensch, nicht Geld, regiert die Welt	*Last issue:*	1890?
Add. lang.:		*Vols. (nos.):*	
First editor:	Robert Schilling*	*Frequency:*	w
First publ.:		*Preservation:*	
Related pubs.:	*Der Reformer*; c *Volksblatt*	*Supplements:*	
Circulation:	1885:3320; 1890:3000	*Category:*	labor

Depositories: Usa-WHi [1883-90]; D-188/144 [1883-1890,m]

Subtitle translation: Man, not Money, Rules the World.

This was the Sunday edition of *Der Reformer*. According to Knoche, the subtitle "Sonntagsausgabe des *Täglicher Reformer*" [Sunday Edition of the Daily Reformer] was added to the *Milwaukee Volksblatt* in 1886 and for the next few years the paper was the "Officielles deutsches Organ der Ritter der Arbeit von Milwaukee" [Official German Organ of the Knights of Labor of Milwaukee]. Its first page contained domestic and foreign news; the other seven pages were filled with serialized novels, local news and gossip, short stories, human-interest stories, jokes, advertisements and announcements. In 1890 the *Milwaukee Volksblatt* was renamed the *Milwaukee Reformer*.

Sources: Arndt/Olson; Knoche, pp. 111-113.

VOLKSBLATT (Sheboygan Volksblatt)   WI Sheboygan   1895-1906

Title trans.:	Sheboygan People's News	*First issue:*	Ja? 1895
Subtitle:	Den Interessen des arbeitenden Volkes gewidmet	*Last issue:*	Mr? 1906//
Add. lang.:	English	*Vols. (nos.):*	
First editor:	Oscar Loebel	*Frequency:*	w, sw
First publ.:		*Preservation:*	4
Related pubs.:		*Supplements:*	
Circulation:	1900:1050; 1905:2400	*Category:*	socialist

Depositories: Usa-WHi [1898,1900-03,1905]; D-188/144 [1898-1905,m]

Subtitle translation: Dedicated to the Interests of the Working People.

Initially a weekly appearing on Saturdays, it was later issued semiweekly on Wednesdays and Saturdays. The editors after Loebel were Anton Hirschberger (May 1901-?), Edmund Deuss (1905), Heinrich Bartel (March 1906). It contained American and foreign news which often consisted of accounts of strange events, curious accidents etc, items such as travelogs, advice for housewives and farmers, poems. One regular feature was "Meik Habersack's Schreibebrief", a humorous letter to the "edithor" (sic!) signed by a "Meik Habersack, Eskweier und Scheriff von Apple Jack, Holie Terrer Kauntie," written in a curious mixture of German and English. After 1905? it had up to one page in English. In 1900 besides the editor and a foreman two female typesetters were employed, one of them belonging to the Typographia, the other being an apprentice. In 1896 the *Sheboygan Volksblatt* asked the German-American Typographias to subscribe to it.

Sources: Arndt/Olson; *BZ* 16 D 1896; 1 Ap 1900; 1 My 1901; 16 Mr 1906.

VOLKSFRONT   IL Chicago   1934-1939

Title trans.:	Popular Front	*First issue:*	N 1935
Subtitle:		*Last issue:*	30 D 1939
Add. lang.:	English	*Vols. (nos.):*	
First editor:	Erich von Schroetter	*Frequency:*	m, w
First publ.:	see below	*Preservation:*	1
Related pubs.:	m *Deutsches Volksecho*	*Supplements:*	
Circulation:		*Category:*	communist

Depositories: D-292

The subtitle of this paper changed: 1) Mitteilungsblatt der Arbeitsgemeinschaft der fortschrittlichen deutschsprachigen Vereine von Chicago [Bulletin of the Action Committee of German Progressive Organizations of Chicago] (November 1935-1936, no 2); 2) Mitteilungsblatt des "Deutschamerikanischen Kulturverbandes Chicago" [German-American League for Culture, Chicago], (1936) (head office: New York), etc.

It was a communist bulletin initially published monthly but after 1938 weekly. The numbering of the volumes is confused (see Maas for details). There were some articles in English. The first editors were Erich von Schroetter, Hans

Weber and Karl Berreitter (Editorial Board), (November-December 1935). Thereafter it was edited by von Schroetter, with Martin Hall as coeditor until 1939. It was published by the Action Committee of Progressive German Societies from 1935 to 1936 (no. 2); the German-American League for Culture from 1936 (no. 3) to 1938 (no. 3); the Cultural Front Press Association, Inc. until December 1939. It contained news from the Action Committee, later from the German-American League for Culture, union news, a women's section and medical advice. In 1939 there was a supplement for young people. Contributions were by Franz Boas, Rudolf Brandl, Bertolt Brecht, Earl Browder, William E. Dodd, Martin Drescher*; Hans Eisler, Lion Feuchtwanger, Felix Frankfurter, Oskar Maria Graf, Stefan Heym, Hermann Kesten, Eva Lips, Heinrich Mann, Thomas Mann, Tom Mooney, Martin Niemöller, Karl Obermann, Otto Sattler, Paul Tillich, Ernst Toller, Franz Carl Weiskopf, Franz Werfel and Stefan Zweig.

It absorbed the *Deutsches Volksecho* on 20 October 1939.

Sources: Arndt/Olson; Cazden, *Exile Literature*, pp. 45, 189; Maas II, pp. 584-589; Maas IV; Ragg, pp. 48-50, 70-79.

DIE VOLKSRECHTE		NY New York	1849?-?
Title trans.:	The People's Rights	*First issue:*	1849?
Subtitle:		*Last issue:*	?
Add. lang.:		*Vols. (nos.):*	
First editor:	Viktor Wilhelm Fröhlich	*Frequency:*	
First publ.:	G. Arnold & V.W. Fröhlich	*Preservation:*	7
Related pubs.:		*Supplements:*	
Circulation:		*Category:*	workers' club

Depositories:

Arndt/Olson call this paper the organ of the Arbeiter Vereine der Vereinigten Staaten [Workers' Associations of the United States].

According to Cazden, the constitution of the Arbeitervereine of the state of New York, whose organ apparently *Die Volksrechte* was, implied that membership was open to any worker, i.e. "any person who through his own intellectual or physical efforts is useful to society." Priority was given to land reform (free homesteads).

Sources: Arndt/Olson; Eberlein 22828; Cazden, *Book Trade*, p. (663).

VOLKSSTIMME	O Toronto	1944-1949?

Title trans.:	Voice of the People	*First issue:*	My 1944
Subtitle:	Anti-Nazi Monthly	*Last issue:*	My 1949?
Add. lang.:		*Vols. (nos.):*	
First editor:		*Frequency:*	m
First publ.:	German-Canadian Federation	*Preservation:*	3
Related pubs.:		*Supplements:*	
Circulation:		*Category:*	antifascist

Depositories: Usa-NN [1944-46]; Cdn-OONL [1944-49]

This paper had 16 pages. The subtitle after May/June 1945 was the "People's Voice." It was published by the German- Canadian Federation, Toronto, which was organized in June 1942. It was illustrated and contained cartoons.

Sources: Arndt/Olson; *Checklist*, p. 147.

VOLKS-STIMME	PA Philadelphia	1925-?

Title trans.:	Voice of the People	*First issue:*	? 1925
Subtitle:		*Last issue:*	?
Add. lang.:		*Vols. (nos.):*	
First editor:	Edmund Thomaser	*Frequency:*	w
First publ.:		*Preservation:*	7
Related pubs.:		*Supplements:*	
Circulation:		*Category:*	socialist-SP

Depositories:

This was an 8-page socialist weekly published on Wednesdays. It was the official organ of the German-language group of the Socialist Party. Thomaser had previously been editor of the *Philadelphia Tageblatt*.

Source: *American Labor Press Directory*, p. 19.

VOLKSSTIMME DES WESTENS	MO St. Louis	1877-1880

Title trans.:	Voice of the People of the West	*First issue:*	3 S 1877
Subtitle:	Organ of the Socialistische Arbeiter-Partei	*Last issue:*	19 Je 1880
Add. lang.:		*Vols. (nos.):*	
First editor:	A. Otto-Walster	*Frequency:*	d
First publ.:	Arbeiter-Press-Verein	*Preservation:*	1
Related pubs.:		*Supplements:*	Sonntagsbeilage; Wochenblatt
Circulation:	1880:3800	*Category:*	socialist-SLP

Depositories: Usa-MoS; D-188/144 (D 1877-D 1878)

This paper was the organ of the St. Louis section of the Socialist Labor Party, which may have been close to the Greenback Party (Ayer).

Its motto was: "Gerechtigkeit für Alle!" [Justice for All!]. In an advertisement the *Volksstimme des Westens* proclaimed that it was guided by the motto: "Nieder mit dem Monopol der Ausbeutung. Es lebe das Recht der Freien Arbeit!" [Down with the monopoly of exploitation. Long live the rights of free labor!).

The paper regularly contained an editorial by Otto-Walster*, news from Europe and America, satires, short stories and serialized novels. In the local news great emphasis was put on reports of suicides, crimes, accidents and cases of women who had become destitute. The *Volksstimme des Westens* attached more importance to women's concerns than most other papers. It denounced harmful panaceas, e.g. a tincture causing abortion, it gave advice on children's education etc. There were also reports and announcements from workers' organizations and their meetings. The issue of 27 May published the platform of the Socialistische Arbeiter-Partei.

Among the contributors were M. Jokai, H. von Lankenau, Moritz Busch.

Sources: Arndt/Olson; Eberlein 22829. On Otto-Walster, see New York *Arbeiterstimme*.

The *Volksstimme des Westens: Sonntagsbeilage* [Sunday Supplement] was edited by Carl Brunneman and Otto Ludwig. Its two pages contained poems, riddles and stories, some of them by Richard Schmidt-Cabanis. The circulation in 1880 was 4500 (Ayer).

Source: Arndt/Olson.

The *Wochenblatt der Volksstimme des Westens* [weekly edition], which seems to be lost, appeared on Wednesdays. It contained eight pages and was published to "cater for the needs of the farmers, of readers living in smaller towns of the state, as well as for workers and political friends living in farther distance." (from the prospectus). The circulation in 1880 was 5500. Arndt/Olson give the dates of appearance as 1878?-1888?

Source: Arndt/Olson.

DER VOLKSTRIBUN	PA Pittsburgh	1850

Title trans.:	The People's Tribune	*First issue:*	Ag 1850
Subtitle:		*Last issue:*	O 1850
Add. lang.:		*Vols. (nos.):*	
First editor:	Karl Peteler	*Frequency:*	
First publ.:		*Preservation:*	7
Related pubs.:		*Supplements:*	
Circulation:		*Category:*	

Depositories:

No further information could be obtained.
Source: Cazden, *Book Trade*, p. (646).

DER VOLKS-TRIBUN	NY New York	1846

Title trans.:	The People's Tribune	*First issue:*	5 Ja 1846
Subtitle:	Organ der deutschen Sozialreform-Association in New York	*Last issue:*	31 D 1846
Add. lang.:		*Vols. (nos.):*	1(1-52)
First editor:	Hermann Kriege	*Frequency:*	w
First publ.:	Deutsche Socialreform-Association in N.Y.	*Preservation:*	1
Related pubs.:		*Supplements:*	
Circulation:		*Category:*	reform

Depositories: Usa-WHi; D-188/144 (1,m)

Subtitle translation: Organ of the German Social Reform Assocation. Later the subtitle changed to Organ der Jugend Amerikas [Organ of the Youth of America]. The motto of nos. 1-25 was "Halt! Die Arbeit hoch! Nieder mit dem Kapital!" [Halt! Long live Labor! Down with Capital!]. On the title-page appeared a vignette of Masaniello: "der große Fischer, der für eine zertretene Unschuld ein ganzes Reich in Flammen setzte". [The big fishermen who set a whole empire in flames for the sake of a trampled innocence]

Der Volks-Tribun was the first German labor newspaper in New York. Kriege* himself called it a continuation of Baboef's *Tribune du peuple*. *Der Volks-Tribun* was an ardent supporter of the Free Soil movement. It advocated separate political actions by workers. Being an organ of the Sozialreform-Association and the German Jung-Amerika-Gemeinde, it was severely criticized by Marx and other German communists at a convention in Brussels in May 1846. They declared in an open letter to Kriege that *Der Volks-Tribun* was not communist, but childish, bombastic and sentimental. Weitling was the only one to vote against this verdict.

The Sozialreform-Association approved of a war between America and Great Britain in 1846 and even organized volunteers. Kriege established contacts to Tammany Hall in order to influence it toward the aims of the Sozialreform-Association. *Der Volks-Tribun* contained reports from the meetings of the Sozialreform-Association and other events of the labor movement, addresses to women, anticlerical articles, poems and letters to the editor. Each edition consisted of four pages and there were no advertisements. Among the contributors were Wilhelm Trautwein, Harro Harring, Karl Heinzen and August Gläser.

Sources: Arndt/Olson; Eberlein 22832; Kamman, pp. 36-37; Schlüter, *Anfänge*, pp. 25-47; Foner, *History* I, p. 77. On Kriege, see Ernst, p. 113.

DER VOLKSVERTRETER	PA Philadelphia	1850-?

Title trans.:	The People's Advocate	*First issue:*	30 Mr 1850
Subtitle:		*Last issue:*	?
Add. lang.:		*Vols. (nos.):*	
First editor:	August Gläser, Nikolaus Schmitt, J.M. Reichart	*Frequency:*	d
First publ.:		*Preservation:*	7
Related pubs.:		*Supplements:*	
Circulation:		*Category:*	radical fortyeighter

Depositories:

Schmitt and Reichart were both refugees of the 1848 Revolution in Germany. They had to suspend publication of their daily after six months. The paper is said to have been directed against world reform schemes such as Weitling's. In the following year Schmitt issued the monthly *Gradaus*.

Sources: Arndt/Olson; Wittke, *Press*, pp. 84, 119, 172; Kamman, p. 39.

VOLKSZEITUNG (Milwaukee Volkszeitung)	WI Milwaukee	1890-1892

Title trans.:	Milwaukee People's News	*First issue:*	1 Ja 1890
Subtitle:		*Last issue:*	31 D 1892
Add. lang.:		*Vols. (nos.):*	vol. 9?-12?
First editor:	Jacob Hunger	*Frequency:*	d
First publ.:	Socialist Publishing Society	*Preservation:*	7
Related pubs.:	c *Milwaukee'r Arbeiter-Zeitung;* s *Wisconsin Vorwärts*	*Supplements:*	Vowärts, Wahrheit
Circulation:		*Category:*	socialist

Depositories:

The numbering was continued from its predecessor, the *Milwaukee'r Arbeiter-Zeitung*. Other editors were Simon Hickler (February-June 1890), Gustav A. Rahn (July-August 1890), Michael Biron (to December 1892). It was the organ of the Federated Trades Council. On 1 January 1890, "the Socialistic Publishing Society absorbed the *Täglicher Reformer* of Robert Schilling, merged it with its own *Milwaukee'r Arbeiterzeitung*, discontinued using either of these titles and commenced publishing a new daily, called the *Milwaukee Volkszeitung*." In 1891 the typesetters of the *Volkszeitung* went on strike, because a foreman had been dismissed. (*BZ* 16 D 1891). Apparently the conflict continued between the typesetters, who were organized in Typographia No. 10 of Milwaukee, and the paper's management: in April 1892

Typographia No. 10 petitioned the Federated Trades Council to refuse to allow the *Volkszeitung* to be their organ any longer. The petition was rejected. In October 1892 the union-cut (union label), which signified that the print shop was operated exclusively by union members, was withdrawn from the paper. (*BZ* 16 Ap, 16 My, 16 O 1892).

Immediately after Biron's resignation, Victor L. Berger* assumed control over the *Volkszeitungs*-papers in January 1893. See *Wisconsin Vorwärts*.

Sunday edition: *Vorwärts*. See there. Weekly edition: *Die Wahrheit*. See there.

Sources: Arndt/Olson; Knoche, pp. 205-206; *BZ*.

VOLKSZEITUNG DER PACIFIC-KÜSTE	CA San Francisco	1891-1894?

Title trans.:	People's Journal of the Pacific Coast	*First issue:*	? 1891
Subtitle:		*Last issue:*	1894?
Add. lang.:		*Vols. (nos.):*	
First editor:	Albert Currlin	*Frequency:*	w
First publ.:	Volks-Zeitungs Publishing Co.	*Preservation:*	6
Related pubs.:		*Supplements:*	
Circulation:		*Category:*	labor

Depositories: Usa-WHi (29 Ag 1891)

This was a labor weekly with 12 pages. In June 1892 a court order prohibited the *Volkszeitung* from continuing to publicize a boycott against certain breweries.

Note: Arndt/Olson give 1891-1892? as dates; Broadbent gives 1891-1894.

Sources: Arndt/Olson; *History of Foreign Journalism in San Francisco* 33; Broadbent, p. 661; *BZ* 1 Jl, 1 Ag 1892.

VOLKS-ZEITUNG	IL Chicago	1877

Title trans.:	People's News	*First issue:*	11 F 1877
Subtitle:		*Last issue:*	26 My 1877
Add. lang.:		*Vols. (nos.):*	
First editor:	Joseph Brucker	*Frequency:*	d
First publ.:	Social-Democratic Printing Co.	*Preservation:*	7
Related pubs.:		*Supplements:*	
Circulation:		*Category:*	socialist

Depositories:

This paper which had been founded by Joseph Brucker was probably sold in April 1877 by the stockholders to the printers and editorial staff of the paper and edited by Hermann Siegel. On 26 May 1877 the printing shop, which had been mortgaged earlier, was sold to Conrad Conzett*, who two days later started using its machinery to publish the *Chicagoer Arbeiter-Zeitung*.

Note: Arndt/Olson mention it as a weekly, and give as the dates of appearance 1874-1876?.

Sources: Arndt/Olson; *BZ* 1 My 1877; "Zur Geschichte der Chicagoer Arbeiter-Zeitung, des Vorboten und der Fackel" [On the History...], *Chicagoer*

Arbeiterzeitung 21 Je 1888. On Conzett, see Chicago *Vorbote*.

DER VORBOTE   IL Chicago   1874-1924

Title trans.:	The Harbinger		*First issue:*	14 F 1874
Subtitle:	see below		*Last issue:*	30 Ap 1924
Add. lang.:			*Vols. (nos.):*	
First editor:	Carl Klings		*Frequency:*	
First publ.:			*Preservation:*	2
Related pubs.:	*Chicagoer Arbeiter-Zeitung*		*Supplements:*	
Circulation:	1876:3334; 1885:8000; 1900:5000;		*Category:*	socialist/
	1915:3500; 1920:8000			anarchist

Depositories: Usa-ICN [1884-1902]; Usa-NN (1874-1907); Usa-WHi ([1874-1891],
1903-24); D-188/144 (1874-1907,1917-24,m)

This was a radically socialist weekly with anarchist tendencies. It was the
weekly edition of the *Chicagoer Arbeiter-Zeitung* from 1 May 1879 to 13
October. This paper was founded by the "Sozial-Politischer Arbeiter-Verein in
Chicago," which was incorporated as a publishing society; the following were
elected as trustees: Carl Klings, Jacob Winnen and C.H. Kraus; as publisher,
Conrad Conzett. Since the costs for paper, typesetting and printing exceeded
the income, loans for $1 were issued and sold to supporters. It was excluded
from Germany under the antisocialist laws in 1881 (Auer); according to the
Buchdrucker-Zeitung of 1 September 1878 it had already been deprived of the
right of sale in that year (1878). It was suspended from 5 to 8 May 1886 during the Haymarket Affair. To some extent the changing subtitles indicate the
changing emphasis of the paper: Organ der Arbeiterpartei für Stadt und Land
[Organ of the Labor Party for City and Country] (14 February 1874-12 August
1876); Organ und Eigentum der Arbeiter-Partei der Vereinigten Staaten
[Organ and Property of the Workingmen's Party of the U.S.] (19 August 1876-9
February 1878); Unabhängiges Organ für die wahren Interessen des Proletari-
ats [Independent Organ for the True Concerns of the Working Class] (16
February 1878-15 May 1880); Wochenausgabe der *Chicagoer Arbeiter-Zeitung*
[Weekly Edition of the *Chicagoer Arbeiter-Zeitung*] (22 May 1880-13 October
1919). It was the organ of the Arbeiterpartei von Illinois (Workingmen's Party
of Illinois) in 1874, the organ of the Internationale Arbeiter-Association
(International Working Men's Association) in 1875, the organ of the SLP in
1876-?. It was edited by Carl Klings* (with Joseph Grünhut, Jacob Winnen and
Conrad Conzett) (14 February-May 1874), Jacob Winnen (March-? 1874), Con-
rad Conzett* (? 1874-June 1878), Paul Grottkau* (July 1878-fall 1880), Liebig
(fall 1880-fall 1881), Paul Grottkau (fall 1881-16 September 1884); the
managing director after 1881 was August Spies and the paper was edited by
August Spies* and Michael Schwab* (September 1884-May 1886), Joseph
Dietzgen* (May 1886-April 1888), Jens L. Christensen* (April 1888-?), Simon
Hickler (December 1889?-1894), Max Baginski* (1894-?) and Adolph Dreifuß (?
April 1924). It was published by Das Presse-Comitee der Buchdruckerei des
Vorbote (Conrad Conzett) (14 February 1874-July 1878), the
Deutschsprechende Sektion der SAP [German-language Branch of the SLP],
i.e. Socialistic Publishing Society (July 1878-1892) and by the Chicagoer
Arbeiter-Zeitung Publishing Co. (1892-1924).

The paper contained political and labor news from America and from abroad,
especially from Germany as well as announcements of unions and

workers'organizations; after 1877 there was a section with humorous articles on exotic countries, tips for farming, gardening, animal-keeping and house-keeping. After 1919 it again published articles of a more political nature as well as news and announcements of the SP. A regular feature after 26 October 1919 was a "Kultur-Sektion," which dealt with art, literature, science and health education. Contributors were Paul Kampffmeyer, Arnold Höllriegel, Ludwig Börne, Robert Degen, Arnold Dodel, Heinrich Bartel, Björnstjerne Björnson, Fritz Mauthner, Carl Fischer, Carl Hauptmann, Otto Walberg, Jakob Wassermann, Kurt Eisner, Paul Keller, Selma Lagerlöf, Peter Rosegger, Robert Reitzel, Ivan Turgenev, Ernst Heckel and many others.

Sources: Arndt/Olson; Eberlein 22849; Schlüter, *Internationale*, pp. 320-325, 370, 393; Morgan, "Einige Daten aus der Chicagoer Arbeiterbewegung," [Some Information on the Chicago Labor Movement], *New Yorker Volkszeitung* 21 F 1903, p. 25; "Zur Geschichte der Chicagoer Arbeiter-Zeitung, des Vorboten und der Fackel," [On the History...], *Chicagoer Arbeiter-Zeitung* 21 Je 1888; Auer, p. 338; *BZ* 1 S 1878; Sorge, p. 151 et passim; Kiesewetter. On Conzett, see Verena Conzett, *Erstrebtes und Erlebtes* [Aims and Achievements], (Zürich, 1929) and obituary in *BZ* 16 D 1897. On Grottkau, see Waltershausen, p. 236; *Geschichte der deutschen Arbeiterbewegung*, p. 173; obituary in Detroit *Herold* 10 Je 1898. On Spies, see Waltershausen, p. 303-307; Foner, *Autobiographies*, pp. 59ff; *Vorbote* 8 S 1886. On Schwab, see Waltershausen, p. 310; Foner, *Autobiographies*, pp. 99ff; *Vorbote* 8 S 1886. On Dietzgen, see Osterroth, p. 64; Marx/Engels, *Werke* XXXVI, pp. 36, 896; *Vorbote* 25 Ap 1888. On Christensen, see Auer, p. 285; *Freiheit* 21 Ap 1888. On Klings, see *Der Deutsche Arbeiter*. On Baginski, see *Sturmglocke*.

VORWÄRTS		NJ Newark	1877-1879?

Title trans.:	Forward	*First issue:*	Jl 1877
Subtitle:		*Last issue:*	1879?
Add. lang.:		*Vols. (nos.):*	
First editor:	Carl Savary	*Frequency:*	w, d
First publ.:	Heymann & Scholvien	*Preservation:*	7
Related pubs.:		*Supplements:*	
Circulation:	1877:1500	*Category:*	socialist-WP

Depositories:

This was a weekly from July to 30 September 1877 when it became a daily. According to the *Freidenker* (20 January 1878) the *Vorwärts* was no longer published at that time. This organ of the Newark section of the Arbeiterpartei der Vereinigten Staaten [Workingmen's Party of the U.S.] was published by Heymann & Scholvien; later by the Journeymen Printing Association.

The New York Typographia criticized the Arbeiterpartei for letting their organ be published in a print-shop where apprentices were employed as cheap labor. "Yes, it has to be cheap, but what will the workers say about such a newspaper, which wants to and should defend their interests?" (*BZ* 1 S 1877).

From Newark came the reply that besides five regular printers only two apprentices were employed. Because of the labor struggles of that year the section had wanted to publish a labor newspaper as cheaply and quickly as possible and therefore they had accepted the offer of Heymann & Scholvien's print-shop which produced 1500 copies for only $33. By the sixth issue the paper already had 1500 subscribers and a very successful workers' festival had yielded so much profit that the Newark section would soon be able to have their own print shop. (*BZ* 15 S 1877).

Sources: Arndt/Olson; Eberlein 22855; Schlüter, *Internationale*, p. 394; *BZ*.

VORWÄRTS (I)		NY New York	1878-1932

Title trans.:	Forward	*First issue:*	? Ja 1878
Subtitle:	Wochenblatt der New Yorker Volkszeitung	*Last issue:*	15 O 1932
Add. lang.:		*Vols. (nos.):*	1 (1)-55 (42)
First editor:	Hugo Vogt	*Frequency:*	w
First publ.:	Socialistic Co-operative Publ. Society	*Preservation:*	1
Related pubs.:	*New Yorker Volkszeitung*	*Supplements:*	
Circulation:	1880:5700; 1900:10,000; 1915:45,000; 1925: 8000; 1930:15,000	*Category:*	socialist

Depositories: Usa-NNRa (1878,1888-1932); D-188/144 (1878-1932, microfilmed with *New Yorker Volkszeitung*)

This weekly edition of the *New Yorker Volkszeitung* appeared Saturdays. The title varied: *Wochenblatt der New Yorker Volkszeitung*, 1878-?. According to the last issue of the *Vorwärts* (New York) (Organ of the SLP 1892-1894), the SLP made a contract with the *New Yorker Volkszeitung* to change the name of its weekly *Wochenblatt* to *Vorwärts* in November 1894. No evidence could be found to prove this. Arndt/Olson give May 1897 as the end of the title *Wochenblatt*, but this could not be confirmed either. The subtitle, usually given in the masthead was Central Organ der Socialistischen Arbeiter-Partei von Nord-Amerika [Socialist Labor Party of North America], later: Organ der Socialist Party.

It contained American and international news. Regular features were "Aus den Neuenglandstaaten" [From the New England States], a women's page, tips for farming, gardening and housekeeping. During World War One there was a special column of war news.

There were contributions by Roda Roda, Paul Heyse, Peter Rosegger and many others.

Sources: Arndt/Olson; Eberlein 22854; *The American Labor Press Directory*, p. 22. On Lore, see DeLeon, p. 140.

VORWÄRTS (II)	NY New York	1892-1894

Title trans.:	Forward	*First issue:*	19 N 1892
Subtitle:	Central-Organ der Sozialistischen	*Last issue:*	17 N 1894
	Arbeiter-Partei von Nord-Amerika		
Add. lang.:		*Vols. (nos.):*	1 (1)-2(52)
First editor:	W.L. Rosenberg	*Frequency:*	w
First publ.:	New York Labor News Co.	*Preservation:*	1
Related pubs.:	c *Der Sozialist*; s *Vorwärts-Wochenblatt*	*Supplements:*	
	der New Yorker Volkszeitung		
Circulation:		*Category:*	socialist-SLP

Depositories: Usa-NN; D-188/144 (1,m)

This paper was edited by Wilhelm Ludwig Rosenberg and then by Hugo Vogt. The first publisher, the New York Labor News Co., was owned by the SLP. The motto (in 1894) was "Wissen ist Macht" [Knowledge is Power]. It succeeded *Der Sozialist*, the numbering of which it continued only in its first issue of 19 November 1892 (vol. 8, no. 47). Its second issue of 26 November 1892 is numbered vol. 1, no. 2. Initially it had 8 pages but from 25 November 1893 the format changed to octavo with 16 pages. The pages are numbered consecutively throughout the second volume.

It contained news from the SLP and its sections, platforms and appeals, articles on the labor movement and the organization of unemployed workers, the progress of socialism in foreign countries, anarchism and diverse scientific subjects. It did not neglect women's issues containing features on matriarchy, women's suffrage, the organization of female workers as well as prostitution. The issue of 24 October 1892 reprinted a lecture by Wilhelm Liebknecht on communism, socialism and anarchism. The second volume contained more literary features and more illustrations. The last number published the contract of the SLP with the *New Yorker Volkszeitung* which agreed to change the name of its weekly *Wochenblatt* to *Vorwärts - Wochenblatt der New Yorker Volkszeitung* and to reserve five columns for the SLP. No evidence could be found to confirm this.

There were contributions by Friedrich Engels, Wilhelm Liebknecht, the late Joseph Dietzgen, Philip Rapaport, Georg C. Stiebeling, Alexander Jonas, Eduard Berg, Adolph Hoffmann; translations from Charles Dickens and Mark Twain.

Source: Arndt/Olson.

VORWÄRTS (MILWAUKEE'R SOCIALIST) (I)	WI Milwaukee	1878-1879

Title trans.:	Forward (Milwaukee Socialist)	*First issue:*	17 Ag 1878
Subtitle:		*Last issue:*	O 1879
Add. lang.:		*Vols. (nos.):*	
First editor:	Hermann Sigel	*Frequency:*	d
First publ.:	Johann Joseph Brucker	*Preservation:*	7
Related pubs.:	s *Milwaukeer Freie Presse*; m (c)? *Der Socialist (Milwaukee'r Socialist)*	*Supplements:*	
Circulation:		*Category:*	socialist

Depositories:

The editors after Sigel were Michael Biron (27 August - September 1878) with Ernst Buhlert (local editor) and Anthony Gfrorner (business manager).

On 24 September 1878 Richard Michaelis purchased the paper from Brucker, the first editor, for $1900. The change in ownership marked the end of the paper as an organ of the social democrats. The tendency was now republican and to indicate this change in policy the *Vorwärts* was renamed the *Milwaukeer Freie Presse* on 29 October 1879. The new owner nevertheless considered the *Freie Presse* as a successor to Brucker's papers and followed the numbering of *Der Socialist*.

Variants: Arndt/Olson give September 1878 - January 1879 as the dates of appearance. Brucker is named as the editor and the Socialist Printing Co. as the publisher. The description follows Knoche.

Sources: Arndt/Olson; Knoche, pp. 181-184.

VORWÄRTS (II)	WI Milwaukee	1887-1932

Title trans.:	Forward	*First issue:*	1 Ja 1887
Subtitle:	Organ der Social-Demokratischen Partei von Wisconsin	*Last issue:*	31 D 1932
Add. lang.:		*Vols. (nos.):*	
First editor:	Victor L. Berger*	*Frequency:*	w
First publ.:	Socialistic Publishing Society	*Preservation:*	1
Related pubs.:	c *Wisconsin Vorwärts*; *Die Wahrheit*	*Supplements:*	
Circulation:	1890:3800; 1910:12,500; 1915:38,000; 1919:4300	*Category:*	social democrat

Depositories: Usa-WM; D-188/144 (1898-1932,m)

Later the subtitle changed: Unabhängige Sozialistische Zeitung [Independent Socialist Weekly].

This paper was the Sunday edition of the *Milwaukee'r Arbeiterzeitung* (1887-1889), of the *Milwaukee Volkszeitung* (1890 - 1 January 1893) and of the *Wisconsin Vorwärts* (8 January 1893 - 1898). See there for editors and publishers.

After the *Wisconsin Vorwärts* was discontinued on 21 August 1898 it became a separate weekly publication. The assistant editors during Berger's editorship until October 1911 were Jacob Hunger, Carl Kleist and Edward Deuss; Heinrich Bartel (November 1911 - 31 December 1932). The publishers were the Vorwärts Publishing Co. (with Hermann W. Bistorius as business manager) (December 1905 - March 1911); the Milwaukee Social-Democratic Publishing Co. headed by V. Berger and Frederic Heath (April 1911 - 31 December 1932). It was printed by the Germania Publishing Co., which in 1901 had 9 Linotype printing machines and 42 employees, all union members except the engineer (*BZ* 16 Ja 1901).

According to Berger, the *Vorwärts* would continue to be a weapon of the progressive proletariat, a paper propagating socialism. (Knoche, p. 207) By 1904 the content of the *Vorwärts* as well as that of the *Wahrheit*, the weekly edition of the discontinued *Wisconsin Vorwärts*, were almost identical. By 1911 the *Vorwärts* was the last remaining German-language socialist newspaper in Milwaukee. In the late 1920s it was operating at a deficit, because due to the economic depression many of its former subscribers were out of work.

It contained political news, party news, news from the labor movement and local news. Other regular features were a women's page, which included reports on the situation of women in foreign countries as well as recipes, announcements of meetings and advertisements, mostly for local businesses.

Sources: Arndt/Olson; Knoche, pp. 206-210; *BZ*. On Berger, see *Wisconsin Vorwärts*. On Bartel, see autobiographical article in *Solidarität*, Jl 1946, pp. 127-128, S 1946, pp. 165-166; O 1946, pp. 183-184.

VORWÄRTS		O Toronto	1948-?

Title trans.:	Forward	*First issue:*	? 1948
Subtitle:	Organ deutscher Sozialdemokraten in Canada	*Last issue:*	?
Add. lang.:	English (?)	*Vols. (nos.):*	
First editor:	Henry Weisbach	*Frequency:*	m
First publ.:	Canadian Club Forward (CCF)	*Preservation:*	3?
Related pubs.:		*Supplements:*	
Circulation:		*Category:*	social democrat

Depositories: Cdn-OONL [1951-71]

This was a mimeographed monthly with 20 leaves. Later, the subtitle changed to Magazine of German Social Democrats in Canada, Monatsschrift; after 1963, Democratic Monthly, Demokratische Monatsschrift. Edited by Henry Weisbach and by a Committee of the Club, it was published by the Canadian Club Forward; in 1963, by the Sudeten Club Forward.

Sources: Arndt/Olson; *Checklist*, p. 147.

VORWÄRTS DER PACIFIC KÜSTE   CA San Francisco   1911-1919

Title trans.:	Forward of the Pacific Coast	*First issue:*	18 Mr 1911
Subtitle:	Officielles Organ der fortschrittlichen deutschen Gewerkschaften und Vereine Kaliforniens	*Last issue:*	?1919
Add. lang.:		*Vols. (nos.):*	
First editor:	Emil Ließ	*Frequency:*	w
First publ.:	California Labor Publishing Association	*Preservation:*	7
Related pubs.:	c Wochenblatt des San Francisco Tageblatt	*Supplements:*	
Circulation:		*Category:*	socialist-SP

Lib. code: title translation: Official Organ of the Progressive German ons and Societies.

Depositories:

This was the organ of the Socialist Party of San Francisco. The first issue commemorated the Commune of Paris.

Sources: Arndt/Olson; Eberlein 22859; *History of Foreign Journalism in San Francisco*, p. 33; *Vorwärts* (Berlin/Germany), 23 Ap 1911; *Le Peuple* (Brussels/Belgium), 14 F 1911.

DIE WAHRHEIT   PA Philadelphia   1901?-?

Title trans.:	The Truth	*First issue:*	1901?
Subtitle:		*Last issue:*	?
Add. lang.:		*Vols. (nos.):*	
First editor:		*Frequency:*	
First publ.:		*Preservation:*	7
Related pubs.:		*Supplements:*	
Circulation:		*Category:*	

Depositories:

This was a "Kampfblatt" [militant newspaper] managed by Julius Weber. It was printed in the same print-shop as the *Philadelphia Tageblatt*.

Sources: Arndt/Olson; *BZ* 16 F 1901.

DIE WAHRHEIT	WI Milwaukee	1889-1910

Title trans.:	The Truth	*First issue:*	Ja 1889
Subtitle:	Organ der Sozialdemokratischen Partei von Wisconsin	*Last issue:*	25 Je 1910
Add. lang.:		*Vols. (nos.):*	1-22 (1-26)
First editor:	Valentin Blatz(?)	*Frequency:*	w
First publ.:	Socialistic Publishing Society	*Preservation:*	2-3
Related pubs.:	*Vorwärts*	*Supplements:*	
Circulation:	1890:2000; 1900:6231; 1919:10,000	*Category:*	social democrat

Depositories: Usa-WHi [1893-1910]; D-188/144 (1,m)

This was the weekly edition of the *Milwaukee'r Arbeiterzeitung* (after January 1889); of the *Milwaukee Volkszeitung* (1890 - 1892); and of the *Wisconsin Vorwärts* (1893 - 1898). After the closing of the *Wisconsin Vorwärts* it continued as a separate weekly publication in August 1898. When it became a separate publication it was enlarged from four to eight pages. See also *Vorwärts*.

Sources: Arndt/Olson; Eberlein 22862; Knoche, pp. 205, 208.

WILDE ROSEN	PA Philadelphia	1851-?

Title trans.:	Wild Roses	*First issue:*	? 1851
Subtitle:		*Last issue:*	?
Add. lang.:		*Vols. (nos.):*	
First editor:	Wilhelm Rosenthal	*Frequency:*	w
First publ.:	Friedrich Wilhelm Thomas	*Preservation:*	7
Related pubs.:		*Supplements:*	
Circulation:		*Category:*	early socialist

Depositories:

According to Wittke, this paper first appeared in 1850 as a weekly paper coming out every Sunday. Its principles championed atheism, socialism and the class struggle. The *Leipziger Charivari* of 16 May 1851 describes its tendency as "rationalistisch."

Sources: Arndt/Olson; Arndt/Olson 2; Wittke, *Refugees*, p. 167.

THE WISCONSIN ADVOCATE   WI Milwaukee   1880-?

Title trans.:		*First issue:*	Mr 1880
Subtitle:	Official Organ of the Ancient Order of United Workmen, Wisconsin	*Last issue:*	?
Add. lang.:	English	*Vols. (nos.):*	
First editor:		*Frequency:*	m
First publ.:	B. Loewenbach & Son	*Preservation:*	?
Related pubs.:		*Supplements:*	
Circulation:		*Category:*	labor union-KofL

Depositories: Usa-WHi [1880-81]

This was a monthly published in large quarto, each issue having 8 pages. It was written in English and German. The subtitle of the German section was Officielles Organ für Wisconsin des A.O.V.A. (Alter Orden der vereinigten Arbeiter ?) Deutsche Abt. and the running title *The Wisconsin A.O.U.W. Advocate* (Ancient Order of United Workmen). The publisher after Loewenbach was H.H. Zahl & Co.

Source: Arndt/Olson.

WISCONSIN VORWÄRTS   WI Milwaukee   1893-1898

Title trans.:	Wisconsin Forward	*First issue:*	1 Ja 1893
Subtitle:	Officielles Organ der American Federation of Labor sowie des Federated Trades Council von Milwaukee	*Last issue:*	17 Ag 1898
Add. lang.:		*Vols. (nos.):*	
First editor:	Victor L. Berger	*Frequency:*	d
First publ.:	Vorwärts Publishing Co.	*Preservation:*	1
Related pubs.:	c *Milwaukee Volkszeitung*; s *Vorwärts*	*Supplements:*	*Vorwärts, Die Wahrheit*
Circulation:		*Category:*	socialist

Depositories: Usa-WM

The issue of this paper of 3 January 1893 is vol. 12, no. 1, indicating that Berger* continued the numbering of the *Milwaukee Volkszeitung* which itself followed the numbering of the *Milwaukee'r Arbeiter-Zeitung* and the *Arminia* before that. (Knoche) Its complete title was *Wisconsin Vorwärts und Milwaukee Volkszeitung, Arbeiter-Zeitung und Täglicher Reformer*.

It was published from 1894 - ? by a stock company for which the Federated Trades Council had contributed $500 and several other unions smaller amounts (*BZ* 16 S 1894).

The *Wisconsin Vorwärts*, as well as its Sunday edition *Vorwärts* and its weekly *Die Wahrheit* expressed the political ideas of the social democrats and also carried news coverage of international and local events as well as items of cultural interest. Financial difficulties forced Berger to suspend the daily, but

he continued the weekly Sunday *Vorwärts* until 1932 and *Die Wahrheit* until 1910.
Note: This description follows Knoche. Arndt/Olson are confusing in their dating and description of the *Wisconsin Vorwärts* and the *Vorwärts*.
Sources: Arndt/Olson; Knoche, pp. 205-207. On Berger, see Knoche, p. 20; Ueberhorst, *Turner und Sozialdemokraten*, p. 21; Miller, pp. 131-134; Sally M. Miller, *Victor Berger and the Promise of Constructive Socialism, 1910-1920* (Westport, CT, 1973).

WOLFSAUGEN		MO St. Louis	1900-1901?
Title trans.:	Wolf's Eyes	*First issue:*	13 O 1900
Subtitle:	Ein Blatt für Freie Geister	*Last issue:*	1901?
Add. lang.:		*Vols. (nos.):*	
First editor:	Martin Drescher*	*Frequency:*	w
First publ.:		*Preservation:*	6
Related pubs.:	c *Der Arme Teufel*; s *Mephisto*	*Supplements:*	
Circulation:		*Category:*	anarchist

Depositories: <§Usa-MWKJA (27 O 1900)

Subtitle translation: A Newspaper for Liberal Minds.
This paper was printed by the Co-operative Printing Co., owned by Philip Morlang. The motto was "Ich bin kein Schaf, ich bin kein Hund/Kein Hofrath und kein Schellfisch./Ich bin ein Wolf geblieben, mein Herz/Und meine Zähne wölfisch." [I'm not a sheep, I'm not a dog/ Not a Privy Councillor nor a haddock./ I have remained a wolf, my heart/ Is still a wolf's and my teeth are fangs]
It was an anarchist paper of individualistic tendency. The editorial of the first issue stated that it would fight for those who bore chains and against those who made them. It was dedicated to those who were hungry for knowledge and beauty. It contained articles on topics such as revolutionary lyrics, gypsies, the German theater in St. Louis, poems and short stories, a letter-box and advertisements for local businesses. It published reprints, e.g. of Iwan Turgeniev and Rudyard Kipling. Drescher's next undertaking was the publication of *Mephisto* in September 1901.
Sources: Arndt/Olson; Arndt/Olson 2, p. 424; *BZ* 1 D 1900. On Drescher, see Kamman, pp. 113-114; Kosch, vol. 3; Poore, p. 221; *BZ* 1 S 1913; Schultz I, p. 348.

YOUTH OUTLOOK	NY New York	1939

Title trans.:	Jugend Wacht	*First issue:*	N 1939
Subtitle:		*Last issue:*	D 1939?
Add. lang.:	English	*Vols. (nos.):*	1 (1-2?)
First editor:		*Frequency:*	m
First publ.:		*Preservation:*	1?
Related pubs.:	c *Das neue Leben*	*Supplements:*	
Circulation:		*Category:*	communist

Depositories: <§ Usa-KyLC

This was a monthly newspaper for young people published by the German-American Youth Federation, an affiliate of the Deutsch-Amerikanischer Kulturverband (see *Volksfront*). The title and entire front page were printed in English, with most of the text in German inside. It advocated the "communist policy of neutrality of its time, i.e. the Hitler-Stalin Pact in August 1939," and was "anti-British, anti-French, and anti-war." (Cazden).

Source: Cazden, *Exile Literature*, pp. 48, 189.

DIE ZEIT	NY New York	1845?-1846?

Title trans.:	The Times	*First issue:*	27 D 1845?
Subtitle:		*Last issue:*	27 Je 1846?
Add. lang.:		*Vols. (nos.):*	
First editor:	Victor Wilhelm Fröhlich	*Frequency:*	w
First publ.:	Charles Müller	*Preservation:*	1?
Related pubs.:		*Supplements:*	
Circulation:		*Category:*	socialist/ freethought

Depositories: Usa-MdBZ

This was reputedly the first socialist newspaper in New York and an organ for freethought ideas. With the issue of *Die Fackel* of 4 April 1846 Samuel Ludvigh transferred the readers of *Die Fackel* to *Die Zeit* which was supposed to gather together the dispersed forces of radicalism while Ludvigh concentrated on publishing his works. This paper did not exist long and Ludvigh resumed publication of *Die Fackel* in 1850.

Sources: Arndt/Olson; Arndt/Olson 2, p. 483; Eberlein 22866.

ZEITGEIST	IL Chicago	1857?-1858?

Title trans.:	Spirit of the Age	*First issue:*	1857?
Subtitle:		*Last issue:*	1858?
Add. lang.:		*Vols. (nos.):*	
First editor:	Görders	*Frequency:*	w
First publ.:	Charles Hess, Görders	*Preservation:*	7
Related pubs.:		*Supplements:*	
Circulation:		*Category:*	radical

Depositories:

No further information could be obtained.

Source: Arndt/Olson.

DER ZEITGEIST	NY New York	1901-?

Title trans.:	The Spirit of the Age	*First issue:*	1 My 1901
Subtitle:	Revolutionäre illustrierte Monatsschrift	*Last issue:*	?
Add. lang.:		*Vols. (nos.):*	
First editor:	Rudolf Großmann	*Frequency:*	m
First publ.:	Zeitgeist Publishing Association	*Preservation:*	?
Related pubs.:		*Supplements:*	Der Tramp
Circulation:		*Category:*	anarchist

Depositories: D-188/144 [My,Je 1901]; D-Bm 41/JGA [My-Jl 1901]

Subtitle translation: Revolutionary Illustrated Monthly.

This paper was an anarchist monthly with 8-10 pages (16 pages including the supplement *Der Tramp*). The title emblem was a terrified young woman being carried away by an old, winged man amidst a cloud. Its publishing association had the same address as Johann Most's *Freiheit*. The front page was taken up by a title drawing; it was printed in black and one other color. The editorial in the first issue stated that *Der Zeitgeist* intended to combine socialism with anarchism and was opposed to social democracy. It contained articles on topics such as pessimism, law, social-democratic thought, articles on Maxim Gorki and Leo Trotsky, book reviews and some advertisements. Contributors included Johann Most, but most articles were written by Großmann himself. For its humorous supplement, see *Der Tramp*.

Note: Eberlein gives 1905 as date and mentions holding of 1905 at the Tamiment Library in New York City.

Sources: Arndt/Olson; Eberlein 22865.

DER ZIGEUNER		IL Chicago	1902-?

Title trans.:	The Gypsy	*First issue:*	Ja? 1902
Subtitle:		*Last issue:*	?
Add. lang.:		*Vols. (nos.):*	1 (1)-?
First editor:	Martin Drescher*	*Frequency:*	w
First publ.:	Zigeuner-Gesellschaft	*Preservation:*	?
Related pubs.:	c *Wolfsaugen*	*Supplements:*	
Circulation:		*Category:*	anarchist

Depositories: D-188/144 [1902]

This was an 8-page paper published weekly except for slight irregularities. It was managed by Georg Meyer. It contained satirical prose and poems, reprints from German newspapers, articles on literature from a class-conscious point of view; on the last page there were advertisements, mostly for saloons and restaurants. Contributions were mostly by Drescher himself; other contributors included Walter Gense and Robert Heymann.

On Drescher, see *Wolfsaugen*.

DIE ZUKUNFT		PA Philadelphia	1884-1885?

Title trans.:	Future	*First issue:*	17 F 1884
Subtitle:	Organ der vereinigten Gruppen der Internationalen Arbeiter-Association von Philadelphia und Umgegend	*Last issue:*	1885?
Add. lang.:		*Vols. (nos.):*	
First editor:	Anton Koberlein	*Frequency:*	w
First publ.:		*Preservation:*	1?
Related pubs.:		*Supplements:*	
Circulation:	1885:2000	*Category:*	anarchist-IWPA

Depositories: Usa-CtY [1884]; D-188/144 (14 Je 1884)

Subtitle translation: Organ of the United Groups of the IWPA of Philadelphia and Vicinity. The motto of this paper was "Arbeiter aller Länder, vereinigt Euch!" [Workers of all countries, unite!]

It contained articles on anarchist militancy, current political events in America and Europe, an almanac reminding readers of the birthdays of (in)famous people in history, announcements of the IWPA-groups and some advertisements.

Sources: Arndt/Olson (they name Henry Grav as editor); Eberlein 22875.

Appendixes

Appendix 1: The Role of the German-American Printers' Union in the Development of the German-American Labor Press

In Europe as well as in the United States the printers were one of the first trades to organize in unions.[1] As early as 1873 the Deutsch-Amerikanische Typographia (DAT), the union of German-American printers was organized and it soon had sections in many larger cities with sizable German population and a German-language press.[2] Since jobs were scarce and because the union wanted to protect its members from additional competition, the DAT through its official organ, the *Deutsch-Amerikanische Buchdrucker-Zeitung* (*BZ*), warned printers in Germany again and again against emigration to America.[3] Nevertheless, after 1880 there was an influx of German printers, partly as a result of the antisocialist laws, partly because of systematic recruitment by American publishers, who made tempting offers to printers willing to emigrate, only to employ them for low wages and under miserable working conditions.[4] The migrants soon joined the DAT whose membership rose from 300 to 1400 during the 1880s.[5]

The German-American printers did not only fear "competition" from outside but they also felt threatened by the large number of female printers. In 1877 the *BZ* pointed out that in no other country were there so many women employed in the printing shops and especially in the composing rooms. According to the article again and again attempts had been made to use women as cheap labor against their male colleagues. However, the writer of the article feels obliged to point out that the attempts to employ women as compositors usually failed since women were less efficient because they were slower, made more mistakes and were less able to work on their own. And besides, they usually got married before they had finished learning the trade.[6]

Considering the long tradition of female printers these male diatribes seem rather absurd. The *BZ* also mentioned that the original Declaration of Independence was printed by a woman.[7] Mathilde Franziska Anneke was probably the first female German-American printer. In the early 1850s she produced her *Deutsche Frauenzeitung* [German Women's Paper] in a printing shop exclusively run by women. During the Civil War, when many printers volunteered for the army, the number of women in the trade rose rapidly.[8]

In 1890 the DAT realized that it did not want to fall behind the position of the Knights of Labor and the English-speaking sister-union with regard to the question of equality of women but on the other hand they did not encourage women to learn the printing trade since it was "unwholesome for the female constitution" and since "much competition was to be expected from the female competition." No information could be found on attempts to unionize women printers.[9]

Were feelings of competition also a reason for the exclusion of Czech workers from the DAT? The Czech-American printers' organization had suggested a fusion of the two unions but DAT members argued that the constitution demanded a "perfect" knowledge of German rather than a relatively good one. While in other instances the printers bitterly complained about the illegible scribbling of editors that made typesetting from a manuscript almost impossible, they in this case pointed out that typesetters had to be able to work from the most difficult manuscripts.[10]

In 1894 the DAT merged with the English-speaking International Typographical Union (ITU), but the German-speaking sections retained a good deal of autonomy. In 1940 they were dissolved completely and absorbed by the ITU. At this time the German sections still had 250 members, but 84 of them were retired printers.[11]

The DAT engaged in numerous labor struggles, primarily over the following types of grievances: - the employment of people who were not union members; - below scale, delayed or completely unpaid wages; - excessive working hours; - poor sanitary conditions in the printing rooms; - Sunday and night work; - the destruction of jobs through the introduction of printing plates and type-setting machines; - illegible copy.

When grievances arose in a profit-oriented capitalist shop such as that of the *New Yorker Staatszeitung* or the *Freie Presse*, the lines of opposition were clearly drawn. But when socialists, anarchists and trade unions sought to publish their organs as cheaply as possible - these papers often had to fight for their bare existence - the controversy took on a moral dimension. Some elements of these struggles will be explained in more detail.

Disputes over the Union Organization of Printers: In the struggle for the "union shop," the DAT like other AFL unions used the "union cut," a union stamp which only organized print shops could obtain.[12] Denial or withdrawal of the union cut was also used as a means of pressure in conflicts with labor newspapers, as in the case of the *Philadelphia Tageblatt* (see below) and the *Buffaloer Arbeiterzeitung*.

Wage Struggles: Inability or unwillingness to pay wages led to work stoppages in several cases, e.g. at the *Buffaloer Arbeiterzeitung*, whose printers struck in 1899 because for weeks they had received no wages,[13] at the Cincinnati *Tageblatt*, which did not observe the wage-scale agreement and at the *Michigan Arbeiterzeitung*, which was unable to pay the printers their outstanding wages when it closed down.

Poor Sanitary Conditions in the Print Shops: The printers worked under bad working conditions. Extreme physical burdens, poor sanitary conditions and long working hours were common.[14] In the 1870s the average working day was 10 hours, and even 12-15 hours for the higher paid night shift. Printers spent all this time standing with their backs bent. This unhealthy posture would lead to a so-called "printer's hump," insufficient oxygen supply and reduced blood circulation. In obituaries, heart disease and especially lung disease are frequently given as causes of death. Continuous standing also produced such deformations as bandy legs, flat feet and varicose veins. All printers' diseases, which often led to early invalidity, were exacerbated by the fact that the printers began their four-year apprenticeship at the age of 14, when their bodies were not yet fully developed, and hence especially subject to damage. Even younger children were often employed as untrained assistant printers at below-scale wages. Additional harm was caused by inadequate equipment and insufficient room. The print shops were frequently located in cellars with poor ventilation. Handling the tiny letters in insufficient light or too much glare led to eye diseases or failing eyesight.[15] Among the print shops which were considered to be especially unhealthy were those of *Cincinnatier Zeitung* and *Freiheit*.[16] While the shop of the *New Yorker Volkszeitung* was considered a model.

Night Work: Because of their unhealthy work rhythm, the DAT bitterly attacked the morning newspapers, which were produced at night. Since it looked upon night work on labor newspapers as especially unjust, it considered the discontinuation of the Louisville *Neue Zeit*, the Chicago *Sozialist* and the *Ohio Volkszeitung* as an appropriate punishment, "since they sought to establish and build the future happiness of the people on the basis of the drudgery of the workers." This article was also directed against plans to publish the *Chicagoer Arbeiterzeitung* as a morning paper.[17]

Technical Innovations: The introduction of printing plates in the 1880s was vehemently discussed in the columns of the *Buchdrucker-Zeitung* and led to conflict and strikes at several labor newspapers. Plates are printing matrices for entire newspaper pages. They can easily be produced in any desired quantity and be sent to newspaper editors. Printing plates were used mainly for inside pages, which contained serialized novels, short stories and world news. The local and editorial portions continued to be set by hand. By the end of the 1880s, socialist newspapers, e.g. the *New Yorker Volkszeitung*, as well as the Democratic and Republican papers were using printing plates produced for their particular political alignment. The DAT resisted the introduction of this device on union and political grounds: jobs were threatened and a monopoly of opinion might be established through the production of plates,[18] but because of the wage savings, printing plates soon also prevailed in labor newspapers.[19]

In contrast to the struggle over printing plates, the introduction of typesetting machines (Mergenthaler's Linotype) in the 1890s [20] did not lead to similarly severe disputes with the labor newspapers, probably because only a few of the large socialist dailies could afford the high investment required.

A DAT investigation in 1901 showed that at least three of the large daily socialist newspapers were produced with typesetting machines:

name	machines	operators	printers	wrk.hours	circulation
Phil.Tageblatt	3	4	3	40	41,000
NY Volksztg.	6	9	8	40	18,000
Chic. Arb.ztg.	4	5	3	48	15,000

In contrast, the Belleville *Arbeiter-Zeitung*, with a circulation of 900 copies, was produced by hand by five typesetters each working 54 hours per week.

Illegible Copy: Illegible or poor copy led to undeserved loss of wages for the printers. An enraged typesetter from the *Freidenker* reported in the *Buchdrucker-Zeitung* that in setting 40 columns of 100 lines almost 60 hours were wasted, because the manuscript was a "Schmierlappen," an illegible dirty rag. The printers received only 20 cents an hour for making corrections which were so tiring that they "send one to the madhouse." Consequently at the *Freidenker* not more than $9.00 could be earned by the average printer for a 54-hour working week. This was a reason why, with a staff consisting of one foreman, three printers and four apprentices, 34 different people were employed during a single year.[21]

A conflict which aroused much contemporary attention was the almost 20-year struggle with the *Philadelphia Tageblatt*, the organ of the city's Central Labor Union. The conflict began in June 1882 with complaints against a foreman who had reduced wages of his own accord and wanted to dismiss DAT members so that non-union "rats" could be employed. A committee of the printers persuaded the management to agree to employ only union members and to dismiss non-union workers. Soon new complaints were heard: wages were not being paid according to the scale; non-union and semiqualified printers were still employed; working conditions were poor; working hours amounted to 12 or more, although the *Tageblatt* was an advocate of the 10-

or 8-hour day. In November 1885 below-scale wages and excessive working hours led to a strike. Representatives of the local German unions reacted by writing to the DAT Central Committee that the demands of the printers were unjustified. They were against the interests of the working class because they threatened the existence of a labor newspaper. The DAT answered in an open letter that the printers of a labor newspaper could not be expected to bear the burden of its financial difficulties. They should be borne by the labor organizations in whose interest the printers worked. A contract between the local association of unions, the Central Labor Union (CLU), and the DAT settled the conflict in January 1886, yet in March it had already broken out again. The *Tageblatt* dismissed all the printers because they would not agree to accept 10 percent of their wages in store-orders and because they had refused to print an advertisement criticizing their refusal. In April 1886, the Central Committee of the DAT declared a boycott of the *Tageblatt* and its *Buchdrucker-Zeitung* appeared with the following notice on the front page. "Closed to Typographia members: the print shop of the Philadelphia Tageblatt (Socialist labor newspaper) because of the firing of union people and hiring of scabs." Negotiations involving DAT members, representatives of the *Tageblatt*'s editors, representatives of various German unions and the Socialist Labor Party remained unsuccessful after heated debates. The *Buchdrucker-Zeitung* called the *Tageblatt* "ein Schandfleck" [a disgrace] to the German-American labor movement. In November 1886 various unions left the German-dominated CLU because the *Tageblatt* was still considered its organ. Finally Hugo Miller, the president of the DAT, wrote an open letter to Samuel Gompers and in March 1887 the conflict was settled through the mediation of the AFL. After various lesser conflicts the *Philadelphia Tageblatt* was allowed to use the union cut again in January 1900.[22]

Notes

1. The term "printer" as used here includes printing machine operators, typesetters and typographers.

2. During the high period of the German-American press the DAT had 23 sections: No.1: Philadelphia; No.2: Cincinnati; No.3: St. Louis; No.4: Buffalo; No.5: Rochester; No.6: Cleveland; No.7: New York; No.8: Newark; No.9: Chicago; No.10: Milwaukee; No.11: Baltimore; No.12: Louisville; No.13: St.Paul; No.14: Indianapolis; No.15: Evansville; No.16: Pittsburgh; No.18: Belleville; No.19: Columbus; No.20: Omaha; No.21: Detroit; No.22: Toledo; No.23: Wheeling (in 1900).

3. See e.g. "Die Einwanderung deutscher Schriftsetzer," *BZ* 1 January 1881; "Die Aussichten für deutsche Setzer in Amerika," *BZ* 1 February 1908; "An Europa-müde Collegen," *BZ* 1 August 1913.

4. Gerhard Beier, *Schwarze Kunst und Klassenkampf. Geschichte der Industriegewerkschaft Druck und Papier und ihrer Vorläufer seit dem Beginn der modernen Arbeiterbewegung*. Band 1: Vom Geheimbund zum Königlich-preußischen Gewerkverein (1830-1890) [The Printers' Craft and Class Struggle: The History of the Industrial Printers' Union and its Predecessors since the Beginning of the Modern Labor Movement. Vol. 1: From Secret Society to Royal Prussian Craft Union], (Frankfurt a. M., 1966).

5. Ibid, p. 448.

6. *BZ* 1 March 1877, 1 August 1878.

7. *BZ* 1 October 1877.

8. Frederick Merk, "The Labor Movement in Wisconsin During the Civil War," *Wisconsin Historical Society Proceedings* (1914), pp. 175-76.

9. *BZ* 16 July 1890, "Die Frauenfrage in der Typographia."

10. *BZ* 1 December 1886.

11. On the history of the DAT, see issues of *BZ* in anniversary years (1883,1893, 1903 ..]; "Typographia No.7 - dreiunddreißig Jahre aus der Geschichte einer Arbeiter-Organisation," *New Yorker Volkszeitung* 21 February 1903.

12. On the union-cut, see e.g. "Unser Union Cut und seine Bedeutung," *BZ* 16 June 1890; "Die Verleihung des UnionCut" *BZ* 1 July 1890; "Eine kleine Abhandlung über das Union Label," *BZ* 1 May 1895; "Der Bankrott der Union Label Propaganda," *BZ* June 1929.

13. See *BZ* 16 January 1899.

14. See articles in the *BZ* on this problem, e.g. "Zur Gesundheitspflege der Typographen," *BZ* 1 May 1879; "Körperliche Missgestaltungen bei Buchdruckern," *BZ* 1 September 1906; "Sanitäre Reformen in New York," *BZ* 16 July 1911; "Die fälligen Krankheiten," *BZ* 16 December 1911.

15. See e.g. "Das Auge- ein Juwel," in *BZ* 1 March 1879.

16. On the *Cincinnatier Zeitung*, see *BZ* 16 February 1893; on *Freiheit*, see *BZ* 15 April 1883.

17. As an illustration, see "Schwere Stunden im Leben eines Zeitungssetzers," in *BZ* 1 September 1878, *BZ* 1 May 1879.

18. On the controversy on printing plates, see issues of *BZ*, e.g. of 16 June, 1 July, 16 July, 1 September 1888, 1 February, 16 February, 16 April 1889.

19. See *BZ* of 16 September 1887, 1 September 1888, 1 July 1889. Labor struggles took place for this reason among others, at the *New Jersey Arbeiterzeitung* and the *Michigan Arbeiterzeitung*, as well as at the *Buffaloer Arbeiterzeitung*, which was temporarily denied the use of the union-cut, because four-fifths of it was produced from plates.

20. See Harry Kelber and Carl Schlesinger, *Union Printers and Controlled Automation* (New York, 1967), chapter 1: "The Impact of the Linotype Machine."

21. See *BZ* 1 October 1888.

22. See *BZ* of August-October 1882, January-April 1886, November 1886, February-March 1887, September and November 1888, September-October 1890, May, July-September 1895, February 1900.

Appendix 2: Short Biographies of Selected German-American Editors and Journalists

Anneke, Mathilde Franziska, née Giesler

born on 3 April 1817 in Blankenstein/Westphalia; supported herself by writing poems, novels and drama after the divorce from her first husband; editor, translator and newspaper correspondent; married Fritz Anneke in 1847; fought in the Palatian revolutionary army, dressed as a man; came to the United States via Switzerland in 1849; wrote and lectured for the cause of women suffrage; editor of *Deutsche Frauenzeitung* and *Newarker Zeitung*; went to Switzerland as a newspaper correspondent, when her husband joined the Union army; returned to Milwaukee in 1865; founded a girls' school, which she conducted until her death on 25 November 1884.

Anneke, Fritz

born on 31 January 1818 in Dortmund; joined the Prussian Army, organized Readers clubs, was dishonorably discharged; joined revolutionary forces in South Germany; came to the United States via Switzerland in 1849 with his wife, M.F. Anneke; edited *Newarker Zeitung* and *New Jersey Zeitung*; returned as a newspaper correspondent to Germany in 1859; returned to the United States when the Civil War broke out; became colonel of Wisconsin Regiment; arrested in 1863 because of criticism of superiors; died in 1870.

Baginski, Max

spokesman of the left wing social democrats in Berlin; accompanied Gerhard Hauptmann on his rounds through the Silesian weaver's district; emigrated via Zurich, Paris, London to the United States; editor of *Sturmglocke*, of *Chicagoer Arbeiter-Zeitung* and *Vorbote*, for which he wrote traveller's reports in 1900; editor of *Freiheit* after John Most's death; lover of Emma Goldman; American delegate to the international anarchist congress in Amsterdam in 1907.

Bartel, Heinrich

born on 9 October 1874 in Reichenberg, North Bohemia; childhood in poverty; worked in textile mill at age of 13; became socialist at age of 15; self-educated; editor of socialist newspaper; imprisoned 12 times for short terms; song-writer; came to the United States in 1904; editor of Sheboygan *Volksblatt*, of *Chicagoer Arbeiter-Zeitung*; of Milwaukee *Vorwärts*; member of Socialist Party, of Arbeiter- Kranken- und Sterbekasse; active in German theater in Milwaukee; died after 1946.

Berger, Victor Louis

born in Nieder-Rehbach, Austria-Hungary, on 28 February 1860; studied philology in Vienna and Budapest; came to the United States in 1878; taught school; became active socialist in Milwaukee; editor of *Wisconsin Vorwärts* and two English-language socialist papers; founded with Eugene Debs the Social Democratic Party, which became the Socialist Party in 1901; was elected to House of Representatives on socialist ticket in 1910; reelected in 1918 but was refused admission because of antiwar stand; was tried for sedition; sentenced to 20 years imprisonment, but released on appeal to higher courts; reelected to Congress in 1922; served three terms; died in Milwaukee on 7 August 1929.

Biedenkapp, Georg

born in 1843 in Londorf, Hessen; came to the United States in 1885; prolific author of stories, drama and songs portraying the misery of the "dispossessed" and the extravagance of the rich (Kamman); editor of *Der Tramp*; many publications in the New York press; died in 1924 at Francfort on the Main.

Christensen, Jens L.

lived in Altona near Hamburg, where he was a teacher; member of Social Democratic Party; forced to emigrate to the United States by antisocialist laws in 1887; edited *Chicagoer Arbeiter-Zeitung* and *Vorbote*; abused by Johann Most as "shadow of Liebknecht" (quoted from Waltershausen, p. 365) and "spineless rogue" (in *Freiheit* 21 April 1888).

Conzett, Conrad

born in 1848 in Switzerland; typesetter; cofounder of Typographia No. 9 of Chicago; founder and editor of *Vorbote* and *Chicagoer Arbeiter-Zeitung*; Marxist; returned to Switzerland when anarchist element in *Chicagoer Arbeiter-Zeitung* gained prevalence; committed suicide by drowning himself in Zurich lake in 1897.

Dietzgen, Joseph

born in 1828 near Cologne, Germany; tanner; self-educated in philosophy and political economy; was called philosopher of the proletariat; forced out of Germany in 1881 by antisocialist laws; came then to the United States for the third time; editor of New York *Socialist*; was courageous enough to take upon him the editorship of *Vorbote* and *Chicagoer Arbeiter-Zeitung* when his predecessors were jailed after Haymarket Affair; prolific author of philosophical works; died on 15 April 1888.

Douai, Carl Daniel Adolf

born on 22 February 1819 in Altenburg, Saxony; studied at University of Leipzig; teacher; participated in 1848 Revolution; was captured, tried and imprisoned; emigrated to Texas in 1852; editor of *San Antonio Zeitung*, *Arbeiter-Union*, *New Yorker Volkszeitung*; contributions to many other newspapers; prolific writer in diverse fields, e.g. philosophy, German grammar, history, education; founded his own school; has been called first popularizer of Marxist ideas in the United States; died on 21 January 1888 in Brooklyn, NY.

Drescher, Martin

born in 1863 in Wittstock in der Mark; studied law in Breslau, Berlin and Göttingen; lived adventurous life as a tramp in the United States, where he arrived in 1891; became interested in socialism; worked for various socialist papers, e.g. Detroit *Herold*, Milwaukee *Vorwärts*; turned towards anarchism; editor of *Der Arme Teufel*, *Mephisto*, *Wolfsaugen*, *Der Zigeuner*; turned away from socialism and edited the Chicago literary magazine *Die Glocke*; died in 1920 in Ottawa.

Fenneberg, Ferdinand Fenner von

born in 1820 in Austria; commanding officer of Viennese National Guard in 1848; for a short time commander of revolutionary army of Palatinate; emigrated to the United States in 1849; in the 1850s editor of several newspapers, e.g. New York *Arbeiterzeitung*, Louisville *Herold des Westens* and *New*

Yorker Abendzeitung; changed jobs so frequently that he was accused of being a mere opportunist (Wittke); died in 1863.

Fischer, Adolf

born in Bremen in 1863; came to the United States at the age of 15; typesetter; employed first at *Volksstimme des Westens*; then as foreman at *Chicagoer Arbeiter-Zeitung*; convicted together with Spies, Schwab and others for the alleged killing of policemen by a bomb thrown during the protest meeting on Haymarket Square in Chicago in May 1886; executed on 11 November 1887; his dying statement: "This is the happiest moment of my life."

Franz, Jacob L.

born in 1846 in Bavaria; typesetter and journalist; had to flee from Munich to Zurich because of lese-Majesty; emigrated to the United States in 1878; successively editor of *Philadelphia Tageblatt, New Yorker Volkszeitung, Brauer-Zeitung*; went back to Germany in 1900, but soon after returned to the United States; killed in a streetcar accident in 1902.

Fritzsche, Friedrich Wilhelm

lived from 1825-1905; social-democratic member of the German Reichstag; worked from the age of nine; influenced by the ideas of Wilhelm Weitling; joined labor groups in the late 1840s; arrested and jailed for participating in 1849 revolution in Dresden; cofounder of the German Cigarmakers Union; fund-raising trip to the United States in 1881 together with L. Viereck, emigrated permanently in the same year; edited *Philadelphia Tageblatt* for some time; settled as innkeeper and withdrew from labor movement; died on 5 February 1905 in Philadelphia.

Grottkau, Paul

born in 1846; descendent of impoverished nobility of the March of Brandenburg; designated architect; came in touch with social-democratic thought during apprenticeship as bricklayer; joined socialist movement; journalist and public speaker; came to the United States in 1878; many lecture tours; editor of *Chicagoer Arbeiter-Zeitung, Vorbote* and later *New Yorker Volkszeitung, Milwaukee Arbeiterzeitung*; opponent of Johann Most; died of pneumonia in June 1898.

Hasselmann, Wilhelm

born in 1884; studied chemistry; joined Lassallean labor movement; member of German Reichstag 1874-76 and 1878-80; came to the United States in 1880 after having embraced anarchism; a lecture tour soon after his arrival was "a complete failure" because he "criticized American conditions sharply without being familiar with them" (Waltershausen); founded in 1885 a "scientific club," for the purpose of introducing its members to the "secrets of chemistry;" anarchist rival of Johann Most; founded the *Amerikanische Arbeiterzeitung*; became an innkeeper around 1889.

Heinzen, Karl

born on 22 February 1809 in Grevenbroich, near Düsseldorf; dismissed from the University of Bonn on account of a revolutionary speech; enlisted in Dutch army; sent to Bavaria in 1829 and entered Prussian civil service; growing hatred against arbitrary authority; fled to Belgium, Switzerland and in January 1848 to New York; editor of *New England Zeitung, Deutsche*

Schnellpost; returned in February 1848 to join revolution in France; to Switzerland; participated in Baden revolution of same year; returned to New York via London in 1850; editor and publisher of *Völkerbund, New York Deutsche Zeitung, Janus* and his most successful and longlived publication: *Der Pionier*; prolific, controversial, radical author, heavily attacked by Karl Marx; early advocate of women's rights; died on 12 November 1880.

Hepner, Adolf (or Heppner)

born on 24 November 1846 in Schmiegel, Posen; son of a baker; studied theology, later philosophy; owned book-store; active member of Social Democratic Party; friend of August Bebel and Wilhelm Liebknecht; editor of Leipzig *Volksstaat*; emigrated to the United States in 1882; edited *Philadelphia Tageblatt* and *St. Louis Tageblatt*; author of "Die Ikarier von Nordamerika," a warning against the founding of communist colonies; returned to Germany in 1908; supported right wing of SPD; died in April 1923 in Munich.

Jonas, Alexander

born on 16 March 1834 in Berlin; of bourgeois background; entered his father's publishing house; read extensively socialist publications; came to the United States in 1869; editor of *Die Arbeiterstimme*; contributor of *Die Neue Zeit*, a German women's paper; cofounder and editor of *New Yorker Volkszeitung*; advocate of women's rights; was put up as candidate for Mayor of New York and later twice for congressman by SLP; a powerful platform speaker, he spoke and wrote only in German; died on 3 February 1912 in New York.

Juchacz, Marie

born on 15 March 1879 in Landsberg a.d. Warthe; worked as domestic servant, industrial worker, nurse and seamstress; joined SPD in 1908; active in organizing women into SPD; founded Arbeiterwohlfahrt, a workers' beneficial organization in 1919; emigrated in 1933 to Saar Territory, in 1935 to France, in 1941 to the United States; editor of *Bulletin. Arbeiterwohlfahrt*; returned to Germany in 1949; honorary chairwoman of Arbeiterwohlfahrt; died on 28 January 1956 in Bonn.

Katz, Rudolf

born on 30 September 1895 in Falkenburg, Pomerania; lawyer; member of SPD; emigrated to China in 1933, to New York in 1935; taught at Columbia University; after 1936 assistant editor of *Neue Volkszeitung*; chairman of German branch of Social-Democratic Federation of America; in 1941 general secretary of German-American Council for the Liberation of Germany from Nazism; returned to Germany in 1946 with AFL-CIO delegation; became vice-president of Federal Constitutional Court; died on 23 July in Baden-Baden.

Keitel, August

born on 15 January 1844 in Berlin; mechanical engineer; deported several times from Germany because of "activities dangerous to the state;" came to the United States in 1881; founded after much hardship the *Clevelander Volksfreund*, which he edited until his death on 4 January 1893; was supported by his wife, Friederike Keitel, who died on 15 January 1905.

Kellner, Gottfried Theodor

born on 27 August 1819 in Kassel; studied and then practiced law; active in the spread of revolutionary publications; member of diet in Hessen; fled to the United States via Belgium after a dramatic jailbreak with the help of his wife; lectured in New York; editor of *Die Reform*; went to Philadelphia in 1856; advocate for cultural endeavors for the workers; leader of a German community in Philadelphia; died on 12 May 1898.

Klings, Carl

born around 1825 in Solingen; cutler; collaborated with Ferdinand Lassalle in founding of the Allgemeiner Deutscher Arbeiterverein in 1863, but supported its affiliation with the First International (IAA) out of work; he emigrated in 1864 via London to the United States; member of Chicago section of IAA; active in organizing German workers in Chicago according to Marx' principles; editor of *Der Deutsche Arbeiter* and *Vorbote*; reprinted Marx' "Communist Manifesto" in an edition of 2,000 copies; died after 1874, probably in Chicago.

Kriege, Hermann

born on 20 July 1820 in Lienen, Westphalia; studied in Leipzig; forced to flee on account of his liberal ideas; arrived in the United States in 1845; edited *Volkstribun*; was associated with Karl Marx and Friedrich Engels but lost their confidence when he unreservedly joined land reform movement; returned to Germany on outbreak of 1848 Revolution; once more exiled; died insane on 31 March 1850 in New York.

Lore, Ludwig and Lily

born in Upper Silesia in 1875; graduated at Berlin University, where he was a pupil of Werner Sombart; came to New York in 1905; joined the *New Yorker Volkszeitung*; became a socialist freelance writer after 1931, well-known for his anti-Nazi writings; joined editorial staff of *New York Post* in 1934; took over a special government assignment in January 1942; died on 8 July 1942 in Brooklyn. His wife Lily Lore, nee Schneppe, was a socialist journalist and editor of the women's page of the *New Yorker Volkszeitung*.

Lyser, Gustav

born in Dresden, Saxony, in 1841; typesetter; social democrat, but expelled from the Party by Eisenach Congress in 1873; emigrated to New York in 1874; editor of New York *Arbeiterstimme*, of *Der Social-Democrat*; coeditor of Milwaukee *Socialist* and editor of its humorous supplements; for a short time assistant editor of *Chicagoer Arbeiter-Zeitung* and later editor of *Die Fackel* "because of his practical abilities," returned to Milwaukee in 1880, where he was active for a time in the labor movement before finally turning his back on it; died in 1909.

Most, Johann

born on 5 February 1846 in Augsburg/Germany; hard childhood which led to deep hatred of any form of tyranny; little formal education, but read extensively; apprenticeship as book-binder; travelled widely; came into contact with the First International in Switzerland; active ever since in the international revolutionary movement; imprisoned several times; expelled from Berlin immediately after the enactment of the antisocialist laws; settled in London, started *Freiheit* there; gradually departed from the principles of social democracy, inclining more and more towards revolutionary anarchism;

opponent of Liebknecht; imprisoned for 16 months hard labor for an article glorifying the assassination of Alexander II; arrived in New York on 18 December 1882, welcomed by an enthusiastic crowd; forceful and popular speaker; lecture tours through the United States; imprisoned in 1883, 1887, 1891 and 1902; died on 17 March 1906 in Cincinnati of erysipelas.

Otto-Walster, August

born on 5 November 1834 in Dresden; studied political science and philosophy; editor of various newspapers; charter member of German Social-Democratic Labor Party; author of novels and stories; came to the United States in 1876 following a request of the Social-Democratic Working Men's Party; editor of *Arbeiterstimme* and *Volksstimme des Westens*; participant of last congress of First International in Philadelphia; returned to Germany in 1891; died on 20 March 1898 in Waldheim/Saxony.

Reitzel, Robert

has been called the "Heine of America;" born in Germany in 1848 or 1849; son of a schoolteacher; educated for ministry, but turned freethinker; emigrated to America in 1871; worked as laborer and then wandered about the country, lecturing, writing, supporting the radical socialist, anarchist and labor movement among the Germans in the Mid-West until 1884, when friends supplied him with money to set up a paper, the *Armer Teufel*; died in 1898.

Rosenberg, Wilhelm Ludwig

born in Hamm, Westphalia in 1850; teacher of Latin and French at Frankfort on the Main; emigrated to the United States in 1880 forced by the antisocialist laws; taught in Boston; editor of *Der Tramp, Die Fackel*, New York *Sozialist*, Cincinnati *Tageblatt*; in the 1880s head of National Executive Committee of SLP; leader of Lassalean faction in the party; excluded from SLP in 1889; prolific author of sketches, drama, songs and poems; strongly concerned for the emancipation of women; contributor to the socialist press until his death sometime in the 1930s.

Sattler, Otto

born in Emmendingen/Baden in 1872; learned book-binders' trade; studied philosophy and literature at University of Zurich; travelled for about 15 years, visiting many parts of the world; came to the United States; journalist and lecturer in New York; editor of *Solidarität*.

Schewitsch, Sergius

born in Russia around 1847; of noble birth; educated in Germany; travels through Europe; spoke and wrote fluently German, English and French; came to the United States in 1877; editor of *New Yorker Volkszeitung*; eloquent platform speaker; on 7 October 1911 he committed suicide together with his wife Helene, former Mrs. Rackowitz, who had been the cause for Lassalle's fatal duel.

Schiele, Friedrich

born on 22 November 1848 in Drossen, Brandenburg; typesetter and teacher in Turner club; emigrated to the United States in 1880 forced by antisocialist laws; cofounder of Typographia No. 2 and of *Cincinnatier Zeitung*; later owner of a print shop and of a hotel in Cincinnati; died in October 1908.

Schilling, Robert

born in Osterburg, Saxony on 17 October 1843; came to the United States in 1848; cooper; in 1871 vice-president, in 1875 president of Coopers' Union; editor of *Coopers' Journal* and *Der Reformer*; active member of Knights of Labor; cofounder of Greenback Party; after 1891 Secretary of Populist Party; opponent of Victor Berger and his Socialist Party; withdrew from politics after 1900; became owner of dairy shop; turned towards spiritualism; died on 26 December 1922 in Milwaukee.

Schlüter, Hermann

born on 8 October 1851 in a village in Sleswick-Holstein; of poor family; formally educated only in a village school; editor, publisher and distributor, organizer of distribution of social-democratic publications: coauthor of Social-Democratic Party platforms; exiled from Germany in 1883, from Switzerland in 1888; went to London, where he became a friend of Friedrich Engels; came to the United States in 1889; editor of *New Yorker Volkszeitung*; author of publications on the labor movement in America, on the Chartist Movement, on Lincoln and on the brewers; died of pneumonia on 26 January 1919.

Schröder, Max

born on 16 April 1900 in Lübeck; studied history of art; joined German Communist Party in 1932; emigrated to France in 1933, to the United States in 1934; substitute editor-in-chief of *The German American*; returned to Germany, East-Berlin, in 1946; died there in January 1958.

Schulze, Moritz

expelled from Switzerland; came to the United States via London; anarchist; editor of *Freiheit* and *Chicagoer Arbeiter-Zeitung*; later said to have become a renegade. As yet no further information could be obtained.

Schwab, Michael

born in 1853 in Bavaria; good schooling; learned bookbinders' trade; supported social-democratic movement; forced out of Germany by antisocialist laws in 1879; in America, joined SLP, worked for *Vorbote* and *Chicagoer Arbeiter-Zeitung* first as journalist, then as assistant editor; jailed after Haymarket; death sentence commuted to life imprisonment and later set free by Governor Altgelt.

Seger, Gerhard

born on 16 November 1896 in Leipzig/Saxony; member of SPD; journalist and editor of diverse social-democratic newspapers; emigrated to England, to New York in 1935; editor-in-chief of *Neue Volkszeitung*; held chairmanship in diverse German-American anti-Nazi organizations; witness in Nuremburg trials; died on 21 January 1967 in New York.

Spies, August

born in Friedenwald in 1855; came to the United States at the age of 17; learned upholsters' trade; owned small shop in Chicago; joined SLP in 1877; became member of Chicago "social revolutionary club," an anarchist split off from the SLP in 1881; editor of *Vorbote* and *Chicagoer Arbeiter-Zeitung*; anarchist of "rather mild and philosophic type" (Hillquit); jailed after Haymarket in May 1886; hanged on 11 November 1887 aged 31. His last words were: "The time will come when our silence in the grave will be more eloquent than our speeches."

Stampfer, Friedrich

born on 8 September 1874 in Brünn/Moravia; social-democrat journalist and politician; editor of Berlin *Vorwärts*, organ of SPD; delegate at Versailles peace negotiations; emigrated to Czechoslovakia in 1933, to France in 1938, to the United States in 1940; editor of *Neue Volkszeitung*; returned to Germany in 1948; died on 1 December 1957 in Kronberg/Taunus.

Struve, Gustav von

born in 1805 in Munich; studied law; lawyer; author of books on phrenology; editor; participant in the 1848 Revolution; came to New York via France and England in 1851; published a successful 6 volume world history; editor of *New Yorker Demokrat* and *Die Sociale Republic*; officer in Civil War; appointed as consul by U.S. government, but Thuringian government denied exequatur; returned to Germany; in 1869 to Vienna, where he died on 21 Agusut 1870.

Urban, William (Wilhelm)

born in Karlsbad/Bohemia in 1858; came to the United States via Austria and Germany in 1878; managing-director of *Chicagoer Arbeiter-Zeitung*, 1892 cofounder of the "Pioneer Aid and Support Association," which was the defence committee for the Haymarket convicts; moved Governor Altgeld to pardon Schwab, Fielden and Neebe; died on 1 July 1915.

Walter, Hilde

born on 4 March 1895 in Berlin; journalist, e.g. for Ossietzky's *Weltbühne*; emigrated to Paris in 1933, to New York in 1941; editor of *Neue Volkszeitung*; founded a literary agency for exiled authors; returned to Germany in 1952; died on 22 January 1976.

Weber, Julius

born on 11 July 1870 in Werdau/Saxony; came to the United States in 1881; started working at *Philadelphia Tageblatt* as errand boy, learned typesetting; worked at different print shops, took possession of *Tageblatt* job print shop in 1897; member of Typographia No. 1 of Philadelphia, of Arbeiter- Kranken- und Sterbekasse, of association for advancement of cremation, of Labor Lyceum Association and several school societies, of Socialist Party and workers' singing societies. Died at the age of 42 of consumption.

Weiss, Samuel

born in Hungary in 1861; learned typesetters' trade there; emigrated to the United States in 1886; joined Typographia, was elected to its executive board; editor of *Buffaloer Arbeiterzeitung*, *Erie Arbeiterzeitung*, of *The People*, the English organ of Populist Party of Erie; active member of International Typographical Union; district-organizer of AFL; died of pneumonia on 1 December 1897.

Weitling, Wilhelm Christian

born on 5 October 1808 in Magdeburg; learned tailor's trade; travelling journeyman; organized cooperative restaurants for journeyman tailors in Paris and Switzerland; member of secret revolutionary societies; influential in founding German workers' communes in Switzerland and other European countries; came to the United States in 1846; returned to participate in German Revolution of 1848; returned to the United States in 1850; edited *Die Republik der Arbeiter*; founded workers' leagues; planned Exchange Bank; founded settlement of "Communia" in Iowa; withdrew disappointedly from public life; became clerk in the Bureau of Immigration; died on 25 January 1871 in New York.

Weydemeyer, Joseph

born on 2 February 1818 in Münster/Westphalia; lieutenant in Prussian Army; discharged because of revolutionary tendencies (or quit ?) in 1845; friend of Marx and Engels; editor of and contributor to socialist newspapers; worked as surveyor; went underground after failed Revolution of 1848; came to the United States via Switzerland in 1851; editor of *Die Revolution* and *Stimme des Volkes*; pioneer of Marxism in the United States; surveyor in Chicago and Milwaukee; served with distinction as colonel in Civil War; afterwards worked for First International and as elected comptroller; died in St. Louis on 20 August 1866 of cholera.

Appendix 3: Newspapers and Broadsheets of the *Deutsch-Amerikanische Typographia*

Title: AGITATOR
Place: IL Chicago
Dates: 1891-1902
Title trans.: Agitator

This four-page weekly was the organ of the Deutsch-Amerkanische Typographia No. 9 of Chicago during several struggles with publishers who tried to prevent the unionization of their newspaper.

Sources: Arndt/Olson; *BZ* 1 N, 1 D 1891, 16 Ja 1892; 16 F 1893; 1 O 1902; "Albert Krumme, Eines Schriftsetzers Laufbahn," in *BZ* Ja 1927.

Title: DER APPELL
Place: MO St. Louis
Dates: 1890-?
Title trans.: The Appeal

This paper was the organ of Typographia No. 3 of St. Louis in a wage dispute with the newspapers *Amerika* and *Anzeiger des Westen*.

Sources: Arndt/Olson; *BZ* 16 Jl, 1 Ag, 16 S 1890.

Title: DER ARBEITSLOSE (I)
Place: IL Chicago
Dates: 1892-?
Title trans.: The Unemployed

This was a pamphlet published annually by the unemployed members of Typographia No. 9 of Chicago.

Sources: Arndt/Olson (who give 1898 as the date of first appearance); *BZ* 1 S 1893; 16 S 1894; 16 Jl 1896; 1 N 1932.

Title: DER ARBEITSLOSE (II)
Place: OH Cleveland
Dates: 1897-?
Title trans.: The Unemployed

This pamphlet was published by unemployed members of Typographia No. 6 of Cleveland.

Source: *BZ* 1 and 16 Ap 1897.

Title: DER GEWERSCHAFTLER/ THE UNIONIST
Place: OH Cincinnati
Dates: 1883-1886?
Title trans.: The Unionist

The paper was published by a so-called "Antagonizing Committee" of Typographia No. 2 of Cincinnati as a boycott-paper against the *Cincinnati Volksfreund*.

Sources: Anrdt/Olson; *BZ* 1 and 16 S 1882; 15 Ja, 1 F, 1 Mr, 15 Jl, 15 Ag, 15 S 1883.

Title: DER MOSQUITO
Place: PA Philadelphia
Dates: 1895

Title trans.:   The Mosquito

This was published by Typographia No. 1 of Philadelphia in protest against the *Philadelphia Gazette*.

Source: *BZ* 16 S 1895.

Title:	NEWARKER VOLKSBLATT
Place:	NJ Newark
Dates:	1888-1889
Title trans.:	Newark People's Journal

The paper was founded as a "weapon" in the conflict of Typographia No. 8 of Newark with the *New Jersey Arbeiter-Zeitung* (see there).

Source: *BZ*.

Title:	O.O.
Place:	NY New York
Dates:	1892
Title trans.:	--

This organ of the Typographia No. 7 of New York was published in a labor dispute with Oswald Ottendörfer, the publisher of the *New York Staatszeitung*, over the unionization of his newspaper's typesetters.

Sources: Arndt/Olson; *BZ* 1 and 16 Je, 16 S 1892; article on "Typographia No. 7 of New York," *New Yorker Volkszeitung* 21 F 1903.

Title:	PITTSBURGER VOLKSZEITUNG
Place:	PA Pitssburgh
Dates:	1894 ?
Title trans.:	Pittsburgh People's News

This paper was founded by some members of the Pittsburgh Typographia who had become unemployed because of the introduction of typesetting machines and a strike at the *Beobachter*.

Sources: Arndt/Olson; *BZ*.

Title:	VORWÄRTS
Place:	PA Philadelphia
Dates:	1886-1887
Title trans.:	Forward

This was published by Typographia No. 1 of Philadelphia during their conflict with the *Philadelphia Tageblatt* (see there).

Sources: Arndt/Olson; *BZ* 1 F and 16 Mr 1887.

Appendix 4: Periodicals Temporarily Taking a Pro-labor Viewpoint

Title: DIE BIENE
Place: OH Cleveland
Dates: 9 Ag 1873 - 1886?
Category: labor:

Title: DER DEUTSCHE REPUBLIKANER *(Cincinnati Republikaner)*
Place: OH Cincinnati
Dates: 28 S 1842 - 23 Mr 1861?
Category: labor:

Title: INDIANA TRIBÜNE
Place: IN Indianapolis
Dates: O 1877 ? - Je 1907
Category: labor:

Title: NEU-ENGLAND ANZEIGER
Place: CN New Haven
Dates: 1877-1886 ?
Category: anarchist:

Title: NEW YORKER DEMOKRAT (*New Yorker Herold*)
Place: NY New York
Dates: 1845 ? -1919
Category: radical fortyeighter:

Sources: Arndt/Olson; Wittke, *Press*.

Appendix 5: English-language Anti-Nazi Publications by German Exiles

Title: AUSTRIAN LABOR NEWS
Place: NY New York
Dates: F 1942 - 1 D 1945
First publ.: Austrian Labor Committee

Source: Cazden, *Exile Literature*, p. 183.

Title: AUSTRIAN REPUBLIC
Place: NY New York
Dates: 1946 - Ap 1948
First publ.: Friends of Austrian Labor

Source: Cazden, *Exile Literature*, p. 183 (probably English).

Title: BULLETIN OF THE COUNCIL FOR A DEMOCRATIC GERMANY
Place: NY New York
Dates: S 1944 - My 1945
First publ.: Paul Tillich*

Source: Maas I, p. 125.

Title: GERMANY TODAY (I)
Place: NY New York
Dates: 1938
First publ.: Endrew Kertesz

Source: Maas III, p. 660.

Title: GERMANY TODAY (II)
Place: NY New York
Dates: 21 Je 1945 - 7 D 1946
First publ.: German American Inc.

Source: Cazden, *Exile Literature*, p. 188

Title: IN RE: GERMANY
Place: NY New York
Dates: F 1941 - Mr 1944
First publ.: Research and Information Service of the American Friends of German Freedom

Sources: Cazden, *Exile Literature*, pp. 185-86; Maas I,
p. 287.

Title: INSIDE GERMANY REPORTS
Place: NY New York
Dates: 15 Ap 1939 - My 1944
First publ.: American Friends of German Freedom

Sources: Cazden, *Exile Literature*, p. 186; Maas IV.

Title: LETTERS ON GERMAN LABOR
Place: NY New York

Dates: 15 Jl - 9 S 1943
First publ.: German Labor Delegation in the United States

Sources: Cazden, *Exile Literature*, p. 186; Maas II, p. 362; Maas IV.

Title: NEW ESSAYS
Place: IL Chicago, NY New York
Dates: O 1934 - Winter 1943
First publ.: Council Communists

Source: Cazden, *Exile Literature*, p. 186.

Title: VICTORY COMMITTEE OF GERMAN-AMERICAN TRADE
 UNIONISTS: ACTION BULLETIN
Place: NY New York
Dates: 1945

Source: Cazden, *Exile Literature*, p.189 (probably English).

Title: BULLETIN. ARBEITERWOHLFAHRT U.S.A
Place: NY New York
Dates: 1945-1946?
First publ.: Relief for the German Victims of Nazism, president:

Sources: Cazden, *Exile Literature*, p. 185; *Jahrbuch der Sozial-demokratischen Partei Deutschlands* (Hannover, 1947), pp. 124-25 (probably English).

Appendix 6: Papers With German or German-Sounding Titles Which Have Been Excluded

Title: ARBEITER WELT
Place: NY New York
Dates: 1904
Title trans.: Labor World

Title: ARBEITERZEITUNG
Dates: 1890-1902
Title trans.: Labor News

Title: FREIE ARBEITER STIMME
Dates: 1946
Title trans.: Free Labor's Voice

Title: FORTSCHRITT
Plcace: NY New York
Dates: 1915-1932
Title trans.: Progress

Title: GERECHTIGKEIT
Place:
Dates: 1919-1957
Title trans.: Justice

Title: LABOR WORLD (Possibly identical with *Arbeiter Welt*, see above)
Place: NY New York
Dates: 1907
Title trans.: --

Reportedly the paper had one German-language page per issue since no. 7, 2 Mr 1907.

Title: UNION ARBEITER
Place: -
Dates: 1925-1927
Title trans.: Union Worker

Title: YUNION ARBEITER (see *Union Arbeiter*)

These papers seem to have been published in Yiddish or Hebrew, see Yiddish section.

Title: NEMESIS
Place: MD Baltimore
Dates: 1884-1885
Title trans.: -

Title: SOCIALDEMOCRAT
Place: IL Chicago
Dates: 1894-1898

These papers were published in English according to the information available.

Title: RITTER DER ARBEIT
Place: MI ST. Charles
On this paper no definite information is available.

Title: BREWER AND MALSTER
Place: IL Chicago
Dates: 1882-1915

Title: GERMAN-AMERICAN BAKERS' AND CONFECTIONERS' JOURNAL
Place: NY New York
Dates: 1897-1904

Title: DER DEUTSCH-AMERIKANISCHE HOLZARBEITER. THE WOODWORKER
Place: IL Chicago
Dates: 1885-1894

These perodicals were published by employers as trade journals

Title Index

Arbeiterfreund, Der (Chicago)
Arbeiter-Freund, Der (Cincinnati)
Arbeiter-Freund, Der (Wheeling)
Arbeiter-Freund, Der (McKeesport)
Arbeiter-Freund, Der (Philadelphia)
    See also *Vorwärts (Philadelphia)*, Appendix 1.
Arbeiter-Freund (Chicago)
Arbeiter-Sport in Amerika
Arbeiter-Stimme (New York)
    See also *New Yorker Volkszeitung.*
Arbeiter-Stimme (Chicago)
Arbeiterstimme am Erie, Die
    See also *Tribüne (Buffalo Tribüne)*
Arbeiter Union (Cincinnati)
    See also *Arbeiter Abendzeitung.*
Arbeiter-Union (New York)
    See also *Der Deutsche Arbeiter, San Antonio Zeitung.*
Arbeiter von Ohio, Die
Arbeiter Welt
    See Appendix 6.
Arbeiterzeitung (Belleville Arbeiterzeitung)
Arbeiterzeitung, Die (New York, I)
Arbeiterzeitung (Philadelphia)
Arbeiterzeitung (New York, II)
Arbeiterzeitung (San Francisco)
    See *California Arbeiter-Zeitung* (San Francisco II).
Arbeiterzeitung (Buffalo)
    See *Buffaloer Arbeiter-Zeitung.*
Arbeiterzeitung
    See Appendix 6.
Arbeiterzeitung und Tageblatt
    See *Arbeiterzeitung (Belleville Arbeiterzeitung).*
Arbeiter-Zeitung (Milwaukee)
    See also *Milwaukee Journal.*
Arbeiter-Zeitung (St. Louis, I)
Arbeiter-Zeitung (Pittsburgh)
Arbeiter-Zeitung (Erie)
Arbeiter-Zeitung (Kansas City)
Arbeiter-Zeitung (St. Louis, II)
    See also *Tageblatt-Abendpost, Volks-Anwalt, Brauer
    Zeitung.*
Arbeiter-Zeitung (Cincinnati Arbeiter-Zeitung)
    See also *Cincinnatier Zeitung.*
Arbeiter-Zeitung (Sheboygan)
Arbeiter-Zeitung und Volksanwalt
    See *Arbeiter-Zeitung* (St. Louis, II).
Arbeitslose, Der (I)
    See Appendix 3.
Arbeitslose, Der (II)
    See Appendix 3.
Arme Teufel, Der
    See also *Wolfsaugen, Libertas, Mephisto.*
Arminia
    See *Milwaukee'r Arbeiter-Zeitung, Wisconsin Vorwärts.*

See *Freidenker, Der Pionier* (Boston).
Freie Arbeiter Stimme
   See Appendix 6.
Freie Blätter
   See *Der Kommunist* (Cleveland).
Freie Presse (Philadelphia)
   See also *Der Kommunist* (Cleveland).
Freie Presse, Die (Aurora)
Freie Tribüne des Internationalen Sozialismus
   See *Austrian Labor Information.*
Freie Wort, Das
   See also *Der Strom.*
Freie Wacht
Freiheit
   See also *Amerikanische Arbeiterzeitung* (New York, II),
   Libertas, New Yorker Arbeiter-Zeitung (II), *Die Parole,*
   Der Sozialist, Sturmglocke, Der Zeitgeist (New York).
Freiheitsbanner
Fur arbeter
   See Jewisch Migrants Section, volume 2.
Furniture Workers' Journal
   See *Möbel-Arbeiter-Journal.*
Gegen den Strom
General Wood Workers' Journal
   See *Möbel-Arbeiter-Journal, International Wood*
   Worker.
Gerechtigkeit
   See Appendix 6.
German American, The
   See also *German-American Emergency Conference. Bulletin,*
   Deutsch-Amerikanische Arbeiterklubs U.S.A.:
   Mitteilungsblatt.
German-American Bakers 'and Confectioners' Journal
   See Appendix 6.
German-American Emergency Conference. Bulletin
   See also *German American, Deutsch-Amerikanische*
   Arbeiterklubs U.S.A: Mitteilungsblatt.
Germany Today (I)
   See Appendix 5.
Germany Today (II)   ·
   See Appendix 5.
Gewerkschafter, Der / The Unionist
   See Appendix 3.
Gewerkschaftszeitung
Glocke am Sonntag
   See *Der Baltimore Herold.*
Gradaus
   See also *Der Volksvertreter.*
Gross-New Yorker Arbeiter-Zeitung
   See also *New Yorker Volkszeitung.*
Habt Acht
Hahnenruf, Der
Halbwöchentlicher Herold des Westens
   See *Herold des Westens.*

Libertas
Liberty
  See *Libertas.*
Lucifer
  See also *Die Revolution* (New York, I).
Luzifer
  See *Lucifer.*
Menschenrechte, Die
  See also *Der Unabhängige* (Cincinnati).
Menschenspiegel, Der
  See *Das Freie Wort.*
Mephisto
  See also *Der Arme Teufel, Wolfsaugen, Der Zigeuner.*
Metallarbeiter, Der
  See also *Der Hammer* (Philadelphia).
Michigan Arbeiterzeitung
  See also *Libertas.*
Milwaukee Freidenker
  See *Freidenker.*
Milwaukee Freie Presse
  See *Arbeiter-Zeitung* (Milwaukee), *Milwaukee Journal,*
  Vorwärts (Milwaukee'r Socialist).
Milwaukee Journal
  See also *Lucifer, Der Freidenker, Arbeiter-Zeitung*
  (Milwaukee).
Milwaukee Reformer
  See *Volksblatt (Milwaukee Volksblatt).*
Milwaukee'r Arbeiter-Zeitung
  See also *Die Wahrheit* (Milwaukee), *Vorwärts* (Milwaukee),
  Volkszeitung (Milwaukee Volkszeitung), Der Reformer
  (Milwaukee).
Milwaukee'r Leuchtkugeln
  See *Der Socialist.*
Milwaukee'r Socialist
  See *Der Socialist.*
Milwaukie Flug-Bätter
  See Czech Section.
Mitteilungsblatt
  See *Der Arbeiter* (New York, III).
Mitteilungsblatt des Deutsch-Amerikanischen Kulturverbands
  See also *Mitteilungsblatt des Deutsch-Amerikanischen*
  Kulturverbands (Ostdistrikt).
Mitteilungsblatt des Deutsch-Amerikanischen
  Kulturverbands (Ostdistrikt)
  See also *Mitteilungsblatt des Deutsch-Amerikanischen*
  Kulturverbands.
Möbel-Arbeiter-Journal
  See also *General Wood Workers' Journal, International Wood*
  Worker.
Mosquito, Der
  See Appendix 3.
National Reformer, Der
  See *Der Reformer* (Milwaukee).
National Socialist

Newarker Post
Newarker Volksblatt
　See Appendix 3, *New Jersey Arbeiter-Zeitung*.
Newarker Zeitung
　See also *New Jersey Zeitung*, *Die Reform* (New York).
Nothblatt
　See *Arbeiterzeitung* (New York, II).
Oestereichische Rundschau
*Official Journal of the Amalgamated Meat Cutters' and
　Butcher Workers of North America*
　See *Butchers' Journal*.
Ohio Staatszeitung
Ohio Volkszeitung
O.O.
　See Appendix 3.
Painter, The
Parole, Die
　See also *New Yorker Volkszeitung*, *New Jersey
　Arbeiter-Zeitung*, *Der Hammer* (Philadelphia), *Freiheit*.
People, The
　See *Gross-New Yorker Arbeiter-Zeitung*.
Philadelphia Gazette-Demokrat
　See *Tageblatt (Philadelphia Tageblatt)*.
Philadelphia Tageblatt Sonntagsausgabe
　See *Tageblatt (Philadelphia Tageblatt)*.
Piano and Organ Workers' Official Journal
　See *Piano, Organ and Musical Instrument Workers'
　Official Journal*.
*Piano, Organ and Musical Instruments Workers' Official
　Journal*
Pionier, Der (Boston)
　See also *Freidenker*.
Pionier (New York)
　See *New Yorker Volkszeitung*.
Pittsburger Beobachter
　See *Der Adoptiv-Bürger*.
Pittsburger Volkszeitung
　See *Der Arbeiter* (Lebanon).
Pittsburger Volkszeitung
　See Appendix 3.
Progress
　See also *Cigar Makers' Official Journal*.
Proletarian Sports
　See *Arbeiter-Sport in Amerika*.
Proletarier, Der
Proletarietis
　See Latvian Section.
Protection
Radikale, Der
Reform, Die (Baltimore)
Reform, Die (New York)
　See also *Newarker Zeitung*.
Reformer, Der (St. Louis)
Reformer, Der (Milwaukee)

See also *Milwaukee'r Arbeiter-Zeitung, Volkszeitung (Milwaukee Volkszeitung), Volksblatt (Milwaukee Volksblatt)*
Republik der Arbeiter
 See also *Die Sociale Republik.*
Révolte, La
 See *Die Parole.*
Revolution, Die (New York, I)
 See also *Lucifer, Die Revolution* (New York, II), *Die Turnzeitung.*
Revolution, Die (New York, II)
 See also *Die Revolution* (New York, I).
Ritter der Arbeit
 See Appendix 6.
Rothe Laterne, Die
 See *Der Sozialist.*
Sänger-Zeitung
San Antonio Zeitung
 See also *Arbeiter-Union* (New York), *New Yorker Volkszeitung.*
Sattler Journal
 See *Sattler und Wagenbauer.*
Sattler und Wagenbauer
 See also *Carriage and Wagon Workers' Journal.*
Schiffahrt
Socialdemocrat
 See Appendix 6.
Social-Demokrat
 See *Arbeiter-Stimme* (New York).
Sociale Republik, Die
 See also *Der Arbeiter* (New York, I), *Republik der Arbeiter.*
Socialist, Der
 See also *Vorwärts (Milwaukee'r Socialist), Chicagoer Sozialist, Die Arbeiter von Ohio.*
Socialistische Arbeiter-Zeitung
 See also *Clevelander Volksfreund.*
Solidarität
Solidarity
 See *Solidarität.*
Sonntagsblatt der Arbeiter-Zeitung
 See *Arbeiterzeitung (Belleville Arbeiterzeitung).*
Sonntagsblatt der Cincinnatier Zeitung
 See *Cincinnatier Zeitung.*
Sonntagsblatt der New Yorker Volkszeitung
 See *New Yorker Volkszeitung.*
Sonntagsblatt des San Francisco Tageblatt
 See *Tageblatt (San Francisco Tageblatt).*
Sonntagsblatt des St. Louis Tageblatt
 See *Tageblatt (St. Louis Tageblatt).*
Sozialdemokratischer Informationsbrief (SIB)
 See also *Sozialistische Informationsbriefe.*
Sozialist, Der
 See also *Vorwärts* (New York, II).

Sozialistische Informationsbriefe
  See also *Sozialdemokratischer Informationsbrief (SIB)*,
  I.B. Berichte.
Spartacist
St. Clair County Volksblatt
  See *Arbeiterzeitung (Belleville Arbeiterzeitung).*
Stimme, Die
  See also *Freidenker.*
Stimme des Volkes
Stimme des Volkes, Die / The Voice of the People
Strom, Der
  See also *Das Freie Wort.*
Sturmglocke
  See also *Freiheit.*
Sturmtrommel
  See *Sturmvogel.*
Sturmvogel
  See also *Der Anarchist* (St. Louis / New York), *Die Brandfackel.*
Tägliche Abend-Presse
  See *Arbeiterblatt (Cincinnati Arbeiterblatt).*
Tägliche Tribüne
  See *Tribüne (Buffalo Tribüne).*
Täglicher Reformer
  See *Der Reformer* (Milwaukee), *Volkszeitung (Milwaukee Volkszeitung).*
Tageblatt (San Francisco Tageblatt)
  See also *Vorwärts der Pacific Küste*, *California Arbeiter-Zeitung* (San Francisco, II).
Tageblatt (St. Louis Tageblatt)
  See also *Tageblatt-Abendpost.*
Tageblatt (Cincinnati Tageblatt)
  See also *Cincinnatier Zeitung.*
Tageblatt (Philadelphia Tageblatt)
  See also *Arbeiter-Zeitung* (St. Louis, II), *Brauer-Zeitung*,
  Volks-Stimme (Philadelphia), *Die Wahrheit* (Philadelphia).
Tageblatt-Abendpost
  See also *Tageblatt (St. Louis Tageblatt)*,
  Arbeiter-Zeitung (St. Louis, II).
Tageblatt und Arbeiterzeitung
  See *Arbeiterzeitung (Belleville Arbeiterzeitung).*
Tailor, The
Tramp, Der (New York, I)
  See also *O.O.* (Appendix 3), *Der Tramp* (New York, II).
Tramp, Der (New York, II)
  See also *Der Tramp* (New York, I), *Der Zeitgeist* (New York).
Tribüne (Buffalo Tribüne)
  See also *Arbeiterstimme am Erie.*
Tribun du Peuple
  See *Der Volks-Tribun.*
Turn-Blatt für die Vereine des socialistischen Turnerbundes von Nordamerika
  See also *Die Turnzeitung.*

Turnzeitung (Milwaukee)
  See *Amerikanische Turnzeitung.*
Turnzeitung, Die (New York)
  See also *Turn-Blatt für die Vereine des socialistischen Turnerbundes von Nordamerika, Baltimore Wecker* (Appendix 1), *Die Revolution* (New York, I).
Unabhängige, Der (Bern)
  See *Der Proletarier.*
Unabhängige, Der (Cincinnati)
  See also *Die Menschenrechte.*
Union
  See *Arbeiter-Union* (Cincinnati).
Union Arbeiter
  See Appendix 6.
Unser Wort
Unsere Zeit
  See also *German American, Deutsch-Amerikanische Arbeiterklubs U.S.A: Mitteilungsblatt.*
Vereins-Organ für die Turnvereine des socialistischen Turnerbundes von Nord-America
  See *Die Turnzeitung.*
Victory Committee of German-American Trade Unionists. Action Bulletin
  See Appendix 5.
Vierteljahres-Berichte des Socialistischen Turner-Bundes von Nord-Amerika
  See *Turn-Blatt für die Vereine des Socialistischen Turnerbundes von Nordamerika.*
Völkerbund, Der
Volks-Anwalt
  See also *Cincinnatier Zeitung, Tageblatt (St. Louis Tageblatt), Arbeiter-Zeitung* (St. Louis, II).
Volksblatt (Milwaukee)
  See also *Volksblatt (Milwaukee Volksblatt).*
Volksblatt (Milwaukee Volksblatt)
  See also *Der Reformer, Volksblatt* (Milwaukee).
Volksblatt (Sheboygan Volksblatt)
Volksfreund und Arbeiterzeitung
  See *Clevelander Volksfreund, Socialistische Arbeiter-Zeitung.*
Volksfront
  See also *Deutsches Volksecho, Youth Outlook.*
Volksrechte, Die
Volksstimme (Toronto)
Volksstimme des Westens
Volksstimme des Westens: Sonntagsbeilage
  See *Volksstimme des Westens.*
Volks-Stimme (Philadelphia)
  See also *Tageblatt (Philadelphia Tageblatt).*
Volkstribun, Der (Pittsburgh)
Volks-Tribun, Der (New York)
Volksvertreter, Der
  See also *Gradaus.*
Volkszeitung (Milwaukee Volkszeitung)

See also *Milwaukee 'r Arbeiter-Zeitung, Wisconsin Vorwärts,
Die Wahrheit* (Milwaukee), *Vorwärts* (Milwaukee).
Volkszeitung der Pacific-Küste
Volks-Zeitung
See also *Chicagoer Arbeiter-Zeitung* (I).
Vorbote, Der
See also *Chicagoer Arbeiter-Zeitung* (I).
Vorwärts (Berlin/Germany)
See *Arbeiter-Zeitung* (St. Louis, II).
Vorwärts (Newark)
Vorwärts (New York, I)
See also *New Yorker Volkszeitung.*
Vorwärts
See Appendix 3.
Vorwärts (New York, II)
See also *Der Sozialist, New Yorker Volkszeitung.*
Vorwärts (San Francisco)
See *Tageblatt (San Francisco Tageblatt).*
Vorwärts (Milwaukee 'r Socialist)
See also *Arbeiter-Zeitung* (Milwaukee), *Der Socialist.*
Vorwärts (Milwaukee)
See also *Milwaukee 'r Arbeiter-Zeitung, Wisconsin Vorwärts,
Volkszeitung (Milwaukee Volkszeitung), Die Wahrheit*
(Milwaukee).
Vorwärts (Toronto)
Vorwärts der Pacific Küste
See also *Tageblatt (San Francisco Tageblatt).*
Vorwärts-Wochenblatt der New Yorker Volkszeitung
See *Vorwärts* (New York, I), *Vorwärts* (New York, II).
Wahrheit, Die (Philadelphia)
See also *Tageblatt (Philadelphia Tageblatt).*
Wahrheit, Die (Milwaukee)
See also *Milwaukee 'r Arbeiter-Zeitung, Vorwärts*
(Milwaukee), *Wisconsin Vorwärts, Volkszeitung (Milwaukee
Volkszeitung).*
Westliche Post
See *Neue Zeit* (St. Louis).
Wilde Rosen
Wisconsin Advocate, The
Wisconsin Vorwärts
See also *Vorwärts* (Milwaukee), *Die Wahrheit* (Milwaukee),
*Volkszeitung (Milwaukee Volkszeitung), Milwaukee 'r
Arbeiter-Zeitung.*
*Wisconsin Vorwärts und Milwaukee Volkszeitung,
Arbeiter-Zeitung und Täglicher Reformer*
See *Wisconsin Vorwärts.*
Wochenblatt der Volksstimme des Westens
See *Volksstimme des Westens.*
Wochenblatt des Clevelander Volksfreund
See *Clevelander Volksfreund.*
Wochenblatt der New Yorker Abend-Zeitung
See *New Yorker Abend-Zeitung.*
Wochenblatt der New Yorker Volkszeitung
See *Vorwärts* (New York, I), *Vorwärts* (New York, II).

Place Index

Canada

ALBERTA
Edmonton
Deutsche Arbeiterzeitung

MANITOBA
Winnipeg
Deutsche Arbeiter Zeitung
Kampf, Der

ONTARIO
Toronto
Einziger, Der
Volksstimme
Vorwärts

United States

CALIFORNIA
San Francisco
Abendpost
California Arbeiter-Zeitung (I)
California Arbeiter-Zeitung (II)
California Freie Presse
Tageblatt (San Francisco Tageblatt)
Volkszeitung der Pacific-Küste
Vorwärts der Pacific Küste

ILLINOIS
Aurora
Die Freie Press

Belleville
Arbeiterzeitung (Belleville Arbeiterzeitung)

Chicago
Anarchist, Der
Arbeiterfreund, Der
Arbeiter-Freund
Arbeiter-Stimme
Carriage and Wagon Workers' Journal
Chicagoer Arbeiter-Zeitung (I)
Chicagoer Arbeiter-Zeitung (II)
Chicagoer Baecker-Zeitung
Chicagoer Sozialist
Chicagoer Volks-Zeitung
Deutsche Arbeiter, Der
Fackel, Die
Illinois Volkszeitung

MASSACHUSETTS
Boston
Libertas
Neu-England Zeitung
Pionier, Der

Holyoke
Biene, Die

MICHIGAN
Detroit
Arme Teufel, Der
Herold, Der
Michigan Arbeiterzeitung

MISSOURI
St. Louis
Anarchist, Der
Arbeiter-Zeitung (I)
Arbeiter-Zeitung (II)
Communist, Der
Kämpfer, Der
Mephisto
Neue Zeit
Parole, Die
Radikale, Der
Reformer, Der
Tageblatt (St. Louis Tageblatt)
Tageblatt-Abendpost
Wolfsaugen

NEBRASKA
Omaha
Nebraska Arbeiterzeitung

NEW JERSEY
Elizabeth
Agitator

Newark
New Jersey Arbeiter-Zeitung
New Jersey Zeitung
Newarker Post
Newarker Zeitung
Protection
Vorwärts

NEW YORK
Brooklyn
Arbeiter-Sport in Amerika
Deutsch-Amerikanische Fleischer-Zeitung
General Wood Workers' Journal

Möbel-Arbeiter Journal
Neue Leben, Das
Neue Volkszeitung
Neue Zeit, Die
New Yoker Abend-Zeitung
New Yorker Arbeiterzeitung (I)
New Yorker Arbeiter-Zeitung (II)
New Yorker Arbeiter-Zeitung (III)
New Yorker Deutsche Zeitung
New Yorker Volkszeitung
Österreichische Rundschau
Painter, The
Progress
Refrom, Die
Republik der Arbeiter
Revolution, Die (I)
Revolution, Die (II)
Sänger-Zeitung
Schiffahrt
Solidarität
Sozialdemokratischer Informationsbrief (SIB)
Sozialist, Der
Sozialistische Informationsbriefe
Spartacist
Strom, Der
Sturmvogel
Tailor, The
Tramp, Der (I)
Tramp, Der (II)
Turnzeitung, Die
Unser Wort
Unsere Zeit
Völkerbund, Der
Volksrechte, Die
Volks-Tribun, Der
Vorwärts (I)
Vorwärts (II)
Youth Outlook
Zeit, Die
Zeitgeist, Der

Syracuse
Butchers' Journal

Williamsburgh
Turn-Blatt für die Vereine des Socialistischen
Turnerbundes von Nordamerika

OHIO
Cincinnati
Arbeiter Abendzeitung
Arbeiterblatt (Cincinnati Arbeiterblatt)
Arbeiter-Freund, Der
Arbeiter Union

TEXAS
Hallettsville
 Habt Acht

San Antonio
 San Antonio Zeitung

WEST VIRGINIA
Wheeling
 Arbeiter-Freund, Der

WISCONSIN
Milwaukee
 Amerikanische Turnzeitung
 Arbeiter, Der
 Arbeiter-Zeitung
 Deutsche Frauen-Zeitung
 Emanzipator, Der
 Freidenker
 Milwaukee Journal
 Milwaukee'r Arbeiter-Zeitung
 Reformer, Der
 Socialist, Der
 Stimme des Volkes, Die / The Voice of the People
 Volksblatt (I)
 Volksblatt (II) *(Milwaukee Volksblatt)*
 Volkszeitung (Milwaukee Volkszeitung)
 Vorwärts (I) *(Milwaukee'r Socialist)*
 Vorwärts (II)
 Wahrheit, Die
 Wisconsin Advocate, The
 Wisconsin Vorwärts

Sheboygan
 Arbeiter Zeitung
 Volksblatt (Sheboygan Volksblatt)

Chronological Index

1840   1850   1860   1870   1880   1890   1900   1910   1920   1930   1940   1950
012345678901234567890123456789012345678901234567890123456789012345678901234567890123

Beobachter am Ohio   KY Louisville
Adoptiv-Bürger, Der   PA Philadelphia
Communist, Der   MO St. Louis
Zeit, Die   NY New York
Neu-England Zeitung   MA Boston
Volks-Tribun, Der   NY New York
Reformer, Der   MO St. Louis
Amerikanische Arbeit   NY New York
Deutsche Schnellpost   NY New York
Freie Presse   PA Philadelphia
Arbeiter-Freund, Der   OH Cincinnati
Arbeiter-Union   OH Cincinnati
Baltimore Herold, De   MD Baltimore
Newarker Zeitung   NJ Newark
Volksrechte, Die   NY New York
Arbeiter Abendzeitun   OH Cincinnati
Demokrat   MD Baltimore
Hochwächter, Der   OH Cincinnati
Kommunist, Der   IL Nauvoo
Lucifer   NY New York
New Yorker Abend-Zei   NY New York
Reform, Die   MD Baltimore
Republik der Arbeite   NY New York
Unabhängige, Der   OH Cincinnati
Völkerbund, Der   NY New York
Volkstribun, Der   PA Pittsburgh
Volksvertreter, Der   PA Philadelphia
Arbeiterblatt, Das   LA New Orleans
Arbeiterzeitung, Die   NY New York
Gradaus   PA Philadelphia

1840   1850   1860   1870   1880   1890   1900   1910   1920   1930   1940   1950
0123456789012345678901234567890123456789012345678901234567890123456789012345678901234567890123

Hahnenruf, Der	NY	New York
Handwerker- und Arbe	OH	Cincinnati
New Yorker Deutsche	NY	New York
Turnzeitung, Die	NY	New York
Deutsche Frauen-Zeit	WI	Milwaukee
Janus	NY	New York
Kommunist, Der	OH	Cleveland
Revolution, Die (I)	NY	New York
Revolution, Die (II)	NY	New York
Communist, Der	LA	New Orleans
Herold des Westens	KY	Louisville
Menschenrechte, Die	OH	Cincinnati
New Jersey Zeitung	NJ	Newark
Ohio Staatszeitung	OH	Columbus
Proletarier, Der	IL	Chicago
Reform, Die	NY	New York
San Antonio Zeitung	TX	San Antonio
Arbeiter, Der	WI	Milwaukee
Pionier, Der	MA	Boston
Arbeiterfreund, Der	NY	New York
Neue Zeit, Die	NY	New York
Turn-Blatt	NY	Williamsburgh
Zeitgeist	IL	Chicago
Arbeiter, Der (I)	NY	New York
Deutsche Republikane	OH	Cincinnati
Sociale Republik, Di	NY	New York
Stimme des Volkes	IL	Chicago
Neue Zeit	MO	St. Louis
New Yorker Arbeiterz	NY	New York
Radikale, Der	MO	St. Louis

1840   1850   1860   1870   1880   1890   1900   1910   1920   1930   1940   1950
012345678901234567890123456789012345678901234567890123456789012345678901234567890123456789012345678901234567890123

Arbeiter-Freund, Der	WV Wheeling
Abendpost	CA San Francisco
Arbeiter-Union	NY New York
Arbeiterzeitung	PA Philadelphia
Deutsche Arbeiter, D	IL Chicago
Coopers' Journal	OH Cleveland
Arbeiter, Der	PA Lebanon
Freidenker	WI Milwaukee
Arbeiterzeitung (II)	NY New York
Dt.-Am. Buchdrucker-	IN Indianapolis
Arbeiterfreund, Der	IL Chicago
Arbeiter-Stimme	NY New York
Newarker Post	NJ Newark
Vorbote, Der	IL Chicago
Cigar Makers' Offici	NY New York
Socialist, Der	WI Milwaukee
Chicagoer Arbeiter-Z	IL Chicago
Chicagoer Sozialist	IL Chicago
Hammer, Der	LA New Orleans
Ohio Volkszeitung	OH Cincinnati
Tribüne	NY Buffalo
Arbeiterblatt	OH Cincinnati
Arbeiter von Ohio, D	OH Cincinnati
Chicagoer Volks-Zeit	IL Chicago
Emanzipator, Der	WI Milwaukee
Neue Zeit	KY Louisville
Tageblatt	PA Philadelphia
Volksstimme des West	MO St. Louis
Volks-Zeitung	IL Chicago
Vorwärts	NJ Newark

1840 1850 1860 1870 1880 1890 1900 1910 1920 1930 1940 1950
01234567890123456789012345678901234567890123456789012345678901234567890123456789012345678901234567890123

Newspaper	State	City
Amerikanische Turnze	WI	Milwaukee
Arbeiterstimme am Er	NY	Buffalo
California Arbeiter-	CA	San Francisco
Freiheitsbanner	OH	Cincinnati
New Yorker Volkszeit	NY	New York
Vorwärts (I)	NY	New York
Vorwärts (Milwaukee'	WI	Milwaukee
Arbeiter-Zeitung	WI	Milwaukee
Fackel, Die	IL	Chicago
Freiheit	NY	New York
Gewerkschaftszeitung	NY	New York
Bulletin of the Soci	NY	New York
California Freie Pre	CA	San Francisco
Familien-Journal	IA	Davenport
Laterne, Die	NY	Buffalo
Milwaukee Journal	WI	Milwaukee
Reformer, Der	WI	Milwaukee
Wisconsin Advocate,	WI	Milwaukee
Carpenter, The	IN	Indianapolis
Hammer, Der	PA	Philadelphia
Progress	NY	New York
Volksblatt (I)	WI	Milwaukee
Volksblatt (II)	WI	Milwaukee
Möbel-Arbeiter-Journ	NY	New York
Arbeiterzeitung	IL	Belleville
Arme Teufel, Der	MI	Detroit
Illinois Volkszeitun	IL	Chicago
Parole, Die	MO	St. Louis
Protection	NJ	Newark
Zukunft, Die	PA	Philadelphia

| 1880 | 1890 | 1900 | 1910 | 1920 | 1930 | 1940 | 1950 | 1960 | 1970 | 1980 |

01234567890123456789012345678901234567890123456789012345678901234567890123456789012345

Newspaper	State	City
Arbeiter-Freund, Der	PA	McKeesport
Dt.-Am. Bäcker-Zeitu	NY	New York
Neue Zeit, Die	IL	Evansville
Sozialist, Der	NY	New York
Amerikanische Arbeit	NY	New York
Anarchist, Der	IL	Chicago
Brauer-Zeitung	OH	Cincinnati
Cincinnatier Zeitung	OH	Cincinnati
Clevelander Volksfre	OH	Cleveland
Milwaukee'r Arbeiter	WI	Milwaukee
New Jersey Arbeiter-	NJ	Newark
New Yorker Arbeiter-	NY	New York
Arbeiter-Freund, Der	PA	Philadelphia
Buffaloer Arbeiter-Z	NY	Buffalo
California Arbeiter-	CA	San Francisco
Küfer-Zeitung	NY	New York
Tailor, The	NY	New York
Vorwärts	WI	Milwaukee
Arbeiter-Zeitung (I)	MO	St. Louis
Chicagoer Baecker-Ze	IL	Chicago
Libertas	MA	Boston
Metallarbeiter, Der	NY	New York
Michigan Arbeiterzei	MI	Detroit
Tageblatt	MO	St. Louis
Tramp, Der (I)	NY	New York
Anarchist, Der	MO	St. Louis
Arbeiter-Stimme	IL	Chicago
Arbeiter-Zeitung	PA	Pittsburgh
Volks-Anwalt	OH	Cincinnati
Wahrheit, Die	WI	Milwaukee

1880   1890   1900   1910   1920   1930   1940   1950   1960   1970   1980
01234567890123456789012345678901234567890123456789012345678901234567890123456789012345

Cooper's Internation	KS Kansas City
New Yorker Arbeiter-	NY New York
Volkszeitung	WI Milwaukee
Arbeiter-Zeitung	PA Erie
General Wood Workers	NY Brooklyn
Sattler und Wagenbau	IL Chicago
Volkszeitung der Pac	CA San Francisco
Vorwärts (II)	NY New York
Agitator	NJ Elizabeth
Brandfackel, Die	NY New York
Illinoiser Volkszeit	IL Chicago
Painter, The	NY New York
Tageblatt	CA San Francisco
Wisconsin Vorwärts	WI Milwaukee
Arbeiter-Zeitung	KS Kansas City
Biene, Die	MA Holyoke
Freie Wacht	PA Philadelphia
Herold, Der	MI Detroit
Freie Presse, Die	IL Aurora
Tageblatt	OH Cincinnati
Volksblatt	WI Sheboygan
Int. Wood Worker	IL Chicago
Kämpfer, Der	MO St. Louis
Sturmglocke	IL Chicago
Buffalo Herold, Der	NY Buffalo
Industrial News, The	NY New York
Sturmvogel	NY New York
Tageblatt-Abendpost	MO St. Louis
Arbeiter-Zeitung (II	MO St. Louis
Gross-N.Y.Arbeiter-Z	NY New York

1880   1890   1900   1910   1920   1930   1940   1950   1960   1970   1980
01234567890123456789012345678901234567890123456789012345678901234567890123456789012345

Butchers' Journal	NY Syracuse
Carriage and Wagon W	IL Chicago
Nebraska Arbeiterzei	NE Omaha
Piano, ...Workers Jo	IL Chicago
Socialistische Arbei	OH Cleveland
Stimme d. Volkes/Voi	WI Milwaukee
Wolfsaugen	MO St. Louis
Mephisto	MO St. Louis
Tramp, Der (II)	NY New York
Wahrheit, Die	PA Philadelphia
Zeitgeist, Der	NY New York
Arbeiter-Zeitung	OH Cincinnati
Neues Leben	IL Chicago
Zigeuner, Der	IL Chicago
Dt.-Am. Fleischer-Ze	NY Brooklyn
Arbeiter, Der (II)	NY New York
Solidarität	NY New York
Freie Wort, Das	NY New York
Arbeiter-Zeitung	WI Sheboygan
Strom, Der	NY New York
Anti-Autoritär, Der	NY New York
Echo	OH Cleveland
Vorwärts der Pacific	CA San Francisco
Habt Acht	TX Hallettsville
Int. Arbeiter-Chroni	NY New York
Einziger, Der	O Toronto
Arbeiter-Freund	IL Chicago
Klassen-Kampf, Der	IL Chicago
Sänger-Zeitung	NY New York
Volks-Stimme	PA Philadelphia

556

```
1880    1890    1900    1910    1920    1930    1940    1950    1960    1970    1980
01234567890123456789012345678901234567890123456789012345678901234567890123456789012345
```

Arbeiter, Der (III)   NY New York
Arbeiter-Sport in Am   NY Brooklyn
Deutsche Arbeiterzei   A Edmonton
Deutsche Arbeiter Ze   M Winnipeg
Kampf, Der   M Winnipeg
Chicagoer Arbeiter-Z   IL Chicago
Kampfsignal   NY New York
Neue Volkszeitung   NY New York
Stimme, Die   PA Philadelphia
Dt.-Am. Arbeiterklub   NY New York
Einheitsfront, Die   NY New York
Volksfront   IL Chicago
Mitteilungsblatt des   NY New York
Deutsche Zentralbüch   NY New York
Schiffahrt   NY New York
Deutsches Volksecho   NY New York
Anti-Faschist, Der   NY New York
Gegen den Strom   NY New York
I.B. Berichte   NY New York
Int. Arbeiterfront   NY New York
Mitteilungsblatt (Os   NY New York
Neue Leben, Das   NY New York
Soz.dem. Information   NY New York
Soz. Informationsbri   NY New York
Youth Outlook   NY New York
Unser Wort   NY New York
Unsere Zeit   NY New York
Austrian Labor Infor   NY New York
German American, The   NY New York
German-Am. Emergency   NY New York

1880   1890   1900   1910   1920   1930   1940   1950   1960   1970   1980
01234567890123456789012345678901234567890123456789012345678901234567890123456789012345

Oestereichische Rund	NY New York
Volksstimme	O Toronto
Int. Freigew. Nachri	NY New York
Vorwärts	O Toronto
Wilde Rosen	PA Philadelphia
Bulletin der Soz. Ar	NY New York
Spartacist	NY New York

Combined Southern and Western Title Index

The italicized page numbers indicate the main entry.

About the Editor

DIRK HOERDER is Professor of the Social History of North America at the University of Bremen, West Germany. His numerous previous works include *Crowd Action in Revolutionary Massachusetts, 1765-1780*; *Plutocrats and Socialists: Reports by German Diplomats and Agents on the American Labor Movement*; *Protest, Direct Action, Repression: Dissent in American Society from Colonial Times to the Present*; *Labor Migration in the Atlantic Economies: The European and North American Working Classes During the Period of Industrialization* (Greenwood Press, 1986), and *The Immigrant Labor Press in North America, 1840s-1970s* (3 vols., Greenwood Press, 1987).